OPICON II 3 HOMER
PHANES 5 HERODO
8 ARISTOTLE II 9 HIPPOCRATES
NICOMACHUS 11 LUCRETIUS
LOTINUS 12 VIRGIL 13 PLUTARCH
NICUS KEPLER 16 AUGUSTINE 17
QUINAS II 19 DANTE CHAUCER 20
22 RABELAIS 23 ERASMUS MON-
SHAKESPEARE II 26 GILBERT
28 FRANCIS BACON DESCARTES
MOLIERE RACINE 32 NEWTON
IME 34 SWIFT VOLTAIRE DIDEROT
DAM SMITH 37 GIBBON I 38 GIB-
TE PAPERS THE FEDERALIST I S.
ARADAY 43 HEGEL KIERKEGAARD
GOETHE BALZAC 46 AUSTEN
MELVILLE TWAIN 49 DARWIN 50
OSTOEVSKY IBSEN 53 WILLIAM
ES BERGSON DEWEY WHITEHEAD
EIN BARTH 56 POINCARE PLANCK
ON BOHR HARDY HEISENBERG
DDINGTON 57 VEBLEN TAWNEY
ZINGA LEVI-STRAUSS 59 HENRY
PIRANDELLO PROUST CATHER
LAWRENCE T. S. ELIOT O'NEILL
HEMINGWAY ORWELL BECKETT

the Western World

Visitors at The Exploratorium Museum examine The Sun Painting *by Bob Miller. This painting was created for the museum through its Artists-in-Residence program. The Exploratorium is located in San Francisco, California.*

The Great Ideas Today

Encyclopædia Britannica, Inc.

Chicago London Paris Rome Seoul Sydney Tokyo

"Applied Anthropology: The State of the Art" by Margaret Mead
from *Perspectives on Anthropology, 1976.* Reproduced by permission
of the American Anthropological Association from *Perspectives on
Anthropology, 1976.* Not for further reproduction.

"The Value of Poetry," "On Discovery," and "The Healing Power of Nature"
are from DEEP PLAY. Copyright © 1998, 1999 by Diane Ackerman.
To be published by Random House, Inc., in Spring 1999.
Reprinted by permission of the publisher.

Library of Congress Number: 61-65561
International Standard Book Number: 0-85229-684-3
International Standard Serial Number: 0072-7288

EDITOR
John Van Doren

CONSULTING EDITOR
Mortimer J. Adler

Assistant Editor
Amanda E. Richards

ART DEPARTMENT

Creative Director
Bob Ciano

Director, Art Production
Melvin Stagner

Art Director
Jon Hensley

Picture Editor
Corrine L. Johns

Production
Ethan Persoff

Systems/Technical
Michael Born, Jr.
Bruce Walters

Art Staff
Michelle R. Burrell   Kimberly L. Cleary   Karen M. Farmer
Carla M. Whittington

Supervisor, Composition/Page Makeup
Danette Wetterer

Composition/Page Makeup Staff
Griselda Cháidez   Carol A. Gaines
Thomas J. Mulligan   Gwen E. Rosenberg
Tammy Yu-chu Wang Tsou

MANAGING DIRECTOR, ART AND CARTOGRAPHY
Barbra A. Vogel

MANAGER, COPY DEPARTMENT
Sylvia Wallace

Copy Supervisor
Julian Ronning

MANAGER, PRODUCTION CONTROL
Mary C. Srodon

Production Control Staff
Marilyn L. Barton

PUBLISHING TECHNOLOGY GROUP
Oleg Barsukov   Steven Bosco
Troy A. Broussard   Peter Davies   Ray Goldberger
Vincent Star   Mary Voss

A NOTE ON REFERENCE STYLE

In the following pages, passages in *Great Books of the Western World* are referred to by the initials "*GBWW*," followed by a roman numeral (indicating the first edition of 1952 [I] or the second edition of 1990 [II]) with volume and page number. Thus, "*GBWW* I: 5, 100; II: 4, 112" refers to a passage from Sophocles' *Oedipus the King,* which is on page 100 in Volume 5 of the first edition, and on page 112 in Volume 4 of the second edition. Sometimes only one reference will be given, since the contents of the first and second editions differ. Also note that passages quoted in an article may differ from the translation of that passage in either the first or second edition, since newer translations of some works are included in the second edition.

Gateway to the Great Books is referred to by the initials "*GGB*," followed by volume and page number. Thus, "*GGB* 10, 39–57" refers to pages 39 through 57 of Volume 10 of *Gateway to the Great Books,* which is James's essay, "The Will to Believe."

The Great Ideas Today is referred to by the initials "*GIT,*" followed by the year and page number. Thus, "*GIT* 1968, 210" refers to page 210 of the 1968 edition of *The Great Ideas Today.*

CONTENTS

Preface

Looking over the contents of this year's volume, we are struck, not for the first time, by the range of the material we have managed to assemble, reaching from quantum theory to fairy tales. The tone varies greatly, too, as it must. Modern physics, considered here by Richard Healey, does not allow the approach that one brings, say, to ancient Hesiod, who is taken up by George Anastaplo; nor would we expect Diane Ackerman, talking about poetry, to sound like Gerald Holton writing about scientific research. Yet there are common elements among the essays, to be observed in a moment, and most of the writers have tried to see through to the other side of their subjects. Thus we find Professor Anastaplo, for example, saying that he cannot write about Beginnings, his chosen topic, without reflecting at the same time upon Endings.

The latter, regrettably, is the concern of our preface as well. We must inform our readers that *The Great Ideas Today,* 1998, will be the last issue of this annual to appear. Encyclopædia Britannica, Inc., our publishers, have determined that after nearly forty years there are not enough subscribers remaining for the book to be profitable, and so it no longer makes economic sense to produce it. This does not mean that it has failed to interest the subscribers it has gained. As yearbooks go, ours has had a strikingly loyal readership, perhaps because it has long since given up the pretense of a strictly annual review of the arts and sciences and has become instead a compendium of more than ephemeral character—with writings, at least some of which seem likely to prove permanent, on books and ideas and the whole field of learning, so far as we could encompass it. But it *has* been sold by subscription, not in stores; the subscribers have been, as they were intended to be, purchasers of *Great Books of the Western World;* buyers of these have not been much sought for some time, whether or not they could have been found; and those who once did buy have died, or moved to Florida, or run out of shelf space, as was to be expected. So the inevitable has occurred. The number of our readers has dropped below what is required, or will have done, with the expected attrition, after next year.

The point about *Great Books of the Western World* is worth making because we hear much these days about the general loss of interest in those writings (or in any books at all), and it would be easy to explain the discontinuance of the annual on that ground. But the evidence does not support such a conclusion, indeed contradicts it. No one has forced our subscribers to buy successive issues of this yearbook; they have done so on their own, as they or others like them have not done, or not done so consistently, with other annual publications; and it is reasonable to suppose that they have done this not because they have lost interest in the Great Books, but because, on the contrary, they find them more interesting than most things. Perhaps they are not quite aware that they do, or quite why.

The authors of the Great Books have not been the direct object of attention for most of our writers. Their presence has been of a more subtle kind. They have presided over *The Great Ideas Today* much as the Muses are said by Thomas K. Simpson in this issue to preside over museums, whether we know it or not. No other book has sounded like this one because no other book has had such tutelary figures. A kind of critical intelligence has been lent by them to its discussions even if it was not always acknowledged. It is a good guess that this is why the publication lasted so long.

Of course it has had remarkable contributors. Anyone who looks over the cumulative index, 1961–1998, at the end of this volume can see that a fair number of the most distinguished intellects of the century have appeared in our pages, apart from those who are represented in the section devoted to reprints, who make the list even longer. Their presence is in part a tribute to the genius of Mortimer J. Adler, who conceived the book in the first place and for many years was its editor in chief. Mr. Adler, as readers know, was also the designer of the Syntopicon, as he was of the 15th edition of the *Encyclopædia Britannica,* and a formative figure generally in the Great Books movement of our time. It was he who insisted on the essentially dialectical character of the annual, which has encouraged its contributors to explore their subjects as deeply as they could but to avoid mere opinion, taking positions only as truth seemed to require.

We have had latitude also from our publishers over whose imprint the volume has each year gone out, but who have never sought to control its content save as, in early days, Senator William Benton, who owned the company, wrote long letters to Mr. Adler taking issue with what some contributors said (Mr. Adler learned to pre-empt these by writing defensive accounts of each issue to the Senator first).

Still, it is the Great Books authors themselves who have been formative of our volumes, organizing much of their content and recalling contributors to their task at many points. That was, and is, the excuse for having such a publication in the first place. This would have been pretentious or absurd as an act of piety, but it has made sense as an enterprise of what might be called inspired exploration and analysis. The Great Books are to be read, if at all, not as jewelry is worn around the neck, because it looks good, but because we cannot take them off: they have formed the minds with which we begin our inquiries. This is so even if we are from the East, where incidentally such books are by no means unknown, and even if we are women, whom they treat unjustly, justice being something they have taught us to define. We remember T.S. Eliot's rejoinder to the objection that we now *know* more than the authors of the Great Books did, which was, "precisely, and they are *what* we know." To pursue such inquiries is to prove the debt. "Wherever I go in my mind I meet Plato coming back," Alfred North Whitehead once remarked. That is so whether we know Plato or not, save if we don't we pass him without knowing what to make of the encounter. George Anastaplo, our regular contributor, has shown us who is *there* for us in the Great Books on many different occasions. The writings of Thomas K. Simpson, another regular contributor and no friend to mindless traditionalism, are an education in how meetings with such sources may become instructive—for both his and our sakes, as writer and readers. Note that neither of these men is a specialist, any more than was Mr. Adler. Professor Anastaplo writes as well on Greek tragedy as he does on philosophy and law; Mr. Simpson has astonishing depth in Marx, Maxwell, and Shakespeare, all of whom he has investigated in our pages. And there have been other frequent contributors of great range, too—Otto Bird in many issues of the book, Jon Elster in this and other recent volumes. The best minds have no departments, though we all understand some things better than others, and probably should.

It remains only to thank our subscribers, of whom some thousands remain after all, and who have stuck with us for so long. We must also thank those—the many members of the staff at Britannica—who over the years have worked hard to put the book into pages and boards, and have found illustrations for it. One hopes that a sense of pride in their undertaking may last. In which connection it should be added that, at this writing, efforts are being made to have the cumulative index in the back of this issue placed also on the Web, so that what has been written for the book will not be lost to the future. If it is secured in this way, we are likely to meet sooner or later on your screens.

—John Van Doren, Editor
The Great Ideas Today

Current Developments in the Arts and Sciences

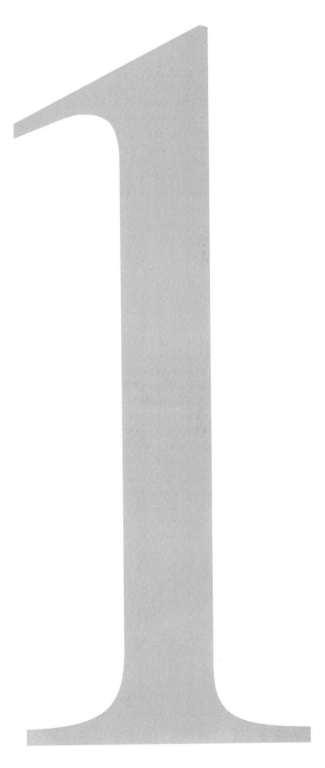

Abode of the Modern Muse: The Science Museum

Thomas K. Simpson

I. Introduction

The museum as grove of the Muses

I n a society suffused with the sciences and their companions, the technologies, it is perhaps time to take our science museums more seriously than we have done in the past. We have always prized and delighted in these halls of wonder and investigation, but we may not have thought enough about their special role as the forum in which we meet to contemplate the sciences and reflect on their role in our past, present, and future lives.

It may be helpful to begin by reconsidering the word *museum*. We inherit it from the Greek *museion,* which means the temple or abode of the Muses initially, more likely a hill or a grove than a building. We are reluctant to admit that ancient words may have force for us today, but the Muses are timeless: we meet them whenever we are moved by music, or moved to compose—and "musics" may take many forms. The range of the ancient Muses was reflected in their titles and responsibilities—Erato, singing of love; Calliope, Homer's Muse, of epic verse; Urania, the astronomer. Dance, comedy, and tragedy all belong to their company; but they all in turn follow in the train of Apollo (who is himself as much tempted as tempter), and they are all, finally, one Muse who entrances and inspires us, whatever channel this inspiration may flow in.

Our modern *science* is distinct enough, perhaps, from anything the ancients knew to deserve a Muse of its own, so without producing a new name out of the hat, let us simply say that this modern Muse is our form in which the old Muse of the human spirit takes brilliant new life. The new Muse is at work throughout our society, wherever the sciences and technologies are flourishing, but the *science museum* is the special place we dedicate to reflection on the sciences, and display and wonder at their works. I will argue that the science museum, for all the fun and celebration it is capable of inducing, is also in the most literal sense a sacred space. In any grove in which one Muse has appeared, we might well be on the lookout for the others, and this caution applies to the science museum as well: for our Muse of the modern sciences keeps close company with Urania, Calliope, and the Muse of tragedy, Melpomene, as well.[1]

Meet the Muses

There was one very special summer's day when Socrates took Phaedrus to meet the Muses, just outside the walls of ancient Athens. To get a closer look at these divinities whose service I believe we still honor, we might well join them; it will be a little like going bird-watching with an expert, for we soon see that Socrates is remarkably familiar with this terrain. The event is reported by Plato in the dialogue simply titled *Phaedrus.*[2] Phaedrus is a young man, full of the passions and enthusiasms of youth; today it might be the prospects of digital technologies or the mystique of black holes; for him it was the wit and intriguing techniques of the new art of rhetoric, the current rage in Athens. Phaedrus thus arrives as a young

(Overleaf) The lobby of the National Museum of Natural History, located in Washington, D.C.

devotee of the Muses; he is carrying a book with him, a prized display of the skills of the orator Lysias, which he is impatient to recount. Together he and Socrates make their way along the stream Ilyssus—the stream of both love and discourse—to the shade of a plane tree favored by the Muses. Lysias' art in this case has been demonstrated in a tricky argument to the effect that it is better to yield to the entreaties of a non-lover than to those of a lover, for the lover will make irrational and enslaving demands, while the non-lover keeps a cool and level head. Phaedrus does not realize that, read in this grove of the Muses, such an argument is blasphemy, as not only Erato, but all the Muses are true lovers—and it is a special offense to Socrates, whose life is one of philosophy, the unwavering love of wisdom.

Socrates, *curator* we might say in this sacred grove, assumes the role of *psychagogos*—leader of souls—to guide Phaedrus' spirit gently but surely to a higher sense of service to the Muses. He first wins Phaedrus' attention and respect by matching Lysias' effort with a far superior speech to Lysias' own point—taking care, however, to first cover his head to make clear that his heart is not in his words. He takes care, as Lysias had not, to define this Eros, the "love" which is being decried. It is the "left-handed" love, charac-

"The Museum as grove of the Muses." An outside view of the Museum of Science and Industry in Chicago, Illinois.

terized by grasping, need, and deprivation. Won by this first speech, Phaedrus is now ready for a reversal in the *palinode,* the second, opposite speech, which Socrates gives, now in behalf of true love. This time Eros is rightly characterized as generous, not acquisitive or transient, but timeless because devoted to what is true, beautiful, and good. Mankind's deep confusion is between lasting devotion and passing delight. If the science museum is indeed the sacred grove, the same confusion will rend us there between the passing delights of fascinating technologies and those things for which we should truly care.

In the branches of the plane tree, cicadas have been singing lustily through the heat of the day: one could succumb to their charms and sleep away the afternoon. These are siren voices with which the Muses test and mock us. The real power of the Muses is something altogether different, awakening our spirits and stirring true devotion to things worthy of our love. This picture is painted by Socrates—and as it unfolds, we recognize that the truer Muse is awakening in Phaedrus' breast—in a myth of the soul as a chariot drawn by two horses. The charioteer, *nous*—intuitive intellect, capable of grasping truth—is devoted to the highest, most beautiful and eternal things, but the chariot is drawn by two very different horses in the everyday world of opinion, one of which serves the charioteer well, while the other fiercely grasps the delights of the moment. Phaedrus is won, at least for this day, and the victory of Socrates in the sacred grove means that the Muses in the highest form have begun to stir in Phaedrus' heart.

It is of the essence of this dialogue that Socrates loves, not only that which is truly beautiful and good, but Phaedrus himself. The grove is a place of friendship and caring; this is the secret working of the Muses, and at the same time, the secret of true teaching and learning. It is a mystery, not something which can be achieved by cleverness or guaranteed by methodical design. And it is not simply a happy tale, for the notes of epic and tragedy sound in that grove as well. Few of Plato's *Dialogues* are as sensitive to the moment and the passage of time as this one; as we turn away, back to the city, we are painfully aware of the likely transience of Phaedrus' insight.

The science museum may be such a mystic grove, and Phaedrus a young visitor arriving at the door. If so, we must bear a heavy curatorial responsibility to offer more than the fascination of a clever exhibit, or graphic attractions, to the wonders of modern technology. Cicadas are everywhere, as we know, in the modern world. There is a *wholeness* about the grove of the Muses which we need to consider carefully, for if the Muses abide in one another's company, then even if our attention is to a new Muse attired in a fresh white lab coat, we know the others are present as well. Thought will be led by the Muses past any boundary by which we may seek to contain it. Despite its name, and however inconvenient, the science museum cannot finally be about "science" alone. If the spell works, then thought will range from the science we offer to all the contexts in which it is embedded, and through all the modes of coloration, from celebration through, it may be, to despair.

The word museum comes from the Greek museion, "which means the temple or abode of the Muses."

II: The Alexandrian museum as paradigm
The Great Museum of Alexandria and its works

What has become known to the world as the "Great Museum of Alexandria," with its even more famous Library, was only one component of a bold concept of Alexander the Great—the concept of a city of a new sort within which a Museum would be the jewel, and of a new world order, of which Alexandria would be the symbol and the focus. This plan, including the detail of the city, Alexander seems to have laid out in one winter in Egypt, at the outset of his campaign to the extreme bounds of the known world. In one of its roles, the Museum of Alexandria was very much a science museum, and a brief consideration of it may be of help in considering what a *museum* may be, and yield in the process certain principles which will aid in characterizing instances of science museums closer to our own time.[3]

As the hub of Alexander's new world order, Alexandria was to be a center of commerce; facing the Mediterranean on one side, and the system of the Nile on the other, it was destined to flourish as a center of trade between the West and the East. At the same time, it was to become a center of commerce in ideas, full counterpart to its economic function and equally important in shaping the new world. Alexander died after the close of his first great cycle of campaigning, and the political world-order he envisioned was never achieved. But, remarkably, Alexandria went on to play that role as intellectual focus of the world in much the way he must have intended, so that for centuries this Museum remained a vital institution of a remarkable kind.

The histories appear to agree that the conception of the city was Alexander's own, and that he laid out the site personally. It joined its commer-

A sixteenth-century representation of the Egyptian city Alexandria

cial, political, religious, and intellectual functions in one coherent and dramatic design. One long axis paralleled the seacoast, while a major cross-street linked the seacoast with the Nile harbor. The result was a grid of four elongated quarters, one being reserved as the center of government. During Alexander's lifetime, it was the palace of the Macedonian governor he had appointed for Egypt; when, following his death, his Macedonian governor, Ptolemy, proclaimed himself king, this quarter became the royal palace. At the far end of the long axis was the Serapeium, the temple which reproduced in Alexandria its predecessor in Memphis, and thus became the spiritual center of Egypt.

The Museum was a prominent feature of the royal quarter of the city; it included accommodations for some thirty members of an academic community, with rooms and colonnades for lectures, thought, and conversation. There were facilities to dine together, and above all perhaps, a library to be gathered, as a resource for thought, from all corners of the world.[4]

From Aristotle to Alexandria

If we ask ourselves how Alexander happened to give such prominent place to this vision of the Museum, we are led back to Athens and to two schools there, the Academy of Plato and Aristotle's Lyceum—and thence, finally, to the grove of the Muses under whose auspices Socrates conversed with Phaedrus. The term "school" is misleading, just as the term "museum" is. The word *schole* means "leisure"—a term even more confusing for moderns. "Leisure" is not a *time* of doing *nothing,* but rather, an activity in which one is doing one's *most;* correspondingly, Aristotle speaks of "waging peace" as one would speak of "waging war."[5] The root sense is of *freedom*—not simply as lack of restraint, but as the fully implemented opportunity to act to our full human capacity, without constraint of necessity. It is not something one thinks of doing alone, but in the polity, or in company and conversation.

The Academy, then, as a school, was a place of such leisure in which students and teachers in fellowship were enabled to pursue to the fullest that conversation between teacher and student which constitutes true teaching, or among the teachers themselves, which constitutes the pursuit of learning at the highest level men can conceive. To close our circle of terms, we need only add that such a *school* is a *museum;* for it is the place in which the presence of that Muse which presides over Socrates' inspired love of learning is most strongly felt. We do not, today, readily think of *reason* as occurring in a sacred place, or involving a sense of mystery; our reductive notion of reasoning draws too much upon computers or the operation of formal logics. In truth, the Muse most of all leads thought, and insight is a matter of grace, not design. These must be thoughts of the kind Alexander had in mind when he envisioned a *museum* as the centerpiece of the new city—a place sacred to the Muses, like the schools of Athens but on a new, world scale.

Though these thoughts link back to the Academy, the connection is far more direct to Aristotle and the Lyceum, equally a fellowship of learning and quite literally named for a sacred grove, that of Zeus Lykeos. The lives of Aristotle and Alexander are woven in a most remarkable way, for Alexander had been Aristotle's student for three highly formative years, apparently between the ages of 14 and 16. It is nearly impossible today to imagine what these meetings would have been like, what curriculum they would have followed. We infer that they read Homer together, for Alexander carried his copy of Homer, edited by Aristotle, through his campaigns; this was not a question of light reading, but empowerment, for Alexander had reason to think of himself as descended from Herakles on his father's side and from Achilles on his mother's. But we can be confident that they followed some serious line of teaching which addressed virtue and led to the politics—for Aristotle would not have treated lightly the responsibility of educating a brilliant young man destined to take up his father's campaigns throughout Greece, and into Persia as well. Without attempting to paint Aristotle as father to Alexander's plan for a rational, peaceful, and unified world-order, we can be sure that Aristotle and Alexander conversed at length about the nature of man as both rational and political. Aristotle's must have been the last words of formal teaching Alexander heard, for he was soon carried off by unhappy affairs at the court; and he was only twenty-one that winter in Egypt when he laid out

Alexandria with its new museum. If we had time, we could trace a fascinating pattern of relations between Aristotle and his former student. Let it
suffice to say here that it was a former student of the Lyceum, Demetrius,
who served as advisor to Ptolemy I of Egypt in bringing the Museum into
being.[6]

It is hard to visualize how the great Museum actually functioned, and
most of all, perhaps, it is difficult to clarify the notion of that crucial
component, the "library." It was apparently a collection of books, rather
than a special building; but then, the term "book" itself may carry misleading suggestions. Homer sang long before anyone thought to write him
down: in this sense, the Muses do not need books. Manuscript books
represented an effort to capture on papyrus an ephemeral stream of
thought; and in vigorously pursuing a search for books for the library
wherever they were to be found, the Ptolemies were perhaps not so much
acting as bibliophiles as attempting to gather the wits of the world as a
resource for new and ongoing thought at the Museum. Vast efforts were
made in copying works, so that Alexandria became a center for the publication of handwritten books, while the traditional art of the Egyptian scribe
must have been co-opted from the elegant production of hieroglyphs to
lowly trafficking in the alphabet. Nobody knows how large the collection
became, nor is a "volume" quite such a stable measure in the world of
scrolls as in that of stacked-up books. Yet it tells us a great deal to hear
informed estimates of a peak of some 500,000 volumes. We should perhaps
think of the library in organic terms, rather as a garden than a depository,

for it must have been in constant flux, and its role was to nourish the work of the members of the Museum and to absorb new thought as it unfolded.[7]

The Alexandrian science museum

The project of the Alexandrian Museum was to bring to light in a single forum as much of the world's ongoing work as it was able to gather, in a company of minds able to bring this immense collection to life in a new order of intellectual advance. Heretofore, schools like the Lyceum and the Academy had gathered what they could from traveling philosophers or the books of other schools. Now, in Alexandria, what had been limited and fragmentary would become organized, on a world scale. A new kind of insight arises, a new perspective of a whole which had not before been visible. Thus just as we have come to see the Library as a living thing, the interplay of lesser treatises and partial contributions would give rise to a new order of intellectual life. Since our concern is with science museums, we might mention three giants of this Alexandrian era, through whose vision we are able today to contemplate as ordered wholes the domains we know as classical geometry and astronomy—Euclid, Apollonius, and Ptolemy. Their work spans more than four hundred years, evidence of the endurance of the Alexandrian project.

It will be enough to consider very briefly the work of Euclid, whose name—if not in truth his great book, the *Elements of Geometry*—is so well known to all.[8] He was there in the first years of the Museum project, and indeed it was to Ptolemy I that he is reputed to have said, tellingly, "There is no royal road to geometry"—for there is no alternative, if one is to know geometry, to bringing one's own mind, step-by-step and sometimes with great difficulty, to perceive the light of truth in the unfolding systems of demonstrations. Most of the world, academia by no means excepted, has elected the "royal road" and thereby missed the geometry; little of the work as a whole is read, or its content understood, in our modern colleges.

Euclid nonetheless provides an excellent window for us into the workings of the Mu-

In this detail from The School of Athens, *a mural by Raphael, Euclid explains a problem in geometry.*

seum, for he was able to draw together there a number of scattered segments into the one dramatic system. The very concept of an ordered deductive structure needed to be seen, displayed in a paradigm of completeness with a beginning, middle, and end. The mystery of the irrational, in one aspect close to the secrets of Eleusis, together with Eudoxus' key which opens this to the contemplation of mind, and Theaetetus' brilliant reconciliation of the irrationals within a system of the rational, a wondrous victory of the mind over chaos—all these Euclid had to gather and give them place within an ordered body. The pieces were there to *be* gathered, but *geometry* as a body of thought had yet to be composed. It is easy to miss the originality of this typically Alexandrian work: not a matter of assemblage, but of conception, at a new level of intellectual insight.

Euclid's achievement throws special light on the concept of the museum more generally: for the sacred grove is a space reserved for such speculative review, for reading works in search of their relations (the meaning, after all, of *collection*). In Alexandria, it meant intellectual adventure, the projection on the intellectual plane of Alexander's political dream of a world fully in touch with itself. The earlier work of ancient learning—of the dramatists, of the Academy, and the Lyceum—is often seen as heroic, and the Alexandrian phase as a kind of mopping-up. In the same way, perhaps, the work of science museums is thought of as second-order, following upon the heroic work of the research centers and universities; no one would claim a Nobel prize for mounting an insightful exhibit! But it goes beyond apologetics to urge that the role of the museum in its serious mode should rise to the highest intellectual plane—when the works it interprets are read through and grasped individually, and the curator's constructive work is ready to begin.

There is an implication here for the museum visitor as well. Just as the Library is an organic center of new growth, so Euclid's work is of no use on the shelf: generations of students read the *Elements* at Alexandria, each making the same voyage Euclid himself had laid out. One such student, at a second generation's remove, was Apollonius of Perga; he in turn became a great composer: for Euclid had not comprehended *geometry,* but only its *elements.* In his own brilliant adventure of the *Conics,* Apollonius, like Euclid a collector, took the mind to a new level of vision; and of course we know that his system was destined ultimately to become the foundation of Newton's own *System of the World.*[9] Every powerful interpretation of the world, assimilated by new generations of minds, becomes a springboard for the insights of the future.

The Alexandrian paradigm

The time has come to consider what the Alexandria Museum may have to tell us about the essence of the concept of the "science museum." Are there principles here, insights concerning the nature of the museum itself, especially in application to science, on which we might ground our inquiry into the science museum in our own time? Let me venture some suggestions, however outrageous they may seem or remote from ready applicability today.

(1)   *The museum is a sacred space.* I begin with what may be the most difficult principle of all, yet critical to each of the museums we have looked at. The museum is defined by its special relation to the Muses, who are collectively the underlying principle inspiring the human mind, spirit, or soul to dance, sing, speak, or compose works of myth or reason. The museum is not a place of merely technical works, produced by the application of system or method, whether an art of rhetoric or our "scientific method," alone. Something fundamental, some love reaching beyond method is summoned inducing fresh production, a new and unpredictable life of the spirit to arise. We know no better today than men did then, the answer to the question of the origin of such vitality, such spontaneity and imagination. Dedicated to the celebration and invocation of this mystery, the museum is inherently a sacred space.

Is this Muse truly a *sacred* source? Moderns might be more inclined to regard such a principle as a matter of genetics or the hormonal system than as a mystery of which we might stand in awe. Yet whatever theories we might contrive out of genetics or physiology to account for such phenomena, our inner feeling of possession by the Muse remains one of mystery and awe. Some force—of creativity, of insight, of memory—is sensed moving among us in a museum, not by our own efforts; and in its presence we are at once humbled and exalted. We may not agree with Homer in ascribing such experiences to the immanence of the gods, and may hesitate to call our museums sacred places, but if in these special halls we invoke something for which we care greatly, and which we cannot simply command, its coming will allow us to share the feeling of mystery. The ancients had a very strong sense of the presence and power of mystery; we may not. But we will have a *museion* only to the extent that we share that ancient sense of awe, and recognize to some degree the sacred character of the groves in which we work.

(2)   *The museum is a fellowship.* In the presence of such mystery the Museum must be, fundamentally and primarily, a fellowship, a community as the Academy and the Lyceum were. This is a difficult lesson for our busy, competitive modern world; we are proficient at creating assemblages of people, but there will be no *museion* unless we are committed to the belief that in this special place we share one Muse, and finally speak, or sing, with a single voice. The museum will then be a place of true conviviality, based on a sense of sharing a common source, and embarking on a common enterprise.

(3)   *The museum is universal.* It is fundamental to the concept of the Alexandrian Museum that it be universal, that it belong to everyone. It belonged to Alexander's brilliant design that Alexandria be the center and focus of the world, in that by its nature it addresses its work to all mankind. Politically Alexander's project was aborted, but the concept remained with the Museum and gave essential life to its work. Euclid produced the *Elements,* not for Ptolemy I, or for Egypt or for Greece, but for the human

race. Whatever the location or specification of a museum, it will partake of the Alexandrian spirit only insofar as it thinks of its work as undertaken on behalf of mankind, deeply and fundamentally searching for our common humanity.

(4) *The museum is political.* Museums, to make institutional life easier, or to avoid serious complications, often assert that they are "non-political"; curators may even imagine that they are being truer to the museum concept when they remove their work from "politics." Alexandria teaches us, on the contrary, that it is of the essence of the museum to *be* political—that it should be, in principle, a function of a body politic. Alexander housed his Museum within a complete city, of which it was an integral, organic part. It is true that his city was meant in turn to be part of a coherent political world, and that in literal terms, he failed to bring that about. Yet the Museum remained a political concept, belonging to its city, which in turn belonged to the world. Otherwise put, the Museum cannot stand alone, and not just because it needs economic support. More deeply, it is political because, in its *universality* is presupposed the common political member-ship of all humanity. As in the case of Alexander's failed political project, that universal polity may yet be unrealized in practice. The museum may well run ahead of the world in this: the museum may harbor the future world government. But if it were not presupposed in principle—if the members of the museum did not feel that they were by the same token members of the common body of mankind—universality would receive only lip-service. This is not romance or illusion; we are speaking of the realities on which the museum must be based, the soil from which it grows. Though we are still far from a political constitution for mankind, yet in a working sense, a functional spirit, every true museum today is a museum of the future and belongs deeply to a real polity still awaiting formal recogni-tion.

(5) *The museum is a place of collection.* As we conceived Euclid as a great collector, one who read many works in order to discover and compose the insight latent in them, the museum more generally provides a place of reflection in which the world can gather to collect its wits. In Alexandria, centuries after Euclid, the astronomer Ptolemy collected data and observa-tions and found in them a System of the World of a new order.[10] The museum's collecting function is easily misunderstood: it does not stop, as it often seems, with conservation, preservation, and display (though these functions of guardianship are important)—the essential meaning of the museum's collecting begins with the stage of interpretation in which the world's treasures begin a new life, revealing their meanings as they are read together, and a whole emerges which is a new revelation of the Muses.

(6) *The museum remembers.* As the Library in Alexandria was an inher-ent component of the Museum, and it must be so with any true museum. A museum cannot be a thing of the moment; it has a mission to tell a story, and thus to reach into the past and remember the elements which will compose the tale. In this sense, Homer is our model; the museum is a place in which the epic of our time is always being spun. The Greek chorus was

always alluding to a past too dark to name, and in the same way the museum reaches for the origin myth which society finds it difficult to confront. Having a library is, as we have seen, not at all a banking operation: we saw that it was more like gardening. The Museum, then, must have an organic library with which the Museum works in its effort to aid us in comprehending the work which the world is doing, and to hold in the balance of thought the future story which we with our lives are attempting to tell. It is unnecessary to remark how much more difficult, and at the same time more important, this responsibility is for the science museum, dealing as it does with the impetuous modern Muse and her siren-song of progress.

(7) *The museum makes music.* If the museum is to follow the ancients in devotion to the Muse, we need hardly add that its ultimate purpose will be to sing as Homer sang. As the song will have sacred and mystic origins, no one will be able to design the outcome. If the sense of the sacred is lively, then the Muse will choose the song. In other words, if the other principles have been attended to, wonderful things will emerge from the museum, and these will be of a sort which we could not design in advance and would not want to. We will recognize this "song" as a stirring within the body of the institution, a stirring which spreads with a thrill of recognition among all who enter its doors. The museum will take organic form as a living thing whose works unfold as insights no one could have specified in advance. Such is the mystery of the Muse, whose immanence is the mark of the true museum.

The history of the human race is written in the history of its song; Euclid's composition, built on elements as mystic as they are clear and strung by threads of insight, is not in the same form as the dances and verses of Aeschylus. But the differences are fewer than the unities. Today, the notes of quantum mechanics are strange, and yet for a while remain in the hands of a priesthood, but its compositions are a music nonetheless and sing of the cosmos in terms strikingly resonant of those of Ptolemy or the *Timaeus.* The Museum must be open to all such song, and must achieve interpretations of even the deepest and widest theories by which all will be able to hear, and share the thrill of comprehension.

(8) *The Muse is one.* We met in the *Phaedrus* the suggestion that there is finally just one Muse, enchanting us in many guises. The departmentalization of the Muses, as the Muse of this or that, is a convenience for the taxonomy of mythologies, but it is deeply misleading. This proposition is companion to that of universality, but appears more directly in our modern scene in the supposed departmentalization of knowledge and the fragmentation of both the university and the arts. I have urged that the members of the Museum must constitute one community; that Euclid be aware of the tragic forms in which irrationality is housed; that Ptolemy be moved by the deepest human reasons for studying astronomy. Every work of the museum, albeit the special responsibility of a few or only one of the members, will be of final interest to all, and will in some sense belong to, and be a work of, the whole.

Alexander's Museum is frequently referred to in texts as a "university," and in the root sense of the term, it was just that. But we have so utterly abandoned the meaning of the term, so lost the unity of our "universities," that the term today means the very opposite of its etymology. Our universities are fragmented, fissured assemblages of people and facilities: they are brought back together by contract, or by good intentions to do things in common, but we have lost the grounds of community. The museum today, by some mystery of rebirth, must defy the university and rediscover our human community. The museum today, just as it must be the world community of the future, must anticipate the university, not simply mirror it, and constitute itself the reunited university of the future.

These "principles" are by no means definitive, are offered merely as suggestions drawn from our ancient models, in the hope that they may serve as guides to reflection on the tangled experience of the science museum in the modern world, to which we turn now.

An early photograph of the Smithsonian Castle (left), located on the Mall in Washington, D.C.

The first Smithsonian

In 1835, a court in England processed a most unusual bequest, that of a certain James Smithson. By virtue of a slender thread of the deaths of other

potential beneficiaries, he had, to everyone's complete surprise, left to the United States of America a very sizable estate, to be used, he said, "for the increase and diffusion of knowledge among men."[11] The Congress of the United States for its part had great difficulty in deciding whether to accept such a benefaction from abroad, but in time it assented and the estate was reduced to a chest of gold sovereigns which was escorted to these shores.

This was a chest of pure potentiality, as no clue had been left for the gold's use beyond the cryptic formula of the will itself. A powerful voice throughout the long period of the ensuing Congressional debate was that of John Quincy Adams, who fought off a stream of pragmatic schemes which would have dissipated the funds, asserting his own historic sense of the importance of science to the growing nation. The ultimate decision of the Congress was to create the Smithsonian Institution, which came into being by an Act of Congress in 1846. That Act created an institution, with the President of the United States and all the cabinet as members, together with a Board of Regents to whom it was left to decide the appropriate use of the funds in accord with the terms of the bequest. The composition of this board, which has undergone only minor change to the present day, reflects the ambivalence of the new Institution itself—at once a public trust of the highest order, its membership to include the Chief Justice and the Vice-President of the United States, yet in its judgments and actions otherwise independent of the United States Government.[12] The first Regents, in turn, were much influenced by the firm convictions of the American scientist Joseph Henry, whom, after they had heard his views, they appointed to be the first Secretary of the Smithsonian.[13]

Some sense of Smithson's own intention, and his conception of the bequest, may be drawn from a review of the scant details we have of his life. Smithson, though born of aristocratic and wealthy parents, was an illegitimate son, and was thereby barred from a career in the church, political service, or the military. Much of his life was spent abroad, and though he graduated from Oxford he could have no position in the aristocracy, nor could he hope for any of the careers to which it was the key. Not surprisingly, he is known to have strongly distrusted the institution of monarchy. He turned to science in search of a path his shadowed status would allow him, his interests being mainly in chemical analysis and geology. He assisted, of all people, the recluse Henry Cavendish; he was early in life a member of the Royal Society, and later he became a founding member of the Royal Institution. It appears that in Paris he was acquainted with leading scientists of the French scene and came to share certain basic convictions of the Revolution, including the prospect of a rational and democratic future for all the members of mankind. His simple characterization of an institution "for the increase and diffusion of knowledge among men" incorporates exactly this conviction. And his making the donation to the United States "to found" this institution, similarly bespeaks a confidence that the future lay with the new experiment in democracy.[14] The notion of "diffusing" knowledge is more important than it may seem: the traditional, aristocratic British schools and colleges had nothing to do with "diffusing" knowledge, but, quite the contrary, confined it to strictly aristocratic channels. Thus the bequest in its aim to *increase* knowledge speaks to a confidence in the progress of mankind, and in its aim to *diffuse* this knowledge affirms faith in a new era of democracy. We sense that Smithson's bequest is deeply political in character.

In Henry's own interpretation of the bequest, formulated as a proposal to the Regents entitled "Plan for the Organization of the Smithsonian Institution," we see this political principle reflected. Like every great oracle, Smithson's bequest reveals the character of its interpreter.[15] Henry's proposal displays a decisive mind, capable of very political insight and strong convictions. The bequest is not a gift, he says, but a trust; it is not intended for national or local purposes. The United States has accepted this trust on behalf of mankind, and Henry's elaboration of means for "increase" and "diffusion" of knowledge is shaped throughout by that initial understanding. A corollary is that the Congress is not called upon to support the Smithsonian financially: the Institution will belong to mankind; its resources will consist of its own gold bars (albeit now recast as coin of the realm), and the interest thereon.

The previous decade of incoherent American debate had shown that any integrity of the institution, or fidelity to its purposes as defined as Henry had delineated them, would depend on the Institution's strict autonomy. The Institution was to *report* to the Congress, and the Congress, in its function as *trustee,* would insure fidelity to the founding Act, but the Smithsonian Institution would go forward, as an activity of mankind, according to the judgment of its own Board of Regents. This world-citizenship, reflected in the Institution's avoidance of designation as a "national" enterprise, has long since been lost, and Henry's insistence upon it now seems prophetic in view of the straits into which the Smithsonian has fallen in recent years, as we shall see.

As the composition of the Board of Regents suggests, the new Institution was accorded great respect. When after great delay the construction of a building was authorized, it was placed directly on the new Mall; presumably in order to announce its exceptional and timeless character, it was built in the form of a late 12th-century castle, and has been known as the "Castle" ever since. This was conceived as the residence of the Secretary, and the Henrys lived and entertained there until his death, in turn possibly suggesting a scientific counterpart to the political White House.

If all of this suggests some cryptic allusion to the Egyptian Alexandria, we might remember that the laying of the cornerstone was declared a public holiday, celebrated with a mile-long civic parade, with the President and his cabinet in formal attendance. Moreover, the cornerstone was laid by a Masonic Grand Master wearing an apron, like that of an Egyptian priest, which had been presented to George Washington by the Grand Lodge of France. It was worn, of course, not as a costume but as a badge of office appropriate to this civic ceremony.

A year later, at the end of the same Mall, the cornerstone of a new obelisk was laid in honor of the Father of his Country. Remembering this, I believe we are justified in thinking that, in its lofty and political conception, its universality as a trust for mankind, and in the strongly mystic allusions at its founding, there was an inner bond between the remarkable creation of the Smithsonian and certain of those principles we found exemplified in the Museum of Alexandria. Some Muse from the past was surely presiding at its inception.[16]

Henry's Plan for the Smithsonian Institution is notable, not only for what it proposes but for the many possible functions which it sheds. On the one hand his Plan is immensely ambitious—in addressing all mankind, but also in taking all knowledge as its province. Although "knowledge" is understood in terms of science, Henry's conception of the spectrum which this entails is arresting. The arts are politely dismissed, envisioning only the provision of an empty room in which other institutions might wish to mount exhibitions. In addition, Henry's delineation of the work of the Library limits it strictly to support of scientific work. Yet within the span of "science" we find a vast horizon, including both a "Physical Class" and a "Moral and Political Class." Although we know that Henry believed deeply in the value of pure science, as distinct from its applications, the first class includes "physic," "natural history, agriculture," and "application of science to arts." The second class ("Moral and Political") is even more Baconian in its inclusiveness, including "ethnology, statistics and political economy," "mental and moral philosophy," and "a survey of the political events of the world."

Henry's own most original and fundamental scientific contribution had been in the investigation of electrical induction and the discovery of self-induction, which he shared with Michael Faraday, though only Faraday is normally credited. But he had had wide experience in other fields, stemming in part from early participation in an exploratory expedition surveying the course for a road across the state from West Point to Lake Erie, and his own interests were wide-ranging. The fact that the new institution was not national did not make it the less American, in taking the new continent as its field of investigation. Henry conceived exploration of this new continent as an investigation on behalf of mankind, just as Smithson must have

understood the American polity to be an experiment in democracy on behalf of the world.

Thus, to look ahead, we will not be surprised to find one of the most appropriate and representative of Henry's ideas to be the investigation of the weather over the American continent: a corps of observers would be established, ultimately ranging from Canada to Mexico, to gather information which would serve as data for the new science of meteorology. This project would introduce the first daily weather maps, bringing crucial advice to farmers. In time, this task was shifted from the Smithsonian to the Weather Bureau, a distinct entity of the United States government, leaving the Smithsonian free to break new ground in other areas.[17]

In the same spirit, the Smithsonian would early embark on the investigation of the mound cultures of the Mississippi—to penetrate the mystery of these obscure human ancestors—while in the category of ethnology the Smithsonian would embark on what would become a massive series of studies of the peoples of this new world. However misconceived, we know that what became the work of the Bureau of Ethnology (still under the Smithsonian) gathered immense bodies of information on cultures which were perceived as rapidly being "lost," together with corresponding studies of the philology of their languages. Some of the work for which the Smithsonian has been best known over the years has been in the area of objective recording and study of these people, recorded as specimens of humanity.[18]

There must be some inner connection between this notion of the scientific study of peoples, and the genocidal operations which were simultaneously underway. How far back, how deep down, does this syndrome of yoked enterprises run: objectively knowing, and viciously destroying? The ethnologists had nothing to do, we might suppose, with the destruction of the peoples they had undertaken to study: quite the contrary, they lived closely with them, and imagined themselves to care for them. The venom must lie with this new principle of *objectivity:* just as the rest of nature is taken as *object,* for systematic ordering, so these peoples were being addressed as taxonomic problems. How far back, indeed, and how far forward, does this problem run? We will meet it again, in various ominous forms.

In many ways, we can find impressive likenesses between Alexander's project and Henry's. Each is political, in the broadest sense of addressing mankind as a whole, and looking to a new, more rational and unified human community. Each is wide-ranging, taking all learning as its scope. Each is the work of an institution created specifically to grant freedom and opportunity to a few who will exercise it on behalf of all, and each in its own way emphasizes widespread diffusion of the result. The difference, it seems to me, marks the watershed between ancient learning and the way in which modern science understands itself. Learning in Alexandria, however it involved observation, came ultimately from within: it was the work, finally and primarily, of thinking *mind,* only aided by observation. The Smithsonian, belonging to a new era, is assembling observations, gathering and dispersing information, but it is not primarily truth-producing. Knowl-

(Left) Visitors in the Lower Main Hall of the Smithsonian Institution Building, 1867.

edge is thought to have become objective, with mind, now merely analytic and logical, playing a noble but secondary role.

There is a more interesting Muse at work, but not in Washington. This Muse presides over the entire West, among the explorers and observers, comprehending a domain of new discovery in which excitement runs high and new findings are everywhere. In its time, Alexandria was the center of its world; Washington in this new prospect merely floats on the civilized tide. Perhaps we should imagine the Museum turned inside-out, and the soul as well. Mind was once, as in Alexandria, the generative center; now energy has shifted to the observing senses, ranging the theater of the world, endlessly recording the peoples it finds and detailing their cultures, as if it were enough for science to observe precisely and analyze, and thereby conclude that it gathered truth.

There remains, however, some sense in which, though such analysis fills volumes, human truth remains invisible in it. James Smithson, we are told, liked to do chemical analyses of the petals of flowers, to learn about their colors. There is a lovely myth that Smithson once analyzed a lady's tear: he was able to catch only half the drop, but it was enough, he soon knew the repertory of salts which it contained. And what was the source of that demi-tear? Was the lady much consoled, we wonder, to have a consort able to explicate exactly the elements in her tear? Truth does not quite lie, it would seem, in the direction of such objectivity.[19]

III. The museum as cabinet of collections
Natural History and the great collections

Joseph Henry, as we have seen, had fended off to the best of his ability the role of collector which was being thrust upon the Smithsonian from all sides. The Patent Office was acquiring a growing collection of inventor's models, and a succession of exploring expeditions was bringing back samples from the far reaches of the new-found West, in unmanageable quantities. Not only was the storage and exhibiting of this aggregation outside the central concept of the Institution's function—it was not, in Henry's view, conceived as a *national* institution, or a museum in the limited sense of a showplace of exhibits—but to take on this role would require a new order of funding, beyond the resources of the Smithson endowment. Henry prized the autonomy of the institution; he wanted to "mingle its operations as little as possible with those of the general government," recognizing, prophetically, that to do so would:

> . . . annually bring the Institution before Congress as a supplicant for government patronage, and ultimately subject it to political influence and control.[20]

The design for the new building, however, contained provision for an exhibit hall which had to be utilized, and Henry brought in for the purpose

The Great
White Heron,
*painted by
John James
Audubon,
1785–1851.*

an assistant with special responsibility for dealing with the collecting and exhibiting function. This was Spencer F. Baird, later to succeed Henry as Secretary of the Smithsonian. Baird brought with him a passion for Nature, and for collecting the productions of Nature, and with his arrival an altogether different phase of the Smithsonian's history began to unfold. Henry in his own work had been doing what we would call "physics" and think of as pure science, experimenting with electricity and magnetism. Baird had by contrast grown up under the spell of the naturalists, Audobon, Titian Ramsey Peale, and John Toerry: as a youth, he had been awed by a portfolio of Audobon's illustrations of birds. He had corresponded with Louis Agassiz at Harvard on the subject of fish, and he had come to Henry with a recommendation from James Dwight Dana at Yale. He brought with him to the Smithsonian a love of Natural History, and he set the Smithsonian on the track of becoming the nation's Natural History museum. It would yield up the autonomy Henry had thought essential, to become in effect the partner and counselor to the government in searching out the resources of the world which was opening up. Without sacrificing fidelity to most of Henry's original convictions, the concept of the science museum was shifting in fundamental ways.[21]

We live in an era in which the great museums of "natural history" are less prized, their carefully organized and labeled cabinets of specimens, their dioramas of creatures in the wild, now spurned and rejected. The very halls of the dinosaurs themselves, which seized the imaginations of so many generations, prove less moving to viewers accustomed to the more literal excitements of ever-new orders of computerized photorealism. Museum professionals and the public alike tend to make this judgment. The director of one of Europe's classic natural history museums, closed for dismemberment at the time he wrote these words, says that they have been left behind by history:

. . . natural history museums . . . did not adapt themselves to the conceptual evolution that accompanied the birth of biology and because of this they became anachronistic institutions. Their exhibitions maintained, and in some cases still do, a poetic and aesthetic view which reflects a way of studying nature that ceased to exist over a century ago.[22]

The Paleontology Hall in the National Museum of Natural History, c. 1932. The exhibit was then known as the "Hall of Extinct Monsters."

The writer of those words was committed to a large-scale replacement of his natural history museum by something of another sort, directed to "concepts" and the imparting of information, a project for which the specimens would no longer be needed.

We, on the other hand, will be interested to know what the natural history museum was in its period of full flourishing, and if we can, to recapture something of the "poetic and aesthetic" view which it is assumed that history has closed to us. The beginning, I think, is in a love which is said to have been lost: Baird, and the natural historians who followed him, loved nature. They prized and cared for the wild things they collected; they

stuffed them only as a way of exhibiting Nature in her plenitude to those who could not join in the trips they themselves were constantly making into the wilderness, or upon the oceans. They formed great study collections, and above all they classified what they and thousands of others brought back. But it would be a mistake to imagine that they preferred the classification scheme, the specimens in their cabinets, to the thing itself. Today, we find only their cabinets, to us perhaps desiccated or boring; but they rejoiced in the life reflected in these same collections. We implied earlier that the Muse deserted Washington for the field and the explorations; perhaps now we should recognize that in this full blossoming of the spirit of natural philosophy, the Muse returned to claim the Castle which had been built for her.

As our critic has pointed out, these scientists of an earlier age were not focusing on questions of physiology, of underlying chemistry or causality; their immense research effort took the form of identifying and classifying what their eyes were seeing. The collections were indeed research tools, but for the purpose of comprehending precisely, by types and clues, what the scope of Nature was proving to include. The resulting scholarship took the form of great, handsome, publications, whether compendia such as Baird's *Mammals of North America* (1859) and *Birds of North America* (1860), or intricate series: the findings of the Wilkes United States Exploring Expedition, which returned from a round-the-world cruise in 1842, were published in a series of twenty volumes, the last of which was not completed until 1876. Enthusiasm for this work was infectious, not least of course for the adventuring involved: Baird gathered his own lyceum, the "Bairdians," some of whom lived for years in the towers of the Castle building when they were not on the trail or on the high seas.[23] There was, it is true, an admixture of sheer competition in the aggregation of these collections. At its best, however, it was indeed as if the very Muse of the Lyceum had returned, to induce once again the ancient admiration of the organism in its wholeness, so lost, and so dreadfully needed, in our own day. Critics who fault these careful observers for their innocent admiration of the appearances of things, and for failing to put Nature to the Baconian torture, are right in perceiving a return to Aristotle, though perhaps quite wrong in faulting it.

Baird came to the Smithsonian in 1850, when the Gold Rush was lending new fervor to the sweep of expeditions to the West. Baird was soon becoming de facto an adviser to the government in the matter of expeditions, counseling on the design of instruments, the plan of observations to be taken, even training scientific members of the expeditions, and then, in the end, absorbing the findings into the Museum's collections and publishing the outcome. In the case of an Alaska expedition, the specimens included copper and gold, and the Institution's testimony was influential in tilting the decision toward William H. Seward's purchase of Alaska. In an age of inventorying a continent, the Smithsonian was proving of service close to the seats of power, and it became feasible for a later Secretary to extract funds from Congress for the construction of a Natural History building. It would take the form of a Grecian temple of Nature with its great rotunda; it would hold generations to come in awe of its dinosaurs, its great, stuffed elephants, and the whale.[24]

The Smithsonian was now walking a precarious ridge line between Smithson's intention of service to humanity, and partisan service to the government of the United States, though for Baird and the Secretaries who followed him, the easy identification of the two may have felt it so natural that it would trouble them very little. They were all, I believe, devout

A taxidermist works on the model of the giant whale at the National Museum of Natural History, c. 1950s.

Christians of one stripe or another, and shared a sense that they were dealing with divine work. The last of this series, Charles D. Walcott,[25] was a prominent geologist; he became a strong defender of Darwin but retained the belief that divine guidance was at work in evolution as well. Science was still conceived as natural philosophy, a body of learning in which one man could become competent and progress. Successive Secretaries were all scholars, each specializing in a special field of interest—ichthyology, ornithology, geology—but each was prepared to address all aspects of the collection as a member of one "natural history" community. In this sense, the tradition of universality we found in Alexandria could be seen to remain intact.

One way to deal with a mystery at second-hand is by way of the words of a witness, so let me testify: I have felt the Muse of natural history, and not so long ago at that. As of this writing, they have not yet got around to destroying the classic collection at the American Museum of Natural History in New York City.[26] I recently visited two galleries at that museum, entering first one of the classic halls, and then deliberately selecting one of the most modern. The older, classic space was the Hall of African Mammals: a broad, darkened hall circling past a sequence of great, luminous glass cases, deep within each one of which stood an animal group, caught in some critical moment of its day. We stand with a pride of lions on a height; they, but now we as well, are looking keenly into the valley below, where a herd of zebras can be made out, grazing. All eyes—theirs, and ours too—are riveted. It is the very point of attack. Yes, the distant scene is quite evidently painted, albeit expertly, on canvas; indeed, the animals are products of the taxidermist's skill, though this is evidently a high art. Lend just a grain of credence, and the experience becomes gripping.

Would a film be better? A television crew zooms readily to real zebras, nature programs in an undying stream permit us to watch as "real" lions leap, and "real" blood runs. Is the "real" thing, seen while eating popcorn in the living room, better? Or, if we lend that credence which the modern world disdains, have we not caught in these dioramas the *virtue,* the life, of those fellow-creatures at the moment which Galen, with a physician's sensibility, calls the *crisis*—and thereby caught the act itself?[27] The act must be ours—high-technology cannot *give* it to us, because we are not speaking of a donation. Old toys had it, unpainted maple buses or simple dolls with faces to be supplied by the imagination: a child provided that, in the "play" of a less literal era. In the same way, the natural history museum invoked the Muse, and the Muse in turn inspired the imagination; the experience was one of presence, wonder, delight, and deep respect.

As I watched, the silence of the little-frequented hall was broken by the arrival of a class of high-school students: full of energy and highly motivated by materials they had firmly in hand. It was a kind of race, a competition quite literally to check off information. In the full spirit of a competitive age, they made short work of their task, full of excited conversation and noticing, *lending,* nothing. Only a loser might have fallen behind, to look.

The modern hall, by contrast, is the latest word in deconstruction. Here old dinosaur displays are disassembled, stripped of tiresome vestiges of mythology; as misguided constructions are taken apart, the principles are intelligently explained by which science now corrects such errors of the past. Put back together, the once-awesome creatures have become instead mechanical constructions of the information age. It is not that the old constructions were not corrected from time to time, but such improvements took us closer to what we could grasp of the ancient living creature. Now, the deconstruction has become the point. The spell has been broken; the exhibit will come apart and be readjusted routinely, as new evidence comes in. For the jaded children, a racy time-lapse sequence on a computer screen suggests how readily these things come together and fall apart.

The Director we spoke of earlier, complaining that people find science boring, planned to replace his banished exhibits with what are called today "conceptual" displays, arranged by media experts and implemented by tested theme-park marketing techniques. Everyone was to get a measured dose of "information," together with a reward of "entertainment." The project must by now have been opened; it was indeed professionally guaranteed to be a success in the terms in which it was conceived. Yet we must wonder if the fickle Muses have remained with it or elected to live in groves more reminiscent of their ancient homes.

The nostalgia of which I am unabashedly guilty will get us nowhere: one cannot live in an era which no longer exists, and it would be poor strategy to make the attempt. Yet we need to inquire earnestly about the presence of the Muse, without whom we have exhibits and visitors, but no museum. Is Nature *something,* or has it been only an illusion? If one who lingers feels something strongly in the presence of the old tableaus, and responds with a

(Left) A view of the Brontosaur Hall at the National Museum of Natural History, 1953.

surge of desire, to speak or write or dance, or scream—is that not evidence of the presence of *something?* We may yet feel this in the wilderness, on a mountain peak, on a quiet night in the backyard if the stars are exceptionally brilliant, or there are northern lights. That wholeness, and the sense of the sacred place—the sense the tableaus conveyed of an alert organism, more than the sum of its parts—which belonged to the early *museion* may still be invoked today; the evidences are everywhere. Museum displays cannot be blindly carried over from the past, but the wisdom of the past need not be abandoned in the designs of the future. An excess of deconstruction wantonly banishes the Muse and leaves us with an enterprise which, however successful, is no museum at all. This is evidently a thought to which we must return.[28]

IV. The didactic museum
The Deutsches Museum

The Smithsonian collection of arts and industries emerged as something of a jumble; like the Science Museum in London, it arose to a large extent as a receptacle of objects left over from great exhibitions, together with a variety of inherited items. No one plan gave rise to it, or impressed any single conceptual form. The case was very different with a museum which came into being a little later, the Deutsches Museum in Munich, first proposed in 1903.[29] Though similarly a product of the industrial revolution, it was the brainchild of one powerful figure, Oskar von Miller, a German electrical engineer whose own field had been the important technology of long-distance power transmission. Germany had been formed into a single nation during his lifetime, and there was a strong impulse to give expression to the new national consciousness through the exhibition of those sciences and industries which were distinctively German accomplishments. Mechanical and civil engineering, with the development of the steam engine and the railroads, belonged to England, but in the natural sciences, and in certain other industries, electrical and chemical, Germany had taken a lead. Von Miller's concept, accordingly, was of a museum which would feature the "masterworks" of German engineering, together with supporting exhibits which would make clear the developments of which they formed a part and the scientific principles on which they were based.

This identification of the Deutsches Museum with German industry was important, not only in the design of the exhibits, but in the support which they received. Individual industries took responsibility for their corresponding halls, funding and maintaining them on a regular basis and contributing new equipment for exhibits. Emphasis was placed throughout on engineering as such, and from the beginning the museum had the special support of engineering societies, which were, during this same period, actively concerned to establish the dignity of the profession of engineering among the academic professions, and not incidentally, to woo engineers away from any potentially disruptive association with unionizing labor.

The exhibits were of a very high quality; many of the machines on display were in working order and provided with electric motors which made it possible to see them spring into action. Exhibits were typically actuated with push-buttons, anticipating the interactive exhibits of the future. It was a highly disciplined museum in the sense that its original charter was clear, the purpose of each exhibit was well-defined and the planning, organization, and funding of the whole

Visitors to the Deutsches Museum in Munich, Germany, examine experiments of "air-reduced rooms."

were achieved through the genius of a single personality. It depended on an interesting mix of private and public support—materials for construction of its building, which was not able to open until after World War I, in 1925, were contributed, and transported without charge by the German railroads. It had early taken this character as an organically *civic* museum, thoroughly identified from the beginning with capitalist industry as well as the engineering societies. This at the same time defined its excellence, and placed an unquestioned boundary around its role. It celebrated industry and engineering in a masterful, intelligent, and unquestioning composition of displays.

The Deutsches Museum became a recognized paradigm of the fully-achieved science and industry museum. The halls were clear and clean, shining with the beauty of the machines which fascinated the eye and delighted the mind with their balanced and intelligible motions. If a science museum is in some special way a sacred grove, a place of reflection apart from the affairs of the city, the Deutsches Museum presented itself as such a grove, a place of dignity, awe, and wonder. It placed triumphs which had already entered history in an orderly, progressive series, and became in turn the paradigm of such arrangement, by which technological history may be presented as an intelligible developmental order.

The difficulty is, of course, that such a series is linear and single-minded—exactly, indeed, the intention of the Deutsches Museum. The message of such an exhibit can be clear, proud, and unambiguous: that of orderly progress through science and engineering. Lifting this principle to the highest plane, it confirmed as an ideal a dogma which becomes the more dangerous as it is the more difficult to question. For this is authoritarian history, an engineer's vision of the role of his industry. It is a comedy of never-ending advancement in a world in which truth demands that the tragic face of this same vision be acknowledged. If the tragedy had not become overwhelming in the first World War, it was certainly destined to become so for the entire world in World War II and its aftermath. The world is dangerously unsafe in the hands of such authoritarian, unquestioning history. In a very telling remark, one author points out the connection this conforming history was to have with National Socialism:

> The [Deutsches Museum's] dependence on industrial money also brought serious disadvantages, especially in the matter of setting industry and technology within their social context. Any suggestion that capitalism might not always work for the common good or that industrial relations in Germany had ever been other than faultless would not have been tolerated by the paymasters on whom the Museum depended, a consideration which became even more important as the National Socialist Party increased its control over the life of Germany. Under these circumstances, the temptation to concentrate on 'pure' technology and to disregard the social implications of technical change were very great.[30]

There must be some warning of more general importance here, for such single-minded and disciplined thinking is of the sort which brought its practitioners before the courts of human justice: it is not humanly permissible to follow single lines of thought without larger and critical explorations, having always to do with justice and human welfare. Machines are not built, and do not function, in sterile isolation from human origins and human applications. In fact, as we shall need to discuss later, technology does not in truth *have* such a linear history: the one-dimensional line of progress is an artifact of the historian too little questioning of the story he is telling. Von Miller began with a strong conviction about the story which his museum *ought* to tell, a story which would celebrate and strengthen the new Reich. It may have done its work all too well. But there is no longer anything specifically German about this paradigm: understandably, it remains a tempting recourse everywhere for museums of science and technology pretending to an "apolitical" stance, or avoiding consideration of the moral implications of their exhibits. The temptation to embrace this simplification is virtually universal; what appears at first a fascinating, sacred grove of "pure" technology all too easily becomes a craven retreat from the full light of human reality, and no true dwelling place for the Muses.

One might well respond that the museum of science and technology is not meant to do *everything,* or to house all thoughts. That might be true if critical thoughts about technology were lively elsewhere. The trouble is that such museums are designed to teach us things that *seem* to be everything but aren't; these are the places we go—and often take great pains to make sure our children go—to meet the world that science and technology create. But this leaves out the question we ought to be asking about what sort of world that is. The Muses do not factor in this way: one cannot think thoughts of one sort about technology on Mondays and Wednesdays, and

The Deutsches Museum "celebrated industry and engineering in a masterful, intelligent, and unquestioning composition of displays."

thoughts of another sort on Tuesdays and Thursdays. These museums are stimulating places, and our thoughts, and those of our children, should race, and do race, while we are under their spell. But the kind of spell they cast, the story they tell, is of the highest importance, and it is not to be left to the engineers to design for us according to a selective vision of progress. We can prize and delight in the classical exhibits of the Deutsches Museum, and in the technologies they presented; we do; but it is the Muses themselves who whisper to us not to let such exhibits, or such technologies, stand alone.

V. The diaspora

The Smithsonian was taking shape at a time when the concept and the practice of science were undergoing immense transformations, driven in the end by the forces of the Industrial Revolution. On the one hand, an upheaval within science was shifting its world from one of natural philosophy, in which science was still to be thought of as a connected whole in which one could hope to be interested and even proficient, into the specialized areas of competence which are the hallmark of our modern academic world. The appearance of specialized graduate schools within academia sealed this separation and at the same time provided a new domain of advanced study in which research could be pursued. Concurrently the modern corporation, another product of the same history movement, was aggregating resources which made possible the great corporate research laboratories of the modern world. Scientific societies proliferated to occupy and certify the new niches appearing in the academic world. Almost at the same time as the Smithsonian Institution, and similarly under the leadership of Joseph Henry, the American Association for the Advancement of Science, late-coming counterpart to the British Association, brought scientists of this new era together in a semblance of the old fellowship. But in the end we must wonder whether the concept of community within the sciences remains sustainable.[31]

All this was in the domain of research and the "expansion" of knowledge. In the field of "diffusion" the phenomena were equally overwhelming: new technologies of printing and mailing made it possible to publish magazines such as *Scientific American* and the *National Geographic*, which served in effect as museums-in-print. Systematic public education, with some rudimentary attention to mathematics and the sciences, became a feeble approximation to the channel of democratic diffusion of knowledge Smithson probably intended. Radio and now television complete this outpouring onto a scattered flood-place of "diffusion," often of little depth, admittedly, but in extent beyond any measuring.

These are all functions which were once embraced in the simple concept of the "museum"—as in the Academy, the Lyceum, the Museum of Alexandria, or even the early Smithsonian. Within the contemporary scene, we may tend to think of the science museum as just one more in a vast range of alternative modes of diffusion, blurred utterly by the modern sophistic of commercial advertising and the "media" industry in general. Within this *diaspora* of what is carelessly termed "information" does the museum have no longer any special role, is it charged with no special responsibility? Might we not argue that the case is precisely the opposite: with the diaspora, the problem of collecting our human wits becomes ever more pressing? Is there not a new urgency to draw upon the long tradition of the museum to bring together the parts of this shattered intelligence into some sort of larger comprehension? Separate readings, specialized conversations, will not do this trick: we need to assemble in that one special forum, the museum—still the sacred grove, still awesome and universal—to revive a larger human conversation in which we may regain some sense of wisdom, some comprehension of what we are doing, and why. By way of only a few, perhaps rather random samples, we will see now some forms this effort has been taking in more recent times.

VI. The new era
Frank Oppenheimer and the Exploratorium

With the launching of the Exploratorium in San Francisco in 1968, something new came into the world of science museums, a fresh vision which has offered an alternative approach to the science museum throughout much of the world. It was very much the product of the vision of one man, Frank Oppenheimer, who in the aftermath of World War II was seriously concerned about the place of the sciences in a democratic society.[32]

The hallmark of the Exploratorium is the interactive exhibit, centering on the visitor's involvement and sense of discovery. Oppenheimer's ambitions for the Exploratorium are revealed in the several levels of the criteria he spelled out by which prospective exhibits were to be judged:

> They must give the viewer the opportunity to react with them and to explore and manipulate them. They must be of value to a broad spectrum of visitors, including young and old, professional and lay, and to people who have lived in both barren and enriched environments. The individual exhibits as well as the Exploratorium as a whole must be of value at a variety of levels which range from relatively superficial sightseeing through a broad and deep understanding. The exhibit material must provide a multiplicity of interlocking threads and pathways which visitors can select.[33]

Ambitious and unrealistic as these goals might seem, Oppenheimer, with an extremely resourceful staff of designers and craftsmen, contrived a museum whose exhibits met them exceedingly well. In part by publishing their designs in detail in "cookbook" fashion, the Exploratorium has exercised a wide and stimulating influence on museums in this new mode throughout the world. The democratic and unifying spirit in this vision—in stark contrast to the rigidity of the Deutsches Museum—is political in the best sense of that term. Going often to intuitive phenomena, simple and perceptually surprising, Oppenheimer circumvented the traps of technology and was able to construct a common meeting ground for naive visitors and scientists alike. This sense of wholeness, both in so-

At the Exploratorium, a young girl plays with the Bernoulli Ball. The ball is kept aloft and centered in the air current by strong forces of air pressure.

ciety and in the body of the sciences, may hark back to the universality we identified in Alexandria; at times it becomes for Oppenheimer an invocation of the unifying concept of "nature," once so prized but now, as we have seen, often forgotten in new trends in museums:

The Exploratorium is about nature, and one of the accomplishments of science has been to demonstrate that there is a unity to the diversity of nature. . . . It is hoped that the visitors to the Exploratorium sense this connectedness.[34]

We may almost recognize an invocation of the Muse in Oppenheimer's suggestion that there is art involved in this process of composition:

A museum can resemble a musical composition, a symphony in which, even though the listeners may not be aware of the structure of the piece, they must sense that it exists because the composer was disciplined in his efforts to achieve the coherence of his composition. Museums, at their best, require their creators to be guided by a similar kind of discipline.[35]

We may see in the Exploratorium one approach to an answer to the problem of the diaspora. Where wholeness can no longer be achieved in

Artist Peter Richards created the Wave Organ for the Exploratorium. The acoustic sculpture is activated by waves.

terms of a comprehension of the whole of science, another form of composition takes its place. If we cannot aspire to a whole in common, each person can aspire to an individual composition, can assemble things in a personal and special way. Similarly, the museum is no longer a coherent display of the body of science, but an arrangement of options among which the visitor can design a personal route. Terms and themes run through, and if there is no community of knowledge, there is in this one great hall a bond of common experience, for we are all in the same position; the scientists themselves are, in their way, in the same condition, for they can no more master their separate fields than we.

The Exploratorium, then, symbolizes the new world of dispersed knowing, and may be the mode in which the Muses (themselves no doubt as baffled as we) summon our spirits to deal with it. It does not address directly the social issues we said earlier that no science museum could afford to neglect; yet it is, on the other hand, specifically intended to empower the citizen to come into dialogue with the scientists. It may thus be, indirectly, the very basis on which the responsible democratic criticism of science must rest.

The visitor's experience may be organized around any one of perhaps uncountable "mini-curricula" which weave exhibits in respect of various themes or scientific principles. But simple sightseeing is equally appropriate. Without, I presume, entertaining any such intention, Oppenheimer seems to invoke the image of the sacred grove, saying of his Exploratorium:

> It is a place for sightseeing, a woods of natural phenomena through which to wander. Sightseeing is more than just pleasurable; it can build the experiences and the intuitions on which other opportunities for learning rely; it can arouse curiosity and, in a broad sense, it can help people determine where they are going and where they want to make their home.[36]

This sense of the aesthetic composition goes beyond the role it plays in the design of the exhibits and their arrangement in the museum, for an explicit invocation of the arts is a parallel and co-equal partner of exhibit design. Artists-in-residence are commissioned to come and work at the Exploratorium where, in close collaboration with the staff, they shape pieces which approach the phenomena of nature from a very different point of view:

> Art is not included just to make things pretty, . . . but primarily because artists make different kinds of discoveries about nature than do physicists or biologists. . . . both artists and scientists help us notice and appreciate things in nature that we had learned to ignore or had never been taught to see. Both art and sciences are needed to fully understand nature and its effects on people.[37]

We sense, again, a breathtaking liberation springing from the spaciousness and generosity of Oppenheimer's vision, breaking the spell of the linear dogmatic or historic exhibits which in an earlier era seemed so inevitable.

One of these commissioned works, the "Sun Painting," well illustrates the way in which the same principles exhibited in the "scientific" experiments appear in different guise, incorporated in works of art. Here, prismatic colors extracted from a sunbeam coming through the roof are arranged to paint ever-changing patterns on a great screen. This confirms our intuitive sense of the beauty of the rainbow; it gives us occasion to contemplate and dwell on this beauty. People will return to the Sun Painting to watch this vibrant pattern, much as we are drawn to gaze at the patterns in a flowing stream. Oppenheimer says that a science museum is a composition, like a symphony. The resulting music, the whole composition, is the central objective of the enterprise. In this easy converse with the Muse, which seemed to come so naturally to Oppenheimer, he not only opens new paths to our wonder and contemplation; he is questioning the limitations of our concept of "science."

It would be difficult to summarize the nature of the exhibits themselves, for they take a great many different forms. Reflecting on what makes a good Exploratorium exhibit work, Oppenheimer likened it at one point to a drama: there is curiosity, or fascination, which builds *tension;* and then, some resolution in which this tension is resolved.

> In some ways, an exhibit resembles a play or a musical composition. A tension is built up by something in the exhibit that elicits curiosity, or an interesting task or a lovely effect, then the tension is resolved as the result of an aesthetic or intellectual payoff.[38]

We recognize here the insight of Aristotle, that all learning begins with *wonder,* just as a plot proposes a problem which must be solved dramatically, or a musical composition develops tone relationships which require resolution. Psychologically, it is Gestalt theory which best reflects this sense of the tension of the unsolved problem, and the release in the "Aha!" But Oppenheimer's principles are those of poetics as well, the very arena of the Muses, and at the same time the foundations of teaching and learning. It was better understood in Athens than it is today how these insights belong together, in a single invocation of the liberating power of the Muse. Though he eschewed the term, Oppenheimer's insight into the true concept of the museum goes far toward incorporating the insights we have gathered in the course of this essay.

Oppenheimer was sensitive to nuances of appropriate and inappropriate means to achieve these ends. We may leave this section with a warning too little observed in our contemporary scene, where concepts of marketing and competition are rapidly eroding the spirit of our museums, thereby defeating their purpose:

> The creation of tension should not involve flamboyance or the high-signal strength of traditional advertising. It should be a quiet affair. . .[39]

Many a science center today, incorporating a projection-dome theater and measuring its drawing power against the theme parks of our time, would do well to reflect on this prophetic observation.

The Experiment Gallery of the Science Museum of Minnesota

Many of the exhibits at the Exploratorium engage the visitor in investigations, an exploratory thought-process closely involved with the apparatus. But they do not normally support what we might call true *experimenting,* in which the visitor might alter the components of an exhibit with real freedom, forming hypotheses and putting them to the test along lines of thought which are entirely personal. Perhaps only with such fully subjective intervention could the visitor fully come into relation to science, in the way in which the Exploratorium itself intends. With the commitment to an experimental idea—a hypothesis—and with the real possibility of failure and hope of recovery with a revised hypothesis, the visitor might come close to whatever is meant by the term, "the experimental method." Such an exhibit would be very nearly impossible to design, however, as it must at the same time be interesting, highly versatile, altogether harmless, and reliably unbreakable!

The design of such exhibits has been an ongoing project at the Experiment Gallery at the Science Museum of Minnesota, and it may be interesting to look at just one product of that effort, a visitor-friendly experimental apparatus which works very much as we might wish. It consists of a large set of modular circuit elements which can be connected very freely in any way one wishes; there is a power supply which meets the criteria of "harmless and unbreakable." The modules, each containing just one circuit element, are provided with paired magnets at each end which permit any circuit element to be connected to any other simply by contact—they stick magnetically, in a way which is secure and aesthetically pleasing: here is a circuit unencumbered with wires and hence satisfyingly clear to the mind's eye. The circuit elements range from a solid length of connecting wire or simple light-bulbs to diodes, light-emitting diodes, a motor, and a voltmeter and ammeter. Every component is elegantly mounted on a uniform base and plainly labeled, so there is an open invitation to a mix of thought and experimental play.

Clumsy accounts of scientific method in terms of "making hypotheses" and "refuting" them quickly dissipate here in the experience of actually experimenting—in that middle-ground of ideas which are tested before they are quite formed, of things which are tried in the absence of any distinct forethought (hypotheses which *follow* the experiment)—all under the guidance of half-shaped mythologies such as that of the "circuit" itself. Unpracticed visitors may make tentative arrangements which seem at first like circuits, but must be rethought and reshaped before they will consent to carry currrents, while more demanding distinctions such as that between "series" and "parallel" circuits emerge dramatically out of mists of initial uncertainty. It is much better if friends work together, for then the conversation fetches out insights and the embarrassing stupidities which are the order of the day, in ways which are dramatic and, simply, fun. We speak of this where, in the context of the vicissitudes of experimenting, it is especially appropriate, but we might well have spoken of it in other contexts as well. Wherever thought is meeting challenges, as in science museums generally, it is often best if two people meet them together, for the proposals, perplexities, and answers of conversation—which Socrates calls *dialectic*—are the medium of the mind's most productive life. Thought proceeds by way of challenge and response; here in the context of the Experiment Gallery, it is two working together, helping to make one another's thinking explicit, who are likeliest to experience true scientific "experimenting."

One of the many "hands-on" experiments at the Experiment Gallery at the Science Museum of Minnesota.

I have been describing an experiment in the Experiment Gallery at the Science Museum of Minnesota, where there are many other experiments as well. It is a very musical space, in which the spirit of inquiry is in some way "in the air." In its old form, in which I knew it, it was a bit dark; there was a gazebo in the center in which the sound of birds could inexplicably be heard. Many of the experiments are beautiful: water waves, sand waves, sound waves, brilliant mathematical tiling patterns on a computer screen involving geometrical problems of a very unfamiliar sort. Here, I am confident, is the very garden of the modern Muse. When two people, sharing any one of these experiences, burst forth in a simultaneous, hard-won mutual insight, it is perfectly evident that the Muse has full control of the situation.

Young people who perhaps ought to do other things with their lives could easily be seduced into becoming scientists here. But the Muse we meet is really less specific. This "experimenting" escapes the bounds we attempt to place around the sciences; one could as well experiment with the plot of a story, the development of the theme in a sonata, alternative modes of communication with one's children, or the control of global warming. We cannot package this mode of thought; where does it begin or end? From the "circuits" experiment, one might take away not so much an insight into the laws of physics, as a new and abiding metaphor. This would satisfy the goals of a science museum as well, if not better.

It is only when the sciences are not lively—as in the most conventional museum displays—that they package well. Once the exhibits spring to life, minds begin to click and the intended fences do not hold. The Muses, we have suspected from the beginning, are finally *one*. This, not the orderly packaging, is the true strength of the Museum as the sacred grove. With conversation and far-ranging thought, the Museum can take giant steps toward reassembling the fractured world. "Science" only pretends to be a defined and limiting discipline; it is really simply a new mode of entry into the full range of human critical thought.

The National Museum of American History

A fundamental and lasting transformation has taken place, during the period since World War II, in our approach to the study of history. Rather than the formal narration of what was traditionally thought of—and is still often referred to—as the "facts" of history, a new approach looks more deeply into the social origins and implications of the developments which make up the formal account. It sometimes takes the form of history "from the bottom up" as it views events from the point of view of the people involved and their interests and practices, rather than recording simply the names of the commanding figures and the "historic" events. The word "culture" figures largely in descriptions of the new approach, often characterized as "cultural history."[40] It is on the whole a welcome development, as it entails an effort to tell the whole story, or to admit that there may be many stories, rather than to supply a single convenient, skeletal, and selective framework. The deep connection between our universities and our museums is evidenced, hearteningly, by the fact that this movement within academia has had its consequences for the museums as well. Once again, it will be helpful to look at this in terms of our Smithsonian Institution as an example, for there, its effects have been dramatic and especially disturbing. It may be well to remind ourselves that, for American readers, events at the Smithsonian are inevitably of special interest, since as a public trust within our democracy, the Smithsonian not only serves, but is the personal responsibility of every voting citizen.

A new component of the Smithsonian Institution was opened in the period after World War II, as the National Museum of History and Technology. On its scientific side it was an American version of the Deutsches Museum, less disciplined by far, but setting out in an intelligible order the development of fundamental sciences and technologies. In its aspect of a "history" museum, it exhibited various memorabilia from a broad expanse of American history. With the coming of the new cultural history, however, this paradigm seemed limiting and restrictive, and a transformation of the museum took place, reflected in a new name, the National Museum of American History. Science and technology continued to be included, now however to be assimilated as elements of a larger history, inclusive of an astonishing range of cultural artifacts and concerns. A major shift was taking place in the concept of the science museum, from the paradigm of the Deutsches Museum to something far broader and evidently closer to the universality of the museum as we saw it asserted in Alexandria.[41]

One example taken from the recent history of the NMAH will exemplify this new approach and the issues it brings with it. For a long while a professional association of scientists, the American Chemical Society—itself an institution of the diaspora of which we have been speaking—had been interested in looking to its own educational role, explicitly taking the Exploratorium as one model, but clearly also with the exhibition of its own science, perhaps in the manner of the Deutsches Museum, in mind as well. It had thought at first in terms of a small science museum within its own headquarters building, but when this proved unfeasible, the Society proposed to carry out its project by way of a contract with the nearby Smithsonian Institution. Accepting a sum which ultimately amounted to $5.3 million, the Institution undertook to mount an exhibit to be called "Science in American Life." The title should perhaps have suggested to the Society the broader approach which lay in store. By agreement, the Society appointed an Advisory Committee of twenty scientists and scholars, but ultimate decision was reserved to the Smithsonian, represented by the exhibit's Curator. An implicit polarization was in store, for the Society wanted a purely "scientific" exhibition which would introduce young people to chemistry in a supportive spirit, while the curatorial staff envisioned a cultural approach to the same science, in a broader and more critical spirit. Yoked by a contract which lawyers agreed could not be broken, they were, it would prove, worlds apart.[42]

A major supporter of the American Chemical Society is the Du Pont Company, and it was precisely the spirit of Du Pont's legendary claim of "Better Things for Better Living Through Chemistry" which the curators wished to bring into thoughtful question. Exhibits, beyond the interactive science area with which the donors were pleased, addressed, among many other topics, the birth control pill, the public adaptation to the era of the nuclear bomb, and environmental problems including DDT and the ozone layer. To the Advisory Committee, the very fact of raising such questions seemed a negative move, or a thrust *against science;* they fought the curators, but though they achieved some slackening of the label texts, they essentially lost the battle, and their funding was completed in an atmosphere of acute bitterness in which they were joined as well by the American Physical Society, whose delegation to the Secretary of the Smithsonian on the issue is said to have included two recipients of the Nobel prize. The ACS vowed that it would never again fund an exhibit over which it did not retain control, a pronouncement which came at exactly the time in which the Smithsonian was being shifted from federal to private support. A new Secretary, I. Michael Heyman, renowned for the fund-raising abilities he demonstrated as Chancellor of the University of California, has made it clear that he welcomes this challenge, and intends to redouble the Smithsonian's private funding.

When a fundamental issue of this sort arises, between narrow and broad understanding of a science museum's role, the autonomy of the institution is called into question, and in part this *becomes* a matter of funding. Even if, as in this case, those who fund an exhibit do not control its content, this same case makes it clear as well that if donors are not satisfied by the Institution's performance, future funding will not become available.

Secretary Heyman has made clear that the Smithsonian "*bears a huge responsibility to the donor community.*"[43] Taken in its apparent sense, this would mean that the donors hold an ultimate veto over the exhibit process; and insofar as the Smithsonian bears the responsibility of formulating science and its history on behalf of the American people, the question can be bluntly but plainly put: "Who owns our history?" In Henry's understanding, the Smithsonian, as a trust on behalf of mankind, would be absolutely independent of external funding. In the succeeding years, dependence on federal funding became a question of submitting an annual request, and with this, the Institution became frankly national and an instrument of the democratic process: the nation "owned" its history and funded its interpretation. The new era will be different yet, in that individuals, corporations, or groups willing to fund exhibitions will "own" the result; in the long run, the wishes of private donors will control the interpretation of science. The possibility remains that private donors may be found who are willing to respect the autonomy of the Institution, and yield control; but we see that that is not the case with even a respected scientific society.

The concept of obligation to funding sources can take very crude form, the more ominous as large science museum projects require increasing levels of funding and join forces with commercial, civic, or federal development projects. In the case of a very large new science center in nearby Baltimore, even government funding has been characterized as "venture capital," with the stark assertion in respect of one exhibit function that donors, whether federal or private, are entitled to "*quid pro quo.*"

Two intertwined issues were raised by the "Science in American Life" exhibit: one is that of funding and the principle of a museum's autonomy; the other is that of the type of exhibit appropriate to a science museum. With respect to the latter, the issue has now been clearly joined between the concept of the "pure" exhibition of science and technology and the broader view of science in its full human context. With the pronouncement of the Chemical Society that it would never again release control of an exhibit it funded, we have seen how ominously these two issues may become identified.[44]

The "Enola Gay" affair

We turn now to the National Air and Space Museum, another component of the Smithsonian Institution, where the issue we have just met has recently taken drastic and more ominous form in the cancellation of an exhibit planned to accompany the display of the "Enola Gay," the aircraft which launched the first atomic bomb over Hiroshima in 1945. The origin of the National Air and Space Museum was significantly different from that of other divisions of the Smithsonian: it was born, not as an offshoot of any pursuits originating within the Institution, but out of a desire on the part of a retired Air Force officer, General Harold "Hap" Arnold, to preserve certain military aircraft following World War II.[45] The aircraft would memorialize those who had fought in them, though no doubt at the same time nourishing support for the ongoing role of military airpower in the future. Quite independently, during that same period arrangements had been completed to return to the United States the original Wright brothers' aircraft, the "Flyer." It, too, was to be memorialized, and other aircraft, including Charles Lindbergh's "Spirit of St. Louis," were added to the collection. It fell eventually to the lot of the Smithsonian to host this new function when, with the advent of space exploration further exhibits were provided by NASA and the new museum opened its doors in 1976 under the name, the "National Air and Space Museum." Only with time would a distinction between those limited *memorial* functions and those of a *museum* come fully to the surface as an open contest of wills.

Initially, under the direction of a retired general expert in aircraft technologies, the display took the form of an uncritical celebration of aeronautical engineering and a depiction of the advance of aircraft technology, in comfortable conformity with the tradition of the Deutsches Museum. Military aircraft, arrayed in linear, developmental sequence, were displayed for appreciation as technical achievements, with no consideration of their essentially lethal mission. With the addition of the famous "moon rocks" and other exhibits from the era of space exploration, the new museum included the work of NASA as well as the Air Force, and thus showcased the products of a large segment of the American military-industrial complex. It was described in a 1981 review as "basically a temple of the glories of aviation," and by one critic as "largely a great advertisement for air and space technology."[46] Primarily as a consequence of its space exhibits, it has become today the most popular museum in the world, with some seven million visitors annually.

The tide began to turn at the NASM following the appointment of a new Secretary of the Smithsonian Institution, Robert Adams, in 1984; the Regents appointed Adams with the intention of raising the academic stan-

(Right) An interior view of the National Air and Space Museum in Washington, D.C.

dards of the Institution, and Adams in turn felt that one of the divisions most in need of attention was the NASM. This opinion was later echoed by the NASM's Advisory Council, which asserted that science literacy must be extended to include cultural interests and meanings.[47] Dr. Martin Harwit, a new director appointed in 1987, came not from the military or the industry, but from academia, with a background in astrophysics; he had participated at Cornell University in the formation of a program in the history and philosophy of science. He shared the belief that the NASM's mission should extend to consideration of the social effects of the technologies it exhibited: "No longer is it sufficient to display sleek fighters," he said, while making no mention of the "misery of war."

In this, the NASM was following the path of the new concern for "cultural history" which we have already encountered in the case of the Museum of American History. From an unquestioning memorial to the exploits of space exploration and flight, the NASM was being transformed into a true museum, which could not by its nature be uncritical. Under Harwit's direction a variety of projects were initiated, one of them a new mounting of a V-2 rocket exhibit which looked now to the rocket's effects as well as to its technology—an exhibit which, in all those halls of lethal instruments, is said to have included the museum's first image of a corpse. A revealing, broad-ranging study of air power in World War I looked unflinchingly at the extremely short lifespans of the pilots whose heroism was so well known, and at the deadly effects of early aerial bombing in its first use against civilians, as well as its role in combat.

Many supposed that with this new approach the museum was turning altogether away from its earlier role in memorializing flight; but I think we must acknowledge that in truth the two functions converge. Every solemn memorial invites reflection on the foundations upon which it rests, in the very spirit of critical thought which is the hallmark of the serious museum; in a sense, such a memorial is by its nature at the same time a grove sacred to the Muses. In striving to become a museum in earnest, the NASM was thus in effect only rising to the full measure of its responsibility as custodian of the nation's icons of space and flight. As we shall see, however, this point was not appreciated by some who were already agitating for a return to the simpler ways of an earlier, unquestioning era.

The occasion was approaching in which the nation would put this issue to the test, for the 50th anniversary of the dropping of the world's first nuclear bombs was at hand. The "Enola Gay," the aircraft which had launched the bomb on Hiroshima, had been stored in the possession of the Smithsonian since 1949, but had never been placed on display. It was evident that this anniversary would constitute the occasion on which a section of the plane should be restored and placed on view, and—in a judgment whose wisdom it must be left to the reader to weigh—it seemed evident to the museum as well that with the lapse of a half-century, the time had come to contemplate the reality of nuclear bombing and to reflect on the thinking which had led to the decision to launch the bomb. The NASM thus resolved to mount such an exhibit, incorporating a careful, reflective discussion of the decision to conduct the nuclear bombing as well as the consequences of this decision for the world. Certainly, if ever an historic decision called for critical reflection and study, this was that case; and it would be reasonable to suppose as well that the nation's Smithsonian Institution would be the appropriate host for such a review.

Those responsible for this decision realized full well that this would be a difficult matter, for the American people had been insulated over the years from confrontation with the reality of this holocaust of their own making.[48] Great care would be taken to introduce the topic to the public gradually, through a series of lectures, panels, and symposia conducted by nationally recognized scholars, and spanning a period of more than a year. The plan for the exhibit itself, and the initial version of the script, would be shared with interested organizations. No preparation, however, could protect the visitor from the experience of confrontation with one element of the exhibit, the "Ground Zero" room. There the visitor would get some sense of the reality on the ground below the Enola Gay, where 100,000 persons, the majority of them women and children, were immolated in an instant. All that would appear would be finely-divided rubble, with a scattering of items, one of them a child's carbonized lunchbox. Is Ground Zero, we may wonder, a fit abode for the Muses? We know that they are made of stern stuff; through the eyes of Sophocles, for example, the Muse has looked, when comprehension required, upon sheer horror.

Shown here is the ground crew of the "Enola Gay." The atomic bomb was dropped on Hiroshima on August 6, 1945.

The B-29 bomber "Enola Gay" on display at the Air and Space Museum.

During the weeks after the first version of the script had been made public, a wave of criticism and growing outrage swept through the media and found voice in the halls of Congress: both the House and the Senate passed resolutions condemning the exhibit. Veterans' organizations, beginning with the Air Force Association, organized widespread opposition; efforts to work with them in revising the script, culminating in one now infamous session in which the curatorial staff at the museum consented to sit down with representatives of the American Legion to revise a script line-by-line, were of no avail. The same organization which agreed to a revised script one day would continue to condemn the exhibit on the next; it became evident that there was no will on the part of these critics to arrive at agreement on any form the exhibit might take; no form of the exhibit would in fact be acceptable.

Many voices of the political right, which had already embarked upon broad attacks on cultural institutions and the academic "elite," simply seized this occasion to beat their familiar drums. But other voices of the media, including some of the most respectable of the nation's newspapers, joined in the chorus of complaint. The Institution was widely accused of engaging in "revisionist history," of "rewriting history," or simply of "questioning" those things which had long been accepted as unquestionable; there was little evidence of understanding that history by its nature is continually in process of being written, or that new documentation had emerged over the years which threw important light on many of the events and decisions of that time. Ultimately the new Secretary of the Smithsonian, I. Michael Heyman, whom we met earlier in connection with the Science in American Life exhibit and who took office in the midst of these events as well, after first defending the exhibit subsequently cancelled it, leaving only the section of the plane itself and the barest of labels where an exhibit should have been.[49] Martin Harwit, given the position in which he then found himself, soon resigned his directorship. Even the book which had been announced, which would have preserved the record of the script and images of the exhibit for those interested in studying it, was cancelled by the Smithsonian Press on the instructions of the Secretary. The conservative Congressional voices which were raised in triumph at this victory demanded a return to "patriotism" and uncritical "commemoration"; since 77% of the funding of the Smithsonian comes from the Congress, and Congress would hold, as we know, a group of seats *ex officio* on the Institution's own Board of Regents, a heavily conservative Congress from this point forward would hold a tight rein on the Smithsonian's future.

The Smithsonian Institution had been driven altogether from the field; whether the engagement itself had been ill-advised and foolish, or whether this was a noble defeat in a worthy cause, may be difficult to decide. Many conclude that it was the wrong exhibit, in the wrong place, at the wrong time; others believe that the museum should have done a far better job of estimating and confronting its opposition, or should have been more realistic in moderating the exhibition itself. Few serious critics seem to claim that the script, as it emerged from its first revision, was faulty from a scholarly point or view, or unbalanced in its presentation.[50] In any case, this defeat of the Smithsonian, as the nation's museum, and on an issue absolutely vital to the national experience, has dealt a devastating blow to museums in general. As a result, it has given rise to a great deal of reflection on the role of the science museum in our society today.

We should perhaps not be too quick to take the attack on the Enola Gay exhibit as genuine evidence of the voice of the American people, who we must believe would support a balanced and thoughtful exhibit in the proper circumstances—else how could we preserve our faith in the future of our democracy? Two subsequent analyses of the Enola Gay affair give grounds for the belief that strong forces other than those of "veterans" were working against the Smithsonian, and that the American people were not receiving a true account of the exhibit to which they were expressing their opposition.

It is important to know, first, that the Air Force Association, whom even Harwit describes as a "veteran's organization," has in fact 199 *corporate sponsors* as well; the pages of its magazine are filled with advertisements for advanced air and space weaponry. The AFA joins with the aerospace industry in promoting shows of advanced weaponry; it has been characterized as the "air wing" of the "military-industrial complex" against which Dwight Eisenhower once warned the nation. The ties between the Association and the Museum, dating from its founding, had been extremely close until the new administration broke the spell of uncritical celebration of the industry. Since the Air Force Association lobbies the Congress for the restoration of cuts in the military budget, it is understandably concerned that the popular image of the industry remain favorable and unquestioned. Thus the battle in which the Smithsonian found itself engaged with the AFA may not have concerned the Enola Gay exhibit alone, but rather may have constituted a struggle for control of the Air and Space Museum, or even of the Smithsonian Institution itself—a struggle for the soul of the museum, as a place of mere celebration, or of serious and critical reflection. It is a sobering consideration that among the corporate sponsors of the AFA one finds Boeing, Du Pont, Martin Marietta, Northrup Grumman, Rockwell, and Lockheed—clearly names on any list to which Secretary Heyman must go to seek future corporate funding for the Institution.[51]

The AFA is long experienced in lobbying, with well-developed ties to the Congress and skillful techniques for dealing with the press—"feeding" the press, in the terms of its own experts. In one case, a mailing of over two thousand pages each was sent to some thousand recipients in the Congress and the press, with guides to call attention to significant passages. It has been shown that the passages selected were taken out of context and misleading, indeed chosen to be as damaging as possible.[52] But even the normally responsible press accepted such handouts, and repeated and editorially amplified them in such a way that neither the press nor the American public in voicing their opinions was reacting to a realistic account of the exhibit. The public was, in Harwit's description, denied an exhibit which many might have wanted to see had they known what the options really were.

This affair of the Enola Gay exhibit is not a clear-cut case. Yet, however one is to evaluate it, it stands directly in the path of any inquiry into the fate of the science museum in our time. It has reverberated throughout the museum world and raised well-founded fears for the future choice and design of socially-sensitive exhibits. We have recognized that the science museum in its essence must be political; not only does its own welfare depend on the health of the political process, but the kind of critical thinking which the museum makes possible is itself essential to the democratic political process. If such thinking can be blocked, as it has been in this case—the exhibit cancelled and the book suppressed—it is not the fate of the museum but through it the fate of the democratic process, which has been crippled. We see in this instance how closely the critical role of museums, large and small, may be bound to the future health of the democratic process.[53]

The Muse in the white lab coat

The time has come to confront a question which we have touched upon over the course of this essay, but saved for proper consideration until more evidence was before us: Who is this "Muse of Modern Science," to whom the world has paid such enthusiastic service for so long? In the first instance, she presides over our laboratories and our institutions of research, and she must certainly take credit for a flood of technologies which have delineated the course of progress of the modern world. She enchants us with visions of progress; it is she who spreads before us series of engineering achievements such as those celebrated in the Deutsches Museum, or the triumphs of technology to which the world beats its path at the Air and Space Museum. She inspires the composition of the great theories of fundamental physics and biology, and stirs the ingenuity which devises the experiments which put them to the task. Whatever the family relationship, she is not simply the ancient Urania who charmed Euclid and Ptolemy, for she incites her followers with a *scientific method* to produce objective truths of a new sort, verifiable in the domain of the senses. No one can deny the power and splendor of the works which this, her method, has produced. She is the Muse in the White Lab Coat, and her vestment symbolizes the objectivity and certainty of the knowledge she offers, untainted with personal opinion or the ephemera of dreams and wishes.

Her domain, however, is apparently considerably larger than her garb suggests, for she is not only to be found in the laboratory. It is hard indeed to know where her method begins and ends. Often enough, we refer to the objective truth of scholarship, not least when the scholarship is that of a curator who has guaranteed the information underlying a museum exhibit. Is it not the case that whenever an historian stands firm upon the facts, or an interpretation is presented as verifiable in the documents and records of an event, these assertions stand as *true* under the authority of our Muse, until they may be refuted by the production of other evidence? Thus the historian, too, and many another scholar of the modern era is using the scientific method, presided over by the same Muse.

Visitors to the Field Museum in Chicago, Illinois, watch as a technician works on excavated fossils.

Perhaps we are ready for a definition of this broad realm. *Whenever reason searches out evidence, builds theories, forms judgments, and is ready to look again and revise or abandon a position in the face of new evidence or a contrary demonstration, there is science, and there is our Muse at work.* This captures, I suspect, the spirit if not quite the letter of the age of modern science. May we not assert, for example, that the curators of the Air and Space Museum, preparing that exhibit which was destined never to be seen, were working under the spirit of the new Muse, as the composition they were preparing was not one of mere opinions but of reasoned and carefully supported positions, designed to invite the same thoughtful spirit on the part of the American public? If so, it was she who was banished when that exhibit was cancelled. "Critical thinking" is perhaps another name for this same domain, that thinking which we saw being cultivated at the Exploratorium and in the Experiment Gallery. We have remarked on the irony of the situation in the "Science in American Life" exhibit, in which the very adherents of critical thinking, the chemists, flinched when that same reasoning was brought to bear on their own case. Our Muse, then, not only unfolds the achievements of the sciences, but inspires that further stage of thought which brings imagination and evidence to bear upon them, to probe their meaning.

It may be Francis Bacon who first introduced the new Muse to the world in the *New Organon;* and if so, the scope of her realm may be just that to which Bacon intends his work to apply. By this test she is everywhere to be found, for Bacon did not name his work the *new* "Organon" without intending his method to be at least as extensive as Aristotle's *old* one. Like Aristotle's, Bacon's *Organon* covers the range of human affairs, though now in a very new spirit. It is this searching spirit and strict method of probing inquiry which is new—overturning idols, as Bacon says, questioning assumptions, and putting all things to the test of firm evidence and reasoned judgment. Bacon was no quantifier—he seems not to have had a head for mathematics, he was a man of vivid rhetorical images—so we should be careful not to identify our Muse too closely with number and measure alone. Still, whenever the need arises, the scientific mind is prepared to deal with qualitative information, incomplete data, and probable judgments. It is not the precision and completeness we associate with physics which is essential, but the spirit of reason and investigation whose scope of application is far broader.

Having seen, then, that this Muse deals in her own way with a vast range of human affairs, we must now ask the further question: does she work alone? It is a striking aspect of the Muses as Socrates introduces them that they constitute a company to such an extent that we can understand them best as aspects of a single Muse. Yet for a long while it has been a commonplace of our modern culture to suppose that it is split into one domain of the humanities and another of the sciences, and that the bridge between the two is difficult or impossible to build—which is to say, that our new Muse does not keep company with the others. The argument to the contrary is not only to be found in the spirit of Bacon's work, which does not admit such boundaries, but in the operations of critical reason itself, which follows a question wherever it leads. Further, we know that the white-coated Muse keeps close company with Erato, for scientists above all people are lovers of their work, and the greatest scientists are those who have pursued it with the most unflinching devotion. We who read their writings or follow their theories share the beauty of the argument, and the delight of grasping it. But retribution is close at hand as well. The Enola Gay and the forbidden image of Ground Zero symbolize well enough the awful embrace in which tragedy holds our sciences today—beautiful in themselves, but doomed, tightly harnessed to war, the ugliest of human activities.

One further question may trouble us. If this new Muse is so busy at the forefront of the sciences, why should she be bothered with visits to such old-fashioned places as sacred groves; will she have any real presence in a science museum? Perhaps her case is like that of Calliope, the Muse of epic, who, it is true, is vivid in the mind of Achilles at Troy, but whose role really begins later, on reflection, when the bard turns these affairs into epic verse. That is, in turn, why Mnemnosyne's role is so central, the Muse of history, for it is only in memory that events find the coherence and meaning of song. The sacred grove is that place of reflection whose mystery endows the fleeting and fragmentary with wholeness, timelessness, and meaning. Our new Muse needs such halls of reflection and retreat all the more, as the events in her world unfold with lightning speed and seeming inexorability. Science needs the science museum. The new Muse works in the greater world, but she is at home, and most in converse with her sisters, and Apollo too, in the quieter halls of the science museum. It is here where thought must be freest and most reflective. As other institutions, increasingly including our universities, reconcile themselves to the pace and measures of the commercial world, the science museum, if it endures, may be the crucial remaining host to the sacred grove.

The human mind, whose spirit we represent in the image of the Muses, is ultimately one and whole, however its attention roves the world among the disciplines and the arts. It is that integrity of the human mind—which sings and loves, reasons, or despairs—which is symbolized in the unity of the Muses and discovers itself only in the retreat of the sacred grove. Everywhere in the world, where thinking is clear and evidence is respected, our Muse has some involvement, but this is normally scattered and fragmentary; only when the Muse is at home, dwelling with her sisters, will things come together, as they once did for Euclid in Alexandria, into a composition which we can grasp, and by which we can be moved. As we have seen, Frank Oppenheimer seems to have had a remarkable intuition of the meaning of the sacred grove for the science museum; but the task remains to press this concept further, to take the full measure of both the sciences as they present themselves, and of that mode of critical thought as well which is the spirit of the sciences in its application in the wider world. It is thus not only within the walls of the traditional science museum that science and its products are to be studied, or that the critical thinking engendered by science is to be brought into play. Industrial archaeology, for example, performs this magic, converting the original scene of a technology into a museum-like reflection upon itself, in which it can be understood after the fact in a way it could never have been while the time-clocks were running and the power was still on.

VII. The object becomes subject
Museums without walls: The Slater Mill

There is a magic in viewing historic things; they bear their legends in their very beings, but these texts tend to remain hidden, only waiting to be read. That, of course, is part of the fascination of the historic displays in a traditional museum, very well exemplified by the planes of the Air and Space Museum. As in the case of those aircraft, their stories sleep within them, to become vivid only when they are somehow set in the context in which they once lived. The same is true of historic sites, which become museums in their own way, without walls—and here, too, their stories sleep, awaiting some wake-up call.

We have seen the science museum entering more boldly upon questions of social history and cultural context, and with this transformation the object may become uncomfortable housed in the museum, crying out to be visited in the very place from which its story radiates. One might hope that the object which had slept within the walls of the museum would yield its story as soon as we visited it in its original home, but this is not necessarily the case. An exhibit may sleep as comfortably when restored to its original site as it did enclosed in a museum. What brings an exhibit to life is not a fine display, even on an original site, but some real question. Only when we meet surprise or perplexity, or when an exhibit strikes home with us in some special or personal way, do we become fully attentive, and then begin to hear the story which it has always been prepared to tell. And curiously, such a story may not prove to be about the old days, when the mill was in full operation or the machines were at their best—it may rather be a story of today, which binds past and present in that vital relation which is the life of history.

This is the secret of industrial archaeology, an extension of the science museum which is drawing increasing attention as the social significance of science and technology becomes better understood. Once in a while now, a covered bridge is rescued in the nick of time, an old mill saved, a railroad line or a canal preserved—typically the achievement of dedicated amateurs with a love of the object or the site, or some memory of the people who had made it or used it.[54] The rescued item is prized, but there may be little understanding of the kind of significance it may harbor, or the ways to bring this significance to light.

One site especially woven into American legend may illustrate these considerations—the Slater Mill on the Blackstone River in Rhode Island, which on plausible grounds defines itself as the "Birthplace of the Ameri-

May 29, 1790

Rhode Island

The United States Postal Service issued this stamp of the Slater Mill.

can Industrial Revolution."[55] Like many another site rescued from an industrial past, it has been tidied up and restored as something of a shrine to an early technology. Surrounded now by a small, tree-shaded park above the river which once powered the mill, it appears the very image of a grove of the Muses; yet we must see whether the Muses will indeed inhabit there. In such a charming setting we might be reminded of the locusts who sang to Socrates and Phaedrus, those Siren voices sent by the Muses to test the souls of men—luring them, if they could, to idleness and sleep. Locust-history is like that, comfortably enclosing the past in a cocoon of unquestioned fable, changing the reassuring music of the theme-park.

Slater's frame building has been carefully restored, emerging pristine after shedding generations of other uses, as once a manufactory of casket hardware, and then again a testing rink for a local purveyor of bicycles. Inside, today is found Samuel Slater's machine on which thread could for the first time in America be wound by mechanical means.[56] There Slater, a good Quaker, launched the era of unskilled labor by giving employment to seven children, four boys and three little girls—not to be thought of as an exploitation, since the work was light and an attractive alternative to farm labor.[57] Here then is food for thought, assuredly, but not yet a living question: the Slater site is if anything too well interpreted, the story is told and the past left sealed. The very cleanliness of the site makes it fresh and strangely new, and yet by the same token infinitely remote; it is nowhere in time, neither "then" nor "now," only a textbook vignette.

Around this gem-like park, however, the eye is met in every direction by evidences of a very different kind, vast abandoned mills of brick or stone which not so long ago were still flourishing but are now only shells, haunting in their emptiness, or in the rubble of their decay. Here indeed *is* a question: what has befallen this home of the Industrial Revolution? It is thus not the manicured Slater Site which draws the Muses. We sense that they do indeed haunt this locale, but it is the ghosts who are speaking, ghosts of mills, ghosts of the thousands whose lives were devoured by the descendants of Slater's fate-laden machine.[58] With all the force of Delphi itself, this place now cries out with a question, "What was that Revolution? What befell it, and what has it left us, today?"

The Slater Site, reproduced as an exhibit, is placed carefully in the *past*—and there it sits. Perversely, the Muses opt for the decaying mills. It is their ghosts who ask the *present* question, for it is *our* time, the new time, which is broken and speaks of loss, while the old time is presented as whole and secure, a mere memorial. Met in tense conjunction with its ruined offspring, however, the old mill breaks its silence and asks a question which bears on us today: "What have we now, what is our case?" In this valley, in the tight space between its beginning and its demise, is embraced the whole intricate history of the Industrial Revolution. This in turn is a question which will strike home for many Americans, for many of our towns today look a little like this one, marred by disturbing symptoms of the same virus. It is our own history, then, which is embraced by this dual vision, of promise and ruin; and with this observation we come to a central realization: this question is *real* precisely because it has *come home*. In this way, all real questions are in some respect personal questions, as all real answers are those in which we have invested something of our own selves.

It happens that we may take our question up-river, where in the same Blackstone Valley, which once teemed with mills built along "the hardest-working river in America," a new museum has sprung up which embraces the question of the fate of the Industrial Revolution. This is the Museum of Work and Culture, devoted to the traditions and the struggling, embattled lives of the thousands of French-Canadian workers once recruited to fill these mills and work the machines—selected as they were for their large families, presumed docility, and linguistic isolation from agitational elements.[59] The Museum of Work and Culture is not conceived to encapsulate a statement about the past, but to launch an empowering proclamation concerning the present and the future: of a people, no longer mill-workers, but present, and proud.

The inversion of past and present implicit in the confrontation between Slater's mill and its surroundings becomes explicit here, where the present becomes, in effect, the exhibit's standpoint from which the world is seen. For *past* we here substitute *present;* but further, for *object* we substitute *subject*—for now the workers are not being *spoken of* (though they are exhibited), but *speaking* (for they are the interested exhibitors). Here, then, is a spirit which is living, something of an answer to the oracular cry from below, "What is our case today?" The Museum of Work and Culture replies, "We are here; and this is who we are." With this, one can truly feel the presence of the Muse. But is this our Muse of science? I believe it is, exactly: for the exhibits, and the mills around them, display in full human extension the technology of the Industrial Revolution and its consequences; while this is posed as a real and powerful question which, as much perhaps as the apparatus of the Minnesota Experiment Gallery, invokes the active

"Unionism is the spirit of Americanism."
Woonsocket French-Canadian skilled worker.

"The Pre... ...s you to join the un... ...L. Lewis, 1935.

"We shall soon be ... from thi... ...the day when poverty ... President Herbert Hoover, ...

"Production for Use and Not for Profit."
Artist Upton ...mber, 1933.

...st July, I ...d man. I ...
John Re... ...ployed Ford

...depressi...
live a more ...

THE GREAT DEPRESSION

involvement of the speculative and critical mind. Since the question is a real one for the social and economic future of our society, we see here again that the science museum gravitates as if by its very nature toward the domain of the political, where it may offer a surprising source of strength.

Visitors to the Museum of Work and Culture study an exhibit about unions and strikes.

Museology as thaumaurgy

The distinctive power of the Muses is to induce us to activity, to dance or sing, to compose, or above all, to speak. In each case it is a question of inspiring us with love, for it is by love of the beautiful that we are moved to perform as artists in any of the spheres of the Muses. Thus, to refer once again to that Dialogue of Plato's with which we began this exploration, the great turning point arrives—that moment in which we see that the magic of the Muses has, through Socrates' inspired speech, begun to work upon him; when Phaedrus is moved to step out of his easy role as *connoisseur,* as mere listener and the object of others' persuasions, when he begins to speak from his own convictions, in which his own active thought is invested. He becomes willing to join in earnest dialogue with Socrates and give voice to thoughts of his own. We tend to think of a museum as a place where things are shown to us, or we are intrigued, entertained or informed: but the Muses have not begun to function fully until we have made the passage

Phaedrus made, and the questions become our own. Such was the question prompted by the stark juxtaposition of the end of the Industrial Revolution to its tidy beginning at the Slater Mill.

It goes hand-in-hand with this observation to notice also that Phaedrus is coming to realize that the Dialogue is not about others, but about himself: that the image of which we spoke earlier, of the soul drawn by two disparate horses, is a description of Phaedrus himself, and of the present moment as well. This is deeply disturbing and more than a little frightening; myth is strong medicine, which Socrates is administering with very specific awareness of its powers in this case. The moment is one of magic, *thauma,* and the treatment Phaedrus is receiving is an instance of the Socratic thaumaturgy, or wonder-working. Strangely, we must admit that the museum— whether its exhibits are about life-forms of millions of years ago, or about steam engines, aircraft, or computers—begins to perform its essential role only when we are struck, by way of some thaumaturgy, with the realization that the exhibits are ultimately of ourselves. So it is for any who recognize in the mills of Rhode Island symptoms of their own home-towns. Everywhere, in all truly successful exhibits, the text is one: *"Know thyself!"* As the artful curator—and who is that but Socrates?—well knows, from being the *object* of the curator's messages, we must be led to become the *subject* who is responding. These subtleties of object and subject, effected in the Dialogue through the many devices of the Socratic thaumaturgy, will help to prepare us for the last, and most mythic, of the museum visits in this essay's odyssey.

Revolution in anthropology

We have seen how, in the early "collecting" phase of the Smithsonian, the Bureau of Ethnology investigated Native American groups in much the same manner as other specimens from the West were being studied and classified. They were treated as *objects* of observation and collection. Now, in an impressive upheaval in the museum process, the Smithsonian has come full circle, and has opened the Heye Collection in New York City, the first phase of a new Museum of the American Indian, as a museum in which those who until now had been *objects* of the study now become *subjects.* They take over the exhibiting process, and speak for themselves, with authentic voices. Native Americans both choose the displays and speak for them, as if in the very voice of the display itself. The collected object has taken voice, and becomes with this reversal of the flow of discourse, in a sense its own interpreter.[60] In the first hall of this new museum we see fascinating artifacts, as we have before, but now in place of the label or the interpretive graphics of the museum designer, we hear voices, very human and yet in some way mythic, speaking gently, firmly, and as if timelessly of the world as it appears from within the culture which they are now exhibiting to us.

The collection itself from which the exhibits are drawn was that of a certain George Gustav Heye, a New York investment banker and a collector in the starkest form of the old mode: over a period of decades he gathered artifacts from Native American communities into what became perhaps the largest collection of such artifacts in the world. The Heye Foundation for many years maintained a small museum in Manhattan, but the greatest part fell into precarious condition in a warehouse in the Bronx. Since 1989, when the collection passed into the hands of the Smithsonian, the warehouse has been repaired, and the new museum in the old Customs House at the Battery in New York City has opened as a branch of the future National Museum of the American Indian, to take its place in the company of Smithsonian buildings on the Mall.

The exhibits to be shown in New York were chosen from that immense collection, not by museum curators in the normal manner, but by Native Americans themselves. To prepare a second hall, "All Roads are Good," twenty-six "selectors" were named, each of whom chose at will a group of artifacts which were in some way appealing, and which the selector wished to display to the world. In a videotape accompanying each exhibit, the same selector speaks quite personally about the special significance of the objects chosen. These voices are distinctive, for not only do they speak authentically for the objects displayed, but as subjective and personal they are remote from the customary objective voice of curatorial authority. For a visitor who listens with sensitivity to these words, this museum is unlike others: this is not cultural information but personal address. Here is a

Sculptor Douglas Coffin, of the Potawatomi tribe, was involved in developing the exhibits at the Heye Center in New York City.

museum which is a human space. We are reminded, yet again, of that grove in Athens in which our inquiry began, with a most human conversation in an aura of mythic forces. Here are the words of one of the Pueblo voices:

> I feel very strongly that Indian people forget—all people forget—those deeper places these objects can remind us of. As a human race we have moments of incredible greatness, not power and control over things, but power to connect with Po-wa-ha, 'water-wind-breath,' the creative energy of the world, the breath that makes the wind blow and the waters flow."[61]

The museum has become a sincere and mythic place. It would be easy to conclude, on the other hand, that this is now *not* a "science museum," were it not that the winds spoken of here sound so much like those of the grove on the Ilyssus, as though we were being reminded of something which our own tradition had in some way once known, but forgotten. We need to ask once more, whether the science museum, taken in its serious and root sense as we have tried to do, might properly include the Heye Collection, and even in the future tend to become more like it. Does not the American Indian, after all, at this late date have something to teach us about *science*?

If it belongs to science to study the peoples of the world and to come to know their cultures, as such sciences as anthropology and ethnology, among others, assume, then we cannot be content to know *about* them, objectively, which is as we have seen, not to know them at all. We must know them for what they are, as subjects, not objects, and with points of view very different from our own. They must speak, and we must listen. Only in this way can any true knowing, or science, arise. But finally as well, once this step has been taken, we see that knowing becomes a two-way street. Who is the knower, and who the known? Science, or knowing, is opened to the same symmetry. This is not so surprising; our science has always been telling stories, and is no stranger to myth. Perhaps we in the West have lacked imagination about our own modern science; very likely our Muse has been waiting patiently for us to catch up with her. In the new global society of a world ever more closely in touch with itself, there is no preferred viewpoint; "we" are all people, we must come to know each other, and to do this authentically—to do this truly scientifically—we must pool our modes of knowing. This is the significance of the Heye Collection for the science museum of the future.

VIII. Conclusion
Toward the science museum of the future

It is hardly given to us to predict what the science museum is apt to be like in the future, but we may draw some conclusions from the excursion we have made among existing instances, and together with rumors we have heard about new developments, draw a picture of the science museum of the future as we might wish to envision it.

It does not seem that great size is advantageous: in fact, the immense requirements for funding of great enterprises tends, as we have seen, to leave them hostage to inherently unfriendly forces. We need to rethink the science museum, to see whether its purposes may not be achievable on a more human and less vulnerable scale. The human feeling, the participatory character and the authentic voices of the Heye collection, suggest one attractive model. Though its own scale is in fact large, it is nonetheless quiet, musical, and thoughtful, and invites translation to a modest, local, or regional level. The places we care most for; and the technologies and industries which most immediately affect our lives are likely to be local. Again, the museum without walls which extended to the entire Blackstone Valley is an interesting paradigm, for we do not need formal temples so much as provocative local sites, about which to think. Indeed, the science museum of the future might well be in anyone's home town. Great exhibits are less important than they used to be: they put us off, make us dependent on exhibit designs and curatorial authority, and in general lock us into syndromes suggestive of the worst, rather than the best of the traditions we have considered. It must be better to summon the best of local resources, in schools, colleges, libraries, local historical societies, and the dedicated amateur labors of students and willing citizens, than to place ourselves in the hands of remote institutions and external authority. What is important is the process of informed, dedicated, and critical thought directed to present questions; and that may often best be brewed at home.[62]

It is very important, however, on the other side of this ledger, to conceive the science museum as a cosmopolitan meeting place which escapes bounds of habit and prejudice and opens up new worlds. That would seem to work directly against the intimate, local nature of the museum I have just suggested. But there is a new mode of global conviviality available to us now, and here we may meet the answer to many of our conundrums. Increasingly, we will have access to other persons and remote places by way of what is today called the "Internet," and will take on new forms and names as time and technology unfold. This offers the prospect of digital electronic communication with sites—with the great, remote exhibits, or more importantly, perhaps, with persons in communities, individually or in groups—in ways we could not have imagined. The science museum of the future, albeit local and limited in resources, may thrive on this mode of human communication, so open to the personal voice and the inquiring mind. Today the world perceives its new digital technologies in terms of "information"; but we do not love information of which no Muse exists. For the science museum as we have described it, communication is a means to insight, with critical and imaginative thinking. For such a museum, the Internet and its descendants will be modes of conversation, dialectical and transforming in ways fit to delight the Muses.

Against these suggestions must be set the abiding value of the great museums we already know. There, unique exhibits, not to be reproduced on local scales or by lesser means, can be visited; one can wander in Oppenheimer's grove of enchanting devices or play freely in an Experiment

Gallery. The challenge becomes that of integrating all of these into one system vibrant with life at all levels. It is too early to spell out what this might be like. But let us hope it will draw upon the best features of the sites we have visited, from Athens to Rhode Island, and that throughout, it will invoke the Muses and rise to the principles we identified first in Alexandria. If so, even the Internet will have contrived to become a sacred space, and there is perhaps no reason why it might not.[63]

1. Strictly transliterated, this term would be *mouseion,* but we avoid a pitfall of English pronunciation by taking the liberty of substituting *museion.* After all, literal application of the same rule would make Homer's Muse a "mouse"! I owe the suggestion that it would be fruitful to pursue the term "museum" to its source with the Muses to Caryl Marsh, "A Neighborhood Museum that Works," *Museum News,* October, 1968.

2. *See GBWW* I: 7, 115–41; II: 6, 115–41

3. There is, of course, a rich literature on Alexander and Alexandria. On Alexander, we may mention first the *Encyclopaedia Britannica* article "Alexander the Great" by Frank W. Wallbank, and Plutarch's *Life of Alexander* (*GBWW* I: 14, 540–76; II: 13, 540–76); then Michael Grant, *From Alexander to Cleopatra* (New York: Charles Scribner's Sons, 1982); Agnes Savill, *Alexander the Great and his Time* (New York: Citadel Press, 1966); and the discussions of Alexander's political vision in Stringfellow Barr, *The Mask of Jove* (Philadelphia: J.B. Lippincott, 1966). On Alexandria, there is first E.M. Forster, *Alexandria, a History and Guide* (Gloucester, Mass.: P. Smith, 1968); Jasper Griffin, "The Library of Our Dreams," *American Scholar,* vol. 65, December, 1996, p. 59; David T. Runia, "Polis and Megalopolis: Philo and the Founding of Alexandria," *Mnemosyne,* vol. 42, fasc. 3–4, 1989, p. 398; and especially André Bernand, *Alexandrie des Ptolémées* (Paris: CNRS Editions 1995). Bernand traces each aspect of Alexander's plan to corresponding passages in Aristotle's *Politics* (*GBWW* I: 9, 445–548; II: 8, 445–548). References specifically concerning the museum and library are given in note 4, below.

4. Sources concerning the Library and the Museum abound: Diana Delia, "From Romance to Rhetoric: The Alexandrian Library in Classical and Islamic Traditions," *American Historical Review,* vol. 97, December 1992, p. 1449; Andrew Erskine, "Culture and Power in Ptolemaic Egypt: The Museum and Library of Alexandria," *Greece and Rome,* vol. 42, April 1995, p. 38; Edward Parsons, *Alexandrian Library, Glory of the Hellenic World* (London: Cleaver-Hume Press, 1952); Mostafa El-Abbadi, *The Life and Fate of the Ancient Library of Alexandria* (Paris: UNESCO/UNDP, 1990).

5. As often, Aristotle's words here are a challenge to translate, though the idea is clear and striking, since "to leisure" is an active verb. He seems to say: "We busy ourselves (we unleisure) in order to carry on leisure (to leisure), as we wage war in order to wage peace," *Nichomachean Ethics,* 1177b4 (*GBWW* I: 9, 432; II: 8, 432).

6. On the life of Aristotle, see Lorenzo Minio-Paluello, "Aristotle and Aristotelianism," *Encyclopaedia Britannica,* ed. 15, vol. 14, p. 55; and W.D. Ross, *Aristotle* (London: Metheun, 1945). On the relation of Aristotle and Alexander, see Bernand, op. cit., p. 6. One wonders, if Alexander and Aristotle had both lived, whether Aristotle might not have been invited to become the first Director of this new Lyceum.

7. Historians have long repeated the tradition that the Library at Alexandria burned as an inadvertent consequence of Caesar's attack on Alexandria. In fact it appears to have been only the copying enterprise or publication department, located at the harbor's edge, which burned, with a loss of some 40,000 volumes, a small percentage of the total. See Luciano Canfora, *Vanished Library* (Berkeley: University of California Press, 1987), and Bernand, op. cit., p. 13ff.

8. See Euclid's *Elements* (*GBWW* I: 11, 1–396; II: 10, 1–396).

9. See Apollonius' *Conics* (*GBWW* I: 11, 603–804).

10. See Ptolemy's *Almagest* (*GBWW* I: 16, 1–478; II: 15, 1–478).

11. A basic source for the history of the Smithsonian, including an account of the Smithson bequest, is Paul H. Oehser, *The Smithsonian Institution* (Washington, D.C.: Praeger Publishers 1970); I have made use of an earlier work by the same author, *Sons of Science* (New York: Henry Schuman, 1949). The Institution's early history is detailed by

Joseph Henry himself, in the sequence of his annual Reports and in other documents assembled in a unique volume as *Account of the Smithsonian Institution* (1854) at the Johns Hopkins University Library, and reviewed in his *Ninth Annual Report to the Board of Regents* (Washington, D.C.: Smithsonian Institution, 1855). His writings are collected in Nathan Reingold, ed., *The Papers of Joseph Henry* (Washington, D.C.: Smithsonian. Institution Press, 1972). John Quincy Adams' proposals for the new museum are contained in Wilcomb E. Washburn, ed., *The Great Design: Two Lectures on the Smithson Bequest by John Quincy Adams* (Washington, D.C.: The Smithsonian Institution, 1965).

12. The Regents originally consisted of 15 members: the Vice-President and the Chief Justice of the United States, and the Mayor of Washington, *ex officio,* three members of the Senate appointed by the President of the Senate, and three members of the House of Representatives, appointed by the Speaker of the House, and six citizen members, appointed by joint resolution of the Senate and the House.

13. Accounts of Joseph Henry are to be found in the works by Oehser cited in note 11 (*Sons of Science,* pp. 26 ff; *Smithsonian,* pp. 26 ff); and the article [by Spencer F. Baird], in the 11th edition of the *Encyclopaedia Britannica.* See also Arthur P. Molella, Nathan Reingold, et. al., eds, *A Scientist in American Life: Essays and Lectures of Joseph Henry* (Washington, D.C.: Smithsonian Institution Press, 1980), and the historical notes throughout *The Papers of Joseph Henry,* cited above.

14. It would not be out of line with my understanding, if it were true that he was influenced by the charter of the Royal Institution (founded, interestingly, by the American, Benjamin Thompson, Count Rumford), for "the general diffusion of knowledge," which in turn is likened to the phrase in George Washington's Farewell Address, urging the founding of institutions for the diffusion of knowledge. This is suggested by Oehser, *Smithsonian,* p. 13.

15. Henry's "Plan" is reproduced in Oehser, *Smithsonian,* p. 256.

16. Many documents testifying to its solemn role, including a copy of the New Testament, were deposited in the cornerstone. Unfortunately, as Oehser points out, no one thought to mention where this is located, and the Institution, custodian over the years of the nation's collections of record, had never, at least at the time of Oehser's account, been able to find its own cornerstone! (Oehser, *Smithsonian,* p. 186)

17. On the Weather Bureau, see Oehser, *Smithsonian,* p. 35. Other functions were incubated and later spun off, among them what was to become the Fish and Wildlife Service (ibid., p. 41).

18. On the Bureau of American Ethnology, see Oehser, op. cit., p. 63, and *Sons,* pp. 81 ff.

19. The episode was related by the president of the Royal Society in an address shortly after Smithson's death (Oehser, *Sons,* p. 6).

20. Oehser, *Smithsonian,* p. 40.

21. On Baird, see Oehser, *Sons,* pp. 60 ff.

22. Pere Alberch, Director of the Museo Nacional de Ciencias Naturales in Madrid, "The Identity Crisis of Natural History Museums at the End of the Twentieth Century," in Roger Miles, Lauro Zavala, *Towards the Museum of the Future* (London: Routledge, 1994), p. 196.

23. On the "Bairdians": Oesher, *Sons,* p, 106.

24. On the founding of the National Museum of Natural History, Oehser, *Smithsonian,* pp. 96 ff. An interesting review written from the same point of view is the article "Museums of Science," by William Holland, in the 11th edition of the *Encyclopaedia Britannica.* See *The Origins of Natural Science in America,* Sally Gregory Kohlstedt, ed., and George Goode (Washington: Smithsonian Institution Press, 1991).

25. Oehser, *Sons,* pp. 140 ff.

26. The Museum is currently at work updating the classic Planetarium, another category of natural history display, whose once awesome effect many readers will have known.

27. Galen, *On the Natural Faculties* I, xiii; 39 (*GBWW* I: 10, 173–77; II: 9, 173–77).

28. On the emergence of the "idea-driven museum," see the Introduction by Amy Henderson and Adrienne L. Kaeppler, eds., to *Exhibiting Dilemmas: Issues of Representation at the Smithsonian* (Washington, D.C.: Smithsonian Institution Press, 1997). Much of the thought "deconstructing" traditional museum concepts derives from the

seminal work of Michel Foucault, *The Order of Things* (New York: Vintage Books, 1973); Eilean Hooper-Greenhill applies this systematically to museums in *Museums and the Shaping of Knowledge* (London: Routledge, 1992); see also "Museums and Communication: An Introductory Essay," in Hooper-Greenhill, ed., *Museum, Media, Message* (London: Routledge, 1995). A provocative discussion prompted by this issue as it arose at the Field Museum in Chicago is reported in William H. Honan, "Say Goodbye to the Stuffed Animals," *New York Times Magazine,* January 14, 1990, p. 35.

29. On the Deutsches Museum, see Wolfhard Weber, "The Political History of Museums of Technology in Germany Since the Nineteenth Century," pp. 13 ff.; Svante Linqvist, "An Olympic Stadium of Technology: Deutsches Museum and Sweden's Tekniska Museet," both in B. Schroeder-Gudehus, *Industrial Society and its Museums* (Chur, Switzerland: Harwood Academic Publishers, 1993), and from a recent perspective, Melanie Quin, "Aims, Strengths and Weaknesses of the European Science Centre Movement," in Mills and Zavala, op. cit., pp. 39 ff.

30. Kenneth Hudson, *Museums of Influence* (Cambridge: Cambridge University Press, 1987), p. 100.

31. See Joseph Henry's address as outgoing president of the American Association for the Advancement of Science in 1850, in Arthur P. Molella et al., eds, *A Scientist in American Life: Essays and Lectures of Joseph Henry* (Washington, D.C.: Smithsonian Institution Press, 1980), p. 35.

32. Sally Duensing, "Science centres and exploratories: a look at active participation," in David Evered and Maeve O'Connor, eds, *Communicating Science to the Public* (New York: John Wiley, 1987), p. 131.

33. Frank Oppenheimer, *Exhibit Planning* (occasional document, March 12, 1971, kindly supplied by Sally Duensing.)

34. Frank Oppenheimer, "Exhibit Conception and Design," in Oppenheimer and the Exploratorium Staff, *Working Prototypes: Exhibit Design at the Exploratorium* (Washington, D.C.: Association of Science-Technology Centers, 1986), p. 5.

35. Loc. cit.

36. Ibid., p. 6.

37. Ibid., p. 9.

38. Ibid., p. 12.

39. Loc. cit.

40. See Bernard S. Finn, "Exhibit Reviews—Twenty Years After," *Technology and Culture,* vol. 30, 4 October 1989, p. 993; Amy Henderson and Adrienne L. Kaeppler, eds., *Exhibiting Dilemmas* (Washington, D.C.: Smithsonian Institution Press, 1997), especially their Introduction to this volume; Michael Wallace, "The Politics of Public History," in Jo Blatti, ed., *Past Meets Present* (Washington, D.C.: Smithsonian Institution Press, 1987) p. 37.

41. Oehser, *Smithsonian.* p. 96; Steven Lubar, "Public History in a Federal Museum: The Smithsonian's National Museum of American History," in Barabara J. Howe and Emory L. Kemp, eds., *Public History: An Introduction* (Malabar, Florida: Robert F. Krieger Publishing Co., 1986), p. 218.

42. Faye Flam, "Privately Funded Exhibit Raises Scientists' Ire," *Science,* vol. 265, no. 5173, August 5, 1994, p. 729; Robert Adams, "Smithsonian Horizons," *Smithsonian,* vol. 25, no. 3, June 1994, p. 8; Sasha Memecek, "Out of the Lab and into the Fire," *Scientific American,* vol. 272, no. 2, February, 1995, p. 21.

43. I. Michael Heyman, "Smithsonian Perspectives," *Smithsonian,* vol. 25, no. 9, December, 1994, p. 12.

44. Steve Olson, "Baltimore's Newest Tourist Attraction—Scientists," *Science,* vol. 275, no. 5308, March 28, 1997, p. 1874.

45. Oehser, *Smithsonian,* op. cit. Alex Roland, "Celebration or Education: The Goals of the National Air and Space Museum," in Schroeder-Gudehus, op. cit., p. 77.

46. Samuel A. Batzli, "From Heroes to Hiroshima: The National Air and Space Museum Adjusts its Point of View," *Technology and Culture,* vol. 31, no. 1, January, 1990, p. 830; Michael Wallace, "The Battle of the Enola Gay," in his *Mickey Mouse History and Other Essays on American Memory* (Philadelphia; Temple University Press, 1996), p. 270. The story of the Enola Gay affair is told by Martin Harwit, the museum's director, himself, in *An Exhibit Denied: Lobbying the History of the Enola Gay* (New

York: Copernicus, 1996), and in Philip Nobile, ed., *Judgment at the Smithsonian* (New York: Marlowe & Co., 1995), a volume which includes an unauthorized printing of the original script, "The Crossroads: The End of World War II, the Atomic Bomb and the Origins of the Cold War." See especially the careful study by Barton J. Bernstein, "The Struggle Over History: Defining the Hiroshima Narrative," in that volume, p. 127.

47. Batzli, op. cit., p. 824.

48. The systematic suppression of images of the actual effects of the atomic bombings is traced by Gary Mitchell, "A Hole in History: America Suppresses the Truth About Hiroshima," *Progressive,* vol. 59, no. 8, August, 1995, p. 22.

49. Before the weight of opposition led him to change his position, Heyman had originally stated, "The Smithsonian, as a meaningful and responsible public educational institution, should seek to present matters in their full dimension. At the same time, we should do our level best to be balanced. . . . This is what we are trying to do with the Enola Gay exhibition. I believe that our final product, to go on display in May, will properly present the record of what happened. . . ." *Smithsonian* vol. 25, no. 8, November, 1994, p. 10.

50. In mid-January, Heyman was still able to write: "I believe the script . . . now strikes the appropriate balance. . . . The development of this script has served as a catalyst for a national discussion about the legacy of the *Enola Gay* and the atomic bombings. Next May we will open an exhibition that I believe will make a positive and thoughtful contribution to this dialogue." Harwit, op. cit., p. 360.

51. Wallace, "Battle of the Enola Gay," p. 286.

52. On the Air Force Association's management of the press, see Harwit, op. cit., p. 320. A very careful critique of the distortion of the public discussion is formulated by Tom Capaccio and Uday Mohan, "Missing the Target: How the Media Mishandled the Smithsonian Enola Gay Controversy," *American Journalism Review,* July-August, 1995, p. 19.

53. The implications of the Enola Gay affair for museums generally have been widely discussed. See for example Lonnie G. Bunch, "Fighting the Good Fight: Museums in an Age of Uncertainty," *Museum News,* March-April, 1995, p. 32; Edward T. Linenthal, "Can Museums Achieve a Balance Between Memory and History?" *The Chronicle of Higher Education,* February 10, 1995; Barton J. Bernstein, "Misconceived patriotism," *Bulletin of the Atomic Scientists,* vol. 51, no. 3, May-June 1995, p. 4. It is perhaps unnecessary to remark that the issue of the use of nuclear weapons is one confined neither to museums, nor to the past; the failure of the Smithsonian in hosting thought about what this means is thus a blow to the present thinking of society generally. One large modern weapon is equivalent to some 1,000 Hiroshima bombs, while the world is presently equipped with some 35,000 nuclear weapons: a situation neither well understood, nor under stable control. See Jonathan Shell, "The Gift of Time," *The Nation,* vol. 266, no. 4, February 2/9, 1998, p. 9.

54. Kenneth Hudson, *World Industrial Archaeology* (London: Cambridge University Press, 1979); Emory L. Kemp, "A Perspective on Our Industrial Past Through Industrial Archaeology," in Barabara J. Howe and Emory L. Kemp, op. cit., p. 174.

55. Theodore Z. Penn, "The Slater Mill Historic Site and the Wilkinson Mill Machine Shop Exhibit," *Technology and Culture* 21 (January 1980), p. 64. The Slater site is described in a National Park Service National Heritage Service brochure, *Blackstone River Valley,* while a number of other sites in the same region are interestingly interpreted in other brochures published by Blackstone River Valley National Heritage Corridor Commission, One Depot Square, Woonsocket, Rhode Island, 02895; see also Paul Rivard, *Samuel Slater, Father of American Manufactures* (Pawtucket, Rhode Island: Slater Mill Historic Site, 1974); Steve Dunwell, *The Run of the Mill* (Boston: David R. Godine, 1978), p. 14; and Gary Kulik and Julia C. Bonham, *Rhode Island: An Inventory of Historic Engineering and Industrial Sites* (Washington, D.C.: Historic American Engineering Record, 1978), p. 143. Regions analogous to the Blackstone Valley are discussed in Brian O'Donnell, S.J., "Memory and Hope: Four Local Museums in the Mill Towns of the Industrial Northeast," *Technology and Culture,* vol. 37, no. 4, October, 1996, p. 817; "deindustrialization" is discussed by Mike Wallace in "Industrial Museums and the History of Deindustrialization," in his book, *Mickey Mouse History,* cited earlier.

56. The original Slater machine is not at the site, but exhibited in the National Museum of American History in Washington, in the very different context of the interesting exhibit, "Engines of Change."

57. Rivard, op. cit., (unpaginated) p. [25]; Ruth Macaulay, *Dull Dejection in the Countenances of them All: Children at Work in the Rhode Island Textile Industry* (Pawtucket, Rhode Island: Slater Mill Historic Site, 1987).

58. The problem of the manicured exhibit is well discussed by Kath Davies in "Cleaning up the Coal Face and Doing Out the Kitchen: The Interpretation of Work and Workers in Wales," in Gaynor Kavanagh, ed., *Making Histories in Museums* (London: Leicester University Press, 1996), p. 105.

59. Announcement of "The Museum of Work and Culture," Woonsocket, Rhode Island, 02895; the museum has taken shape under the guidance of Dr. Scott Molloy of the University of Rhode Island's Labor Research Center. On the experience of French-Canadian workers in the mills, see Gerald J. Brault, *The French-Canadian Heritage in New England* (Hanover, New Hampshire: University Press of New England, 1986).

60. Ian Fitzgerald, "America's Indian Renaissance, *History Today,* vol. 44, no. 11 (November, 1994), p. 4; Joseph Bruchac, "The Heye Center Opens in Manhattan," *Smithsonian,* vol. 25, no. 7, October, 1994, p. 40.

61. Bruchac, op. cit., p. 47.

62. The Anacostia Museum, in southeast Washington, D.C., has long been a paradigm of the local neighborhood museum. See Caryl Marsh, "A View from the Anacostia Museum Board," *Curator,* June, 1996, p. 86; and her article cited in note 1, above.

63. My own further thoughts concerning computers in museums are expressed in "The Vision Machine," in Natalie Rusk and Anna Slafer, guest editors, "Digital Media in Museums: Preparing for the Post-Hype Era," *Journal of Museum Education,* vol. 22, no. 1, Winter, 1997, p. 7.

Thomas K. Simpson has been a long-time contributor to *The Great Ideas Today*. He is a tutor emeritus at St. John's College in Annapolis, Maryland, and Santa Fe, New Mexico, where he continues to teach on occasion in the Graduate Institute. His education was at Rensselear Polytechnic Institute, St. John's College, Wesleyan University, and Johns Hopkins University.

Recently, Mr. Simpson has been engaged in a project with the NEH and the Association of Science-Technology Centers, leading Great Books seminars with science museum personnel. Mr. Simpson works with special fascination on the visualization of objects in four-dimensional space. In his most recent work, *Maxwell on the Electromagnetic Field* (1997), he traces the emergence of the concept of the electromagnetic field through a dramatic succession of three papers by James Clerk Maxwell. Mr. Simpson's book is reviewed elsewhere in this volume.

Fellowship of Reason: The American Association for the Advancement of Science at 150

Thomas K. Simpson

I t is a privilege, and something of a thrill, to attend any annual meeting of the American Association for the Advancement of Science (AAAS). For here, as in the many rings of a great circus, one can observe performances in the immense range of topics of the modern scientific arts. This time, however, the event was special, for the AAAS had arrived at the 150th year of its founding and was very much interested in taking stock of its progress, appraising its present and future status. Since the association's president, Mildred Dresselhaus, herself a physicist, generously welcomed amateurs as well as experts to its ranks, it seems appropriate that readers of *The Great Ideas Today* be introduced to the event by way of a review of the impressions of one inquiring visitor, a Pierre Buzukhov on the field of these vast modern operations.[1]

The association was founded in 1848 as a fellowship of scientists, eager to establish for themselves an academic status equal to that of traditional professions such as medicine and law. Although science was then still in the early stages of a transition from a branch of philosophy pursued by gentleman amateurs to a profession on which one might found a career, there was little doubt that *science* was a well-defined department of our intellectual life and that the members of the new association, in their common dedication to science, shared an evident bond.

Today the situation may not be so clear. As this year's meeting made more vivid than ever before, the sciences today have spread over a vast plane of human endeavor to which we can make out no visible bounds, either in subject matter or in method. The question thus asks itself whether, beneath the conventions of established social practice, there is today in truth any one common principle, rightly to be called *science,* which all members share, and which might thus bind this association as a well-founded, coherent body.

One thing seems clear: our older, tidy notions of science, with its logical closure of a well-defined method, will not suffice. In a session on the human genome, a domain in which the production of vast quantities of patentable information is being pursued with industrial intensity, one speaker was explicitly searching for new benchmarks and framed a contrast between the old mode of science and the new. In the old, one could frame an hypothesis, perform an experiment, get an answer of confirmation or disconfirmation, and move on. Now, an hypothesis entails an investigation generating immense amounts of data, shared, perhaps over the Internet, with colleagues who contribute volumes of data in their turn, all culminating in the meeting of a committee to appraise the outcome and propose new inquiries with a range of possible implications. This is not bad science, but science directed to a new order of things, to a world of a different kind.

Another speaker at the same session weighed the relation of genomic patterns to human behavior. The initial problem lay in the characterization of the modes of behavior themselves, a problem long familiar to behavioral psychologists, yet still fraught with the ambiguities of alternative definitions, scales, and subjective judgments. When now, assemblages of such data are to be correlated with a maze of patterns encountered in the human genome, the methods become doubly indirect and the investigator gropes for correlations. The resulting connections prove altogether real and of the first order of significance, and yet the science which produced them is of a sort which would once have been called "soft." The speaker was quick to acknowledge this, yet was able to insist upon the scientific character of the new mode of work. Old criteria of "hard" and "soft" no longer help. Science cannot wait for the establishment of tidy causal links; indeed, in systems of this new order of complexity, the very image of a causal chain can easily mislead: we are looking at woven patterns of relations, structures of information from which no linear pattern of causality can be teased. In a range of areas throughout this meeting, systems of comparable orders of complexity were reported on—of oceanographic and atmospheric phenomena, of climate change, of the operations of the mind.

Indeed, new studies of the operation of our minds are exercises in such patterning. To the method today familiar as the "PET" scan has been joined a high-resolution, multi-electrode version of the encephalograph. The combination can track, at a new level of detail, patterns which reveal just those regions of the human brain which are active in the performance of successive stages of very specific mental tasks. Here we see one domain of patterning throwing light on another, for as in a mirror, images which picture the invocation of successive regions within the brain suggest new understandings of the organization and typology of our mental operations themselves.

In instances such as these we sense that science has undergone an inversion: systems grasped from the outset in their wholeness, as patterns, take priority; less often is it a question of building up the whole by way of mastery of its parts. The light shines brightest now on these very areas which not long since were still seen as shrouded and avoided as science's gray and questionable outer fringe.

Again we are thrown back to our initial question: "What is it which is distinctive of the work of these scientists?" We know that economists, securities traders, pollsters, and artists work rigorously with patterns as well. It can no longer be their subject matter which distinguishes scientists, for the topics of their sessions ranged from the flavors of chocolate to the forecasting of the futures of whole nations. Do the members of this association have at least some common rule or method which the rest of us do not share?

Let us put on the table just one more piece of evidence, this one of a somewhat different sort. An especially interesting session—little-enough attended, it must be confessed, for all that it was described in its literature as "high-profile"—was devoted to "Water Management in Africa." We might say more concerning the general neglect of the few international sessions within this altogether celebratory party of the American association. Our purpose at the moment, however, is to note on the one hand the spectrum of disciplines and concerns during that one morning session, and at the same time an ominous, intractable wall against which the work of the scientists was brought up short. A very long history of the African water regime, extending over some ten thousand years, has been derived from the artful study of lake sediments, yielding evidence of immense, devastating, and sometimes strikingly rapid swings. Europeans, it would seem, formed their image of a "wet" Africa in part from the coincidence of their arrival near a peak of precipitation. A parallel study of carbonaceous rocks serves to relate precipitation to atmospheric carbon dioxide, yet even here we are warned against oversimple conclusions, for the energetics of monsoon winds are implicated as well. Traced back in time, this tale is suspected to lead, breathtakingly, to dynamic instabilities in the orbit of the Earth. Followed in the other direction, however, the story of these same changes leads, as one might expect, to drastic consequences for modern biota and the coupled fate of human occupation. Finally, we find ourselves in direct confrontation with present issues of social and political policy, and here I suspect the question raised earlier in terms of systems, patterns, and bodies of information takes new form. One speaker, examining the consequences of industrial pollution and what we still presume to call economic "development," dared cry out from a deep despair at the "wall" which splits scientific studies of a ruined lake from the realm of policy in the hands of others, indifferent to the evidence of the scientists, who persist in their destructive programs. That unwelcome outcry from the Horn of Africa spoke to a problem which ran like a silent thread through many sessions this reporter attended. It forces our initial question to a new formulation. "What," we must now ask, "is that magic seal which splits the thinking of mankind into two domains: one, the disciplined, courageous reasoning of the scientist; the other the habitual reactions and unreasoned routines of the politician and the marketplace?"

A perhaps startling answer to this question came in Philadelphia from one of the plenary session speakers, a keen observer of the contemporary scene whose insight, invited from outside the sciences themselves, may penetrate to their core as others did not. This was Esther Dyson, known for her entrepreneurial talents and perceptive insights in the field of the Internet—a field, incidentally, of intense interest to the scientists in their new preoccupation with large systems and huge information flows.[2] She told the scientists that a crucial feature of communication on the Internet is the equal voice it gives to all participants and the consequent empowerment of all to question the *official story*. This critical thinking, she said, was the essence of science itself, for scientists are those who, by stratagems which change as their methods evolve, are ready to bring accepted assumptions to the test of evidence and critical reason. Bacon must have been making the same point in saying that his new, universal *Organon* would serve to dethrone established idolatries, wherever they were found.

Here, then, we have a possible answer to our question: the common principle binding this fellowship of the scientists may be simply creative, critical thinking, open to the judgment of the evidence and unconstrained by any official story. If this is indeed the essence of science and the bond of the AAAS, it must be one and the same wherever it may be found. The seal, that wall, which dismayed the African scientist, is an artifact, a Baconian idol in our midst which we have not thought to question. Such critical, creative thinking must be as fully appropriate on one side of that wall as on the other—the side we call "science," or the side we assign to "policy." In sharing it, we constitute, as human, one fellowship of reason. Yet that wall, and our too-ready acceptance of it, rises everywhere and disables our reasoning in the very areas which need it most. The shallowness of our public debate, the superficiality of our social and political discourse, the banality of our journalism, do not consort well with our devotion to the standards of reason on the scientific side of the wall. As the sciences dramatically broaden their scope and expand their methods, in ways which this AAAS meeting has made so evident, it makes no sense to defer to an unreal barrier, preventing equally clear and systematic thought at the very point at which all of humanity suffers most from its absence.

One noble and long-standing interest of the AAAS has been its program in "science literacy," to which a retrospective session at the Philadelphia meeting was devoted. This goal, first articulated in a document titled *Science for All Americans,* has been understood primarily to mean the education of citizens in those aspects of the sciences which they most need to understand in order to make sound judgments as citizens in the modern world. Yet if the insight we have just met is correct, if science is in essence the responsible implementation of critical thinking, understood as we have described, then science literacy means not only knowing *about* science but acquisition of the power to reason in other areas to the standard the sciences set. Can it be that that noble company assembled in Philadelphia is not in principle divided, in being scientific, from the rest of the American citizenry? If this is true, the boundary which traditionally separates the sciences from the rest of our human endeavors is one of practice and prejudice, a sociological and habitual barrier, but neither a feature of the world nor a truth of our human nature.[3]

For a very long time we have labored with the problem of our "two cultures" and have struggled to bridge the abyss which separated the sciences from the humanities. Now, as we survey the range of concerns, and the boldness and openness of the methods of the scientists, we see how far they have, unnoticed, advanced in the direction of the humanities. Even the wall at the point of "policy" of which we have been speaking was breached in certain sessions of the meeting. A session on "Foresight" studies, carried out in Japan, Germany, and England, though not yet in this country, joins minds from all sectors of society, not merely to predict but to plan, to set priorities of human need and to estimate the possibilities and timetables of attainment in all areas of society. Another session was devoted to the social costs of fossil fuel consumption, with the aim of steering society toward alternative modes of energy supply.

These are strong evidence that science is restless in its traditional confinement to the laboratory, and is, on its own initiative, making its way past that once-defining wall. We have worried that such advances on the part of the sciences would prove reductive, that the sciences would bring with them a devotion to materialism, because they dealt with "fact," and not with "value." How different the reality is proving to be! It is clear now that the sciences are not reductive; they deal with systems, whole and organic, far better than the rest of us do; and we can only wish that the concern for truth and the human good, the powers of wit and imagination and the dedication to fellowship with which the sciences are infused, might be found in any equal measure on the unscientific side of the purported abyss.

There is a corollary of this line of thought which points, regrettably, to a darker side of the Philadelphia meeting. The exercise of reason, in the way I have described, is inherently an affair of humanity itself; in a world community so acutely aware today of being *global,* science above all is by its nature an enterprise which cannot stop at national borders. It was therefore dismaying to this observer to note the complacency, bordering on chauvinism, with which American science was celebrated, as if science were a competitive contest and not inherently a cooperative endeavor. Seldom did the leading voices give emphasis to the role of science in moving mankind toward a more humane world order. Further, I could find little discussion of a sort that was once a feature of these meetings, in which the gathered scientists considered the problems of the social management of the weapons of mass destruction, whose conception and production is still, unfortunately, very close to the center of their work. As we know well, the uncontrolled proliferation of technological weapons since the end of the Cold War is a matter of urgent current concern, and not least the possibility of their use in combat by forces of the United States. It is not popular to discuss these matters, and they went nearly unnoticed in Philadelphia.

The president of the United States spoke to the meeting; his visit was acclaimed, and his arrival was warmly greeted, but his address, though it spoke encouragingly of new funding for the sciences, was devoid of statesmanship. It was a poignant detail of the program that Benjamin Franklin was very effectively personated and spoke briefly in several plenary sessions. Not only was he by far the most eloquent of the orators, but when he said that, on hearing that the president was to appear, he had looked for George, but could nowhere find him, he was suggesting perhaps more than he intended. A great deal of satisfaction was expressed by the speakers over the several days, but in this world so fraught with human distress, and so desperately in need of the kind of thinking in which the sciences excel, remarkably little concern was expressed on a broader human scale. Here, as in other aspects of the American experience today, there are evident material grounds for complacency, but it is not attractive, and it does not bode well for the human future, global or American.

It is important, however, in closing this report to recall our earlier, more positive note. A century and a half after its founding the AAAS is evolving ever-more rapidly, and it may be expected soon to overcome any limitations we perceive today. In this searching development on its own part, and in its vigorous concern for the spreading of public literacy in the arts it practices, it may implicitly be inviting all of us to join in a fellowship of clear and courageous reason, in the process setting new standards for our very conception of social and political discussion.

1. The 150th annual meeting of the American Association for the Advancement of Science was held in Philadelphia from February 12–17, 1998. The program is published under the title *Exploring Frontiers—Expanding Opportunities: AAAS Annual Meeting* (Washington, D.C., American Association for the Advancement of Science, 1998).

2. Esther Dyson's overview of the Internet has been published in *Release 2.0: A Design for Living in the Digital Age* (New York: Broadway Books, 1997). We should note that she has an insider's view as well, as her father is Freeman Dyson whose book, *Imagined Worlds,* is reviewed elsewhere in this volume.

3. *Science for All Americans: A Project 2061 Report on Literacy Goals in Science, Mathematics, and Technology* (Washington, D.C.: American Association for the Advancement of Science, 1989). See also, *Benchmarks for Science Literacy: Project 2061 American Association for the Advancement of Science* (New York: Oxford University Press, 1993).

The Meaning of
Quantum Theory

Richard Healey

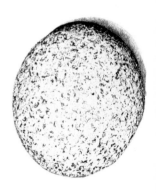

Illustrations by Ivan Chermayeff

I. Why quantum theory needs interpreting

Some scientific ideas are great because of their enormous practical import. Think, for example, of the steam engine, electric power, antibiotics, or the computer. Others owe their great significance to the way in which they transform our view of the world and our relation to it. Copernican astronomy irrevocably altered our perspective on the physical universe, and Darwin's theory of evolution through natural selection produced a similar reevaluation of the place of humankind in the living world.

Two great theories have dominated twentieth century physics—relativity and quantum theory. Each theory initiated a revolution in physical science, and the ideas associated with these theories have provided a new foundation for physics. Building on this foundation, twentieth century physics has produced many practical applications of tremendous significance. The relativistic equivalence of mass and energy has been made manifest in nuclear weapons as well as controlled nuclear fission. Practical applications of quantum theory include lasers, semiconductors, superconductors, and the electron microscope.

But what of the broader intellectual significance of relativity and quantum theory? Does either of them prompt a radical transformation of our world-view, and if it does, what is the resulting view of the world and our relation to it? Two types of answer to these questions seem to have insinuated themselves into popular consciousness, but the answers are hard to reconcile with each other. Though relativity is generally acknowledged to have profound implications for our most basic concepts of space, time, and motion, the theory is popularly (though in my opinion incorrectly) believed to be too technical to be understood by any but highly trained professionals, so these implications can never be expected to be widely disseminated and incorporated into a world-view of any kind. Quantum theory is popularly supposed to maintain that it will never be possible to predict the future behavior of an object with certainty, or even to describe its present state in a way that is independent of our means of observing it, which would seem to have profound implications for a world view. But does the theory really have such implications? If we ask the experts, we are likely to get a variety of different answers, for even the experts seem to have difficulty in understanding quantum theory. In a semipopular lecture, the late, great physicist Richard Feynman brought out the particular difficulty in fathoming its meaning:

> There was a time when the newspapers said that only twelve men understood the theory of relativity. I do not believe there ever was such a time. There might have been a time when only one man did, because he was the only guy who caught on, before he wrote his paper. But after people read the paper a lot of people understood the theory of relativity in some way or other, certainly more than twelve. On the other hand, I think I can safely say that nobody understands quantum mechanics.[1]

But how can it be that even its creators fail to understand quantum mechanics, when it has proved enormously successful in yielding highly accurate predictions of particular events and satisfying explanations of entire classes of otherwise puzzling phenomena? If not even the experts understand the theory, what hope is there for the rest of us?

The answer, in a nutshell, is that the widespread agreement in the scientific community on how to apply quantum theory conceals a significant lack of consensus on its exact content. Moreover, different attempts to articulate this content reflect radically divergent accounts of the world portrayed by quantum theory—and even of whether quantum theory can or should be taken to portray a world at all. It is customary to speak of such an attempt as an *interpretation* of quantum mechanics.

Debates about its correct interpretation began even before the basic formal structure of the theory became clear, and have been going on ever since. Fascinating though it was, the early debate between rival interpretations advocated by Niels Bohr and Albert Einstein ended inconclusively. More recently, new ideas of many physicists, philosophers, and mathematicians have sharpened the issues and provoked a reassessment of the available options for interpretation. While no interpretation has either warranted or won universal acceptance, those involved in the hunt for the meaning of quantum theory have certainly caught tantalizing glimpses of some extraordinary possibilities! To appreciate these possibilities, it is necessary to have some acquaintance with the basic formal features of the subject.

II. Quantum theory: Bohr vs. Einstein

Before the turn of the twentieth century it had already become apparent that serious difficulties arose when physicists attempted to apply the classical physics of Newton and Maxwell to atomic-sized objects. Classical physics predicted, for example, that atoms should collapse spontaneously within a millionth of a second as their orbiting electrons spiraled into the central nucleus. It is a clear consequence of classical electromagnetic theory that a charged particle in orbit must radiate away energy—and this can only be supplied by the decay of the orbit itself (just as the orbit of an earth satellite must decay as it loses energy when it encounters the earth's atmosphere). It was not until the 1920s that a theory emerged which seemed capable of replacing classical mechanics in its treatment of atoms and, at least in principle, in all other domains. The new mechanics quickly proved its empirical success, both in accounting for general phenomena such as the stability of atoms and in predicting quantitative details, like the wavelengths and intensities of the light which atoms are observed to emit when excited. But the underlying theory possessed certain features that set the new mechanics apart from classical mechanics and indeed all previous physical theories.

In classical mechanics, the state of a system at any one time is completely specified by giving the precise position and momentum of each of its constituent particles. This state fixes the precise values of all other dynamical quantities (for example the system's kinetic energy, or its angular momentum). The state typically changes as the system is acted upon by various forces. The theory specifies how it changes by means of equations of motion. At least in the case of simple isolated systems, the solutions to these equations uniquely specify the state of a system at all later times, given both its initial state and the forces acting on it. In this sense, the theory is *deterministic:* the future behavior of the system is determined by its present state.

While any particular method of observing a system may disturb its state, there is no theoretical reason why such disturbances cannot be made arbitrarily small. An ideal observation of a system's state would then not only reveal the precise position and momentum of each of its constituent particles at one time but also permit exact prediction of their future state (given the forces that will act on it, and setting aside computational difficulties).

Although it uses almost the same dynamical quantities, quantum mechanics does *not* assign a system to which it applies (such as an electron) a state in which all these quantities have precise values. Instead, the state of an isolated system at any given time is represented by an abstract mathematical object called a *wave-function.* The state of a single electron, for example, may be represented by a wave-function that assigns a number to each region in which it may be found—the bigger the number, the greater the chance of finding it there. A collection of wave-functions, each representing a different state in which a system can exist at a given time, can be simply added together to give a new wave-function. According to the *superposition principle,* the sum of these states represents another state in which that system may exist at that time.

As long as a system neither interacts with other systems nor is observed, its wave-function changes in a way that is determined by its initial wave-function. But the wave-function specifies only the *probability* that measuring any dynamical quantity such as the position of an atom in a box will yield a particular result; and not all such probabilities can equal zero or one: the atom, for example, may as likely be found in one half of the box as the other. Moreover, no attempt to establish a system's initial state by measuring dynamical quantities can provide more information than can be represented by a wave-function. It follows that no measurement, or even theoretical specification, of the present state of a system suffices within the theory to fix the value that would be revealed by later measurement of a dynamical quantity. In this deeper sense the theory is *indeterministic.*

A famous two-slit experiment illustrates these features of quantum mechanics. If a suitable source of electrons is separated from a detection screen by a vertical barrier in which two closely spaced horizontal slits have been cut, impacts of individual electrons on different regions of the screen may be detected. Quantum mechanics is able to predict the probability that an electron will be observed in a given region of the screen. The resulting probability distribution is experimentally verified by noting the relative frequency of detection in different regions, among a large collection of electrons. The resulting statistical pattern of hits is characteristic of

phenomena involving interference between different parts of a wave, one part of the wave passing through the top slit and the other part through the bottom slit.

Now, according to quantum mechanics, the electrons are indeed represented by a wave-function at all times between emission and detection. But the theory does not predict, and experiment does not allow, that any given electron splits up, with part of it passing through each slit. The electrons' wave-function specifies no path by which any particular electron travels from source to screen: it specifies only the probability that an electron will be detected in a given region of the screen. The theory neither predicts just where any electron will be detected on the screen, nor has anything to say about how individual electrons get through the slits.

After heated discussions at Bohr's Institute for Theoretical Physics in Copenhagen in the 1920s, there emerged a rough consensus among many physicists that became known as the *Copenhagen interpretation.* The central tenet of this interpretation is that the quantum mechanical representation provided by the wave-function is both predictively and descriptively complete. This is held to be the case even though description of a system at a given time permits only probabilistic predictions of its future behavior; the indeterminism of the theory reflects the underlying indeterminism of the processes to which it applies. Such a description is held to be complete, notwithstanding that it fails to assign a precise value to each dynamical quantity. As an example, if a system's wave-function makes it practically certain to be located within a tiny region of space, the system's momentum must be indefinite. A quantitative measure of the reciprocal precision with which quantities such as position and momentum are simultaneously defined is provided by the Heisenberg indeterminacy relations. According to the Copenhagen interpretation, these relations do not just represent an inherent limit on our knowledge of the definite position and momentum of an electron (say) at a time—rather, they specify how definite such quantities can actually be.

Some, including Einstein, have objected to the Copenhagen interpretation of quantum mechanics because of its rejection of determinism in physics. But Einstein's main objections to the Copenhagen interpretation sprang from his conviction that it was incompatible with realism. In its most general form, realism is the thesis that there is an objective, observer-independent reality that science attempts (with considerable success) to describe and understand. To an outsider this may seem so obviously true as to be hardly worth saying. But see how the Copenhagen interpretation seems to conflict with such a contention when it is applied to the two-slit experiment.

If one performs an observation capable of telling which slit each individual electron passes through, one will indeed observe each electron passing through one slit or the other. But performing this observation will alter the nature of the experiment itself, so that the pattern of detections on the screen will look quite different from what it did before. The characteristic interference pattern will no longer be observed: in its place will be a pattern which, ideally, corresponds to a simple sum of the patterns resulting from closing first one slit, then opening it and closing the other.

Observation of the electrons passing through the slits therefore affects their behavior. The Copenhagen interpretation further implies that it is only when this observation is made that each electron does actually pass through one slit or the other! The observed phenomenon then so far depends on its being observed that its objective reality is threatened. Yet quantum mechanical probabilities explicitly concern results of just such observations. Quantum mechanics, on the Copenhagen interpretation, thus appears to be a theory not of an objective world, but merely of our observations. If there is an objective world somehow lying behind these observations, quantum mechanics seems notably unsuccessful in describing and understanding it.

It is not altogether surprising that Bohr, reflecting on such phenomena, once remarked:

> There is no quantum world. There is only an abstract quantum physical description. It is wrong to think that the task of physics is to find out how nature *is*. Physics concerns what we can *say* about nature.[2]

It seems to have been Bohr's idea that even though an objective physical world exists, it is of such a nature that, at least on the atomic scale, the limitations on both our observational access to that world and the concepts in terms of which we are forced to describe it make us unable simply to say what it is like, independent of our means of observing it. One may legitimately speak of the position of an electron only in the context of a precisely specified experimental arrangement capable of yielding some more or less approximate value for this position, and in such a context it may be legitimate to ascribe a wave-function to a collection of similarly prepared electrons so as to permit correct predictions of how these values will be found to be statistically distributed among the electrons in the collection. But the ascription of neither wave-function nor position constitutes a description of the intrinsic properties of any electron in the collection. In Bohr's view, the acceptance of quantum theory requires us to give up the attempt to describe any such properties.

For Einstein, to do so would be to abandon the task of physics—a task he characterized as follows:

> Physics is an attempt conceptually to grasp reality as it is thought independently of its being observed. In this sense one speaks of "physical reality."[3]

At the deepest level, the dispute about the meaning of quantum theory between Bohr and Einstein turned on this disagreement about the aims and limits of science. The disagreement has never been entirely resolved. But seventy years of success have encouraged quantum physicists to regard their theory as transcending the limits prescribed by Bohr to which Einstein objected, and to espouse instead a version of the Copenhagen interpretation initiated by Paul Dirac and John von Neumann that does take quantum theory as making objective claims about intrinsic properties of systems like electrons.

III. The standard interpretation and its problems

According to this version of the Copenhagen interpretation, which may now be considered to be standard, the wave-function yields a description of the real properties of an individual system even when they are not observed—and moreover the description is complete. In this view, a system has exactly those properties which would be revealed on measurement. These properties are assigned probability one by its wave-function; hence I shall call this interpretative principle the *wave-to-property link*.[4] Accepting this link makes it tempting to endow the superposition principle with a puzzling new significance. When the wave-function of a system equals the sum of some set of wave-functions, the system may be thought to exist in each of the states represented by each of these wave-functions—in some sense it participates in all their properties, even when these are incompatible. One may think, for example, of a hydrogen atom whose wave-function is the sum of two wave-functions, each associated by the wave-to-property link to a different energy, as itself having an energy that is indeterminate between these two different amounts. Einstein's detailed arguments against the Copenhagen claim of the completeness of quantum mechanics may be seen as attempts to show that the wave-to-property link is false. A sketch of his two main arguments will set the stage for what loom today as the major obstacles to any satisfactory interpretation of quantum mechanics.

Einstein developed a version of the first argument in consultation with his colleagues Boris Podolsky and Nathan Rosen, and the paper they published in 1935 (known as "EPR") became a classic.[5] The paper described a thought-experiment in which quantum mechanics implies the possibility of establishing either the position or the momentum of one particle with arbitrary accuracy, solely by means of a measurement of the corresponding quantity performed on a second particle. They argued that such a measurement would not affect the state of the first particle, given that the two particles are physically separated. They concluded that the first particle *has* both a precise position and a precise momentum, even though (as Einstein came to accept) these quantities are not comeasurable—that is, they cannot both be precisely measured on the same particle at the same time. If this is so, however, the wave-to-property link must be false, since it implies that no particle in itself ever does have both a precise position and a precise momentum.

Here is Einstein's second argument against the wave-to-property link. The link implies that many properties of a quantum system are often indeterminate. But if quantum mechanics is a universal theory, it must apply not only to atoms and subatomic particles, but also to ordinary objects like beds, cats, and laboratory apparatus. Now, while it may seem unobjectionable for an electron to have an indeterminate position, it is surely ridiculous to suppose that my bed is nowhere in particular in my bedroom. The wave-to-property link seems to commit quantum mechanics to just such absurd suppositions.

One can attempt to avoid this absurdity by representing the initial state of a macroscopic object like a bed by a wave-function that is extremely small everywhere except in a certain bed-sized region where it is located. Because the bed is so heavy, it follows that this wave-function will remain very small everywhere outside such a region for an enormously long time. It may seem that one can thus reconcile the determinate location of the bed with its quantum mechanical description.

But the attempt is unsuccessful, since it is possible to transfer the alleged indeterminateness of a microscopic object's state to that of a macroscopic object by means of an appropriate interaction between them. Indeed, this is exactly what happens when a macroscopic object is used to observe some property of a microscopic object.

In Schrödinger's famous example, a cat is used as an unconventional (and ethically questionable) apparatus to observe whether or not an atom of a radioactive substance has decayed. The cat is sealed in a box containing a sample of radioactive material. A Geiger counter is connected to a lethal device in such a way that if it detects a radioactive decay product, then the device is triggered and the cat dies. Otherwise, the cat lives. The size of the sample is chosen so that there is a 50% chance of detecting a decay within an hour. After one hour the box is opened.

Quantum mechanics takes the wave-function representing the radioactive atoms and the wave-function representing the cat and forms a single wave-function representing them both at once. The fact that the atomic wave-function is indeterminate between decay and no decay implies that the wave-function representing the total coupled system after one hour is indeterminate between the cat's being alive and dead. If this wave-function completely describes the state of the cat, it follows that the cat is then neither alive nor dead! This is hard to accept, since cats are never observed in such an absurd state. Indeed, when an observer opens the box he will observe either a dead cat or a live cat. But, in the present view, if he finds a corpse he is no mere innocent witness: rather his curiosity killed the cat!

Now it is possible to reconcile the wave-to-property link with our observations of cats if one supposes that observation of the cat discontinuously alters, or "collapses," the wave-function of the coupled system (including the cat) so that it now describes either a live cat or a dead cat. Such a change, however, is very different from the kind of continuous change the theory postulates while the system remains unobserved. Moreover, it raises the question of just what it was about the process of observation that induced such discontinuous change. Most proponents of the Copenhagen interpretation would claim that an observation had already taken place as soon as the decay of a radioactive atom produced an irreversible change in a macroscopic object (such as the Geiger counter), thus collapsing the wave-function and causing the death of the cat. However, this response is

satisfactory only if it can be backed up by a precise account of the circumstances in which an observation occurs, thereby leading to a determinate
result.

The problem of explaining just why and when a measurement of a
quantum mechanical quantity yields some one determinate result has come
to be known as the *measurement problem*. The problem arises, because if
quantum mechanics is a universal theory, it must apply also to the physical
interactions involved in performing quantum measurements. But if the
Copenhagen interpretation is correct, a quantum mechanical treatment of
the measurement interaction is either excluded in principle (as Bohr
claimed), or else leads to absurd or at least ambiguous results. In recent
years, attempts to give a quantum mechanical treatment of measurement
interactions have given rise to several alternatives to the Copenhagen interpretation. Before examining some of these alternatives, I shall explain how
further reflection on the EPR argument has presented any would-be interpretation of quantum mechanics with a second significant challenge.[6]

IV. Quantum nonlocality: Einstein's problem

In the course of their argument, EPR applied quantum mechanics to a
scenario in order to draw out some consequences of the theory. They then
used these consequences to argue that the quantum mechanical description
of the scenario is incomplete. In his own textbook presentation of the EPR
argument in the early 1950s, the physicist David Bohm appealed to a
different and in some ways simpler scenario. Rather than position or momentum, Bohm's scenario involved measurements on either of two different non-comeasurable quantities on one of a pair of separated particles—
call these quantities A and B.[7] One advantage of Bohm's modified scenario
was that quantities like A and B were readily measurable on certain particles in actual experiments, so an analog to the EPR thought-experiment
could be carried out in the laboratory. In 1964, the physicist John Bell
noticed a second, theoretical, advantage of Bohm's scenario. In that scenario, there are, for each particle, more than just two mutually non-comeasurable quantities of the kind considered by Bohm. Hence one can consider
many different pairs of quantities A, B, C, . . . in which one quantity is
measured on one particle, while the other quantity is measured on the other
particle. Quantum mechanics predicts statistics for the results of measurements on each such pair.

Now suppose that quantum mechanics is predictively incomplete, and
that the result of any measurement of any of these quantities on either
particle is in fact determined ahead of time by some characteristic of the
set-up. (This might be simply the prior value of the quantity itself, or it
might be some quite new physical property of the particle pairs or the
instruments used to conduct the measurements on them.) In that case, the
statistics for measurements of these quantities on the particle pairs will
result from a kind of averaging over all the different possible determining

characteristics. If one could select a set of pairs and measuring instruments, all with the same determining characteristic, the results of any possible measurements of these quantities on the two particles in each pair would be the same, and one could predict them with certainty. In that case, quantum mechanics, which excludes this possibility, could be shown to be predictively incorrect for such sets of pairs. The assumption that no such set can in fact be selected makes it appropriate to call the determining characteristics "hidden variables." What Bell showed in 1964 was that no such hidden variable theory can give rise to all the quantum-mechanically predicted statistics on averaging over the different possible values for the hidden variables unless it violates the following condition: *the result of a measurement on one particle in a pair does not depend on the setting of the instrument used to perform the measurement on the other particle.* Not only was this condition implicitly assumed in the EPR argument, but also Einstein independently articulated the following closely related condition:

> But on one supposition we should, in my opinion, absolutely hold fast: the real factual situation of the system S_2 is independent of what is done with the system S_1, which is spatially separated from the former.[8]

These are known as *locality* conditions, and theories that satisfy them are called local. What Bell showed is that no local hidden variable theory is compatible with all the predictions of quantum mechanics for the results of measurements on quantities like A, B, C. His initial proof applied only to deterministic hidden variable theories, i.e., those in which a precise specification of the hidden variable state of a system would uniquely determine the result of any relevant measurement on that system. It was subsequently strengthened to apply also to stochastic local hidden variable theories, i.e., those local hidden variable theories in which a precise specification of the hidden variable state of a system would determine only a probability for the result of any relevant measurement on that system. The precise form and justification of the assumptions one has to make to strengthen the result in this way have been matters of intense discussion in recent years.[9]

What are the implications of Bell's results for the interpretation of quantum mechanics? Since these results show that any theory satisfying certain apparently plausible locality conditions must, in certain circumstances, conflict with the statistical predictions of quantum mechanics, it became important to test these predictions to see whether they were correct. Many such tests have now been carried out, and the relevant predictions have by now been very well confirmed. This presents any interpretation of quantum mechanics with the challenge of reconciling quantum mechanics itself with the failure of at least one of these apparently plausible locality conditions. But just what are these conditions, and what can be said in their defense?

Einstein's assumption that what is done to a system cannot directly affect the state of a spatially distant system may be decomposed into two very plausible principles, which I shall call Locality and Separability. *Separability* requires that spatially separated systems have their own intrinsic properties, and these wholly determine the properties of the system they compose. *Locality* requires that if S_1 and S_2 are spatially separated, the intrinsic properties of S_2 cannot be immediately affected by anything that is done to S_1 alone.

This Locality principle may be thought of as an expression of the requirement that there can be no instantaneous action at a distance. The whole history of physical thought prior to quantum mechanics seems to support this principle. Action-at-a-distance theories like Newton's theory of gravity and early theories of electricity and magnetism were superseded in the nineteenth and early twentieth centuries by Einstein's general theory of relativity and Maxwell's electromagnetic theory, both of which postulate the transmission of physical influence across "empty" space by fields that propagate with high, but finite, velocity. The principle of Locality may be further justified by appeal to relativity's requirement that causal influences cannot propagate faster than light. The idea that the structure of the whole is determined by the way it is put together out of its parts is fundamental to our ordinary ways of thinking of the world, and Separability seems to capture that idea. Moreover, Separability holds for the states of systems in classical physics.

What locality condition does quantum mechanics violate, if any? Different interpretations of quantum mechanics give different answers to this question. Consider first the Dirac/von Neumann version of the Copenhagen interpretation. On that interpretation, the state of a two-particle system is completely described by its wave-function in accordance with the wave-to-property link. The whole system may be in one state rather than another, corresponding to different wave-functions, even though each of its constituent particles has exactly the same intrinsic properties in one state as it has in the other. Hence Separability fails. But the Dirac/von Neumann version of the Copenhagen interpretation postulates wave-function collapse such as we saw in the case of the cat. And besides helping to reconcile the wave-to-property link with the observation of determinate measurement results, this interpretation also renders unobservable the conflict between that link and Separability. For, if observing one of a pair of particles collapses the pair's wave-function, then, after such an observation, each of the particles will have its own state specified by its own wave-function, and the state of the pair will indeed be wholly determined by the states of its constituents. Unfortunately, this attempt to reconcile the wave-to-property link with Separability can succeed only at the cost of bringing that link into conflict with Locality! If observation of one particle collapses the joint wave-function, the wave-to-property link implies that it immediately alters the properties of the other particle, no matter how far apart the particles are, and how well they are shielded from one another. The interpretation abandons a principle on which Einstein thought we should absolutely hold fast.

What if we accept EPR's own conclusion, that quantum mechanics is descriptively incomplete? This naturally suggests a simple realist interpretation, according to which a quantum system always has a precise value of every dynamical quantity like position and momentum, while the wave-function incompletely describes a large number of similarly prepared systems by specifying the fraction that may be expected to have each value of any given quantity. Measurement simply reveals the preexisting value of the measured quantity, and the statistics of measurement results reflect the way these values are in fact distributed independently of measurement. The Heisenberg relations are understood as constraints on these distributions, which indicate how a distribution that is sharp in position is never sharp in momentum, and vice versa. This simple realist interpretation has seemed perennially attractive, especially to those who agree with Bell that "The concept of 'measurement' becomes so fuzzy on reflection that it is quite surprising to have it appearing in physical theory at the most fundamental level."[10]

However, suppose we apply the simple realist interpretation to Bohm's scenario for the EPR argument itself. According to the simple realist interpretation, the quantities A, B, C, . . . all have precise values on each particle in each pair, and the wave-function for the pairs just specifies what frac-

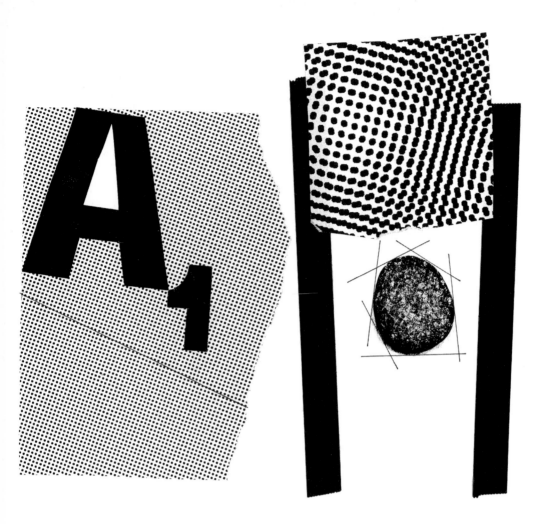

tions of the pairs can be expected to have particular values for each comeasurable combination of quantities. But it is a consequence of Bell's results that some pairs of particles have a wave-function for which this cannot be true. The fractions of these particle pairs that the simple realist interpretation takes to have precise values for each comeasurable combination of quantities cannot all match the statistics quantum mechanics predicts if one measures these values on a large number of pairs. Moreover, these statistics have been confirmed by experiment. Ironically, an interpretation naturally suggested by the conclusion to the EPR argument is in fact ruled out by Bell's extension of that very argument!

The following analogy may help to convey the essential content of Bell's result. Suppose you were presented with many poker hands, and told to pick a card at random from one of these hands. And suppose you were also told (correctly) that the chance you will end up with a black ace is greater than the chance you will end up with either a club or a major suit ace. It is quite easy to show that there is no set of poker hands in which the frequencies of black aces, clubs, and major suit aces match these chances. It follows that at least some cards in these poker hands, before you pick, do not have the properties you would find that they had after picking one of them! So the fact that you always end up with a card with quite determinate properties does not entitle you to conclude that it must have had those (or indeed any) determinate properties before you picked it.

This is not the only powerful objection to the simple realist interpretation of quantum mechanics. The way values have to be assigned to quantities to match the results of any possible measurement of these quantities turns out to be inconsistent with features of the mathematical representation of quantities in the theory.[11] It is unfortunate that the simple realist interpretation fails so decisively, since it does have the great advantage of offering a simple resolution of the measurement problem: Measurement plays no fundamental role within the theory, and measurement results are determinate because all quantities are always determinate.

V. Collapsing waves or multiplying worlds?

Neither the simple realist interpretation nor the Dirac/von Neumann version of the Copenhagen interpretation offers satisfactory solutions to both the measurement problem and the problem of nonlocality. Is there any interpretation that can do better? The measurement problem is the more serious of the two. Experimental verification of the relevant quantum mechanical predictions seems to show that it is not just the theory of quantum mechanics but the world itself that is nonlocal. But if this is right, no interpretation of quantum mechanics, and no successor theory to quantum mechanics, can account for the experimental results without violating some extremely plausible locality principle, so the fact that it violates such a principle cannot be sufficient grounds for rejecting any interpretation of quantum mechanics. But if an interpretation of quantum mechanics is unable to give a satisfactory account of how it is even possible to measure basic quantities like position or momentum, why should we believe quantum mechanics in the first place, since the evidence for it comes ultimately from just such measurements? Provision of a satisfactory account of the possibility of such measurements therefore seems a minimal necessary condition for acceptance of an interpretation of quantum mechanics.

The standard Dirac/von Neumann version of the Copenhagen interpretation cannot succeed without wave-packet collapse. But the interpretation provides no precise specification of when this collapse is supposed to occur, and no way of reconciling its occurrence with the requirements of the theory of relativity. In recent years a number of attempts have been made to answer these objections to "standard Copenhagen" by offering a detailed dynamical theory of collapse. The status of such theories is rather peculiar. One may regard them as attempts to defend the Copenhagen interpretation of quantum mechanics against serious objections. However, there is no unique way to do this—alternative dynamical theories are mutually incompatible, and none clearly captures the content of Copenhagen quantum mechanics. Indeed, from another perspective, all these dynamical

collapse theories are incompatible with quantum mechanics itself, since each allows that collapse can occur even when no actual observation is made. But it turns out to be very difficult to design experiments to discriminate among different collapse theories, and between any of these and quantum theory *without* collapse. If such an experiment were nevertheless to yield convincing evidence for some particular dynamical collapse theory and against standard quantum theory without collapse, there would be some temptation to take this as an empirical refutation of quantum mechanics rather than as a successful defense of the standard Copenhagen interpretation of that theory.

Can the measurement problem be solved within an interpretation of quantum mechanics which denies that the collapse of the wave-function ever occurs as a physical process? One radical response to the measurement problem is given by the *many-worlds interpretation,* offered originally by Everett (1957). It is to deny that a quantum measurement has a single result: rather, every possible result occurs in some actual world! This implies that every quantum measurement produces a splitting, or branching, of worlds. A measurement is just a physical interaction between the measured system and another quantum system (call this the *observer-apparatus*) which, in each world, correlates the result with the observer-apparatus's record of it.

This correlation comes about as follows. The wave-function of the combined measured system + observer-apparatus after the interaction is a superposition of waves, each of which is associated via the wave-to-property link to a (different) determinate result in the system and corresponding record of that result in the observer-apparatus: each different result/record combination is supposed to occur in a different world. One can show that the records built up after a sequence of measurement interactions by an observer-apparatus in a world will display just that pattern which would have been expected if each measurement had actually had a single result. Human observers are sentient observer-apparatus, whose records underlie their memories.

Two consequences of the many-worlds interpretation deserve special mention. Since every possible result actually occurs in every quantum measurement, the evolution of the physical universe is *deterministic* on this interpretation: indeterminism is a kind of illusion resulting from the inevitably restricted perspective presented by the world of each observer-apparatus. Second, while it may seem to each observer-apparatus that locality is violated, this too turns out to be an illusion, which arises as follows. In order to "investigate" the results of an experiment based on Bohm's EPR scenario, an observer-apparatus must interact with each of the spatially separated measuring devices in that scenario. These interactions leave a pattern of "records" of the experimental outcomes that can conform to the quantum mechanically predicted statistics even though the measurement devices themselves actually record results that, taken together, violate those statistics! No actual violation of locality is involved in the formation of any of these records. The illusion of nonlocality arises when the observer-apparatus's records are taken to reflect faithfully the actual results recorded by the spatially separated measuring devices with which it must interact to produce its records.

Unfortunately, the many-worlds interpretation faces severe conceptual difficulties. It must distinguish between the physical universe and the "worlds" corresponding to each observer-apparatus. But the status of these "worlds" is quite problematic. If they are objective, they can scarcely all coexist in the one space occupied by the physical universe. But if each world has its own space, then how are all these spaces related to one another?

Suppose instead that a "world" is just a mental representation of a sentient observer-apparatus. Then the wave-function of a typical system does not describe its physical state at all, but is rather a device for describing how a sentient observer's mental state represents that system, and predicting likely changes in that representation. Moreover, such "worlds" are subjective, in that different sentient observers will have different, and apparently conflicting, representations. A realist may well find this last view even less acceptable than the Copenhagen interpretation.

VI. Bohm: determinism restored?

After writing a classic textbook exposition of the Copenhagen interpretation, Bohm (1952) rejected its claims of completeness and proposed an influential alternative which sought to restore determinism. On this alternative, a particle always has a precise position. Changes in its position are produced by a physical force generated by a field described by the wave-function of the entire system of which the particle is a component. Other dynamical quantities are of secondary significance: the particle's state does not specify all their values, and their measurement is analyzed into observations of some system's position. On this interpretation, it is because every particle always has a precise position that each such measurement produces a determinate result. That result is indicated by the determinate position of some part of the apparatus (its final "pointer position").

Quantum mechanics is understood as offering probabilities for the results of these measurements. Since on Bohm's view each result is actually determined, in part by the initial positions of measured system and apparatus (which are not described by the wave-function), quantum indeterminism is just a consequence of the incompleteness of the quantum description, as Einstein suspected. Every measurement leads to a definite final pointer position that is uniquely determined by the wave-function, the initial positions of the apparatus, and the measured system, together with the forces acting on these. Provided that the initial positions of a collection of similarly prepared systems are distributed randomly, in a way that corresponds to the probability distribution generated by the wave-function, the distribution of final pointer positions will be that specified by quantum mechanics for measurements of the chosen quantity. Moreover, if one assumes that the positions of a collection of systems are appropriately distributed at one time, it follows that they will continue to be distributed that way as the systems evolve.

Bohm's interpretation clearly involves interactions which violate Locality (indeed, it was by reflecting on these violations that Bell was led to his more general results on nonlocality). A measurement on one particle can instantaneously affect the behavior of a distant particle by altering the force acting on it. This instantaneous effect makes the interpretation particularly hard to reconcile with the theory of relativity. But even if the interpretation is correct, it turns out that this instantaneous action at a distance cannot be exploited to transmit signals instantaneously. Thus the nonlocality inherent in the interpretation remains hidden.

VII. New ideas: decoherence

The Bohr-Einstein debate was cut short by Einstein's death. Bohm's hidden-variable interpretation was published in 1952, and Everett's interpretation in 1957. Since then, the work of Bell and others has contributed significantly to an articulation of the problems any successful interpretation must solve. In the past twenty years or so a variety of proposals have been made as to how an interpretation might succeed in solving these problems, especially the most serious of them—the measurement problem.

Such interpretations tend to be motivated more by the need to give a clear statement of the theory which resolves the measurement problem than by any desire to return to a classical or deterministic world-view. Their common strategy of attempting to give a purely quantum mechanical account of the measurement process without invoking wave-function collapse conceals a significant divergence in tactics. Physicists have tended to appeal to technical consequences of quantum mechanics (such as decoherence, an idea I shall shortly explain) whose interpretative significance has, they claim, been insufficiently appreciated. Their idea has been to use these consequences further to develop and refine existing interpretative approaches so as to render these immune to various objections. Philosophers, on the other hand, have been more ready to develop new interpretative approaches by rejecting central principles of previous approaches (such as the wave-to-property link) and replacing them by alternative principles that physicists have been reluctant to consider. This has given rise to a variety of what have come to be known as modal interpretations.

On the Copenhagen interpretation, the measurement problem arises when one applies quantum mechanics to the interaction between measured system and measuring apparatus. If the system is initially represented by a wave-function that is a superposition corresponding to distinct values of the measured quantity, then the wave-function of the combined system after the interaction will also be a superposition. The wave-to-property link then implies that the apparatus ends up recording no determinate measurement result—its pointer points to no particular place on the dial! Bohr's response to this problem was to declare by fiat that quantum mechanics cannot be applied to the measurement process. In his view, a measurement is an interaction between a system described by quantum mechanics and an apparatus that must be described classically. Landau and Lifshitz expressed this view as follows in their influential textbook *Quantum Mechanics:*

> quantum mechanics . . . contains classical mechanics as a limiting case, yet at the same time it requires this limiting case for its own formulation.[12]

Contemporary advocates of the Copenhagen interpretation are eager to free quantum mechanics from any such dependence on theories they take it to have superseded. Many believe that the key to its liberation is the recognition that an exclusively quantum mechanical treatment of the measuring process is indeed possible, provided one pays careful attention to the character and situation of a measuring apparatus.

If we are to be capable of perceiving the result it records, any measuring apparatus must include some component that is enormous on an atomic scale— this will typically contain something like 1,000,000,000,000,000,000,000,000 atoms! Even if the state of such an object can be represented quantum mechanically, it cannot be represented simply by a wave-function. For one thing, it would be impossible in practice to acquire the detailed knowledge needed to decide which of a vast collection of candidate wave-functions correctly represents this system. Physicists have developed a technique that enables them to factor their ignorance of a system's wave-function into its quantum mechanical representation by a kind of averaging over all the wave-functions that are consistent with what they know about the system. This is called a *mixture,* and the system is then represented by a *mixed state*—a mathematical object that is neither a wave-function nor a sum of these, but a different kind of combination of all the candidate wave-functions. The representation yields a convenient way of calculating the probabilities for the results of measure-ments in a situation in which one does not know just which wave-function correctly represents a system, but one does know how likely it is to be each of a set of possible candidates. Even if a measuring apparatus does come to acquire a property that records a determinate measurement result, one would not expect to represent its state by a single wave-function correlated to this property by the wave-to-property link, but rather by a mixture of an enormous number of such wave-functions.

Not only does a measuring apparatus include vast numbers of atoms, most details of whose behavior we neither know nor care about: it is also in

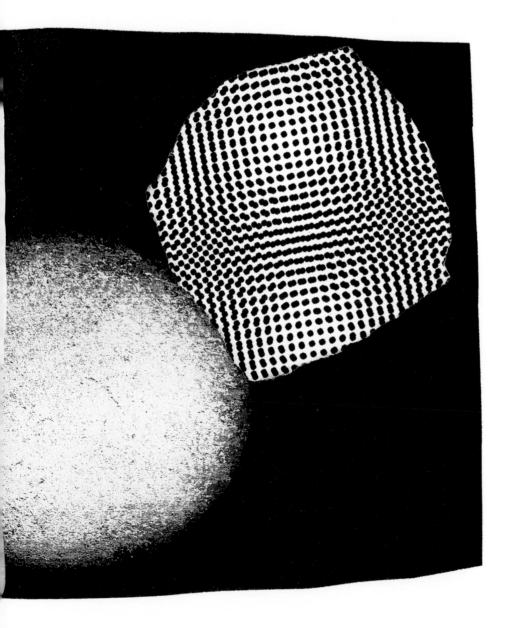

constant interaction with its environment through its contact with the bench on which it rests, its bombardment by air molecules, the light that strikes it so that it can be seen, and so forth. One can represent the state of a system by a wave-function in quantum mechanics only on the assumption that it is isolated. Almost any interaction with a system renders such a representation impossible—it is only the combination of all the systems that are involved in the interaction whose state can be thus represented. But this does not mean that there is no way of representing the state of any component of this combined system. Indeed, there is a uniquely appropriate way of representing a component by a mixed state. This mixed state representation is possible insofar as the probabilities for the possible results of measuring any quantity on the component calculated from the mixed state coincide with the probabilities calculated from the wave-function of the combined system of which it is a part. Taking into account its interaction with its environment is therefore going to involve an independent reason to represent the state of a measuring apparatus as a mixture.

What happens if we incorporate these new insights into a more realistic quantum mechanical description of a measurement interaction? Over the past twenty years or so, physicists have applied quantum mechanics to a hypothetical measurement in the context of a variety of models of an apparatus and its interaction with its environment. These applications have yielded some intriguing results. Suppose one simplifies by taking a measurement to proceed in two stages. In the first stage, a measured system in a superposed state interacts with an apparatus whose state is represented by a wave-function. Their combined wave-function becomes a superposition of waves, each of which corresponds to a different precise value of the measured quantity correlated to an appropriate record of that value in the apparatus. In the second stage, the apparatus interacts with its environment. As a result, the total system + apparatus + environment state evolves into an enormously complicated superposition. But the combined state of just the measured system and measuring apparatus may at any time then be represented as a mixture. If that is done, two significant facts about this mixed state emerge. First, it assumes a particular form in a very short time, and retains that form thereafter. This process is called *decoherence*. Second, the form is special because each component wave in the mixture corresponds, via the wave-to-property link, to a state in which the measured system has some determinate value for the measured quantity and the measuring apparatus has recorded that value.

Now, recall the way that mixed states were first introduced as representations of our ignorance of the actual wave-function representing a system. If this is the significance of the mixed state of the combination of system and apparatus, it follows that, during the second stage of the measurement interaction, the actual wave-function of this combined system very rapidly evolves so as to represent a state in which the measured system has some determinate value for the measured quantity, while the determinate state of the measuring apparatus correctly records that value. That appears to be exactly what was needed to solve the measurement problem.

Unfortunately, it seems that this cannot be the correct way of understanding the mixed state of system + apparatus. The problem is that the total system + apparatus + environment state is not a mixture but a superposition. Applied to this superposition, the wave-to-property link implies that the measured quantity does not *have* a determinate value on the measured system, and the measuring apparatus does not faithfully *record* such a value. Therefore, it cannot be correct to understand the mixed state of system + apparatus as simply representing our ignorance of their actual determinate conditions. Indeed, both physicists and philosophers have been warning against just this way of misunderstanding the significance of this kind of mixed state for the past twenty years.[13]

Still, the technical result that environmental interactions can induce extremely rapid decoherence is too pretty to be ignored, and some physicists have tried to find a more congenial home for this result outside of the standard Copenhagen interpretation of quantum mechanics.[14] Specifically, Wojciech Zurek has proposed what he calls an "existential interpretation" of quantum mechanics, which he takes to be a development of Everett's ideas made possible by the exploitation of decoherence. He characterizes this interpretation as follows:

> Memory is the stable existence of records—correlations with the state of the relevant branch of the universe. The requirement of stable existence and the recognition of ultimate interdependence between the identities of the observers (determined in part by the physical states of their memories) and their perceptions define the *existential interpretation* of quantum mechanics.[15]

Recall that on Everett's interpretation a measurement interaction is associated with a process that gives rise to many branches, in each of which a different result occurs and is recorded. This presents the technical problem of specifying in quantum mechanical terms what it is that defines the branches. Everett himself postulated a very special form for a measurement interaction which can solve this problem for the severely restricted set of measurement interactions of that form. Decoherence may provide a better solution, because it applies to a much wider and more realistic class of measurement interactions; indeed, the form of the measurement interaction itself is quite unimportant, compared to the form of the interaction with the environment. Moreover, decoherence can help to explain why the records contained in a branch are stable, and thus fit to serve as "memories." But what about the "ultimate interdependence between the identities of the observers . . . and their perceptions"? The idea seems to be that an observer is to be identified not with a physical observer-apparatus, but rather with what one might call an observer-process, where many different observer-processes are associated with each observer-apparatus. Different observer-processes associated with the same observer-apparatus branch off from one another as they acquire their different memories, and hence identities, through the physical interactions corresponding to quantum measurements.

While this application of decoherence may help the Everett interpretation overcome some of its technical difficulties, daunting questions remain. Two of these loom large. Is there any good reason to believe in the existence of an enormous collection of entities—observer-processes—of a wholly unfamiliar kind, over and above the ordinary physical objects and conscious observers (if these are more than simply physical objects of a very special kind) to whose existence our experience of the quantum world already commits us? How can we make sense of the probabilities quantum mechanics generates if every possible measurement result actually occurs in some branch of it?

VIII. More new ideas: modal interpretations

Quantum mechanics has long attracted the attention of philosophers of science eager to understand it so that they could come to appreciate its implications for their subject. Rather than expecting some formal consequence of the theory to yield the key to such understanding, they have tended to look more carefully at the informal principles wielded by its practitioners. One such principle has already been highlighted here, namely the wave-to-property link. Recall that, according to this link, a system has just those properties which would certainly be revealed on measurement, since its wave-function assigns them probability one. At first sight this link appears to embody a confusion about the application of probability. Interestingly, it was Schrödinger, a physicist and codiscoverer of quantum mechanics, who pointed that out in a letter to Einstein in 1950, in which he wrote:

> It seems to me that the concept of probability is terribly mishandled these days. Probability surely has as its substance a statement as to whether something *is* or *is not* the case—an uncertain statement, to be sure. But nevertheless it has meaning only if one is indeed convinced that the something in question quite definitely either *is* or *is not* the case. A probabilistic assertion presupposes the full reality of its subject.[16]

Confusion arises if one makes the following fallacious inference: If a statement is quite definitely either true or false, then it is either certainly true or certainly false. Suppose one uses this inference to reason as follows. If quantum mechanics assigns a probability to a hydrogen atom's being located in its lowest energy, or ground state, then that atom is quite definitely either in its ground state or not in its ground state. In that case it is either certainly true or certainly false that such an atom is in its ground state. But this is consistent only with assignment of probability 1 or 0 to its being in its ground state, and if the probability is 0 then the assertion is certainly false. Hence, a hydrogen atom is certainly in its ground state if and only if quantum mechanics assigns probability 1 to its being in that

state, which is just what the wave-to-property link maintains. But this creates confusion when one remembers that quantum mechanics typically assigns probabilities *other* than 0 and 1 to a hydrogen atom's being in its ground state. Moreover, as Schrödinger noted, it only compounds the confusion if one tries to square the wave-to-property link with such probability assignments by supposing that they correspond to conditions in which it is neither true nor false that the hydrogen atom *is* in its ground state.

Having diagnosed the error in this piece of reasoning, may we simply reject the wave-to-property link which the reasoning supports? No, that link is too deeply embedded in physicists' practice to be abandoned for this reason. And one can reconcile the link with Schrödinger's criticism by taking, as "the substance" of quantum mechanical probability statements, not whether or not some hydrogen atom *is* in its ground state, but whether or not it will be *observed* to be in its ground state, supposing that a measurement of its energy is to be performed.

But there is a much better reason for exploring the prospects of replacing the wave-to-property link by alternative interpretative principles. It is the wave-to-property link that makes the measurement problem so intractable. Accordingly, in recent years philosophers of science have explored a variety of proposed replacements for the wave-to-property link. Such views have come to be known as *modal interpretations.* The term modal is used by philosophers to refer to the way (or mode) in which an object may be considered to have a property. For example, will the weather be sunny in Los Angeles next July 4th? Some confident Californians may think the weather there must be sunny then, others merely that it will in fact be sunny, while the cautious few may venture only that it is possible for it to be sunny then. Bas van Fraassen originally introduced the term modal into discussions of quantum mechanics to describe an interpretation according to which a quantum system must have every quantum mechanical dynamical property to which its wave-function assigns probability 1, yet actually has additional quantum dynamical properties to which its wave-function assigns probabilities between 0 and 1. But the term has come to be used to denote any interpretation that rejects the wave-to-property link—even those that deny that a system must have every quantum dynamical property assigned probability 1 by its wave-function.

Three varieties of modal interpretation have been proposed recently. Each variety offers an account of a quantum measurement which treats it as an ordinary physical interaction between quantum systems involving no wave-function "collapse."

The first variety[17] is closely related to Bohm's interpretation. Just as Bohm took the systems' positions to be always determinate, so this variety singles out some one privileged quantity as always having precise values, in violation of the wave-to-property link. The idea is to solve the measurement problem by reinterpreting the significance of the final superposed state of system + apparatus. While the wave-to-property link implies that the apparatus records no determinate result in this state, the new interpretative rule implies rather that, in this state, a determinate result is indeed recorded by the value of the privileged quantity on the apparatus. This variety of modal interpretation inherits many of the difficulties of Bohm's view, including in particular the difficulty of reconciling the kind of nonlocality it involves with the requirements of relativity theory.

A second variety[18] revises the wave-to-property link in a way that has empirical significance only at the conclusion of a measurement interaction. Van Fraassen spells out in detailed quantum mechanical terms the conditions he takes to be necessary for an interaction between a pair of systems to count as a measurement interaction. When these conditions are met, he is then able to pick out certain quantities on one of the interacting systems—the "apparatus" system—which are postulated as having precise values at its conclusion, along with corresponding quantities on the other system, whose values the interaction is then taken to measure.

Van Fraassen presents his interpretation as a way of "cleaning up" the Copenhagen interpretation, even though it diverges significantly from both Bohr's and the Dirac/von Neumann version of that interpretation. The interpretation offers no new insights into quantum nonlocality—indeed, in van Fraassen's view, this is an inappropriate label for phenomena we find puzzling only because we cling to outmoded concepts of causal explanation whose inadequacy quantum mechanics serves to dramatize. In addition, its treatment of the measurement problem is open to objections. Van Fraassen's conditions do not seem to apply to actual laboratory measurements of quantum quantities, so it is not clear why those measurements provide us with any good reason to believe quantum mechanics as he interprets it. Moreover, on van Fraassen's interpretation, quantum mechanics seems unable to account for the stable behavior of the properties of macroscopic systems (including, but not confined to, measuring apparatus).

A third variety of modal interpretation was first proposed by Simon Kochen. Interpretations later developed by Dieks and myself are similar in that they make use of the same key mathematical result.[19] Like van Fraassen, and unlike Bub, Dieks and I treat all quantities in quantum mechanics democratically—which of them are taken to have precise values in a given situation depends on the appropriate quantum mechanical description of that situation, rather than on some universal external decree. But as Bub maintains, and van Fraassen does not, precise values are ascribed to particular quantities in circumstances other than those obtaining at the end of a measurement interaction. The way in which this is done depends on a certain well-known mathematical result concerning a wave-function representing the state of a pair of systems in quantum mechanics. It would be inappropriate to enter into technical details here, particularly since different interpretations deploy this mathematical result in different ways. Instead, I shall simply outline some key features of my own interpretation.

I call this interpretation interactive because, like Everett's interpretation as well as other modal interpretations, it treats measurements as a particular class of interaction between physical systems that follow the normal course for such interactions prescribed by quantum mechanics without "collapse." The measurement problem is addressed by means of the revised rules governing the ascription of determinate properties to systems. The idea is that, for the special class of measurement interactions, these rules suffice to guarantee that one system (the "apparatus") will acquire and retain a determinate property that serves as a record of the measurement's outcome. It is an additional intended consequence of these rules that macroscopic systems display the kind of stable behavior that we observe, whether or not they are used as quantum measuring apparatus.

In order to secure these desirable consequences, it is necessary to appeal to formal results that show how interactions with the environment induce decoherence. But these results do not themselves solve the measurement problem and the broader problem of the observed stable behavior of macroscopic systems. They contribute to this interpretation of quantum mechanics only as an essential adjunct to the basic interpretative move of replacing the wave-to-property link by interpretative rules that allow for more determinacy of properties, though not so much more as to run into conflict with the results that eliminate the simple realist interpretation.

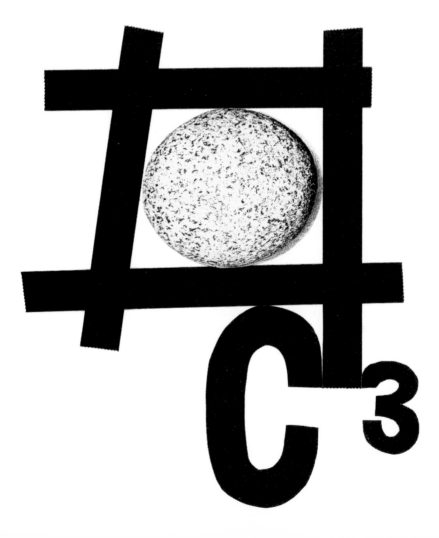

My interactive interpretation is not an exception to the earlier generalization that no interpretation of quantum mechanics yet offered has either won or warranted universal acceptance. Technical objections have been raised to the rules proposed as replacements to the wave-to-property link, and it is not clear whether these can be met by further developing the interpretation. It is also unclear how the interpretation may be brought into conformity with all the requirements of relativity theory. But what view of the quantum world emerges if one steps back from these technical details?

On this interactive interpretation, quantum theory describes an objective physical world by ascribing properties to physical objects whether or not they are observed. But the objects and properties are very different from what our everyday experience leads us to expect. On this view, the physical world consists of a vast collection of elementary quantum systems like electrons, continually interacting with one another. Groups of these form compound quantum systems such as atoms, EPR pairs, measuring apparatus and human bodies. Both compound and elementary systems have intrinsic dynamical properties even when unobserved, so an electron has position-like properties whether or not it is observed. But at any moment, many dynamical properties are indeterminate. If, for example, one thinks of the interior of a box as being divided up into many small regions, then an electron in the box often fails to occupy any one of these small regions to the exclusion of the others. Moreover, the physical interactions required for us to observe these systems typically alter their dynamical properties, and for this reason our observations of the quantum world involve active intervention and not mere passive registration of its features. The indeterminateness of properties and their sensitivity to observing interactions become manifest only in the case of isolated systems, and usually only if these are of microscopic dimensions. That is why typically quantum behavior strikes us as so odd—even unimaginable.

The interpretation incorporates a kind of holism that leads to a novel treatment of quantum nonlocality. A pair of systems may have properties as a whole that are not fixed by the intrinsic properties of the systems that make it up. This implies the failure of Separability; but since Locality still holds, it is easier to see how quantum mechanics may be reconciled with relativity. On this interpretation, quantum mechanics does indeed conform to the idea that doing something to one system has no immediate effect on a distant system. But we are able to hold on to this idea only by giving up the deep-seated prejudice that what an object is like depends only on the nature of its parts and the way it is built up out of them.

1. Richard P. Feynman, *The Character of Physical Law* (Cambridge, Mass.: MIT Press, 1967), p. 129.

2. The remark is quoted by Aage Petersen in "The Philosophy of Niels Bohr," *Bulletin of the Atomic Scientists* 19 (1963), p. 12.

3. Albert Einstein, "Autobiographical Notes," in Paul Arthur Schilpp ed. *Albert Einstein: Philosopher-Scientist* (La Salle, Illinois: Open Court, 1949), p. 81.

4. The name eigenvalue-eigenstate link employed in contemporary interpretative discussions is technically preferable, but may put some readers off unnecessarily!

5. Albert Einstein, Boris Podolsky, and Nathan Rosen, "Can Quantum-Mechanical Description of Physical Reality be Considered Complete?" *Physical Review,* 47 (1935), pp. 777–780. This paper (along with an English translation of Schrödinger's cat paper and other important papers by Bohm, Bell and Everett referred to later) is reprinted in the collection *Quantum Theory and Measurement,* John Archibald Wheeler and Wojciech Hubert Zurek (eds.) (Princeton, N.J.: Princeton University Press, 1983).

6. David Mermin treats both the EPR argument and Bell's development of it in more detail in his article "Spooky Actions at a Distance: Mysteries of the Quantum Theory" in *The Great Ideas Today,* 1988.

7. Each quantity was the spin-component of a spin 1/2 particle along a particular axis: for different axes, these spin-components constitute "incompatible" (i.e., noncomeasurable) quantities.

8. Albert Einstein, in *Albert Einstein: Philosopher-Scientist,* op. cit., p. 85.

9. See especially the essays in James T. Cushing and Ernan McMullin (eds.), *Philosophical Consequences of Quantum Theory: Reflections on Bell's Theorem* (Notre Dame, Indiana: University of Notre Dame Press, 1989).

10. Bell "Quantum Mechanics for Cosmologists," reprinted in *Speakable and Unspeakable in Quantum Mechanics* (Cambridge: Cambridge University Press, 1987), p. 117. The philosopher Karl Popper has endorsed this simple realist interpretation in "Quantum Mechanics Without 'The Observer'," in *Quantum Theory and Reality,* Mario Bunge (ed.) (New York: Springer Verlag, 1967), pp. 7–44.

11. Suppose that all quantities always had precise values, and, indeed, the very values that measurement turns up. Since the measured values of related comeasurable quantities (such as momentum and the square of momentum) always satisfy the same relations as those quantities themselves (e.g., the measured value of the square of momentum is always the square of the measured value of momentum), it would follow that these relations are also always satisfied by the values of unmeasured quantities. But sets of comeasurable quantities in quantum mechanics are interrelated in so many different ways that this turns out to be provably impossible.

12. See Landau and Lifshitz's *Quantum Mechanics* (Reading, Ma.: Addison-Wesley, 1965), p. 3.

13. See especially Bernard d'Espagnat's *Conceptual Foundations of Quantum Mechanics (2nd edition)* (Reading, Ma.: W.A. Benjamin Advanced Books Program, 1976).

14. Besides Zurek, these include Roland Omnès (see his *The Interpretation of Quantum Mechanics* [Princeton: Princeton University Press, 1994]) and Gell-Mann and Hartle "Quantum Mechanics in the Light of Quantum Cosmology," in Zurek, W. (ed.) *Complexity, Entropy, and the Physics of Information* (Redwood City, Calif.: Addison-Wesley, 1990), pp. 425–459. The latter, in particular, use the term decoherence to apply to a somewhat different, though closely related, technical concept. Omnès sees decoherence as the most important missing ingredient in the standard Copenhagen interpretation, while Gell-Mann and Hartle take it to be necessary to successful implementation of Everett's interpretation.

15. Zurek, "Negotiating the Tricky Border Between Quantum and Classical," *Physics Today,* 46 (1993), p. 88.

16. Erwin Schrödinger, from a letter to Einstein dated 18 November, 1950. The letter appears in K. Przibram (ed.) *Letters on Wave Mechanics* (New York: Philosophical Library, 1967), p. 37.

17. See Jeffrey Bub, *Interpreting the Quantum World* (Cambridge: Cambridge University Press, 1997).

18. See Bas C. van Fraassen, *Quantum Mechanics: an Empiricist View* (Oxford: Clarendon Press, 1991).

19. See Simon Kochen, "A New Interpretation of Quantum Mechanics," in Pekka Lahti and Peter Mittelstaedt, eds., *Symposium on the Foundations of Modern Physics 1985* (Singapore: World Scientific, 1985), pp. 151–69; D. Dieks, "Quantum Mechanics Without the Projection Postulate and Its Realistic Interpretation," *Foundations of Physics* 19, pp. 1397–1423; Richard Healey, *The Philosophy of Quantum Mechanics: an Interactive Interpretation* (Cambridge: Cambridge University Press, 1989).

Richard Healey grew up in London, England, and received his bachelor's degree from the University of Oxford. After taking a master's degree in theoretical physics from Sussex University, he went on to Harvard University where he received a doctorate in philosophy in 1978. Professor Healey's book *The Philosophy of Quantum Mechanics: an Interactive Interpretation* was published in 1989. He edited *Reduction, Time and Reality* (1981) and (with Geoffrey Hellman) *Quantum Measurement: Beyond Paradox* (1998). His research interests lie at the intersection of metaphysics and the philosophy of science, and he has published many articles on the philosophy of physics.

Before coming to the University of Arizona, Professor Healey taught at both the Los Angeles and Davis branches of the University of California and also taught and researched at the University of Cambridge and the University of Pittsburgh. He was married to Professor Jean Hampton and edited her posthumous work, *The Authority of Reason* (1998). Professor Healey and his son Andrew Hampton-Healey live in Tucson, Arizona, where they share common interests in music, hiking, horseback riding, and discussing philosophy.

What Kinds of Science Are Worth Supporting?

Gerald Holton

A New Look, and a New Mode

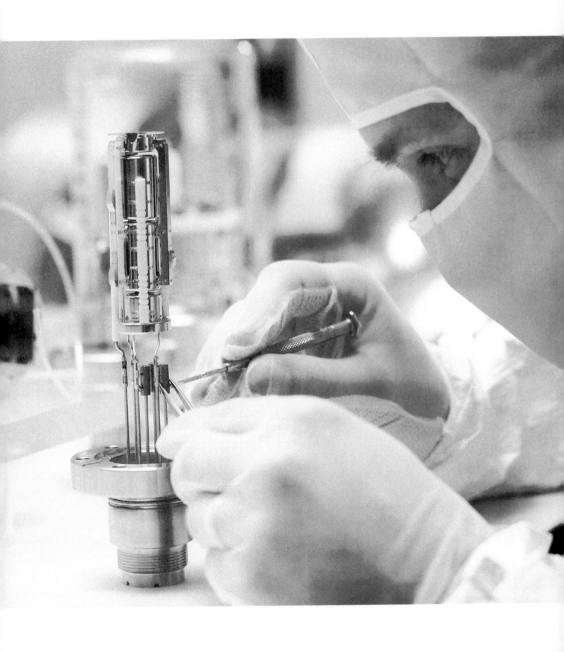

What Kinds of Science Are Worth Supporting? A New Look, and a New Mode

108

From time to time, the nation and its leaders return to an old question—what kinds of science are worth supporting with public funds? Should priority be given to research driven by the pure "curiosity" of the specialists, or more to the development and practical applications of already known scientific results? Moreover, which of the hundreds of specialties—from the study of black holes in astrophysics to problems of cognitive psychology in early childhood to the vast problems concerning the biomedical research community—should be favored? How to set the priorities among competing claimants from vastly different areas? And through what institutional arrangement should such decisions be made?

Such considerations are again very timely, particularly as federal funding for research and development is projected to change significantly over the next few years in the United States. Congress has been struggling to outline what one of its members has called recently "a new contract between science and society." Whatever the outcome, the way science has been supported during the past decades, the priorities, and the motivation for such support are likely to undergo changes, with consequences that may well test the high standing that American science has achieved over the past half century.

At such a turning point, it is wise to try to learn from historical precedents. Even a brief look at some past practices and solutions can help order our thoughts on how to deal with present dilemmas, and may even lead us to recognize the wisdom of adding a new rationale for the support of certain sorts of urgently needed scientific research. First, however, we have to characterize the seemingly opposite two main types of science research projects that have been vying for support in the past and to this day—those often called "curiosity driven" versus "mission oriented." Then we shall have to recognize that there are two flaws in these common characterizations. The first is that in actual practice these two contenders are usually tightly interacting and collaborative rather than clear-cut antitheses and inherently opposed in claims for support, despite what their most fervent advocates think. The second important flaw is that these two widespread and ancient modes of thinking about science have tended to displace and derogate another, third way of rationalizing support for science. My argument is that this third mode of scientific research is not an empty dream. On the contrary, it has had a fascinating tryout at the highest level, now almost forgotten but eminently worth remembering and restarting.

I. The "Newtonian mode" of Scientific Research

(Overleaf)
The scientist at work in the lab: an image of one type of scientific research.

The concept of pursuing scientific knowledge for its own sake, letting oneself be guided chiefly by the sometimes overpowering inner necessity to follow one's curiosity, has been associated with the names of many of the greatest scientists, but most often with that of Isaac Newton. His grand work, the *Principia* (*GBWW* I: 34, 1–372; II: 32, 1–372), may well be said to have given the 17th-century Scientific Revolution its strongest forward thrust. It can indeed be seen as the work of a scientist motivated by the abstract goal of eventually achieving complete intellectual "mastery of the world of sensations" (using Max Planck's phrase). Newton's program has been identified with the search for *omniscience* concerning the world accessible to experience and experiment, and hence with the development of a scientific world picture within which all parts of science cohere.

In the *Principia,* Newton postulated four laws of mechanics—the three laws of motion, and the law of general gravitation—and he succeeded in explaining, through their use, an infinity of observable phenomena, from the way objects move on earth to the movement of the bodies in our solar system. Within his structured system of ideas, the behavior of material objects could not only be understood but predicted, from the reappearance of comets to the tides of the ocean.

Of course, an infinity of other phenomena was *not* included, among them optics, chemistry, and the operation of the human senses, all of which were problems that fascinated Newton. With a hint of disappointment, he wrote in the *Principia,* "I wish we could derive the rest of the phenomena of nature by the same kind of reasoning from mechanical principles." (*GBWW* I: 34, 371; II: 32, 371) Ever since, subsuming the whole world of experience ultimately under one unified theoretical structure has been the Holy Grail of those scientists who are driven by their demon of curiosity. Einstein too thought that the "noblest aim" of science was to grasp the "totality of empirical facts," not leaving out "a single datum of experience."

That approach to science can be called the *Newtonian mode.* Within the much more limited horizon of ambition of the specific projects most research scientists undertake, the term also characterizes the life of laboratories and theoretical centers in the largest part of academe, though by now the explanatory models are of course not merely mechanics; and the indi-

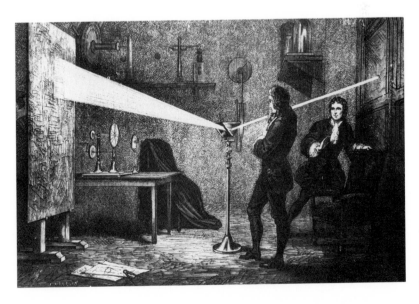

Newton examines a ray of light deflected through a prism.

What Kinds of Science Are Worth Supporting? A New Look, and a New Mode

110

vidual researcher may not have in mind some grand unification of all parts of the sciences, being satisfied to prepare one more brick for the building of a Temple of Science. The ascent to the Acropolis from which one will be able to look over all sciences is left to relatively few; but there is intense activity in the plains below, without which the upward movement would never be possible.

Science is still divided into various well-marked areas, although the boundaries are capable of penetration. While optics, chemistry, and mechanics (to take the examples Newton had in mind) are now largely fused at the fundamental level, Newton was unsuccessful in understanding the operation of the human senses—or of biology as such—in the same way. The Newtonian mode of progress has revealed that science, as the philosopher Willard Van Ortman Quine put it, is not an assemblage of "isolated bits of belief, but an interconnected system which is adjusted as a whole to the deliverance of experience." To be sure, our present ignorance is probably far greater than the areas scientific knowledge has already mapped out. We have yet to discover why matter exists, what the life cycle of the universe is, what causes some of the most severe diseases of living things and, indeed, of societies. Few scientists, however, doubt that as long as their imaginative curiosity is allowed to be unfettered, and their practical means are reasonably assured, progress will continue without foreseeable end, and that the best is just over the horizon. Moreover, they rightly feel that investment in even the most esoteric science may in the long run turn out to be the wisest move.

In all this past and present activity in the Newtonian mode, the hope for practical and benign *applications* of the knowledge gained in this way is a real but secondary consideration. Such applications occur constantly—and they help explain why citizens in the United States think of basic science as usually leading to beneficent uses. Those unanticipated social gains stemming from pure science have so far supported the implied contract between science and society.

II. The Baconian mode of Scientific Research

We turn now to the second main style of scientific research, popularly identified with mission-oriented or applied. We find ourselves not among those in the Newtonian mode, who essentially were in pursuit of omniscience, but among those who claim to follow the call of Francis Bacon, best known for his work *Novum Organum,* published in 1620. He urged the use of science not only for "knowledge of causes, and secret motion of things," but also in the service of *omnipotence,* "the enlarging of the bounds of human empire, to the effecting of all things possible." Even stripped of its overarching and overextended rhetoric, the latter aspect of Bacon's approach is characteristic not of those whose search proceeds without prime regard for applications, but of those to whom the "effecting of all things possible" is the main prize.

Such scientific research in what might be called the "Baconian mode" is carried out more likely in the laboratories of industry rather than in those of academe. Among the prototypical examples is the targeted-research project in the late 1940s by John Bardeen, Walter H. Brattain, and William B. Shockley at the Bell Telephone Laboratories that led to the invention of the transistor. From that advance sprang the possibility of making

Shown from left to right are: John Bardeen, William Shockley, and Walter H. Brattain, the Bell Laboratories scientists who invented the transistor.

ever more effective and powerful electronic devices in everything from heart pacemakers to computers, for commerce as well as for the science labs themselves. One might well say that the transistor initiated the new electronics- and information-based technological shift that has changed our culture and civilization.

A study of the transistor research case reveals that the applied result of prior scientific knowledge depended on many factors that typify mission-oriented research. For example, the official policy of the Bell Telephone Laboratories included "the development of completely new...elements of communications systems." These laboratories belonged to an industry dependent upon them for continuous improvements in communication devices. There had been pressure to find those "new elements." Amplifiers dependent on vacuum tubes were at the heart of the communication system of the day, but were limited by power drain. The switching devices in systems such as that of the telephone network had problems of corrosion and slow response that called urgently for remedy.

The work of the three Bell scientists was quite "problem focused," and the expectation was that there would be a practical payoff within a relatively short time, a working process very unlike that of scientific researchers in the Newtonian mode. The case of the transistor also illustrates that the intended as well as unintended changes brought about by progress in engineering and technology are apt to penetrate fairly quickly into such widely varied fields as medicine or the world of financial transactions. Unlike the results seen with basic research, it is clear that mission-oriented research by its very definition results in very practical, and preferably rapid, applications.

What Kinds of Science Are Worth Supporting? A New Look, and a New Mode

112

III. The Bush Report

Any historical study will, I believe, show that both the Newtonian and Baconian types of research, whether they exist in pure or somewhat modified form, are equally important for the health of the total research and development system of science. Indeed, as we shall see below, each system needs the other for its progress, and they tend to blend together at the edges. Yet policy makers often battle over which of the two modes should have higher priority when it comes to funding and setting up scientific institutions. For example, in late 1993, a report on the future of the National Science Foundation, prepared and published by the Senate Appropriations Committee chaired by Senator Barbara Mikulski, amounted to an edict that federal funding for basic or curiosity-driven research should be cut back, in favor of supposedly quick-payoff strategic research; the document even warned the NSF not to "shroud" Newtonian mode research under the guise of Baconian mode research. More recently, many representatives in prominent Congressional positions have turned against strategic research, declaring that support for applied research through government agencies should be cut back. As Representative Bob Walker stated, subsidizing applied research was equivalent to corporate welfare payments to private industry, which should fund most of such research through its own budgets.

Perhaps the most famous occasion where public support for only one mode of research was urged and the other left to its own fate was the 1945 report to the President by the director of the Office of Scientific Research and Development, Vannevar Bush. It was entitled, *Science, the Endless Frontier* (dated July 1945).[1] It is worth examining here some key aspects of this report—a document which has had an enormously beneficent effect on the United States system of science, despite its one-sided position. Any essay on the topic "What Kinds of Science are Worth Supporting" must acknowledge that the Bush Report was a quantum leap in the evolution of 20th-century science policy.

The Bush Report stands as an elegant and memorable manifesto of what scientists believed at the time, and it has become a classic which has endured beyond its own time. (My definition of a classic is a work that has survived both its imitations and its refutations.)

Despite some internal contradictions and other flaws, many of which Vannevar Bush recognized, its cumulative impact on science, on technology, on universities and other institutions, and on our society has hardly begun to be properly estimated. It is not merely a celebratory remark to say that without the Bush Report and the alternatives it generated (such as those authored by Senator Harry Kilgore and by John Steelman), America—and the world—would now be in a much reduced position.

The Report is really two books in one. President Roosevelt had originally commissioned the work, and Bush starts the Report with a thirty-four page summary intended for the President, Congress, and the American people. With almost hypnotic effect, Bush continually emphasizes a few major ideas under headings such as "Scientific Progress is Essential"; "Science is a Proper Concern of Government"; "Action is Necessary." Above all, the Report called for public patronage, for funding of basic research and science education by the federal government on a large scale—an idea quite contrary to tradition and common practice at the time. Bush put the case succinctly: "Scientific progress is one essential key to our security as a nation, to our better health, to more jobs, to a higher standard of living, and to our cultural progress."[2]

The rest of the 182-page booklet was called "Appendices." This section constitutes, so to speak, the second book, consisting of the reports of Bush's working committees, totaling forty persons. While their work provided the raw material upon which Bush drew for his own part of the Report, we can believe Bush's later comment that few in Congress would actually have read those appendices with care, if at all.

Vannevar Bush, during his tenure as Director of the Office of Scientific Research and Development.

What Kinds of Science Are Worth Supporting? A New Look, and a New Mode

114

Using a system developed by Harvard research scientists, packets of "window" are ejected from a B-17 plane. Each "window" contains thousands of thin aluminum strips that, upon release, jam the German anti-aircraft radars by giving false indications on the radar screens.

Writing during the period between November 1944 and June 1945, Bush and his colleagues knew that World War II was ending. They believed deeply in the fundamental proposition announced in the letter of November 17, 1944, signed by the President, asking for the drafting of the Report: "New frontiers of the mind are before us, and if they are pioneered with the same vision, boldness, and drive with which we have waged this war we can create a fuller and more fruitful employment and a fuller and more fruitful life."[3] The document is imbued with the optimism of a victorious people who have gone through hellish battles to rescue Western civilization from its sworn enemies—thus, seemingly thrust by fate to become at least for a time the primary shapers of a new world order. The psychology showing through the prose is therefore rather utopian.

By 1944, American research scientists had already made great achievments in applied scientific and technological work (such as radar, synthetic rubber, and medical advances) that were essential components in achieving the victory, and they were now looking forward to returning to basic research. Bush himself wrote later: "I was as anxious to get out of government, as were nearly all of those who manned the war laboratories."[4] They all had to make up for lost time. In addition, many were chafing under the threat that the military control of research would continue in peacetime.

For an illustration, we need only look at the editorial page of the *New York Times* of August 7, 1945, a few weeks after the publication of the Bush Report, and on the day after the release of the atomic bomb over

Hiroshima. The whole edition is full of unmixed praise for the bombing. The editorial page called the bomb "the most stupendous military and scientific achievement of our time. It may even be the most stupendous ever made in the history of science and technology." It followed with a significant paragraph that sternly spelled out a model for science policy by which all future science progress might be achieved, the kind of science worth supporting:

> University professors who are opposed to organizing, planning, and directing research after the manner of industrial laboratories because in their opinion fundamental research is based on 'curiosity,' because great scientific minds must be left to themselves, have something to think about. A most important piece of research was conducted on behalf of the Army, by precisely the means adopted in industrial laboratories. And the result? An invention was given to the world in three years which it would have taken perhaps half a century to develop if we had to rely on prima-donna research scientists who work alone. The internal logical necessities of atomic physics and the war led to the bomb. A problem was stated. It was solved by teamwork, by planning, by competent direction, and *not* by a mere desire to satisfy *curiosity*.[5]

In 1945, this opinion largely reflected the public's perception of how scientists should be directed, i.e., to the Baconian mode; and as we have seen from Senator Mikulski's directive, issued half a century later, the same kind of battle is still being fought over the federal role in supporting those research projects that are motivated chiefly by curiosity. The Bush Report, siding strongly with the Newtonian mode, issued the dictum that "In order to be fruitful, scientific research must be free...free from the necessity of producing immediate practical results...."[6]

Among the positive general remarks about the Bush Report, we must add two. One is that it had a long life, despite the many changes in implementation. In terms of visionary ideas, the Report not only had quick influence—as in helping to establish the Office of Naval Research in 1946—it has also remained the standard against which to measure its would-be successors. The other point worth remembering is that the Report by no means asked for unreasonable autonomy for the pursuit of science. While noting that the special requirements of research make necessary "adjustment in procedure," e.g., curbing red tape, it declared that the proposed agency for the increased support of research science "must be responsible to the President and the Congress. Only through such responsibility can we maintain the proper relationship between science and other aspects of a democratic system."[7]

The main criticisms of the Bush Report are not minor. Its scope did not include the social sciences or, as some critics would wish, the humanities. The possibilities of later developments in the conduct of science were not considered in the report. The Bush proposal to concentrate almost all federal research support for all fields in one agency was happily not implemented. Instead, later plans allowed for a diversity of funding by different

Recycling rubber was a large part of the recycling efforts during World War II. Shown here is seven acres of scrap rubber tires know as "war tires."

What Kinds of Science Are Worth Supporting? A New Look, and a New Mode

118

agencies. There was no conception of environmental dangers accompanying such triumphs as DDT—a substance singled out, along with penicillin, as one of the great advances of science—or for that matter, the problem of nuclear wastes quietly piling up in the wake of the bomb programs. There was no inkling of the exponentiation of science into Big Science and beyond, with the corresponding increase of costs. (How could Bush have predicted, for example, that the recent publication of the discovery of the top quark lists about 400 co-authors?)

The downgrading of federal support for applied research or *technological* progress (except in a proposed non-profit "technical clinics for small business enterprise") is usually considered to be due in part to an incompletely developed idea, current at that time, of how modern basic science relates to technology. One commentator has written that in 1945, and even later,

> an implicit argument took place in which the policy makers based their policies on a simple but incorrect model [of the relationship of science and technology], while the historians began to gather the pieces for a new model not yet built.

> The oversimplified model favored by the policymakers depicted science and technology as an assembly line. The beginning of the line is an idea in the head of the scientist. At subsequent work stations along that assembly line, operations labeled applied research, invention, development, engineering, and marketing transform that idea into an innovation. A society seeking innovations should, in the assembly-line view, put money into pure science at the front end of the process. In due time, innovation will come out of the other end.[8]

Bush was above all a superb engineer and his view was not simply linear. He clearly feared, however, that too much pressure for applied research would drive out pure research, and that not enough basic science would be performed in the U.S. to provide the "scientific capital [that] creates the fund from which the practical applications of knowledge must be drawn."[9] In his view, therefore, research was the pacemaker of technological progress.

According to the figures given in Bush's report, the projected cost for all that was to be accomplished was, in hindsight, quite low: in steady state $122.5 million (in 1945 dollars) of government support for all research and development in natural science, medical research, science education, and long-range national defense development. Financial restraint won public consent for the Report in initiating federal support of science. Not until the Vietnam War did substantial popular disenchantment over federal control of research and development arise, signaling a profound change from the earlier, rather euphoric phase in the relation of science and society. The end of the Cold War further focused a reconsideration of federally-funded science.

IV. Beyond the Bush Report

Perhaps in part as an answer to these more recent voices against increased federal support for basic science, a report was unveiled by the Executive branch in August 1994. It adopted the stance of being a successor to the Bush Report. Entitled "Science in the National Interest," it indicates its authority by putting the seal of the President of the United States on its cover and the signatures of President Bill Clinton and Vice President Al Gore on the covering letter. The connection with the Bush Report was made clear in the very first paragraph, in which Bush is credited with setting forth an "investment strategy" by which "the Government should accept new responsibilities for promoting the flow of new scientific knowledge and the development of scientific talent in our youth"; that was still the "bedrock wisdom."[10]

Indeed, upon its publication, the brochure was quickly hailed as the successor document, one commentator writing that it will "do for science policy in the post-Cold War era what Vannevar Bush's *Science, the Endless Frontier* provided for the post-World War II era—a strong rationale for federal support for basic or fundamental science."

In fact, basic differences between the two reports are only acknowledged twice in the 1994 document. The first difference is that the words "the social and behavioral sciences" are included—at least in one sentence which speaks about "fundamental science" that must remain "integral to the agency planning activities." Another passage reads that "research is also essential in social and behavioral sciences for preventing disease." But these brief remarks do not hide the continuing ambivalence about the "soft sciences."

The second difference is more explicit. The model for translating science into benefits for society has changed. In the Bush report there was an implied progression from basic to applied research and then development into a product. The 1994 report states,"We depart here from the Vannevar Bush canon, which suggested a competition between basic and applied research. Instead, we acknowledge the intimate relationships among and interdependence of basic research, applied research and technology, and appreciate that progress in any one depends on advances in the others...."[11] Indeed, according to Vice President Gore, this first White House statement on science policy in fifteen years held that "technology is the engine of economic growth; science fuels technology's engine." The new metaphor for the relation of basic science to development, in the words of the report, is "an eco-system [rather] than a production line." Or, as the scientist-statesman Harvey Brooks appropriately commented, we are now really talking about a "seamless web."

It remains to be seen whether that report of 1994—still the most authoritative of recent official documents on the reasons for and ways of supporting science at the federal level—will become a new manifesto, rallying contending forces to a common cause. Perhaps the best advice for those who are now engaged in the vigorous debate over a new vision for science

What Kinds of Science Are Worth Supporting? A New Look, and a New Mode

120

In 1997, President Bill Clinton and Vice President Al Gore participated in a Presidential Forum on the Environment at Lake Tahoe.

policy is an observation recorded in Bush's autobiography: "The question before us is whether men in power can become reasonable before they become exterminated."[12] In this contentious era, lacking in the optimism of the early post-World War II days, Bush's stern warning is part of the heritage he left to us. Still, the development of greatest interest is the newly emerged vision of the total enterprise of scientific and technological advance as an "eco-system" (Gore's phrase), with interacting parts of equal importance. Or, to change the metaphor, one should now recognize that the variously labeled activities are all threads forming Brooks' "seamless web."

That vision is justified by recent cases of scientific achievement. The following summary of one such case will show how, in the new era, important scientific discoveries are achieved using the *combined* Newtonian and Baconian modes.

V. The "seamless-web" view of science: an example from the frontier of research

Two young co-workers, Hasok Chang and Edward Jurkowitz, and I have found that the lessons of science policy emerge clearly when one looks carefully at the actual conditions that made possible a major leap forward—in this case the discovery, in 1986, of the existence of superconductivity at high temperatures.[13]

The phenomenon of superconductivity itself—that is, the loss of electrical resistance below a critical temperature (T_c) characteristic of the material—had long been known. It had been found first by the Dutch physicist Heike Kamerlingh Onnes (a professor of experimental physics at the University of Leiden) in 1911 in a sample of mercury when cooled to just 4.2 degrees above absolute zero (4.2 K, degrees Kelvin). Soon many investigators joined in the search for electrical conductors that would have higher critical temperatures—materials that would be easier and cheaper to keep resistance-free—because achieving lower temperatures involves complex and expensive apparatus. To be sure, the superconductivity researchers were aware of possibly creating enormous new efficiencies in the transmission of electricity, but their original and main motivation was curiosity.

Here and there, small progress was made, but by 1973, over six decades after the discovery of the phenomenon of superconductivity, the best materials that had been found had a T_c of only 23.3 K. The continual frustration in failing to break through this barrier was crystallized in a remark by Bernd Matthias, a highly respected physicist at the Bell Laboratories in New Jersey. He said that in the absence of successful theories to guide one, it would be best to give up the search, or "all that is left in this field will be these scientific opium addicts, dreaming and reading one another's absurdities in a blue haze."[14]

All this changed practically overnight with the discovery of superconductivity at a significantly higher temperature, about 30 K, announced in 1986 by Karl Alex Müller and his former student Johannes Georg Bednorz, both working at the IBM Zürich Research Laboratory (Switzerland). Their announcement became an instant sensation, in part because the materials used by the Swiss team were distinctly different from all previously known superconductors. They used a ceramic, a mixed oxide, of barium, lanthanum, and copper. It was relatively easy to prepare and it could be modified by chemical substitution. No new technology was involved in this groundbreaking discovery; the particular ceramic had been available for decades, but had never been considered a candidate for high-temperature superconductivity research.

The news of the discovery caused the so-called "Woodstock of Physics," an impromptu session at the 1987 meeting of the American Physical Society; more than 3,500 researchers crowded into the meeting rooms to hear about the new achievement, and the excited discussions went on into the early morning hours. The Nobel committee, citing Müller and Bednorz's papers from about 1986 describing their achievement, awarded the 1987 Nobel Prize for Physics with maximum possible speed. Even President Ronald Reagan took notice, greeting the "new age" of superconductivity as a "revolution," with great promise for eventual practical applications.

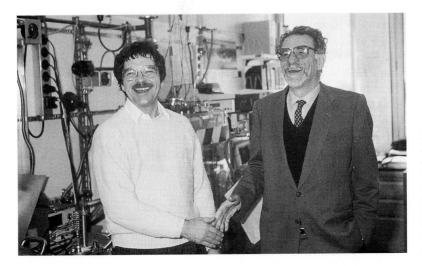

Karl Alex Müller (left) and Johannes Georg Bednorz (right) after winning the Nobel Prize for their work in physics.

What Kinds of Science Are Worth Supporting? A New Look, and a New Mode

122

All over the world, researchers could now look in new directions for potential superconductors at ever-higher temperatures. The record currently stands at over 160 K—a temperature that is quite inexpensive to maintain (the freezing point of water is 273.16 K). Hope persists that eventually a superconductor will be found that works at room temperature.

Quite apart from the hopes for the future, and indeed from the ever-growing practical applications of high-temperature superconductivity even at the present levels of T_c, the most interesting question is what the elements were that made the scientific discovery of Müller and Bednorz possible in the first place. Their work was not spun out of thin air. Their success depended not only on their own imagination and skills, but on the work of others who had preceded them and on whose findings or inventions they built. These findings were the strands in the web in which their own work was a nodal point.

One way of finding the "ancestors" of the Müller-Bednorz innovation is a method known as citation studies. As in most scientific papers, theirs published during 1986-87, specifically cited in their footnoted references the main resources on which they had been relying, as previously published in the literature. In addition to explicit references, there are others implicit throughout their papers; for example, a concept or a piece of apparatus generally known in the field need not be "footnoted" in writing for scientific publication—the informed reader knows where such a concept or apparatus originated.

These explicit and implicit citations form, so to speak, the "first generation" in a genealogy of resources that constituted the essential core of the Swiss team's discovery. The citations can be grouped together into at least four *types of resources*: the theoretical framework within which the scientists proceeded (such as the idea of electron-photon coupling); the experimental techniques and material resources for producing the superconducting compound (such as the existence of cryostats, the equipment for achieving very low temperatures); the means of observing, gathering, and analyzing the data while studying the compound's properties (such as x-ray diffractions and thermometers); and the theoretical concepts needed to interpret the data obtained (such as "zero resistance").

Reference to a wide range of prior studies are found in Müller and Bednorz's first five papers. We find physicists who had worked entirely in the Newtonian mode, such as the important theoreticians John Bardeen, Leon Cooper, and Robert Schrieffer, publishing in the *Physical Review* of 1957, and, of course, Onnes in 1911. There are, however, also references that document their reliance on what we have called the fruits of Baconian-mode research, such as the perfection of the x-ray devices they used, going back to work published many decades earlier, and the platinum thermometer they used, putting them in debt to its inventor H.C. Callendar, who described it in a publication in1887.

We already begin to see that the Swiss researchers depended, according to their own published statements, on a great variety of modes of prior research—basic, applied, technology-directed; pure and mission-oriented—and spread over a full century by the labors of their intellectual "parents."

That crucial point becomes even more striking when we then turn to *these* parents, and look in the same way for *their* antecedents, i.e., the second, third, and even earlier generations of citations. The whole family tree of resources on which Müller and Bednorz were relying explicitly or implicitly, reaches far back, literally to centuries of previous findings in science and technology.

Clearly, successful scientists are "borrowers." The borrowing of resources routinely takes place between different traditions within a conventionally defined discipline; for instance, among the theoretical ancestors of Müller and Bednorz are ideas from thermodynamics, statistical mechanics, the old quantum theory, quantum mechanics, and quantum field theory. In addition, borrowing also routinely occurs across traditional boundaries between disciplines; thus the Swiss team used concepts and equipment that originated in physical chemistry, material science, crystallography, metallurgy, electronics, and low-temperature technology.

Of greatest importance to us, however, is that such a study shows that in the course of history basic research borrows resources from applied research, and applied research borrows resources from basic research. This can be proven by looking into the ancestry of every scientific and technological advance. Even Newton's *Principia* can be subjected to such an examination, with the same result. Newton said of himself that he saw further because he was standing on the shoulders of giants. In effect, he was relying on a great diversity of earlier achievements, ranging from the theoretical ideas of Kepler and Galileo, to the practical accomplishments of geographical expeditions (for such needed data as the size of the earth), the ancient technology of preparing glass (making possible the lenses of the telescopes), and so forth. In short, far from being separate and distinct, the seemingly initially unrelated pursuits of basic knowledge, technology, or instrument-oriented developments are, in the eye of the historian, revealed in practice to be the weaving of a single, tightly-woven fabric.

In the light of such findings, what can the scientist or science administrator do to encourage the scientific enterprise? One answer is to support the most promising projects in both the Newtonian and Baconian modes. It has historically been the case, and it will be so even more in the future, that the two modes interact and reinforce each other. Support for both types of projects is essential. The balance may differ in various disciplines—there is less interaction in pure mathematics and more in biomedical research. Indisputably, the trained intuition of the scientist and policy maker will always be needed to make decisions in each specific case.

Here, however, we come to an important new point. There is a mode of research, a kind of science worth supporting, that does not quite fall under the headings discussed so far. It may open a new window of opportunity in the current reconsiderations of what kinds of science are worth supporting, not least in Congress and the federal agencies. We noted that the purely Newtonian mode on a discipline-oriented base seeks knowledge regardless

What Kinds of Science Are Worth Supporting? A New Look, and a New Mode

124

of future applications, and Baconian science looks essentially for practical applications in a problem-oriented mode, of science *already known*. But there is a third mode: It is a combination of aspects of both previous modes, best characterized by the following formulation: *The project is suggested by and targeted at an area of basic scientific ignorance at the heart of a social problem.*[15] The main point is to combat basic ignorance in some uncharted area of science by bringing research to bear on a persistent, debilitating national (or international) problem.

VI. The Jeffersonian Research Program

An early and impressive case of this sort was Thomas Jefferson's decision to launch the Lewis and Clark expedition (lead by Captian Meriwether Lewis and Lieutennant William Clark) into the western parts of the North American continent. Jefferson, who declared himself most happy when engaged in some scientific pursuit, correctly understood that the expedition would serve basic science by bringing back maps and samples of new fauna and flora. In addition, it would

provide observations on the native inhabitants of that blank area on the map (including knowledge of their habits and languages, which to Jefferson was perhaps the most precious part of the knowledge to be gained). In that sense, Lewis and Clark's expedition into the unknown was rather analogous to our exploration of Mars and space generally.

At the same time, however, Jefferson realized that such knowledge would eventually be needed for such practical purposes as establishing relations with the indigenous peoples. In addition, this knowledge would further the expansion westward of the burgeoning United States population.

Shrewdly, Jefferson touted the commercial potential to Congress to back the expedition. To the Spanish authorities, however, from whom Jefferson required permission to pass through their territories, he described it as a purely scientific mission. In fact, that mixture of motivations was correct. This dual-purpose style of research contributed basic scientific study of the sort that would be recognized in the federal science funding agencies today: there was no sure short-time pay-off, and the investigation was targeted at an area where there was a recognized problem affecting society. We might call this style of research the "Jeffersonian mode." This mode should not be thought of in competition with the others discussed above, but as an additional advancement of an alternative way to approach science.

To be sure, the science of plate tectonics did not arise out of an effort to predict earthquakes, nor genetics out of a desire to create a better harvest in the vegetable garden. On the contrary, it happened the other way around, and there are innumerable examples in the history of science and technology that could be collected under a heading such as "How basic research reaps unexpected rewards." The third way of looking at the conduct of science that we are proposing here can provide a way to avoid the dichotomy of "ivory tower" versus "quick payoff" styles of research and in the process make public support of all types of research more palatable to policy makers and taxpayers alike.

The Lewis and Clark expedition consisted of about forty men whose skills ranged from navigation to Indian languages.

What Kinds of Science Are Worth Supporting? A New Look, and a New Mode

126

It is not hard to imagine research that holds the key to alleviating well-known societal dysfunctions. Even the "purest" scientist is likely to agree that much remains to be done in cognitive psychology, the biophysics and biochemistry of conception, the neurophysiology of hearing and sight, and molecular transport across membranes, to name a few. Such basic work, one could expect, will give us a better grasp of complex social tasks such as childhood education, family planning, improving the quality of life for the handicapped, and the design of food plants that can use inexpensive (brackish) water. Other basic research examples might include the physical chemistry of the stratosphere; the complex and interdisciplinary study of global changes in climate and in biological diversity; that part of the theory of solid state which makes the more efficient working of photovoltaic cells still a puzzle; bacterial nitrogen fixation, and the search for symbionts that might work with plants other than legumes; the mathematics of risk calculation for complex structures; the physiological processes governing the aging cell; early learning; the sociology underlying the anxiety of some parts of the population about mathematics, computers, and science itself; and the anthropology of ancient tribal behavior that underlies genocide, racism, and war in our time.

It should be said that in the biomedical area there have already been instances of the success of such Jeffersonian-mode research, from Pasteur to the successes of the NIH Institutes. But such research has in a sense been easier to start and support in the biomedical field, partly because of the immediate self-interest of the patrons. The successes there, in fact, support a mandate that the research system should expand the Jeffersonian mode to fields both inside and outside the biomedical area.

It is fairly easy to imagine a consultative body that could identify the research areas that could benefit from cultivation. One mechanism, a non-governmental "National Forum on Science and Technology Goals," is among the recommendations in the Carnegie Commission report, *Enabling the Future: Linking Science and Technology to Societal Goals* [1992]. Of course, the effort would require the full and continuing participation of a wide spectrum of experienced and trusted scientists, engineers, and policy makers.

VII. The Jimmy Carter-Frank Press initiative toward the Jeffersonian mode of research

A fascinating attempt was made some twenty years ago at the highest level to expand the spectrum of research projects that the government found worthy of support to attend to what we have described as the third mode.

Long neglected, that effort is eminently worth remembering as the contract between science and society is being re-evaluated. During the presidency of Richard Nixon, federal science support had decreased substantially and the science infrastructure had deteriorated greatly. President Jimmy Carter, who considered himself a man of science (and even hoped to be remembered as the "basic research president") was determined to reverse this decline.

Carter enlisted Frank Press, a distinguished geophysicist, as Science Adviser and Director of the Office of Science and Technology Policy in 1977. Press became a major force in making the revival of American science a key federal priority.

Press ordered a survey of government agencies, with the goal of obtaining a list of basic research needs. The composite list would reveal those areas in which the various agencies needed help in order to fulfill their essentially practical commitments to the public. It was exactly the type of inquiry that we have identified by the term Jeffersonian.

Press sent a memorandum to Vice President Walter Mondale on June 10, 1977, making the case for increasing federal funding for research. Mondale wrote a memorandum to Carter on July 21 that proposed, among other things, to ask Press and Bowman Cutter, of the Office of Management and Budget (OMB), to undertake an initial study on the issue that would result in a report and recommendations to the President. In his approval note, Carter added the comment: "Do not overemphasize University concern. I'm not interested in a 'college aid fund' concept. J[immy]."[16] Clearly, Carter was more interested in basic research and its national benefits than in supporting specific research institutions. Instead of the monolithic funding institution recommended in the Bush report, there was now in place an ingenious and fruitful alternative, thanks in good part to two of Frank Press's predecessors, Science Advisers Jerome Wiesner and George Kistiakowski. They had helped to build serious science research capacities into the various federal mission agencies, thus assuring both advisers' intellectual and political interests.

Carter's true concerns manifested themselves also in the planning process for the budget of fiscal year 1979. As Bert Lance, the director of the OMB, reminded the heads of executive departments and agencies on August 15, 1977:

The President has expressed his interest in having Federal de-

In 1979, President Jimmy Carter (left) and his energy advisor, Dr. Frank Press (right), attended an enerty symposium sponsored by the White House.

What Kinds of Science Are Worth Supporting? A New Look, and a New Mode

128

partments and agencies examine their research and development programs to assure an appropriate balance between basic or long-term research and shorter-term applied research and development. The President is particularly concerned with the identification of critical problems currently or potentially faced by the Federal Government where basic or long-term research could assist in carrying out Federal responsibilities more effectively or where such research would provide a better basis for decision-making....

We are asking that in the context of developing your 1979 budget you identify whether there are specific problems in your area of responsibility that might be better addressed through basic research and then use the results of your review to determine whether available resources can be better applied to basic or long-term research associated with those problems....

There is a tendency to defer needed basic or long-term research to meet more pressing near-term problems. We urge that in developing budget proposals for your agency you take a balanced view in dealing with your R&D programs and be sensitive to this tendency....[17]

In a 1978 *Science* article, entitled "Science and Technology: The Road Ahead," Press himself summarized the complex process. Various government agencies, such as the Office of Management and Budget, NASA, and NSF, as well as science representatives of universities, industry, and government installations, did provide their response. Then the initiative reached its decision-point in a Cabinet meeting in November 1977 at which the Carter Administration research policy was discussed. As Press recalled in the article cited above,

[The process] started during a recent preview when certain issues were identified in the Office of Management and Budget (OMB) planning sessions with the President. Subsequently, there were a number of meetings

A scientist examines young plants in a green house. Basic research can make improvements such as "the design of food plants that can use inexpensive (brackish) water."

in which OMB and OSTP [Office of Science and Technology Policy] met with leaders in science and engineering from universities, industry, and the government to review their impressions of trends, issues, and alternatives. We also worked with the Vice President, Cabinet members, and the heads of NASA and NSF.... During the course of our interactions on research with the departments and agencies, the President queried the Cabinet members on what they thought some of the important research questions of national interest were. Here are a few examples cited by the Cabinet officers: Can simple chemical reactions be discovered that will generate visible radiation? How does the material pervading the universe collect to form complex organic molecules, stars, and galaxies? What are the physical processes that govern climate?... What are the factors—social, economic, political, and cultural—which govern population growth?... How do cracks initiate and propagate in materials? How do cells change during growth and development? What are the mechanisms responsible for sensory signal processing, neural membrane phenomena, and distinct chemical operations of nerve junctions?... What predisposing factors govern cellular differentiation and function in plants and animals?[18]

Carter approved Press's and Cutter's recommendations on research policy at this Cabinet meeting, and asked Press to send out a list of research questions, which Press had prepared, to the heads of various government agencies and "to solicit additional examples of basic research whose support might be important to the needs of the country"[19] (Press, Memorandum of Nov. 14, 1977). From Press's original list of research questions and from the agency responses, a master list was assembled that contained all the basic research questions whose solutions were expected to help the federal government significantly in fulfilling its mission.

A novel link was being forged between the investigators' curiosity-driven, pure research, and the government's interest in furthering applications. No longer was the link provided merely by chance and providence (unpredictable spin-offs). At the same time, Press's model resisted public pressure to spend taxpayers' money chiefly on "useful," i.e., applied, research, and to cut back further on "useless" basic research. The new link was to be secured by looking for basic research questions in areas of scientific ignorance that could be identified as obstacles to practical benefits—thus connecting basic research with probable, if not certain, social payoffs. In effect, Press asked the government agencies to "take one step back"—to look beyond their immediate problems and applied research interests, and to identify basic research questions whose solutions in the long run would be likely to have a positive impact on them.

This procedure of course selected only a subgroup of possible "pure" research questions that could be generated in a curiosity-driven mode; but it legitimated federal funding for basic research in a novel and impressive way. In this concrete historical case, President Carter's and Frank Press's initiative turned up a long and varied list of questions, many of the sort that would engage the attention of the "purest" scientists. In addition, the list showed that such a model would to a substantial degree preserve the scientists' own ultimate aims as well as their opportunities for obtaining

What Kinds of Science Are Worth Supporting? A New Look, and a New Mode

130

Storms resulting from the effects of El Niño wreaked havoc in communities across the United States. Here, a California neighborhood clings to the edge of a mudslide.

federal funding for "pure research," while at the same time raising concrete hopes for the solution of problems of national importance.

The master list of research questions that resulted from the Carter-Press initiative is an astounding document; it is a comprehensive collection of the research questions which the heads of federal government agencies (including the Departments of Agriculture, Defense, Energy, State, and NASA) at that time considered good science—good, here, in the sense of expected eventual practical payoffs—but which were, at the same time, basic enough so as to resonate with the intrinsic standards of good science within the scientific community.

The same spirit informed one of the items that was originally part of the list which James Nielson, deputy assistant secretary of agriculture, communicated to Press on January 10, 1978:

What are mechanisms within body cells which provide immunity to disease? Research on how cell-mediated immunity strengthens and relates to other known mechanisms is needed to more adequately protect humans and animals from disease.

This question, framed in 1978 as a basic research question, was to become a life-and-death issue for millions only a few years later, with the onset of the AIDS epidemic. While this issue might serve as a justification for "unpredictable spin-off" benefits of basic research, it illustrates that Press's Jeffersonian mode initiative was able *in advance* to target a basic research issue whose potential benefits were understood in principle at the time, but whose dramatic magnitude could not have been foreseen (and might well not have been targeted in a narrowly application-oriented research program).

A related question emerged from the Department of Defense:

Can we discover anti-viral agents to combat viral diseases? The development of such drugs would have as large an effect on mankind as did the discovery of antibiotics.

This demonstrates a certain convergence at the level of basic research questions between government agencies whose immediate missions are very different. Also significant for our argument, the research questions submitted by the Department of Defense included the following:

Can materials be found that exhibit superconductivity at room temperature? Such a discovery would be extremely important to our energy needs as well as revolutionize all technology using electrical energy.

Almost a decade before the sensational breakthrough in this area, which we described above in detail, the Jeffersonian mode was able to identify this field of basic inquiry as one that deserved support.

What Kinds of Science Are Worth Supporting? A New Look, and a New Mode

132

Among the submissions from the Department of State was a question that focused on disaster prediction in various disciplines—another question that has become more relevant today than one would have wished:

> To what extent can the occurrences of natural hazards such as fire, flood, earthquake, and pestilence be foreseen sufficiently in advance to permit mitigation of their effects? The problems of prediction and of mitigation are different for each hazard, but for each, research offers promise of reducing human and physical costs.

The following question submitted by the Department of Energy expressed concern for the environment:

> At what rate will atmospheric carbon dioxide concentrations increase as a result of increased use of fossil fuels? What effect will increasing carbon dioxide levels have on climate? How will this change the global social, economic and political structure? How might the impact be ameliorated?[20]

It was the NASA contribution, however, that distinguished itself from the others through its closeness to the "Golden Age of Science" postulate of the unpredictable spin-offs of basic research, in the wake of the Bush Report. The NASA list started out in grand style with "What is the nature of the universe?," and then went on to more specialized questions of the caliber "What is the nature of life?," "What is the nature of gravity?," "What is the nature of intelligence?," and "What is the nature of matter?"

Notably absent from the NASA list were any statements of the expected societal benefits that would derive from solving these questions. It may have been the intention, however, to connect the work of basic researchers with the often forgotten fascination many laypersons feel in following the pursuit of fundamental scientific advances. NASA activities in space exploration, in particular, were able to capture the imagination of wide segments of the American public, perhaps partly because they resonate with the frontier and pioneer mythology deeply embedded in the American psyche.

Linking basic research to perceived national need also underlay the reorganization of the NSF's applied research programs in 1978. A division of Integrated Basic Research (IBR) was formed as part of the new Directorate for Applied Science and Research Applications, which encouraged and accelerated the application of existing basic scientific knowledge for a wide range of potential users. IBR intended to provide "support for basic research that has a high relevance to major problems" in selected topic areas in the basic research directorates.

The same ideas pervaded the tenth annual report of the National Science Board of the NSF, released in 1978, which was entitled *Basic Research in the Mission Agencies: Agency Perspectives on the Conduct and Support of Basic Research*. In the now familiar vein, the report contained a catalog of basic research topics keyed to national needs and thus meriting government support. Sixteen agencies, ranging from the Department of Agriculture to the NSF, and from the Department of Housing and Urban Development to the Veterans' Administration, had contributed basic research questions whose solution, in their view, would benefit their missions.

Further momentum was added two years later, in 1980, with the release of the two-volume NSF report *Five-Year Outlook: Problems, Opportunities, and Constraints in Science and Technology.* Again, long and detailed lists of fundamental research that must be encouraged were compiled, lists that showed considerable overlap with those prepared in the earlier report.

The promising new initiatives did not fare well at the outset. President Carter's budget proposal for FY79 recommended a real growth (net of inflation) in basic research expenditure of almost 5%, but by the time the budget was approved by Congress, almost nothing of the proposed growth remained. Efforts in the following years similarly fell short of achieving a substantial increase in basic research funding. In 1980, Eliot Marshall wrote in a *Science* article that "the Administration's actual spending on basic research over the last 3 or 4 years has just stayed ahead of infla-

In 1997, NASA sent a rover vehicle named Sojourner to Mars. The rover sent back thousands of images of the planet.

What Kinds of Science Are Worth Supporting? A New Look, and a New Mode

134

tion."[21] Finally, hopes to boost federal spending on basic research as well as the Jeffersonian mode initiatives in agencies like the NSF were quashed with the election of Ronald Reagan in 1979.

The Carter-Press initiative quickly slid into oblivion, but it does not deserve to be forgotten. On the contrary, a revitalization of the Jeffersonian mode of science would provide a promising, additional model for future science policies, one that would be especially relevant in the current state of unclarity and disorientation about the role of science in society. Undoubtedly, identifying problems that require research can now be expanded beyond the mechanisms in place during the Carter days. For example, proposals might be sought not only from federal agencies, but also from informed sections of the public, such as the focus groups assembled by organizations like Public Agenda and the American Association for the Advancement of Science. In addition, the search might be expanded to provide input from organizations outside the United States. Such modifications can only enrich the process rather than change its goal.

Epilogue: These considerations have covered a wide range, scanning the main spectrum of answers to the question what science is worth supporting today, and why. We are at a time when the answers from various directions are often not based on a historically informed study, and are in profound conflict. This discord is made more ominous by the attacks from parts of academia outside the sciences, which have been aggressively questioning the very existence of the moral authority of science.

Against these confusions and objections, the reinstatement of the Jeffersonian research program could well serve as an immunization against the increasing charges that science is not sufficiently concerned with the national welfare. This "third mode" of research is precisely targeted at the national welfare. As mentioned, biomedical and related research has always been seen to be already active in that mode, and hence has become a model that other sciences may well adopt—as the Carter-Press initiative had tried to put into place, before it was set aside by political misfortune.

Acknowledgment: I am indebted to my Research Associate, Dr. Gerhard Sonnert, for his help in the preparation of this article, and I gratefully acknowledge partial support for the research leading to this essay from the William F. Milton Fund of Harvard University.

1. Vannevar Bush, *Science, the Endless Frontier* (Washington: National Science Foundation, 1960).

2. Ibid. p. 2.

3. Ibid. p. 4.

4. Vannevar Bush, *Pieces of the Action* (New York: William Morrow & Company, Inc., 1970), p. 64.

5. *The New York Times,* Tuesday, August 7, 1945.

6. Bush Report, op. cit., p. 107

7. Ibid., p. 33.

8. George Wise, "Science and Technology," *Osiris* (Philadelphia: History of Science Society, Inc., 1985) Second Series, v. 1, 1985, p. 229.

9. Bush Report, op. cit., p. 83.

10. President William J. Clinton and Vice President Albert Gore, Jr., *Science in the*

National Interest (Washington, D.C.,: Executive Office of the President, Office of Science and Technology, 1994), p. 1.

11. Ibid., pp. 17–18.

12. *Pieces of the Action,* p. 68.

13. *See* Gerald Holton, Hasok Chang, and Edward Jurkowitz, "How a Scientific Discovery is Made: A Case History," *American Scientist,* vol. 84, no. 4 (June 1996), pp. 364–75.

14. Ibid., p. 364.

15. I have treated aspects of this third mode previously, for example in chapters 9 and 14 of my book *The Advancement of Science, and Its Burdens* (New York: Cambridge University Press, 1986; second edition Cambridge: Harvard University Press, 1998).

16. This and the following quotations are from the Frank Press Papers, MC 159, Institute Archives and Special Collections, MIT Libraries, Cambridge, Mass. All quotations from the Press Papers are with the kind permission of Dr. Press and the MIT Archives. Carter quote, MC 159, Box 62.

17. Press Papers: MC 159, Box 40.

18. Frank Press, "Science and Technology: The Road Ahead," *Science,* vol. 200, no. 43, May 19, 1978, p. 740-1.

19. Press Memorandum, January 10, 1978, MC 159, Box 36.

20. Press Papers: MC 159, Box 40.

21. Eliot Marshall "Frank Press's Numbers Game," *Science,* vol. 210, no. 4468, October 24, 1980, p. 406.

What Kinds of Science Are Worth Supporting? A New Look, and a New Mode

136

Gerald Holton is Mallinckrodt Professor of Physics and Professor of the History of Science at Harvard University. His chief research interests are in the history and philosophy of science, and in the physics of matter at high pressure.

Among his books are: *Thematic Origins of Scientific Thought: Kepler to Einstein* (1988), *Science and Anti-Science* (1993), *Einstein, History, and Other Passions* (1996), *The Scientific Imagination: Case Studies* (1998, 2nd ed.), and *The Advancement of Science, and Its Burdens* (1998, 2nd ed.).

Professor Holton is a Fellow of the American Philosophical Society, the American Physical Society, the American Academy of Arts and Sciences, the Academie Internationale d'Histoire des Sciences, the Akademie Internationale de Philosophie des Sciences, and the Deutsche Akademie der Naturforscher Leopoldina. The honors he has received include the Sarton Medal, the Millikan Medal, the Oersted Medal, a Presidential Citation for Service to Education, and selection by the National Endowment for the Humanities as the tenth annual Jefferson Lecturer, described by the N.E.H. as "the highest honor the federal government confers for distinguished intellectual achievement in the humanities."

Reconsiderations of Great Books and Ideas

On Beginnings

George Anastaplo

Introduction

Our sampling of accounts of beginnings includes, on this occasion, a poem by Hesiod, a book of the Hebrew Bible, and the work of a contemporary scientist.[1] Before we discuss these beginnings we should consider, however briefly, what usually permits the beginning of a recognition of the very idea of beginning. The variety in the more or less inspired accounts of beginnings collected in this article suggests what if anything is constant if not "always" about beginnings.

It seems that an *end* is implicit in the notion of *beginning*.[2] *End* can refer to something temporal, something at the other extremity of the process which starts with the beginning. *End* can refer as well to the purpose for which something exists or is done. The end of a thing, in both senses of *end,* may thereby be implied in its beginning.

The beginning of a thing may assume not only an end or conclusion. It may assume as well something prior to the beginning, something which brought about a beginning, or for the sake of which something begins. We venture here upon the theology of our ancients, both Greek and Judaic.

Language seems to be needed if there is to be the recognition, to say nothing of the examination, of any beginning. Poets draw upon, as well as shape, language. Poetry, however much it charms audiences by its mode of expression, depends upon and serves an opinion of what the world is like.

Before we delve into particular poets, we should notice (and not only in anticipation of Part Three of this article) the understanding of things advanced by scientists dedicated to the study of nature. The nature which is studied—the apprehension of which permits scientific inquiry—may imply perpetuity.

A reliance upon nature could mean that there is no temporal beginning to the things of the world. Matter and the universe could be regarded as are, say, numbers and geometrical relations. That is, there are some things always available to be discovered, separated out, and studied, if not to be manipulated and otherwise used.

Does *nature* also suggest *purpose* or *meaning*? Some argue that nature can guide us in how we should act. We can, it is said, be helped by nature to make sense of things not only by what we study but also by how we are shaped by the way we conduct ourselves.[3]

The poet is usually to be distinguished from the scientist in these matters. We can see here an opposition similar to if not quite the same as that identified by Moses Maimonides as existing between the philosophers and those faithful to the Law of Moses—an irreconcilable opposition which rests (it seems) on an opinion whether the world had a beginning in time by having been brought into existence out of nothing by God.[4] In these matters, the poets tend to be the allies of the faithful, especially those poets who undertake to describe the bearing of the divine upon human affairs.

With these observations we are prepared to turn to the Greek writer Hesiod, a poet who, like the authors of the Hebrew Bible, never uses the word *nature*.[5]

(Overleaf) An artist's conception of Space. Shown are the planets Earth and Saturn, a comet, the Orion Nebula (top left), and a spiral galaxy (top right).

Part One. Hesiod's *Theogony*

The noble voice of Calliope, whom Hesiod called chieftest of the
Muses, has sounded steadily since Homer. It has not sounded all of the
time, but whenever it has sounded it has given strength to those through
whom it spoke. It is the source of great poetry—of great story . . .

—Mark Van Doren[6]

I.

Although little is known about Hesiod, we may know more about his
personal life—as a resident of that part of Greece known as the Boeotia to
which his father had emigrated from Asia Minor—than we do about any
other author of his time. An encyclopedist records the following additional
information:

> *Hesiod* (Gr., Hesiodos; fl. c. 730–700 BCE), one of the earliest recorded
> Greek poets. The earlier of his two surviving poems, *Theogony,* is of
> interest to students of Greek religion as an attempt to catalog the gods in
> the form of a genealogy, starting with the beginning of the world [this may
> not be quite so] and describing the power struggles that led to Zeus's
> kingship among the gods. . . .

> Hesiod's other poem, *Works and Days,* is a compendium of moral and
> practical advice. Here Zeus is prominent as the all-seeing god of righ-
> teousness who rewards honesty and industry and punishes injustice.

> Also attributed to Hesiod was a poem that actually dated only from the
> sixth century BCE, the *Catalog of Women,* which dealt with heroic geneal-
> ogies issuing from unions between gods and mortal women. It enjoyed a
> status similar to that of the *Theogony,* but it survives only in fragments.[7]

A much earlier introduction to Hesiod is provided us by Herodotus, in
Fifth Century Greece. He says in his *History:*

> But whence each of [the gods to whom the Greeks sacrifice] came into
> existence, or whether they were for ever, and what kind of shape they had
> were not known until the day before yesterday, if I may use the expression;
> for I believe that Homer and Hesiod were four hundred years before my
> time—and no more than that. It is they who created for the Greeks their
> theogony; it is they who gave to the gods the special names for their
> descent from their ancestors and divided among them their honors, their
> arts, and their shapes. Those who are spoken of as poets before Homer and
> Hesiod were, in my opinion, later born.[8]

It should be noticed that Herodotus does not say that Homer and Hesiod
invented or even discovered the gods, but only that they offered the Greeks
a clear picture of the forms, functions, and relationships of the gods. It
should also be noticed that there remains to this day some uncertainty as to

A mosaic depicting the Greek poet Hesiod.

who was earlier, Homer or Hesiod. There may be an instructive uncertainty here: in one sense, Homer is prior, but in another, Hesiod is.

It should be noticed as well that there is in Homer no systematic account of the beginning of the gods, to say nothing of the beginning of the universe or of cosmic forces. He does not pay much attention even to the beginning of the Great War in which the Achaeans and the Trojans find themselves fighting. Rather, there is in the *Iliad* a detailed account of the beginning of a quarrel (between Achilles and Agamemnon) late in a very long war. This leads to a detailed account of one episode in that war, an episode which says much about the overall war if not also about the world itself.

Why is not Homer concerned about the beginning of things? Is it partly because this does not seem to be a concern of his characters? *They* take the world, including the gods, as *given*. Whether the gods are really *given* for Homer personally, he is willing to make them seem so, even as he presents events and results in such a way that few if any of them may require the much-spoken-of gods for them to be understood in human terms. This does not deny that Homer presents events and their consequences in the terms of human beings who are very much open to the gods.

Much of what Homer (or a particularly gifted predecessor) does can be understood to prepare the way for Hesiod: the language is developed, a poetic meter (the hexameter) is established, the audience is shaped. This can be said even though Hesiod seems more primitive and hence earlier than Homer in some respects, especially with his cataloguing of gods and others.[9]

II.

We can now look more directly at Hesiod and his beginnings by returning to the account of the *Theogony* in our encyclopedist:

The cosmogony begins with Chaos ("yawning space"), Earth, [Tartarus,] and Eros (the principle of sexual love—a precondition of genealogical development). The first ruler of the world is Ouranos ("Heaven"). His persistent intercourse with Earth [who had generated him on her own] hinders the birth of his children, the Titans, until Kronos, the youngest, castrates him. Kronos later tries to suppress his own children by swallowing them, but Zeus, the youngest, is saved and makes Kronos regurgitate the others. The younger gods [led by Zeus] defeat the Titans after a ten-year war and consign them to Tartarus, below the earth, so that they no longer play a part in the world's affairs.[10]

Our encyclopedist then adds:

This saga of successive rulers is evidently related to mythical accounts known from older Hittite and Babylonian sources. Hesiod's genealogy names some three hundred gods. Besides cosmic entities (Night, Sea, Rivers, etc.) and gods of myth and cult, it includes personified abstractions such as Strife, Deceit, Victory, and Death. Several alternative theogonies came into existence in the three centuries after Hesiod, but his remained the most widely read.[11]

Hesiod's account of the origins of the things which he can see and has heard about culminates in the emergence of the supreme and now supposedly unchallengeable rule of Zeus. Here, as elsewhere, the end may help shape the beginning, providing that by which the poet takes his bearings. Other gods than those Hesiod mentions are worshiped elsewhere, such as the Egyptian divinities, but these, whatever Hesiod may have heard about them, are ignored by him.

Hesiod works, then, with what he observes: the earth beneath, the heaven above (which always keeps its distance), perhaps the under-earth, and those erotic relations among living beings which are so critical for "peopling" the world. Along with these can be observed human beings and "evidences" among the Boeotians, if not among the Greeks at large, of the divine, such as shrines, altars, and stories about the gods, as well as their names. Also to be observed is how things do not stay the same: sometimes considerable effort is needed in order to keep them going; sometimes all the effort immediately available cannot be used effectively to preserve them as they have been. This may suggest that the element of chaos is always near, if not with, us. Among the vulnerable things, Hesiod could notice, are the gods themselves, as memories and other signs remain of divinities which have been eclipsed.

It can be taken from Hesiod's account that it was difficult if not impossible to celebrate properly any divinities who appeared before Zeus and his colleagues. Zeus is recognized as responsible for the song and perhaps the poetry critical to any celebrations that are likely to depend upon and endure as extended if not comprehensive accounts of the gods. Thus, in order for Hesiod to present his account of the beginnings (or birth) of the gods, he must describe, however briefly, how he himself got *to be*—that is, how *he* began as a singer (or, as we would say, poet). Without the inspiration

Saturn De-
vouring One
of His Sons,
c. 1819–1823,
by Francisco
de Goya.

available from the Muses, daughters of Zeus, Hesiod would be like most if not all human beings everywhere, merely a "belly" living as little more than an animal dominated by pleasure, fear, and pain.[12]

Piety in Hesiod's time consists, then, of celebrating the regime of Zeus, which is comprehensive in its ministering to the potential that human beings have for maturation, understanding, and justice.

III.

Why does not Hesiod say that the divine is always? Can this be said, with any degree of sustainable plausibility, only about a single unchanging god? Hesiod inherits a theology which includes not only Zeus as dominant but also a history both of other divinities and of how Zeus' ascendancy was established. Perhaps any divine history that is going to be interesting as a story requires a variety of named gods who rise and fall. Almighty Zeus himself first comes to view in the *Theogony* as Kronion ("son of Kronos"); even he cannot be understood completely on his own.[13]

It has been noticed that the "Succession Myth" forms the backbone of Hesiod's *Theogony*: "It relates how Ouranos was overcome by Kronos, and how Kronos with his Titans was in his turn overcome by Zeus." An account is given by Hesiod of Ouranos' eighteen children by Earth and Kronos' six children by Rhea, before the poet turns to the struggles of Zeus to establish himself, and thereafter to secure himself in his rule.

The overall account begins, as has been said, with Chaos, Earth, Tartarus, and Eros somehow emerging, evidently each of the four separately from the other three, into effective being.[14] Nothing is said by Hesiod about what was prior to these four. Nor is anything said by him about what caused Chaos, Earth, Tartarus, and Eros to come into being (if that is what they did) or to manifest themselves when and where they did.

There is about Chaos, Earth, Tartarus, and Eros something more durable, if not eternal, than there is about the divinities that come to view, beginning with Ouranos, who is produced by Earth on her own, and followed by the children of Earth and Ouranos, especially Kronos, and followed in turn by the children of Kronos and his sister Rhea, especially Zeus. The sequence begins with Earth's production of Ouranos—that is, Heaven or Sky: this makes sense, not only in that the Earth provides the stage upon which all this action takes place, but also in that what the sky is, as distinguished from all the vastness of the universe, is somehow keyed to the dimensions of the earth, though with Ouranos completely covering Earth.[15]

Nothing is said about "the place" where all of these beings appear. Does their very appearance, "wherever," establish *the* place?[16] Does Earth emerge to provide a place for gods as well as for human beings? She does produce Ouranos on her own, but not Tartarus and Eros, which emerge after her, perhaps in relation to her. Tartarus' location is defined by Earth's. Eros exerts an influence among beings on or near the earth, including among the Olympian gods. Chaos is always there, it seems, as an alternative. It is after Chaos, or alongside Chaos (but not necessarily out of

Chaos), that the generations of divinities and human beings manifest themselves.

We are left to wonder what it may be, what it is that is "always," which accounts for the emergence of Chaos and Earth, each of which has the capacity to produce others on her own, others who will then be able to help engender still others.

IV.

The gods, including those who are supreme for awhile, do not emerge independently as Earth seems to do (along with Chaos, Tartaros, and Eros). Instead, the gods who are shown as in turn supreme (Ouranos, Kronos, and Zeus), are generated by others.[17] We wonder whether only generated beings can have fates. Certainly in their susceptibility to fate the generated gods resemble human beings. Ouranos, Kronos, and perhaps Zeus were fated to be overthrown—and each took measures which (in the case of Ouranos and Kronos) might have made their overthrow even more likely.[18]

The vulnerability of these deathless gods—Ouranos, Kronos, if not also Zeus—may be related to their having been generated: that is, each has come out of another; they were, before they manifested themselves, confined in another. Perhaps this makes them susceptible to being confined thereafter by adversaries—most obviously so in the case of Kronos. Kronos and his siblings are confined by their father Ouranos in the womb of their mother, Earth; Kronos in turn swallows and thereby confines his children—all but Zeus—in his womb-like stomach.

What about the fate of Zeus? He, like Kronos before him, is warned by Earth and Ouranos that a son of his would surpass him. He, like Ouranos and Kronos before him, takes preventive measures, using in effect the technique relied upon by his grandfather and father, but doing it more effectively. Here is how this is summed up:

> Zeus is now elected king of the gods. He apportions their functions, and undertakes a series of marriages to establish order and security in the new regime. His first wife, Metis, is destined to bear a son stronger than Zeus; but Zeus, instead of waiting to swallow the child, as Kronos had done, swallows Metis, thus halting the cycle of succession. (881–929)[19]

We are left to wonder precisely how the prophecy to Zeus had been put. For instance, did it say that *if* he had a son by Metis, he would be overthrown by him?[20] Hesiod does not address this question: one is left to wonder whether it interested him. We do learn that Metis, when she was swallowed by Zeus, was already with child by him—and this is what leads to Athena being born from the head of Zeus.

Perhaps Zeus, in swallowing Metis (or *Cleverness?*), incorporates prudence within himself, thereby personally becoming something other than what he had been. Perhaps, indeed, Zeus can even be said to have been supplanted in this sense. Does Hesiod understand that the reign of Zeus,

An amphora from Eturia (6th century BCE) showing the birth of Athena from the head of Zeus.

perhaps because of his defensive prudence, is dedicated to justice much more than the preceding reigns (by Ouranos and Kronos) had been?

V.

It has been said, as we have seen, that succession struggles among the gods dominate the *Theogony*. Other stories are told, some at considerable length, but the successor struggles provide the core around which the others are organized. We see in Homer's *Iliad* how Zeus can "physically" threaten the other Olympian gods effectively.[21]

But Earth cannot be overcome in the way that, say, Ouranos can be. Earth provides the stage upon or around which all of the named gods act. And it is on Earth that *we* have seen the eclipse of Zeus since the time of

Hesiod and Homer. Does this suggest that Zeus never "really" existed? Or is it a fulfillment of the prophecy about any son that Zeus may have by Metis? Did that son somehow get conceived, in one sense or another of *conceived?*

There is here a way of accounting for the prophecy to Zeus which a Christian Hesiod might try to do something with. Something mysterious can be said to have gone on here of which the pagans could have had no more than intimations, something consistent perhaps with the deification of the *Logos* recorded in the opening chapter of the *Gospel of John,* a gospel in which Greek influences are quite evident.

VI.

Human beings are secondary in the account laid out in the *Theogony:* there is not evident in that poem the concern with human beings that can be seen elsewhere in inspired texts, such as in the Christian Gospels. The life of human beings is described more in Hesiod's *Works and Days,* with much said there about everyday life. A different succession story may be seen there, with five stages of mortals described.

Five seems to be an inauspicious number for Hesiod, with the fifth stage of mortals on Earth representing quite a decline from the opening golden and silver ages. Perhaps *five* can be seen as well in the development of *Theogony,* which is a kind of "works and days" survey for the gods: these are the stages, in turn, of (1) Chaos, Earth, Tartarus, and Eros, (2) Ouranos and his progeny, (3) Kronos and his progeny (which may have been, in some ways, the best time for human beings), (4) Zeus and his divine wives and progeny (as well as the progeny of Zeus and other divinities with mortals), and (5) the career, perhaps yet to come, of Zeus' son by Metis (which would be a departure, if not a decline, from that age of Zeus which Hesiod is commissioned by the Muses to celebrate).

Thus, the correspondences between Hesiod's two great poems are worth exploring. Further correspondences include the fact that there is in both poems the suggestion that femaleness is an affliction among human beings, if not also among the gods. Still, does not femaleness testify to male incompleteness and hence to the vulnerability of human beings? Is not the female, more than the male, able to produce offspring alone? Furthermore, Earth and Rhea are critical to the overthrow of Ouranos and Kronos. The Biblical parallels here, going back to the Garden of Eden, can be intriguing.

The correspondences between *Theogony* and *Works and Days* may include indications that the gods are in some ways dependent upon human beings, and not only for sacrifice and worship. When human beings change, especially in the opinions they hold, so may the gods change, if not even disappear. Besides, the gods of Hesiod and Homer are said to have the physical forms and all too often the passions of human beings.

We can again be reminded of Maimonides, not least for his insistence that the God of the Bible should never be understood to have a human form or human attributes. In addition, we have been taught that "The Bible is the document of the greatest effort ever made to deprive all heavenly bodies of all possibility of divine worship."[22]

VII.

We return, as we prepare to close the first part of our inquiry, to the question touched upon at the outset of this article about whether an end is implied by any beginning. Is there expected, in the temporal sense, an end to the gods depicted by Hesiod and Homer? And is there, in the sense of the purpose of their existence, an end or aim?

Little if anything is suggested in Hesiod about the immortality of human souls, whatever may be understood about those rare mortals, such as Zeus' son, Heracles, who are transformed into immortals. What should be expected of the cosmos that is described in the *Theogony?* Should it be expected to continue forever?

Chaos and Earth, the *Theogony* seems to say, came into view, if not into being, on their own. Might they somehow go away eventually, perhaps to return and leave again, over and over? Is there, for example, something about Chaos, Earth, and Eros, if not also about the particular gods generated in Hesiod's account which endures, however hidden from view these beings may be from time to time, just as can be said about the Ideas which are perpetually available to be discovered and to shape and nourish reason?

Although Hesiod and Homer do not seem to recognize and address such questions explicitly, they can be said to have helped prepare the ground for the philosophers who would first discover these and like questions to be so much in the very nature of things that they are properly the end of the account which an inspired poet may offer as a beginning.[23]

Part Two. *The Bible*

> And Gideon said unto God, "If Thou wilt save Israel by my hand, as Thou hast spoken, behold I will put a fleece of wool on the threshing-floor; if there be dew on the fleece only, and it be dry upon all the ground, then shall I know that Thou wilt save Israel by my hand, as Thou hast spoken." And it was so; for he rose up early on the morrow, and pressed the fleece together, and wrung dew out of the fleece, a bowlful of water. And Gideon said unto God, "Let not Thine anger be kindled against me; and I will speak but this once: let me make trial, I pray Thee, but this once more with the fleece; let it now be dry only upon the fleece, and upon all the ground let there be dew." And God did so that night; for it was dry upon the fleece only, but there was dew on all the ground.
>
> —*Judges* 6: 36–40

We need do no more on this occasion than briefly remind the reader of beginnings in the Bible, thereby pointing up aspects of the Hesiodic account in Part One of this article and preparing the ground for the scientific account in Part Three. Our principal source here is the *Book of Genesis,* the very name of which refers to origins or beginnings.[24]

Seven forms of beginnings are either described or anticipated in *Genesis.* First, there is the beginning of the world itself, as set forth in the first chapter. Then there is the beginning of the human race, with its twofold creation and its indelible experiences in the Garden of Eden. Then there is the beginning of the troubled career of the human race outside of the Garden, starting with the fatal conflict between Cain and Abel and ending with the devastating Flood attributed to human wickedness.

A new beginning for the human race follows in *Genesis* after the Flood, leaving the descendants of Noah subject to the Noahide Law which can be said to continue to govern most of mankind. Then there is the beginning of the people of Israel, the descendants of Abraham, Isaac, and Jacob, who are to have a special relation with God (with profound implications for the rest of the human race). Then there is, in *Genesis,* an anticipation of the beginning, or liberation from Egypt and Egyptian ways and hence the revitalization, of the people of Israel under the leadership of Moses and his successors who promulgate and administer a comprehensive system of laws for the life and well-being of a designated people.

Finally there is, also as an anticipation in *Genesis,* the beginning of the career of the people of Israel in the Promised Land and thereafter, with exiles and returns, with priests and kings, with triumphs and disasters.

In all seven of these accounts, it seems to be assumed that things cannot be properly understood without some recognition of whatever beginnings they may have had. Each of these accounts has inspired libraries of commentaries, which testifies both to their richness and to their elusiveness.

The first two words of the Septuagint, a pre-Christian Greek translation of the Hebrew Bible, are *En arché* ("In the beginning").[25] Christian theology evidently drew upon this *Genesis* account by using the same Greek words to open the *Gospel of John*—but there, instead of the making of the world by God being "in the beginning," the Word (*Logos,* or the divine itself) was "in the beginning."[26]

This reminds us, if reminder we need, that there is no account in *Genesis* of the beginning of the divine: the divine seems to have been regarded as

An illustration by William Blake (1757–1827): Elohim Creating Adam.

existing "always"—and hence as mysterious. We have seen in the *Theogony* (as we can see in many other such accounts elsewhere) how the gods came into being, whatever there may have always been "somewhere" or "somehow" before the birth of the named gods described by Hesiod.

The world of the Bible, whether the Hebrew Bible or the Greek, is more or less orderly, especially when compared to the worlds of the great non-Biblical religions of the human race. Due recognition should be given to

Expulsion
from Paradise
by Alexandre
Cabanal
(1824–1889).

the considerable physical stability as well as to the challenging shrewdness evident in the Bible both of which elements may be seen in the career of Gideon. Both of these—in the forms of an acceptance of the idea of nature, developed among the Greeks, and of a respect for rational discourse, evident in the Bible—are very much taken for granted by modern science, as well as by its predecessors.[27]

I turn now, not without an awareness of my limitations as a layman here, to the way that modern science can approach these matters—that way of accounting for things which combines somehow the emergence of the idea of nature in Classical Greece and the almost instinctive respect for rationality in the Bible.

Part Three. Modern Science

It can scarcely be denied that at the present time physics and philosophy, two sciences of recognized durability, each handed down in a continuous tradition, are estranged from one another; they oppose one another more or less uncomprehendingly. By the nineteenth century a real and hence effective mutual understanding between philosophers and physicists concerning the methods, presuppositions, and the meaning of physical research had already become basically impossible; this remained true even when both parties, with great goodwill and great earnestness, tried to reach a clear understanding of these issues.

—Jacob Klein[28]

I.

There is in modern cosmology far less of an opportunity than in other sciences to have theories guided and validated either by experiments or by how attempted applications "work." There is, instead, an unleashing among cosmologists of an imagination, poetic or rhetorical in some respects, that can be a key to professional success. The layman rarely senses how little the cosmologists have available to go on and how much something akin to fantasy has to be relied upon by them. Although most physics today is much more sober, a glance at contemporary cosmology can help the layman (who can be quite uncritical in response to spectacular announcements by scientists) to notice some of the temptations to which all of modern science may be subject.[29]

Consider, as a particularly dramatic illustration, a remarkably popular book by an English cosmologist, Stephen Hawking's *A Brief History of Time*.[30] Hawking's book comes to us with the authority (or is it the burden?) of more than two years on the *New York Times* bestseller list.

A Brief History of Time (first published in 1988) and its remarkable author have been conveniently described for us with some extravagance by the publisher in words that echo the author's. I draw here upon the opening and closing paragraphs of the book's dust jacket:

Stephen W. Hawking has achieved international prominence as one of the great minds of the twentieth century. Now, for the first time, he has written a popular work exploring the outer limits of our knowledge of astrophysics and the nature of time and the universe. The result is a truly enlightening book: a classic introduction to today's most important scientific ideas about the cosmos, and a unique opportunity to experience the intellect of one of the most imaginative, influential thinkers of our age.

From the vantage point of the wheelchair where he has spent the last twenty years trapped by Lou Gehrig's disease, Professor Hawking himself has transformed our view of the universe. His groundbreaking research into black holes offers clues to that elusive moment when the universe was born. Now, in the incisive style which is his trademark, Professor Hawking shows us how mankind's "world picture" evolved from the time of Aristotle through the 1915 breakthrough of Albert Einstein, to the exciting ideas of today's prominent young physicists.

A BRIEF HISTORY OF TIME is a landmark book written for those of us who prefer words to equations. Told by an extraordinary contributor to the ideas of humankind, this is the story of the ultimate quest for knowledge, the ongoing search for the secrets at the heart of time and space.

STEPHEN W. HAWKING is forty-six years old. He was born on the [three-hundredth] anniversary of Galileo's death, holds Newton's chair as Lucasian Professor of Mathematics at Cambridge University, and is widely regarded as the most brilliant theoretical physicist since Einstein.

The contents of the Hawking book are further suggested by the following passage on its dust jacket:

Was there a beginning of time? Will there be an end? Is the universe infinite? Or does it have boundaries? With these fundamental questions in mind, Hawking reviews the great theories of the cosmos—and all the puzzles, paradoxes and contradictions still unresolved. With great care he explains Galileo's and Newton's discoveries.

Next he takes us step-by-step through Einstein's general theory of relativity (which concerns the extraordinarily vast) and then moves on to the other great theory of our century, quantum mechanics (which concerns the extraordinarily tiny). And last, he explores the worldwide effort to combine the two into a single quantum theory of gravity, the unified theory, which should resolve all the mysteries left unsolved—and he tells why he believes that momentous discovery is not far off.

Professor Hawking also travels into the exotic realms of deep space, distant galaxies, black holes, quarks, GUTs, particles with "flavors" and "spin," antimatter, the "arrows of time"—and intrigues us with their unexpected implications. He reveals the unsettling possibilities of time running backward when an expanding universe collapses, a universe with as many as eleven dimensions, a theory of a "no boundary" universe that may replace the big bang theory and a God who may be increasingly fenced in by new discoveries—who may be the prime mover in the creation of it all.

Many of the things said here by the publisher about the Hawking book are of general interest to us, commenting as they in effect do upon the modern scientific approach. Hawking's special interests and theories may pass in time, but the scientific project continues. We may usefully consider that project by observing various features of it, as exhibited in this book.

Professor Stephen W. Hawking, the Lucasian Professor of Mathematics at Cambridge University.

A prominent feature of the scientific project today is its abandonment—perhaps from its point of view its necessary abandonment—of what is generally regarded as common sense. The ancient scientist was much more respectful of that common sense, and this is sometimes seen today to have contributed to his limitations. Modern physical scientists consider themselves liberated from such restraints.[31]

Still, common sense continues to be relied upon, for much is inherited from our predecessors without our recognizing it. But since we do not notice what is indeed inherited, we sometimes make inadequate use of it, if only in our efforts to understand what we are doing. Modern scientists can seem rather amateurish, therefore, in explaining the basis or presuppositions for the wonderful things they come up with.

Consider how much common sense, as commonly understood, is still with us even in the most exotic scientific activities today. Elementary observing and counting depend upon ordinary experience. Common sense is needed to direct us to the relevant observations, to determine how many observations suffice, even to assure us that a particular collection of data is from our laboratory assistant, not from, say, our stock broker. Common sense is needed as well in hooking up equipment, in reading dials, in deciding how accurate one has to be, in sorting out aberrations. In addition, common sense has to be drawn upon in what is to be understood as cause and effect and in what is to be understood as a contradiction, if not also in what the significance of contradictions is.[32]

I now put my common-sense point in another form: what is the role of judgment in science? Albert Einstein's old-fashioned reservations about critical modern theories should be taken more seriously than younger scientists today evidently do. God, he insisted, does not throw dice.[33] If one does *not* have deep common sense and good judgment, can one be "in tune" with nature and the universe? I will have more to say about this further on.

The ancients seem to have been more sober than modern scientists in assessments of the alternatives they confronted. The practical judgment of the ancients was more evident even in theoretical matters. We may be more accustomed than they to a kind of madness in speculative work, from which our proliferating science-fiction literature and fantasy films are derivations. One consequence of the differences here between ancients and moderns is that the rate of change, for reigning theories as well as for everyday practice, was much lower for the ancients than it is for us.

The modern propensity for innovation may be seen in the series of novelties conjured up by Hawking in his relatively short career, some of which have already had to be repudiated by him. Another way of putting this reservation is to say that Hawking is astonishingly brilliant, especially as a puzzle-solver, but not truly thoughtful. Still another way of putting all this is to observe that I do not recall another book from a man of his stature with so many questionable comments in it.[34] One does not always have the impression of a mature mind at work here. This may be related to the prominence in these matters, as noticed on the dust jacket and reported in the book, of young physicists. The role here of mathematics may also contribute to the overall effect.

II.

It is important to notice the contributions of modern technology, itself dependent upon and permitted by modern science, in developing scientific discoveries.[35] In fact, the character of "discoveries" is likely to be affected by the "character" of the technology relied upon. There may be a self-perpetuating spiral here; whether it is up or down remains to be seen.

We should be reminded again and again of how slim the evidence is that is exploited for the most fanciful cosmological speculations. We should also be reminded that the fundamental alternatives about the cosmos, including with respect to its extent and its origins, may have been noticed long, long ago. It does not seem to me that Hawking and his associates appreciate what their predecessors routinely faced up to, and in a sophisticated way.

One consequence of the volatility of modern scientific thought is that bizarre things tend to be promoted—which should not be surprising whenever ingenuity and innovation are encouraged—and rewarded. Radical changes can be made, as with respect to Hubble's Constant—changes which require stupendous curtailment or enlargement of the estimated age, extent, or "population" of the universe. These changes, which are consistent with a large body of established mathematical theory, can be made without blinking an eye.

Hawking does caution against jumping to conclusions; he encourages people to admit their mistakes. But is not much of modern science susceptible to rashness and consequent bad judgment?[36] Again, one wonders whether all this is conducive to the sobriety and thoughtfulness that may be necessary for a sound grasp of fundamental issues in science, just as in, say, theology.

Hawking may be most obviously a modern in his inability to grasp what predecessors such as Aristotle said, an inability that reveals his own limitations. Whenever he reaches back—if not even to Isaac Newton, certainly to before Newton—he is apt to be sloppy if not simply wrong.

Consider, for example, his remarks about why Aristotle believed the earth to be at rest. Aristotle is seen, here as elsewhere, to have been "mystical." There is no recognition of what we have long been told about the parallax with respect to the fixed stars expected to be observed if the earth is really in a great orbit around the sun, and about the significance of the inability of observers of Aristotle's day and for centuries thereafter, with their equipment, to detect such parallax. Much of what is said by Hawking about predecessors such as Aristotle and Ptolemy is trivial stuff, evidently picked up from unreliable "pop" history. Yet various experts seem to have let him get away with this sort of thing, both before and after publication of this book. Why is that? Because they do not know better themselves? Or because they do not believe it matters? I suspect there is something of both explanations here.

It is a sign of bad judgment not to be more careful in these matters, not to check things out, and perhaps most important not to be aware of how much one does not know. It is this bad judgment which contributes to a mode of

An artist's interpretation of the Big Bang, the explosion cosomologists believe created the universe.

scientific endeavor that permits if it does not encourage all kinds of wild things to be tossed around and regarded as profound efforts. All too many competent scientists today do not appreciate that the best of their ancient predecessors may have been at least as intelligent as they are.

The three biographies appended to Hawking's book confirm that his limitations are not confined to reports on the ancients. In those biographies three of the modern heroes of science, Einstein, Galileo, and Newton, are dealt with.[37] For many readers, the Hawking biographies may be the only extended accounts they will ever have of these men. This is not fair either to these men or to the typical reader. Newton, for example, is dramatized as a sadistic self-seeker.[38]

An intelligent high school student with access to standard reference works could be expected to do better than Hawking (or his research assistant) does here. Such a student might also ask himself what the purpose of such biographies might be, something which is far from clear in this book. The "history" thereby provided is flimsy.

What, according to Hawking, are scientists really after? One thing that scientists seem to be after, he indicates, is the Nobel Prize. The reader is surprised by how often Hawking feels compelled to mention that this or that discovery earned a Nobel.

Related to this may be the use he makes of chance relations, such as the fact that he was born three hundred years after Galileo died.[39] Similar connections are made with Newton. We can suspect here the spirit of astrology, perhaps not surprising in an age when so much is made (and not only by pollsters) of numbers.

Even as Hawking connects himself with Galileo and Newton, he shows himself "with it" in comments and illustrations which draw upon passing fancies. In all this, a lack of seriousness may be detected.

I have touched upon various things that contribute to the popular success of the book, a success which may be a tribute as well to the recognized eminence of Hawking as a physicist. The successful mixture here of the high and the low is similar to what we can observe in other surprising bestsellers from recognized scholars. In such cases, the authors can have previously shown themselves to be capable of much more competent work.[40]

What *do* readers get from the Hawking book? They are both flattered and reassured. They are led to believe that they now understand things that they did not understand before or, at least, that they have been exposed to some wonderful things.

But I must wonder if a great deal is gained in the way of a serious understanding of things. There is much in the book which is serious-sounding, but a good deal of that is really incomprehensible. Indeed, much of the book must be simply unintelligible for most of its purchasers.[41] Furthermore, the typical reader is likely to be misled as to what the fundamental alternatives are in facing the cosmological questions that are glanced at in the Hawking book, fundamental alternatives that have been developed long ago and far more competently elsewhere.

III.

Hawking and his colleagues, I have suggested, do not appreciate how naive they can be. They are certainly intelligent, even gifted, hardworking, and imaginative. Yet, I have also suggested, they all too often lack the kind of productive sobriety that obliges one to take the world seriously and that disciplines flights of fancy. They sometimes seem far from accomplished in their grasp of how the thoughtful investigate serious matters, and how they promulgate their discoveries and conjectures.

Another way of putting my reservations is to suggest that Hawking and his associates do not know what a real book is like.[42] One who is not practiced in reading carefully is unlikely to write with the greatest care.[43] Is the cosmos of the modern cosmologist as shallow as his book? If it is not, then the modern cosmologist may not be equipped to have a soulful encounter with the cosmos. No doubt, competent scientific work can be done without the utmost seriousness—but are not great souls required for the highest activities?

It may not be possible to read or write with the greatest care if one is imbued with our modern prejudices. One such prejudice is that of the Enlightenment, as illustrated in the concluding paragraph of the Hawking volume. It is suggested there that "if we do discover a complete theory [which concerns both the extraordinarily vast and the extraordinarily tiny], it should in time be understandable in broad principle by everyone, not just a few scientists." Hawking goes on, "Then we shall all, philosophers, scientists, and just ordinary people, be able to take part in the discussion of the question of why it is that we and the universe exist."[44]

Such egalitarian sentiments are found elsewhere in the volume as well. This hope or expectation is very much in the Enlightenment tradition, and it may be reflected in the intriguing popularity of this volume. It is not recognized, however, what the limits are as to how many can grasp the most serious things. That is, the limits placed here by nature as well as by circumstances are not taken into account.

Related to this can be the irresponsibility exhibited by all too many intellectuals in how they present what they come to believe. The social, moral, and psychic consequences of ideas are not properly assessed.

We have been told that eighty-five percent of all the scientists who have ever lived are alive today. Their influence is evident and so are their marvelous works. But since they are usually no more thoughtful than most of their fellow-citizens, the dubious consequences of many of their innovations, in their intellectual as well as in their technological manifestations, are also evident.

The immaturity, even the not-infrequent juvenile cast of expression, among contemporary scientists may be sanctioned if not encouraged by the insulating effects of the mathematics so critical to modern scientific activity. The spirit here is very much that of games, especially of those sports in which much is made of record-keeping and of statistics.[45] The childishness evident in contemporary scientific enterprises may well be accompanied by, and depend for success upon, considerable ingenuity and a laudable integrity.

Childishness is not unrelated to the self-centeredness that sometimes seems to be, in principle, at the heart of the scientific method today. Self-centeredness may be seen in the anthropic-principle explanations of the universe as understood by contemporary scientists. It sometimes seems to be believed that things exist only if there is, in principle, a human observer.[46]

Is it true what is often said by cosmologists, that we cannot possibly know anything about what happened before the Big Bang? May there not have been, for instance, an extraordinary compacting then of the matter that resulted in the Big Bang? What can be known about that? It will not do to say as Hawking does that "events before the big bang can have no consequences," for conjectures about such events, however difficult they may be to grasp "scientifically" and thus "verify," can affect the grasp we have of the whole.

To argue, as some do, that only the measurable exists so as to be knowable is to make too much of the way—the remarkably productive way—we happen to approach scientific inquiries today. Hawking recognizes "In effect, we have redefined the task of science to be the discovery of laws that will enable us to predict events. . . ."[47] Various animals effectively "predict" events—and yet they surely do not understand what is going on.[48]

The earth, we are often reminded, is no longer regarded as at the center of the universe. It sometimes seems, however, that the earth has been replaced by the scientist: for whatever *he* cannot measure does not exist, at least for practical purposes if not also for human understanding. The predictability made so much of by the scientist does rely altogether upon measuring.[49]

I conclude my primary critique of Hawking's volume by saying that it is hard for me to see that we know more because of it. It does not seem to be generally appreciated, I have argued, how slim the evidence is that Hawking builds upon, or how much slimmer is all too many scientists' understanding of what it means *to know*. The approach and spirit of current cosmology may effectively cut us off from the most thoughtful awareness of the fundamental issues posed by the inquiries touched upon here. There may be something unnatural in making so much of so little in the way that modern cosmologists "have" to do, exciting though it may sometimes be.[50]

IV.

What, one may well ask, does nature suggest here? Although I will continue to comment upon the Hawking volume, it is only fair, after the criticisms I have presumed to make, to put myself at risk by venturing now some "cosmological" speculations of my own.

Nature, taken by herself, means that there need be neither a beginning nor an end to the universe.[51] This in turn means, as Hawking sometimes seems to recognize, that there need be no beginning of time, however limited the means may be in one set of circumstances or another for noticing or measuring the passage of time. Nature seen in this way is opposed, at least in spirit, to the professional (not necessarily personal) self-centeredness of modern scientists. Thus, nature and self-centeredness contend for the central position in the soul of man, if not in the universe.

A somewhat different, perhaps laudable, kind of self-centeredness may also be seen in the goal set by Hawking, which is "to know why we are here and where we came from." Much is made here and elsewhere of the universe as a place in which human beings live. But, as both Hesiod and the Bible have taught us, human beings may not be the highest things in the universe, and to understand the universe primarily in human terms may not give it its due.

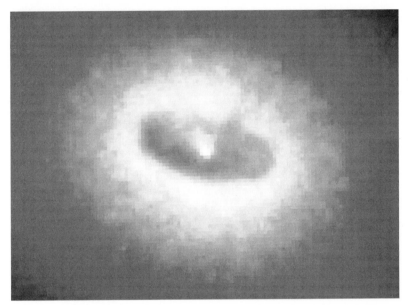

An image retrieved from the Hubble telescope of a possible black hole.

Nor may it do to frame a study of the universe, or even of physics, as a history of *time*. To put it thus may make far too much of process and of human perceptions, not enough either of substance or of principles. This is not to deny that it is natural for time to be made so much of by human beings who regard themselves as personally vulnerable.

But does not nature also direct us to look for those enduring things by which we can take our bearings as we notice and deal with the transitory? Hawking has in his volume a brief account of the origins of life on earth, with the eventual emergence of mammals. This seems to me far easier to grasp than the astronomical, or cosmological, conjectures he and his colleagues offer us, and it was fairly easy to grasp as well when first developed by Charles Darwin a century ago.[52] It also seems to me that this greater ease depends in part upon the fact that nature and a common-sense awareness of things may be closer to the surface of this evolutionary account than

they are to the surface of many of the cosmological and other speculations of our physicists.

Is it not easier to believe that life on earth had a beginning, and even that the earth itself had a beginning, than it is to believe that the universe did? Aristotle evidently believed that the human understanding of things depends upon the opinion that the visible universe is eternal—that is, more or less unchanging.[53] Since this evidently is not so, Aristotle seems to be vulnerable. But perhaps a sound intuition was at work in Aristotle, which may be appreciated when we recognize that "visibility" may extend far beyond what he could be immediately aware of in his circumstances.[54]

Things may always have been as they are now, with a variety of forms evolving and available for the enduring substance of the universe. The ancients who looked to cycles—ancients such as some of the Platonists, and perhaps Lucretius—may also have been sound in their intuition.

V.

Hawking talks at times about a beginning of time with the Big Bang, at other times only about an ascertainable time beginning with the Big Bang. More seems to be made of the former than of the latter, as is reflected in the dust-jacket summary I have quoted. Would not the tenor and force of Hawking's argument change significantly if *the* beginning he makes so much of were simply recognized as merely the *most recent* cataclysmic "beginning," and as such no more than a useful starting point for our inquiries?

If we take the Big Bang seriously, must we not also consider the implications of something that has been called the Big Crunch, that concentration of matter which eventually led to the Big Bang? And why should we believe that we happen to be the beneficiaries of, or "tuned in" to, the only occasion that this sequence came about? Is not this too self-centered or otherwise unimaginative on our part?[55]

If, on the other hand, a cyclical pattern of Big Crunches and Big Bangs is assumed, what follows? Whether there was a beginning of time may be intimately related to whether there is a beginning of space. Here we can be reminded of Lucretius and his tireless spear-thrower, repeatedly pushing back the "frontiers" of the universe.[56]

However beginning-less both time and space may be, it is hard, perhaps impossible, to imagine infinite matter. Do our cosmologists try to imagine that? I am not sure. They talk about infinite density (the Big Crunch concentration of all matter into one point) at the time of (that is, culminating in) the Big Bang. If their calculations show all matter in the universe compacted to virtually a point—and if they mean that literally—my natural inclination is to suggest that they had better calculate again. Lucretius was particularly insistent upon the good sense of recognizing what cannot be.[57]

We are investigating, in effect, the nature of science. We should not forget that science must, like all reasoning, begin with premises which cannot themselves be demonstrated. Related to this is the fact that Newton, for example, does not define the matter that he makes so much of. No doubt he could have done so, but the thing(s) in terms of which he did define matter would in turn have had to be left undefined. Perhaps he preferred to leave as his principal undefined premises those things which are sufficiently available to us by our natural grasp of the everyday world.

The comprehensive account of the universe that the modern cosmologist aims at (as seen in the loose talk at the end of the Hawking volume about knowing "the mind of God") may be, in principle, impossible to attain. I suspect that it is also impossible to comprehend either the smallest element in the universe or the universe itself. To try to comprehend them is like trying to demonstrate the premises that one uses.

I suspect that we see in the celebrated Uncertainty Principle of Werner Heisenberg a reflection of the impossibility of avoiding a dependence upon premises. The ambition of modern cosmologists makes them less thoughtful than they might otherwise be, for it keeps them from recognizing the premises they must inevitably depend upon.

VI.

Critical to our Hawking volume is a discussion of Black Holes. One can become particularly aware, upon considering the basis for the imaginative discourses we have had in recent years about Black Holes, how slim the basis for much scientific speculation has had to be.

Perhaps related to this state of affairs is what is said by modern cosmologists about chaos. It is difficult to see, especially if the stuff of the universe

does move back and forth between Big Crunch and Big Bang, that any state can be considered truly chaotic. Is it not possible, if not even probable, that matter or at least the idea of matter has always *been,* and hence has always been susceptible to the same "rules"? Why would the rules ever change, except in accordance with a Rule of Rules?

Chaos may be, therefore, only a way of talking about our unsettling ignorance about any particular state of things. Among the things implicit in each state of things is the eventual emergence not only of life but even of reason. The potential for reason, if not even an "inclination" toward the emergence of reasoning, is thus always present in the universe.

But to say that reason always *is,* in some form or other, does not mean that reason should be able on its own to understand the whole, including why the whole exists at all. The eternity of the universe probably cannot be demonstrated. But it does seem to be conceivable, whatever that may mean. And it may be vain (if not maddening) to wonder, or to insist upon wondering, why things "have" to exist at all. That is, there may be no place to stand upon in answering such a question. In any event, it is prudent to leave open the possibility of what genuine revelation may be able to teach us about such matters.

Is it not possible that matter has to be as it is, just as number has to be as it is, and perhaps reason as well? To what extent, or in what way, reason depends upon matter is another question better left perhaps for another occasion.

It is possible that even God, however conceived, might be obliged to accept matter as well as number for what they are. One reading of the opening chapter of the *Book of Genesis* finds matter already in existence when the creation described there begins. Also, when the days are being counted during Creation Week, it does not seem that the numbers drawn upon there (culminating in *seven*) are being created as well.

It may not make sense, therefore, to pursue very far the inquiry of why matter exists. Number can be used in describing the operations of matter—but, I again venture to suggest, we should be careful not to assume that the most important things to be known about anything, including matter, come to view only by way of measurements, with or without experiments.

Numbers can give us the appearance of orderliness and even of comprehensiveness, especially as they are projected indefinitely. But an awareness of important aspects of things may be sacrificed in the process. Consider, for example, the limitations of a census-taker in grasping the spirit of a people. Consider, also, this suggestion by Bertrand Russell: "Physics is mathematical not because we know so much about the physical world, but because we know so little: it is only its mathematical properties that we can discover."[58]

(Left) An artist's interpretation of a binary star system made up of a red giant star (upper right) and a black hole (lower right).

VII.

One defect to be guarded against, especially by the more clever and talented among us, *is* presumptuousness. Presumptuousness is dependent, in part, upon a failure to appreciate what is assumed or presupposed—or, more generally speaking, upon a failure to recognize what has gone before or is always.

As mentioned earlier in this essay, thoughtfulness is needed for the most serious grasp of things. An awareness of one's limitations can contribute to, even if it does not guarantee, thoughtfulness. Such an awareness is far less likely to be secured if one is presumptuous—if, for example, one has been imbued with scientific doctrines which hold out the prospect of a comprehensive understanding of everything, including the very process and form of that understanding.

Why are people today as interested in cosmology as they evidently are? No doubt they simply want to know about the grandest things. That is natural enough. Perhaps also they seek material confirmation or reassurance about eternal matters, including the standards by which they live and understand. But does modern cosmology provide the means to grasp these things? Is there not a limit to what can be learned, even by a select few, about such things in this way?

The appeal for us of Hawking's fortitude and perseverance in the face of great personal adversity is a reflection of our own awareness of, and respect for, the significance and enduring worth of various virtues. Do we not have from him, here, access to something much more solidly magnificent than the cosmological doctrines spun out of the flimsy data that even the most gifted scientists seem destined to have to settle for—and to replace from time to time?

It is instructive here to be reminded that Socrates moved, in the course of his career, from such inquiries as contemplation of the heavens to a concern primarily with human things.[59] It is hardly likely that access to such instruments as electron microscopes and radio telescopes would have induced him to conduct himself otherwise.

To turn to human things, as Socrates evidently did, includes an effort to know oneself. Unless one knows oneself it may be difficult, if not impossible, to know reliably any other thing, for how can one be certain that one's own psyche does not distort what one believes one sees or how one reasons about such things?

But as one comes to know oneself and hence what it means to know, one may also learn that the whole cannot be truly and fully known by human beings. This is one reason Socrates can speak of *philo*sophy or *love* of wisdom, not of wisdom itself, as that which characterizes the thoughtful human being.[60]

The evident limitations of even the most thoughtful may encourage many human beings to look to some faith in the divine as a way of providing for them a meaningful universe. But if one is unsettled by the prospect of a universe without beginning, how does recourse to a God without beginning take care of one's sense of groundlessness?

It may be said that God is unchanging, while matter, and hence the universe, is always changing. There is a sense, however, in which an eternal material universe, however varied its forms, is as unchanging as a divinity which is forever. One may have to look elsewhere, then, for justification of that faith in the divine which has meant so much to so many for so long.

The "mind of God" talk of which so much is made in the Hawking volume and elsewhere can seem the essence of presumptuousness. It may be intended as a kind of piety, of course, however misconceived it may be.

The perhaps unbridgeable gulf, and hence the prudence of a truce, between Reason and Revelation may not be generally appreciated these days, however fundamental that gulf has been for millennia in Western thought. The popular appeal of the Hawking volume may rest in part upon its being perceived as siding, in the name of science, with theology against philosophy.

Something of the divine is elicited by the enormous numbers invoked by the cosmologist. Thus we can be told, as if we are being told something that should mean something to us, that a thousand billion stars have already been accounted for.[61] Are not such numbers, whether applied to stars or galaxies or distances or time, simply incomprehensible, if not literally nonsense?

Numbers of this scope do suggest the extent of the divine. But they may not suggest the awesomeness of the truly divine, partly because they are numbers which are repeatedly being revised, almost (it can sometimes *seem*) at the whim of the cosmologist.

How does the mythology of the modern cosmologists compare with the theology of our ancients, whether Greek or Judaic? We have to understand the old better than we now do in order to be able to answer—and for that understanding, a grasp of what each of these ways of thinking takes to be the *beginning* should be useful, if not even essential.

Conclusion

Morale among physical scientists can be high, however much their efforts can remind one at times of the highminded but ill-fated Children's Crusade. The enthusiasm of gifted students is stimulated, in large part, by the great talents and obvious dedication of their teachers, by the noble hope that the general understanding as well as the material conditions of mankind will be enhanced, and by the plausible perception that much has already been accomplished because of the technology generated by science. The more thoughtful scientists are not unaware of some of the reservations I have sketched on this occasion about the modern scientific project. Particularly challenging is the question of what it is that the scientist is entitled to believe and to say on the basis of the evidence that happens to be available to him.[62]

To what extent should the evidence that can be mustered in support of scientific speculation include the technology to which these speculations have contributed? We can still see, in various parts of Europe, North Africa, and the Middle East, Roman aqueducts (perhaps often repaired since antiquity) that carry water as they did thousands of years ago. The technology of the Romans has continued to work long after the natural sciences of their day were superseded if not even discredited. It is instructive thus to notice that a "theory" may "work"—it may have substantial practical applications—even if not strictly or fully true. Many are the marvels associated with modern science—not least with the technology inspired by and otherwise keyed to modern science—but these marvels should not be taken to validate that science, certainly not to validate it unqualifiedly when it speculates about the beginnings of things. Similar comments can be made about the religious foundations upon which great enterprises have been reared and sustained for centuries, if not even for millennia.

A story I once heard at the weekly physics colloquium at the University of Chicago, which I have attended regularly for decades, assures us that some scientists are alert to the follies to which unbridled speculation can lead: Two American engineers who had made fortunes developed a passion for archaeology. This led them to purchase villas in Rome where they could excavate to their hearts' content. Their zeal was rewarded. One of the engineers came to the other with exciting news. Excavations on his grounds had turned up some ancient metal strings. This proved, he was pleased to report, that the ancient Romans had invented the telephone as well as the aqueducts for which they were already admired by everybody. The other engineer was inspired by this report to dig further on his own grounds. Eventually, he too had exciting news to report. He had dug all over and had found nothing. "Then why are you so excited?" his friend asked. "Don't you realize what this means?" came the reply. "The Romans must have invented the radio also!" Scientists intend to remind us by such stories about the difficulty, as well as the allure, of discovering the true beginnings (and hence the very nature) of things, even as we keep in mind these propositions:

> Philosophy in the strict and classical sense is quest for the eternal order or for the eternal cause or causes of all things. It presupposes then that there is an eternal and unchangeable order within which History [including the "history" of Big Crunches and Big Bangs?] takes place and which is not in any way affected by History.[63]

1. Our scientist, a cosmologist (discussed in Part Three of this article), is not representative of physical scientists today, whose speculations tend to be much less spectacular. But cosmology does fit in nicely with the poetic and Biblical accounts considered in Parts One and Two of this article. Although cosmology may not be representative of disciplines such as "ordinary" physics, it does suggest the direction in which science is moving, with speculations about the most minute and immediate things matching, in their inventiveness, speculations about the grandest and remotest things. See the text at note 36, below.

2. Quintillian, Seneca, and many others have observed that everything ends that has a beginning. Consider, also, the opening line of T.S. Eliot's *East Coker:* "In my beginning is my end." Consider, as well, the opening lines of his *Burnt Norton.*

3. See, e.g., Leon John Roos, *Natural Law and Natural Right in Thomas Aquinas and Aristotle* (University of Chicago doctoral dissertation, 1971); Anastaplo, "Natural Law or Natural Right?" 38 *Loyola of New Orleans Law Review* 915 (1993).

4. See Maimonides, *The Guide of the Perplexed,* II, 15 sq.

5. Homer uses *nature* only once, and that use is curious. See *Odyssey*, X, 303 (*GBWW* I: 4, 239; II: 3, 401). See also the text at note 27, below.

6. Mark Van Doren, *The Noble Voice: A Study of Ten Great Poems* (New York: Henry Holt and Company, 1946), p. xi. See Anastaplo, *The Artist as Thinker: From Shakespeare to Joyce* (Athens: Ohio University Press, 1983).

7. *Encyclopedia of Religion* (New York: Macmillan, 1987), vol. 6, pp. 307–08.

8. Herodotus, *History*, II, 53 (David Grene translation). *GBWW* I: 6, 60; II: 5, 60.

9. The Catalogue of Ships, in Book II of Homer's *Iliad*, can be seen as a Boeotian element adopted by Homer (*GBWW* I: 4, 14–18; II: 5, 22–29). See Anastaplo, *The Thinker as Artist: From Homer to Plato & Aristotle* (Athens, Ohio: Ohio University Press, 1997), pp. 23, 37–39, 375–77.

10. *Encyclopedia of Religion*, vol. 6, pp. 307–08.

11. *Ibid.*, vol. 6, p. 308. See, on the Babylonian and Hittite sources, Anastaplo, "An Introduction to Mesopotamian Thought" (*GIT:* 1986, 288).

12. See *Theogony*, 26 sq.

13. See *Theogony*, 4.

14. Eros is critical to the generating to be done later by divine as well as by human couples; Tartarus becomes important later as a place to be used by Zeus to confine permanently his defeated challengers. See *Theogony* 713 sq. See also Virgil, *Aeneid*, Book VI (*GBWW* I: 13, 211–35; II: 12, 174–96).

15. See *Theogony* 126 sq.

16. We recall that God could be referred to, in ancient Hebrew, as "the place."

17. *Theogony*, 126 sq., 453 sq., 491 sq.

18. They are in this respect like Oedipus, whose presumptuous efforts to avoid his fate may have made that fate come about in the worst possible way. That too, by the way, is a Boeotian story, and one in which, like the story of Ouranos, a son mates with his mother to produce a much-troubled dynasty.

19. M.L. West, ed., Hesiod, *Theogony* (Oxford: Clarendon Press, 1966), p. 19.

20. Was this the kind of prophecy that Laius, the father of Oedipus, had had?

21. *Iliad*, XV, 48 sq., (*GBWW* I: 4, 98; II: 3, 175).

22. Leo Strauss, *Jewish Philosophy and the Crisis of Modernity*, ed., Kenneth Hart Green (Albany: State University of New York Press, 1997), p. 293. (This book is reviewed elsewhere in this *Great Ideas Today* volume.)

23. Parmenides helped open up the West to nature and hence philosophy. He shows himself in a Homeric-style poem introduced to his subjects by a goddess. This reminds the reader of Hesiod's initiation by the Muses. See, on Parmenides "as the first extant author deserving to be called a philosopher in a present-day sense of the word," David Gallop, ed., *Parmenides of Elea* (Toronto: University of Toronto Press, 1984), p. 3. The evident coextensiveness for Parmenides of *thinking* and *being* suggests that "beginning," as distinguished from that which is "always" or eternal, may be for him little more than an illusion, except that the process of change itself may be eternal.

24. The traditional Hebrew name for this book is *In the Beginning*. The title *Genesis* was a much later addition from the Greek. The other four books of the Torah are also called traditionally by the word or words that appear first in the text. See note 63, below.

25. *Arché* is the term evident in such English words as *archetype, architect,* and *architectonic*.

26. Should this be understood as God speaking or thinking? Goethe has his Faust open a book and begin to speak thus:

It says: "In the beginning was the *Word*."
[Geschrieben steht: "Im Anfang war das Wort!"]
Already I am stopped. It seems absurd.
The *Word* does not deserve the highest praise,
I must translate it otherwise
If I am well inspired and not blind.
It says: In the beginning was the *Mind* [der Sinn].
Ponder that first line, wait and see,
Lest you should write too hastily.
Is mind the all-creating source?

It ought to say: In the beginning there was *Force* [die Kraft].
Yet something warns me as I grasp the pen,
That my translation must be changed again.
The spirit helps me. Now it is exact.
I write: In the beginning was the *Act* [die Tat].

Goethe, *Faust,* Walter Kaufman, trans. (Garden City, New York: Anchor Books, Double-day & Company, 1963), p. 153.

27. Compare Robert Graves, "Introduction," *Larousse Encyclopedia of Mythology* (New York: Prometheus Press, 1959), p. v:

> Mythology is the study of whatever religious or heroic legends are so foreign to a student's experience that he cannot believe them to be true. Hence the English adjective 'mythical,' meaning 'incredible'; and hence the omission from standard European mythologies, such as this, of all Biblical narratives even when closely paralleled by myths from Persia, Babylonia, Egypt and Greece; and of all hagio-logical legends.

Most of the major religions of the world, when compared to those grounded in the Bible, can seem rather "wild" to us in the West. An exception, although it may not really be a "religion," is the Confucian way. See, e.g., Anastaplo, "An Introduction to Confucian Thought" (*GIT*: 1984, 124). See, on the Bible, note 63, below.

28. Jacob Klein, *Lectures and Essays* (Annapolis, Md.: St. John's College Press, 1985), p. 1.

29. A mature physicist, who is not himself a cosmologist, has told me that one did not hear much if any talk, forty years ago, about the age of the universe; there was little talk then of a "beginning." But, he insists, observational evidence is now available, primarily because of the work earlier of Edwin Hubble (arguing for the steady expansion of the universe) and because of the discovery in the 1960's of the cosmic radiation background, that suggests a beginning of time—that is, the Big Bang. This "beginning of time," we shall see further on, seems to mean to cosmologists today the beginning of *knowability.* It is hard, this physicist can add, to fathom either a finite universe (in time or space) or an infinite universe (in time).

30. The full title of the Hawking book is *A Brief History of Time: From the Big Bang to Black Holes.* It was first published, by Bantam Books, in 1988. A revised edition should come out soon.

31. Has our "common sense," if not even our "intuition," been shaped by such grand innovations as Newton's system of the world? For example, what we accept as his law of inertia defied "common sense": that is, everyday observation is that things moving on earth come to a stop unless pushed or pulled further.

32. See the text at note 57, below. The Hawking career puts to a severe test the ancient prescription of *mens sana in corpore sano.* Hawking himself has had to compen-sate for a dreadful disease for which he was in no way responsible. See Hawking, *Black Holes and Baby Universes* (New York: Bantam Books, 1993), pp. 21–26. It is a disease which has made him, in key respects, very much a creature of modernity—not only in his reliance upon more and more technology for survival and communication but also in his being able to divorce his mental activity to a remarkable degree from bodily activity and hence from the material element.

33. Consider, e.g., this comment by Einstein in a letter to Max Born, December 12, 1926:

> Quantum mechanics is certainly imposing. But an inner voice tells me that it is not yet the real thing. The theory says a lot, but does not really bring us any closer to the secret of the Old One. I, at any rate, am convinced that He does not throw dice.

Ronald W. Clark, *Einstein: The Life and Times* (New York: World Publishing Company, 1971), p. 340. See also, ibid., p. 396 ("God is subtle but he is not malicious.")

34. He starts well enough, on page 1, with the charming story about the tower of

turtles; but he is all too often flip thereafter. Consider, for example, what he says about astronauts falling into black holes, about the risks run at a Vatican conference, about such things as *Penthouse* and *Private Eye*, about various of the ancients, and about the biographies of great predecessors. I will return to some of these matters.

35. See Hawking, *A Brief History of Time*, p. 85. Engineering seems to be a vital part of contemporary physics.

36. A particularly dramatic instance was the Cold Fusion scandal of the late 1980s. But the scientific community itself dealt with *this* aberration decisively. See, e.g., John R. Huizenga, *Cold Fusion: The Scientific Fiasco of the Century* (Rochester: University of Rochester Press, 1992).

37. Consider these observations by Jeremy Bernstein, "Cosmology," *New Yorker,* June 6, 1988, pp. 121–22:

> As much as I like Hawking's book [*A Brief History of Time*], I would be remiss if I didn't point out an important way in which it might be improved. Hawking has a somewhat impressionistic view of the history of recent science. Very few active scientists—Steven Weinberg is an exception, and that is one of the reasons why his book [*The First Three Minutes*, note 50, below] is so good—actually take the trouble to read the papers of their early predecessors. A kind of folklore builds up which bears only a tangential relationship to reality, and when someone with the scientific prestige of Hawking repeats these legends it gives them credibility.

38. *A Brief History of Time*, pp. 181–82. Compare, for the grandeur of Newton's work, Subrahmanyan Chandrasekhar, *Newton's Principia for the Common Reader* (Oxford: Clarendon Press, 1995); Anastaplo, book review (*GIT:* 1997, 448).

39. *A Brief History of Time*, p. 116.

40. See, e.g., Hawking, "The Unification of Physics," (*GIT:* 1984, 2–10), 1984. Compare ibid., p. 4:

> Einstein spent most of the last forty years of his life trying to construct a unified theory of physics. He failed partly because not enough was known about nuclear forces and partly because he could not accept the limits on our ability to predict events, limits which are implied by the quantum mechanical uncertainty principle. He said: "God does not play dice." Yet, all the experimental evidence suggests that God does. In any case, we now know a lot more than Einstein did and there are grounds for cautious optimism that a complete, unified theory is in sight. Were I a gambling man, I would bet even odds that we can find such a theory by the end of this century, if we do not blow ourselves up first.

41. Compare Hawking, *Black Holes and Baby Universes*, p. 38.

42. This limitation is reflected in how the typical physics colloquium is presented these days, with an inordinate reliance upon visual aids.

43. See Leo Strauss, *Persecution and the Art of Writing* (Glencoe, IL: The Free Press, 1952).

44. *A Brief History of Time*, p. 175.

45. An illuminating anticipation of the Hawking volume in this respect is James D. Watson's *The Double Helix* (New York: Atheneum, 1986), in which the contest for winning the Nobel Prize awaiting the description of the DNA molecule is vividly presented by one of the exuberant winners.

46. Thus, Hawking can observe (*A Brief History of Time*, p. 46), "As far as we are concerned, events before the big bang can have no consequences." This can seem an inverse of that aspect of the Uncertainty Principle which has the object observed altered by the very act of observing it.

47. *A Brief History of Time*, p. 173. The sentence quoted concludes, "up to the limits set by the uncertainty principle."

48. Human beings, too, can predict events, or can proceed confidently with the predictions by others, that they do not understand.

49. Compare Plato, *Republic* 602D sq., (*GBWW* I: 7, 431; II: 6, 431).

50. The most cautious, and hence reliable, of the popular accounts here still seems to

be Steven Weinberg, *The First Three Minutes: A Modern View of the Origin of the Universe* (New York: Basic Books, 1977).

51. See, e.g., Plato, *Timaeus* 27C sq., (*GBWW* I: 7, 446–7; II: 6, 446–7); Anastaplo, *The Thinker as Artist,* p. 279f.

52. The National Academy of Sciences has recently recommended that evolution should be taught in public schools as "the most important concept in modern biology." "Scientific Panel Urges Teaching of Evolution," *Chicago Tribune,* April 10, 1998, sec. 1, p. 13. See also Larry Arnhart, *Darwinian Natural Right* (Albany: State University of New York, 1998); Anastaplo, *The Artist as Thinker,* p. 482f. Can the advocates of "creation science" justify settling on any particular story of Creation among the many that have long been available around the world?

53. Hawking himself seems open to the possibility, if not even to the likelihood, of a universe without a beginning or an end.

54. Does the discovery that light has a velocity play a role here? Thomas Aquinas and others, including perhaps Galileo, basing themselves on experience, seem to have considered light's action as instantaneous.

55. Recent conjectures by some cosmologists have the universe expanding indefinitely, thereby making another Big Crunch unlikely. See, e.g., George Johnson, "Once Upon a Time, There Was a Big Bang Theory," *New York Times,* March 8, 1998, p. 3 (WK). But even more recent conjectures about the mass of neutrinos suggest otherwise.

56. See Lucretius, *On the Nature of Things,* I, 958 sq. (*GBWW* I: 12, 12–3; II: 11, 13–4).

57. See Lucretius, *On the Nature of Things,* I, 72 sq. (*GBWW* I: 12, 1-2; II: 11, 1). See also, *ibid.,* I, 536 sq., V, 55 sq. (*GBWW* I: 12, 7, 61–2; II: 11, 8, 59). See, as well, the text at note 32 above.

58. See Anastaplo, *The Artist as Thinker,* p. 252.

59. This redirection of his thought is recalled by Socrates on his last day, as recorded in Plato's *Phaedo.* But had he not been obliged to think through a notion of the whole, however provisional, which allowed or accounted for the rationality, however limited it may be, found in the human things?

60. See, on what Socrates did know, Anastaplo, "Freedom of Speech and the First Amendment," 21 *Texas Tech Law Review* 1941, 1945f (1990).

61. See *A Brief History of Time,* p. 37. Others can speak with apparent confidence of fifty billion *galaxies,* still others of a million million galaxies.

62. See, e.g., Hellmut Fritzsche, "Of Things That Are Not," in John A. Murley, Robert L. Stone, and William T. Braithwaite, eds., *Law and Philosophy: The Practice of Theory* (Athens: Ohio University Press, 1992), p. 3f.

63. Strauss, *Jewish Philosophy and the Crisis of Modernity,* p. 471. See note 23, above. An expanded version of this article on Beginnings, with additional documentation, is appended to my 1998 *Oklahoma City University Law Review* collection, "Law & Literature and the Bible."

George Anastaplo is a professor of law at Loyola University of Chicago, lecturer in the liberal arts at the University of Chicago, and professor emeritus of political science and philosophy at Dominican University. Professor Anastaplo is widely known as an author and lecturer on law and public morality, most notably in constitutional matters.

Among his books are *The Constitutionalist: Notes on the First Amendment* (1971), *The Artist as Thinker: From Shakespeare to Joyce* (1983), and *The American Moralist: Essays on Law, Ethics, and Government* (1992). A recent book, *The Amendments to the Constitution* (1995), includes a commentary on the Emancipation Proclamation and a defense of affirmative action programs. This is a companion volume to *The Constitution of 1787* (1989). Both of these commentaries have as a foundation Professor Anastaplo's book *Human Being and Citizen: Essays on Virtue, Freedom, and the Common Good* (1975). His latest book is *The Thinker as Artist: From Homer to Plato and Aristotle* (1997).

In 1992, Professor Anastaplo was honored by the publication of a *festschrift, Law and Philosophy: The Practice of Theory* (1992). In addition, the 1997 volume of the *Political Science Reviewer* includes six articles concerning his scholarship.

Natural Rights

James O'Toole

Illustrations by Philippe Lechien

True law is right reason in agreement with nature; it is of universal application, unchanging and everlasting; it summons to duty by its commands,
and averts from wrongdoing by its prohibitions. And it does not lay its
commands or prohibitions upon good men in vain, though neither have
any effect on the wicked—We cannot be freed from its obligations by
senate or people, and we need not look outside ourselves for an expounder
or interpreter of it. And there will not be different laws at Rome and at
Athens, or different laws now and in the future, but one eternal and
unchangeable law will be valid for all nations and all times, and there will
be one master and ruler, that is, God, over us all, for he is the author of this
law, its promulgator, and its enforcing judge. Whoever is disobedient is
fleeing from himself and denying his human nature, and by reason of this
very fact he will suffer the worst penalties, even if he escapes what is
commonly considered punishment.

—Cicero, *The Republic,* 52 B.C.[1]

merican society is ensnared in endless debate about a set of highly contentious social issues. These issues often are framed in terms of "rights." For
decades, Americans have debated whether individuals have

- a right to a job
- a right to education
- a right to medical care.

Today, even more contentiously, Americans ask,

- Does a person have a right to free speech (even if this entails produc-
  ing pornography, burning the flag, or inflaming racial passion)?
- Does a homosexual have a right to marry?
- Does a woman have a right to abort a fetus (or, does a fetus have a
  right to life)?
- Does a fatally ill person have a right to choose when to die?
- Do trees and animals have rights (as some conservationists and
  animal rights activists claim)?

While Americans debate these difficult issues in terms of "rights," the
arguments they offer make it clear that they have lost sight of the underlying philosophical principles that give rise to the rights they take for granted.
For example, Judge Robert H. Bork and philosopher Russell Hittinger
recently joined other conservative intellectuals in a symposium published
in *First Things 67* concerned with current applications of the doctrine of
natural law. The symposium participants adopted Pope John Paul II's philosophical perspective, especially his view that "Law and decrees enacted in
contravention of the moral order, and hence of the divine will, can have no
binding force in conscience." In reference to recent American federal court
rulings on abortion and euthanasia, the *First Things 67* participants reached
the conclusion that, because these rulings violated rights implicit in natural
law as understood by the Pope, the rulings brought into question "the
legitimacy of law in the present [American] regime." In sum, their particu-

lar interpretation of natural law led the participants to ask if "The End of Democracy" was nigh in America.[2]

When leading intellectuals misinterpret natural law in ways that lead them to question the legitimacy of the American "regime," it is not surprising that average Americans are also confused about what rights they have and why they have them. Although most Americans are vaguely aware that there is a doctrine of Natural Rights, they do not understand how to decide whether or not they possess a right, or how to define the limits to whatever rights they may possess. The purpose of this article is to clarify the central principles of the doctrine of Natural Rights in order to enhance that understanding. The doctrine has applications in three distinct arenas: personal ethics, law, and political philosophy. While these overlap considerably, our focus here is on the third category, which relates to the question of creating a good society.

At its heart, the doctrine of Natural Rights posits that all members of the human species are inherently equal, that they all possess certain rights by virtue of being human—or as granted by God or the gods—and that those rights should be secured by a just system of government. This is the core of a simple but powerful argument about the nature of men and women, and the nature of the laws by which they are entitled to be governed. Significantly, Natural Rights was the central philosophic principle upon which the government of the United States was predicated. The Founders (in particular, Thomas Jefferson, James Madison, Benjamin Franklin, John Adams, Alexander Hamilton, and Jefferson's friends, Thomas Paine and George Mason) embraced the Enlightenment's change-oriented notion that a good society could be built on a new social contract, the foundation of which would be the "laws of nature and of Nature's God," which prescribed for each individual certain "inalienable rights." The Founders understood that if one is enslaved—or, in their case, subject to the whims of a tyrant—it is futile to appeal for relief to existing "civil" or "positive" law. When constrained by outmoded custom or unjust law, one's strongest recourse is to reason and to what is known as "natural" law.[3]

The tension between the laws of men and the laws of God has been recognized for over 2,500 years. In *Antigone,* Sophocles dramatically illustrated that king-made law was not always just, and that it is the risky duty of men and women to obey the higher law of the gods when there is conflict between the two. In modern fiction, Herman Melville's *Billy Budd* revolves around two protagonists, each of whom is committed to a different set of laws: Starry Vere, a British warship captain during the War of 1812, sees his allegiance entirely to the man-made laws of Britain; Billy Budd, an American sailor, represents the natural law orientation of the New World. When Budd is impressed into service on Vere's ship, he poignantly bids adieu to his appropriately named American merchant vessel: "And goodbye to you too, old *Rights-of-Man!*" Indeed, it was Melville's intent to show American readers that the Enlightenment ideas found in the Declaration were not mere philosophical abstractions, but imperatives with practical consequences for how they lived their lives. To both Sophocles and

Melville, people risk becoming enslaved by tyrants when they ignore their duty to obey the higher law of nature and the gods.

The beliefs laid out in the Declaration—as well as in the Constitution, the Federalist Papers, and the Gettysburg Address—constitute a coherent philosophical testament based on Enlightenment thought.[4] This body of ideas was crystallized in 1651 in the brilliant mind of Thomas Hobbes in *Leviathan.*[5] Hobbes built on the contributions of Aristotle, Cicero, Aquinas, and Gotius.[6] In turn, the hard, anti-democratic edges of Hobbes' thinking were softened by significant refinements made by Locke, Rousseau, and Kant.[7] By the time the Founders put ink to paper in July of 1776, the basic ideas of Natural Rights were well understood by all educated people in Western Europe and the American colonies.

The origins of these beliefs are rooted in an Edenic "state of nature," a world that anthropologists today call pure fantasy, but that moral and political philosophers then and now see as a convenient first assumption on which to predicate a theory of justice.

Men and Women in the State of Nature:
The Foundation of the Doctrine of Natural Rights

Natural law philosophers posit that, once upon a time, before there were laws or governments—even before there was the hint of society with structure, rules, customs, or conventions—men and women lived like other wild animals. (They lived, as in the song, "as free as the summer breeze/without pajamas and without chemise."[8]) In this natural state, all men and women were equal. They were equal in the way one might say all wild bears are equal: *There are no kings among bears.* No bear has inherent social or political power, privilege, or status that differs from that possessed by other bears. Clearly, some bears are stronger than other bears, and they may use that strength to exert dominance over the others—to steal their food, their territory, and their mates. But such dominance, if achieved, is ephemeral. It lasts for only as long as it can be defended; that is, until a fiercer bear comes along. Indeed, there is a constant struggle among bears for dominance over others because the differences that distinguish the strength of one from another are so slight that, in most instances, every bear eventually will have his day.

Similarly, there are no natural monarchs among humans. No man or woman is genetically a king or queen; no one is hard-wired from birth to be an aristocrat (or, for that matter, a serf or a slave). The differences in strength among members of the human species are slight. Where one brutish man might be able to exert his strength over another man or woman, almost any two or more people working in concert can overcome the strength of even the strongest individual. Among humans there is, of course, a normal distribution of intelligence over a limited range. Nonetheless, among men and women born without mental defects, intellectual abilities are clustered around the mean, with only a few truly exceptional individuals (whose very special mental abilities tend to be specific rather than general).[9]

More important than these differences are the obvious similarities that all humans share, and that distinguish our species from all others. Humans are capable of rational thought. They use language to form abstract ideas. They create knowledge which they share with future generations, much as present generations build on the knowledge of those from the past. Indeed, humans, alone among species, are aware of the existence of past generations, and are aware of the fact that there will be a future that extends beyond their own lifetimes. While the capacity to reason varies, all men and women possess that general ability and, to a greater or lesser extent, they all possess the ability to make choices: They can distinguish right from wrong, good from bad, and thus choose what is good for themselves. In short, all humans can decide what is in their own self-interest.

Additionally, all members of the human species have a limited set of common needs. Along with other animals, all humans share the need for food and shelter. More than any other animal, all share the need of protection during a prolonged period of infancy. Peculiar among animals, all humans share a need for clothing and, especially, a need for education—whether taught by their parents to hunt, to gather, and to care for their young, or taught in school the specific human skills of reading, writing, and calculation. In this way, all members of the species *Homo sapiens* are said to be equal in the state of nature.

By observation of this natural state, it can be concluded that all animals, including humans, possess a right to self-preservation: no animal freely bares its neck to a predator; all struggle to live to the biological limit of their species. From this behavior, we deduce a natural right to life shared by all animals.[10]

But humans alone have a natural right to liberty by virtue of their ability as rational beings to make choices. Whether we believe this special ability is God-given or a gift of beneficent nature, our ability to choose was clearly not a human bequest. Philosophers posit that, since the gods (or nature) give us only that which we are intended to use, our right to choose is, in fact, our essence—that which distinguishes us as individuals, and that which makes us human. We cannot give up our freedom to choose, because to do so would be to deny our nature. No one can take that freedom from us because to do so would be to rob us of our humanity.[11]

The right to liberty is also a means to the highest good of life: happiness. Happiness is called the highest good to which all humans aspire because it is always an end in itself and never a means to anything else.[12] We say, "I want to be rich (or famous, or powerful, or beautiful) in order to be happy"; we do not say "I want to be happy to be rich (famous) (powerful) (beautiful)." Happy people are those who have achieved their highest-order human potential, who have developed their capacity to reason and applied it to the arts, sciences, and professions. Happy people have no regrets over what might have been, over roads not taken, over potential unreached, over talent undeveloped, or over promise unfulfilled. When a happy person is on his deathbed, he will be content with the life he lived and will not say "I could have been," or "I should have done." The natural right to pursue happiness means that no one—no person, no monarch, no government, no class or category of humans—is entitled to arbitrarily stand in the way of any individual who wishes to strive for happiness, that is, who strives to fulfill his God-given potential.[13]

Humans also possess a right of property. In the state of nature, an individual will hunt for, or gather, food. He or she will be entitled to the possession of that food because it is the fruit of his or her labor. Similarly, if a man and woman marry, and fence in a bit of property, farming it and raising domestic animals on it, all of the bounty produced will be theirs by right because it has become an extension of their selves. By investing their labor in their land, crops, and animals, they have made their property a part of themselves, and thus are entitled to it as a matter of right, much as they have a right to do with their own persons as they choose. They also have a right to share this property with their children.[14]

Hence, it is said that humans in the most primitive, preliterate state— starting from the day the species was blessed with the divine spark of reason—possessed the right to life, to liberty, to the pursuit of happiness, and to the possession of their property by virtue of their equal standing as members of the human race.

But there were, and are, problems with the securing or enforcement of these rights. While all humans are capable of reason, they are also driven by animal emotion. Where cooperation, altruism, and interdependence grow from the exercise of reason, it is also true that greed, fear, and envy emanate from the species' baser instincts. In the state of nature, the biggest and strongest man thus may attempt forcibly to take the possessions of the smallest and weakest. Then, groups of men may conspire to retake this stolen property from the solitary brute and, once having done so, will fall into conflict among themselves over the distribution of the spoils. Hence, through the exercise of animalistic force, there is a continuing war over property, with lives endangered in the process—and no hope for men or women that they will enjoy the safety and security needed to pursue happiness.[15]

The lessons of nature are thus mixed: While men and women are naturally free and equal, they find no security for their lives or property because there is no earthly power to enforce the laws of God. In the state of nature, rights are not enforceable except as individuals have power to protect themselves: no law exists to which they can appeal.

But men are not animals; they do not accept the fate of beasts. After a prolonged struggle to maintain life and property by precarious dint of self-preservation, man's reason will overcome his animal passion. Alone among the higher mammals, humans can see beyond their first condition. To gain security, men and women will forsake the law of the jungle and form a social compact—a contract in which they each abandon the right of self-preservation in exchange for laws that collectively guarantee their lives and property.[16] In this, they seek to have their cake and eat it, too. Securing safety of person and security of property, they also insist on maintaining their natural liberty, equality, and right to pursue happiness.[17]

In short, the goal of humans in civilized societies is to create a government in which man-made laws conform to the laws of God. The clearest expression of this is found in the opening two paragraphs of the Declaration of Independence, where the American founders announced that they were writing a new social contract. They declared that their goal was to create a government the long-term justice of which would be measured by the extent to which its civil laws secured Natural Rights.[18]

"Nonsense On Stilts"

Not every great philosopher has accepted this intellectual construct. Jeremy Bentham, the father of utilitarianism—a pragmatic reaction to the excesses of the age of revolution that grew out of the Enlightenment—called Natural Rights "nonsense on stilts." He wrote:

> How stands the truth of things?…that there are no such things as Natural Rights. No such things as rights anterior to the establishment of government. No such things as Natural Rights opposed to, and in contra-distinction to, legal rights. Natural Rights is simple nonsense.[19]

Bentham was not alone in asking such questions as "How do we know God's will?" and "Aren't rights culturally determined?" Today, the doctrine is opposed by a powerful, albeit improbable, melange of utilitarians, economic conservatives, Marxists, and moral and cultural relativists. Over the last two centuries, skeptical philosophers from those schools of thought have raised the following objections to the doctrine of Natural Rights:

1. There is no way to prove the existence of such rights (How can one presume to know the will of God?).
2. Natural Rights are unenforceable (There is no power on earth charged with guaranteeing the rights granted by God).
3. The doctrine results from a subjective confusion of what some people feel *should be* (natural law) with what *is* (civil law).
4. Natural Rights are limitless and arbitrary, a blank check written on society.
5. Rights are a cultural by-product of a particular place (the West) and time (the Enlightenment) and, hence, not universal.
6. The notion of Natural Rights is absolute and, therefore, potentially tyrannical because it may lead to its imposition on non-believers.

Bentham's objections to the natural law doctrine were more than a self-serving defense of British Crown Rule. He was correct in noting that, when defining the source of America's rights, the Founders had been vague in the extreme. In 1785, Madison wrote that Natural Rights are "the gift of nature," and Hamilton hadn't been much more precise ten years earlier when he had said that

> the sacred rights of mankind are not to be rummaged for, among old parchments, or musty records. They are written, as with a sunbeam, in the whole volume of nature, by the hand of divinity itself.[20]

Even anti-royalists in America saw the obvious shortcomings of such pale arguments. Boston's James Otis called natural law "a piece of meta-physical jargon and systematic nonsense." Yet, Otis himself vigorously subscribed to the doctrine because there was no alternative justification for freedom. Even if the state of nature was pure fiction, he conceded that "the natural and original rights of each individual may be illustrated and ex-plained in this way better than in any other."[21]

In the final analysis, Madison, Hamilton, and Otis believed the doctrine of Natural Rights was indispensable in the war against tyranny for the simple reason that these champions of freedom possessed no other con-vincing weapon. The King had declared the rebellious colonists outlaws because they broke the legitimate civil laws of England, a charge that was undeniably true. The colonists only retort was an appeal to a higher law: the laws of nature and of Nature's God. To understand their perspective, imagine the following situation: You live in a small island society with 20 individuals governed by a constitution that requires a 2/3 plurality for the passage of a law. Punctiliously following the procedures prescribed in the constitution, 95 per cent of the populace—the other 19 citizens—vote to enslave you. From your point of view, this is clearly wrong and unjust! But the rub is, it is *legal*. It is also a rough form of utilitarian justice because the happiness of the majority has been enhanced: it is in the self-interest of all the others to have you serve them. What recourse do you have? What argument can you make to convince them that what they have done is, in fact, wrong and unjust as you claim? This is the analogous situation to that faced by the American colonists (and everyone else in the Western world at that time who was subject to the whims of tyrannical monarchs).

Paradoxically, it also was to be the plight of American slaves for some ninety years after the Founders penned the Declaration, and for nearly eight decades after the ratification of the U.S. Constitution (a document that guaranteed the property rights of slave holders). Lincoln, in seeking to free the slaves, was faced with a nearly intractable obstacle: When he called on his fellow Americans to abolish slavery, many answered, "It is my civil right to own slaves." Since the Constitution he had sworn to uphold vio-lated one of his most deeply held principles, his only recourse was to appeal to the nation's founding document and its roots in natural law. In 1861, in an impromptu speech at Philadelphia's Independence Hall, Lin-coln explained the priority of the Natural Rights orientation of the Declara-tion over the flawed civil-law Constitution:

> I have never had a feeling politically that did not spring from the senti-

ments embodied in the Declaration of Independence. I have often pondered over the dangers which were incurred by the men who assembled here and adopted that Declaration of Independence—I have pondered over the toils that were endured by the officers and soldiers of the army, who achieved that Independence. I have often inquired of myself, what great principle or idea it was that kept this Confederacy so long together. It was not the mere matter of the separation of the colonies from the mother land; but some-thing in that Declaration giving liberty, not alone to the people of this country, but hope to the world for all future time. It was that which gave promise that in due time the weights should be lifted from the shoulders of all men, and *all* should have an equal chance. This is the sentiment embod-ied in that Declaration of Independence.[22]

Ten years earlier, Harriet Taylor Mill (the wife of Bentham's illustrious student, J.S. Mill) had studied the U.S. Declaration and concluded that its call for the recognition of Natural Rights was *universal* and, hence, applied to men *and* women of all colors everywhere:

> We do not imagine that any American democrat will evade the force of these expressions by the dishonest or ignorant subterfuge, that 'men,' in this memorable document, does not stand for human beings, one sex only; that 'life, liberty, and the pursuit of happiness' are 'inalienable rights' of only one moiety of the human species; and that 'the governed,' whose consent is affirmed to be the only source of just power, are meant for that half of mankind only, who, in relation to the other, have hitherto assumed the character of *governors*.[23]

Harriet Mill's argument convinced John Stuart Mill to abandon the utili-tarianism of his teacher, Bentham, and develop a more inclusive philosophy that was as responsive to the rights of each single person as it was to the "greatest good for the greatest number." He argued that utilitarianism can never be a total safeguard against totalitarianism, because there are in-stances when protecting a right is too costly—that is, when its protection does not maximize the sum total of happiness—but is nevertheless proper to protect. Thus, in his later works, Mill called for recognition of the rights of women, the poor, and such "eccentric" individuals as entrepreneurs and non-believers because it was "just" to do so even when it wasn't "useful" in the Benthamite sense.[24]

A hundred years later, Martin Luther King, Jr. also appealed to the Declaration's doctrine of Natural Rights in his struggles to overturn the legal system of racial segregation found in the South:

> We can never forget that everything Hitler did in Germany was 'legal' and everything the Hungarian freedom fighters did in Hungary was 'illegal.' It was 'illegal' to aid and comfort a Jew in Hitler's Germany. But I am sure that if I had lived in Germany during that time I would have aided and comforted my Jewish brothers even though it was illegal. If I lived in a Communist country today where certain principles dear to the Christian faith are suppressed, I believe I would openly advocate disobeying these anti-religious laws.[25]

And he, of course, openly advocated breaking the segregationist laws of his own time:

> One may well ask, 'How can you advocate breaking some laws and obeying others?' The answer is found in the fact that there are two types of laws: there are *just* and there are *unjust* laws. I would agree with Saint Augustine that 'an unjust law is no law at all.'
>
> Now, what is the difference between the two? How does one determine when a law is just or unjust? A just law is a man-made code that squares with the moral law or the law of God. An unjust law is a code that is out of harmony with the moral law. To put it in the terms of Saint Thomas Aquinas, an unjust law is a human law that is not rooted in eternal and natural law. Any law that uplifts human personality is just. Any law that degrades human personality is unjust.[26]

Like Harriet Mill, King thought that Jefferson meant "all men are created equal" to be an inclusive concept and, thus, African-Americans possessed Natural Rights even "before the pen of Jefferson etched across the pages of history the majestic words of the Declaration of Independence," although they lacked the civil rights to enforce them.[27]

The Minimal Presumption: The Right to Equal Liberty

Who is correct, the advocates of natural law, or their positive law opponents? To weigh the two, it is useful to start with an analysis of the weakest assertion of Natural Rights, the liberal Kantian proposition, as amended by J.S. Mill: *All humans capable of choice have the right to take any action that does no harm to others.*

Is there anything prescriptive, culture-based, or time-bound about this basic proposition of Natural Rights? It appears to give to no person any special privileges or claims on others or on society; and there is in it no implied legal code or set of commandments, no oughts, no goods and bads, no social entitlements. This limited right is not a question of individual virtue or ethics—it does not tell us how a person should lead a good life—it merely establishes the freedom of every individual from coercion by each and all. Significantly, no moral obligations accompany this right other than, perhaps, the responsibility *not* to coerce others (Kant suggested that all individuals have a moral responsibility *not* to enter into any social contract in which the basic right to liberty is denied to anyone).[28] Even adding Kant's proviso, these are *negative* duties; no one is under obligation to *do* anything in this minimalist view.

Moreover, if anyone does have obligations, this does not signify that those who benefit from them have accompanying rights.[29] For example, we may have duties to protect children and animals (or, at least, a duty not to mistreat them) but that does not mean that infants and beasts have rights to good treatment. Merely because a party stands to benefit from the performance of a duty does not signify that the beneficiary possesses a right to any special treatment. The question then arises: to whom does one owe the obligation of performing the duty of protection of infants and beasts? The answer may be one or more of the following: we owe this duty to (a) God, (b) nature, (c) ourselves.

In the Kantian proposition, our right to exercise our will in our own interest is inalienable and unalterable—that is, it is not subject to amendment or option. Here we see a crucial characteristic of Natural Rights: They come to us by virtue of our ability to make rational decisions about our own lives. Our treatment of children and animals, in contrast, has nothing to do with the free-exercise of *their* wills: The will in question is ours, not theirs. The obligation to care for them is more akin to obeying the Ten Commandments. We may have an obligation to do so; but it is absurd to say that the beneficiaries of my obeying the decalogue have a *right* to my doing so. Rights are owned, or possessed, by individuals; but duties do not belong to the recipients. My father has no right to my honor, my neighbor has no right to my not coveting his wife. (An exception is the Sixth Commandment, which protects the Natural Right to life.) Nine of the ten commandments are clearly matters of conscience and choice, instances to which one can imagine exceptions (or, at least, they are subject to moral deliberation). While I have the right to choose whether to obey these moral injunctions, you have no right to my doing so. Whether I respect these moral precepts or not is part of my deciding how I will live my own life. Indeed, it is *that* right to choose how to live one's life that is inalienable; everything else has moral, legal, or social contingencies and consequences that vary from time to time, place to place, depending on circumstances, culture, and other variables.

One of the paradoxes of a Natural Right is that it is both absolute and limited, absolute in that it is inviolable and inalienable by government, but limited by the extent to which a right comes into conflict with other rights. Even liberty, the most basic of all rights according to Kant, Locke, and Rousseau, has its limits. Unlimited liberty—untrammeled, unrestrained, untamed—exists only in the state of nature. The very act of creating a

social contract—joining a community, accepting its laws, morality, and customs—limits individual freedom. Obeying traffic lights, calling on the police to deal with a criminal rather than taking the law in one's own hands, not needlessly crying fire in a crowded theater, these and countless other limitations on freedom are necessary trade-offs to gain the security of a social order. The most basic example of waiving certain aspects of liberty was offered by Hobbes: In signing a social contract an individual will give up his freedom to the extent that all others do likewise; for example, we forgo our individual right to self-preservation in exchange for collective protection by the state. By extension, we may be willing to give up lesser freedoms (the freedom to jaywalk) in exchange for what we perceive to be a greater one (personal safety). Our guide in such exchanges will be our rational reckoning of our own self-interest (no rational person will freely enter into a contract the terms of which are detrimental to his self-interest). A collective sequence of such decisions leads, of course, to the rules and laws of a polity. All are obliged to obey such laws because every one who is a party to the social contract—that is, every member of society—has implicitly agreed to do so, even though there is some sacrifice of liberty.[30]

This provision for giving up certain categories of liberty makes social life possible. Following Aristotle's observation about the political nature of the human species, giving up the liberty of the jungle allows for civilization, for the creation of a community, and for the social and economic activities that require voluntary cooperation. It provides for the common good, allowing for mutual defense, police, courts, and collective response to common problems.

While an individual's liberty is thus limited in the non-essential ways suggested above, the doctrine of Natural Rights nonetheless implies an absolute protection of one's essence as an individual. A right, according to Locke, is an extension of one's self, as indivisible and inalienable as one's arm. We thus possess an absolute right to our beliefs and to express our wills in matters relating to our own consciences. In the United States, such rights are protected by the Preamble and the First and Fourteenth Amendments to the Constitution. Using a natural law interpretation of the Constitution, legal scholar Ronald Dworkin has examined such issues as abortion, pornography, affirmative action, homosexuality, and euthanasia.[31] Dworkin believes that the Founders sought to create a framework for a community in which the rights of individuals to take personal responsibility for their own moral decisions concerning such questions were secured absolutely. For example, while the subject of abortion never arose in the minds of the Founders, the broader question of the inherent right to freedom of choice was foremost among the concerns of Madison and the framers in their overall construct of the Constitution. Denying the liberty of the individual by removing her exercise of choice was exactly what the Founders wished to avoid in all instances.

Dworkin concedes that the ascendant view since the 1980's—as expressed by such jurists as Justices Rehnquist, Scalia, and White (and Judge Bork)—is far narrower and, often, exactly the opposite. These judges claim that the rights of Americans are limited to the specific examples cited by the politicians who created them, and that the Constitution, therefore, must be strictly interpreted to comply with the political ideas and concerns of the times in which the various amendments were first adopted. Moreover, if one offers a broad reading of the rights inherent in the Constitution—the right to privacy, for example—the ascendant jurists' claim that such a reading offends democracy because it introduces the worst of all legal sins: "judge-made law."

Dworkin, too, is against judge-made law. He insists that the Constitution always must be interpreted in light of the original Natural Rights orientation of the Enlightenment which informs the entire spirit of the document, and in light of the two-hundred-year judicial tradition that has, in the main, interpreted the document in that spirit. He reminds us that, over history, Constitutional change has been introduced incrementally and in the spirit of preserving the original philosophy of freedom. What is, in fact, anti-democratic to Dworkin is the ascendant view of interpreting the Constitution in light of *current* economic theories and *current* political/religious agendas:

> the point of integrity—the point of law itself—is exactly to rule out politi-
> cal compromises of that kind. We must be one nation of principle: our
> Constitution must represent conviction, not the tactical strategies of jus-
> tices anxious to satisfy as many political constituencies as possible.[32]

Dworkin's Ciceronian conclusion is that "the Bill of Rights can only be understood as a set of moral principles." The American ideal is "government not only under law but under principle." His argument rests finally and firmly on what he terms a "moral reading" of the Constitution. Instead of interpreting each word, phrase, and provision as a separate, unrelated, and historically distinct legal point, he suggests that judges—and we—should understand the great document as a piece, a coherent whole that advances a powerful philosophical context in which to interpret each new issue as it arises.

If one reads the Constitution as a coherent philosophical document, it is clear that on the great issues of the day—yesterday, today, and tomorrow—the unifying principle is that we must all be free to choose:

> Someone who believes in his own responsibility for the central values of
> his life cannot yield that responsibility to a group even if he has an equal
> vote in its deliberations. A genuine political community must therefore be
> a community of independent moral agents. It must not dictate what its
> citizens think about matters of political or moral or ethical judgment, but
> must, on the contrary, provide circumstances that encourage them to arrive
> at beliefs on these matters through their own reflective and finally individ-
> ual conviction.[33]

Thus, like Justice Holmes, Dworkin concludes that we must protect even speech that we loathe. Here he parts company with radical feminists, minority leaders, and others who wish to ban pornography, racist literature, and hate talk on the grounds it offends or harms individuals and vulnerable groups. Dworkin argues that the first amendment protects bigots, sexists, and even Nazis and the Ku Klux Klan. Their lies, propaganda, and hate

> should be refuted publicly, thoroughly, and contemptuously wherever it appears. But censorship is different. We must not endorse the principle that opinion may be banned when those in power are persuaded that it is false and that some group would be deeply and understandably wounded by its publication… The hoodlums remind us of what we often forget: the high, sometimes nearly unbearable, cost of freedom. But freedom is important enough even for sacrifices that really hurt.[34]

Dworkin argues that freedom is threatened most in America by those, ironically, who act in the name of freedom. America's unique gifts to the world—the Declaration and the Bill of Rights—are under constant threat from those who most vociferously claim to love liberty. Dworkin reminds us of something else that we too often forget: around the world, governments have copied the American Declaration and Constitution exactly because they present a coherent, principled view of how a good or just society should be organized and governed. The genius of the Constitution is not in its details—which are mostly absent—but in its primary philosophical purpose to protect individuals from tyranny. The U.S. Constitution, and the Declaration, better than any documents governing any other country, enhance the liberty of citizens by limiting the power of government to interfere in the exercise of their most fundamental rights—in particular, as Dworkin says, the exercise of their own moral judgment.

The alternative to this comprehensive philosophical approach would be a programmatic, piecemeal, list of specific rights and responsibilities—dos and don'ts, rules and regulations that attempt to cover all contingencies but, in fact, lead to inflexibility as conditions change. As judges today try to make the U.S. Constitution into such a narrower document through an amoral, historical reading of its intent, their efforts fly in the face of what much of the rest of the world knows and appreciates. The unique genius of the American system is that it provides a lasting, flexible framework in which all who are subject to its dominion have "equal moral and political status:"

> [the Constitution] must respect whatever individual freedoms are indispensable to those ends including, but not limited to the freedoms more specifically designated in the document.[35]

Who Has Natural Rights?

The issue arises: At what point in life does a person acquire *Natural* Rights? Clearly, infants have no such rights because they cannot yet exercise their deliberative faculties. At age eighteen, the law grants full *legal* rights. Between infancy and legal adulthood there presumably comes a point at which the individual's sense of his own self-interest becomes sufficiently developed so that we may conclude he should be free to choose to exert his own will. This is a troublesome issue in practice because cultural and familial customs are impossible to eliminate from the decision. In some societies—in *most* societies, throughout most of history, in fact—puberty was seen as the onset of adulthood. In modern times, Western society has prolonged adolescence far beyond the onset of sexual maturity; but, prior to the twentieth century, many young boys and girls were "orphaned" in their pre-teens and allowed to fend for themselves in cities and villages in Europe and America. When forced out on their own, most humans of seven or eight could, in fact, care for themselves. Indeed, even today, children of that age reveal a rather clear, if short term, sense of their own self-interest. (Judges today recognize this: the desires of pre-teens are often taken into account when deciding child custody cases.)

For purposes of applying the doctrine of Natural Rights, one may thus assume that children gradually acquire rights as their capacity for rational thought develops. Although the pace of acquisition varies from culture to culture, and child to child, the sense of possessing rights—that is, the desire to exercise one's will in determining what is best for oneself—begins at an early age and can be said to be fully developed at the point the individual understands the necessity for education in achieving his long-term self-interest (or "happiness"). Hence, a youngster of seven or eight who insists, "Hey, I've got my rights," to that extent has acquired them! The kind of rights to which the young person refers are the general, Natural Rights shared equally by all persons by virtue of their humanity. To assert such rights is to recognize that one possesses the capacity to make a moral choice, and that he or she alone is the best judge of his or her own self-interest. It is an assertion of one's moral claim to be free of coercion from the will of another or (others).

But are such rights "inalienable"? While one can transfer or void one's legal or contractual rights, one cannot alienate one's right to life, liberty, and the pursuit of happiness, nor can they be alienated by others or by the state. These rights cannot be alienated because to do so is to deny one's personhood, one's equal membership in the species, one's humanness. Before Madison became President—even before he penned the Bill of Rights—he wrote that Americans not only possessed a God-given "right to property" but, equally important, they had "a property in rights."[36] As Locke had claimed before him, property—from the Latin cognate of the word for "self" (as in the French *propre*) —was by right one's own when it was an extension of one's self: thus, to Locke, property was an indivisible part of the individual because one had created it with one's own hands or effort. Similarly, to Madison, our God-given, natural, and "inalienable" rights to freedom are a part of who we are, and thus cannot be sundered by any mortal being, sovereign, or state action.

In sum, the essential, minimal characteristics of Natural Rights are as follows:

1. They are possessed equally by all humans capable of rational choice.
2. They come by virtue of one's membership in the species (not because they are granted by human or human institutions).
3. They are the same for all humans everywhere at all times.
4. They are few and limited.
5. We understand these rights *not* because they have been revealed by God; rather, they are "self-evident" because they are based on the few universals that all humans share in common.

Do the Chinese Have Natural Rights?

Opponents of the doctrine of Natural Rights include cultural relativists whose prime tenet of belief is that there are no universal ideas or principles. Relativists are concerned with pluralism and with respecting the differences among humans. Paradoxically, they do not appreciate that the doctrine of Natural Rights is the best defense of the right to be different. Each of us *is* different: we have different interests, aspirations, values, thoughts, and capacities. Since these aspects of the self vary, they are not universals. Therefore, none of them entails a Natural Right because we have such rights only to those things all humans possess in common. Thus, I have no Natural Right *to be* an opera singer. Instead, what *is* universal is that all people have desires, interests, aspirations, values, thoughts, and capacities. Thus, we each have a right to the possession and pursuit of our own individuality on these matters; we all have the Natural Right *to pursue* our self-interests as we each define them, whether it is to be an opera singer, a vegetarian, or a flat earther. Similarly, when we speak of respect for individuals, we mean that we recognize the right of each individual to that which is his or her own—our different personhoods. Importantly, this also includes the right to belong to a group, the right for members of that group to exercise their unique customs and behaviors, and for all members of all groups to be treated with equal respect.

Such differences were not, until recently, respected in much of the world. In Europe, until this century, a serf's aspiration to attend university, a woman's aspiration to own property, a Jew's desire to practice his faith, a Puritan's desire to practice Christianity according to his conscience, an intellectual's desire to express unorthodox political values, even a wealthy merchant's desire to have his life and property free from risk of the arbitrary will of a monarch, were not secure. That is, the Natural Right to pursue those ends was without legal protection. But Rousseau, Locke, and Kant recognized that these individuals, in fact, possessed such a right even though it was denied by the sovereign or the state. They argued that the possession of a Natural Right is prior to, superior to, and separate from, the provision of a legal right. Indeed, the Enlightenment philosophers' demands for legal rights to freedom were predicated on the existence of Natural Rights that were not only inalienable but *universal*.

Yet, today, the right-wing dictator Lee Kwan Yew in Singapore, and the Marxist tyrants who rule the People's Republic of China, both claim that Natural Rights are not universal. In particular, they claim that the doctrine is alien to Chinese culture. In effect, they argue that only Westerners have human rights. Moreover, certain Western defenders of cultural relativism agree that the doctrine is only concerned with the Enlightenment values of the West; they thus ask, who are we to say that China should respect such Western notions as liberty, individualism, and human rights?

Such extreme cultural relativism is what philosopher Mary Midgley terms "moral isolationism." She writes, "People usually take it up because they think it is a respectful attitude to other cultures. In fact, however, it is not respectful." For example, how is it respectful to Chinese to say that we in the West will accept nothing less than full human rights, but they are "different"? And who says that Chinese—at least some of them—do not want human rights? Midgley illustrates this latter point with reference to the classical Japanese verb *tsujigiri,* which was used in the ancient samurai tradition to mean "trying out one's new sword on a chance wayfarer":

> A samurai sword had to be tried out because, if it was to work properly, it had to slice through someone at a single blow, from the shoulder to the opposite flank. Otherwise, the warrior bungled his stroke. This could injure his honor, offend his ancestors, and even let down the emperor. So tests were needed, and wayfarers had to be expended. Any wayfarer would do—provided, of course, that he was not another Samurai...Now, when we hear of a custom like this, we may well reflect that we simply do not understand it; and therefore are not qualified to criticize it at all, because we are not members of that culture.[37]

But Midgley asks us to reconsider this facile response—do we really think that no one in feudal Japan ever asked, "Whoa, is this a healthy tradition?" Here is her test of the relativist's proposition: Do we really think that the poor peasant who got sliced in half thought it was morally acceptable to use *him* as a razor strop? Midgley asks, "Did he consent?"

We may apply Midgley's test to other human rights issues. For example, relativists argue that the contemporary rejection of slavery is time-conditioned: that is, *slavery is wrong now, but it wasn't wrong then.* Indeed, prior to the Civil War, American slave owners argued that it was a peculiar custom of their society: They argued that Northern abolitionists were, in effect, cultural imperialists attempting to impose Yankee morality on the South. In response, we ask Mary Midgley's question: Did the slaves consent? If not, slavery was a transgression of a human's right to be free, a violation of Natural Rights even in times and places where slavery was legal and culturally accepted. That is, as Martin L. King, Jr., argued, slaves possessed the Natural Right to freedom long before there was any effort to emancipate them. Otherwise, one could say that slavery is justified wherever it exists, and wrong only where it is illegal. That would be absurd, and would be nothing more than a justification of tyranny and the belief that might makes right.

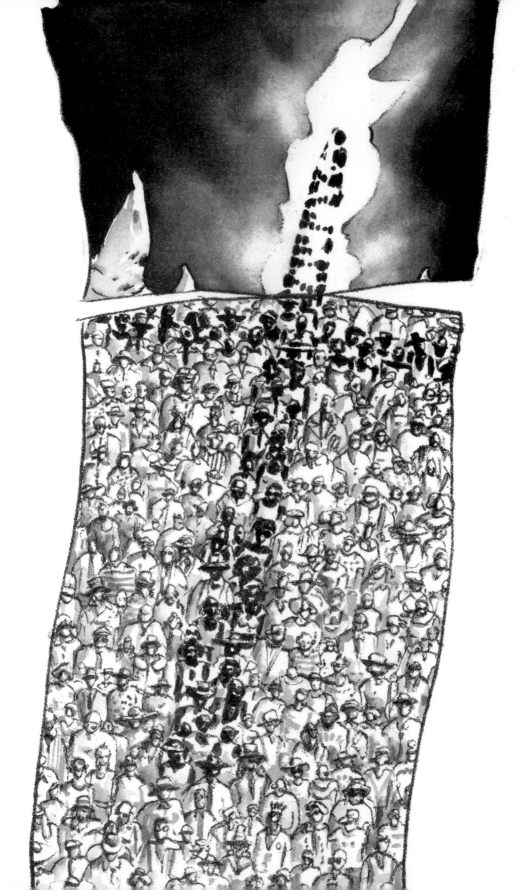

The principles implied in the universal moral prohibition against slavery can be extended to other human rights issues. Like slavery, any activity that inflicts intense pain on others is a violation of Natural Rights. Similarly, it is wrong to apply this universal principle selectively. As A.M. Rosenthal recently noted on the op-ed page of the *New York Times,* it was morally bankrupt to use the relativistic argument—"Flog Asians only"—in defense of an American who had been sentenced to be caned in Singapore. Midgley would say, instead, "Flog no one."

Female circumcision (genital mutilation) is another case in point. The practice, widespread in parts of Africa, is designed to make women submissive to male dominance by denying them sexual satisfaction. It is defended by relativists on the grounds that it is a traditional cultural practice and, consequently, Westerners have no right to pass judgment on it. In a letter published in the *New York Times* on November 14, 1993, a history instructor at Lehigh County Community College in Pennsylvania wrote that, even though female circumcision is unhealthy and painful and ushers in a lifetime of torture, it does so only "from the Western liberal tradition, and certainly from a feminist perspective. However, from the African viewpoint, the practice can serve as an affirmation of the value of women in traditional society." The writer goes on to grant that many women become infected when their clitoris and labia are removed in painful surgery— "there were even reports of elder women using their teeth to perform the ritual. Yet, whatever the degree of tissue removed, there is little doubt that for the girls it was a joyous occasion." Why? Because they become marriageable after the operation; without it, they would be social outcasts. Thus, the professor concluded, to condemn "a tradition central to many Africans and Arabs is the height of ethnocentrism."

Cultural relativists, like the professor quoted above, thus argue that female clitorectomy is moral by Midgley's test because (at least some) African women consent to the practice. But there is a further test of the difference between a legitimate cultural tradition and a violation of human rights: After a cultural practice has been abolished, would people then say it was a mistake to have abolished it, and that it was still essential to the culture of the group? For example, do people in cultures once based on slavery want to reintroduce the practice? Since it is clearly the case that individuals in all cultures appreciate the immorality of past practices once they have become aware of the alternatives, could we imagine a time in the future when African women would long for the "good old days" when their clitorises were amputated?

The notion of Natural Rights corresponds with the common sense that all humans share. While people around the world eat different things, marry at different ages, worship with different customs, they share the same practical wisdom (for example, all societies find it necessary to have specific rules about such matters of social organization as political structure, marriage, kinship, and religion). Moreover, in most places and at most times, most people will make the same moral judgments *if* free from coercion (that is, if convinced there will be no social reprisals or punishments). Hence, it is reasonable to suppose that African women are willing to undergo clitorectomy only because they are convinced that they will be unmarriageable social outcasts if they fail to do so. Remove the socially imposed constraint, and no reasonable woman will choose to have the body mutilated.

The relativistic argument is as false as it is hoary. As we have seen, prior to the Civil War, the claim was made that the practice of slavery was a tradition central to Southern culture (as *tsujigiri* was no doubt to samurai traditions). Yet, today, no Southerners (or Japanese) would defend either practice or claim that it is central to their cultures. Although many Southerners in the past did not realize that slavery was wrong, and many samurai did not acknowledge that slicing people in half was immoral, that did not make those practices right—not now, and not even then. In the future, it is safe to predict that the thinking of the descendants of the current practitioners of female circumcision will similarly arrive at the point where they understand that the ritual is, and was, barbaric.

Though most issues in social life are subjective and relative, not all are. The list of moral absolutes is small. It includes only a few moral principles based on natural law. Slavery and torture are invasions of the liberty and personal autonomy to which all humans have an equal right by virtue of their common humanity. That is why rape is always wrong. Further, because disrespect of the will of others violates this principle, it is always wrong everywhere to physically or psychologically abuse people. Put positively, there is a universal moral imperative to respect the dignity and autonomy of others, which includes, regardless of their culture, their irrevocable rights to their own opinions, values, and bodies.

Thus, the Natural Rights theorist concludes that Chinese people do, indeed, possess human rights; what they lack are the civil rights needed to protect them, much as African slaves possessed Natural Rights for the hundreds of years that civil laws were lacking to secure those rights. If natural law was, in fact, culture bound, one would have to argue as follows: *Slavery was morally right until the day it was abolished.*

Even though they deny it, Chinese leaders themselves offer de facto acknowledgment of the universality and timelessness of Natural Rights. When the Communists came to power in China, they abolished two ancient practices, the foot-binding of young women (to make them "attractive" for marriage) and the castration of young men (to make them "fit" for service in the Emperor's harem). The Communist authorities who banned these practices called them cruel and inhumane, and the test of the cruelty was that no young person would voluntarily undergo either painful operation if given a free choice. (Both operations occurred *after* the age at which a child could reasonably choose.) Significantly, the Communist authorities did not argue that these ages-old Chinese practices had *suddenly* become cruel and unacceptable when Mao assumed power in 1948. The Communists recognized that the practices had *always* been cruel, even when they were socially sanctioned. Thus, while the Communists did not use the language of Natural Rights, they clearly understood that the concept was universal. In fact, the doctrine is compatible with the traditional teachings not only of Christians and Jews, but of Moslems, Hindus, Zoroastrians, Sikhs, Buddhists, and Confucians, as well. All of those systems of belief, in one way or another, contain the basic concept of loving one's neighbor as one's self—that is, respecting the dignity of our fellow beings by virtue of the fact that they also are human. Mao and his political cadres were, of course, familiar with the Natural Rights argument. The reason they (and their fellow communists in Europe) did not use it as justification when they abolished such terrible practices as castration, foot-binding, concubinage, and serfdom is that they were not happy about where the argument led: to civil rights and individual freedom.

Paradoxically, freedom-loving descendants of Bentham, down through such influential critics of Natural Rights as Ronald Reagan, Newt Gingrich, and Milton Friedman, similarly adopt parts of the doctrine selectively without acknowledging the overall construct because they, too, are unhappy with where it leads. While they are passionate believers in political and economic liberty, they are uncomfortable with notions of free choice on social issues—and even more uncomfortable with the notion of governments being constituted for the purpose of securing economic rights to the pursuit of happiness.

The Maximal Position: Economic Rights

Most of the rights discussed thus far are "negative," in that they protect the individual's property from arbitrary seizure, and protect the individual's liberty from infringement by the state. The United States Bill of Rights is a catalog of such negative rights, which are basically prohibitions against the state. Related are certain positive legal rights. These are rights to protection by the state against thieves and murderers who would steal our property and do harm or injury to our bodies. Such rights also protect us by preventing private individuals and organizations from infringing on our basic rights and liberties. These two categories of rights cost society little to guarantee (other than the cost of courts and police).[38]

But a third category of rights is particularly controversial because they entail economic costs. In his 1944 State of the Union Address, President Franklin D. Roosevelt argued that the time finally had come to make good on the promise made in the Declaration (later reiterated by Lincoln) to secure every individual's right to pursue happiness:

> This republic had its beginning, and grew to its present strength, under the protection of certain inalienable political rights—among them the right of free speech, free press, free worship, trial by jury, freedom from unreasonable searches and seizures. They were our rights to life and liberty. As our nation has grown in size and stature, however—as our industrial economy expanded—these political rights proved inadequate to assure us equality in the pursuit of happiness.

We have come to a clear realization of the fact that true individual freedom cannot exist without economic security and independence. "Necessitous men are not freemen." People who are hungry and out of a job are the stuff of which dictatorships are made. In our day these economic truths have become accepted as self-evident. We have accepted, so to speak, a second Bill of Rights under which a new basis of security and prosperity can be established for all—regardless of station, race, or creed.

Among these are:
The right to a useful and remunerative job in the industries or shops or farms or mines of the nation;
The right to earn enough to provide adequate food and clothing and recreation;
The right of every farmer to raise and sell his products at a return which will give him and his family a decent living;
The right of every businessman, large and small, to trade in an atmosphere of freedom from unfair competition and domination by monopolies at home or abroad;
The right of every family to a decent home;
The right to adequate medical care and the opportunity to achieve and enjoy good health;
The right to adequate protection from the economic fears of old age, sickness, accident, and unemployment;
The right to a good education.[39]

These are the rights that appal contemporary conservatives, both minimalist libertarians and Benthamite utilitarians. The strongest argument against the possession of such economic rights was presented by the grandfather of modern American conservatism, William Graham Sumner, in 1914:

The notion of Natural Rights is destitute of sense, but it is captivating, and it is the more available on account of its vagueness. It lends itself to the most vicious kind of social dogmatism, for if a man has Natural Rights, then the reasoning is clear up to the finished socialistic doctrine that a man has a natural right to whatever he needs, and that the measure of his claims is the wishes which he wants fulfilled.[40]

Sumner thus equated the limited, basic needs common to all humans with the unlimited and different *wishes* found among individuals. Hence, to Sumner, and generations of conservatives who followed him, the Declaration's Natural Rights were a promissory note to be cashed in by unworthy individuals who had not earned their own keep. Worse, rights are a "slippery slope," and those who ask for bread and water today will demand steak and wine tomorrow—and will not be satisfied until they have spent the entire wealth of hard-working taxpayers.

But, clearly, this is a misinterpretation of the doctrine of Natural Rights. As we have seen, to the extent that anyone can be said to have a Natural Right, that right must be the same for everyone and based on characteristics common to all humans. As discussed, humans are all equal in that they have certain needs in common, ranging from those shared by animals (food, sleep) to those that are uniquely human (for extended parental care, shelter, clothing, and education). For *all* people to live a good life—to be happy as Aristotle and Jefferson meant that word—these basic needs must be fulfilled. Thus, in order to pursue happiness—that is, to be able to devote one's efforts to the full realization of one's God-given potential— every individual must first have adequate and sufficient food, clothing, shelter, and education. Jefferson recognized this and devoted much of the twenty years remaining to his life after leaving the Presidency to encouraging the creation of public education for those who could not afford private schooling and universities.

Sumner's unstated assumption was that Jefferson and his followers were either fools or Marxists. In fact, they were neither. The doctrine of Natural Rights opens the door only so far as to enable each individual true equality of opportunity; that is, a fair chance to develop his or her potential. Necessitous individuals are entitled only to what they *need* (which is limited) and not, as Sumner claims, to what they *desire* (which is unlimited). Thus, extremely poor citizens are entitled to help from society only in meeting their basic needs of food, clothing, shelter, health care, and education— much as FDR said in 1944.

Doubtless, Sumner was correct that Jefferson was silent on the issue of where exactly to draw the line concerning how much is enough to satisfy one's needs. That lack of specificity is both a weakness and a virtue of the Natural Rights doctrine. It is a weakness in that it is imprecise; it is a strength in that it is non-prescriptive and allows for future generations to decide how much can be provided based on the economic capacity of the nation. Jefferson felt that reckoning was a prime, on-going task of a democracy.

Curiously, the manifestly non-Sumnerian Marx also attacked the notion of economic Natural Rights (in *The Jewish Question*). But Marx argued that Locke's right to property was no more than a justification of bourgeoisie society by granting, in effect, the "rightness" of the existing—and grossly unequal—distribution of property. Marx had it wrong. In fact, Locke, and those who followed him (including Rousseau, Jefferson, and Mill) had never spoken of an *absolute* right to property. Locke, following Aristotle, thought that the right to property was limited by one's natural needs—not unlimited to one's boundless desires. Jefferson, an Aristotelian, saw property (along with life and liberty) as the *means* to a higher end: happiness. And one of Jefferson's most visible co-authors of The Declaration of Independence, Benjamin Franklin, argued that because property rights beyond those created by one's own hand are *legal* rights (the right to issue stock in a corporation is granted and protected by the state) such rights could be morally relinquished "down to the last farthing" to protect the overall public good.[41] Indeed, all authors in the natural law tradition conceived of a hierarchy of rights in which, when one came into conflict with another, the interests of the higher (happiness) would take precedence over the lower (money).

Locke, Mill, Samuel Johnson, Franklin, and Adam Smith—perhaps the greatest defenders of liberty in human history—shared the belief that economic systems must exist within a moral order. Within this order they all saw that the concerns of the community, of human dignity, of morality, came higher than economic concerns. Hence, Marx clearly was wrong to assume that Enlightenment scholars with all their prodigious candle power would equate the highest rights (freedom of speech, conscience, and religion) with the lowest (freedom from taxation).

As Franklin, Mill, and Samuel Johnson—among others—argued, it is not a violation of our basic liberties to contribute to the overall good of society. This opening makes taxation legitimate when the proceeds are used for the collective good. A societal, democratic decision to tax—within limits and for specific purposes—is not an infringement on liberty, and is not tantamount to infringing one's right to pursue happiness. From the perspective of Franklin, Mill, and Johnson, when government takes property (that is, when it taxes) the effect is not tantamount to the taking of one's self. Clearly, to tax to the point where an individual cannot pursue happiness—when government takes away the wherewithal needed to pursue a good life in terms of fulfilling one's human potential—would constitute a violation of Natural Rights. But, to contemporary advocates of the doctrine of Natural Rights, for government to take even half of the property of a rich woman is not morally tantamount to limiting a smidgen of her right to exercise her conscience.

Is Natural Rights an Absolutist Doctrine?

The strongest argument against Natural Rights—brought forward by Karl Popper, Isaiah Berlin, Hannah Arendt[42] and others who have understandably recoiled from the horrors of mid-twentieth century totalitarianism—is that the doctrine is dangerous, per se, in that it is absolutist. In particular, it is often characterized as part of Roman Catholic dogma, and thus unacceptable to Protestants, Jews, and individuals from non-Western cultures. This is particularly ironic because the Enlightenment was, in the main, a reaction *against* Roman Catholic doctrine, and few of those most associated with the development of the doctrine in the eighteenth century were Christians by any accepted standard.[43] Yet, Natural Rights is broad enough, general enough, and flexible enough to have attracted a wide range of adherents whose varying interpretations create confusion about its core tenets. As we have seen, at one extreme are Kantian minimalists who hold that freedom is the *only* natural right. At the other end of the spectrum are maximalists, like Roosevelt, who offer an expansionist interpretation that includes economic rights. Indeed, the concept easily accommodates the full spectrum from least to most.

However, the concept is less readily shoe-horned into ideological or religious constructs such as the Roman Catholic attempt to square Natural Rights with other teachings of the church. Pope John Paul II, for example, stretches the scope of the concept to the breaking point when he claims that the right of freedom must be limited by "certain moral truths about the human person and human community." Since not all of the truths he has in mind are derived from natural law—and, thus, are not universal by the logic of the doctrine—the Pope's conclusion about rights conflicts with the minimalist position. For example, minimalists hold that individuals should be free even to use heroin as long as they do not infringe on the rights of others (that is, as long as they alone bear all the costs and consequences of their actions). In the minimalist position, one is thus free to be an addict but, if one becomes a public nuisance, neglects one's children, or becomes a welfare burden, the state is entitled to limit one's behavior (for example, by forcing the individual to internalize the costs of his actions through making him pay for whatever social services he receives, or compensate others for whatever damages she causes). With these provisos, civil libertarians in the tradition of Kant and Mill conclude that society has no right to create civil laws that contravene the autonomous individual's right to choose.

The Pope would disagree. He argues that for a good society to function individuals must perforce subscribe to a particular code of morality. Heroin addicts—because they are less-than-fully participating members of the community—are outside the bounds of freedom even if they are law-abiding citizens. To the Pope, individuals must choose to be virtuous, that is, to meet their full responsibilities as members of a moral community. Moreover, in the Pope's eyes, individuals do not have a right to abuse the mind and body given to them by God. To him, a civil law that permitted drug use would be in contradiction of natural law and, thus, unjust.

In most such instances, the differences between the Catholic and the civil libertarian positions can be reconciled. Society can devise ways to preserve individual choice while at the same time bolstering responsible behavior—as in laws that permit adults the freedom to choose to smoke tobacco, but prohibit them from irresponsibly passing the costs and effects of their actions on to others in public places. In another example, the Catholic church condones the freedom of its adult members to drink alcohol, even as it supports government actions to limit such irresponsible behavior as driving while intoxicated.

The key concepts in both of those examples are "adults," "free to choose," and "responsibility." We see the centrality of those concepts when we move to issues like abortion, where no such easy accommodation between the values of freedom and community have been found. In the case of abortion, the civil libertarian and Catholic views are in irreconcilable conflict, and we must return to the assumptions about the state of nature to understand why. In the state of nature, as posited above, only "adults" who are "rationally able to choose" possess Natural Rights. Hence, we saw that infants (and fetuses), by definition, do not have such rights. At the same time, adults have "responsibilities" for such living beings. Thus while mothers have the *right* to choose whether to bear a child or not, they carry a moral responsibility for the children they conceive. It is

thus the mother who possesses Natural Rights—and moral responsibilities—not the fetus which is incapable of exercising either rights or responsibilities.

Likewise, since trees and animals are incapable of making rational decisions, they cannot be said to possess Natural Rights. Therefore, the responsibility falls on adult humans to make the difficult decisions concerning their proper treatment. It is not only illogical to argue that animals have Natural Rights, to do so is to let humans off the hook morally and to allow them to shirk their responsibility to care for animals. For example, among Hindus, to whom animals have the same rights as humans, we can see the consequences of this moral misunderstanding. In India, when an old cow no longer is able to produce milk, its owner sets it "free." What this freedom amounts to is the right to slow and cruel starvation for the animal while its erstwhile owner unloads an economic burden. The confusion of an animal's supposed rights with a human's responsibility for God's creatures is also found in the West. In America, a defender of animal rights will choose to castrate a dog "for its own good"—implicitly acknowledging that, in fact, the dog has no rights; but, instead, its owner has a moral responsibility to decide what is in the animal's best interests.

Conclusion: A Minimalist Belief for Non-Believers

The doctrine of Natural Rights is not a fairy tale, even if it is founded on the myth of an idyllic past. It requires us to make hard, tough choices and to assume personal and social responsibility for those humans and other creatures of God who are unable to make such decisions themselves. The doctrine gives us guidance on how to make these decisions, but no certainty.

The doctrine is neither prescriptive nor all-inclusive. Australian philosopher Stephen Buckle differs sharply with some advocates of Natural Rights who hold to "the wistful belief that there is a moral code inscribed somewhere in the heavens." Indeed, to the philosophers who developed the concept of Natural Rights, the doctrine "was not generally understood to be a fixed, unalterable set of rules which could be simply applied to human conduct or society irrespective of the circumstances."[44] It is not prescriptive, nor will it help to resolve all our moral dilemmas. For example, while the doctrine might help to inform discussion of such questions as "Is war ever justifiable?" "Is human cloning a violation of natural law?" and "Is artificial insemination moral?" it certainly will not provide definitive answers.

In sum, Natural Rights is a minimalist belief for non-believers. It is a moral anchor in a relativist world. While relativists are correct in claiming that Natural Rights are in a sense absolute, they are wrong in confusing rights with values (or social goals). A prime characteristic of rights is that they are constraints. As such, they are not subjective, nor are they open to differences of opinion. Values, on the other hand, are not absolute. They

may be good or bad, a reckoning which is inherently subjective. Values thus can be compromised (where there is demonstrated reason). Rights can never be compromised. And while the domain of values is very large, the domain of rights is extremely small. It is, in fact, limited to the protection of the individual's freedom to choose among many competing, subjective, relative values.

It is easy to confuse rights with values, particularly for those relativists who are sensitive to the fact that a world in which values were absolute would be totalitarian. But a world in which rights are absolute is one in which relativists are free to be relativists. One cannot have a society in which there is protection of pluralism if there are no absolute rights. Ultimately, what defends the relativists' freedom to choose is a civil constitution in which their Natural Rights are inalienable. Natural Rights are thus the *de minimis* of morality in an otherwise relativistic world.

This article is dedicated to Dr. Mortimer Jerome Adler, who has taught three generations of Americans how to read the Declaration of Independence and the Constitution of the United States.

1. Cicero, *De Re Publica,* III.xxxii.

2. "The End of Democracy?: The Judicial Usurpation of Politics" in *1996 First Things 67,* November 1996, pp. 18–42. Quotes p. 19.

3. The distinction is between *jus naturale* (natural law, innate rights, the laws of God) on the one hand, and *jus civile* or *jus gentium* (civil law, positive rights, the laws of men) on the other hand. See Hobbes *Leviathan,* Chapter XIX (*GBWW* I: 23, 71–76; II: 21, 71–76), and Kant *The Science of Right* (*GBWW* I: 42, 400–02; II: 39, 400–02).

4. Mortimer J. Adler and William Gorman, *The American Testament,* (New York: Praeger Publishers, 1975), and Mortimer J. Adler, *We Hold These Truths,* (New York: Macmillan, 1987).

5. *GBWW* I: 23, 49–283; II: 21, 49–283.

6. In particular, Aristotle's *Nicomachean Ethics* and *Politics* (*GBWW* I: 9, 335–548; II: 8, 335–548), Cicero's *De Re Publica,* and Aquinas' *Summa Theologica* Part I of Second Part (*GBWW* I: 19, 609–826, 20, 1–378; II: 17, 609–826, 18, 1–378).

7. In particular, Locke's *Concerning Civil Government* (*GBWW* I: 35, 25–36; II: 33, 25–36), Rousseau's *The Social Contract* Book I (*GBWW* I: 38, 387–94; II: 35, 387–94), and Kant's *The Science of Right* (*GBWW* I: 42, 395–458; II: 39, 395–458). The description of men and women in the state of nature that follows is a distillation based primarily on the descriptions in Hobbes, Locke, Rousseau, and Kant found in the *Great Books.*

8. C.Y. Harburg's lyrics from *Finian's Rainbow,* 1947.

9. This paragraph is a modern restatement of Hobbes Chapter XIII (*GBWW* I: 23, 84–86; II: 21, 84–86).

10. Hobbes and Rousseau agree on this point.

11. Here, I leave Hobbes behind and draw on Locke, Rousseau, and Kant.

12. The concept of "happiness" comes from Aristotle's *Nicomachean Ethics.* Adler explains its meaning in the context of Natural Rights in *We Hold These Truths,* pp. 51–61.

13. It is worth noting that Aristotle's hierarchy of needs, the highest of which is "happiness," corresponds with Maslow's similar hierarchy, the highest of which is "self-actualization." Abraham H. Maslow, *Toward a Psychology of Being,* (Princeton, N.J.: Van Nostrand, 1962).

14. This is Locke Chapter V, parts 25–51 (*GBWW* I: 35, 30–36; II: 33, 30–36).

15. This is Hobbes (*GBWW* I: 23, 85; II: 21, 85).

16. This is a point of agreement among all natural law philosophers.

17. This is Rousseau.

18. Lincoln called this the "promise" of the Declaration. Adler and Gorman, op. cit. p. 122. See note 4, above.

19. Bentham, "Anarchical Fallacies" in *The Works of Jeremy Bentham,* ed. John Bowring, (Edinburgh: W. Tait; London: Simpkin, Marshall, 1843), vol.2.

20. Madison, Hamilton, and Otis quoted in James H. Hutson, "A Nauseous Project," *Wilson Quarterly,* Winter 1991, 15 p. 60.

21. Ibid., p. 61.

22. Quoted in Adler and Gorman, op. cit., p. 121.

23. Harriet Taylor Mill, "The Enfranchisement of Women," in *Dissertations and Discussions,* John Stuart Mill, (New York: Huskell House Publishers Ltd, 1973) vol. 2 p. 416. This is reprinted elsewhere in this volume.

24. See, in particular, Mill's "On Liberty," (*GBWW* I: 43, 267–327; II: 40, 267–323) "On The Subjection of Women," (*GIT* 1966: 454–528) and "Political Economy."

25. Martin Luther King, Jr., "Letter from a Birmingham Jail," 1963.

26. Ibid.

27. Ibid.

28. Kant, *The Science of Right,* op. cit.

29. H.L.A. Hart, "Are There Any Natural Rights?" *Philosophical Review,* 64 (1955) pp. 175–191.

30. Ibid.

31. Ronald Dworkin, *Taking Rights Seriously,* (Cambridge: Harvard University Press, 1978).

32. Dworkin, *Freedom's Law,* (Cambridge, Mass.: Harvard University Press, 1996), p. 103.

33. Ibid., p. 26.

34. Ibid., pp. 225, 226.

35. Ibid., p. 8.

36. James Madison, "The Rights to Property and Property in Rights," 1772.

37. Mary Midgely, *Heart and Mind,* (New York: St. Martin's Press, 1981), pp. 69–74.

38. Arthur M. Okun, *Equality and Efficiency: The Big Tradeoff,* (Washington, D.C.: The Brookings Institution, 1975).

39. Adler and Gorman, op. cit., pp. 106–7.

40. William Graham Sumner, "The Challenge of Facts," in *The Challenge of Facts and Other Essays,* ed. Albert Galloway Keller, (New Haven: Yale University Press, 1914), pp. 33–4.

41. Franklin, "Hints for the Members of [the] Convention," *Federal Gazette,* November 3, 1789 in "On the Legislative Branch," from *Representation and Suffrage* in *The Complete Works of Benjamin Franklin,* ed., John Bigelow, (New York and London: G.P. Putnam's Sons, 1988), vol. X.

42. Karl L. Popper, *The Open Society and Its Enemies;* Isaiah Berlin, *Four Essays on Liberty,* and Hannah Arendt, *The Origins of Totalitarianism.*

43. Peter Gay, *The Enlightenment: The Rise of Modern Paganism,* Norton, 1977.

44. Stephen Buckle, "Natural Law," in Peter Singer, ed., *A Companion to Ethics,* (Cambridge, Mass.: Blackwell, 1991), pp. 165–66.

James O'Toole retired from the University of Southern California (USC) in 1994 after a career of over twenty years on the faculty of the Graduate School of Business, where he held the University Associates' Chair of Management. At USC he had most recently been Executive Director of the Leadership Institute. For six years, he was Director of the Twenty-Year Forecast Project, where he interpreted social, political, and economic change for top management of thirty of the fifty largest American corporations.

Mr. O'Toole's research and writings have been in the areas of planning, corporate culture, and leadership. He has addressed dozens of major corporations and professional organizations, and has published over seventy articles. Among his twelve books, *Vanguard Management* was named "one of the best business and economics books of 1985" by the editors of *Business Week.* His latest book, *Leading Change,* was published in the spring of 1995.

From 1994 through 1997, Mr. O'Toole was Executive Vice President of The Aspen Institute, where he headed all seminar programs, including the renowned Executive Seminar. He continues to serve The Aspen Institute as Chairman of the Institute's distinguished Board of Overseers and as Senior Fellow of the Institute. He has won a coveted Mitchell Prize for a paper on economic growth policy, and has served on the prestigious Board of Editors of the *Encyclopædia Britannica.* A graduate of the University of Oxford, Mr. O'Toole is editor of *The American Oxonian.*

Special Features

Shakespeare's Fairy Tales: Is All Well That Ends Well in Shakespeare's Comedies?

Cynthia L. Rutz

Shakespeare's Fairy Tales: Is All Well That Ends Well in Shakespeare's Comedies?

210

T he inspiration for this lecture came from a performance of *All's Well That Ends Well* (*GBWW* I: 27, 142–173; II: 25, 142–173) that I attended some time ago. At the final resolution of the play, I missed that satisfied "all's well with the world" feeling I associate with Shakespeare's comedies, when all the right people have been neatly paired off and any erring Dukes or Kings have been completely reformed offstage. Instead, an intrepid heroine had been reconciled with an unredeemed cad who does not deserve her. Moreover, the fairy-tale plot of the play did not seem to fit with this ending, for it was not at all likely that the couple would live happily ever after. This disturbing ending led me to explore further some of the unequal pairings both in Shakespeare's comedies and in fairy-tale plots. In the following reflections, I take *All's Well* as my starting point, but examine the question of endings in other comedies as well.

The plot of *All's Well* is a fairy tale, and I will tell the story to you as such. It contains many standard fairy-tale elements as well as some that do not seem to fit the fairy-tale pattern:

> Once upon a time there was a king who became very ill. He was attended by the best physicians in the kingdom, but none could cure him, and so he grew sicker and sicker. In this kingdom there also lived a beautiful but poor young maiden, the daughter of a famous physician now dead. This maiden lived with a noble family and grew up with the son of the house, whom she loved dearly but felt she could never marry because of her lowly state. When the maiden heard of the king's illness she re-solved to cure him and ask for the hand of her beloved as her reward. She journeyed to the capital and obtained an audi-ence with the king. The king was doubtful that a cure could come from such a source, but agreed to let her try on the condition that she forfeit her life if the cure should fail. She succeeded in healing the king, who grate-fully rewarded her with a rich dowry and the hand of any young man in his kingdom she chose, and she of course chose her be-loved.

(Overleaf) Helena and the King from All's Well That Ends Well. *(Right) Act 2, scene 3. After Helena cures the King, she asks for Bertram's hand in mar-riage.*

Here is where the story ought to end, given all our fairy-tale instincts. The young man of course agrees, and the two live happily ever after, possibly even ruling the kingdom after their patron dies. That is not exactly how it goes in Shakespeare, however. Let me continue:

> The young man does not agree to the maiden's proposal and only marries her because the king demands it. Immediately after the wedding he deserts his wife to go to foreign wars, leaving her a note saying he will only accept her as his wife when she can procure the ring which never leaves his finger and produce a child he is father to. After many trials and tribulations our heroine manages these two seemingly impossible tasks. First she gives out that she is dead, and then follows her husband and cleverly substitutes herself in his bed in place of a local girl he has been trying to seduce and to whom he has given his ring as a lovetoken. His wife thereby procures from him both the ring and the pregnancy without his knowledge. When confronted with these proofs he begs her forgiveness and accepts her as his wife.

So finally we seem to reach happily ever after; simply by a more circuitous route. Here too, however, Shakespeare denies fairy-tale expectations. Bertram, the man the heroine Helena loves, does not behave very heroically, to say the least. He publicly refuses to marry Helena for class reasons—"A poor physician's daughter my wife! Disdain / Rather corrupt me ever!" (*GBWW* I: 27, 152; II: 25, 152) He only *pretends* to accept the king's arguments that her virtue makes up for her low birth, and then proceeds to use the king's gift of wedding dower for the wars and abandons Helena. He is also a poor judge of character, his bosom friend being a

Falstaffian soldier named Parolles who is all bombast, empty boasts, and slanderous talk. And finally, Bertram is only prevented from taking advantage of Diana, another dowerless young girl, by his wife's bed trick. In short, Bertram is a perfect example of that wonderful old English word *cad*, and we cannot help but be sorry to see Helena end up with him. Indeed, Shakespeare actually makes Bertram's character appear worse than in his source story, a tale from Boccaccio's *Decameron*, by providing a long-drawn out dénouement in which, as the

Act 2, scene 3: Bertram's rejection of Helena before the court.

Shakespeare's Fairy Tales: Is All Well That Ends Well in Shakespeare's Comedies?

212

truth begins to come out, Bertram viciously slanders Diana (who had helped his wife with her bed trick) by first calling her a liar, then claiming she is a camp-follower and prostitute. Moreover, Bertram's counterpart in Boccaccio embraces his wife at the end, and we are told that "from that time forth, never failing to honour the Countess as his lawful wedded wife, he loved her and held her in the greatest esteem."[1] Shakespeare, on the contrary, gives us no convincing proof of any reformation on his part, only a brief "Oh, pardon" when Helena finally appears. Bertram's final words in the play, spoken in answer to Helena's "Will you be mine, now are you doubly won?" are conditional, and spoken not to her but to the king: "If she, my liege, can make me know this clearly, / I'll love her dearly, ever, ever dearly." (*GBWW* I: 27, 173; II: 25, 173) This "if" of Bertram's prompts the king to utter the final couplet of the play proper as a conditional too: "All yet *seems* well; and *if* it end so meet, / The bitter past, more welcome is the sweet," (*GBWW* I: 27, 173; II: 25, 173) (emphasis added).

Why, then, does Shakespeare marry the resourceful Helena, a woman everyone else in the play considers beautiful, accomplished, and intelligent, to such a man? Though Bertram is an extreme case, one could ask that question about many, if not most of the heroines in Shakespeare's comedies. The comedies abound in strong, witty, interesting female characters such as Portia, Rosalind, and Viola who often end up with rather weak, sometimes fickle men who seem unworthy of them. We are often hard put even to remember the names of their beloved when the play is over, but we do not forget the women. In *As You Like It*, Rosalind's lover Orlando, is upright and true but no match for her keen wit, so she is able to tease him endlessly to our great amusement. In *The Merchant of Venice*, Portia's Bassanio, while generous and warm-hearted, loses his friend Antonio's money, and then foolishly allows him to contract his life in order to get even more money and is at a loss to get his friend out of trouble until Portia saves the day. Viola's beloved in *Twelfth Night* languishes for another woman throughout the play, talking endlessly about the depth of his devotion, then instantly switching his affections to Viola as soon as he sees his cause is hopeless. Even in the case of Benedict and Beatrice, that seemingly well matched duo of sparring partners from *Much Ado About Nothing,* Shakespeare is careful to show us Benedict's chagrin that Beatrice always bests him in their verbal battles. The great exception to this rule is Kate and Petruchio in *The Taming of the Shrew,* where it seems clear that Petruchio rules the roost. By and large, however, in order to make the inequality among couples even more apparent, Shakespeare often has his women test their lovers in some way, whether by disguising themselves as men or giving them a ring that is never to leave their finger, and when the men invariably fail the test the women take them back anyway.

Stories of such clever women matched with hapless men are quite common in fairy tales, including many that bear a striking resemblance to some of Shakespeare's comic plots, as we shall see. *The Arabian Nights* in particular, portrays many clever women who are forever getting good-looking and good-hearted but dull-witted men out of jams. The most famil-

Orlando (right) and Rosalind (center) from As You Like It, *act 3, scene 2.*

Orlando. What were his marks?
Rosalind. A lean cheek,—which you have not; a blue eye and sunken,—which you have not.

Act III. Scene II.

iar examples are Ali Baba's servant girl Morgiana, whose quick thinking saves him from the wrath of the forty thieves and Scheherezade herself who saves the sultan from his worse self by curing his hatred of women with her stories. This is all done in a comic vein, of course, but we are compelled to ask what Shakespeare is trying to accomplish by setting up such unequal matches in these fairy tales.

Shakespeare's Fairy Tales: Is All Well That Ends Well in Shakespeare's Comedies?

214

The servant girl Morgiana from Scheherezade's tale, "Ali Baba and the Forty Thieves."

First, I would like to say a bit more about the uniqueness of Shakespeare's comic heroines. Aristotle claimed that the comedies in Greek drama show us characters worse than ourselves, while tragedies show us our betters.[2] While it is indeed true that Shakespeare's best and greatest *male* figures, noble though faulty, appear in the tragedies—Hamlet, Lear, Macbeth, Othello—his best and most noble women he generally saves for his comedies. If the importance of a role is partly dependent upon how much stage time it receives, then it is clear from merely noting the number of lines assigned to women that Shakespeare's comic women talk far more than those in his tragedies, with Helena, Portia, and Rosalind in particular dominating their respective plays.

In Greek drama, on the other hand, the memorable women are all tragic—Clytemnestra, Antigone, Alcestis. Through Aristotle's remarks about comedy and tragedy, we can see that while it is funny to see low characters ridiculed, tricked and mocked, it would not be so funny if these characters were noble. Shakespeare's comedies demonstrate the truth of Aristotle's observations, for he both complicates and enriches these plays by showing the trials and tribulations of women better than ourselves. We laugh at the comic confusion of male lovers when, for example, women like Rosalind or Portia disguise themselves to tease the men or set them up for failure with impossible tasks. But we do not laugh in *Measure for Measure* when we see the soon-to-be nun Isabella threatened by the Duke's deputy Angelo with rape and the death of her brother, nor do we laugh when Helena is publicly repudiated and deserted by Bertram, nor in *Much Ado About Nothing* when Claudio abandons the chaste Hero at the altar after brutally and publicly denouncing her for her supposed infidelity. Such scenes seem more suited to a tragedy; they are certainly terrible moments for the heroines. In the wake of such scenes we may hope, along with the king quoted above, that all *may* be well that ends well, but it is hard to think that what he called "the bitter past" can all be forgiven and forgotten so easily. Yet by the end of the play all three of these men are rehabilitated and wed, two of them to the very women whom they had humiliated. By contrast, Shakespeare's purely comic heroines, who have a well-developed sense of humor, tend to be spared such scenes, for they make light of such potentially humiliating tasks as Viola's carrying love messages from her beloved to her rival in *Twelfth Night*.

To examine the question why Shakespeare's comedies have so many unequal pairings of strong women with weak men, it is useful to look at the folk and fairy-tale tradition he draws upon. The popular conception of a fairy-tale romance is that of a passive princess being rescued from peril or death by a prince on a white charger—hardly a scenario that fits such capable heroines as Rosalind or Portia. This notion of fairy tales is, however, a stereotype fostered by the selective use we have made of them in America, where the Disney studio's depiction of passive heroines as Snow White, Sleeping Beauty, and Cinderella have been our models for fairy-tale females. But there exists a much wider world of other stories where women are anything but passive, and the Disney studios are finally beginning to explore some of these other tales with their recent heroines such as Beauty, the gypsy Esmeralda, and The Little Mermaid. To explore further this kind of fairy tale and the use Shakespeare makes of it, let me return to the fairy-tale plot of *All's Well That Ends Well*.

The plot of *All's Well* falls into two parts, both of which have many fairy-tale precedents, which I shall call (1) The Curing of the Royal Problem and (2) The Performing of Seemingly Impossible Tasks. As we have seen, the "Curing of the Royal Problem" plot ends abruptly with Bertram's refusal to marry Helena because she is not of his social standing. Our expectation based on limited experience with fairy tales would be that this is not supposed to happen to the hero or heroine who has "Cured the Royal Problem." In one typical tale, for example, a king has issued a decree that anyone who can make the princess cry will win her hand. The simpleton who cures the princess by making her chop onions does indeed marry her, and they live happily ever after.

Other variations on this tale-type, however, share Bertram's attitude, with a princess who is none too happy to be saddled with a commoner. For

example, in the Brothers Grimm version of *The Brave Little Tailor*, after the hero has performed various tasks and won the princess, she overhears him talking in his sleep one night and for the first time realizes that she has married a common tailor. She then plots with her courtiers to have them kill him while he sleeps, but he discovers the plot and pretends to talk in his sleep again, saying "I've slain seven with one blow, killed two giants, captured a unicorn, and trapped a wild boar. Do you think those fellows waiting outside my door could ever scare me?" This frightens the men away, and the princess is obliged to accept her commoner husband. The tale does not try to claim that the couple share wedded bliss thereafter; it merely ends: "none of them ever dared to do anything to him after this. Thus the tailor reigned as king and remained king for the rest of his life."[3]

(Left) Sophocles' tragic heroine, Antigone.

Similar class conflict occurs in the version of *Beauty and the Beast*, published in 1740 by Madame de Villeneuve.[4] This mini-novella is the original source for the version of the tale that is best known in the west. In Madame de Villeneuve's story the virtuous Beauty cures the royal problem by agreeing to marry the Beast, who is really an enchanted prince who must remain a Beast until some woman will love him despite his appearance. After the prince returns to his original form, however, his mother arrives, and while she is thankful for Beauty's efforts, she firmly quashes any prospect of a wedding because Beauty is merely the daughter of a merchant, the kind of behavior one would expect from Bertram. A sympathetic fairy, who arrives with the mother, argues with her to no avail about the true meaning of nobility, just as the king had argued with Bertram that Helena's deeds and worth made her noble. Madame de Villeneuve then takes the easy way out of this dilemma by having the fairy at last reveal that Beauty is of noble birth after all, being a princess who was left with the merchant's family for safe-keeping at birth.

As we have seen then, Bertram is actually *not* acting outside fairy-tale tradition when he reveals his snobbery. Fairy tales by and large take the sympathetic fairy's position, best stated by the king in *All's Well* when he is trying to persuade Bertram of Helena's worth: "From lowest place when virtuous things proceed, / The place is dignified by th' doer's deed." Yet the tales do not expect everyone in the story to agree with the view that good deeds glorify humble origins. Along with tales of snobbish wives or husbands there are stories containing the far more dangerous snobbish mother-in-law who often does harm to her new daughter-in-law of dubious social origins as soon as her son has gone off to war, though of course she is always thwarted in the end. The implication of such fairy tales seems to be that although there are always those who will disapprove of the hero or heroine's lowly origins, they may finally reach a position where their virtue is unassailable. This, finally, is all that Helena can expect. If she never has Bertram's love she may at least have forced a grudging respect from him. Like the tailor with his class-conscious princess, at least Helena is, in the end, acknowledged Countess and will remain so the rest of her life.

The second plot in *All's Well*, after the "Curing of the Royal Problem," is the "Performing of Seemingly Impossible Tasks." This is such a common

Shakespeare's Fairy Tales: Is All Well That Ends Well in Shakespeare's Comedies?

218

motif in European fairy tales that one can open almost any page of a collection and find it. In most stories, as in Bertram's case, the tasks are set by someone who expects that no one could ever accomplish them. In some Cinderella stories, for instance, her stepmother pours a bowlful of lentils into the ashes on the hearth and tells her she can go to the ball only if she can pick them all out in two hours. When Cinderella, with the help of some friendly birds, is able to perform the task, her stepmother still will not let her go to the ball.[5] Similarly, Bertram does not believe that Helena can ever get his ring or get a child by him, so his letter implies: I will be your husband when hell freezes over.

The "impossible task" fairy tales most relevant to Helena's case are those involving a woman's quest for her lost true love. One of the oldest written tales in the Western world is one such. It is the story of Cupid and Psyche, first recorded by the Roman Apuleius in the second century A.D.[6] In the story the goddess Venus is furious to discover that mortals are beginning to offer the worship due to her beauty to an astoundingly beautiful mortal girl named Psyche. (Here we are reminded of Snow White's jealous stepmother.) Venus instructs her son Cupid to create a passion between the girl

Cupid and Psyche (1798), painted by François Gérard.

and some horrible beast (shades of *Beauty and the Beast*), but instead he is smitten with her himself. Cupid whisks Psyche off to a mysterious castle where, in order to conceal the match from his mother, he appears only at night and warns Psyche never to look at his face. When her jealous sisters persuade her to disobey by playing on her fears that she has perhaps married a beast, Cupid abandons her. Psyche then goes on a long quest to get him back, finally throwing herself on the mercy of Venus, who, still furious at the match, sets Psyche such impossible tasks as obtaining a box of beauty from Persephone in the Underworld. In the end Cupid begins to pity Psyche and pleads with Jupiter to reconcile her to his mother. Jupiter assures Venus that he will make this a match of social equals, just as the king had assured Bertram that he could enoble Helena, saying "if thou canst like this creature as a maid, / I can create the rest. Virtue and she / Is her own dower; honor and wealth from me." (*GBWW* I: 27, 153; II: 25, 153) Jupiter creates the equality by having Psyche drink some nectar so that she becomes an immortal and concludes by telling Psyche he hopes she will be able to control her wayward husband. Like Helena, then, Psyche is reunited with her repentant husband, though the future prospects for Love and Soul (the English translation for Cupid and Psyche) look better than those for Helena and Bertram.

Tales of such female quests are in fact relevant to most of Shakespeare's comedy heroines. Male seekers in fairy tales, if they do not set out in response to some edict of the king's regarding a princess in distress, often set out, as many of them put it, just to make their way in the world. Many find a profession that stands them in good stead for the tasks they are later asked to perform. The women who leave home in fairy tales, however, often leave for one of two reasons: (1) like Psyche, they are seeking a lost love, or (2) they are running away from a bad situation at home, as Snow White did. Among Shakespeare's heroines seeking a lost love are Helena from *All's Well* and also Helena of a *Midsummer Night's Dream* (another Helena not merely abandoned by but actually hated by her man), and Julia and Silvia from *Two Gentlemen of Verona*. Among his heroines who are running away from bad situations at home are Rosalind and Celia from *As You Like It*.

When I say that Shakespeare's heroines are seeking their lost loves I do not mean to say that the loss is anything mysterious or magical; mostly these are men who have been unfaithful and have transferred their affections to another woman. In the fairy-tale versions this is sometimes softened to the notion that the wayward man has been bewitched by a rival female. In Disney's *Little Mermaid* for example, the prince is exonerated for abandoning his growing love for the mermaid because he is seduced by the voice of the evil sea witch, a voice the witch had extorted from the mermaid as the price of making her human.

Lest we mistake any of these male changes of mind for second thoughts being better thoughts, Shakespeare is quite clear, actually formulaic, in fact, about what he means by true love. We can state his position, what I shall call Shakespeare's Law of True Love, as the following: First love is true love so long as either (a) the love is mutual or (b) the woman loves with no return at first. Men who love with no return, on the other hand, must eventually be disabused of their folly. We see the law operating in *Two Gentlemen of Verona* when the wandering Proteus must return to his first love Julia by the end of the play so that mutual lovers Valentine and Silvia can be together. For women, however, even when their love is at first unrequited, the man must eventually end up with them, as with Helena and Bertram in *All's Well*, or Viola who wins Count Orsino, even though he claims to love another woman until the very last scene of *Twelfth Night*. Among the men who love unrequitedly and must, according to Shakes-

Shakespeare's Fairy Tales: Is All Well That Ends Well in Shakespeare's Comedies?

220

The ring scene between Proteus (left), the disguised Julia (center), and Silvia (far right) in Two Gentlemen of Verona.

peare's Law, be returned to the women who first loved them are Count Orsino who pines for Olivia, *Measure for Measure's* Angelo, who lusts after the postulate Isabella, *Two Gentlemen's* Proteus who falls for his best friend's girl, and of course Bertram's love for Diana. Shakespeare even holds tragic hero Romeo to this rule; he must forget his unrequited love for Rosalind (for whom he is pining when the play begins) to end up with his mutual and true love Juliet.

In the case of *Measure for Measure,* Shakespeare is so conservative about his rule that he reunites Angelo with the woman he broke an engagement with five years before the play begins.

More evidence of Shakespeare's conservative rule of true love is seen in his comedies. Often, as in fairy tales, a promise is as good as a wedding. In addition, tokens that are exchanged even outside marriage, especially rings, are regarded as binding. His use of these tokens in the comedies is very revealing of relations between his comic males and females. I will take us through several examples. One use he makes of such tokens is as a means of recognizing true love. In *Two Gentlemen of Verona,* the faithful Julia, who has been following her wayward Proteus in the disguise of a page, discovers that he is going to give his ring, a love token which had been given to him by Julia, to his current love Silvia. Later Julia hears Proteus' friend actually offer Silvia to Proteus, whereupon Julia faints away. Proteus recognizes her when he sees his own ring that he had given her as a token. Only then does he come to his senses and take her back. This scene closely parallels one in another fairy tale about a woman's quest for her true love, the Brothers Grimm tale, "The Twelve Huntsmen." In this story, the abandoned betrothed girl has disguised herself as a huntsman to be near her wayward lover, but faints when she hears news of his new bride coming. The sight of his ring on her finger disenchants him and he recognizes and marries his true bride.[7]

Though in Shakespeare rings are never magical, they have an important symbolic power that figures in several comedies. In the folktale sources of the *All's Well* story, Bertram's ring, which Helena wins through trickery, is hinted at as being near-magical. When Bertram's current love Diana demands his ring as proof of his love he answers her thus: "I'll lend it thee, my dear, but have no power / To give it from me. / ....It is an honor 'longing to our house, / Bequeathed down from many ancestors; / Which were the greatest obloquy i' the world / In me to lose." Her response makes one of the symbolic meanings of the ring crystal clear: "Mine honor's such a ring. / My chastity's the jewel of our house, / Bequeathed down from many ancestors; / Which were the greatest obloquy i' the world / In me to lose." Bertram then gives her the ring, which she passes on to his wife who sleeps with him in place of Diana. (*GBWW* I: 27, 163; II: 25, 163)

Thus rings for Shakespeare, as well as in numerous fairy tales, can represent male honor and sexual innocence. Once given away, even through trickery, the giver is irrevocably affected. One fairy-tale example is the

Bertram gives his ring to Diana.

Alls well that ends well

Act 4. Sc.2.

Shakespeare's Fairy Tales: Is All Well That Ends Well in Shakespeare's Comedies?

222

frame story to the Arabian Nights.[8] The story begins with two sultans, brothers whose wives have been unfaithful to them. After dispatching both their wives and their lovers, the brothers decide to set forth, never to return home until they find a worse cuckold than themselves. Nearing a great ocean they see a horrible genie approaching from the waters, and they quickly hide themselves in a tree. When the genie reaches the tree he sets down the iron box he is carrying, unlocks and unbinds seven heavy chains around the box, opens it and brings forth a beautiful maiden. The genie lays his head in her lap and the maiden begins to delouse him until he falls asleep. Upon seeing the two men in the tree, she gestures for them to come down and forces them to make love to her on the spot, threatening to wake the genie if they refuse. Afterwards she demands their rings from them, and adds the two rings to a necklace she keeps in a little bag, a necklace which already contains five hundred seventy rings from other men she has slept with. Once they escape, the two brothers go home, having concluded that the genie is a worse cuckold than they, despite his great efforts to keep his love under lock and key. The lesson they might have drawn from this incident, but did not, was an understanding and tolerance of human weakness, since they both had lost their own honor easily. Instead, one of the two brothers marries a new wife every night and cuts off her head every morning, avoiding further infidelities. It takes Scheherazade 1001 nights of stories illustrating human foibles to teach this sultan the understanding and tolerance he could have learned from the loss of his ring. Even then the deciding argument for him is that, like Shakespeare's Helena, Scheherazade presents her husband with the fait accompli of three children begotten by him over the course of those three years of stories.

Here, then, is where the true significance of the impossible tasks Bertram set for Helena lies. He will be a husband to his wife only if she can procure his ring, that is, his honor and his family's past, and also have a child by him, that is, provide for the family's future. In doing so, he takes from her, however unwittingly, her chastity or honor. After such an exchange their bond is unbreakable and they must be husband and wife, whether Bertram likes it or not. A Biblical version of such an exchange is illuminating here. Chapter 38 of the Book of Genesis contains a story about Judah, one of the brothers of Joseph of the many-colored coat. Judah marries his eldest son to a woman named Tamar, but we are told that this son "was wicked in the sight of the Lord and the Lord slew him." According to the custom of the time Judah then marries Tamar to his next oldest son, Onan. However, Onan realizes that according to custom any children he has with Tamar will be considered not his but rather his dead brother's. Therefore when he sleeps with Tamar he "spills his seed on the ground" so as not to raise up children for his brother. Again the Lord is angry and smites this young man dead as well. Knowing it is his duty to then give Tamar in marriage to his youngest son, Judah nevertheless puts it off, claiming that his son is still too young, "for he feared that he would die, like his brothers." After some time has passed Tamar realizes that Judah may never make good on his promise, for his youngest son has already grown up and she has not been

given to him in marriage. Tamar then takes matters into her own hand. When Judah leaves on a journey she follows him in disguise and poses as a temple prostitute. When Judah wishes to sleep with her she demands his staff and ring to be redeemed later for a goat from his flock. After the encounter, however, she makes off with these objects and returns home. Months later Judah is told that Tamar is pregnant by some unknown man and he determines to have her burned. As she is being taken away, she produces the ring and staff and tells

Judah and Tamar. "And he said, What pledge shall I give thee? And she said, thy signet, and thy bracelets, and thy staff." Genesis 38.

him that the owner of these is the father of her child. He then understands what she has done and ends the story by saying that "she is more righteous than I." The Lord seems to agree with the judgment, for one of the children she gives birth to proves to be the ancestor of His beloved King David.

Both Tamar and Helena confront the man with his own failure. The women shame the men by procuring through a trick what should have been theirs by right: both the family honor and the right of the marriage bed. Women who marry and are expected to live with their husband's family are quite vulnerable to the sense of honor of those in power in that family. We find this even today when we hear about dowry killings in India, where young women have been murdered by their new in-laws because they have not provided a sufficient dowry. Tamar and Helena are thus left seemingly defenseless by Judah and Bertram. However, having obtained the symbol of family authority in the ring and staff, and the actual family future in a child, they must be and are respected, if not loved, by those in power in their adopted households.

In a lighter vein, rings and tokens are also used by Shakespeare as matters for comic testing of men by women. In the *Merchant of Venice,* when Portia weds Bassanio she gives him a ring and tells him never to take it off on peril of losing her love. Then when she is disguised as the male law clerk who argues so well that she saves Bassanio's friend Antonio's life, she asks for this very ring in payment for her services. Bassanio is reluctant to give it after his promise to Portia, but is persuaded to do so by his friend Antonio. When back in her woman's clothes, Portia insists that he explain the loss of the ring and she pretends that she believes Bassanio is

Shakespeare's Fairy Tales: Is All Well That Ends Well in Shakespeare's Comedies?

224

lying and must have really given it to another woman. After teasing him that she will retaliate by sleeping with this law clerk herself if he be male, she relents and reveals her trick to Bassanio. As with Bertram's ring and the rings of the two sultans, the loss of the ring here is comically equated with the loss of the male's honor, even literally his chastity. In fact, as Bassanio points out, even Portia would have to agree that it may really have been more honorable to give the ring away to one who had saved his friend's life. In other words, it is not so clear that Portia really wanted him to pass this test or imagined that he could, attached as he is to his friend Antonio. In this comic mode, however, the test of the ring serves more to show Bassanio, as it should have shown the sultan, his own frailty. If Bassanio learns anything from this, it is that the extravagant oaths and promises he is wont to make, to friends as well as to Portia, will not be accepted at face value by his wife. She may love him, but she has shown that she is not blind to his weaknesses.

The King of Navarre and the French Princess (center) with their attending lords and ladies.

Another comic testing with love tokens occurs in *Love's Labour's Lost*. In that play, the King of Navarre and three of his lords make a vow to live as scholars for three years and to forswear the company of women for all that time. Immediately afterwards, however, an embassy arrives from France and all four men are smitten by the French princess and three of her

attending ladies. Each lady receives a love token from her beloved, but during some revels where all the lovers are masked, the women switch their tokens so that each man makes love to the wrong lady. Each lady extracts promises from her lover such that when the trick is revealed the men are chagrined to be forced to recant their extravagant promises. At the end of the play the princess is called back to France because of the death of her father. The men ask the ladies to grant them their love at this "latest minute of the hour" before they leave, but they do not receive the expected response. Instead the princess says, "A time, methinks, too short / To make a world-without-end bargain in. / No, no, my lord, your grace is perjured much, / Full of dear guiltiness; and therefore this:" (*GBWW* I: 26, 283; II: 24, 283). She goes on to propose that the men spend a year in a hermitage, and if they can endure that trial then they may have the ladies' hands. This oddly deferred ending makes *Love's Labour's Lost* the only Shakespeare comedy that does not contain a wedding. Perhaps Shakespeare felt that French women, more circumspect than their English counterparts in matters of the heart, are less willing to believe in love at first sight from men already forsworn and require the proof of time. However, if we extrapolate to the end of that year of waiting using Shakespeare's "Law of True Love," I think we can assume that the men will not pass this new test and that the women will marry them anyway.

All these failed tests of love tokens involving male honor prompt us to raise again the question of why Shakespeare's comic heroines put their men to the test in the first place, other than for our amusement? To put it simply, the answer must be to show them who is in control. By the time these ring trials are complete, it is clear, for example, that law-clerk Portia is going to win every argument she and Bassanio have, that the princess and her ladies are more than a match in wits with Navarre and his lords, and that Helena can easily foil any future attempt Bertram might make at adultery. These are women who know they have a limited realm—Portia would not really be allowed to practice law, nor Helena medicine—but within that limited realm they have secured their rule partly by showing their men their own frailty through these tests.

To highlight the importance, perhaps even the necessity, of this testing of male honor, Shakespeare provides a foil for Portia and Bassanio in the *Merchant of Venice* with the untested love duo of Shylock's daughter Jessica and her Lorenzo. It is Jessica who plans the details of her elopement with Lorenzo, and she brings with her gold and jewels from her father's house, "gilding" herself as she calls it. Lorenzo thus does nothing but go along with her plans and Jessica has never tested him to know whether he would have her, gold or no gold. In fact, there are ominous hints to the contrary in their later love duet where, whether consciously or not, the lovers keep invoking the names of loves that ended badly, including famous women who were abandoned by their lovers after rescuing them, such as Dido and Medea, abandoned by Aeneas and Jason, respectively. Jessica also shows her lack of understanding of the binding power of the ring, by trading her own family ring for a monkey.

Shakespeare's Fairy Tales: Is All Well That Ends Well in Shakespeare's Comedies?

226

If it is true that Shakespeare's comic heroines by and large wish to rule, and choose their husbands accordingly, then *Twelfth Night*'s Olivia may come closest to admitting that desire. At the start of that play we learn that the countess Olivia has been spurning the advances of neighboring Count Orsino for some time though she admits to an emissary of his that "I suppose him virtuous, know him noble, / Of great estate, of fresh and stainless youth; / In voices well divulged, free, learn'd, and valiant; / And in dimension and the shape of nature / A gracious person: but yet I cannot love him;" (*GBWW* I: 27, 7; II: 25, 7). After this list of virtues it is hard to see what fault Olivia finds with the Count, but we learn the possible reason from her uncle Toby, who tells another suitor of Olivia's that "She'll none o' the Count: she'll not / match above her degree, neither in estate, years, / nor wit; I have heard her swear't." (*GBWW* I: 27, 3; II: 25, 3)

Twelfth Night, act 1, scene 5. Olivia unveils her face to the disguised Viola.

The reason for this vow of hers is made clear by an observation made by Count Orsino himself. In giving advice about why women should marry older men he says: "let still the woman take / An elder than herself: so wears she to him, / So sways she level in her husband's heart." (*GBWW* I: 27, 10; II: 25, 10) Olivia's inverted interpretation of this advice would be that a woman should marry beneath herself in degree, years, and wit so that her husband might adapt himself to her and keep steady in his wife's heart. She may, of course, be looking for one who is equal to her in all these respects, but that is not what she gets. Instead she comically falls for Viola, a young woman dressed in men's clothes who has come to woo her for Count Orsino. Viola certainly seems beneath the countess in years and degree but is more than her match in wit and is thus able to deflect Olivia's increasingly direct advances. When Viola's identical twin brother Sebastian arrives in town and is mistaken by everyone for the disguised Viola, however, Olivia sees that he will be ruled and takes every advantage of it, even to being forward enough to bring in a priest hastily and get him to marry them before the mistake in Sebastian's identity is even discovered. He, on his part, goes along with Olivia to church, having been impressed on their short acquaintance, by the way she can "sway her house, command her followers, / Take and give back affairs and their dispatch / With such a smooth, discreet, and stable bearing...." (*GBWW* I: 27, 23; II: 25, 23) Even when the mistake is discovered Sebastian stands by his marriage contract, saying to Olivia: "So comes it lady you have been mistook: / but nature to her bias drew in that. / You would have been contracted to a maid; / Nor are you therein, by my life, deceived, / You are betroth'd both to a maid and man." (*GBWW* I: 27, 26; II: 25, 26) This riddle of how Sebastian is both maid and man is partly solved by the Elizabethan connotation of maid as being virgin. In another sense, however, Sebastian may be saying that he is a maid in that he is as mild and tractable as a woman, as he has indeed shown himself to be with Olivia, though he is man enough to best her uncle in a sword fight. Thus Olivia does in the end get her wish, to marry someone who will be ruled by her.

Olivia, then, holds the key to why it is that many of Shakespeare's great comic heroines are willing to accept husbands who have proved themselves to be their inferiors, certainly in wit and constancy. These are superior women who wish, and most likely by temperament need, to rule within their households and they choose men who will certainly let them do so. This also does much to explain Shakespeare's invariable rule of true love. Where *women* love there will be a union. Where *men* love there will be a union only if the woman wishes it too. From this point of view the detested Bertram begins to seem a little to be pitied. In this comic world of Shakespeare's, Bertram's main offense is that he wished to choose his own wife, not to have one thrust upon him. Failing that, he wished to choose his own lover, and was not allowed that consummation either.

Is all well that ends well in Shakespeare's comedies then? His answer seems to be that as long as wise and good women can rule, all is well. I would like to close with another fairy tale which I think exemplifies Shakespeare's attitude toward his comic heroines. The tale is from Chaucer, whom Shakespeare greatly admired and borrowed from. We recall the Wife of Bath's tale, in which a knight of the Round Table callously raped a woman and was sentenced to death. Guinevere takes pity on him and declares that he will not die if in the course of a year he can discover what it is that women really want. He travels far and wide and gets many answers: Women want "Honour," or "Jollity and pleasure." Some say "Gorgeous clothes," others "Fun in bed." He knows none of these is the right answer. Finally he meets an old hag who tells him that she will give him the correct answer if he will marry her. He has no choice, so he brings the woman back to Camelot with him and at a great gathering of the court declares the answer she has given him: "A woman wants the self-same sovereignty / Over her husband as over her lover, / And master him; he must not be above her." Guinevere and all the other women present agree that this is the correct answer and his life is spared. Thereupon the knight goes through with the marriage to the old crone. On their wedding night she tells him she has the power to grant him two choices. He can have her ugly but faithful, or young and beautiful and take his chances as to her virtue. The knight replies by giving *her* the choice, and thus gets her both

Shakespeare's Fairy Tales: Is All Well That Ends Well in Shakespeare's Comedies?

228

The Wife of Bath.

The lively Wife of Bath from Chaucer's The Canterbury Tales.

beautiful and faithful. The Wife of Bath ends her tale with the prayer: "May Christ Jesus send / Us husbands meek and young and fresh in bed, / And grace to overbid them when we wed."[9] Shakespeare, the god of his comic universe, grants that prayer to his favorite comic heroines.

1. Giovanni Boccaccio, *The Decameron,* trans. G.H. McWilliam, (London: Penguin Books, 1972), p. 314. (The is the Ninth Story of the Third Day.)

2. Aristotle, *Poetics,* 1448a17–18. (*GBWW* I: 9, 682; II: 8, 682)

3. *The Complete Fairy Tales of the Brothers Grimm,* trans. Jack Zipes, (New York: Bantam Books, 1987), #20, *The Brave Little Tailor,* pp. 80–86.

4. Gabrielle-Suzanne de Villeneuve, "The Story of Beauty and the Beast," in *Beauties, Beasts and Enchantment: Classic French Fairy Tales,* trans. Jack Zipes, (Markham, Ontario: New American Library, 1989), pp. 153–229.

5. Grimm, *op.cit.,* #21, *Cinderella,* pp. 86–92.

6. Apuleius, *The Golden Ass,* trans. Robert Graves, (New York: Pocket Books, Inc., 1951), pp. 87–130.

7. Grimm, *op.cit.,* #67, *The Twelve Huntsmen,* pp. 265–67.

8. *The Book of the Thousand Nights and One Night,* trans. Dr. J.C. Mardrus and Powys Mather, (London: Routledge, 1989), pp. 1–5.

9. Geoffrey Chaucer, *The Canterbury Tales,* trans. Nevill Coghill, (London: Penguin Books, 1977), pp. 281–92.

Cynthia L. Rutz is a lecturer in liberal arts with the Basic Program of the University of Chicago, from which she has an M.A., and where she is writing a dissertation examining the origins of Shakespeare's source tales. A graduate of St. John's College, Santa Fe, New Mexico, she has been an editorial assistant with *The Great Ideas Today* and a coordinator for Mortimer J. Adler of the Paideia Program of Basic Schooling, which she now serves elsewhere as a consultant, administering Great Books seminars for elementary and high school students in the city of Chicago. The essay printed here was originally a Basic Program lecture, one of a number Ms. Rutz has given on the subject of her research.

Aristotle on the Emotions

Jon Elster

Illustrations by Istvan Banyai

ARISTOTLE

FREUD

I. Introduction

Aristotle's *Rhetoric* is the founding work of psychology. It offers, in particular, an account of the emotions that remains, more than two thousand years later, utterly fresh and illuminating. Unlike his treatises on physics or biology, it has not been superseded. Although modern scientific psychology has done much to advance our understanding of the emotions, Aristotle's basic framework remains intact. Moreover, some of his insights have not yet been fully exhausted.

In this article, I set myself three goals. First and foremost, I shall expound Aristotle's theory of the emotions.[1] Second, I shall relate his account to modern theories, to indicate convergences as well as divergences. Third, I shall try to bring out how Aristotle's analyses can illuminate the nature of emotions among the ancient Greeks. Although most of his observations transcend boundaries of space and time, some of them point to emotional patterns that, even if not unique to the Greek, differ from those of modern Western societies.

I shall proceed as follows. Section II is a brief introduction to the study of the emotions. Section III is an equally brief introduction to the *Rhetoric*, with a few comments on other works by Aristotle that are relevant for his view of the emotions. Section IV is an attempt to reconstruct Aristotle's answer to one of the two basic questions in this area: *What are emotions?* In Section V I discuss his answer to the other basic question: *What emotions are there?* In Section VI I draw on Aristotle's analyses to discuss the nature and role of the emotions in ancient Greece more generally. Section VII offers a brief conclusion.

II. The study of the emotions
Sources of knowledge about the emotions

The psychological analysis of the emotions is little more than a hundred years old. Charles Darwin's *Expression of the Emotions in Man and Animals* (1872) and William James's "What is an Emotion" (1884) are the first studies of the emotions using scientific methodology. Before these writings the emotions were investigated mainly by philosophers, moralists, and—in a very different way—by playwrights and novelists. The scientific study of physical phenomena dates from the seventeenth century. Up to that time, physics (apart from astronomy) was not an empirical and mathematical discipline as it is today, but rather a form of "natural philosophy." Once it had acquired a firm footing in experimental and deductive methods, the earlier speculative style of doing physics simply died away. Nobody today reads Aristotle or Descartes in the hope of coming across novel physical conjectures to be tested experimentally. Similar comments apply, although less strictly, to biology.

With regard to the emotions, the pre-scientific writings retain much more of their interest and validity. At the same time there are severe limits to what can be done using current scientific methodology. In the light of earlier ill-fated attempts to legislate a priori what science can and cannot explain, it would be foolhardy to assert that the emotions will forever remain outside the scope of rigorous scientific study. Yet the obstacles to experimental analysis of the emotions are so severe that I feel confident at least in asserting that they will not be removed in the near future. Although animal studies can be useful for many purposes, they are limited by the fact that animals are incapable of harboring emotions that depend on complex cognitions. Even if animals are capable of feeling envy—an unresolved question—they are incapable of feeling anger triggered by the belief that another animal is trying to make them feel envious. Laboratory studies on humans are limited in other respects and for other reasons. Financial and ethical constraints limit the possibility of creating high-stake emotional situations in the laboratory. More fundamentally, the experimental situation may itself be incompatible with some of the emotions one might want to study, such as spontaneous joy or romantic love. Finally, even if the emotions themselves may eventually be mapped neurophysiologically, it seems doubtful that one will be able to assign exact neurophysiological correlates to the beliefs that trigger them.

Under these circumstances the observations of wise men and women in the past retain all their importance. With respect to the more complex human emotions one can learn more from Aristotle, Montaigne, Jane Austen, or Proust than from psychological and neurophysiological studies. Also, historical works provide a repertoire of observations that can suggest causal hypotheses—or undermine them. Studies of dueling, feuding, and vendettas help us understand the causes of pride, anger, hatred, fear, and shame, as well as their behavioral expressions.[2] Analyses of witchcraft in seventeenth-century England or of social mobility in eighteenth-century France can make important contributions to our understanding of envy and malice.[3] Although in some ways less reliable than controlled studies, such works have the immense advantage of showing strong emotions at work in real-life settings.

Aspects of the emotions

In Section IV below I consider the fine grain of emotional reactions in some detail. Here, I raise a few more general issues: the relation between occurrent emotions and emotional dispositions; the relation between emotions and other motivations; the relation between emotion and cognition; and the question whether emotions are universal or culture-bound.

When we say that a person is angry, we are referring to an occurrent emotional episode. When we say that the person is irascible, we are referring to an emotional disposition, i.e., a disposition to be angry. A person is ashamed if he is currently experiencing shame; he is shameless if he lacks the disposition to be ashamed. A pronounced disposition to have a certain emotion does not necessarily imply frequent occurrences of that emotion. People may learn not to offend an irascible person, thus reducing the number of occasions that will trigger his temper. A person who is prone to strong feelings of shame will learn how horribly unpleasant they can be and do everything to avoid behavior that might cause others to blame him.

The question whether emotions can be chosen must be answered differently in the two cases. Typically, one cannot decide to be angry or happy, even though it might be useful or pleasant to be in one of these states; nor can one decide not to grieve or to feel guilty. (One can seek out or avoid situations that will predictably produce those emotions, but that is another matter.) By contrast, it has often been argued that one can choose to develop certain emotional dispositions, or to rid oneself of them. Buddhism, stoicism, and psychotherapy are all, in different ways, based on this idea.

Emotions serve as a motivation for behavior. An important aspect of the study of emotions, therefore, is the relation of emotion to other motivations. Although there is no generally accepted way of classifying human motivations, a fruitful trichotomy is suggested in a maxim by La Bruyère: "Nothing is easier for passion than to overcome reason; its greatest triumph is to conquer interest."[4] By reason, he probably meant something like an impartial concern for the common good, and by interest the pursuit of individual or group advantage. For an example of how these motivations may suggest different courses of behavior, consider trials of the agents of an authoritarian regime after transitions to democracy, as in German-occupied countries after World War II or ex-Communist countries after 1989.[5] Those suspected of collaborating obviously had a direct interest in not being prosecuted or, failing that, in mild sentences. Members of the opposition or resistance movements were often animated by strong emotions of anger and hatred, and demanded swift and harsh punishments. Some political leaders took a larger view. For them, the paramount concern was to establish the rule of law, even if it meant proceeding more slowly and accepting more acquittals than the second group wanted. For many of those who insisted on harsh punishments, emotion overcame reason. It could even conquer interest, in cases where the collaborators possessed economic or administrative expertise that could be useful in rebuilding the country. For the sake of satisfying their passion for vengeance, some may have been willing to sacrifice their material interest.

A central issue in the study of emotion is the relation between emotion and cognition. The question has three aspects. (i) Cognitions can serve as the cause of emotions. In fact, it has been widely argued that *all* emotions are caused by a cognitive appraisal of some kind.[6] Although it has now been shown that emotions such as fear can also be triggered by mere perception,[7] the more complex human emotions are in fact usually caused by a prior belief. (ii) Emotions can influence cognition. Although the standard view has been that emotions tend to cloud or distort cognition, as in wishful thinking, recent studies claim that they can actually improve cognition and decision-making.[8] (iii) Emotions can themselves form the object of cognitions. Although one can be angry, envious, or infatuated without being aware of it, it is obviously also possible to know that one is currently subject to one of these emotions. Moreover, in light of (i), this cognition may itself trigger a second-order emotion. Furthermore, in light of (ii), that emotion can modify the initial cognition and the accompanying first-order emotion. Thus, because the emotion of envy is usually seen as a shameful one, the perception of oneself as envious may trigger a transmutation of this emotion into righteous indignation.[9]

Another important—and unresolved—issue is whether emotions are universal or culture-specific.[10] This issue must be distinguished from the question whether all societies conceptualize emotions in the same way. Patricia Spacks has argued, for instance, that the *phenomenon* of boredom is universal, but that the *concept* of boredom is relatively modern, adding that the phenomenon itself is transformed when it is raised to the level of conscious awareness.[11] Similarly, Robert Levy has argued that among the Tahitians, behavior that we would see as a sign of depression is characterized in terms of physical fatigue.[12] To some extent, the debate over the universality of the emotions may have been confused with the universality of emotion-language. Although it has not been proved that the behavioral and physiological expressions of emotion are the same in all cultures, there is considerably more uniformity than one would think if one identified the emotions solely by verbal labels.

III. The Rhetoric

The *Rhetoric* (*GBWW* I: 9, 593–675; II: 8, 593–675) presents itself as a study of the art of persuasion through speech, and occasionally as a handbook of political manipulation. It is also, and perhaps above all, "the earliest systematic discussion of human psychology" in Western thought.[13] In this work Aristotle distinguishes three kinds of speech and three means of persuasion. There is political speech, i.e., deliberation in the assembly about "ways and means, war and peace, national defence, imports and exports, and legislation" (*Rhetoric* 1359[b] 20–21).[14] There is forensic speech, i.e., speeches before the court by plaintiffs and defendants in a suit. Finally, there is epideictic speech, or speech in praise or censure of somebody. The means deployed in rhetoric are *ethos, pathos,* and *logos:* "the first kind depends on the personal character of the speaker; the second on putting the audience into a certain [emotional] frame of mind; the third on the proof, or apparent proof, provided by the words of the speech itself" (*Rhetoric* 1356[a] 2–4).

As Aristotle observes, the third kind of speech and the first kind of means are closely related: "the ways in which to make [our hearers] trust the goodness of other people are also the ways in which to make them trust our own" (*Rhetoric* 1366[a] 26–28). He also asserts that the first kind of speech relies exclusively on the third kind of means:

> In a political debate the man who is forming a judgement is making a
> decision about his own vital interests. There is no need, therefore, to prove

anything except that the facts are what the supporter of a measure maintains they are. In forensic oratory this is not enough; to conciliate the
listener is what pays here. It is other people's affairs that are to be decided,
so that the judges, intent on their own satisfaction and listening with
partiality, surrender themselves to the disputants instead of judging between them (*Rhetoric* 1354ᵇ 31–1355ᵃ 1).

In this passage, Aristotle makes two controversial claims. First, emotion
does not matter if the agent has a personal interest in the outcome or, to put
it differently, emotions can never override interest. This starkly contradicts
La Bruyère's maxim cited above. Second, he claims that jurors have no
interest in the outcome of law cases, contradicting what he asserts in the
Politics (*GBWW* I: 9, 439–584; II: 8, 439–584). Here he notes that "The
demagogues of our own day often get property confiscated in the law-
courts in order to please the people" (*Politics* 1320ᵃ 4–5) because the
people have a direct financial interest in the size of the state coffers. He
then goes on to recommend

a law that the property of the condemned should not be public and go into
the treasury but be sacred. Thus offenders will be as much afraid, for they
will be punished all the same, and the people, having nothing to gain, will
not be so ready to condemn the accused. (*Politics* 1320ᵃ 6–10)

In the terminology used above, Aristotle seems to assume that disinterested
jurors would judge according to *reason*. According to his own account in
the *Rhetoric*, however, the removal of interest would leave the people open
to the influence of *emotion*. Specifically, the citizens might impose confis-
catory fines out of envy.[15]

The passions occur in two different contexts in the *Rhetoric*. In Book I
they are treated as independent variables in order to explain behavior. Here,
Aristotle considers three aspects of wrong-doing: the motives of wrong-
doers, their states of mind, and the individuals to whom they do wrong.
Among the motives he cites anger as the cause of revenge (*Rhetoric* 1369ᵇ
11–12). Among their states of mind he cites their belief of being able to
stave off a trial, or have it postponed, or corrupt the judges (*Rhetoric* 1372ᵃ
33–34). To identify the kind of people to whom they do wrong he mentions
that "a man may wrong his enemies, because that is pleasant: he may
equally wrong his friends, because that is easy" (*Rhetoric* 1373ᵃ 3–5). As
these examples indicate, the analysis is not exactly systematic.

In Book II, which shall mainly concern me here, the emotions are treated
as dependent variables to be explained in terms of three aspects of the
person who is subject to them.[16] "Take, for instance, the emotion of anger:
here we must discover (1) what the state of mind of angry people is, (2)
who the people are with whom they usually get angry, and (3) on what
grounds they get angry with them" (*Rhetoric* 1378ᵃ 23–26). Among the
grounds for anger Aristotle cites the fact of being deliberately slighted (see
Section V below). The state of mind of the angry man is "that in which any
pain is being felt" (*Rhetoric* 1379ᵃ 10–11) as a result of his desire being

frustrated in some way. The persons with whom he gets angry include "those who laugh, mock, or jeer at us" (*Rhetoric* 1379ᵃ 29).

From these and other examples, it appears that emotions, for Aristotle, have two sets of antecedents. On the one hand, they have cognitive preconditions. The relevance of the persons with whom we get angry, for instance, is mediated by our beliefs about them. On the other hand, and this is for us a more unusual insight, they are facilitated by certain non-cognitive antecedents, such as being already in a state of distress or pain; Aristotle cites the states of thirst, sickness, poverty, and love.[17] Like the emotions, these states may have cognitive antecedents and intentional objects, but, again like them, they are not themselves cognitive states. Nor, as shown by the inclusion of thirst and illness among the examples, are they necessarily themselves emotions in the full-blown sense of the term.

As mentioned, the *Rhetoric* is not a systematic treatise, but rather a catalogue of examples from which a more systematic account can be more or less reliably reconstructed. In doing so, one also has to take into account other texts in which Aristotle touches on the emotions, the most important being the *Nicomachean Ethics* (*GBWW* I: 9, 335–436; II: 8, 335–436) and the *Politics*. I have already given an example of an apparent inconsistency between the *Rhetoric* and the *Politics*. Below, I cite passages on shame from the *Rhetoric* and the *Ethics* that, while not inconsistent with one another, present quite different perspectives on that emotion. By and large, nevertheless, Aristotle is quite consistent in his treatment of the emotion.

IV. What are emotions?

Earlier, I distinguished between occurrent emotions and emotional dispositions. The latter are obviously defined in terms of the former: to be irascible, for instance, is to have a disposition to be angry. Although I shall mainly focus on what Aristotle says on occurrent emotions, I begin by noting that he frequently refers to emotional dispositions. These references all occur in the *Ethics,* where he is concerned with assessing—praising or blaming—conduct as well as the dispositions from which it springs. With regard to many of these dispositions—emotional as well as behavioral—he asserts the principle of the mean. Just as the behavioral disposition of courage is the mean between rashness and cowardice (*Ethics* 1115ᵇ–1116ᵃ), the proper degree of pride is the mean between empty vanity and undue humility (*Ethics* 1107ᵇ 22) and that of anger the mean between irascibility and its nameless converse (*Ethics* 1125ᵇ–1126ᵃ). The case of shame is more complex, as we shall see: although it is bad to be shameless, the good man is one who never behaves badly rather than one who feels the proper degree of shame when he does. Rather, the mean between "the bashful man who is ashamed of everything" and the shameless man who is ashamed of nothing, is *modesty* (*Ethics* 1107ᵇ 32–35).

In assessing behavior that springs from our dispositions, Aristotle asserts a two-stage theory: "to the unjust and to the self-indulgent man it was open at the beginning not to become men of this kind, and so they are unjust and self-indulgent voluntarily; but now that they have become so it is not possible for them not to be so" (*Ethics* 1114ª 20). Similarly, if we blame people who act out of irascibility, vanity, or shamelessness (or their opposites) it is not because they could have behaved differently at the time but because they could have cultivated other dispositions. Aristotle does not tell us, though, how one should go about developing specific emotional dispositions. Emotional character planning is perhaps more difficult or less frequent than he thought.[18]

I turn now to Aristotle's characterization of occurrent emotions. According to his explicit definition found in the *Rhetoric*, "the emotions are those things through which, by undergoing change, people come to differ in their judgments, and which are accompanied by pain and pleasure, for example, anger, pity, fear, and other such things and their opposites" (*Rhetoric* 1378ª 21–22). In the context of Aristotle's other writings, this definition of occurrent emotions is too wide, incomplete, and misleading. The definition is too wide, because it also covers physiological disturbances such as headaches.[19] It is incomplete, because it fails to mention other invariant features of the emotions (see below). It is misleading, finally, because it defines emotions by their impact on cognition rather than by the fact of being shaped by cognition (see below). When Aristotle considers specific emotions in his writings he consistently analyzes them in terms of their cognitive antecedents rather than in terms of their consequences for cognition. The latter causal connection is contingent: people may be angry or ashamed without having their judgment distorted by the emotion. The former connection is—with qualifications mentioned above—a necessary one: emotions such as anger are unable to arise without an antecedent belief about another person.

The implicit definition of emotion that can be reconstructed from Aristotle's specific analyses is amazingly close to the idea of emotion found in recent writers. Drawing upon the work of Paul Ekman and Nico Frijda,[20] I believe the modern conception of the emotions can be captured by the following features:

- Unbidden occurrence
- Brief duration
- Inducing physiological changes ("arousal")
- Physiological expressions
- Cognitive antecedents
- Intentional objects
- Accompanied by pleasure or pain ("valence")
- Inducing specific action tendencies

I shall not here discuss the adequacy of this conception, except to say that each of the eight features may be missing in some occurrent emotions.[21] Instead, I shall use the list as a device for organizing the discussion of Aristotle's views.

Unbidden occurrence

Aristotle never explicitly says that all emotions are involuntary—passively undergone rather than actively chosen. Nor, however, does he assert that they are voluntary. Although he does say that actions undertaken out of anger are voluntary—for "it would surely be odd to describe as involuntary the things one ought to desire; and we ought . . . to be angry at certain things" (*Ethics* 1111ᵃ 30)—he does not say that anger itself is voluntarily produced. In fact, he always seems to proceed on the implicit common-sense assumption that anger is outside the control of the will (see, for instance, *Ethics* 1147ᵃ 15–16). To be sure, people can repress their anger (*Ethics* 1126ᵃ 20), but that does not imply that they can choose whether to be angry or not. For there to be any anger to repress, it first has to arise spontaneously in the mind.

Brief duration

Once again, most of the relevant passages concern anger. Unlike some modern writers,[22] Aristotle does not assert that anger always subsides spontaneously. Rather, he argues that the duration of the emotion depends on whether the angry man is allowed to act on his feelings

> *hot-tempered* people get angry quickly and with the wrong persons and at the wrong things and more than is right, but their anger ceases quickly— which is the best point about them. This happens to them because they do not restrain their anger but retaliate openly owing to their quickness of temper, and then their anger ceases. . . . *Sulky* people are hard to appease, and retain their anger long; for they repress their passion. But it ceases when they retaliate; for revenge relieves them of their anger. (*Ethics* 1126ᵃ 12–21)

The tendency for anger to abate when it has found expression in action can explain inconsistencies in behavior:

> men become calm when they have spent their anger on someone else. This happened in the case of Ergophilus: though the people were more irritated against him than against Callisthenes, they acquitted him because they had condemned Callisthenes to death the day before. (*Rhetoric* 1380ᵇ 11–13)

The war trials after WWII in countries that had been occupied by Germany showed similar patterns of inconsistency, the same crimes being judged more leniently in 1947 than in 1945.[23]

Arousal

In *De Anima* (*GBWW* I: 8, 629–68; II: 7, 629—68), Aristotle points to the fact that affections of the soul such as "passion, gentleness, fear, pity, courage, joy, loving, and hating" are also affections of the body, and goes on to say that "hence a physicist would define an affection of soul differently from a dialectician; the latter would define, e.g., anger as the appetite for returning pain for pain, or something like that, while the former would define it as the boiling of the blood or warm substance surrounding the heart" (403^a 17, 29–32). We may note, for future reference, that the "dialectical" definition includes the action tendency of returning pain for pain. To use Aristotelian categories, *De Anima* highlights the material cause as well as the final cause of the emotions, while not citing the efficient cause which takes center place in Book II of the *Rhetoric*.[24]

Physiological expressions

In the *Categories* (9^b 27–30; *GBWW* I: 8, 3–21; II: 7, 3–21) Aristotle draws a distinction between properties such as pallor and darkness, which are permanent qualities, and those that "result from something that easily disperses. . . . Thus a man who reddens through shame is not called ruddy, nor one who pales in fright pallid." In the *Ethics* (1128^b 11–13) he similarly defines shame "as a kind of fear of dishonour, and produces an effect similar to that produced by fear of danger; for people who feel disgraced blush, and those who fear death turn pale." Although he clearly knew—how could he not?—that emotions have specific physiological expressions, this feature has no role in his more substantive discussions. He does not mention, for instance, how the expressions of the emotions might be perceived by others and affect their behavior. Nor does he mention the possibility of simulating or suppressing emotional expressions, a neglect that is quite natural given his emphasis on involuntary expressions, as distinct from more voluntary expressions such as smiling.

Cognitive antecedents

According to W.W. Fortenbaugh, Aristotle achieved something like a cognitive revolution in the study of the emotions, in that he clearly and decisively "construes the thought of outrage as the efficient cause" of pain.[25] Before Aristotle "it was easy to think of emotions as diseases whose victims suffer a misfortune curable only by drugs and inspired incantations."[26] If, however, emotions do not act like charms or enchantments but depend on beliefs, they are amenable to rational argument designed to change the beliefs. Moreover, one can use the cognitive antecedents to distinguish among the emotions:

> By building the thought of personal insult into the essence of anger Aristotle could draw a logical distinction between this emotion and the emotion of hate. For the occurrence of hate it is not necessary to believe in personal outrage. It is only necessary to think of someone as a certain kind of person—for example, a thief or a sycophant. In other words, the efficient cause became a powerful tool for distinguishing the logical boundaries between related emotions.[27]

Although these two emotions also differ in other ways (see below), their cognitive antecedents may be the only features that yield *sufficient* grounds for distinguishing them from each other.

It is not entirely clear, however, that Aristotle thought emotions were triggered by beliefs in the usual sense.[28] The words he uses to denote the antecedents of the emotions may sometimes be rendered by "impression" rather than "belief," as when I have an impression that the sun is a foot in diameter while at the same time believing it is not (*De Anima* 428[b] 1–2). According to Martha Nussbaum, in the context of the *Rhetoric* we are entitled to render these words as "belief."[29] John Cooper, however, praises Aristotle for being "alive to the crucial fact about the emotions, that one can experience them simply on the basis of how, despite what one knows or believes to be the case, things *strike* one."[30] Independently of Aristotelian exegesis, *is* that a crucial fact about the emotions? The fact that we can experience strong emotions when reading about fictional characters suggests that this is in fact the case.[31] In the *Poetics* (1452[b] 32 ff; *GBWW* I: 9, 679–699; II: 8, 679–699) Aristotle himself underlines how tragedy is designed to evoke the emotions of pity and fear.

Intentional objects

As I have previously noted in this essay, Aristotle's general strategy in characterizing the emotions includes the identification of the person with whom we get angry or of whom we are afraid, envious, and the like. The object of an emotion need not be a person, however, and persons may play other roles in the emotions besides that of being their objects. For example, the case of shame illustrates both points. The disapproval of others causes us to feel shame, an emotion whose intentional object is some act we have done (or the character revealed by that action). If, however, the other person acts (or is believed to act) for the *purpose* of making us feel ashamed, the reaction tends to be one of anger directed at that individual (see the discussion of *hybris* below). This fact shows, incidentally, why attempts to substitute "shaming" for punishment in dealing with criminal offenders is unlikely to succeed.[32]

Pleasure and pain

Modern writers tend to think of an emotion as associated with pleasure *or* pain.[33] Aristotle, by contrast, seemed to think that an individual emotion typically is associated with pleasure *and* pain. What for us is the exceptional case of "mixed emotions" was, for Aristotle, closer to being the typical case.[34] The case of anger is paradigmatic. It "may be defined as a desire accompanied by pain, for a conspicuous revenge for a conspicuous slight at the hands of men who have no call to slight oneself or one's friends. . . . It must always be attended by a certain pleasure—that which arises from the expectation of revenge" (*Rhetoric* 1378[a] 31–33). In fact, "no one grows angry with a person on whom there is no prospect of taking vengeance, and we feel comparatively little anger, or none at all, with those who are much our superiors in power" (*Rhetoric* 1370[b] 12–13).

According to this analysis, the mixed emotion of anger is caused by the presence of two beliefs: the belief that the other insulted me and the belief that I can take revenge. One belief causes pain, the other pleasure.[35] In many cases this analysis seems exactly right. I wonder, though, whether we cannot feel angry even when there is no prospect of taking vengeance. Aristotle is aware of the problem. Noting that some might deny that the angry man desires vengeance, "because we become angry with our parents, but we do not desire vengeance on them," he refutes them by observing that "upon some people it is vengeance enough to cause them pain and make them sorry" (*Topics*, 156[a] 37–39; *GBWW* I: 8, 139–223; II: 139–223). Yet even if our parents may indeed suffer when we get angry at them, I do not believe the anticipation of their suffering *invariably* contributes an element of pleasure to our anger, although it may do so on occasion. To such counterexamples we might answer with Fortenbaugh, (i) that "there is no reason why Aristotle's conception of . . . anger must be exactly like our own," and (ii) that Aristotle "does not deny that [an angry] man may on occasion be in a hopeless position and either not realise it or cling to some quite irrational fantasy of safety or revenge."[36] We might add that the anger could itself enter into the causal history of the irrational belief in the possibility of revenge.

Aristotle's claim about anger as a mixed emotion is part of a wider context.[37] Plato had observed that some appetites involve both pain and pleasure, as when the distressing sensation of thirst and the pleasant anticipation of quenching it occur at the same time (*Philebus* 36[b]; *GBWW* I: 7, 609–39; II: 6, 609–39). The interruption of the normal state of the body is painful and the restoration of the normal state is pleasant; hence, through learning, the anticipation of that restoration itself becomes a source of pleasure. This idea is then generalized to "anger, fear, longing, lamenting, love, emulation, malice, and so forth": they, too, are both "pains of the soul" and "replete with immense pleasures" (ibid., 47[e]). Like Aristotle, Plato cites the Homeric lines about the sweetness of wrath; and like Aristotle he refers to "the pleasures mixed up with the pains in lamentation and longing."

These are phenomenological observations; no explanation is offered. Aristotle, by contrast, suggests an explanation in terms of two simultaneous cognitions. We have seen how this works in the case of anger. "Similarly there is an element of pleasure even in mourning and lamentation for the departed. There is grief, indeed, at his loss, but pleasure in remembering him" (*Rhetoric* 1370[b] 24–26). This might be read as a statement of the endowment-contrast mechanism: grief over the person who is dead is mingled with pleasant memories of what he was like when alive.[38] To get the analogy with anger right, however, another reading is required: the person who is mourned is absent rather than dead, and the pain of his absence is mingled with the pleasure of the memory-triggered *anticipation* of seeing him again.

The idea may be further generalized. Fear and pity are painful, but there may also be a pleasurable element in the thought of salvation. (But the dreaded outcome might be certain. In that case, Aristotle says [*Rhetoric* 13083[a] 5–8], no fear will be felt.) Envy is distressful but may go together with the pleasurable anticipation of the destruction of the envied object or its possessor. (But the costs of destruction might be prohibitively high.) If we disregard Aristotle's implausible claim that hatred is a painless feeling (see below), this emotion may also be analyzed as involving pain combined with the pleasurable anticipation of the destruction of its object. (But the hated tyrant might be invulnerable.) Guilt is horrible but can be alleviated by the prospects of confession and reparation. (But the person whom we wronged may be dead.)

Rather than viewing emotional life as a simple succession of experiences, we may see it as a succession of episodes, each of which has an internal structure. The disturbance of an initial equilibrium generates a negative emotion, which in turn induces an action tendency, a desire to reestablish the equilibrium, the fulfillment of which generates a positive emotion. Plato and Aristotle took the further step of assuming that the last step can be *foreseen* and thus generate pleasures of anticipation simultaneously with the occurrent pains. But as indicated in the parenthetic observations in the previous paragraph, the restoration of equilibrium may be impossible or prohibitively costly. In such cases, and perhaps also when restoration is possible but unlikely, there may not be any pleasures of anticipation. Conversely—a more controversial point—when the future satisfaction is *certain* there may be *no* pain in the present. The analysis clearly does not have the full generality that Aristotle claimed for it. It is simply not true that all emotions are mixed.

I believe, nevertheless, that the analysis captures an important aspect of emotional experience. When an emotion generates an action tendency, the mind may race ahead of itself and consume the outcome of the action even when effective action is blocked. Observing the greater fortune of another, I may feel a brief pain of envy and an equally fleeting joy at the thought of destroying his possessions, before I come to my senses and dismiss the former as unworthy and the latter as both unworthy and impractical. In some cases, as Fortenbaugh notes, daydreams and fantasies about revenge or destruction may persist for longer periods.

Action tendencies

The intimate relation between anger and revenge shows that Aristotle believed action tendencies to be features of some emotions. Because the most extensive discussion of the emotions occurs in the part of the *Rhetoric* that deals with the relation between judgment and emotion, rather than between emotion and action, it is more difficult to say whether he ascribed this tendency to all emotions. Among the emotions discussed below, action tendencies are explicitly associated with anger, fear, emulation, envy, and hatred, but not with the others. Aristotle certainly does not say about any specific emotion that it has no action tendency, or desire, associated with it.[39] It has been claimed that some of the emotions he discusses, such as shame, pity, or indignation, do not or need not have any action tendency associated with them.[40] This might seem puzzling. Shame, for instance, is strongly linked with the urge to hide or to disappear. The solution to the puzzle may lie in Fortenbaugh's comment that "in extreme cases an ashamed man may commit suicide, but in doing this he is not rectifying the past."[41] This suggests that an action tendency, for Aristotle, would always have to be a tendency to restore the natural equilibrium that has been interrupted by the emotion-generating event. It is hard for us to see, however, how that argument would apply to a positive emotion such as love or joy, which induce a tendency to prolong their causes rather than to end them. Given Aristotle's silence on the subject, however, these are somewhat idle speculations.

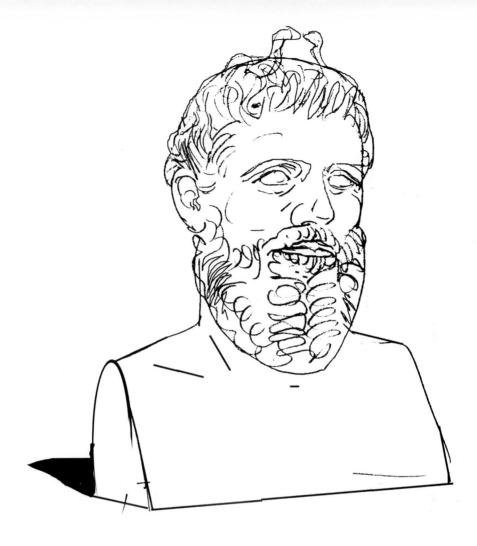

Summary

Overall, Aristotle's conceptualization of the emotions is very much on target. If we compare his discussions with recent treatments of this subject, there is very little that he misses. He did not and could not have a full understanding of the physiology of the emotions, but his treatment of their mental aspects is penetrating. In fact, several of Aristotle's insights go beyond what is available to us in the modern literature. These insights include notably his discussion of the non-cognitive antecedents of the emotions; his analysis of how emotions can be relieved through action; and the importance he attaches to mixed emotions. In addition, Aristotle may also have been alert to the possibility of emotions being triggered by cognitive states that involve fictional characters and hence fall short of full-blown beliefs.

V. What emotions are there?

Having discussed Aristotle's view of what emotions are, let us now consider his account of which emotions there are. I shall disregard his comments on the states that we call emotions but which he does not refer to as *pathe*, such as pride (*Nicomachean Ethics* 1123ᵃ–1125ᵃ), or two of the motives that are said to trigger anger in others, viz. spite and *hybris* (*Rhetoric* 1378ᵇ 16–31). Although for us the latter might seem to be emotions when viewed from the point of view of the subject who is experiencing them, Aristotle considers only how their expression through behavior may induce emotions in others.

In the *Ethics* (1105ᵇ 21–24; see below for a discussion of *hybris*), Aristotle offers the following list of the passions: "appetite, anger, fear, confidence, envy, joy, love, hatred, longing, emulation, pity, and in general the states of consciousness that are accompanied by pleasure or pain." The list is overly inclusive, as it allows us to count as passions pleasurable or painful states not triggered by cognition, such as hunger or thirst. The discussion in Book II of the *Rhetoric* is more consistent. Here Aristotle discusses how the orator can induce the following psychic states: anger, calmness, friendship, hatred, fear, confidence, shame, kindness, unkindness, pity, indignation, pleasure-at-the-deserved-misfortune-of-another (gloating), envy, delight-at-the-misfortune-of-another (malice), emulation, and contempt.[42] It is not clear whether all of these are emotions as we would use the term. Calmness and confidence, for instance, seem to be defined more by the absence of their opposites than by any positive features. Be that as it may, I shall disregard them, as they are less important for my purposes. In fact, I shall limit myself to anger, hatred, fear, shame, pity, indignation, gloating, envy, malice, and contempt. For the analysis of social and political phenomena with which Aristotle was mainly concerned, these (mostly dark) emotions seem to have the greatest explanatory relevance.

Anger

This emotion is said to be triggered by an undeserved slight or belittling, and in turn to trigger the desire for revenge (see above).[43] Although mere desire-frustration without intent to slight can also trigger anger, it is less likely to give rise to the desire for revenge. Hence Aristotle's anger may be a different emotion from what we call anger, and may more accurately be captured by the term "wrath."[44] As noted above, the slighting can take the form of contempt, spite, or insolence. I discuss contempt below. Spite is defined as "thwarting another man's wishes, not to get something for yourself but to prevent his getting it. The slight arises just from the fact that you do not aim at something for yourself: clearly you do not think that he can do you harm, for then you would be afraid of him instead of slighting him, nor yet that he can do you any good worth mentioning, for then you would be anxious to make friends with him" (*Rhetoric* 1378ᵇ 16–22). A's anger, in other words, is induced by what he perceives to be B's malicious

frustration of his wishes. Anger can also be induced by the perception of B's contempt for an *independently* caused state of wish-frustration: "people who are afflicted by sickness or poverty or love or thirst or any other unsatisfied desires are prone to anger are easily roused: especially against those who slight their present distress" (*Rhetoric* 1379^a 15–18). As this statement would make little sense if the distress was itself caused by the offending person, as is the case with spite and *hybris,* I infer that Aristotle here is referring to contempt.

Insolence (*hybris*) is an even more intensively interactive phenomenon. Rather than merely frustrating the wish of the other, it embodies deliberate humiliation of the other—"doing and saying things that cause shame to the victim, not in order that anything may happen to yourself, or because anything has happened to yourself, but simply for the pleasure involved. (Retaliation is not insolence, but vengeance.) The cause of the pleasure of the insolent man is that he thinks himself greatly superior to others when ill-treating them" (*Rhetoric* 1378^b 24–26).[45] *Hybris* is when you give offense neither for profit nor in revenge,[46] but simply because you delight in inflicting shame on the other. It follows from Aristotle's analysis that the victim of *hybris* feels both shame and anger: shame before third parties at what has been done to him, and anger at the person who has done it.[47]

Another connection between anger and shame is that they involve exposure before (roughly) the same categories of persons. We feel anger when slighted before "(1) our rivals, (2) those whom we admire, (3) those whom we wish to admire us, (4) those for whom we feel reverence, (5) those who feel reverence for us" (*Rhetoric* 1379^b 25–27). We feel shame if thought badly of by "those who admire us, those whom we admire, those by whom we wish to be admired, those with whom we are competing, and those whose opinion of us we respect" (*Rhetoric* 1384^a 27–29). Anger, for Aristotle, is an intensely social emotion. Although it can occur in dyadic encounters, the central cases involve the triadic relation of *being slighted before an audience*. Although Aristotle's Athens may not have been a full-blown "culture of honor," it certainly had many of the elements that characterize such cultures (see Section VI below).

The social aspect of anger is also brought out by Aristotle's curious (to us) notion of what constitutes a "justified" slighting. The Greek text in the definition of anger (*Rhetoric* 1378^b 1) is ambiguous, as shown by comparing the Oxford and Loeb translations. The former says that anger is caused by a slight "at the hands of men who have no call to slight one," the latter that it is caused "when such a slight is undeserved."[48] For a modern reader, the latter idea is the more natural. We get angry if someone slights us and we have done nothing that would justify the treatment. Aristotle, by contrast, thinks that we get angry when someone offends us who is not in a (social) position to do so. He notes, namely, that "we feel particularly angry with men of no account at all, if they slight us. For, *we have supposed* that anger caused by the slight is felt towards people who are not justified in slighting us, and our inferiors are not thus justified" (*Rhetoric* 1379^b 11–12 my italics).

Hatred

Aristotle offers insightful but puzzling discussions of hatred, differentiated from anger as follows:

> Enmity may be produced by anger or spite or calumny. Now whereas anger arises from offences against oneself, enmity may arise even without that; we may hate people merely because of what we take to be their character. Anger is always concerned with individuals—a Callias or a Socrates—whereas hatred is directed also against classes: we all hate any thief and any informer. Moreover, anger can be cured by time; but hatred cannot. The one aims at giving pain to its object, the other at doing him harm; the angry man wants his victim to feel; the hater does not mind whether they feel or not. . . . And anger is accompanied by pain, hatred is

not; the angry man feels pain, but the hater does not. Much may happen to make the angry man pity those who offend him, but the hater under no circumstances wishes to pity a man whom he once hated: for the one would have the offenders suffer for what they have done; the other would have them cease to exist. (*Rhetoric* 1382ᵃ 2–16)

A similar analysis is offered in the *Politics:*

There are two chief motives which induce men to attack tyrannies— hatred and contempt. Hatred of tyrants is inevitable, and contempt is also a frequent cause of their destruction. Thus we see that most of those who have acquired, have retained their power, but those who have inherited, have lost it, almost at once; for living in luxurious ease, they have become contemptible, and offer many opportunities to their assailants. Anger, too, must be included under hatred, and produces the same effects. It is often-times even more ready to strike—the angry are more impetuous in making an attack, for they do not follow rational principle. And men are very apt to give way to their passions when they are insulted. To this cause is to be attributed the fall of the Peisistratidae and of many others. Hatred is more reasonable, for anger is accompanied by pain, which is an impediment to reason, whereas hatred is painless. (1312^b 19–34)

In anger, my hostility is directed towards another's action and can be extinguished by getting even—an action that reestablishes the equilibrium. In hatred, my hostility is directed toward another person or a category of individuals who are seen as intrinsically and irremediably bad. For the world to be made whole, they have to disappear. This distinction is valuable, and largely neglected by modern emotion theorists. Of six authoritative texts on emotions that I consulted only one characterizes hatred;[49] and among the others only one of them mentions it at all.[50] The two texts that discuss the closely related idea of prejudice spell it out in terms of contempt rather than hatred.[51]

The puzzling feature of Aristotle's analyses is the assertion that hatred is unaccompanied by pain. Concerning the first of the two passages that I cited above, it has been suggested that Aristotle here treats hatred as an emotional disposition rather than as an occurrent emotion;[52] concerning the second, that it "makes one almost think he is talking about no emotion or passion at all, but a fully reasoned dispassionate rejection and dislike."[53] Yet as these commentators recognize, these observations do not do away with the problem: Aristotle explicitly says that hatred is a *pathos* and that a *pathos* is accompanied by pain and pleasure. If we assume, more than plausibly, that hatred is not accompanied by pleasure, there is a stark contradiction.

Whatever solution one adopts to the exegetical issue, understanding hatred merely as a disposition does not make substantive sense. It follows from first principles that the immediate cause of behavior must be an occurrence rather than a disposition. My irascibility does not serve as a direct cause of behavior, although it might enter indirectly into the causation of my action, e.g., through my awareness of it. Only the occurrent emotion of anger can serve as a direct cause of behavior. Similarly, my misogyny—a disposition to hate women—cannot be the proximate cause of my behavior. What causes me to act must be an occurrent emotion that has the same relation to misogyny that anger has to irascibility—but what emotion is that? "Hatred" may do as well as any other term, as long as we keep in mind that the word is also used in the dispositional sense. Although Aristotle's statement that hatred is unaccompanied by pain makes sense if applied to the disposition rather than to its occurrent manifestations, the contrast with anger is misleading, as irascibility is not accompanied by pain either.

Finally, it would seem that hatred does involve pain. For the prejudiced or the fanatic, the thought that the earth is inhabited by what he perceives as evil creatures—members of another race, ethnic group, or religious community—can be intensely painful. One can imagine, to be sure, that the

offending category is viewed with "fully reasoned dispassionate rejection and dislike." Some of those who advocate the death penalty for certain crimes may believe, dispassionately, that those who commit such crimes ought to die. But given the undeniable reality of passionate hatred, it is confusing to use the same word about dispassionate reasoning that happens to yield similar conclusions.

The other contrasts that Aristotle draws here between anger and hatred are more valid. Compared to anger, hatred is more compatible with rational calculation. One of the greatest acts of hatred in history, the Holocaust, was organized and carried out in a methodical and systematic way. Despite the fact that hatred is painful, it does not cloud the mind as anger or fear do. Although frequently based on irrational beliefs, the behavior hatred triggers need not be irrational, given those beliefs. For this reason, I cannot fully accept Aristotle's argument that

> Of those who attempt assassination they are the most dangerous, and require to be most carefully watched, who do not care to survive, if they effect their purpose. Therefore special precaution should be taken about any who think that either they or those for whom they care have been insulted; for when men are led away by passion to assault others they are regardless of themselves. As Heracleitus says, 'It is difficult to fight against anger; for a man will buy revenge with his soul'. (*Politics* 1315ᵃ 25–31)

Although the angry man may indeed be willing to take risks that a calculating hater would avoid, his lack of instrumental rationality detracts from his chances of success. The net impact on how dangerous he is for the ruler, compared to someone motivated by hatred, could go either way.

The statement that anger wants the offender to suffer whereas hatred wants him to cease to exist also makes good sense. Commenting on the genocidal tendencies of the Spanish Inquisition, B. Netanyahu writes that "the extreme, irreparable evil which allegedly inhered in the Jewish nature had to be treated in an extreme manner: since it was incorrigible, it had to be annihilated."[54] Torture, in the Inquisition, was used not for the purpose of making the victims (Jews converted to Christian faith) suffer, but to coerce them into fictitious confessions of being secret "Judaizers" that would justify their persecution and execution. The Holocaust, too, was based on the desire to extinguish the Jews, not to make them suffer.

Although talk about hatred is not unusual in everyday life, it often means nothing but a strong feeling of anger. "I hate him for what he did to me." In my opinion hatred, in Aristotle's technical sense, is a crucially important emotion in explaining many forms of behavior, notably political behavior. What allows us to differentiate it from other emotions is, as Aristotle said, the belief that a certain person or a certain category of people are intrinsically bad. The link to behavior is not that "because they do bad things, they are bad," but the converse, "because they are bad, they do bad things." Thus, evidence about their actual behavior will not affect the belief that they are bad, any more than evidence about the apparently mature behavior of a small child will affect our policy of assuming that he or she is likely to behave childishly. "Their true nature will come out." Thus according to the racist theory underlying the Spanish inquisition, "the Jewish moral propensities, inherited by the Marranos from the Jews, must sooner or later determine their religion—which means that those who are *racially* Jews are also, or will be, *religiously* Jews."[55]

Fear, pity, envy, indignation, gloating, malice

I treat these emotions together because of their close relations to one another. They are characterized by three pairs of concepts: whether something good or bad that is deserved or undeserved is predicated about oneself or others. Here, "undeserved" should be distinguished from "non-deserved." If I get rich by stealth, it is undeserved. If I get rich by hard work, to use a non-Aristotelian example, it is deserved. If I win the big

prize in the lottery, it is neither deserved nor undeserved, it is non-deserved (and non-undeserved). Similarly, if I am punished for a crime I committed, my fate is deserved. If I am punished for a crime I did not commit, it is undeserved. If I am hit by a meteor, it is neither deserved nor undeserved.

The notion of desert used here is spelled out in Aristotle's discussion of indignation, caused by the sight of the undeserved good fortune of others. From his discussion it is clear that my example of desert (wealth achieved by hard work) is indeed non-Aristotelian. Although this *topos* does occur in speeches from the period,[56] Aristotle does not mention it. Instead, he elaborates as follows:

> Indignation is roused by the sight of wealth, power, and the like—by all those things, roughly speaking, which are deserved by good men and by those who possess the goods of nature—noble birth, beauty, and so on.

Again, what is long established seems akin to what exists by nature; and therefore we feel more indignation at those possessing a given good if they have as a matter of fact only just got it and the prosperity it brings with it. The newly rich give more offence than those whose wealth is of long standing and inherited. . . . Further, it is not any and every man that deserves any given kind of good; there is a certain correspondence and appropriateness to such things; thus it is appropriate for brave men, not for just men, to have fine weapons, and for men of family, not for parvenus, to make distinguished marriages. Indignation may therefore properly be felt when any one gets what is not appropriate for him, though he may be a good man enough. (*Rhetoric* 1387ᵃ 14–32)

This passage, which could have been used as an epigraph by Proust or Edith Wharton, reflects very much an upper-class attitude. Although Aristotle himself may not have shared it, he seems to be advising speakers about how to address an upper-class audience, or at least an audience for which upper-class values had some appeal.[57] Yet Aristotle also entertained the more natural (to us) idea that desert is related to behavior: "If you are pained by the unmerited distress of others, you will be pleased, or at least not pained, by their merited distress. Thus no good man can be pained by the punishment of parricides or murderers" (*Rhetoric* 1386ᵇ 26–28). Note the acute observation that the sheer passage of time can give rise to a belief in entitlement.

Fear is produced when something bad is about to happen to oneself. Although Aristotle does not mention desert in this context, one might imagine a finer differentiation according to which the bad thing is deserved, undeserved, or neither. *Pity* is produced when an undeserved bad happens to another. Although Aristotle asserts (*Rhetoric* 1382ᵇ 26, 1386ᵃ 28) that that which causes fear if it happens to ourselves is also what causes us to feel pity when it happens to another, this claim is somewhat undermined by the lack of reference to desert in the definition of fear. *Envy* is produced when another possesses a good that I lack. *Indignation* is produced when an undeserved good is possessed by another. In the case of envy, therefore, the good must be either deserved or non-undeserved, two cases that might give rise to subtle differences in the envy that is felt. *Malice* is produced by the distress of another. *Gloating* is produced when the other's distress is deserved. Malice, therefore, will occur only when the bad is undeserved or non-deserved. Again, the two cases might yield different emotional nuances. Although Aristotle does not mention hope, i.e., the emotion or emotions that arise when a deserved, undeserved or non-deserved good is about to happen to oneself, the analyses of anticipated pleasure referred to above may partly fill this gap.

The conditions under which we feel fear include (beliefs about) both the motives and the opportunities of those whom we fear. We need not fear them, obviously, if they have no power to harm us. Their motives to do us harm include hatred, anger and, strikingly, fear. People fear "those who have done people wrong, if they possess power, since they stand in fear of retaliation" (*Rhetoric* 1382ᵇ 11–12). Aristotle does not mention envy or malice in others as a reason for fearing them. The reason might be that envy is felt by inferiors and that inferiors rarely have the power to harm one. Yet one person might have reason to fear the envy of many inferiors when joined together, as Aristotle recognizes in the *Politics* (1304ᵃ 37).

The conditions under which we feel pity and envy also include similarity of situation with the pitied or envied man. With regard to pity Aristotle says that "we pity those who are like us in age, character, disposition, social standing, or birth; for in all these cases it appears more likely that the same misfortune may befall us also" (*Rhetoric* 1386ᵃ 25–27). With regard to envy he says that "we feel it towards our equals . . . ; and by 'equals' I mean equals in birth, relationship, age, disposition, distinction, or wealth" (*Rhetoric* 1387ᵇ 23–26). Or again, "we envy those who are near us in time, place, age, or reputation" (*Rhetoric* 1388ᵃ 6). In both cases, then, the cognitive antecedents for the emotions include the thought "it could have been me." A similar condition obtains, as we shall see, in some cases of shame.

Shame

In the *Nicomachean Ethics* Aristotle writes that shame

> is not becoming to every age; but only to youth. For we think young people should be prone to shame because they live by passion and therefore commit many errors, but are restrained by shame; and we praise young people who are prone to this passion, but an older person no one would praise for being prone to the sense of disgrace, since we think he should not do anything that need cause this sense. For the sense of disgrace is not even characteristic of a good man, since it is consequent on bad actions . . . ; and it is a mark of a bad man even to be such as to do any disgraceful action. To be so constituted as to feel disgrace if one does such an action, and for this reason to think oneself good, is absurd; for it is for voluntary actions that shame is felt, and the good man will never voluntarily do bad actions. But shame may be said to be conditionally a good thing; *if* a good man did such actions, he would feel disgraced; but the excellences are not subject to such qualifications. And if shamelessness— not to be ashamed of doing bad actions—is bad, that does not make it good to be ashamed of doing such actions. (*Ethics* 1128ᵇ 10–33)

This austere passage can be read in conjunction with two others, which create a more nuanced picture:

> Citizens seem to face courage because of the penalties imposed by the laws and the reproaches they would otherwise incur, and because of the honours they win by such action; and therefore those peoples seem to be bravest among whom cowards are held in dishonour and brave men in honour. . . . This kind of courage . . . is due to shame and to desire of a noble object (i.e. honour) and avoidance of disgrace, which is ignoble. One might rank in the same class even those who are compelled by their rulers; but they are inferior, inasmuch as they act not from shame but from fear, and to avoid not what is disgraceful but what is painful. (*Ethics* 1116ᵃ 18–32)

[While arguments] seem to have the power to encourage and stimulate the generous-minded among the young, and to make a character which is gently born, and a true lover of what is noble, ready to be possessed by excellence, they are not able to encourage the many to nobility and goodness. For these do not by nature obey the sense of shame, but only fear, and do not abstain from bad acts because of their baseness but through fear of punishment. (*Ethics* 1179^b 7–12)

Although the reading of these and related passages is difficult, the following propositions may, perhaps, be defended. "The many," although shameless, are kept in check by the fear of physical punishment. Aristotle makes it clear that shame operates through the immediate feeling of disgrace rather than through any material sanctions that might accompany it. Second, among the young and immature, shame acts as a useful passion that counteracts other passions. Third, shame may serve the role of fixing the end of action rather than that of shaping each and every action. Commenting on the second passage, Myles Burnyeat writes that "the only thing that is 'second best' about this form of courage is that the citizen soldier takes his conception of what is noble from the laws and other people's expectations rather than having his own internalized sense of the noble and disgraceful."[58] Fourth, shame may be a stage in moral learning—Burnyeat calls it "the semivirtue of the learner."[59] Finally, once that learning has been accomplished, shame plays no further role. Acting courageously then flows from one's nature, like water seeking its natural downhill course. In battle, some soldiers refrain from cowardly behavior because of the fear of being punished by their superiors, whereas others are held in check by the shame they would feel before their equals. The truly excellent man thinks neither of his superior nor of his equals.

In the *Ethics,* shame is induced by the fear of disgrace from acting ignobly. The *Rhetoric* covers a wider range of grounds. In general, "Shame may be defined as pain or disturbance in regard to bad things, whether present, past, or future, which seem likely to involve us in discredit" (*Rhetoric* 1383^b 15–16). Here, too, it is clear that the pain is internal rather than consequential: "we shrink from the disgrace itself and not from its consequences" (*Rhetoric* 1384^a 24–25). Some of the things that induce disgrace are, as in the *Ethics,* due to badness: cowardliness, licentiousness, meanness, flattery, boastfulness, and so on. In addition, "another sort of bad thing at which we feel shame is, lacking a share in the honourable things shared by every one else, or by all or nearly all who are like ourselves. . . . Once we are on a level with others, it is a disgrace to be, say, less well educated than they are; and so with other advantages: all the more so, in each case, if it is seen to be our own fault" (*Rhetoric* 1384^a 9–15). Here, shame shades over into envy, which is also felt of "those whose possession of or success in a thing is a reproach to us: these are our neighbours and equals; for it is clear that it is our own fault we have missed the good thing in question" (*Rhetoric* 1388^a 17–19). As already noted, shame can also shade over into anger, if we are submitted to hybristic behavior (e.g., rape). In this section, however, Aristotle adds that the shame arises when we submit to *hybris* without resisting, for such behavior is "due to unmanliness or cowardice" (*Rhetoric* 1384ᵃ 21). I do not know whether he means to suggest that in such cases our co-complicity in the act defuses anger so that only shame remains.

Contempt

Shame and contempt are correlated emotions. We feel shame if and only if we are the targets of the actual or anticipated contempt of others. Although Aristotle discusses both emotions, he does not draw this connection. Rather, as we have seen, he cites (what we translate as) contempt as a source of anger in the target. Quite possibly, he had a somewhat different emotion in mind. This interpretation is also supported by the fact that he cites contempt, along with hatred, as a source of opposition to tyrants. In fact, he does not state that the persons whose disapproval causes us to feel shame feel any emotion at all.

Aristotle's explicit discussion of contempt as an emotion occurs in his discussion of emulation, an emotion related to envy but different in that "it is felt not because others have [highly valued goods], but because we have not got them ourselves . . . Emulation makes us take steps to secure the good things in question, envy makes us take steps to stop our neighbour having them" (*Rhetoric* 1388ᵃ 33–36). In his enumeration of those who are the object of emulation, Aristotle includes

> those who have . . . courage, wisdom, public office . . . Also those whom many people wish to be like; those who have many acquaintances or friends; those whom many admire, or whom we ourselves admire; and those who have been praised and eulogized by the poets or prose-writers. Persons of the contrary sort are objects of contempt: for the feeling and notion of contempt are opposite to those of emulation. Those who are such as to emulate or be emulated by others are inevitably disposed to be contemptuous of all such persons as are subject to those bad things which are contrary to the good things that are the objects of emulation: despising them just for that reason. Hence we often despise the fortunate, when luck comes to them without their having those good things which are held in honour. (*Rhetoric* 1388ᵇ 15–28)

Like hatred, contempt is triggered by the belief that a person is intrinsically bad. Whereas the badness of the person we hate is related to his ineradicably evil character, the badness of the person towards whom we feel contempt is based on his utter lack of worth. In Aristotle's case the lack of worth was expressed as lack of honor, but that is a contingent feature. Lord Chesterfield, writing to his son, certainly thought women were inferior, but not because they lacked honor:

> Women, then, are only children of a larger growth; they have an entertaining tattle, and sometimes wit; but for solid reasoning, good sense, I never knew in my life one who had it, or who reasoned or acted consequentially for four and twenty hours together. . . . A man of sense only

trifles with them, plays with them, humors and flatters them, as he does a
sprightly forward child; but he neither consults them about, nor trusts them
with serious matters, though he often makes them believe that he does
both; which is the thing in the world that they are most proud of . . .
Women are much more like each other than men; they have in truth but
two passions, vanity and love; these are their universal characteristics.[60]

If I hate another and I have the power to harm him, he is likely to be
afraid (*Rhetoric* 1382^a 32). If I express my contempt for him, he is likely to
be angry. (That presumably is why Lord Chesterfield thought one should
make women believe they were trusted.) Hate can be symmetrical, as
shown by the fact that Aristotle sometimes uses "hatred" and "enmity" as
near-synonyms (*Rhetoric* 1382^a 1–3). It can also be asymmetrical, as
shown by the hatred of thieves and informers. Contempt, by contrast, is
usually asymmetrical: If I believe another to be utterly lacking in worth or
honor, he is unlikely to think the same of me. As mentioned above, prejudice can take the form either of hatred or contempt. When President Ronald
Reagan referred to the U.S.S.R. as "the evil empire," he expressed hatred,
not contempt. Lord Chesterfield expresses contempt for women, not hatred.
Followers of Hitler thought Jews evil but Slavs inferior.[61]

The emotion of contempt is likely to be particularly strong if the person
or group believed to be inferior is also seen as more powerful than oneself.
An example is found in Aristotle's comment on the contempt for tyrants.
Another example occurs when a regime change propels into power a group
viewed as inferior by the traditional elite. Thus Aristotle cites several
examples to show that contempt can cause the fall of democracies, "when
the wealthy despise the disorder and anarchy which they see prevalent"
(*Politics* 1302^b 29–30). In this case, contempt is close to resentment, defined by Roger Petersen as "the emotion that stems from the perception that
one's group is located in an unjust subordinate position on a status hierarchy."[62]

Summary

The antecedents of these emotions are quite varied. They include (beliefs
about) *actions* and the motivations behind them (anger, shame, pity, fear),
possessions (envy, indignation, emulation, gloating, malice), and *character
traits* (hatred, contempt). More simply, they include (beliefs about) what
people—others or oneself—do, have, and are. In addition, some emotions
(pity, fear) can be triggered by *events,* i.e., by what happens in the non-
human world. The actions, possessions, traits, and events may lie in the
past (one is ashamed of what one has done), in the present (one is angry
when struck by another), in the future (one is afraid of something that is
about to happen) or extend over time (one hates people for constant character traits). Often the emotion-triggering beliefs have moral components, as
when we feel pity because of someone's undeserved misfortune or indignation at his undeserved fortune. Aristotle also takes account of counterfac-
tual beliefs: when he observes that we feel shame and envy by failing to

achieve what others like us have achieved, it is presumably because we think that we, being like them, could have done what they did. Among his specific analyses, his account of hatred is more penetrating than any of the few modern discussions of that emotion. His analysis of shame, although somewhat ambiguous (see below), is also very illuminating.

VI. The emotional life of the Greeks

The role of emotions among the ancient Greeks—which usually means the Athenians—has been extensively studied. A general overview is Kenneth Dover's *Greek Popular Morality*. On specific emotions one may cite Peter Walcot: *Envy and the Greeks*, N.R.E. Fisher: *Hybris*, Bernard Williams: *Shame and Necessity*, and Douglas Cairns: *Aidos: The Psychology and Ethics of Honour and Shame in Ancient Greek Literature*. The primary sources for these and similar studies are the Greek tragedies and comedies, the speeches of the Athenian orators, and the historical works of Herodotus, Thucydides, and Xenophon. By drawing on these primary and secondary sources one can add relief and detail to Aristotle's very succinct and compact analyses, and raise some issues that are implicit rather than explicit in his texts.

Guilt and shame

In modern Western societies, the emotional reactions of guilt and shame coexist. These two emotions differ in several respects. With regard to their cognitive antecedents, shame is triggered by the belief that one has been seen to violate a social norm, whereas guilt is caused by the belief that one has violated a moral norm, whether or not anyone else knows about it. With regard to their intentional objects, guilt and shame are related to each other as anger to hatred. In guilt and anger, the emotion is directed towards an *action* performed by oneself or by another person. But emotion can also be directed towards the *character* of the person, one's own in the case of shame or another's in the case of hatred. The paradox of shame is that it "involves taking a single unworthy action or characteristic to be the whole of a person's identity."[63] With regard to action tendencies, guilt typically induces a desire to undo the bad one has done or, if that is impossible, to confess or to impose a suffering upon oneself that matches the suffering one has caused. Shame, by contrast, makes one wish to disappear, to hide or even kill oneself.

Ancient Greece was a "shame culture." People sought to be *seen* to be good and to avoid being *seen* to be bad, rather than to *be* good or to avoid *being* bad. For them, "goodness divorced from a reputation for goodness was of limited interest."[64] The inner gnawings of conscience and self-reproach are not prominent in Greek writings.[65] To see how much this attitude differs from (one strand of) modern thinking we may cite Montaigne to the effect that "The more glittering the deed the more I subtract from its moral worth, because of the suspicion aroused in me that it was exposed more for glitter than for goodness: goods displayed are already halfway to being sold."[66] At the limit the only good acts are those that never come to light. Along the same lines Pascal wrote that "the finest things about [fine deeds] was the attempt to keep them secret" and that "the detail by which they came to light spoils everything."[67]

Yet from the absence of explicit references to guilt we should not conclude to the absence of the emotion itself. As noted in Section II above, a culture may display the characteristic physiological and behavioral expressions of an emotion even if it does not have a cognitive and linguistic label. Thus, according to Bernard Williams, the Greeks were concerned with many of the things that we associate with guilt rather than shame, such as indignation, reparation and forgiveness. What they lacked, was the concept of this concern: "What people's ethical emotions are depends significantly on what they take them to be. The truth about Greek societies . . . is not that they failed to recognize any of the reactions that we associate with guilt, but that they did not make of those reactions the special thing that they became when they are separately recognized as guilt."[68]

Williams also observes that in ancient Greece something like the shame-guilt distinction reappears within the concept of shame itself. "By the later fifth century the Greeks had their own distinctions between a shame that merely followed public opinion and a shame that expressed inner personal conviction."[69] The idea is illustrated with examples from Euripides' *Hippolytus*. We find a related distinction in Aristotle's treatment of shame.[70] He writes that we are not "ashamed of the same things before intimates as before strangers, but before the former of what seem genuine faults, before the latter of what seem conventional ones" (*Rhetoric* 1384[b] 25–27). Also, he notes, we feel friendly "towards those with whom we are on such terms that, while we respect their opinions, we need not blush before them for doing what is conventionally wrong: as well as towards those before whom we should be ashamed of doing anything really wrong" (*Rhetoric* 1381[b] 19–21). There is no conception of guilt here, but a distinction between types of spectators and a distinction between types of acts. Something like the shame-guilt distinction appears here, then, as a distinction between shame before strangers and shame before friends, or, equivalently, between shame for conventionally wrong actions and shame for genuinely wrong actions. (For the latter distinction see also *Ethics* 1128[b] 23–5.) The picture would have been even clearer if shame before friends or for genuine faults was associated with indignation, reparation and forgiveness, but Aristotle does not make this connection.

Honor and glory

The other side of the fear of being seen to be bad is the desire to be seen to be good. In fact, for the Greeks, merely being seen as good was not what mattered: they wanted to be seen as *better* than others, or as unique in some other way. To heighten the effect of praise, Aristotle says (*Rhetoric* 1368[a]

11–13) we may "point out that a man is the only one, or the first, or almost the only one who has done something, or that he has done it better than any one else; all these distinctions are honorable." Once again, we may draw a distinction between emotions that are directed towards an action and those that are directed toward a person's character as a whole. The emotion of *pridefulness* comes from the belief that one is a good person (or better than others); that of *pride* stems from the belief that one has acted well (or better than others) on some particular occasion.[71]

The Greeks were extremely competitive, and *philotimia* or "love of glory" was a pervasive motivating force. Dover writes that "the Greeks tended to judge people not on a 'pass or fail' criterion, but by deliberately imparting a competitive character to as many aspects of life as possible (e.g., plays, songs and dances at festivals), and the wide difference between the treatment of winners and the treatment of losers augmented the incentive to excel."[72] Aeschylus, for instance, "wrote his plays for performance at a dramatic competition with the hope presumably of securing first prize"; hence when he left Athens for Sicily "it will occasion no surprise that one reason advanced in antiquity for his departure from Athens was professional chagrin, defeat at the hands of the young Sophocles or at the hands of Simonides."[73] Losing is always shameful; in fact "defeat is *aischron* [shameful] even when the gods cause it."[74] The value attached to glory in the Greek world was so strong that shame could attach not only to losers but also to non-contestants. Thus in Xenophon's *Memorabilia* (III.7.1) Socrates and Charmides agree that "a man who was capable of gaining a victory in the great games and consequently of winning honour for himself and adding to his country's fame, and yet refused to compete," could only be a coward.

The desire for glory is the desire to be seen as the best in competitive interactions. Yet, competition is a fairly weak form of interaction. Two authors who compete for the same literary prize may not even have met one another. Even two athletes running side by side do nothing they could not have done in the absence of the other. A stronger form of interaction is found in battles and combats. The man who risks his life, health or fortune in trying to subjugate another gains *honor*. Feuding and dueling are common means deployed to this end,[75] but they are not the only ones. In Athens, for instance, litigation was often a form of legal feuding, a way of humiliating the opponent and achieving honor for oneself.[76]

Yet the humiliation of another can also be sought for its own sake rather than as a means to honor. The peculiarly Greek phenomenon of *hybris* must be understood in this light. As N.R.E. Fisher has shown, conclusively as far as I can judge, *hybris* was not the phenomenon of excessive self-confidence with which we associate the term today. Rather, it must be taken in Aristotle's sense, as the deliberate humiliation of others for the sheer pleasure of the act.[77] Although *hybris* typically refers to a specific kind of behavior, I shall also use the term to refer to the emotion associated with that behavior. It is closely related to pridefulness, in the full-blown variety which involves the belief that one is intrinsically superior to all others. It involves the pleasure of being able to do evil with impunity, the most potent of all the rewards of wealth and power; the malicious pleasure of watching another squirm or shrink in shame; and the sadistic pleasure of being the one who makes him suffer. A paradigm of *hybris* is Meidias' public slapping of Demosthenes, expounded and condemned at length in the latter's speech against the former. A temporally extended paradigm is offered by the life of Alcibiades, "the most hybristic of those who lived under the democracy," in Xenophon's words (*Memorabilia* 1.2.12).

Envy

In *Democracy in America* Tocqueville makes a distinction between envy, which is a "debased taste for equality," and the "legitimate passion for equality which rouses in all men a desire to be strong and respected." (*GBWW* II: 44, 57) Aristotle makes a similar distinction when he writes in the *Rhetoric* that emulation is "a good feeling felt by good persons, whereas envy is a bad feeling felt by bad persons. Emulation makes us take steps to secure the good things in question, envy makes us take steps to stop our neighbour having them" (*Rhetoric* 1388ª 34–35). Tocqueville also claimed that envy is "the democratic sentiment." (*GBWW* II: 44, 44–310) There is no direct textual basis for imputing this view to Aristotle. Yet we may ask, more conjecturally, whether it does not flow from his idea that democracies are subject to *status inconsistency,* i.e., that most citizens are high on one status dimension while low on another. In the *Politics* Aristotle writes, "For the one party [i.e., oligarchs], if they are unequal in one respect, for example wealth, consider themselves to be unequal in all; and the other party [i.e., democrats], if they are equal in one respect, for example free birth, consider themselves to be equal in all" (*Politics* 1280ᵇ 23–25). In his study that explores the subject of envy among the ancient Greeks, author Peter Walcot makes a connection between status inconsistency and envy:

> Equality among the full Spartan citizens was something consciously adopted, or so the ancient sources imply, in order to reduce envy among these citizens and thus prevent a Helot revolt. Athenian democracy had no such origin—but a consequence of the development of democracy at Athens was a restriction on the scope offered for feelings of envy because of an equality of voting rights. In one respect at least a citizen could feel himself to be as good as the next citizen, and this was in an area of the greatest importance, political life. But perhaps democracy actually intensified rather than reduced feelings of envy: the very fact that all citizens were equal as voters in the assembly simply may have made some that much more aware of their inequality in birth or wealth or even good luck, and so Plutarch refers frequently to envy in his biographies of fifth-century Athenians. To put it another way, if one is 'entitled' to an equality of rights as a voter, this is a strong inducement to expect a comparable equality across the board. In fact if equality is to curb envy it must be a full equality which covers all of life, and the Spartan system did attempt to be comprehensive.[78]

If envy may be curbed by equality across the board, it can also be mitigated by *in*equality—provided the differences of situation are large rather than small. Aristotle states very clearly the principle of "neighborhood envy," according to which "we envy those who are near us in time, place, age, or reputation" (*Rhetoric* 1388ª 5–6).[79] Conversely, we do not envy "those whom, in our opinion or that of others, we take to be far below us or far above us" (*Rhetoric* 1388ª 11–12). The orator Isocrates implicitly appeals to this idea when he argues that "those who live in monarchies, not having anyone to envy, do in all circumstances so far as possible what is best" (3.18). We may contrast this statement with Aristotle's assertion that "those who have secured power to the state, whether private citizens, or magistrates, or tribes, or any other part or section of the state, are apt to cause revolutions. For either envy of their greatness draws others into rebellion, or they themselves, in their pride of superiority, are unwilling to remain on a level with others" (*Politics* 1304ª 34–36). Envy is directed towards those who have recently acquired some superiority, not towards those whose superiority is so firmly entrenched that they appear to be "far above us."

Misrepresentation of emotion

In a given society some emotions may be viewed as more objectionable than others. Because different emotions may give rise to similar behaviors, people may have an incentive to substitute a more acceptable emotion for the one that actually moved them to act. In ancient Greece, the unavowability of envy and *hybris* induced commoners as well as kings to present actions thus motivated in a different light.

In "On envy and hate," Plutarch writes that "men deny that they envy . . . and if you show that they do, they allege any number of excuses and say they are angry with the fellow or hate him, cloaking and concealing their envy with whatever other name occurs to them for their passion." In Classical Athens, this tendency was revealed by the practice of denouncing others who claimed to act for the sake of revenge of being really motivated by envy. In David Cohen's summary, the orator Lysias

> argues that his opponent will falsely claim that he brings the prosecution out of enmity so as to get revenge, but in fact it is only out of envy because the speaker is a better citizen. . . The desire for revenge apparently would be seen by the judges as a legitimate reason for prosecuting, so the speaker must deny that this is the case. Meanspirited envy, on the other hand, reflects badly upon the accuser's character and indicates that the suit is unreliable.[80]

In ancient Greece, *hybris* was a punishable offense and, moreover, a strongly disapproved form of behavior. There was a legal category, *graphe hybreos,* which enabled victims (or others) to prosecute hybristic behavior. Against accusations of *hybris* therefore, it was expedient to represent one's behavior as motivated by a more acceptable urge. In the *Politics* (1311ᵇ 20),

Aristotle tells a story about a tyrant, Archelaus, who was killed (among other reasons) because one of his boyfriends decided that their association had been based on "*hybris* not on erotic desire." Aristotle then offers the following advice to tyrants who want to stay in power. Aristotle recommends that in their acquaintances with youth, the tyrants should appear to be acting from desire rather than from *hybris*.[81] In other contexts, those accused of *hybris* represent their behavior as motivated by revenge. Although there may have been truth in their allegations of having been wronged, they might still be guilty of *hybris* if the revenge was disproportionate to the offense.[82]

One could also try to deflect accusations of *hybris* by arguing that one had been drunk, or even get drunk so as to be able to insult an enemy without laying oneself open to the charge of *hybris*. The following passage from N.R.E. Fisher's treatise entitled *Hybris*, indicates some of the complexities involved:

> One 'ideal type' of *hybris* as an act like that of Meidias in the theatre, where no excuse of drink, sudden onrush of hatred or anger, or pressure from intense competition or conflict could mitigate the outrage, or suggest that he did not reveal a cold, premeditated, intention to insult Demosthenes, for the pleasure it would give him to display his ability to so act. But other cases are imaginable, where some of these mitigating elements are present, yet the act is still *hybris;* and the [speech against] Meidias in fact offers a useful selection of possibilities. . . . First, Euaion killed Boiotos when angered and dishonoured by the blow from Boiotos and by the *hybris* which he felt accompanied it; but Boiotos was drunk and they were at a dinner party (21.7 1 ff.). The same possibility was felt by the jury to be relevant to the whipping by Ctesicles of his enemy at the festival procession (21.180); but the feeling was that he had acted 'in *hybris* and not in wine'; the same phrase is used of Meidias in contrast with Boiotos; and presumably Boiotos therefore could be said in some way to have acted 'in wine.' But in fact each case is different, and that of Boiotos less serious than either that of Ctesicles and that of Meidias. Boiotos and Ctesicles were both drunk, and both assaulted and insulted another. But one can distinguish between cases of drunken assault: some may be cases where the drink and the occasion might have induced any ordinary man to engage in fighting and insults; cases where the drink greatly exacerbated an existing tendency to insult others; and cases where the drink was little more than a cover to hide a deliberate decision to insult an enemy. Ctesicles was held by the jury to fall into the last category, and *hybris* was the main cause of his act, and the drink contributed little or nothing. Boiotos may have been thought by Euaion to fall into that category but the neutral observers would place him in the second, or even the first.[83]

In modern legal systems, passion can only be an extenuating circumstance, never (to my knowledge) an aggravating one. For the Greeks, it could be either. Because revenge was attenuating, it could be used as an excuse. Because *hybris* was aggravating, it had to be excused away by appeals to various passions such as revenge, sexual desire or, as above, to drunkenness.

VII. Conclusion

Karl Marx remarks that in the realm of art the Greeks were like "normal children."[84] It is tempting to apply a similar characterization to the emotional life of the Greeks. By "childlike" I mean only a frankness and lack of self-consciousness that in modern societies is more frequently found in children than in adults. The passages I have cited from Aristotle and others suggest in fact an emotional world that differs from our own. It is intensely confrontational, intensely competitive, and intensely public; in fact, much of it involves confrontations and competitions before a public. It is a world in which everybody knows that they are constantly being judged, nobody hides that they are acting as judges, and nobody hides that they seek to be judged positively. It is a world with very little hypocrisy, or "emotional tact," a world in which a man was not afraid to express disapproval of others merely because they were born ugly or poor—just as a child in our own society may express disgust at the sight of a disfigured person. Although—as we have seen—people did occasionally try to hide or misrepresent their emotions, they did so to a smaller extent than in modern societies. Also, the Athenians were relatively unselfconscious about their emotions. They did not have the idea that emotions could be the object of cognition, nor, a fortiori, the idea that emotions might give rise to second-order emotional reactions. As far as we can tell from the texts that have come down to us, being ashamed of one's envy was not a typical Greek reaction. Shame, for the Greeks, was limited to behavior that could be observed by others and did not extend to unobservable mental states.

In spite of the stunning accuracy and penetrating insight of many of his observations, there are lacunae in Aristotle's treatment of the emotions. I have mentioned the absence of the idea that emotions may be the object of cognition which can trigger second-order emotions. By and large, Aristotle also neglects the causal effect of emotions on cognition. This statement may seem paradoxical, given that the impact on cognition is part of Aristotle's definition of emotion (see Section IV above). Yet in his specific analyses of emotion, this idea does not have the central place it came to have in later discussions. Consider for instance the idea captured in a phrase from Seneca's *On Anger:* "Men whose spirit has grown arrogant from the great favor of fortune have this most serious fault—those whom they have injured they also hate (*quos laeserunt et oderunt*)."[85] The scenario behind this observation can be reconstructed as follows. First, I injure somebody who has done nothing to deserve it. Second, because the incipient feeling of guilt or shame resulting from this behavior is incompatible with my self-esteem, I invent a story that justifies what I did. Third, the cognition embodied in this story causes me to hate the person whom I injured. In a variant of the scenario, I may interpret the offended reaction of the person I injured as a deliberate attempt to make me feel guilty and thus to injure *me*—a perceived intention that provokes and justifies my anger.

As is evident from his remarks on anger cited in Section V above, Aristotle was aware that emotion might *cloud* cognition. Yet he seems to have been unaware of the extent to which it may *distort* and *shape* cognition so as to serve our emotional needs, notably our need for self-esteem. It was left to the French moralists to explore this idea. In the words of La Rochefoucauld, "The head is always fooled by the heart (*L'esprit est toujours la dupe du coeur*)."[86] Although Aristotle was fully aware of the direct role of the emotions in triggering behavior through spontaneous action tendencies (see Section IV above), he neglected their ability to modify cognition and thus to shape behavior indirectly.

This article draws heavily on the fuller discussions of the emotions in general and in ancient Greece in particular offered in my *Alchemies of the Mind,* forthcoming from Cambridge University Press. I am grateful to Bernard Manin, Amélie O. Rorty and Bernard Williams for their comments on the section on Aristotle in that book. References to the classical orators are given in the standard format, with the number of a speech in the corpus of an orator followed by the number of the section within the speech.

1. I do not read Greek. Although I have tried to compensate for this deficiency by consulting several translations of the *Rhetoric* and the other works by Aristotle that I cite, there are likely to be nuances that have escaped me.

2. François Billacois, *The Duel* (New Haven, Conn.: Yale University Press, 1990); David Cohen, *Law, Violence, and Community in Classical Athens* (New York: Cambridge University Press, 1995); William Ian Miller, *Bloodtaking and Peacemaking* (Chicago: University of Chicago Press, 1990); Stephen Wilson, *Feuding, Conflict, and Banditry in Nineteenth-Century Corsica* (New York: Cambridge University Press, 1988).

3. Keith Thomas, *Religion and the Decline of Magic* (Penguin: Harmondsworth, 1973); Alexis de Tocqueville, *The Old Régime and the French Revolution* (New York: Anchor Books, 1955).

4. *The Characters* IV. 77.

5. For a fuller discussion, see my "Coming to terms with the past," *Archives Européennes de Sociologie* 39 (1998), 7–48.

6. See for instance Richard S. Lazarus, *Emotion and Adaptation* (New York: Oxford University Press 1991).

7. Joseph E. LeDoux, *The Emotional Brain* (New York: Simon and Schuster, 1996).

8. Antonio R. Damasio, *Descartes' Error* (New York: G.P. Putnam, 1994). For critical comments, see Ch.IV.3 of my *Alchemies of the Mind.*

9. For discussion of such transmutations, see my "Montaigne's Psychology," (*GIT* 1996; 108-55).

10. For different views on this issue, see the essays in Robert A. Shweder and Robert A. LeVine (eds.), *Culture Theory: Essays on Mind, Self, and Emotion* (Cambridge: Cambridge University Press, 1984).

11. Patricia Ann Meyer Spacks, *Boredom* (Chicago: University of Chicago Press, 1995).

12. Robert I. Levy, *The Tahitians* (Chicago: University of Chicago Press, 1973).

13. Editorial remark in G.A. Kennedy, (ed.), *Aristotle on Rhetoric* (New York: Oxford University Press, 1991), p. 122.

14. I have mainly used the translations in GBWW 8. The page references are in the standard Aristotelian format, also used in the GBWW. References to the Athenian orators and historians are also in the standard format of these texts.

15. Thus in a part of a speech where he defends his own character, Isocrates cites the following comment by a friend who was afraid that praising himself might have the opposite effect of what he wanted: "Some men," he said, "have been so brutalized by envy and want and are so hostile that they wage war, not on depravity, but on prosperity; they hate not only the best men but the noblest pursuits; and, in addition to their other faults, they take sides with wrong-doers and are in sympathy with them, while they destroy those whom they have cause to envy. They do these things, not because they are

ignorant of the issues on which they are to vote, but because they intend to inflict injury and do not expect to be found out." (4.142–43)

16. For discussions of the relation between the treatments of emotions in Books I and II, see Dorothea Frede, "Mixed Feelings in Aristotle's *Rhetoric,*" in Amélie Oksenberg Rorty (ed.), *Essays on Aristotle's Rhetoric* (Berkeley and Los Angeles: University of California Press, 1996), pp. 258–85, esp. pp. 265–72 and Gisela Striker, "Emotions in Context: Aristotle's Treatment of the Passions in the *Rhetoric* and His Moral Psychology," ibid., pp. 286–302, esp. pp. 288–93.

17. In his discussion of "stimulus conditions that facilitate elicitation of emotion without themselves being stimuli for such an emotion," Nico H. Frijda, *The Emotions* (New York: Cambridge University Press, 1986), p. 283 does not mention preexisting distress.

18. J. Sabini and M. Silver, "Emotions, responsibility, and character," in Ferdinand Schoeman (ed.), *Responsibility, Character, and the Emotions* (New York: Cambridge University Press, 1987), pp. 165–75 comment that they "do believe that some people at some moments have been responsible for their emotions—although perhaps this responsibility is iatrogenic, limited to those who have studied Aristotle's theory."

19. William W. Fortenbaugh, (1970), "Aristotle's *Rhetoric* on Emotions," cited after the reprint in Jonathan Barnes, Makolm Schofield and Richard Sorabji (eds.), *Articles on Aristotle,* vol. 4: Psychology and Aesthetics (London: Duckworth, 1979).

20. Paul Ekman, "An Argument for Basic Emotions," *Cognition and Emotion* 6 (1992), 169–200; Frijda, *The Emotions.*

21. For discussion, see Ch. IV. 3 of *Alchemies of the Mind.*

22. Frijda, *The Emotions,* p. 43.

23. For examples and references, see my "Coming to terms with the past."

24. W.W. Fortenbaugh, *Aristotle on Emotion* (London: Duckworth, 1975), p. 15.

25. Ibid., p. 12.

26. Ibid., p. 17.

27. Ibid., p. 15.

28. Amélie Oksenberg Rorty, "Structuring Rhetoric," in Amélie Oksenberg Rorty (ed.), *Essays on Aristotle's Rhetoric,* pp. 1–33, esp. pp. 17–20.

29. Martha Craven Nussbaum, "Aristotle on Emotions and Rational Persuasion," ibid., pp. 303–23, at p. 307.

30. John M. Cooper, "Rhetoric, Dialectic, and the Passions," in C.C.W. Taylor (ed.), *Oxford Studies in Ancient Philosophy* XI (Oxford: Oxford University Press, 1993), pp. 175–98, at p. 191.

31. See notably Robert J. Yanal, "The Paradox of Emotion and Fiction," *Pacific Philosophical Quarterly* 75 (1994), 54–75.

32. June Tangney, interviewed in the *New York Times* January 16, 1997; see also my "Emotions and Economic Theory," *Journal of Economic Literature* 36 (1998), 47–74.

33. See for instance James A. Russell, "A Circumplex Model of Affect," *Journal of Personality and Social Psychology* 39 (1980), 1161–1178.

34. See notably Frede, "Mixed Feelings in Aristotle's *Rhetoric.*"

35. By contrast, the treatment of anger as a mixed emotion in A. Ortony, G.L. Clore and A. Collins, *The Cognitive Structure of the Emotions,* Cambridge University Press 1988, pp. 146–53 breaks it down into two *negative* components: disapproving of someone else's blameworthy action, and being displeased about an undesirable event.

36. Fortenbaugh, *Aristotle on Emotion,* p. 80 note 1.

37. The following draws heavily on Fortenbaugh, *Aristotle on Emotion,* and Frede, "Mixed Feelings in Aristotle's *Rhetoric.*"

38. Amos Tversky and Dale Griffin, "Endowment and Contrast in Judgments of Well-being," in Richard J. Zeckhauser (ed.), *Strategy and Choice* (Cambridge, Mass.: M.I.T. Press, 1991), pp. 297–318; see also examples from Montaigne in my "Montaigne's psychology."

39. Fortenbaugh, *Aristotle on Emotion,* p. 82 claims that "Aristotle is . . . clear that [indignation] need not be manifested in action," but the passage from the *Rhetoric* that he cites to support this view does not speak to the issue.

40. Fortenbaugh, *Aristotle on Emotion,* pp. 15, 81–82; Striker, "Emotions in Context," p. 293. Striker also cites the fact that emotions such as pride and relief, while

based on desire-fulfillment, are not themselves desires. These do not, however, belong to the Aristotelian list of emotions (see below).

41. Fortenbaugh, *Aristotle on Emotion*, p. 81.

42. Although a far from ideal term, "gloating" is the closest word I could find for pleasure-at-the-deserved-misfortune-of-another. It is embodied in a famous description by Tertullian of the joys of the saved in heaven when they contemplate the sufferings of the damned; (cited in Frederich Nietzsche, *The Birth of Tragedy* and *The Genealogy of Morals*, (New York: Anchor Books, 1956), p. 183–85.

43. Aristotle is concerned with a slight *to oneself.* In *Les Passions de l'âme* (Art. 195), Descartes observes that there is a characteristic emotion, which he calls "indignation," which arises when A observes B slighting C. When A loves C, this indignation is indistinguishable from anger (Art. 201).

44. Nico H. Frijda, "The Lex talionis: on vengeance," in Stephanie H. M. Goozen, Nanne E. Van De Poll and Joe A. Sergeant (eds.), *Emotions: Essays on Emotion Theory* (Hillsdale, N.J.: Lawrence Erlbaum, 1994), pp. 263–90, at p. 265. Aristotle also claims, however, that wish-frustration as a state of mind may induce anger (*Rhetoric* 1379^a 10–22). Cooper, "Rhetoric, Dialectic, and the Passions," p. 196 argues that this is a case of one emotion (distress) preparing the ground for another (anger). To render Aristotle consistent with himself, one would have to assume that in addition to the cause for distress (wish-frustration) a separate cause of anger (intentional slighting) has to be present. Some of the things Aristotle says in this passage support this reading; others suggest that wish-frustration by itself is enough to induce anger. Cooper seems to have the second idea in mind when he writes that "The upset feeling that belongs to anger in all these cases is an offshoot of the antecedent upset feeling the person has been experiencing in having some aroused, but unsatisfied appetite. It is as if a pre-existent energy, the appetite, gets redirected when one feels oneself blocked or obstructed in satisfying it, and becomes or gives rise to this new feeling of distress, the anger."

45. The Loeb and Kennedy translations render the last sentence by the more general idea that people feel superior when ill-treating others, without specifying (as in the Oxford translation that I cite in the text) that they feel superior *to those whom they are mistreating.* Some recorded instances of *hybris* can plausibly be understood in the more restricted sense (Meidias slapping Demosthenes in public), whereas in other cases the structure is that A feels superior to B because unlike B, A can get away with ill-treating C. The case of Alcibiades committing *hybris* against his wife by bringing his *hetairai* into the house illustrates this idea.

46. We shall see below, however, that excessive revenge could be interpreted as a form of *hybris.*

47. See M. Lewis, *Shame* (New York: The Free Press, 1992), pp. 149–53 for a recent discussion of anger triggered by shame (and sometimes triggering shame in return). It is not clear, though, that the concepts of anger and shame are those that Aristotle had in mind.

48. The rendering in Edward Meredith Cope, *The Rhetoric of Aristotle* (New York: Cambridge University Press, 1877) is the same as in the Loeb translation, which makes it hard to understand why in his rendering of 1379^b 11–12 Cope refers back to the definition given in 1378^b 1. The translation in Kennedy, *Aristotle on Rhetoric,* preserves the ambiguity of the original.

49. Frijda, *The Emotions,* p. 212 argues that hatred is based on an "object evaluation," anger on an "event evaluation." Hatred says that "he is bad," anger that "he did something bad to me." This is close to Aristotle's view. Unlike Aristotle, however, Frijda does not note that the two emotions differ in their action tendencies.

50. These are Silvan S. Tomkins, *Affect, Imagery, Consciousness,* vols I–IV (New York: Springer Publishing Co., 1992); Paul Ekman and Richard J. Davidson, *The Nature of Emotion* (New York: Oxford University Press, 1994); Michael Lewis and Jeannette M. Haviland, (eds.), *Handbook of Emotions* (New York: The Guilford Press, 1993); Carroll E. Izard, *The Psychology of Emotions* (New York: Plenum Press, 1991); Keith Oatley and Jennifer M. Jenkins, *Understanding Emotions* (Cambridge, Mass.: Blackwell Publishers, 1996). The last text makes a few references to hatred, but does not try to characterize it. Perhaps one can reconstruct their idea of hatred from the claim that "envy is hatred arising from comparison of oneself with another person" (p. 88). The hostility

in envy, however, differs from the hostility in hatred as, following Aristotle, I construe it here.

51. Izard, *The Psychology of Emotions,* p. 274, Oakley and Jenkins, *Understanding Emotions,* p. 308.

52. Stephan R. Leighton, "Aristotle and the Emotions," in A.O. Rorty (ed.), *Essays on Aristotle's Rhetoric,* pp. 206–37, at p. 232–33 note 14.

53. Cooper, "Rhetoric, Dialectic, and the Passions," p. 193.

54. B. Netanyahu, *The Origins of the Inquisition* (New York: Random House, 1995), p. 990.

55. Ibid., p. 983.

56. J. Ober, *Mass and Elite in Democratic Athens* (Princeton, N.J., Princeton University Press, 1989), p. 221.

57. For this distinction, see Kenneth Dover, *Greek Popular Morality* (Indianapolis: Hackett, 1994), p. 34–35; also, at greater length, Ober, op. cit., p. 141 (the social composition of the Athenian jury was representative of the population at large), and p. 287 (the jurors were not hostile to the idea of personal superiority), and *passim.* His explanation of the suspicion of the nouveaux-riches differs from Aristotle's: "Basic to the topos was the assumption that since they had started with nothing, the newly wealthy politicians must have accrued their wealth dishonestly" (Ober, op. cit., p. 235).

58. Myles Burnyeat, "Aristotle on Learning to be Good," in A. Rorty (ed.), *Essays on Aristotle's Ethics* (New York: Cambridge University Press, 1980), pp. 69–92, at p. 89, note 13; see also Elizabeth S. Belfiore, *Tragic Pleasures* (Princeton University Press, 1992), p. 202 and Douglas L. Cairns, *Aidos: The Psychology and Ethics of Honour and Shame in Ancient Greek Literature* (New York, Oxford University Press, 1993), p. 419.

59. Burnyeat, "Aristotle on learning to be good," p. 78.

60. Cited in Gordon W. Allport, *Prejudice* (Reading, Mass.: Addison-Wesley, 1979), p. 33–34.

61. Daniel Jonah Goldhagen, *Hitler's Willing Executioners* (New York: Alfred A. Knopf, 1996), p. 469.

62. R. Petersen, *Fear, Hatred, Resentment: Delineating Paths to Ethnic Violence in Eastern Europe* (Manuscript, Department of Political Science, Washington University, St. Louis). As an example, he cites the resentment felt towards Jews by the general Lithuanian population during the period of Soviet occupation in 1940–41, when Jews briefly acquired positions of political influence they had never had before.

63. Janice Lindsay-Hartz, Joseph de Rivera, and Michael F. Mascolo, "Differentiating Guilt and Shame and Their Effects on Motivation," in June Price Tangney and Kurt W. Fischer (eds.), *Self-Conscious Emotions* (New York: The Guilford Press, 1995), pp. 274–300, at p. 297.

64. Dover, *Greek Popular Morality,* p. 226.

65. In his discussion of "conscience" Dover, *Greek Popular Morality,* pp. 220–223, by and large agrees that the Greeks did not have our concept of guilt, but also cites "passages which seem to carry a suggestion (perhaps in some cases illusory) that self-respect and the prospect for self-contempt are genuine motives," p. 221.

66. Montaigne, *The Complete Essays,* tr. M.A. Screech (Harmondsworth: Penguin, 1991), p. 1157–58.

67. Pascal, *Pensées* (Ed. Sellier), #520.

68. Bernard Williams, *Shame and Necessity* (Berkeley: University of California Press, 1993), p. 91.

69. Ibid., p. 95.

70. As Williams points out to me, the distinctions, although related, are not quite identical. Aristotle does not, for instance, entertain the idea that the audience before which one feels shame may be oneself.

71. June P. Tangney, "Assessing Individual Differences in Proneness to Shame and Guilt: Development of the Self-Conscious Affect and Attribution Inventory," *Journal of Personality and Social Psychology* 59 (1990), 102–11, refers to these emotions as alpha and beta pride, respectively. Lewis, *Shame,* p. 78–79 refers to them as hybris and pride. Montaigne draws a similar distinction between vainglory and glory in *Essays* II. 17 and II. 16.

72. Dover, *Greek Popular Morality,* p. 232.

73. Peter Walcot, *Envy and the Greeks* (Warminster, England: Aris and Phillips, 1978), pp. 50, 51.

74. A.W.H. Adkins, *Moral Values and Political Behaviour in Ancient Greece* (New York: Norton, 1972), p. 60.

75. See references in note 2 above.

76. David Cohen, *Law, Violence and Community in Classical Athens* (New York: Cambridge University Press, 1995).

77. N.R.E. Fisher, *Hybris* (Warminster, England: Aris and Phillips, 1992).

78. Walcot, *Envy and the Greeks*, p. 64.

79. I take the term "neighborhood envy" from D. Bös, D. and G. Tillman (1985), "An 'envy tax': Theoretical principles and applications to the German surcharge on the rich," *Public Finance/Finances Publiques* 40 (1995), 35–63.

80. David Cohen, *Law, Violence and Community in Classical Athens*, p. 82–83.

81. *Politics* 1315ª 23; see also Cohen, *Law, Violence and Community in Classical Athens*, p. 145 and Fisher, *Hybris*, p. 30–31.

82. Fisher, *Hybris*, p. 509 (summarizing his analyses in earlier chapters notably Ch. XI).

83. Fisher, *Hybris*, p. 57–58.

84. In the "Introduction" to *Grundrisse* (Harmondsworth: Penguin, 1973).

85. Seneca, *On Anger,* II. xxiii.

86. La Rochefoucauld, *Maxims* #102. See *Alchemies of the Mind,* Ch. II. 3 for a fuller discussion.

Jon Elster is the Robert K. Merton Professor of Social Science at Columbia University. He has also taught at the University of Chicago, and divides his time between New York, Norway, and France. Professor Elster describes himself as a "methodological individualist," and his various writings have made substantial contributions to contemporary economics and political theory from the perspective of a social scientist.

His numerous books include *Ulysses and the Sirens* (1979), *Making Sense of Marx* (1985), *The Cement of Society* (1989), *Political Psychology* (1993), *Alchemies of the Mind* (1999), and (as editor) *Local Justice in America* (1995). Three previous articles by Professor Elster have appeared in *The Great Ideas Today:* "Egonomics: The Economics of Personal Conflict" (1993), "The Psychology of Tocqueville's *Democracy in America*" (1994), and "Montaigne's Psychology" (1996).

On Discovery,
The Value of Poetry,
and
The Healing Power
of Nature

Diane Ackerman

On Discovery

When I read of the just-discovered *Symbion pandora,* a radically new life-form that's pinpoint small, trisexual (it will try anything), and lives on the lips of lobsters, my first thought was: Do lobsters have lips? But that was quickly followed by a renewed sense of wonder at the quirky fantasia of life on earth. With a mouth like a hairy wheel, and other anatomical oddities, pandora is so outlandish that a special phylum was created for it— *Cycliophora,* of which *pandora* is the sole member.

I must admit, I get a devilish delight when the miraculous appears right under my nose. After all, the marvelous is a weed species. One can glimpse it on one's doorstep. People often ask me where they might go to find adventure. Adventure is not something you must travel to find, I tell them, it's something you take with you. The astonishing can turn up in the leaf clutter, or even at a neighborhood restaurant, in a dingy tank, on the lips of lobsters.

We forget that the world is always more and stranger than we guess. Or can guess. Instead, we search for simple answers, simple laws of nature, in a sleight of mind that makes us uniquely human. Just as we're addicted to rules, home-truths, and slogans, we're addicted to certain ways of explaining things. There's bound to be a simple answer to everything, we insist. Maybe not. Maybe complexity frightens us. Maybe we fear becoming as plural as all we survey. Maybe we still tacitly believe that the universe was created for our pleasure, that we pint-sized demigods are its sole audience and goal. Then something like *pandora* turns up, a minute being with a sex life even stranger than our own, a creature that breaks all the rules and gives biologists a jolt.

Because we have swarmed across the world with our curious and agile minds, we sometimes think that nature had been fully explored, but that's far from true. Plants and animals are going extinct at an appalling rate— some estimates are as high as 300 species a day—and many of them are vanishing mysteries. The riches of the natural world are slipping through our fingers before we can even call them by name. Hanging on by a suction cup, and reaching around to vacuum up fallen morsels from a dining lobster's lips, *pandora* reminds us that we share our planet with unseen hordes, and it hints at the uniqueness of our own complex niche.

Recently, a graduate student strolling through the woods happened upon a fungus in a curious state of arousal. Odder still, it was sprouting behind the head of a beetle grub. Intrigued, she took it to a laboratory, studied it carefully, asked the right questions, and soon realized that she had made an astounding discovery: a sexual form of *Cordyceps subsessilis,* a mold that produces cyclosporin, an immunosuppressant used to combat organ rejection. We know the tropics contain a rich pharmacopeia, but for many organisms our backyards are still unexplored, too.

(Overleaf) "Most people find nature restorative, cleansing, nourishing in a deeply personal way."

Variety is the pledge that matter makes to living things. Think of a niche and life will fill it, think of a shape and life will explore it, think of a drama and life will stage it. I personally find pampas grass an unlikely configuration of matter, but no stranger than we humans, the lonely bipeds with the giant dreams.

At the heart of the word "discovery" is a boomerang. It literally means to uncover something that's hidden from view. But what really happens is a change in the viewer. The familiar offers a comfort few can resist, and fewer still want to disturb. But as relatively recent inventions such as the telescope and microscope have taught us, the unknown has many layers. Every truth has geological strata, and for some truths the opposite may be equally true (for example, you can't have an orthodoxy without a heresy).

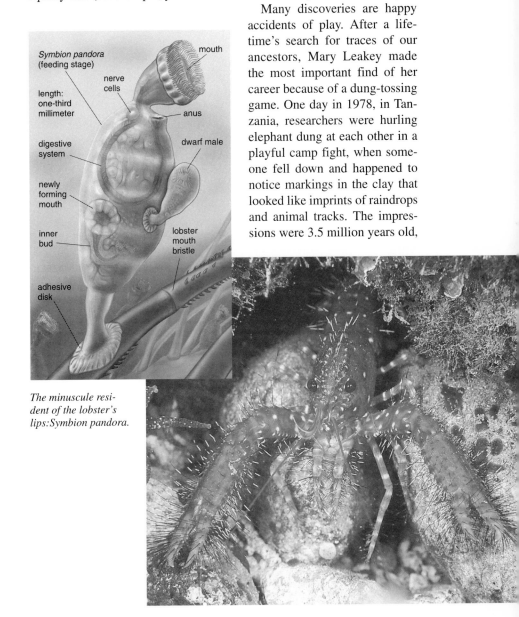

Symbion pandora (feeding stage)

length: one-third millimeter

nerve cells

mouth

anus

digestive system

dwarf male

newly forming mouth

inner bud

lobster mouth bristle

adhesive disk

The minuscule resident of the lobster's lips: Symbion pandora.

Many discoveries are happy accidents of play. After a lifetime's search for traces of our ancestors, Mary Leakey made the most important find of her career because of a dung-tossing game. One day in 1978, in Tanzania, researchers were hurling elephant dung at each other in a playful camp fight, when someone fell down and happened to notice markings in the clay that looked like imprints of raindrops and animal tracks. The impressions were 3.5 million years old,

and preserved in hardened ash that had eroded over the years. Only partial tracks were visible, so it was difficult to tell what left them. In time, Mary Leakey uncovered a trail of footprints left by three humans—male, female, and child—that led across the volcanic plain. As the footprints clearly showed, the female paused at one point and turned to her left. The child's footprints sometimes dawdled behind those of the adults and sometimes overlapped; the child may have been stepping in its parents' footprints on purpose, a game children still play. Mary Leakey was profoundly moved by possibly our earliest glimpse of human behavior: the female's pausing to turn. "This motion, so intensely human, transcends time," she wrote in National Geographic. "A remote ancestor—just as you or I—experienced a moment of doubt." Or of discovery. Perhaps the female heard a relative call, or sensed a dangerous predator. Volcanoes spurted ash onto those plains; she may have been monitoring a threatening plume in the distance. Maybe she was simply enjoying the scenery—the changing stir of sun and shadow, a whiff of newly risen plants, an unusual land animal or bird taking flight—as she strolled happily with her mate and child. We know her life made relentless physical and emotional demands, as ours does, and she felt the basic emotions we do. She would have enjoyed family comforts; she would have feared; she would have played; she would have been curious about the world.

The moment a newborn opens its eyes, discovery begins. I learned this with a laugh one morning in New Mexico, where I worked through the seasons of a large cattle ranch. One day, I delivered a calf. When it lifted up its fluffy head and looked at me, its eyes held the absolute bewilderment of the newly born. A moment before it had enjoyed the even black nowhere of the womb, and suddenly its world was full of color, movement, and noise. I've never seen anything so shocked to be alive. Discoverers keep some of that initial sense of surprise lifelong, and yearn to behold even more marvels. Trapped in the palatial rut of our senses, we invent mechanical extensions for them, and with each new attachment more of the universe becomes available. Some of the richest moments in people's lives have come from playing with a mental box full of numbers or ideas, rotating it, shaking it, while the hours slip by, until at last the box begins to rattle and a revelation spills out. And then there are those awkward psychological mysteries. I suspect human nature will always be like mercury, a puzzle to grasp. No matter how much of the physical universe we fathom, what makes us quintessentially human eludes us to some degree, because it's impossible for a system to observe itself with much objectivity. When it comes to powerful emotions such as love, for instance, each couple rediscovers it, each generation redefines it. Of course, that makes studying human nature all the more sporting.

(Left) The trail of hominid footprints found by Mary Leakey's team in Laetoli, Tanzania.

I rarely dwell on this when I go biking through the countryside each day. I don't worry about the mites that live among my eyelashes either. I have other fish to fry: the local land trust's campaign for acreage, the plight of endangered animals and landscapes, what will become of the residents of a local psychiatric institution who were kicked out because of recent state cutbacks, not to mention all the normal mayhems of the heart. But I get a crazy smile when I think of *pandora.* I like knowing the world will never be small enough to exhaust in one lifetime. No matter how hard or where we look, even under our own or a lobster's nose, surprise awaits us. There will always be plenty of nature's secrets waiting to be told. This is one of those tidy, simple-sounding truths I mentioned, the sort of thing humans crave. And I believe it because I got it straight from a lobster's lips.

The Value of Poetry (How Artists Play)

All language is poetry. Each word is a small story, a thicket of meaning. We ignore the picturesque origins of words when we utter them; conversation would grind to a halt if we visualized flamingos whenever someone referred to a *flight* of stairs. But words are powerful mental tools invented through play. We clarify life's confusing blur with words. We cage flooding emotions with words. We coax elusive memories with words. We educate with words. We don't really know what we think, how we feel, what we want, or even who we are until we struggle "to find the right words." What do those words consist of? Submerged metaphors, images, actions, personalities, jokes. Seeing themselves reflected in one another's eyes, the Romans coined the word *pupil,* which meant "little doll." Orchids take their name from the Greek word for testicles. Pansy derives from the French word *pensée,* or "thought," because the flower semed to have such a pensive face. "Bless" originally meant to redden with blood, as in sacrifice. Hence "God bless you" literally means "God bathe you in blood."

We inhabit a deeply-imagined world that exists alongside the real physical world. Even the crudest utterance, or the simplest, contains the fundamental poetry by which we live. This mind fabric, woven of images and illusions, shields us. In a sense, or rather in all senses, it's a shock absorber. As harsh as life seems to us now, it would feel even worse— hopelessly, irredeemably harsh—if we didn't veil it, order it, relate familiar things, create mental cushions. One of the most surprising facts about human beings is that we seem to require a poetic version of life. It's not just that some of us enjoy reading or writing poetry, or that many people wax poetic in emotional situations, but that all human beings of all ages in all cultures all over the world automatically tell their story in a poetic way, using the elemental poetry concealed in everyday language to solve problems, communicate desires and needs, even talk to themselves. When people invent new words, they do so playfully, poetically—computers have *viruses,* one can *surf* the internet, a naive person is *clueless.* In time, people forget the etymology or choose to disregard it. A plumber says he'll use a gasket on a leaky pipe, without considering that the word comes from *garçonette,* the Old French word for a little girl with her hymen intact. We dine at chic restaurants from porcelain dinner plates, without realizing that when smooth, glistening *porcelain* was invented in France long ago, someone with a sense of humor thought it looked as smooth as the vulva of a pig, which is indeed what *porcelain* means. When we stand by our scruples we don't think of our feet, but the word comes from the Latin *scrupulus,* a tiny stone that was the smallest unit of weight. Thus a scrupulous person is so sensitive he's irritated by the smallest stone in his shoe. For the most part, we are all unwitting poets.

Just as the world of play exists outside of ordinary life, the poetic world of humans exists within—but separate from—ordinary reality. So play lives at two removes from the real world (whatever that is), except when we play through the artform we call poetry. Then we stare straight at our inherently poetic version of life, make it even more vigorous and resourceful. Poetry speaks to everyone, but it cries out to people in the throes of vertiginous passions, or people grappling with knotty emotions, or people trying to construe the mysteries of existence. At a stage of life remarkable for its idealism, sensitivity, and emotional turbulence, students tend to respond for all three reasons.

Sometimes when I pass a basketball court I'm transported, thanks to the flying carpet of memory, back to my first real teaching job in the early eighties. At the University of Pittsburgh, I taught various undergraduate writing and literature courses, but I remember most dearly the graduate poets I taught. Not much older than most of them, younger than a few, I found their blue-collar enthusiasms a tonic. All the elements of their lives breathed with equal intensity. They played as hard as they worked as hard as they loved as hard as they wrote. It was typical of them to discuss Proust in the stands before a hockey game. They also bought poetry, read poetry, wrote poetry in the seams between work and family, met at a bar after class to drink Iron City beer and continue talking about poetry.

After class one evening, we all went to a nearby basketball court so that one of the students could teach us "fade away jump shots," an image he had used beautifully in a poem. Sometimes I went with them to the Pitt Tavern after class, where we would continue talking late into the night. With an unselfconscious fervor that amazed me then, and in retrospect still does, they demanded to be well-taught. My job was to keep pace with their needs. I had no choice but to teach them everything I knew, learn with fresh energy, then teach them even more if I could.

At the end of one semester, in the closing hour of the final seminar, I asked if there were anything we hadn't talked about that needed to be addressed. One of the best writers raised his hand. "How to make love stay," he said simply. For the remaining hour, that is what we discussed. As I write this, I can see his soulful face. Smart, romantic, unpredictable—he was all poet. Even now, a dozen years later, I worry about him, hope he survived the intensity he craved but could not live with. I hope he continued writing. I see the faces of the others, too, and wonder how they've fared. Although I could not tell them so at the time, I knew where some of their emotional travels might lead them. They were intense young poets. In vital ways, we were similar. I had already endured some of the struggles they were yet to face, and we shared a common currency—we understood the value of poetry.

When I was a freshman at Boston University in the late sixties, I used to stroll beside the Charles River with a copy of Dylan Thomas's poems in one pocket and Wallace Stevens's in another. I was drawn to the sensuous rigor of Thomas and the voluptuous mind of Stevens. Together they opened the door for me into a realm of ideas, song, word play, idea play, discovery, and passion. What I loved about Thomas (and still do) is the way his poems provide a fluid mosaic in which anything can lose its identity in the identities of other things (because, after all, the world is mainly a "rumpus of shapes"). By mixing language and category with a free hand, he seems to know the intricate feel of life as it might come to a drunk, or a deer, or a devout astronomer freezing to death at his telescope. His poems throb with an acute physical reality. No poet gives a greater sense of the *feel of life*.

Then he goes even further, to recreate the *process* of life through a whole register of intricate and almost touchable images and events. Working himself into a state of neighborly reverence, he invents metaphors that don't so much combine A and B as trail A and B through a slush of other phenomena. He ardently weds himself to life's sexy, sweaty, chaotic, weepy, prayerful, nostalgic, belligerent, crushing, confused vitality in as many of its forms as he can find, in a frenzy that becomes a homage to Creation. In this way, he seems to create a personal physics to match his ideas, so that the language of his best poems echoes the subject matter, and both suggest the behavior deep in our brains, hearts, and cells. He really does nibble the oat in the bread he breaks, intuit the monkey in the newborn baby, see the shroudmaker in the surgeon sewing up after an operation.

Sometimes he's cryptic ("Foster the light nor veil the manshaped moon"), sometimes a clear-eyed observer ("the mousing cat stepping shy, / The puffed birds hopping and hunting"), sometimes lyrically emphatic ("The hand that signed the paper felled a city"). Sometimes he's a maker of schoolboy jokes, sometimes a celebrant seer. But, above all, he can transform the Saturday afternoon reputation of the planet—a couple of imposing-sounding topics, its being called a "star," the pyramids, Jesus, Adam, illness, birth, death, sex—into something sacramental. Not neat. Not well-behaved. Not explicit. Not always argued or even structured. But bold, wild, and tenderly voluptuous. How could I resist all that?

Other poets took my fancy, too. I loved the way poets illuminated life like a holy text, drawing my attention to how dreams were made, and to the beauty at the heart of the most commonplace dramas and things. Poetry had a way of lifting a feeling or idea out of its routine so that it could be appreciated with fresh eyes. In "the foul rag and bone shop of the heart," as William Butler Yeats called it, I knew poetry had everything to teach me about life.

Poetry was all I knew to write at eighteen. Much has happened in my writerly life since then. Although I still write poetry, I've learned to write prose, too, and that brought its own frustrations and freedoms. In both genres, writing is my form of celebration and prayer, but it's also the way in which I inquire about the world, sometimes writing about nature, sometimes about human nature. I always try to give myself to whatever I'm writing about, with as much affectionate curiosity as I can muster, in order to understand a little better what being human is, and what it was like to have once been alive on the planet, how it felt in one's senses, passions and contemplations. In that sense, I use art as an instrument to unearth shards of truth. Writing is also the avenue that most often leads me to deep play.

These days, I do that more often in prose. But the real source of my creativity continues to be poetry. I've just finished a new collection. I love to read books of poetry. My prose often contains what are essentially prose-poems. Why does poetry play such an important role in my life? For centuries, poetry was vital to the life of nearly everyone. In the 19th century, poets such as Byron and Tennyson were superstars of Hollywood status. Movies and television may draw more viewers now, but poetry continues to inspire us, reveal us to one another, and teach us important truths about being human.

The reason is simple: Poetry reflects the heart and soul of a people. There is nothing like poetry to throw light into the dark corners of existence and make life's runaway locomotive slow down for a moment so that it can be enjoyed. Science and technology explain much of our world. Psychology tells us more about human behavior; all three succeed by following orderly rules and theories. Poetry offers truths based on intuition, a keen eye, and the tumultuous experiences of the poet. Long ago in India, for example, Urdu poets writing in the verse form known as a *ghazal* were also trying to figure out the universe. A ghazal was the technology they used to make sense of their world, and no doubt they felt as sonneteers and composers of villanelles do, that there are truths only to be learned when you're dancing in chains.

The craft of writing poetry is a monklike occupation, as is a watchmaker's, tilting tiny cogs and wheels into place. It's ironic that poets use words to convey what lies beyond words. But poetry becomes most powerful where language fails. How can we express in words that are human-made emotions that aren't? How can we express all the dramas and feelings that are wordless, where language has no purchase? Words are small shapes in the gorgeous chaos of the world. But they *are* shapes, they bring the world to focus, they corral ideas, they hone thoughts, they paint watercolors of perception. Truman Capote's *In Cold Blood* chronicles the drama of two murderers who collaborated on a particularly nasty crime. A criminal psychologist, trying to explain the event, observed that neither one of them would have been capable of the crime, but together they formed a third person who was able to kill. Metaphors, though more benign, work in the same way. The chemical term for what happens is *hypergolic:* You can take two inert substances, put them together and produce something powerfully different (table salt), even explosive (nitroglycerine). The charm of language is that, though it's human-made, it can on rare occasions capture emotions and sensations which aren't.

The best poems are rich with observational truths. Above all, we ask the poet to teach us a way of seeing, lest one spend a lifetime on this planet without noticing how green light sometimes flares up as the setting sun rolls under.

When a friend and I were cycling the other day, she mentioned that reading poetry frightens her.

"What if I don't get the real meaning?" she asked. "What if I read 'a ghostly galleon' and think it's referring to a ship, when it's really referring to the lost innocence of America?" I was dumbfounded. Someone had taught her (and nearly everyone else) that poems work like safes—crack the code and the safe opens to reveal its treasure.

"There are many ways to read a poem," I said, "After all, you don't really know what was going through the poet's mind. Suppose he was having a tempestuous affair with a neighbor, and once when they were alone he told her that her hips were like a *ghostly galleon.* He might then have used the image in a poem he was writing because it fit well, but also as a sly flirtation with his neighbor, whose hips would be secretly commemorated in verse."

"Do poets do that?" she asked, slightly scandalized that noble thoughts might be tinged with the profane.

"I've done it," I admitted with a grin. "I presume other poets do."

I went on to explain, as teachers of the writerly arts do, that poems dance with many veils. Read a poem briskly, and it will speak to you briskly. Delve, and it will give you rich ore to contemplate. Each time you look, a new scintillation may appear, one you missed before.

The apparent subject of a poem isn't always an end in itself. It may really be an opportunity, a way for the poet to reach into herself and haul up whatever nugget of the human condition distracts her at the moment, something that can't be reached in any other way. It's a kind of catapult into another metaphysical country where one has longer conceptual arms. The poet reminds us that life's seductive habits of thought and sight can be broken at will. We ask the poet to shepherd us telescopically and microscopically through many perspectives, to lead us like a mountain goat through the hidden, multi-dimensionality of almost everything.

We expect the poet to know about a lot of strange things, to babysit for us, to help us relocate emotionally, to act as a messenger in affairs of the heart, to provide us with an intellectual calling card, to rehearse death, or map escape routes. As many have pointed out, poetry is a kind of knowing, a way of looking at the ordinary until it becomes special and the exceptional until it becomes commonplace. It both amplifies and reduces experience, paradoxical though that may sound. It can shrink an event teeming with disorder to the rigorous pungency of an epigram. It can elasticize one's perspective until, to use an image of John Donne's, a drop of blood sucked by a single flea accommodates the entire world of two lovers. Few views of life are as panoramic as the one seen through John Milton's cosmological eye. Milton could write "All Hell broke loose" because he knew where (and what) Hell was; he had sent his wife and daughters there often enough, and his vision encompassed it, just as it did the constellations (many of which he introduces into *Paradise Lost*). He could write "Orion rose arm'd" because he'd observed Orion often enough when the arms weren't visible.

Poetry, like all imaginative writing, is a kind of attentiveness that permits one both the organized adventure of the nomad and the armchair security of the bank-teller. Poetry reminds us of the truths about life and human nature that we knew all along, but forgot somehow because they weren't yet in memorable language.

If a poet describes a panther's cage in a certain vivid way, that cage will be as real a fact as the sun. A poem knows more about human nature than its writer does, because a poem is often a camera, a logbook, an annal, not an interpreter. A poem may know the subtlest elisions of feeling, the earliest signs of some pattern or discord. A book of poems chronicles the poet's many selves, and as such knows more about the poet than the poet does at any given time, including the time when the book is finished and yet another self holds her book of previous selves in her hands. A poem knows a great deal about our mental habits, and about upheaval and discovery, loneliness and despair. And it knows the handrails a mind clings to in times of stress. A poem tells us about the subtleties of mood for which we have no labels. The voluptuousness of waiting, for instance: how one's whole body can rock from the heavy pounding of the heart. It knows extremes of consciousness, knows what the landscape of imagination looks like when the mind is at full-throttle, or beclouded, or cyclone-torn. Most of all, it tells us about our human need to make treaties. Often a poem is where an emotional or metaphysical truce takes place. Time slow-gaits enough in the hewing of the poem to make a treaty that will endure, in print, until the poet disowns it, perhaps in a second treaty in the form of a poem. There is even a technical term for that: a "palinode." A poem knows about illusion and magic, how to glorify what is not glorious, how to bankrupt what is. It displays, in its alchemy of mind, the transmuting of the commonplace into golden saliences. A poem records emotions and moods that lie beyond normal language, that can only be patched together and hinted at metaphorically. It knows about spunk, zealousness, obstinacy, and deliverance. It *accretes* life, which is why different people can read differ- ent things in the same poem. It freezes life, too, yanks a bit out of life's turbulent stream, and holds it up squirming for view, framed by the white margins of the page. Poetry is an act of distillation. It takes contingency samples, is selective. It telescopes time. It focusses what most often floods past us in a polite blur.

We read poems in part, I think, because they are an elegant, persuasive form of reasoning, one that can glorify a human condition feared to be meaningless, a universe feared to be "an unloving crock of shit," as philos- opher Henry Finch once said off-handedly. To make physical the mystery is in some sense to domesticate it. We ask the poet to take what surpasses our understanding and force it into the straitjacket of language, to rinse the incomprehensible as free of telltale ambiguity and absurdity as possible. That's not to say that we don't find nature ambiguous or life absurd, only that the temptation to play and land the mystery like a slippery salmon, to freeze it in vocabularic aspic, is irresistible. Surely this is not far from the hunting magic of the cave drawings at Lascaux.

We ask the poet to reassure us by giving us a geometry of living in which all things add up and cohere, to tell us how things buttress one another, circle round and intermelt. Once the poet has broken life into shards, we ask him to spin around and piece it back together again, making life seem even more fluid than before. Now it is a fluency of particulars instead of a nebulous surging. We ask the poet to compress and abbreviate the chaos, so we don't overload from its waterfall of sensations, all of which we nonethe- less wish somehow to take in.

Like surgeons, mathematicians, composers, and physicists, poets seem to do their best work when they're young. Once, after a lecture, a woman asked why accomplished scientists and prose writers (such as Loren Eise- ley), who turned to poetry late in life, were such poor poets. Is it easier to switch from poetry to prose than from prose to poetry? she wondered. I don't think the genre is what matters, but the time of life. If you read the first book by famous scientists—J.B.S. Haldane, Werner Heisenberg, Fran- cis Crick, Fred Hoyle—you find a mind full of passion and wonder. Those books are thrilling to read because mystery is alive in them. But in later books these same people become obsessed with politics and sociology; their books are still of intellectual interest, but they've lost the sense of marvel. It may be that young surgeons are at the height of their careers for the same reason—not because of their reflexes, eyesight, fresh knowledge, or youthful skills—but because they're at a stage of life when enthusiasm flows freely, a stage when people most often write poetry. "Every child is an artist," Pablo Picasso observed. "The problem is how to remain an artist once he grows up." Those who stay poets all of their lives continue to live in that early state, as open and vulnerable and potentially damaging as it can be.

I suppose what most people associate with poetry is soul-searching and fiercely-felt emotions. We expect the poet to be a monger of intensity, to feel for us, to reach into the campfire so that we can linger in the woods and watch without burning ourselves or grubbying up our clothes. Then, even if we don't feel the fire, we can see the poet's face illuminated by light, hear her flushed chatter, the blazing wood crackle, and imagine well enough what the fire feels like from our safe remove. Though one can't live at red-alert from day to day, we expect the poet to, on our behalf, and to share that intensity with us when we're in the right mood. And if we become frightened or bored, we can simply put the poem back on the shelf. Really, we are asking the poet to live an extravagantly emotional life for us, so we can add her experiences to our own.

Because poets feel what we're afraid to feel, venture where we're reluctant to go, we learn from their journeys without taking the same dramatic risks. We cherish the insights that poets discover: We'd love to relish the moment and feel rampant amazement as the seasons unfold. We yearn to explore the subtleties, paradoxes, and edges of emotions. We long to see the human condition reveal itself with spellbinding clarity. Think of all the lessons to be learned from deep rapture, danger, tumult, romance, intuition—but it's far too exhausting to live like that on a daily basis, so we ask artists to feel and explore for us. Daring to take intellectual and emotional chances, poets live on their senses. In promoting a fight of his, a boxer once said: "I'm in the hurt business." In a different way, poets are too.

And yet, through their eyes—perhaps because they risk so much—we discover breath-taking views of the human pageant. Borrowing the lens of a poet's sensibility, we see the world in a richer way—more familiar than we thought, and stranger than we knew, a world laced with wonder. Sometimes we need to be taught how and where to seek wonder, but it's always there, waiting, full of mystery and magic. Much of my own duty as a poet is to open those doors of vision, shine light into those dark corners of existence, and search for fountains of innocence.

The poet Heinrich Heine once said: "Life is the best teacher, but the tuition is high." So true. That's why it's important to find time for poetry. Poetry is an education in life. It's also an act of pure play. As Huizinga points out, to call poetry "a playing with words and language is no metaphor: it is the precise and literal truth." Every poem is a game, a ritual dance with words. In the separate world of the artwork, the artist moves in a waking trance. According to Freud, a lot of play is projection, in which bad motives and feelings may be attributed to others, conflicts may be re-enacted in order to master them, and fantasies and wishes may be fulfilled. The same is true of many artworks. By its nature, all art is ceremonial, which we sometimes forget, except perhaps when we think of the Neolithic cave painters in the *mysterium tremens* of their task. Intent on one feature of life, exploring it mentally, developing it in words, pigments, or sounds, an artist follows the rules of the game. Sometimes artists change the game, impose their own rules and disavow everyone else's.

Whatever artform one chooses, whatever materials and ideas, the creative siege is the same. One always finds rules, always tremendous concentration, entrancement and exaltation, always the tension of spontaneity caged by restriction, always risk of failure and humiliation, always the drumbeat of rituals, always the willingness to be shaken to the core, always an urgent need to stain the willows with a glance. For me this becomes most personal in poetry.

A poem is a ceremony. It teaches us a way of seeing and feeling, lest we spend a lifetime on this planet without noticing the unfurling of a dogwood blossom, the gauzy spread of the Milky Way on a star-loaded summer night, or the translucent green of a dragonfly's wings. A ceremony refuses to let things merge, lie low, succumb to habit. It hoists events from their routine, plays with them a while, and lays them out in the sunshine for us to celebrate and savor.

The Healing Power of Nature

When summer blows through the willows, I love to ramble in an open field near my house, where Queen Anne's lace flutters like doilies beside purple coneflowers. Although I've never harvested the carrot-like roots of Queen Anne's lace, I have taken essence of coneflower (*echinacea*) as a tonic to keep colds at bay. Many people practice such homeopathy— swallowing minute amounts of herbs as curatives for an assortment of ills—and in a sense that's what most of us do, psychologically, when we go out into nature. We drink briefly from its miracle waters. We inoculate ourselves against the aridity of a routine, workaday life.

When we spend most of our lives indoors, what becomes of our own wilderness? Safe and dry in our homes, clean and well-lit, at arm's length from the weedy chaos outside, no longer prey to weather and wild, we can lose our inner compass. Nearly two years ago, for instance, when I first broke my foot, it took a year and a half, four months in a wheelchair, and finally a bonegraft and titanium screw to heal. For an active person, being so helpless and limited is a nightmare. But the hardest thing about that injury was how it separated me from nature, whose green anthem stirs me, whose moods fascinate me, whose rocks and birds help define my sense of belonging, whose mysteries provide me with rich moments of deep play. Even if I'm feeling low, I can always find solace in nature, a restorative when dealing with pain. Wonder heals through an alchemy of mind. But, exiled from Paradise, where could I turn? Once knitted into nature, I felt myself slowly unraveling. Standing upright may be our hallmark and a towering success, but sometimes bone, joint, and spine can't live up to the challenge and act subversive. A house of bones, the Elizabethans called the body. Imprisoned by my need to heal, I craved the outdoors. To heal I needed to rest, lie low, shelve things, restrict myself, be willing to sacrifice pleasure for recovery. But I only managed it with grace when I rented an electric scooter, climbed aboard, and crept out into the sunlight and among the birds and trees for an hour or so each day. I also had friends drive me out into the country. Those doses of sunlight and wildlife were my salvation. Even a small park or yard can be wilderness enough.

For the most part, when we go to psychologists, we don't discuss how divorced we feel from nature, how destructive that can be, or the tonic value of reacquainting ourselves with nature's charms, the charms we fell in love with when we were children, when nature was a kingdom of wonder, play, self-discovery, and freedom. A special loneliness comes from exiling ourselves from nature. But even my saying that will strike many people as a romantic affectation. After all, we are civilized now, we don't play by nature's rules anymore, we control our own destiny, we don't need nature, right? That attitude is so deeply ingrained in our culture that most people take it for granted, assume it's a given, and don't worry about nature when they consider improving the important relationships in their lives. It's a tragic oversight, but I can understand why the attitude is so appealing. Nature is crude and erotic, chaotic and profuse, rampant and zealous, brutal and violent, uncontrollable despite our best efforts, and completely unin-

"Our human habitat encompasses rolling veldts and mown lawns, remote deserts...all 'natural' eco-systems."

hibited. Small wonder the natural world terrifies many people and also embarrasses the prim Puritans among us. But most people find nature restorative, cleansing, nourishing in a deeply personal way. To have peak experiences, mystics, prophets, and naturalists have travelled into the wilderness.

Wild is what we call it, a word tottering between fear and praise. Wild ideas are alluring, impulsive, unpredictable, ideas with wings and hooves. Being with wild animals—whether they're squirrels in the backyard, or heavily-antlered elk in Yellowstone—reminds us of our own wildness, thrills the animal part of us that loves the feel of sunlight and the succulence of fresh water, is alert to danger and soothed by the familiar sounds of family and herd. It's sad we don't respect the struggles and talents of other animals, but I'm more concerned about the price we pay for that haughtiness. We've evolved to live tribally in a kingdom of neighbors, human neighbors and animal neighbors.

When I'm in a rain forest I caress it with all my senses, and am grateful for the privilege, but I also love temperate forests, scrublands, lake shores, glaciers, even city parks. One doesn't have to leave home to encounter the exotic. Our human habitat encompasses rolling veldts and mown lawns, remote deserts and the greater wilderness of cities—all "natural" ecosystems. Many animals inhabit the small patch of woods in my backyard, for example, from deer, raccoons, skunks, wild turkeys, garter snakes, and other large fauna down to spiders, moths, and swarming insects. The animals all seem busy, feeding themselves and their families, running one urgent errand or another. Their behaviors remind us of our own, their triumphs teach us about the indomitableness of life.

Although I've had the privilege of travelling the world to behold some fascinating animals and landscapes, one needn't go to the ends of the earth to find an abundance of life, or to feel connected to nature through deep play. I felt rapture recently while riding a bike along a country road just as a red-tailed hawk flew very low overhead, showing me the brown-and-white speckled bloomers of its legs and a bright red tail through which the sun shone as through stained glass. We're lucky to be alive at a time when whales still swim in the oceans, and hawks fly through the skies. One day, through our negligence, they may be gone.

There are noble reasons for protecting the environment—one might argue that it's our moral duty, as good citizens of the planet, not to destroy its natural wonders. There are also mercenary reasons—the vanishing rainforests contain pharmaceuticals we might need; the Antarctic holds a vast store of fresh drinking water; thick forests insure that we'll have oxygen to breathe. But another reason is older and less tangible, a matter of ecopsychology. We need a healthy, thriving, bustling natural world so that *we* can be healthy, so that *we* can feel whole. Our word "whole" comes from the same ancient root as "holy." It was one of the first concepts that human beings needed to express, and it meant the healthy interrelatedness of all things. "Mother Earth," we often call the planet. If earth *is* our mother, then we have many siblings among the other animals, many rooms in our home.

"We need a healthy, thriving, bustling natural world so that we can be healthy, so that we can feel whole."

Most of the time we forget that simple truth and even pretend we could live outside of nature, that nature doesn't include us.

We really are terribly confused about our relationship with nature. On the one hand, we like to live in houses that are tidy and clean, and if nature should be rude enough to enter—in the form of a bat in the attic, or a mouse in the kitchen, or a cockroach crawling along the skirting boards—we stalk it with the blood-lust of a tabby-cat; we resort to chemical warfare. We don't even like dust around us. In fact, we judge people harshly if their house is full of dust and dirt. And yet, on the other hand, we just as obsessively bring nature indoors. We touch a switch and light floods the room. We turn a dial and suddenly it feels like summer or winter. We live in a perpetual breeze or bake of our devising. We buy posters and calendars with photographs of nature. We hang paintings of landscapes on our walls.

We scent everything that touches our lives. We fill our houses with flowers and pets. We try hard to remove ourselves from all the dramas and sensations of nature, and yet without them we feel lost and disconnected. So, subconsciously, we bring them right back indoors again. Then we obsessively visit nature—we go swimming, jogging, or cross-country skiing, we take strolls in a park. Confusing, isn't it?

Sometimes it's hard for us collectors of such rarities as paintings, buttons, china, or fossils, to understand that we ourselves are rare. We are unique lifeforms not because of our numbers, but because of the unlikeliness of our being here at all, the pace of our evolution, our powerful grip on the whole planet, and the precariousness of our future. We are evolutionary whizz-kids who are better able to transform the world than to understand it. Other animals cannot evolve fast enough to cope with us. If we destroy their future, we may lose our own. But because vast herds of humans dwell on the planet, we assume we are invulnerable. Because our cunning has allowed us to harness great rivers, and fly through the sky, and even add our artifacts to the sum of creation, we assume we are omnipotent. Because we have invented an arbitrary way to frame the doings of nature, which we call "time," we assume our species will last forever. But that may not be true.

Off and on over the past few years, I've been working with endangered animals and ecosystems, which has kindled precious moments of deep play. But, as part of the species responsible for their downfall, I also feel an urgent need to witness and celebrate them before they vanish. There are little-known species alive among us right now, which have lived on the planet for millions of years longer than we have but will perish without our noticing, without our chronicling their ways and habits. I find that thought unbearable.

Playing in nature rejuvenates the spirit while deepening insight. One can learn there, as Heraclitus did, that "conflict is common to all, and strife is

"One doesn't have to leave home to encounter the exotic."

justice, and that all things come into being and pass away through strife." One can achieve a stance that minimizes the finite self in the vast sprawl of the universe, and identifies with unseen forces supreme in power and reality, exalted and mysterious, yet completely non-rational. As many artists have found, nature is an ideal place for creative play. Among the Kwakiutl Indians, a song-maker (also known as "a man of understanding") and a "word-passer" compose music in the woods. Sometimes a novice musician (known as "sitting-close-beside-the-head") joins them. Here is a typical account of an improvisatory song-making circle in the woods, which a Kwakiutl Indian told an ethnologist in 1915:

> The song-maker draws inspiration chiefly from the sounds of running or dropping water, and from the notes of birds. Sitting beside a rill of falling water, he listens intently, catches the music, and hums it to himself, using not words but the vocables *hamamama*. This is his theme. Then he carries the theme further, making variations, and at last he adds a finale which he calls the "tail." After a while he goes to the word-passer, constantly humming the tune, and the word-passer, catching the air, joins in, and then sets a single word to it. This is called "tying the song," so that it may not "drift away" like an unmoored canoe. Then gradually other words are added, until the song is complete. The novice sits a little apart from the

master, and if he "finds" a melody, he "carries" it at once to the song-maker, who quickly catches the theme and proceeds to develop it. Many songs are obtained from the robin, some from the waterfowl which whistles before diving, and from other birds. An informant saw a song-maker, after employing various themes, coil a rope and then compose a song representing it. On a certain occasion when the singers were practicing new songs in the woods, the song-maker lacked one to complete the number, and he asked the others if they had a song. The other composers present said they had none. One of them looked across at a visiting woman song-maker and said to the presiding song-maker, "I will ask her." She heard the phrase, caught the inflection of the rising and falling syllables, and began to sing *hamamama*. As the sound left her lips, those on the opposite side of the circle heard it and at once began to hum, and together they composed the necessary song. This manner of catching a melody is called "scooping it up in the hands."

Karl von Frisch, the zoologist, once described his study of the honeybee (which he adored) as a magic well which replenishes itself endlessly. The same is true for any facet of nature. However much water you draw from it, you always find more waiting for you. Lose yourself in its miracle waters and time will shimmy, the world recede, and a sense of harmony enter your bones. It is fall in North America. The well of nature is full today. Time to go outside and take a drink.

Diane Ackerman, poet, essayist, and naturalist, was born in Waukegan, Illinois. She received an M.A., M.F.A., and Ph.D. from Cornell University. Her works of nonfiction include, *On Extended Wing* (1987), the best-seller *A Natural History of the Senses* (1990), *The Moon by Whale Light, and Other Adventures among Bats, Crocodilians, Penguins, and Whales* (1992), *The Rarest of the Rare* (1995), *A Natural History of Love* (1995), and her latest work, *A Slender Thread* (1997).

Her poetry has been published in leading literary journals, and in the books *Wife of Light* (1978), *Lady Faustus* (1983), *Reverse Thunder: A Dramatic Poem* (1988), *Jaguar of Sweet Laughter: New and Selected Poems* (1991), and *I Praise My Destroyer* (1998). She is coeditor (with Jeanne Mackin) of a Norton anthology, *The Book of Love* (1998).

Ms. Ackerman has received many prizes and awards, including the John Burroughs Nature Award and the Lavan Poetry Prize, and has been honored as a Literary Lion by the New York Public Library. She has taught at a variety of universities, including Columbia and Cornell. Her essays about nature and human nature have appeared in *Parade, National Geographic, The New York Times, The New Yorker,* and other journals, where they have been the subject of much praise. A five-hour PBS television series, inspired by *A Natural History of the Senses,* aired in 1995, with Ms. Ackerman as host.

Additions to the Great Books Library

Hesiod

Not nearly so celebrated as Homer, the other poet of ancient Greece whose work survives, Hesiod is known for two long poems, the *Theogony,* which tells of the birth of the Greek gods, and the *Works and Days,* which describes the grim reality of peasant life as the poet knew it in the part of Greece called Boeotia, where he lived sometime during the eighth century BC. We have little in the way of historical record either of him or the age, and that little is provided by poets such as himself. But before we decide that this means his account must be false we should remember that poets then combined in themselves functions we have long since divided among the historian, the reporter, and the social scientist, and that they can be regarded as authorities on who people were, what beliefs they held, and how they lived. Aristotle regularly quotes them, for example, in the first book of his *Politics,* as those we must consult if we wish to know the character and institutions of human kind.

Boeotia, of which the most famous city, long even before Hesiod lived, was Thebes (from which Oedipus fled to his ruin), lies in a region of harsh climate north of the Gulf of Corinth. It was an otherwise agricultural area which nevertheless later produced a people of some importance. Unhappily for them, they sided with the Persians when the latter invaded Greece in 480–479, thinking to save themselves in the likely event of Persian success, and when this failed they suffered at the hands of the victorious Greeks. Subsequently, in the fourth century, they managed to ally themselves first with Sparta and then with Athens in an effort to regain their independence, which they finally lost, as did the rest of Greece, when they were conquered by the Macedonians.

All this was well after Hesiod's time (*c.* 800 BC), yet to remember it is to realize that that part of the world was one in which from the beginning great events could take place, and did, and in which social institutions and artistic works were well developed. Hesiod himself, for example, is known to have participated in a contest of songs at funeral games for a certain Amphidamas of Chalcis on the island of Euboea and this could hardly have been the only such occasion for such sophisticated activities in his lifetime.

That he should have undertaken an account of the birth of the gods in the *Theogony* is interesting, not least because the gods, who are by nature immortal, would not appear ever to have had a beginning, and partly because, if they did, it would presumably not be such as any human being could relate. We may take the poem as an attempt to provide some account of the origin or beginning of *things*, in which respect it is discussed elsewhere in this volume by George Anastaplo. Again, we may dismiss what Hesiod tells us as fanciful, for, while it claims revelation in the authority of the Muses, it does not offer anything that we would call science. Yet it tells of things we now accord *to* science, such as the emergence from Chaos of Gaea, or Earth, and the subsequent formation of mountains, seas, and skies, and we may recognize in it the effort that human beings have made everywhere and at nearly all times to make sense of themselves and their situation.

The poem was known in the western world as long as classical writings were commonly read, which means until some two centuries ago. References to the Nereids, daughters of the sea god Nereus, which are found in poetry through the eighteenth century and some after, evoke Hesiod, as do descriptions of Pandora, the first woman, who is here considered as having been sent by Zeus to bedevil man. She appears also in the *Works and Days* where the story of the unluckily-opened jar is told, and where Hesiod explores the decline of mankind since the Golden Age. In both poems there is evident a peculiarly Greek reverence for Justice—the favorite daughter of Zeus, Hesiod insists in the *Works and Days*—on the treatment of whom the happiness of both individuals and human communities is held to depend. And we can understand why at least the *Works and Days* became a moral source for later ages, seeing that it extols the virtues of hard and honest toil. "Before success," the poet says, "the immortal gods have placed the sweat of our brows."

In both poems may be detected something of an opposition to Homer, whose works Hesiod certainly knew. Speaking for humble people—for law, not glory—he celebrates truthfulness, oath-keeping, righteousness, and good behavior, with notions of sin and retribution quite absent in Homer and far in advance of their time. It is said that his works were of prime importance in shaping the morals of Greece and Rome. "A people educated only in Homer would not be nearly so ready to accept Christian ethics," Moses Hadas writes, "as one informed by Hesiod." To which he adds, "Homer is the classic of the ancients; Hesiod their Bible." There are signs that Hesiod accepted this rivalry and enjoyed such triumphs as he occasionally gained. The contest for song at Chalcis is described in the *Works and Days* as one at which he inscribed a tripod "dedicated to the Muses of Helicon" because he "overcame divine Homer," meaning just possibly the poet himself, more likely a rhapsode who visited him.

The Theogony
or
The Birth of the Gods

Hesiod

Illustrations by Cathie Bleck

Begin we from the Muses, O my song!
Whose dwelling is the vast and holy hill
Of Helicon; where aye, with delicate feet,
Fast by Jove's altar, and the fountain, dark
From azure depth, they tread the measured round;
And bathing their soft bodies in the brook
Permessus, or in that divinest spring
Olmius, or the well of Hippocrene,
O'er Helicon's smooth topmost height they wont
To thread their dances, graceful, kindling love,
And, with fast feet rebounding, smite the earth.
Thence rushing forth tumultuous, and inwrapt
In air's deep mist, they pass, with all their train,
On through the mount by night, and send abroad
A voice, in stilly darkness beautiful.
They hymn the praise of ægis-bearer Jove,
And Juno, named of Argos, worshipp'd queen,
Who walks in golden sandals; her whose eyes
Shine with cerulean light, the maid who sprang
From th' ægis-bearer Pallas; Phœbus, too,
And Dian gladden'd by the arrow's flight;
Earth-shaker Neptune, earth-enclasping god;
And Themis, name adorable in heaven;
And Venus, twinkling bland her tremulous lids;
And Hebe, who with golden fillet binds
Her brow, and fair Dione, and the Morn,
And the great sun, and the resplendent moon;
Latona, and Iapetus, and him
Of mazy counsel, Saturn; and the earth,
And the vast ocean, and the sable night;
And all the holy race of deities
Existing ever.
                    They to Hesiod erst
Have taught their stately song, the while he fed
His lambs beneath the heavenly Helicon.
And thus the goddesses, th' Olympian maids,
Whose sire is Jove, first hail'd me in their speech:—
'Shepherds! that tend the fold afield, base lives,
Mere fleshly appetites, the Muses hear!
We know to utter fictions, veil'd like truths,
Or, an we list, speak truths without a veil.'
  So spake the daughters of great Jove, whose speech
Is undisguised; and gave unto my hand
A rod, a bough of laurel blooming fresh,
Of goodly growth; and in me breathed a voice
Divine; that I might know, with listening ears,
Things past and future; and enjoin'd me praise

The race of blessed ones, that live for aye,
And first and last sing ever of themselves.
But why these idle words, like tales oft told
Around the sheltering oak, or shadowing rock?
Begin we from the Muses, O my song!
Who the great spirit of their father Jove
Delight in heaven; whose voice symphonious breathes
The present, and the future, and the past.
Sweet, inexhaustible, from every mouth
That voice flows on: the palaces of him,
Who hurleth the loud thunder, laugh with sounds
Scatter'd from lilied breath of goddesses;
Olympus echoes from its snow-topt heads,
The dwellings of immortals. They send forth
Th' imperishable voice, and in their song
Praise first the venerable race of gods,
From the beginning, whom the spacious heaven
And earth produced, and gods who sprang from these
Givers of blessings: then again to Jove,
Father of gods and men, those goddesses
Give praise, or when they lift the choral hymn,
Or when surcease; how excellent he is
Above all gods, and mightiest in his power.
Once more, recording in their strain the race
Of men and giants strong, they soothe the soul
Of Jupiter in heaven: Olympian maids;
The daughters they of ægis-bearer Jove:
Whom to th' embrace of Jove, Mnemosyne,
Queen of Eleuther's fallows, bare of old
In the Pierian mount: to evils they
Yield an oblivious balm, to torturing cares
Rest: thrice three nights did Jove, of counsel deep,
Embrace her, climbing to the sacred couch
Apart from all immortals; and when, now
The year was full, when moons had wax'd and waned,
And seasons run their round, and many days
Were number'd, she, some distant space from where
Olympus highest rears its snow-capt head,
Brought forth the thrice three maids, whose minds are knit
In harmony; whose thought is only song;
Within whose bosoms the free spirit dwells.
Theirs on the mount are the smooth pomps of dance,
And beautified abodes: their mansions nigh
The Graces hold, and elegant Desire,
And share the feast. So they through parted lips
Send forth a lovely voice: they sing the laws
Of universal heaven; the manners pure

Of deathless gods; and lovely is their voice.
Anon they bend their footsteps towards the mount,
Rejoicing in their beauteous voice and song
Unperishing; far round, the dusky earth
Rings with their hymning voices, and beneath
Their many-rustling feet a pleasant sound
Ariseth, as they take their onward way
To their own father's presence. He in heaven
Reigns; the red lightning and the bolt are his;
Since by the strong ascendant of his arm
Saturn his father fell: hence Jove to all
Disposes all things; to th' immortal gods
Ordering their honors. So the Muses aye,
Indwellers of th' Olympian mansions, use
To sing; nine daughters, born to mighty Jove:
The chiefest of them all, Calliope:
For she alone with kings majestical
Walks; whomsoever of the race of kings,
The foster-sons of Jove, Jove's daughters will
To honor, on whose infant head, when first
Usher'd to light, they placid gaze from high,
Upon his tongue they shed a balmy dew;
And words, as honey sweet, drop from his lips.
To him the people look: on him all eyes
Wait awful, who, distinguishing the laws,
Gives upright judgments; he, haranguing firm,
With prudence makes the strife on th' instant cease,
When mightiest. Lo! in this are kings discreet;
That, in their judgment-hall, they from th' oppress'd
Turn back the tide of ills, retrieving wrongs
With mild accost of soothing eloquence.
Him, when he walks the city-ways, all hail
With a bland worship, as he were a god:
And in the great assembly first is he.
   Such is the Muses' goodly gift to men.
Yea, from the Muses and the god, who sends
His darts from far, Apollo, rise on earth
Minstrels and men of song; but kings arise
From Jove himself. O blessed is the man
Whome'er the Muses love. Sweet is the voice
That from his lip flows ever. Is there one
Who hides some fresh grief in his wounded mind,
And mourns with aching heart? but he, the bard,
The servant of the Muse, awakes the song
To deeds of men of old and blessed gods
That dwell on Mount Olympus. Straight he feels
His sorrow stealing in forgetfulness;

Nor of his griefs remembers aught; so soon
The Muses' gifts have turn'd his woes away.
Children of Jove, all hail! but deign to give
Th' enchanting song! record the sacred race
Of ever-living gods; who sprang from earth,
From the starr'd heaven, and from the murky night,
And whom the salt deep nourish'd into life.
Declare how first the gods and earth became;
The rivers and th' immeasurable sea
Raging in foamy swell; the glittering stars,
And the wide heaven above; and who from these
Of deities arose, dispensing good;
Say how their treasures, how their honors each
Allotted shared; how first they fix'd abode
Amidst Olympus' many-winding vales;
Tell, O ye Muses! ye, who also dwell
In mansions of Olympus, tell me all
From the beginning; say who first arose.
First Chaos was; next ample-bosom'd Earth,
The seat immovable for evermore
Of those immortals, who the snow-topt heights
Inhabit of Olympus, or the glooms
Tartarean, in the broad-track'd ground's abyss.
Love, then, arose most beautiful amongst
The deathless deities; resistless he
Of every god and every mortal man
Unnerves the limbs; dissolves the wiser breast
By reason steel'd, and quells the very soul.
From Chaos, Erebus and ebon Night:
From Night the Day sprang forth and shining air,
Whom to the love of Erebus she gave.
Earth first produced the Heaven; whose starry cope,
Like to herself immense, might compass her
On every side, and be to blessed gods
A mansion unremoved for aye. She brought
The lofty mountains forth, the pleasant haunts
Of nymphs, who dwell midst thickets of the hills.
And next the sea, the swoln and chafing sea,
Apart from love's enchantment. Then, with Heaven
Consorting, Ocean from her bosom burst
With its deep-eddying waters. Cæus then,
Creus, Hyperion, and Iapetus,
Themis and Thea rose; Mnemosyne
And Rhea; Phœbe, diadem'd with gold,
And love-inspiring Tethys; and of these
Youngest in birth the wily Saturn came,
The sternest of her sons, for he abhorr'd

The sire who gave him life. Then brought she forth
The Cyclops brethren of high daring heart,
Brontes, and Steropes, and Arges fierce,
Who forged the lightning shaft, and gave to Jove
His thunder. They were like unto the gods,
Save that a single ball of sight was fix'd
In the mid-forehead: Cyclops was their name,
For that one circular eye was broad infix'd
In the mid-forehead: strength was theirs, and force,
And craft in curious works. Then other sons
Were born of Earth and Heaven: three mighty sons
And valiant; dreadful but to name; for they
Were haughty children; Cottus, Briareus,
And Gyges: from whose shoulders sprang at once
A hundred hands, defying all approach;
And o'er whose shoulders fifty heads upgrew,
Cresting their sinewy limbs. A vigor strong,
Immeasurable, fill'd each mighty frame.
Of all the children sprung from Earth and Heaven
The fiercest these; and they, e'en from the first,
Drew down their father's hate: as each was born
He seized them all, and hid them in a cave
Of earth, nor e'er released to open light.
Heaven in his deed malign rejoiced: vast Earth
Groan'd inly, sore aggrieved; but soon devised
A strategem of mischief and of fraud.
Sudden, creating for herself a kind
Of whiter adamant, she cunning forged
A mighty sickle; and address'd her sons:
She spake emboldening words, though grieved at heart.
'My sons! alas! ye children of a sire
Most impious, now obey a mother's voice;
So shall we well avenge the fell despite
Of him your father, who the first devised
Deeds of injustice.' While she said, on all
Fear fell; nor utterance found they, till, with soul
Embolden'd, wily Saturn huge address'd
His awful mother. 'Mother! be the deed
My own. Thus pledged, I will most sure achieve
This feat, nor heed I him, our sire, of name
Detested, for that he the first devised
Deeds of injustice.' Thus he said, and Earth
Was gladden'd at her heart. She planted him
In ambush dark and secret: in his grasp
The rough-tooth'd sickle placed, and tutor'd him
In every wile. Vast Heaven came down from high,
And with him brought the gloominess of night

On all beneath: desiring Earth's embrace,
He lean'd above her, and lay now diffused
In his immensity. The son stretched forth
His weaker hand from ambush; in his right
He took the sickle, huge, and long, and rough
With teeth, and from his natural sire the limbs
Reap'd, hastily cut sheer, and cast behind
So to be borne away; but not in vain
Escaped they from his hold; for Earth received
The blood-drops, and, as years roll'd round, she teem'd
With the strong furies and the giants huge,
Shining in arms, and holding length'ning spears
Within their grasp: and wood-nymphs, named of men
Dryads, o'er all th' unbounded space of earth.
   So severing, as was said, with edge of steel
The limbs, he hurl'd them from the continent
Amidst the boisterous sea: and thus full long
They drifted, floating o'er the distant deep.
Till now swift-circling a white foam arose
From that immortal substance, and a maid
Was nourish'd in the midst. The wafting waves
First bore her to Cythera's heaven-bless'd coast;
Then reach'd she Cyprus, girt with flowing seas,
And forth emerged a goddess, beautiful
In modesty. Green herbage sprang around
Beneath her slender feet. Her gods and men
Name Aphrodite, goddess of the foam,
Since in the sea-foam nourish'd; and again
Wreathed Cytherea, for that first she touch'd
Cythera's coast; and Cypris, for she rose
On Cyprus, 'midst the multitude of waves.
Love track'd her steps, and elegant Desire
Pursued, while soon as born she bent her way
Towards heaven's assembled gods; her honors these
From the beginning; whether gods or men
Her presence bless, to her the portion fell
Of virgin whisperings and alluring smiles,
And smooth deceits, and gentle ecstasy,
And dalliance, and the blandishments of love.
   The father, the great Heaven, upbraiding now
The sons, whom he had form'd, new-named the race
Titans: he said their full-blown insolence
Vindictive wrought a mighty crime, which they
Should rue hereafter; vengeance was behind.
   Abhorred Fate and dark Necessity
And Death were born from Night; by none embraced,
These gloomy Night brought, self-conceiving, forth:

And sleep and all the hovering host of dreams:
Momus and wo-begone Anxiety;
Th' Hesperian maids, who watch, beyond the verge
Of sounding ocean, apples fair of gold,
Trees bearing golden fruitage; and the Fates
And Destinies; relentless punishers;
Clotho and Lachesis, and Atropos;
Who, at the birth of men, dispense the lot
Of good and evil. They of men and gods
The crimes pursue, nor ever pause from wrath
Tremendous, till destructive on the head
Of him that sins the retribution fall.
Then Nemesis, the scourge of mortal man,
Rose from pernicious Night: and after her
Fraud, wasting Age and stubborn Strife. From Strife,
Odious, rose painful Toil; Forgetfulness;
Famine and weeping Sorrows; Combats, Wars,
And Slaughters, and all Homicides; and Brawls,
And Bickerings, and delusive Lies; with them
Came Lawlessness and Wrong, familiar mates,
And the dread Oath, tormentor of the wretch,
Midst earthly men, that wilful is foresworn.
The sea gave Nereus life, unerring seer,
And true; most ancient of his race, whom all
Hail as the sage, for mild and blameless he:
Remembering still the right; still merciful
As just in counsels. Then embracing Earth,
He fashion'd the great Thaumas, Phorcys strong,
And blooming Ceto and Eurybia; her
Whose soul within her breast is adamant.
From Nereus and the long-hair'd Doris, nymph
Of ocean's perfect stream, there sprang to light
A lovely band of children, goddesses
Dwelling within th' uncultivable main.
They from the blameless Nereus sprang to light,
His fifty daughters, versed in blameless tasks.
  Thaumas the daughter of deep-flowing Ocean
Espoused, Electra: she gave Iris birth,
The swift Aello and Ocypetes,
The sister Harpies with long streaming locks;
On fleetest wings upborne, they chase aloft
The hovering birds and wandering winds, and soar
Into the heaven. Then Ceto, fair of cheek,
To Phorcys bare the Graiæ: grey they were
From their birth-hour; and hence their name with gods
And men that walk the earth: Pephredo, clad
In flowing vesture, saffron-robed Enyo;

And Gorgons, dwelling on the brink of night
Beyond the sounding main; where silver-voiced
Th' Hesperian maidens in their watches sing;
Euryale and Stheno and Medusa.
Sad is her lot, since mortal; but the two
Immortal and of undecaying youth.
    Yet her alone the blue-hair'd god of waves
Enfolded, on the tender meadow-grass,
And bedded flowers of spring. When Perseus smote
Her neck, and snatch'd the sever'd bleeding head,
The great Chrysaor then leap'd into life,
And Pegasus the steed, who, born beside
Old Nilus' fountains, thence derived a name.
Chrysaor, grasping in his hands a sword
Of gold, flew upward on the winged horse;
And left beneath him Earth, mother of flocks,
And soar'd to heaven's immortals; and there dwells
In palaces of Jove, and to the god
Deep-counsell'd bears the bolt and arrowy flame.
    Chrysaor with Calliroe blending love,
Daughter of sounding Ocean, stamp'd with life
Three-headed Geryon: him, th' Herculean strength
Slew and despoil'd, among his hoof-cloven herds,
On Orythia, girdled by the wave;
What time those oxen ample-brow'd, he drew
To sacred Tirynth, the broad ocean-frith
Once pass'd, and Orthos, the grim herd-dog, stretch'd
Lifeless; and, in their murky den, beyond
The billows of the long-resounding deep,
The keeper of those herds, Eurytion, slain.
    Another monster Ceto bare anon
In the deep-hollow'd cavern of a rock;
Stupendous, nor in shape resembling aught
Of human or of heavenly: monstrous, fierce,
Echidna: half a nymph, with eyes of jet
And beauty-blooming cheeks: and half, again,
A speckled serpent, terrible and vast,
Gorged with blood-banquets, trailing her huge folds
Deep in the hollows of the blessed earth.
There in the uttermost depth her cavern is
Beneath a vaulted rock: from mortal men,
And from immortal gods, alike, remote:
There have the gods allotted her to dwell
In mansions rumor'd wide. So pent beneath
The rocks of Arima, Echidna dwelt
Hideous; a nymph immortal, and in youth
Unchanged for evermore. But legends tell

That with the jet-eyed maid Tiphaon mix'd
His fierce embrace; a whirlwind rude and wild;
She, fill'd with love, gave children to the light
Of an undaunted strain: and first she bore
Orthos, the watch-dog of Geryon's herds;
And next, a monstrous birth, the dog of hell:
Blood-fed, and brazen-voiced, and bold, and strong,
The fifty-headed Cerberus: third, she gave
To birth the dismal Hydra, Lerna's pest;
Whom Juno, white-arm'd goddess, fostering rear'd
With deep resentment fraught, insatiable,
'Gainst Hercules: but he, the son of Jove
Named of Amphitryon, in the dragon's gore
Bathed his unpitying steel, by warlike aid
Of Iolaus, and the counsels high
Of Pallas the despoiler. Last came forth
Chimæra, breathing fire unquenchable;
A monster grim, and huge, and swift and strong;
Hers were three heads: a glaring lion's one:
One of a goat: a mighty snake's the third:
In front the lion threaten'd, and behind
The serpent, and the goat was in the midst,
Exhaling fierce the strength of burning flame.
But the wing'd Pegasus his rider bore,
The brave Bellerophon, and laid her dead.
    She, grasp'd by forced embrace of Orthos, gave
Depopulating Sphynx, the mortal plague
Of Cadmian nations; and the lion bare
Named of Nemæa; him, Jove's glorious spouse
To fierceness trained, and placed his secret lair
Among Nemæa's hills, the pest of men.
There, lurking in his haunts, he long ensnared
The roving tribes of man; and held stern sway
O'er cavern'd Tretum, o'er the mountain heights
Of Apesantus, and Nemæa's wilds:
But he sank quash'd beneath th' Herculean strength.
    Ceto, with Phorcys blending love, now bare
Her youngest born; the dreadful snake, that, couch'd
In the dark earth's abyss, his wide domain,
Holds o'er the golden apples wakeful guard.
Such race from Ceto and from Phorcys sprang.
    To ocean Tethys brought the rivers forth
In whirlpool waters roll'd: Eridanus
Deep-eddied, and Alpheus, and the Nile:
And the divine Scamander. Bare she then
A sacred race of daughters, who on earth
With king Apollo and the rivers claim

The first-shorn locks of youth; their dower from Jove.
Three thousand slender-ankled ocean nymphs,
Long-stepping, tread this earth; and, scatter'd far,
Haunt every where alike the depth of lakes;
A glorious sisterhood of goddesses.
As many rivers, also, yet untold,
Rushing with hollow-dashing sound, were sons
Of ocean, to majestic Tethys born:
To name them all were hard for mortal man,
Yet known to all who on their borders dwell.
   Now the great sun, and the refulgent moon,
And morn, that shines to men, who walk the earth,
And all immortal gods, who dwell above
The spacious firmament, received their birth
From Thia, yielding to Hyperion's arms.
Eurybia, noble goddess, blending love
With Crius, gave the great Astræus birth,
Pallas the god, and Perses, wise in lore.
   The morning to Astræus bare the winds
Of spirit untamed; east, west, and south, and north,
Cleaving his rapid course; a goddess thus
Embracing with a god. Last Lucifer
Sprang radiant from the dawn-appearing morn,
And all the glittering stars that gird the heaven.
Styx, ocean nymph, with Pallas blending love,
Bare Victory, whose feet are beautiful
In palaces; and Zeal, and Strength, and Force,
Illustrious children. Not apart from Jove
Their mansion is; nor is there seat nor way
But he before them in his glory sits
Or passes forth: and where the Thunderer is
Their place is found for ever. So devised
Imperishable Styx, the ocean nymph,
What time the lightning-sender call'd from heaven,
And summon'd all th' immortal deities
To broad Olympus' top: then thus he spake:
'Hear, all ye gods! that god, who wars with me
Against the Titans, shall retain the gifts
Which Saturn gave, and honors heretofore
His portion midst th' immortals; and whoe'er
Unhonor'd and ungifted has repined
Under Saturnian sway, the same shall rise,
As meet it is, to honors and rewards.'
   Lo! then, imperishable Styx the first,
Sway'd by the careful counsels of her sire,
Stood on Olympus, and her sons beside.
Her Jove received with honor, and endow'd

With goodly gifts: ordain'd her the great oath
Of deities: her sons for evermore
Indwellers with himself. Alike to all,
E'en as he pledged that sacred word, the god
Perform'd; so reigns he, strong in power and might.
   Now Phœbe sought the love-abounding couch
Of Cæus; and embracing with a god,
Conceived the goddess; and to her was born
Latona, robed with azure, ever mild;
Placid to men and to immortal gods;
Mild from the first beginning of her days;
Gentlest of all in heaven. Anon she bare
Fair-famed Asteria; her whom Perses erst
Led to his ample palace, with the name
Of bride. She, fruitful, teem'd with Hecate,
Whom o'er all others the Saturnian Jove
Hath honor'd and endow'd with splendid gifts;
With power on earth and o'er th' uncultured sea.
Nor less from under starry heaven she shared
Of glory, midst th' immortals honor'd most.
If one of earthly men, with custom'd rite,
Offers fair sacrifice, appeasing Heaven,
He calls on Hecate: him honor straight
Accompanies, whose vows the goddess prompt
Accepts, and affluence, for the power is hers.
The many, sprung from heaven and earth, received
Allotted dignity; she shares alone
The privilege of all: nor aught has Jove
Invaded or revoked of that decreed
Her portion, midst the old Titanic gods;
As was the ancient heritage of power,
So hers remains, e'en from the first of things.
Nor less distinction has the singly born
Obtain'd, and power o'er earth and heaven and sea;
But more abundant far, since her doth Jove
Delight to honor. Lo! to whom she wills
Her presence is vouchsafed, and instant aid
With mightiness: whoe'er she wills, amidst
The people in the great assembly shines.
And when men don their armor for the fight,
Waster of mortals, comes the goddess prompt
To whom she wills, bids rapid victory
Await them, and holds forth the wreath of fame.
She sits upon the sacred judgment-seat
Of venerable monarchs. She is found
Propitious, when in the gymnastic strife
Men struggle: there the goddess still is nigh

With succor. He, whose hardiment and strength
Conquer, the goodly chaplet bears away,
And glad brings glory to his parents' age.
She, an she lists, is nigh to charioteers,
Who strive with steeds, and voyagers, who cleave
Through the blue watery vast th' untractable way.
They call upon the name of Hecate
With vows, and his, loud-sounding god of waves,
Earth-shaker Neptune. Easily at will
The glorious goddess yields the woodland prey
Abundant; easily, while scarce they start
On the mock'd vision, snatches then in flight.
She too, with Hermes, is propitious found
To herd and fold; and bids increase the droves
Innumerable of goats and woolly flocks,
And swells their numbers, or their numbers thins.
The sole-begotten of her mother's love,
She thus is honor'd with all attributes
Amongst immortals. Her did Jove appoint
The nursing mother bland of infant youth,
Of all who thenceforth to the morn's broad light
Should raise the tender lid: so from the first
The foster-nurse of babes: her honors these.
Embraced by Saturn, Rhea gave to light
A glorious race. She Vesta, Ceres, bare,
And Juno, golden-sandal'd; and, of heart
Ruthless, the mighty Pluto; him who dwells
In mansions under earth: and Neptune, loud
With dashing waves, and Jove in counsel wise;
Father of gods and men; whose thunder-peal
Rocks the wide earth in elemental war.
    But them, as issuing from the sacred womb
They touch'd the mother's knees, did Saturn huge
Devour: revolving in his troubled thought
Lest other of celestials should possess
Amidst th' immortals kingly sway: for he
Had heard from earth and from the starry heaven,
That it was doom'd by Fate, strong though he were,
To his own son he should bow down his strength.
Jove's wisdom this fulfill'd. No blind design
He therefore cherish'd, and in crooked craft
Devour'd his children. But on Rhea prey'd
Never-forgotten anguish. When the time
Was full, and Jove, the sire of gods and men,
Came to the birth, her parents she besought,
Earth and starr'd Heaven, that they should counsel her
How secretly the babe may spring to life:

And how the father's furies 'gainst his race,
In subtlety devour'd, may meet revenge.
They to their daughter listen'd and complied,
Unfolding what the Fates had sure decreed
Of kingly Saturn and his dauntless son:
And her they sent to Lyctus; to the clime
Of fallow'd Crete. Now, when her time was come,
The birth of Jove her youngest born, vast Earth
Took to herself the mighty babe, to rear
With nurturing softness in the spacious isle
Of Crete. So came she then, transporting him
Through the swift dusky night, to Lyctus first;
And thence, upbearing in her hands, conceal'd
In sunless cave, deep in the blessed ground,
Within th' Ægean mountain, shadow'd thick
With woods. Then swathing an enormous stone,
She placed it in the hold of Heaven's huge son,
The ancient king of gods; that stone he snatch'd,
And in his ravening maw convey'd away:
Wretch! nor bethought him that the stone supplied
His own son's place; survivor in its room,
Unconquer'd and unharm'd: the same, who soon,
Subduing him with mightiness of arm,
Should drive him from his state, and reign himself,
King of immortals. Swiftly grew the strength
And hardy limbs of that same regal babe;
And, when the great year had fulfill'd its round,
Gigantic Saturn, wily as he was,
Yet foil'd by Earth's considerate craft, and quell'd
By his son's arts and strength, released his race;
The stone he first disgorged, the last devour'd:
This Jove on widely traversable earth
Fix'd in bless'd Pythos, underneath the chasm
Of cleft Parnassus; to succeeding times
A monument, and miracle to man.
The brethren of his father, too, he loosed,
Whom Heaven, their sire, had in his frensy bound:
They the good deed in grateful memory bore,
And gave the thunder and the glowing bolt,
And lightning, which vast Earth had heretofore
Hid in her central caves. In these confides
The god, and reigns o'er deities and men.
    Iapetus the ocean damsel led,
Light-footed Clymene, and shared her couch.
She bare to him a son, magnanimous,
Atlas: anon Menœtius arrogant;
Prometheus changeful, artful in designs,

And Epimetheus of misguided mind;
Who was a mischief to inventive men
From olden time; for he the first received
The clay-form'd virgin-woman sent from Jove.
   Wide-seeing Jove struck with his smouldering flash
Haughty Menœtius, and cast down to hell,
Shameless in crime and arrogant in strength.
   Atlas, enforced by stern necessity,
Props the broad heaven; on earth's far borders, where
Full opposite th' Hesperian virgins sing
With shrill sweet voice, he rears his head and hands
Aye unfatiguable: heaven's counsellor
So doom'd his lot. But with enduring chains
He bound Prometheus, train'd in shifting wiles,
With galling shackles fixing him aloft
Midway a column. Down he sent from high
His eagle, hovering on expanded wings:
She gorged his liver; still beneath her beak
Immortal; for it sprang with life, and grew
In the night-season, and repair'd the waste
Of what the wide-wing'd bird devour'd by day.
But her the fair Alcmena's hardy son
Slew; from Prometheus drave the cruel plague,
And freed him from his pangs. Olympian Jove,
Who reigns on high, consented to the deed;
That thence yet higher glory might arise
O'er peopled earth to Hercules of Thebes:
And, in his honor, Jove now made to cease
The wrath he felt before, 'gainst him who strove
In wisdom ev'n with Saturn's mighty son.
   Of yore, when strife arose for sacrifice
'Twixt gods and men within Mecona's walls,
Prometheus, a huge ox with ready thought
Dividing, set before the god, and thus
Sought to delude his knowledge: for in this
Portion he stow'd within the covering hide
Flesh, entrails, unctuous fat; in that again,
Covering with snowy fat, he stow'd the blanch'd
Bones of the bullock, laid with cunning skill.
Then spake the father of the gods and men:
'Son of Iapetus! most famed of kings!
Sweet friend! how partially thy lots are shared!'
So tauntingly spoke Jupiter, whose thoughts
Of wisdom perish not. Then answer'd him
Wily Prometheus, with a laugh suppress'd,
And not forgetful of his cunning craft;
'Hail, glorious Jove! thou mightiest of the gods,

That shall endure for ever: choose the one
Which now the spirit in thy breast persuades.'
He spoke, devising treachery. Jove, whose thoughts
Of wisdom perish never, knew the guile,
Not unforewarn'd, and straight his soul foresaw
Evil to mortals, that should surely be.
He raised the snowy fat with both his hands,
And felt his spirit wroth: yea, anger seized
His spirit, when he saw the blanch'd bones hid
With cunning skill: and thence, ev'n from that hour,
The tribes of earth, before th' immortal gods
Burn the blanch'd bones, when fragrant altars smoke.
    Him then with anger unendurable
Cloud-gatherer Jove bespake: 'Contriver arch
O'er all the rest, son of Iapetus!
Hast thou not yet, sweet friend, thy guile forgotten?'
So spake incensed the god, whose wisdom yields
To no decay; and from that very hour,
Remembering still the treachery, he denied
The strength of indefatiguable fire
To all the dwellers upon earth. But him
Iapetus' brave son deluded still:
For in a hollow reed he stole from high
The far-seen splendor of unwearied flame.
Then deep resentment stung the thunderer's soul;
And his heart chafed in anger, when he saw
The fire far gleaming in the midst of men:
And for the flame restored he straight devised
A mischief to mankind. At Jove's behest
Famed Vulcan fashion'd from the yielding clay
A bashful virgin's likeness; and the maid
Of azure eyes, Minerva, round her waist
Clasp'd the broad zone, and dress'd her limbs in robe
Of flowing whiteness; placed upon her head
A wondrous veil of variegated threads;
Entwined amidst her hair delicious wreaths
Of verdant herbage and fresh-blooming flowers;
And set a golden mitre on her brow,
Which Vulcan framed, and with adorning hands
Wrought, at the pleasure of his father Jove.
Rich-labor'd figures, marvellous to sight,
Inclosed the border; forms of beasts that range
The earth, and fishes of the rolling deep;
Of these innumerable he there had graven,
(And exquisite the beauty of his art
Shone in these wonders) like to animals
Moving in breath, with vocal sounds of life.

Now when his plastic hand instead of good
Had framed this beauteous bane, he led her forth
Where were the other gods and mingled men.
She went exulting in her graced array,
Which Pallas, daughter of a mighty sire,
Known by her eyes of azure, had bestow'd.
On gods and men in that same moment seized
The ravishment of wonder, when they saw
The deep deceit, th' inextricable snare.
From her the sex of tender woman springs:
Pernicious is the race: the woman tribe
Dwell upon earth, a mighty bane to man:
No mates for wasting want, but luxury:
And as, within the close-roof'd hive, the drones,
Co-operative in base and slothful works,
Are pamper'd by the bees, these all the day,
Till sinks the ruddy sun, haste on the wing,
'Their murmuring labors ply,' and still cement
The white and waxen comb; those lurk within
The close hive, gathering in their maw the fruit
Of others' labors; such are womankind:
They, whom the Thunderer sent, a bane to men,
Ill helpmates of intolerable toils.
Yet more of ill instead of good he gave:
The man who, shunning wedlock, thinks to shun
The vexing cares that haunt the woman state,
And lonely waxes old, shall feel the want
Of one to foster his declining years:
Though not his life be needy, yet his death
Shall scatter his possessions to strange heirs,
And aliens from his blood. Or, if his lot
Be marriage, and his spouse of modest fame,
Congenial to his heart, e'en then shall ill
For ever struggle with the partial good,
And cling to his condition. But the man,
Who gains the woman of injurious kind,
Lives bearing in his secret soul and heart
Inevitable sorrow: ills so deep
As all the balms of medicine cannot cure.
Therefore it is not lawful to elude
The eye of Heaven, nor mock th' omniscient mind:
For not Prometheus' self, howe'er benign,
Could shun Heaven's heavy wrath; and vain were all
His arts of various wisdom, vain to 'scape
Necessity, or loose the mighty chain.
    When Heaven their sire 'gainst Cottus, Briareus,
And Gyges felt his moody anger chafe

Within him; sore amazed with that their strength
Immeasurable, their aspect fierce and bulk
Gigantic, with a chain of iron force
He bound them down, and fix'd their dwelling-place
Beneath the spacious ground: beneath the ground
They dwelt in pain and durance, in th' abyss
There sitting, where earth's utmost bound'ries end.
Full long, oppress'd with mighty grief of heart,
They brooded o'er their woes: but them did Jove
Saturnian, and those other deathless gods
Whom fair-hair'd Rhea bare to Saturn's love,
By policy of Earth, lead forth again
To light. For she successive all things told,
How with the giant brethren they should win
Conquest and splendid glory. Long they fought
With toil soul-harrowing; they, the deities
Titanic and Saturnian; each to each
Opposed, in valor of promiscuous war.
From Othrys' lofty summit warr'd the host
Of glorious Titans: from Olympus they,
The band of gift-dispensing deities
Whom fair-hair'd Rhea bare to Saturn's love.
So waged they war soul-harrowing: each with each
Ten years and more the furious battle join'd
Unintermitted: nor to either host
Was issue of stern strife or end: alike
Did either stretch the limit of the war.
    But now when Jove had set before his powers
All things befitting, the repast of gods,
The nectar and ambrosia, in each breast
Th' heroic spirit kindled; and now, all
With nectar and with sweet ambrosia fill'd,
Thus spake the father of the gods and men:
'Hear me, illustrious race of Earth and Heaven!
That what the spirit in my bosom prompts
I now may utter. Long, and day by day,
Confronting each the other, we have fought
For conquest and dominion, Titan gods
And we, the seed of Saturn. Still do ye,
Fronting the Titans in funereal war,
Show mighty vigor, irresistible hands;
Remembering that mild friendship and that state
Of suffering, when ye trod the upward way
Back to the light, and, by our counsels, broke
That irksome chain and left the murky gloom.'
He spake, and Cottus, free from stain, replied:
'O Jove august! not darkly hast thou said;

Nor know we not how excellent thou art
In counsel and in knowledge: thou hast been
Deliverer of immortals from a curse
Of horror: by thy wisdom have we risen,
O kingly son of Saturn, from dark gloom
And bitter bonds, unhoping of relief.
Then with persisting spirit and device
Of prudent warfare, shall we still assert
Thy empire midst the furious fray, and still
In hardy conflict brave the Titan foe.'
   He said: the gods, the givers of all good,
Heard with acclaim; nor ever till that hour
So burn'd each breast with ardor to destroy.
All on that day stirr'd up the mighty strife,
Female and male: Titanic gods, and sons
And daughters of old Saturn; and that band
Of giant brethren, whom, from forth th' abyss
Of darkness under earth, deliverer Jove
Sent up to light; grim forms and strong, with force
Resistless: arms of hundred-handed gripe
Burst from their shoulders: fifty heads upgrew
From all their shoulders o'er their nervy limbs.
They 'gainst the Titans in fell combat stood,
And in their sinewy hands wielded aloft
Precipitous rocks. On th' other side, alert
The Titan phalanx closed; then hands of strength
Join'd prowess, and display'd the work of war.
Tremendous then th' immeasurable sea
Roar'd; earth re-echoed; heaven's wide arch above
Groan'd shattering; broad Olympus reel'd throughout
Down to its rooted base beneath the rush
Of those immortals: the dark chasm of hell
Was shaken with the trembling, with the tramp
Of hollow footsteps and strong battle-strokes,
And measureless uproar of wild pursuit.
So they against each other through the air
Hurl'd intermix'd their weapons, scattering groans
Where'er they fell. The voice of armies rose
With rallying shout through the starr'd firmament,
And with a mighty war-cry both their hosts
Encountering closed. Nor longer then did Jove
Curb down his force; but sudden in his soul
There grew dilated strength, and it was fill'd
With his omnipotence. His whole of might
Brake from him, and the godhead rush'd abroad.
The vaulted sky, the mount Olympus flash'd
With his continual presence, for he pass'd

Incessant forth, and lighten'd where he trod.
Hurl'd from his nervous grasp, the lightnings flew
Reiterated swift, the whirling flash
Cast sacred splendor, and the thunderbolt
Fell. Then on every side the foodful earth
Roar'd in the burning flame, and far and near
The trackless depth of forests crash'd with fire.
Yea, the broad earth burn'd red, the streams of Nile
Glow'd, and the desert waters of the sea.
Round and around the Titans' earthy forms
Roll'd the hot vapor on its fiery surge;
Stream'd upward, and in one unbounded blaze
Swathed the celestial air. Keen rush'd the light,
Quivering from thunder's writhen flash, each orb,
Strong though they were, intolerable smote
And scorch'd their blasted vision. Through the void
Without, th' enormous conflagration burst,
And snatch'd the dark of Chaos. But to see
With human eye and hear with ear of man
Had been, as on a time the heaven and earth
Met hurtling in mid-air: as nether earth
Crash'd from the centre, and the wreck of heaven
Fell ruining from high. Not less, when gods
Grappled with gods, the shout and clang of arms
Commingled, and the tumult roar'd from heaven.
Shrill rush'd the hollow winds, and roused throughout
A shaking and a gathering dark of dust,
With crashing; and the livid lightning's gleam,
And thunder and its bolt, the enginery
Of Jove; and in the midst of either host
They bore upon their blast the cry confused
Of battle and the shouting. For the din
Of sight-appalling strife immense uprose;
And there the might of deeds was shown, till now
The fight declined. But first with grappling front
Steadfast they stood, and bore the brunt of war.
Amid the foremost, towering in the van,
The war-unsated Gyges, Briareus,
And Cottus, bitterest conflict waged; for they,
Thick following thrice, a hundred rocks in air
Flung from their sinewy hold; with missile storm
The Titan host o'ershadowing, them they drove,
Vain-glorious as they were, with hands of strength
O'ercoming them, beneath th' expanse of earth,
And bound with galling chains; so far beneath
This earth, as earth is distant from the sky:
So deep the space to darksome Tartarus.

A brazen anvil, falling from the sky,
Through thrice three days would toss in airy whirl,
Nor touch this earth, till the tenth sun arose;
Or down earth's chasm precipitate revolve;
Nor till the tenth sun rose, attain the verge
Of Tartarus. A fence of massive brass
Is forged around: around the pass is roll'd
A night of triple darkness; and above
Impend the roots of earth and barren sea.
There the Titanic gods in murkiest gloom
Lie hidden; such the cloud-assembler's will:
There, in a place of darkness, where vast earth
Has end: from thence no egress open lies;
Neptune's huge hand has closed with brazen gates
The mouth; a wall environs every side.
There Gyges, Cottus, high-soul'd Briareus,
Dwell vigilant; the faithful sentinels
Of ægis-bearer Jove. Successive there
The dusky earth and darksome Tartarus,
The sterile ocean and the starry heaven,
Arise and end, their source and boundary.
A drear and ghastly wilderness, abhorr'd
E'en by the gods–a vast vacuity;
Might none, the space of one slow-circling year,
Touch the firm soil, that portal enter'd once,
But him the whirls of vexing hurricanes
Toss to and fro. E'en by immortals loath'd
This prodigy of horror. There, too, stand
The mansions drear of gloomy night, o'erspread
With blackening vapors; and before the doors
Atlas, upholding heaven, his forehead rears,
And indefatigable hands. There Night
And Day, near passing, mutual greeting still
Exchange, alternate as they glide athwart
The brazen threshold vast. This enters, that
Forth issues; nor the two can one abode
At once constrain. This passes forth, and roams
The round of earth: that in the mansion waits
Till the due season of her travel come.
Lo! from the one the far-discerning light
Beams upon earthly dwellers; but a cloud
Of pitchy blackness veils the other round,
Pernicious Night; aye leading in her hand
Sleep, Death's half-brother; sons of gloomy Night,
There hold they habitation, Death and Sleep—
Dread deities: nor them the shining sun
E'er with his beams contemplates, when he climbs

The cope of heaven, or when from heaven descends.
Of these the one glides gentle o'er the space
Of earth and broad expanse of ocean waves,
Placid to man. The other has a heart
Of iron; yea, the heart within his breast
Is steel, unpitying; whom of men he grasps
Stern he detains, e'en to immortal gods
A foe. The hollow-sounding palaces
Of Pluto strong, the subterraneous god,
And awful Proserpine, there full in front
Ascend: a grisly dog, implacable,
Keeps watch before the gates: a stratagem
Is his, malicious: them who enter there
With tail and bended ears he fawning soothes;
But suffers not that they with backward step
Repass: whoe'er would issue from the gates
Of Pluto strong and awful Proserpine,
For them with marking eye he lurks: on them
Springs from his couch and pitiless devours.
    There, hateful to immortals, dreaded Styx
Inhabits: refluent Ocean's eldest born:
She from the gods apart for ever dwells
In mansions known to fame, with arching roofs
O'erhung of loftiest rock, and all around
The silver columns lean upon the skies.
Swift-footed Iris, nymph of Thaumas born,
Takes with no frequent embassy her way
O'er the broad main's expanse, when haply strife
Has risen, and controversy 'midst the gods.
If there be one 'midst those who dwell in heaven
That utters falsehood, Jove sends Iris down,
To bring from far in golden ewer the wave
Of multitudinous name, the mighty oath,
That from a high rock inaccessible
Glides cold. Beneath the widely traversed ground
Full from the sacred ocean-river flows
The Stygian branch, through the black shade of night:
A tenth is set apart. In nine-fold stream
Round earth and the wide surface of the sea
Rolling its silver whirlpools on, it falls
Into the main; one gushes from the rock,
To gods a great calamity. For he,
Of those immortals who inhabit still
Olympus topp'd with snow, pours out the stream
And is forsworn, he one whole year intire
Lies reft of breath, nor once draws nigh the feast
Of nectar and ambrosia, but reclines

Breathless and speechless on the tapestried couch
Buried in mortal lethargy; but when
With the great round of the revolving year
His malady remits, most irksome woe,
One following fast the other, holds him still.
Nine years from ever-living gods apart
His lot is cast; in council nor in feast
Once joins he, till nine years intire are full:
The tenth again he mingles with the bless'd
Societies that fill th' Olympian courts.
So great an oath the deities of heaven
Decreed the water incorruptible
Of Styx; the ancient stream, that sweeps along
A rugged region; where of dusky Earth
And darksome Tartarus and Ocean waste
And starry Heaven, the source and boundary
Successive rise and end; a dreary wild,
And ghastly, e'en by deities abhorr'd.
There gates of marble brightness rise: of brass
The threshold; unremoved; fast on its deep
Foundations; self-constructed. In the front,
On th' outer side of heaven and all the gods,
The Titans dwell, beyond the dark abyss.
There the renown'd auxiliaries of Jove,
Who rolls the pealing thunder, in their house
Under the roots of ocean aye reside,
Cottus and Gyges. But the god, who rocks
Earth with hoarse-dashing surge, hail'd Briareus,
For his brave bearing, son, and made his bride
Cymapolia. Now, when Jove from heaven
Had cast the Titans forth, huge earth embraced
By Tartarus, through golden Venus, bare
Her youngest-born, Typhœus: he whose hands
Of strength are fitted to stupendous deeds;
And indefatigable are the feet
Of the strong god: and from his shoulders rise
A hundred snaky heads of dragon growth,
Horrible, quivering with their black'ning tongues:
In each amazing head, from eyes that roll'd
Within their sockets, fire shone sparkling; fire
Blazed from each head, the whilst he roll'd his glance
Glaring around him. In those fearful heads
Were voices of all sound, miraculous:
Now utter'd they distinguishable tones
Meet for the ear of gods: now the deep cry
Of a wild bellowing bull, untamed in strength;
And now the roaring of a lion, fierce

In spirit; and anon the yell of whelps
Strange to the ear; and now the monster hiss'd,
That the high mountains echoed back the sound.
Then had a dread event that fatal day
Inevitable fallen, and he had ruled
O'er mortals and immortals, but the sire
Of gods and men the peril instant knew,
Intuitive; and vehement and strong
He thunder'd: instantaneous all around
Earth reel'd with horrible crash; the firmament
Roar'd of high heaven, the streams of Nile and seas
And uttermost caverns. While the king in wrath
Uprose, beneath his everlasting feet
The great Olympus trembled and Earth groan'd.
From either side a burning radiance caught
The darkly-azured ocean, from the flash
Of lightnings, and that monster's darted flame,
And blazing bolts and blasts of fiery winds:
All earth and heaven steam'd hot, and the sea foam'd
Around the shores, and waves dash'd wide and high
Beneath the rush of gods. Concussion wild
And unappeasable uprose: aghast
The gloomy monarch of th' infernal dead
Recoil'd: the sub-tartarean Titans heard
E'en where they stood, and Saturn in the midst;
They heard appall'd the unextinguish'd rage
Of tumult, and the din of dreadful war.
But now when Jove had roused his strength, and grasp'd
The thunder and the flash and bickering bolt,
His weapons, he from Mount Olympus' top
Leap'd at a bound, and smote him: hiss'd at once,
The grisly monster's heads enormous, scorch'd
In one conflagrant blaze. When thus the god
Had quell'd him, thunder-smitten, mangled, prone
He fell: the vast earth groan'd beneath the shock.
Flame from the lightning-stricken prodigy
Flash'd, midst the mountain-hollows, rugged, dark,
Where he fell smitten. Far and near, vast earth
With that portentous vapor glow'd intense,
And melted; e'en as tin by art of youths
Below the well-bored furnace simmering glows,
Or iron, hardest of the mine, subdued
By burning flame amidst the woody dales,
Melts in the sacred cave beneath the hands
Of Vulcan, so earth melted in the glare
Of blazing fire. He down wide hell's abyss
His victim hurl'd in bitterness of soul.

Lo! from Typhœus is the strength of winds
Moist-blowing; save the south, north, east and west;
These born from higher gods, a mighty aid
To men; those other gusts upon the sea
Breathe unavailable: fall suddenly
Upon the blacken'd deep, to mortal souls
A great destruction, and, now here, now there,
Blow in sore hurricane: the rolling barks
Scatter abroad and wreck the mariners:
An evil without help to all the sons
Of men, who cross them where they scour the seas.
They, too, o'er all th' expanded flowery earth
Waste the fair works of earth-born men, and fill
All things with eddying dust and rustling drear.
But when the blessed gods had now fulfill'd
Their toil, against the Titans battling strong
For glory, they by Earth's persuasions urged
Wide-seeing Jove to rule with kingly sway
Th' immortals. He assign'd them honors due.

First as a bride the monarch of the gods
Led Metis; her o'er deities and men
Versed in all knowlege. But when now the time
Was full, that she should bear the blue-eyed maid
Minerva, he with treacheries of smooth speech
Beguiled her thought and hid his spouse away
In his own breast: so Earth and starry Heaven
Had counsell'd: him they both advising warn'd,
Lest, in the place of Jove, another seize
The kingly honor o'er immortal gods.
For it was in the roll of Fate, from her
Children of highest wisdom should be born:
The head-sprung virgin first, the azure-eyed,
Of equal might and prudence with her sire:
And then a son, king over gods and men,
Had she brought forth, invincible of soul,
But Jove before that hour within himself
Deposited the goddess: evermore
So warning him of evil and of good.

Next led he comely Themis; and she bare
Eunomia, Dice, and Irene blithe,
The Hours by name, who shed a grace o'er all
The works of men. Anon Eurynome,
Old Ocean's daughter, of enchanting form,
Bare to him the three Graces, fair of cheek,
Euphrosyne, Aglaia, and Thalia,
Desire of eyes: their eyelids, as they gaze,
Drop love, unnerving; and, beneath the shade

Of their arch'd brows, they steal the sidelong glance
Of sweetness. To the couch anon he came
Of many-nurturing Ceres: Proserpine
She bare, the snowy-arm'd: her Pluto snatch'd
From her own mother, and wise Jove bestow'd.
Next loved he the fair-hair'd Mnemosyne;
From her were born the Muses nine, whose brows
Are knit with golden fillets; and to them
Are banquets pleasing and the charm of song.
In mingled love with ægis-bearer Jove
Latona shaft-rejoicing Dian bare,
And Phœbus, loveliest of the heavenly tribe.
He last the blooming Juno led as bride,
And she, embracing with the king of gods
And men, bare Mars, and Hebe, and Lucina.
   He from his head himself disclosed to birth
The maid of azure eyes, the head-born maid:
Terrible, stirring up the battle din,
Leader of armies, unfatiguable,
Awful, whom war-shouts, wars and battles charm.
   Without th' embrace of love did Juno bear
(And so provoked to emulation strove
With her own spouse) illustrious Vulcan, graced
With arts o'er all the habitants of heaven.
   From Amphitrite and th' earth-shaking god,
Loud with the crash of waves, great Triton rose
Wide-ruling, who the sea-depths habiteth
By his loved mother and his kingly sire
In golden mansion, a majestic god.
   Now to shield-riving Mars did Venus bear
Terror and consternation: dreadful they
Confuse in rout of war, that numbs the veins,
The phalanx throng'd of men, with Mars who lays
Cities in ruinous heaps: Harmonia last,
Whom for a bride impassion'd Cadmus took.
Daughter of Atlas, Maia bare to Jove
The glorious Hermes, herald of the gods,
The sacred couch ascending. Semele,
Daughter of Cadmus, blending her embrace
With Jove, bare to him an illustrious son,
The jocund Bacchus: thus a mortal maid
Bare an immortal: both are now divine.
Alcmena bare strong Hercules, embraced
By cloud-assembling Jove. Renown'd in arts
The crippled Vulcan made the youngest Grace,
Aglaia, his gay bride. With golden locks
Bacchus sought Ariadne, auburn-hair'd

Daughter of Minos, as his blooming spouse.
Her, Jove immortal made, and free from age.
The brave son of Alcmena, light of foot,
Strong Hercules, when he had now fulfill'd
His agonising conflicts, led the maid
Born from great Jove and golden-sandal'd Juno,
Hebe, upon Olympus' snowy top
His modest bride. Bless'd, who a mighty work
Accomplishing before th' immortals' eyes,
Dwells all his days unhurt and free from age.
Perseis, the famed ocean nymph, bare Circe
And king Æetes to th' unwearied Sun.
Æetes, from the world-enlightening Sun
Descended, by the counsels of the gods,

Wedded the nymph of ocean's perfect stream,
Idya, fair of cheek: and she to him
Bare the light-paced Medea; so in love
Yielding, through influence of Love's golden queen.
    And now farewell, ye heavenly habitants!
Ye islands, and ye continents of earth!
And thou, O main! of briny wave profound!
O sweet of speech! Olympian muses! born
From ægis-bearer Jove! sing now the tribe
Of goddesses, whoe'er, by mortals clasp'd
In love, have borne a race resembling gods.
    Ceres, most excellent of goddesses,
Blending sweet passion with Iasius brave,
Bare Plutus, in the thrice-till'd fallow field
Of Crete's rich glebe, benignant: for he roams
All earth, and the broad surface of the sea;
Who meets him on his way, whose hands he grasps,
Him he makes rich, and ample bliss bestows.
Harmonia, golden Venus' daughter, bare
To Cadmus, in the tower-engirded Thebes,
Ino and Semele; and, fair of cheek,
Agave, and Antinoë, the bride
Of Aristæus with the clustering locks,
And Polydorus. To Tithonus Morn
Bare Memnon of the brazen helm, the king
Of th' Ethiopians, and, alike a king,
Emathion: and anon to Cephalus
Brought forth a noble son, brave Phaëton:
A man resembling gods. Him, while a youth,
E'en in the tender flower of glorious prime,
A boy with childish thoughts, love's smiling queen
Ravish'd away: and in her bless'd fane placed,
The nightly priest and genius of the shrine.
Jason, the son of Æson, by design
Of aye-existing gods, took from his sire
The daughter of Æetes, Jove-rear'd king:
When he had once achieved the weary toils
Which, numberless, the proud great king enforced,
Fierce Pelias, flown with insolence and wrong:
These having once achieved, enduring much,
He reach'd Iolchos, wafting on swift deck
The black-eyed maid, and made her his gay bride.
She, to the shepherd of his people, Jason,
Thus yielding, bare a son, Medeus; him
Chiron, the son of Philyra, uprear'd
Upon the mountains: so great Jove had will'd.
The damsels, who from Nereus drew their birth—

The old man of the sea;—first Psamathe,
The noble goddess, through love's golden queen,
Bare Phocus to the love of Æacus:
And Thetis, silver-footed goddess, next
Yielding to Peleus, brought Achilles forth,
Breaking the ranks of men, the lion-soul'd.
But Cytherea of the blooming wreath
Brought forth Æneas, with th' heroic swain
Anchises blending gentle love upon
The woody heights of Ida, many-valed:
And Circe, too, the daughter of the Sun,
Named of Hyperion, to the patient-soul'd
Ulysses' love bare Adrius and Latinus,
Blameless and brave: who far away forsook
The sacred islands and their secret haunts,
And wide o'er all the glorious Tuscans ruled.
Anon Calypso, noble goddess, bare
Nausithous and Nausinous, with the man
Ulysses mingling in the kind embrace.
Lo! these were they who, sharing their soft couch
With mortal men, themselves immortal, gave
Children like gods. Sing now of womankind,
Olympian muses, ye! whose words are sweet,
The daughters loved of ægis-bearer Jove!

Elizabeth Cady Stanton

When we look back nowadays on the struggle to establish the rights of women, which toward the end of the nineteenth century became focussed on the question of suffrage but which also had to challenge many other legal, social, and moral barriers, we wonder how they did it—those extraordinary individuals who with tireless argument and determined organization achieved a revolution. Not a complete revolution, certainly. Inequalities remained and remain still as between men and women; we hear of them all the time, or we should. Still, a revolution was basically accomplished, and by women—they were mostly women—who as they liked to point out were in the ordinary sense powerless and certainly lacked the military resources usually found necessary to achieve such a result.

The Grimké sisters, Lucretia Mott, Elizabeth Cady Stanton, Susan B. Anthony, and Sojourner Truth are among those in the United States who figured in the movement and in one way or another led it. What inspired them? What gave them the strength to do what they did? What did they actually do?

The third question is easiest to answer. By words—in speeches, in writing, before bodies of powerful men, before the public at large—they made their case, which was finally unarguable for all that it was endlessly argued; indeed, it may be doubted that they could have prevailed had anything else been so. The words had been used by men before them in other causes—William Lloyd Garrison, for example, in the abolitionist movement, and before him Thomas Jefferson in the Declaration of Independence. They were words that had prevailed in war and established themselves in the conscience of the country. What better ones could have been chosen by Elizabeth Cady Stanton than Jefferson's when she spoke at the Seneca Falls Convention in New York in 1848—that year of revolution round the world—and how few of them, at least in the crucial passages, had to be changed? Except that in this case the revolutionaries had no army, and could not make war, and did not in the usual sense even wish to.

But the words of the women's rights movement had other sources besides political ones. Their inspiration, indeed, was not so much political as religious. Of the women listed above, all but Susan B. Anthony came to their conviction through religious example, and the example in each case was that of the Quakers. We can guess what it was in Quakerism that struck them—its absolute individualism, its perfect equality, the rejection of all authority that denied either of those principles. Here was the last of the old Protestant sects to retain its fervor, to mean what it said not in parochial but in comprehensive terms. The Quakers have no church. Whatever they mean must be in the individual, ordinary lives of their members. This could seem to include women, and did, to these pioneers of women's rights.

As for strength, apart from that which must be attributed to character it would appear to be what for lack of a better phrase may be called the democratic process, observed in the 1830's by Toqueville as the source of power in those who learned to wield it. The women's rights leaders were in some degree politicians who learned what we nowadays call the ropes of legislatures and other public bodies, and pulled hard on them. This was what they had to do, but they learned what it was from their antagonists. America, as Toqueville said, has been the trainer of politics for its people, even as, Pericles tells us, Athens was for ancient Greece. Lucretia Mott is noted as "an effective reformer." In this sense she simply became the functional American she wished to be.

The remarks by Elizabeth Cady Stanton reprinted here are not perhaps quite the best that the movement produced, but they have their eloquence. The first is from that Seneca Falls Convention which was organized by Stanton and Mott, the latter mindful of the fact that eight years before she had not been allowed to attend the World Anti-Slavery Conference in England because she was a woman. The second speech was made more than forty years later, before a Congressional Committee, in pursuit of women's suffrage. The note of individualism is struck very determinedly for that group of lawmakers, and the necessary Constitutional Amendment was not passed for almost thirty years.

Elizabeth Cady Stanton (1815–1902) was the daughter of a New York Supreme Court judge from whom she learned of the discriminatory laws under which women lived. She married a lawyer and abolitionist, Henry Stanton, in 1840; in 1848 she helped to secure passage of a New York law giving property rights to married women; that same year she drew up the resolutions that were adopted by the 1848 Convention, including, against the judgment of everyone else, one that called for women's suffrage. In 1850 she began an association with Susan B. Anthony, who took care of business matters for the movement while Stanton did most of the writing. Among her works were at least the first three volumes of *The History of Woman Suffrage* (6 volumes, 1881–1922), which she edited with Anthony and Matilda Joslyn Gage. She also wrote an autobiography which appeared four years before she died.

Selections from Elizabeth Cady Stanton

Elizabeth Cady Stanton

Address Delivered at the Seneca Falls Convention

We have met here today to discuss our rights and wrongs, civil and political, and not, as some have supposed, to go into the detail of social life alone. We do not propose to petition the legislature to make our husbands just, generous, and courteous, to seat every man at the head of a cradle, and to clothe every woman in male attire.

None of these points, however important they may be considered by leading men, will be touched in this convention. As to their costume, the gentlemen need feel no fear of our imitating that, for we think it in violation of every principle of taste, beauty, and dignity; notwithstanding all the contempt cast upon our loose, flowing garments, we still admire the graceful folds, and consider our costume far more artistic than theirs. Many of the nobler sex seem to agree with us in this opinion, for the bishops, priests, judges, barristers, and lord mayors of the first nation on the globe, and the Pope of Rome, with his cardinals, too, all wear the loose flowing robes, thus tacitly acknowledging that the male attire is neither dignified nor imposing.

No, we shall not molest you in your philosophical experiments with stocks, pants, high-heeled boots, and Russian belts. Yours be the glory to discover, by personal experience, how long the kneepant can resist the terrible strapping down which you impose, in how short time the well-developed muscles of the throat can be reduced to mere threads by the constant pressure of the stock, how high the heel of a boot must be to make a short man tall, and how tight the Russian belt may be drawn and yet have wind enough left to sustain life.

But we are assembled to protest against a form of government existing without the consent of the governed—to declare our right to be free as man is free, to be represented in the government which we are taxed to support, to have such disgraceful laws as give man the power to chastise and imprison his wife, to take the wages which she earns, the property which she inherits, and, in case of separation, the children of her love; laws which make her the mere dependent on his bounty. It is to protest against such unjust laws as these that we are assembled today, and to have them, if possible, forever erased from our statute books, deeming them a shame and a disgrace to a Christian republic in the nineteenth century. We have met to uplift woman's fallen divinity upon an even pedestal with man's. And, strange as it may seem to many, we now demand our right to vote according to the declaration of the government under which we live.

(Overleaf) "We now demand our right to vote according to the declaration of the government under which we live."

This right no one pretends to deny. We need not prove ourselves equal to Daniel Webster to enjoy this privilege, for the ignorant Irishman in the ditch has all the civil rights he has. We need not prove our muscular power equal to this same Irishman to enjoy this privilege, for the most tiny, weak, ill-shaped stripling of twenty-one has all the civil rights of the Irishman. We have no objection to discuss the question of equality, for we feel that the weight of argument lies wholly with us, but we wish the question of equality kept distinct from the question of rights, for the proof of the one does not determine the truth of the other. All white men in this country have the same rights, however they may differ in mind, body, or estate.

The right is ours. The question now is: how shall we get possession of what rightfully belongs to us? We should not feel so sorely grieved if no man who had not attained the full stature of a Webster, Clay, Van Buren, or Gerrit Smith could claim the right of the elective franchise. But to have drunkards, idiots, horse-racing, rum-selling rowdies, ignorant foreigners, and silly boys fully recognized, while we ourselves are thrust out from all the rights that belong to citizens, it is too grossly insulting to the dignity of woman to be longer quietly submitted to.

The right is ours. Have it, we must. Use it, we will. The pens, the tongues, the fortunes, the indomitable wills of many women are already pledged to secure this right. The great truth that no just government can be formed without the consent of the governed we shall echo and re-echo in the ears of the unjust judge, until by continual coming we shall weary him.

There seems now to be a kind of moral stagnation in our midst. Philanthropists have done their utmost to rouse the nation to a sense of its sins.

A crowd of men listen attentively to a woman speaking about women's rights. "Man cannot fulfill his destiny alone, he cannot redeem his race unaided."

War, slavery, drunkenness, licentiousness, gluttony, have been dragged naked before the people, and all their abominations and deformities fully brought to light, yet with idiotic laugh we hug those monsters to our breasts and rush on to destruction. Our churches are multiplying on all sides, our missionary societies, Sunday schools, and prayer meetings and innumerable charitable and reform organizations are all in operation, but still the tide of vice is swelling, and threatens the destruction of everything, and the battlements of righteousness are weak against the raging elements of sin and death.

Verily, the world waits the coming of some new element, some purifying power, some spirit of mercy and love. The voice of woman has been silenced in the state, the church, and the home, but man cannot fulfill his destiny alone, he cannot redeem his race unaided. There are deep and tender chords of sympathy and love in the hearts of the downfallen and oppressed that woman can touch more skillfully than man.

The world has never yet seen a truly great and virtuous nation, because in the degradation of woman the very fountains of life are poisoned at their source. It is vain to look for silver and gold from mines of copper and lead.

It is the wise mother that has the wise son. So long as your women are slaves you may throw your colleges and churches to the winds. You can't have scholars and saints so long as your mothers are ground to powder between the upper and nether millstones of tyranny and lust. How seldom, now, is a father's pride gratified, his fond hopes realized, in the budding genius of his son!

The wife is degraded, made the mere creature of caprice, and the foolish son is heaviness to his heart. Truly are the sins of the fathers visited upon the children to the third and fourth generation. God, in His wisdom, has so linked the whole human family together that any violence done at one end of the chain is felt throughout its length, and here, too, is the law of restoration, as in woman all have fallen, so in her elevation shall the race be recreated.

"Voices" were the visitors and advisers of Joan of Arc. Do not "voices" come to us daily from the haunts of poverty, sorrow, degradation, and despair, already too long unheeded. Now is the time for the women of this country, if they would save our free institutions, to defend the right, to buckle on the armor that can best resist the keenest weapons of the enemy—contempt and ridicule. The same religious enthusiasm that nerved Joan of Arc to her work nerves us to ours. In every generation God calls some men and women for the utterance of truth, a heroic action, and our work today is the fulfilling of what has long since been foretold by the Prophet—Joel 2:28:

> "And it shall come to pass afterward, that I will pour out my spirit upon all flesh; and your sons and your daughters shall prophesy."

We do not expect our path will be strewn with the flowers of popular applause, but over the thorns of bigotry and prejudice will be our way, and

"We do not expect our path will be strewn with the flowers of popular applause..." *Indeed, not all women supported the cause. The National Association Opposed to Woman Suffrage was one such group of women.*

on our banners will beat the dark storm clouds of opposition from those who have entrenched themselves behind the stormy bulwarks of custom and authority, and who have fortified their position by every means, holy and unholy. But we will steadfastly abide the result. Unmoved we will bear it aloft. Undauntedly we will unfurl it to the gale, for we know that the storm cannot rend from it a shred, that the electric flash will but more clearly show to us the glorious words inscribed upon it, "Equality of Rights."

The Seneca Falls Declaration (1848)
I. Declaration of Sentiments

When, in the course of human events, it becomes necessary for one portion of the family of man to assume among the people of the earth a position different from that which they have hitherto occupied, but one to which the laws of nature and of nature's God entitle them, a decent respect to the opinions of mankind requires that they should declare the causes that impel them to such a course.

We hold these truths to be self-evident: that all men and women are created equal; that they are endowed by their Creator with certain inalienable rights; that among these are life, liberty, and the pursuit of happiness; that to secure these rights governments are instituted, deriving their just powers from the consent of the governed. Whenever any form of government becomes destructive of these ends, it is the right of those who suffer from it to refuse allegiance to it, and to insist upon the institution of a new government, laying its foundation on such principles, and organizing its powers in such form, as to them shall seem most likely to effect their safety and happiness. Prudence, indeed, will dictate that governments long established should not be changed for light and transient causes; and accordingly all experience hath shown that mankind are more disposed to suffer, while evils are sufferable, than to right themselves by abolishing the forms to which they were accustomed. But when a long train of abuses and usurpations, pursuing invariably the same object evinces a design to reduce them under absolute despotism, it is their duty to throw off such government, and to provide new guards for their future security. Such has been the patient sufferance of the women under this government, and such is now the necessity which constrains them to demand the equal station to which they are entitled.

The history of mankind is a history of repeated injuries and usurpations on the part of man toward woman, having in direct object the establishment of an absolute tyranny over her. To prove this, let facts be submitted to a candid world.

He has never permitted her to exercise her inalienable right to the elective franchise.

He has compelled her to submit to laws, in the formation of which she had no voice.

He has withheld from her rights which are given to the most ignorant and degraded men—both natives and foreigners.

Having deprived her of this first right of a citizen, the elective franchise, thereby leaving her without representation in the halls of legislation, he has oppressed her on all sides.

He has made her, if married, in the eye of the law, civilly dead.

He has taken from her all right in property, even to the wages she earns.

He has made her, morally, an irresponsible being, as she can commit many crimes with impunity, provided they be done in the presence of her husband. In the covenant of marriage, she is compelled to promise obedience to her husband, he becoming, to all intents and purposes, her master—the law giving him power to deprive her of her liberty, and to administer chastisement.

He has so framed the laws of divorce, as to what shall be the proper causes, and in case of separation, to whom the guardianship of the children shall be given, as to be wholly regardless of the happiness of women—the law, in all cases, going upon a false supposition of the supremacy of man, and giving all power into his hands.

After depriving her of all rights as a married woman, if single, and the owner of property, he has taxed her to support a government which recognizes her only when her property can be made profitable to it.

He has monopolized nearly all the profitable employments, and from those she is permitted to follow, she receives but a scanty remuneration. He closes against her all the avenues to wealth and distinction which he con-

Three suffragists put up posters in New Jersey, c. 1915.

siders most honorable to himself. As a teacher of theology, medicine, or law, she is not known.

He has denied her the facilities for obtaining a thorough education, all colleges being closed against her.

He allows her in Church, as well as State, but a subordinate position, claiming Apostolic authority for her exclusion from the ministry, and, with some exceptions, from any public participation in the affairs of the Church.

He has created a false public sentiment by giving to the world a different code of morals for men and women, by which moral delinquencies which exclude women from society, are not only tolerated, but deemed of little account in man.

He has usurped the prerogative of Jehovah himself, claiming it as his right to assign for her a sphere of action, when that belongs to her conscience and to her God.

A poster from 1915 addresses the women's rights issue from the children's point of view. "You can't have scholars and saints so long as your mothers are ground to powder between the upper and nether millstones of tyranny and lust."

He has endeavored, in every way that he could, to destroy her confidence in her own powers, to lessen her self-respect and to make her willing to lead a dependent and abject life.

Now, in view of this entire disfranchisement of one-half the people of this country, their social and religious degradation—in view of the unjust laws above mentioned, and because women do feel themselves aggrieved, oppressed, and fraudulently deprived of their most sacred rights, we insist that they have immediate admission to all the rights and privileges which belong to them as citizens . . .

In entering upon the

great work before us, we anticipate no small amount of misconception, misrepresentation, and ridicule; but we shall use every instrumentality within our power to effect our object. We shall employ agents, circulate tracts, petition the State and National legislatures, and endeavor to enlist the pulpit and the press in our behalf. We hope this Convention will be followed by a series of Conventions embracing every part of the country.

2. Resolutions

WHEREAS, The great precept of nature is conceded to be, that "man shall pursue his own true and substantial happiness." Blackstone in his Commentaries remarks, that this law of Nature being coeval with mankind, and dictated by God himself, is of course superior in obligation to any other. It is binding over all the globe, in all countries and at all times; no human laws are of any validity if contrary to this, and such of them as are valid, derive all their force, and all their validity, and all their authority, mediately and immediately, from this original; therefore,

Resolved, That such laws as conflict, in any way, with the true and substantial happiness of woman, are contrary to the great precept of nature and of no validity, for this is "superior in obligation to any other."

Resolved, That all laws which prevent woman from occupying such a station in society as her conscience shall dictate, or which place her in a position inferior to that of man, are contrary to the great precept of nature, and therefore of no force or authority.

Resolved, That woman is man's equal—was intended to be so by the Creator, and the highest good of the race demands that she should be recognized as such.

Resolved, That the women of this country ought to be enlightened in regard to the laws under which they live, that they may no longer publish their degradation by declaring themselves satisfied with their present position, nor their ignorance, by asserting that they have all the rights they want.

Resolved, That inasmuch as man, while claiming for himself intellectual superiority, does accord to woman moral superiority, it is pre-eminently his duty to encourage her to speak and teach, as she has an opportunity, in all religious assemblies.

Resolved, That the same amount of virtue, delicacy, and refinement of behavior that is required of woman in the social state, should also be required of man, and the same transgressions should be visited with equal severity on both man and woman.

Resolved, That the objection of indelicacy and impropriety, which is so often brought against woman when she addresses a public audience, comes with a very ill-grace from those who encourage, by their attendance, her appearance on the stage, in the concert, or in feats of the circus.

Resolved, That woman has too long rested satisfied in the circumscribed limits which corrupt customs and a perverted application of the Scriptures have marked out for her, and that it is time she should move in the enlarged sphere which her great Creator has assigned her.

Resolved, That it is the duty of the women of this country to secure to themselves their sacred right to the elective franchise.

Resolved, That the equality of human rights results necessarily from the fact of the identity of the race in capabilities and responsibilities.

Resolved, therefore, That, being invested by the creator with the same capabilities, and the same consciousness of responsibility for their exercise, it is demonstrably the right and duty of woman, equally with man, to promote every righteous cause by every righteous means; and especially in regard to the great subjects of morals and religion, it is self-evidently her right to participate with her brother in teaching them, both in private and in public, by writing and by speaking, by any instrumentalities proper to be used, and in any assemblies proper to be held; and this being a self-evident truth growing out of the divinely implanted principles of human nature, any custom or authority adverse to it, whether modern or wearing the hoary sanction of antiquity, is to be regarded as a self-evident falsehood, and at war with mankind.

Resolved, That the speedy success of our cause depends upon the zealous and untiring efforts of both men and women, for the overthrow of the monopoly of the pulpit, and for the securing to women an equal participation with men in the various trades, professions, and commerce.

The Solitude of Self

(Delivered before the Judiciary Committee of the House,
January 17, 1892)

Mr. Chairman and gentlemen of the committee: We have been speaking before Committees of the Judiciary for the last twenty years, and we have gone over all the arguments in favor of a sixteenth amendment which are familiar to all you gentlemen; therefore, it will not be necessary that I should repeat them again.

The point I wish plainly to bring before you on this occasion is the individuality of each human soul; our Protestant idea, the right of individual conscience and judgment—our republican idea, individual citizenship. In discussing the rights of woman, we are to consider, first, what belongs to her as an individual, in a world of her own, the arbiter of her own destiny, an imaginary Robinson Crusoe with her woman Friday on a solitary island. Her rights under such circumstances are to use all her faculties for her own safety and happiness.

Secondly, if we consider her as a citizen, as a member of a great nation, she must have the same rights as all other members, according to the fundamental principles of our Government.

Thirdly, viewed as a woman, an equal factor in civilization, her rights and duties are still the same—individual happiness and development.

Fourthly, it is only the incidental relations of life, such as mother, wife, sister, daughter, that may involve some special duties and training. In the usual discussion in regard to woman's sphere, such men as Herbert Spencer, Frederic Harrison, and Grant Allen uniformly subordinate her rights and duties as an individual, as a citizen, as a woman, to the necessities of these incidental relations, some of which a large class of woman may never assume. In discussing the sphere of man we do not decide his rights as an individual, as a citizen, as a man by his duties as a father, a husband, a brother, or a son, relations some of which he may never fill. Moreover he would be better fitted for these very relations and whatever special work he might choose to do to earn his bread by the complete development of all his faculties as an individual. Just so with woman. The education that will fit her to discharge the duties in the largest sphere of human usefulness will best fit her for whatever special work she may be compelled to do.

The isolation of every human soul and the necessity of self-dependence must give each individual the right, to choose his own surroundings. The strongest reason for giving woman all the opportunities for higher education, for the full development of her faculties, forces of mind and body; for giving her the most enlarged freedom of thought and action; a complete emancipation from all forms of bondage, of custom, dependence, superstition; from all the crippling influences of fear, is the solitude and personal responsibility of her own individual life. The strongest reason why we ask for woman a voice in the government under which she lives; in the religion she is asked to believe; equality in social life, where she is the chief factor; a place in the trades and professions, where she may earn her bread, is because of her birthright to self-sovereignty; because, as an individual, she must rely on herself. No matter how much women prefer to lean, to be protected and supported, nor how much men desire to have them do so, they must make the voyage of life alone, and for safety in an emergency they must know something of the laws of navigation. To guide our own craft, we must be captain, pilot, engineer; with chart and compass to stand at the wheel; to match the wind and waves and know when to take in the sail, and to read the signs in the firmament over all. It matters not whether the solitary voyager is man or woman. Nature having endowed them equally, leaves them to their own skill and judgment in the hour of danger, and, if not equal to the occasion, alike they perish.

To appreciate the importance of fitting every human soul for independent action, think for a moment of the immeasurable solitude of self. We come into the world alone, unlike all who have gone before us; we leave it alone under circumstances peculiar to ourselves. No mortal ever has been, no

"The strongest reason for giving woman... higher education...is the solitude and personal responsibility of her own individual life."

mortal ever will be like the soul just launched on the sea of life. There can never again be just such environments as make up the infancy, youth and manhood of this one. Nature never repeats herself, and the possibilities of one human soul will never be found in another. No one has ever found two blades of ribbon grass alike, and no one will ever find two human beings alike. Seeing, then, what must be the infinite diversity in human character, we can in a measure appreciate the loss to a nation when any large class of the people is uneducated and unrepresented in the government. We ask for the complete development of every individual, first, for his own benefit and happiness. In fitting out an army we give each soldier his own knapsack, arms, powder, his blanket, cup, knife, fork and spoon. We provide alike for all their individual necessities, then each man bears his own burden.

Again we ask complete individual development for the general good; for the consensus of the competent on the whole round of human interest; on all questions of national life, and here each man must bear his share of the general burden. It is sad to see how soon friendless children are left to bear their own burdens before they can analyze their feelings; before they can even tell their joys and sorrows, they are thrown on their own resources. The great lesson that nature seems to teach us at all ages is self-dependence, self-protection, self-support. What a touching instance of a child's solitude; of that hunger of heart for love and recognition, in the case of the little girl who helped to dress a christmas tree for the children of the family in which she served. On finding there was no present for herself she slipped away in the darkness and spent the night in an open field sitting on a stone, and when found in the morning was weeping as if her heart would break. No mortal will ever know the thoughts that passed through the mind of that friendless child in the long hours of that cold night, with only the silent stars to keep her company. The mention of her case in the daily papers moved many generous hearts to send her presents, but in the hours of her keenest sufferings she was thrown wholly on herself for consolation.

In youth our most bitter disappointments, our brightest hopes and ambitions are known only to ourselves, even our friendship and love we never fully share with another; there is something of every passion in every situation we conceal. Even so in our triumphs and our defeats.

The successful candidate for Presidency and his opponent each have a solitude peculiarly his own, and good form forbids either to speak of his pleasure or regret. The solitude of the king on his throne and the prisoner in his cell differs in character and degree, but it is solitude nevertheless.

We ask no sympathy from others in the anxiety and agony of a broken friendship or shattered love. When death sunders our nearest ties, alone we sit in the shadows of our affliction. Alike mid the greatest triumphs and darkest tragedies of life we walk alone. On the divine heights of human attainments, eulogized and worshiped as a hero or saint, we stand alone. In ignorance, poverty, and vice, as a pauper or criminal, alone we starve or steal; alone we suffer the sneers and rebuffs of our fellows; alone we are hunted and hounded through dark courts and alleys, in by-ways and high-ways; alone we stand in the judgment seat; alone in the prison cell we lament our crimes and misfortunes; alone we expiate them on the gallows. In hours like these we realize the awful solitude of individual life, its pains, its penalties, its responsibilities; hours in which the youngest and most helpless are thrown on their own resources for guidance and consolation. Seeing then that life must ever be a march and a battle, that each soldier must be equipped for his own protection, it is the height of cruelty to rob the individual of a single natural right.

To throw obstacles in the way of a complete education is like putting out the eyes; to deny the rights of property, like cutting off the hands. To deny political equality is to rob the ostracised of all self-respect; of credit in the market place; of recompense in the world of work; of a voice among those who make and administer the law; a choice in the jury before whom they are tried, and in the judge who decides their punishment. Shakespeare's play of Titus and Andronicus contains a terrible satire on woman's position in the nineteenth century—"Rude men" (the play tells us) "seized the king's daughter, cut out her tongue, cut off her hands, and then bade her go

A woman homesteader receives the deed to her land. By 1910, ten percent of all homesteaders were women.

call for water and wash her hands." What a picture of woman's position. Robbed of her natural rights, handicapped by law and custom at every turn, yet compelled to fight her own battles, and in the emergencies of life to fall back on herself for protection.

The girl of sixteen, thrown on the world to support herself, to make her own place in society, to resist the temptations that surround her and maintain a spotless integrity, must do all this by native force or superior education. She does not acquire this power by being trained to trust others and distrust herself. If she wearies of the struggle, finding it hard work to swim upstream, and allows herself to drift with the current, she will find plenty of company, but not one to share her misery in the hour of her deepest humiliation. If she tries to retrieve her position, to conceal the past, her life is hedged about with fears lest willing hands should tear the veil from what she fain would hide. Young and friendless, she knows the bitter solitude of self.

How the little courtesies of life on the surface of society, deemed so important from man towards woman, fade into utter insignificance in view of the deeper tragedies in which she must play her part alone, where no human aid is possible.

The young wife and mother, at the head of some establishment with a kind husband to shield her from the adverse winds of life, with wealth, fortune and position, has a certain harbor of safety, anchors against the ordinary ills of life. But to manage a household, have a [desirable] influence in society, keep her friends and the affections of her husband, train her children and servants well, she must have rare common sense, wisdom, diplomacy, and a knowledge of human nature. To do all this she needs the cardinal virtues and the strong points of character that the most successful statesman possesses.

An uneducated woman, trained to dependence, with no resources in herself must make a failure of any position in life. But society says women do not need a knowledge of the world, the liberal training that experience in public life must give, all the advantages of collegiate education; but when for the lack of all this, the woman's happiness is wrecked, alone she bears her humiliation; and the attitude of the weak and the ignorant is indeed pitiful in the wild chase for the price of life they are ground to powder.

In age, when the pleasures of youth are passed, children grown up, married and gone, the hurry and hustle of life in a measure over, when the hands are weary of active service, when the old armchair and the fireside are the chosen resorts, then men and women alike must fall back on their own resources. If they cannot find companionship in books, if they have no interest in the vital questions of the hour, no interest in watching the consummation of reforms, with which they might have been identified, they soon pass into their dotage. The more fully the faculties of the mind are developed and kept in use, the longer the period of vigor and active interest in all around us continues. If from a lifelong participation in public affairs a woman feels responsible for the laws regulating our system of education, the discipline of our jails and prisons, the sanitary conditions of our private homes, public buildings, and thoroughfares, an interest in commerce, finance, our foreign relations, in any or all of these questions, here solitude will at least be respectable, and she will not be driven to gossip or scandal for entertainment.

The chief reason for opening to every soul the doors to the whole round of human duties and pleasures is the individual development thus attained, the resources thus provided under all circumstances to mitigate the solitude that at times must come to everyone. I once asked Prince Krapotkin, the Russian nihilist, how he endured his long years in prison, deprived of books, pen, ink, and paper. "Ah," he said, "I thought out many questions in which I had a deep interest. In the pursuit of an idea I took no note of time. When tired of solving knotty problems I recited all the beautiful passages in prose or verse I have ever learned. I became acquainted with myself and my own resources. I had a world of my own, a vast empire, that no Russian jailor or Czar could invade." Such is the value of liberal thought and broad culture when shut off from all human companionship, bringing comfort and sunshine within even the four walls of a prison cell.

As women oftentimes share a similar fate, should they not have all the consolation that the most liberal education can give? Their suffering in the prisons of St. Petersburg; in the long, weary marches to Siberia, and in the mines, working side by side with men, surely call for all the self-support that the most exalted sentiments of heroism can give. When suddenly roused at midnight, with the startling cry of "fire! fire!" to find the house over their heads in flames, do women wait for men to point the way to safety? And are the men, equally bewildered and half suffocated with smoke, in a position to more than try to save themselves?

At such times the most timid women have shown a courage and heroism in saving their husbands and children that has surprised everybody. Inasmuch, then, as woman shares equally the joys and sorrows of time and eternity, is it not the height of presumption in man to propose to represent her at the ballot box and the throne of grace, do her voting in the state, her praying in the church, and to assume the position of priest at the family altar.

Nothing strengthens the judgment and quickens the conscience like individual responsibility. Nothing adds such dignity to character as the recognition of one's self-sovereignty; the right to an equal place, every where conceded; a place earned by personal merit, not an artificial attainment, by inheritance, wealth, family, and position. Seeing, then that the responsibilities of life rests equally on man and woman, that their destiny is the same, they need the same preparation for time and eternity. The talk of sheltering woman from the fierce storms of life is the sheerest mockery, for they beat on her from every point of the compass, just as they do on man, and with more fatal results, for he has been trained to protect himself, to resist, to conquer. Such are the facts in human experience, the responsibilities of the individual. Rich and poor, intelligent and ignorant, wise and foolish, virtuous and vicious, man and woman, it is ever the same, each soul must depend wholly on itself.

Whatever the theories may be of woman's dependence on man, in the supreme moments of her life he can not bear her burdens. Alone she goes to the gates of death to give life to every man that is born into the world. No one can share her fears, no one mitigate her pangs; and if her sorrow is greater than she can bear, alone she passes beyond the gates into the vast unknown.

From the mountain tops of Judea, long ago, a heavenly voice bade His disciples, "Bear ye one another's burdens," but humanity has not yet risen to that point of self-sacrifice, and if ever so willing, how few the burdens are that one soul can bear for another. In the highways of Palestine; in prayer and fasting on the solitary mountain top; in the Garden of Gethsemane; before the judgment seat of Pilate; betrayed by one of His trusted disciples at His last supper; in His agonies on the cross, even Jesus of Nazareth, in these last sad days on earth, felt the awful solitude of self. Deserted by man, in agony he cries, "My God! My God! why hast Thou forsaken me?" And so it ever must be in the conflicting scenes of life, on the long weary march, each one walks alone. We may have many friends, love, kindness, sympathy and charity to smooth our pathway in everyday life, but in the tragedies and triumphs of human experience each mortal stands alone.

But when all artificial trammels are removed, and women are recognized as individuals, responsible for their own environments, thoroughly educated for all the positions in life they may be called to fill; with all the resources in themselves that liberal thought and broad culture can give; guided by their own conscience and judgment; trained to self-protection by a healthy development of the muscular system and skill in the use of weapons of defense, and stimulated to self-support by the knowledge of the business world and the pleasure that pecuniary independence must ever give; when women are trained in this way they will, in a measure, be fitted for those hours of solitude that come alike to all, whether prepared or otherwise. As in our extremity we must depend on ourselves, the dictates of wisdom point to complete individual development.

In talking of education how shallow the argument that each class must be educated for the special work it proposed to do, and all those faculties not needed in this special walk must lie dormant and utterly wither for want of use, when, perhaps, these will be the very faculties needed in life's greatest emergencies. Some say, Where is the use of drilling girls in the languages, the Sciences, in law, medicine, theology? As wives, mothers, housekeepers, cooks, they need a different curriculum from boys who are to fill all positions. The chief cooks in our great hotels and ocean steamers are men. In large cities men run the bakeries; they make our bread, cake and pies. They manage the laundries; they are now considered our best milliners and dressmakers. Because some men fill these departments of usefulness, shall we regulate the curriculum in Harvard and Yale to their present necessities? If not why this talk in our best colleges of a curriculum for girls who are crowding into the trades and professions; teachers in all our public schools rapidly filling many lucrative and honorable positions in life? They are

Stanton believed that women belonged in all walks of life, in all professions and trades. Shown here is a woman policeman in 1916.

showing, too, their calmness and courage in the most trying hours of human experience.

You have probably all read in the daily papers of the terrible storm in the Bay of Biscay when a tidal wave wreaked such havoc on the shore, wrecking vessels, unroofing houses and carrying destruction everywhere. Among other buildings the woman's prison was demolished. Those who escaped saw men struggling to reach the shore. They promptly by clasping hands made a chain of themselves and pushed out into the sea, again and again, at the risk of their lives until they had brought six men to shore, carried them to a shelter, and did all in their power for their comfort and protection.

What especial school of training could have prepared these women for this sublime moment of their lives. In times like this humanity rises above all college curriculums and recognises Nature as the greatest of all teachers in the hour of danger and death. Women are already the equals of men in the whole of realm of thought, in art, science, literature, and government. With telescope vision they explore the starry firmament, and bring back the history of the planetary world. With chart and compass they pilot ships across the mighty deep, and with skillful finger send electric messages around the globe. In galleries of art the beauties of nature and the virtues of humanity are immortalized by them on their canvas and by their inspired touch dull blocks of marble are transformed into angels of light.

In music they speak again the language of Mendelssohn, Beethoven, Chopin, Schumann, and are worthy interpreters of their great thoughts. The poetry and novels of the century are theirs, and they have touched the keynote of reform in religion, politics, and social life. They fill the editor's and professor's chair, and plead at the bar of justice, walk the wards of the hospital, and speak from the pulpit and the platform; such is the type of womanhood that an enlightened public sentiment welcomes today, and such the triumph of the facts of life over the false theories of the past.

Is it, then, consistent to hold the developed woman of this day within the same narrow political limits as the dame with the spinning wheel and knitting needle occupied in the past? No! no! Machinery has taken the labors of woman as well as man on its tireless shoulders; the loom and the spinning wheel are but dreams of the past; the pen, the brush, the easel, the chisel, have taken their places, while the hopes and ambitions of women are essentially changed.

We see reason sufficient in the outer conditions of human being for individual liberty and development, but when we consider the self dependence of every human soul we see the need of courage, judgment, and the

"The right is ours. Have it we must. Use it, we will." *In 1920, women finally take their hard-earned places at the polls.*

exercise of every faculty of mind and body, strengthened and developed by use, in woman as well as man.

Whatever may be said of man's protecting power in ordinary conditions, mid all the terrible disasters by land and sea, in the supreme moments of danger, alone, woman must ever meet the horrors of the situation; the Angel of Death even makes no royal pathway for her. Man's love and sympathy enter only into the sunshine of our lives. In that solemn solitude of self, that links us with the immeasurable and the eternal, each soul lives alone forever. A recent writer says:

> "I remember once, in crossing the Atlantic, to have gone upon the deck of the ship at midnight, when a dense black cloud enveloped the sky, and the great deep was roaring madly under the lashes of demoniac winds. My feelings were not of danger or fear (which is a base surrender of the immortal soul), but of utter desolation and loneliness; a little speck of life shut in by a tremendous darkness. Again I remember to have climbed the slopes of the Swiss Alps, up beyond the point where vegetation ceases, and the stunted conifers no longer struggle against the unfeeling blasts. Around me lay a huge confusion of rocks, out of which the gigantic ice peaks shot into the measureless blue of the heavens, and again my only feeling was the awful solitude."

And yet, there is a solitude, which each and every one of us has always carried with him, more inaccessible than the ice-cold mountains, more profound than the midnight sea; the solitude of self. Our inner being, which we call ourself, no eye nor touch of man or angel has ever pierced. It is more hidden than the caves of the gnome; the sacred adytum of the oracle; the hidden chamber of eleusinian mystery, for to it only omniscience is permitted to enter.

Such is individual life. Who, I ask you, can take, dare take, on himself the rights, the duties, the responsibilities of another human soul?

Harriet Taylor Mill

That there was general interest, well over a century ago, in the question of women's rights, and particularly women's suffrage, is suggested by the fact that an essay called "Enfranchisement of Women" appeared in the *Westminster Review*. This was an English periodical devoted to the consideration of public questions, and regarded as radical for its interest in forming alliances between the middle and working classes against the aristocracy. The essay, given as the work of John Stuart Mill (1806–73) but subsequently asserted by him to have been written by his wife, Harriet Taylor, took account of an Ohio Convention of Women held in the spring of 1850, and may even be said to have been inspired by it, though "the woman question" had been much talked of in liberal English circles of the time.

Of Harriet Mill, so little is really known apart from the fact that she was idolized by her husband, who gave her credit for many of his ideas and insisted on her frequent contribution to his writings, that it is difficult if not impossible to say what her authorship really meant. Scholarship has struggled with the question of whether her importance to his work was as large as Mill maintained, as if it made much difference in the absence of any significant personal impression left by her on others during her lifetime, or any certain record that remains of her apart from some correspondence. Presumably their collaboration was a close one, and there is no reason to doubt that Harriet Mill was a woman of intelligence and ideas, but where her ideas began and Mill's ended, or when we can hear her voice speaking in his works, as distinct from his, is hard to determine. Granting her every influence, the fact remains that the books and essays written by Mill with her acknowledged help sound very like those written without it—maintain much the same judicious, forensic style of argument on behalf of positions known to have been held by Mill himself—and if we insist upon her presence we find ourselves dealing with a cypher, a ghost; whereas, if we attribute what is said to Mill, we can at least fit it among productions of a mind we know.

Mill, though not a democrat in his sympathies—he feared the influence of the ignorant in political affairs—was deeply interested in the question of the franchise generally, which notwithstanding the reform of 1832 was still in England very restricted. When in 1865 he was persuaded to stand for Parliament, he used the brief interval he stayed there to help in the passage of the Second Reform Bill of 1867, which greatly increased, though it did not extend to all, the number of citizens who could vote in British elections. Mill wished that women could be included, and said so, and the "Enfranchisement" essay in which he said it first may well have been inspired and even written by his wife. But, again, she had no influence; he did, and his support of the idea was what counted—counted perhaps to the proposal's disadvantage, for his last published work, "The Subjection of Women" (1869), was badly received even by influential British women from considerations we recognize as those of class: why would respectable women wish to mix with the green-grocer at the polls, asked Mrs. Oliphant, the novelist, implying that it was bad enough the green-grocer himself had got, since 1867, the vote. If it comes to that, it appears Harriet Taylor was rather more of Mrs. Oliphant's persuasion than her husband on this particular point, being in fact an elitist, which he, who believed in the power of education to raise the intelligence of the citizenry, was not.

It was not, however, the demand for the franchise, which indeed occupied only a small part of the "Enfranchisement" (as it did subsequently of the "Subjection"), that created opposition to the essay in its time, but its questioning of the position of women in the institution of marriage and the laws that regulated it. This challenged not only male domestic dominion; it also envisioned the establishment of sexual equality, and that was something the Victorian psyche was not prepared to accept. Harriet Mill (if it was she) did not perhaps quite realize how radical the proposal was that she was making. We ourselves cannot be as sure as she (or her husband) was that such an alteration in the relations between men and women would result in their being really "companions." Nor can we be so confident that child-bearing and child-rearing are no more than incidental female occupations, if properly regarded—an idea which only a childless couple could perhaps have conceived.

Still, the "Enfranchisement" must seem to us now as having got most things right, and if it gets some of them wrong, it provokes thought with a clarity of statement which time cannot diminish. Not nearly so well known as the "Subjection," it strikes us today as more trenchant in its exposition, avoiding Mill's tendency to be too fair, to say everything that can be said on both sides of every question. If its directness is the sign that much of the "Enfranchisement" was written by Harriet Mill, we must be glad she did so, as Mill claimed.

Enfranchisement of Women

Harriet Taylor Mill

Introduction by John Stuart Mill to the reprinting of *Enfranchisement of Women* (1851) in his collection *Dissertations and Discussions* (1859).

All the more recent of these papers were joint productions of myself and of one whose loss, even in a merely intellectual point of view, can never be repaired or alleviated. But the following Essay is hers in a peculiar sense, my share in it being little more than that of an editor and amanuensis. Its authorship having been known at the time, and publicly attributed to her, it is proper to state, that she never regarded it as a complete discussion of the subject which it treats of: and, highly as I estimate it, I would rather it remained unacknowledged, than that it should be read with the idea that even the faintest image can be found in it of a mind and heart which in their union of the rarest, and what are deemed the most conflicting excellences, were unparalleled in any human being that I have known or read of. While she was the light, life, and grace of every society in which she took part, the foundation of her character was a deep seriousness, resulting from the combination of the strongest and most sensitive feelings with the highest principles. All that excites admiration when found separately in others, seemed brought together in her: a conscience at once healthy and tender; a generosity, bounded only by a sense of justice which often forgot its own claims, but never those of others; a heart so large and loving, that whoever was capable of making the smallest return of sympathy, always received tenfold; and in the intellectual department, a vigour and truth of imagination, a delicacy of perception, an accuracy and nicety of observation, only equalled by her profundity of speculative thought, and by a practical judgment and discernment next to infallible. So elevated was the general level of her faculties, that the highest poetry, philosophy, oratory, or art, seemed trivial by the side of her, and equal only to expressing some small part of her mind. And there is no one of those modes of manifestation in which she could not easily have taken the highest rank, had not her inclination led her for the most part to content herself with being the inspirer, prompter, and unavowed coadjutor of others.

THE
CONSTANT.

The present paper was written to promote a cause which she had deeply at heart, and though appealing only to the severest reason, was meant for the general reader. The question, in her opinion, was in a stage in which no treatment but the most calmly argumentative could be useful, while many of the strongest arguments were necessarily omitted, as being unsuited for popular effect. Had she lived to write out all her thoughts on this great question, she would have produced something as far transcending in profundity the present Essay, as, had she not placed a rigid restraint on her feelings, she would have excelled it in fervid eloquence. Yet nothing which even she could have written on any single subject, would have given an adequate idea of the depth and compass of her mind. As during life she continually detected, before any one else had seemed to perceive them, those changes of times and circumstances which ten or twelve years later became subjects of general remark, so I venture to prophesy that if mankind continue to improve, their spiritual history for ages to come will be the progressive working out of her thoughts, and realization of her conceptions.

M ost of our readers will probably learn from these pages for the first time, that there has arisen in the United States, and in the most civilized and enlightened portion of them, an organized agitation on a new question— new, not to thinkers, nor to any one by whom the principles of free and popular government are felt as well as acknowledged, but new, and even unheard-of, as a subject for public meetings and practical political action. This question is, the enfranchisement of women; their admission, in law and in fact, to equality in all rights, political, civil, and social, with the male citizens of the community.

It will add to the surprise with which many will receive this intelligence, that the agitation which has commenced is not a pleading by male writers and orators for women, those who are professedly to be benefited remaining either indifferent or ostensibly hostile. It is a political movement, practical in its objects, carried on in a form which denotes an intention to persevere. And it is a movement not merely *for* women, but *by* them. Its first public manifestation appears to have been a Convention of Women, held in the State of Ohio, in the spring of 1850.* Of this meeting we have seen no report. On the 23rd and 24th of October last, a succession of public meetings was held at Worcester in Massachusetts under the name of a "Women's Rights Convention," of which the president was a woman, and nearly all the chief speakers women: numerously reinforced, however, by men, among whom were some of the most distinguished leaders in the kindred cause of negro emancipation. A general and four special committees were nominated, for the purpose of carrying on the undertaking until the next annual meeting.

(Overleaf) "The Constant" illustrates the narrow confines of a woman's life in the 19th century.

*Mill seems to have been unaware of the Seneca Falls Convention of 1848.

An American cartoon from 1920 shows the gradual progression of women's rights. The same year, West Virginia became the 34th of the 36 states necessary to ratify the Nineteenth Amendment granting women the vote.

According to the report in the *New York Tribune,* above a thousand persons were present throughout, and "if a larger place could have been had, many thousands more would have attended." The place was described as "crowded from the beginning with attentive and interested listeners." In regard to the quality of the speaking, the proceedings bear an advantageous comparison with those of any popular movement with which we are acquainted, either in this country or in America. Very rarely in the oratory of public meetings is the part of verbiage and declamation so small, that of calm good sense and reason so considerable. The result of the Convention was in every respect encouraging to those by whom it was summoned: and it is probably destined to inaugurate one of the most important of the movements towards political and social reform, which are the best characteristics of the present age.

That the promoters of this new agitation take their stand on principles, and do not fear to declare these in their widest extent, without time-serving or compromise, will be seen from the resolutions adopted by the Convention, part of which we transcribe.

> *Resolved*—That every human being, of full age, and resident for a proper length of time on the soil of the nation, who is required to obey the law, is entitled to a voice in its enactment; that every such person, whose property or labour is taxed for the support of the government, is entitled to a direct share in such government; therefore,

> *Resolved*—That women are entitled to the right of suffrage, and to be considered eligible to office,...and that every party which claims to represent the humanity, the civilization, and the progress of the age, is bound to inscribe on its banners equality before the law, without distinction of sex or colour.

> *Resolved*—That civil and political rights acknowledge no sex, and therefore the word "male" should be struck from every State Constitution.

> *Resolved*—That, since the prospect of honourable and useful employ-

ment in after-life is the best stimulus to the use of educational advantages, and since the best education is that we give ourselves, in the struggles, employments, and discipline of life; therefore it is impossible that women should make full use of the instruction already accorded to them, or that their career should do justice to their faculties, until the avenues to the various civil and professional employments are thrown open to them.

Resolved—That every effort to educate women, without according to them their rights, and arousing their conscience by the weight of their responsibilities, is futile, and a waste of labour.

Resolved—That the laws of property, as affecting married persons, demand a thorough revisal, so that all rights be equal between them; that the wife have, during life, an equal control over the property gained by their mutual toil and sacrifices, and be heir to her husband precisely to that extent that he is heir to her, and entitled at her death to dispose by will of the same share of the joint property as he is.

The following is a brief summary of the principal demands.

1. *Education* in primary and high schools, universities, medical, legal, and theological institutions.

2. *Partnership* in the labours and gains, risks, and remunerations, of productive industry.

3. *A coequal share* in the formation and administration of laws—municipal, state, and national—through legislative assemblies, courts, and executive offices.

It would be difficult to put so much true, just, and reasonable meaning into a style so little calculated to recommend it as that of some of the resolutions. But whatever objection may be made to some of the expressions, none, in our opinion, can be made to the demands themselves. As a question of justice, the case seems to us too clear for dispute. As one of expediency, the more thoroughly it is examined the stronger it will appear.

That women have as good a claim as men have, in point of personal right, to the suffrage, or to a place in the jury-box, it would be difficult for any one to deny. It cannot certainly be denied by the United States of America, as a people or as a community. Their democratic institutions rest avowedly on the inherent right of every one to a voice in the government. Their Declaration of Independence, framed by the men who are still their great constitutional authorities—that document which has been from the first, and is now, the acknowledged basis of their polity, commences with this express statement:

We hold these truths to be self-evident: that all men are created equal; that they are endowed by their Creator with certain inalienable rights; that among these are life, liberty, and the pursuit of happiness; that to secure these rights, governments are instituted among men, deriving their just powers from the consent of the governed.

We do not imagine that any American democrat will evade the force of these expressions by the dishonest or ignorant subterfuge, that "men," in this memorable document, does not stand for human beings, but for one sex only; that "life, liberty, and the pursuit of happiness" are "inalienable rights" of only one moiety of the human species; and that "the governed," whose consent is affirmed to be the only source of just power, are meant for that half of mankind only, who, in relation to the other, have hitherto assumed the character of governors. The contradiction between principle and practice cannot be explained away. A like dereliction of the fundamental maxims of their political creed has been committed by the Americans in the flagrant instance of the negroes; of this they are learning to recognise the turpitude. After a struggle which, by many of its incidents, deserves the name of heroic, the abolitionists are now so strong in numbers and in influence that they hold the balance of parties in the United States. It was fitting that the men whose names will remain associated with the extirpation, from the democratic soil of America, of the aristocracy of colour, should be among the originators, for America and for the rest of the world, of the first collective protest against the aristocracy of sex; a distinction as accidental as that of colour, and fully as irrelevant to all questions of government.

Not only to the democracy of America, the claim of women to civil and political equality makes an irresistible appeal, but also to those Radicals and Chartists in the British islands, and democrats on the Continent, who claim what is called universal suffrage as an inherent right, unjustly and oppressively withheld from them. For with what truth or rationality could the suffrage be termed universal, while half the human species remained excluded from it? To declare that a voice in the government is the right of all, and demand it only for a part—the part, namely, to which the claimant himself belongs—is to renounce even the appearance of principle. The Chartist who denies the suffrage to women, is a Chartist only because he is not a lord: he is one of those levellers who would level only down to themselves.

Even those who do not look upon a voice in the government as a matter of personal right, nor profess principles which require that it should be extended to all, have usually traditional maxims of political justice with which it is impossible to reconcile the exclusion of all women from the common rights of citizenship. It is an axiom of English freedom that taxation and representation should be co-extensive. Even under the laws which give the wife's property to the husband, there are many unmarried women who pay taxes. It is one of the fundamental doctrines of the British Constitution, that all persons should be tried by their peers: yet women, whenever tried, are tried by male judges and a male jury. To foreigners the law accords the privilege of claiming that half the jury should be composed of themselves; not so to women. Apart from maxims of detail, which represent local and national rather than universal ideas; it is an acknowledged dictate of justice to make no degrading distinctions without necessity. In all things the presumption ought to be on the side of equality. A reason must be given why anything should be permitted to one person and interdicted to another. But when that which is interdicted includes nearly everything which those to whom it is permitted most prize, and to be deprived of which they feel to be most insulting; when not only political liberty but personal freedom of action is the prerogative of a caste; when even in the exercise of industry, almost all employments which task the higher faculties in an important field, which lead to distinction, riches, or even pecuniary independence, are fenced round as the exclusive domain of the predominant section, scarcely any doors being left open to the dependent class, except such as all who can enter elsewhere disdainfully pass by; the miserable expediencies which are advanced as excuses for so grossly partial a dispensation, would not be sufficient, even if they were real, to render it other than a flagrant injustice. While, far from being expedient,

A Currier & Ives cartoon from 1869 shows the "triumphs of Woman's Rights."

we are firmly convinced that the division of mankind into two castes, one born to rule over the other, is in this case, as in all cases, an unqualified mischief; a source of perversion and demoralization, both to the favoured class and to those at whose expense they are favoured; producing none of the good which it is the custom to ascribe to it, and forming a bar, almost insuperable while it lasts, to any really vital improvement, either in the character or in the social condition of the human race.

These propositions it is now our purpose to maintain. But before entering on them, we would endeavour to dispel the preliminary objections which, in the minds of persons to whom the subject is new, are apt to prevent a real and conscientious examination of it. The chief of these obstacles is that most formidable one, custom. Women never have had equal rights with men. The claim in their behalf, of the common rights of mankind, is looked upon as barred by universal practice. This strongest of prejudices, the prejudice against what is new and unknown, has, indeed, in an age of changes like the present, lost much of its force; if it had not, there

would be little hope of prevailing against it. Over three-fourths of the habitable world, even at this day, the answer, "it has always been so," closes all discussion. But it is the boast of modern Europeans, and of their American kindred, that they know and do many things which their forefathers neither knew nor did; and it is perhaps the most unquestionable point of superiority in the present above former ages, that habit is not now the tyrant it formerly was over opinions and modes of action, and that the worship of custom is a declining idolatry. An uncustomary thought, on a subject which touches the greater interests of life, still startles when first presented; but if it can be kept before the mind until the impression of strangeness wears off, it obtains a hearing, and as rational a consideration as the intellect of the hearer is accustomed to bestow on any other subject.

In the present case, the prejudice of custom is doubtless on the unjust side. Great thinkers, indeed, at different times, from Plato to Condorcet, besides some of the most

Leaders of the women's rights movement were sometimes sharply reminded that not all women supported them.

eminent names of the present age, have made emphatic protests in favour of the equality of women. And there have been voluntary societies, religious or secular, of which the Society of Friends is the most known, by whom that principle was recognised. But there has been no political community or nation in which, by law and usage, women have not been in a state of political and civil inferiority. In the ancient world the same fact was alleged, with equal truth, in behalf of slavery. It might have been alleged in favour of the mitigated form of slavery, serfdom, all through the middle ages. It was urged against freedom of industry, freedom of conscience, freedom of the press; none of these liberties were thought compatible with a well-ordered state, until they had proved their possibility by actually existing as facts. That an institution or a practice is customary is no presumption of its goodness, when any other sufficient cause can be assigned for its existence. There is no difficulty in understanding why the subjection of women has been a custom. No other explanation is needed than physical force.

That those who were physically weaker should have been made legally inferior, is quite conformable to the mode in which the world has been governed. Until very lately, the rule of physical strength was the general law of human affairs. Throughout history, the nations, races, classes, which found themselves the strongest, either in muscles, in riches, or in military discipline, have conquered and held in subjection the rest. If, even in the most improved nations, the law of the sword is at last discountenanced as unworthy, it is only since the calumniated eighteenth century. Wars of conquest have only ceased since democratic revolutions began. The world is very young, and has but just begun to cast off injustice. It is only now getting rid of negro slavery. It is only now getting rid of monarchical despotism. It is only now getting rid of hereditary feudal nobility. It is only now getting rid of disabilities on the ground of religion. It is only beginning to treat any *men* as citizens, except the rich and a favoured portion of the middle class. Can we wonder that it has not yet done as much for women? As society was constituted until the last few generations, inequality was its very basis; association grounded on equal rights scarcely existed; to be equals was to be enemies; two persons could hardly cooperate in anything, or meet in any amicable relation, without the law's appointing that one of them should be the superior of the other. Mankind have outgrown this state, and all things now tend to substitute, as the general principle of human relations, a just equality, instead of the dominion of the strongest. But of all relations, that between men and women being the nearest and most intimate, and connected with the greatest number of strong emotions, was sure to be the last to throw off the old rule and receive the new: for in proportion to the strength of a feeling, is the tenacity with which it clings to the forms and circumstances with which it has even accidentally become associated.

When a prejudice, which has any hold on the feelings, finds itself reduced to the unpleasant necessity of assigning reasons, it thinks it has done enough when it has re-asserted the very point in dispute, in phrases which appeal to the pre-existing feeling. Thus, many persons think they have sufficiently justified the restrictions on women's field of action, when they have said that the pursuits from which women are excluded are *unfeminine,* and that the *proper sphere* of women is not politics or publicity, but private and domestic life.

We deny the right of any portion of the species to decide for another portion, or any individual for another individual, what is and what is not their "proper sphere." The proper sphere for all human beings is the largest and highest which they are able to attain to. What this is, cannot be ascertained, without complete liberty of choice. The speakers at the Convention in America have therefore done wisely and right, in refusing to entertain the question of the peculiar aptitudes either of women or of men, or the limits within this or that occupation may be supposed to be more adapted to the one or to the other. They justly maintain, that these questions can only be satisfactorily answered by perfect freedom. Let every occupation be open to all, without favour or discouragement to any, and employments will fall into the hands of those men or women who are found by experience to be most capable of worthily exercising them. There need be no fear that women will take out of the hands of men any occupation which men perform better than they. Each individual will prove his or her capacities, in the only way in which capacities can be proved—by trial; and the world will have the benefit of the best faculties of all its inhabitants. But to interfere beforehand by an arbitrary limit, and declare that whatever be the genius, talent, energy, or force of mind of an individual of a certain sex or class, those faculties shall not be exerted, or shall be exerted only in some few of the many modes in which others are permitted to use theirs, is not only an injustice to the individual, and a detriment to society, which loses what it can ill spare, but is also the most effectual mode of providing that, in the sex or class so fettered, the qualities which are not permitted to be exercised shall not exist.

We shall follow the very proper example of the Convention, in not entering into the question of the alleged differences in physical or mental qualities between the sexes; not because we have nothing to say, but because we have too much; to discuss this one point tolerably would need all the space we have to bestow on the entire subject.* But if those who assert that the "proper sphere" for women is the domestic, mean by this that they have not shown themselves qualified for any other, the assertion evinces great ignorance of life and of history. Women have shown fitness for the highest social functions, exactly in proportion as they have been admitted to them. By a curious anomaly, though ineligible to even the lowest offices of State, they are in some countries admitted to the highest of all, the regal; and if there is any one function for which they have shown a decided vocation, it is that of reigning. Not to go back to ancient history, we look in vain for abler or firmer rulers than Elizabeth; than Isabella of Castile; than Maria Teresa; than Catherine of Russia; than Blanche, mother of Louis IX of France; than Jeanne d'Albret, mother of Henri Quatre. There are few kings on record who contended with more difficult circumstances, or overcame them more triumphantly, than these. Even in semibarbarous Asia, princesses who have never been seen by men, other than those of their own family, or ever spoken with them unless from behind a curtain, have as regents, during the minority of their sons, exhibited many of the most brilliant examples of just and vigorous administration. In the middle ages, when the distance between the upper and lower ranks was greater than even between women and men, and the women of the privileged class, however subject to tyranny from the men of the same class, were at a less distance below them than any one else was, and often in their absence represented

---

*An excellent passage on this part of the subject, from one of Sydney Smith's contributions to the Edinburgh Review, we will not refrain from quoting: "A great deal has been said of the original difference of capacity between men and women, as if women were more quick and men more judicious—as if women were more remarkable for delicacy of association, and men for stronger powers of attention. All this, we confess, appears to us very fanciful. That there is a difference in the understandings of the men and the women we every day meet with, everybody, we suppose, must perceive; but there is none surely which may not be accounted for by the difference of circumstances in which they have been placed, without referring to any conjectural difference of original conformation of mind. As long as boys and girls run about in the dirt, and trundle hoops together, they are both precisely alike. If you catch up one-half of these creatures, and train them to a particular set of actions and opinions, and the other half to a perfectly opposite set, of course their understandings will differ, as one or the other sort of occupations has called this or that talent into action. There is surely no occasion to go into any deeper or more abstruse reasoning, in order to explain so very simple a phenomenon." (*Sydney Smith's Works,* vol. i, p. 200.)

An American cartoon from 1894 implies that fashionable clothing also prevented women from gaining the vote.

A SQUELCHER FOR WOMAN SUFFRAGE.

How Can She Vote, when the Fashions Are so Wide, and the Voting Booths Are so Narrow?

them in their functions and authority—numbers of heroic châtelaines, like Jeanne de Montfort, or the great Countess of Derby as late even as the time of Charles I, distinguished themselves not only by their political but their military capacity. In the centuries immediately before and after the Reformation, ladies of royal houses, as diplomatists, as governors of provinces, or as the confidential advisers of kings, equalled the first statesmen of their time: and the treaty of Cambray, which gave peace to Europe, was negotiated in conferences where no other person was present, by the aunt of the Emperor Charles the Fifth, and the mother of Francis the First.

Concerning the fitness, then, of women for politics, there can be no question: but the dispute is more likely to turn upon the fitness of politics for women. When the reasons alleged for excluding women from active life in all its higher departments are stripped of their garb of declamatory phrases, and reduced to the simple expression of a meaning, they seem to be mainly three: first, the incompatibility of active life with maternity, and with the cares of a household; secondly, its alleged hardening effect on the character; and thirdly, the inexpediency of making an addition to the already excessive pressure of competition in every kind of professional or lucrative employment.

The first, the maternity argument, is usually laid most stress upon: although (it needs hardly be said) this reason, if it be one, can apply only to mothers. It is neither necessary nor just to make imperative on women that they shall be either mothers or nothing; or that if they have been mothers once, they shall be nothing else during the whole remainder of their lives. Neither women nor men need any law to exclude them from an occupation, if they have undertaken another which is incompatible with it. No one proposes to exclude the male sex from Parliament because a man may be a soldier or sailor in active service, or a merchant whose business requires all his time and energies. Nine-tenths of the occupations of men exclude them *de facto* from public life, as effectually as if they were excluded by law; but that is no reason for making laws to exclude even the nine-tenths, much less the remaining tenth. The reason of the case is the same for women as for men. There is no need to make provision by law that a woman shall not carry on the active details of a household, or of the education of children, and at the same time practice a profession, or be elected to parliament. Where incompatibility is real, it will take care of itself: but there is gross injustice in making the incompatibility a pretence for the exclusion of those in whose case it does not exist. And these, if they were free to choose, would be a very large proportion. The maternity argument deserts its supporters in the case of single women, a large and increasing class of the population; a fact which, it is not irrelevant to remark, by tending to diminish the excessive competition of numbers, is calculated to assist greatly the prosperity of all. There is no inherent reason or necessity that all women should voluntarily choose to devote their lives to one animal function and its consequences. Numbers of women are wives and mothers only because there is no other career open to them, no other occupation for their feelings or their activities. Every improvement in their education, and enlargement of their faculties, everything which renders them more qualified for any other mode of life, increases the number of those to whom it is an injury and an oppression to be denied the choice. To say that women must be excluded from active life because maternity disqualifies them for it, is in fact to say, that every other career should be forbidden them in order that maternity may be their only resource.

But secondly, it is urged, that to give the same freedom of occupation to women as to men, would be an injurious addition to the crowd of competitors, by whom the avenues to almost all kinds of employment are choked up, and its remuneration depressed. This argument, it is to be observed, does not reach the political question. It gives no excuse for withholding from women the rights of citizenship. The suffrage, the jury-box, admission to the legislature and to office, it does not touch. It bears only on the industrial branch of the subject. Allowing it, then, in an economical point of view, its full force; assuming that to lay open to women the employments now monopolized by men, would tend, like the breaking down of other monopolies, to lower the rate of remuneration in those employments;

let us consider what is the amount of this evil consequence, and what the compensation for it. The worst ever asserted, much worse than is at all likely to be realized, is that if women competed with men, a man and a woman could not together earn more than is now earned by the man alone. Let us make this supposition, the most unfavourable supposition possible: the joint income of the two would be the same as before, while the woman would be raised from the position of a servant to that of a partner. Even if every woman, as matters now stand, had a claim on some man for support, how infinitely preferable is it that part of the income should be of the woman's earning, even if the aggregate sum were but little increased by it, rather than that she should be compelled to stand aside in order that men may be the sole earners, and the sole dispensers of what is earned. Even under the present laws respecting the property of women, a woman who contributes materially to the support of the family, cannot be treated in the same contemptuously tyrannical manner as one who, however she may toil as a domestic drudge, is a dependent on the man for subsistence.* As for the depression of wages by increase of competition, remedies will be found for it in time. Palliatives might be applied immediately; for instance, a more rigid exclusion of children from industrial employment, during the years in which they ought to be working only to strengthen their bodies and minds for after-life. Children are necessarily dependent, and under the power of others; and their labour, being not for themselves but for the gain of their parents, is a proper subject for legislative regulation. With respect to the future, we neither believe that improvident multiplication, and the consequent excessive difficulty of gaining a subsistence, will always continue, nor that the division of mankind into capitalists and hired labourers, and the regulation of the reward of labourers mainly by demand and supply, will be for ever, or even much longer, the rule of the world. But so long as competition is the general law of human life, it is tyranny to shut out one-half of the competitors. All who have attained the age of self-government have an equal claim to be permitted to sell whatever kind of useful labour they are capable of, for the price which it will bring.

The third objection to the admission of women to political or professional life, its alleged hardening tendency, belongs to an age now past, and is scarcely to be comprehended by people of the present time. There are still, however, persons who say that the world and its avocations render men selfish and unfeeling; that the struggles, rivalries, and collisions of business and of politics make them harsh and unamiable; that if half the species must unavoidably be given up to these things, it is the more necessary that the other half should be kept free from them; that to preserve

---

*The truly horrible effects of the present state of the law among the lowest of the working population, is exhibited in those cases of hideous maltreatment of their wives by working men, with which every newspaper, every police report, teems. Wretches unfit to have the smallest authority over any living thing, have a helpless woman for their household slave. These excesses could not exist if women both earned, and had the right to possess, a part of the income of the family.

women from the bad influences of the world, is the only chance of preventing men from being wholly given up to them.

There would have been plausibility in this argument when the world was still in the age of violence; when life was full of physical conflict, and every man had to redress his injuries or those of others, by the sword or by the strength of his arm. Women, like priests, by being exempted from such responsibilities, and from some part of the accompanying dangers, may have been enabled to exercise a beneficial influence. But in the present condition of human life, we do not know where those hardening influences are to be found, to which men are subject and from which women are at present exempt. Individuals now-a-days are seldom called upon to fight hand to hand, even with peaceful weapons; personal enmities and rivalities count for little in worldly transactions; the general pressure of circumstances, not the adverse will of individuals, is the obstacle men now have to make head against. That pressure, when excessive, breaks the spirit, and cramps and sours the feelings, but not less of women than of men, since they suffer certainly not less from its evils. There are still quarrels and dislikes, but the sources of them are changed. The feudal chief once found his bitterest enemy in his powerful neighbour, the minister or courtier in his rival for place: but opposition of interest in active life, as a cause of personal animosity, is out of date; the enmities of the present day arise not from great things but small, from what people say of one another, more than from what they do; and if there are hatred, malice, and all uncharitableness, they are to be found among women fully as much as among men. In the present state of civilization, the notion of guarding women from the hardening influences of the world, could only be realized by secluding them from society altogether. The common duties of common life, as at present constituted, are incompatible with any other softness in women than weakness. Surely weak minds in weak bodies must ere long cease to be even supposed to be either attractive or amiable.

But, in truth, none of these arguments and considerations touch the foundations of the subject. The real question is, whether it is right and expedient that one-half of the human race should pass through life in a state of forced subordination to the other half. If the best state of human society is that of being divided into two parts, one consisting of persons with a will and a substantive existence, the other of humble companions to these persons, attached, each of them to one, for the purpose of bringing up *his* children, and making *his* home pleasant to him; if this is the place assigned to women, it is but kindness to educate them for this; to make them believe that the greatest good fortune which can befall them, is to be chosen by some man for this purpose; and that every other career which the world deems happy or honourable, is closed to them by the law, not of social institutions, but of nature and destiny.

When, however, we ask why the existence of one-half the species should be merely ancillary to that of the other—why each woman should be a mere appendage to a man, allowed to have no interests of her own, that there may be nothing to compete in her mind with his interests and his

THE WALL STREET HIPPODROME.

HOW TO MANAGE A BALKY TEAM.
New York Evening Telegraph, February 18th, 1870.

pleasure; the only reason which can be given is, that men like it. It is agreeable to them that men should live for their own sake, women for the sake of men: and the qualities and conduct in subjects which are agreeable to rulers, they succeed for a long time in making the subjects themselves consider as their appropriate virtues. Helvetius has met with much obloquy for asserting, that persons usually mean by virtues the qualities which are useful or convenient to themselves. How truly this is said of mankind in general, and how wonderfully the ideas of virtue set afloat by the powerful, are caught and imbibed by those under their dominion, is exemplified by the manner in which the world were once persuaded that the supreme virtue of subjects was loyalty to kings, and are still persuaded that the paramount virtue of womanhood is loyalty to men. Under a nominal recognition of a moral code common to both, in practice self-will and self-assertion form the type of what are designated as manly virtues, while abnegation of self, patience, resignation, and submission to power, unless when resistance is commanded by other interests than their own, have been stamped by general consent as pre-eminently the duties and graces required of women. The meaning being merely, that power makes itself the centre of moral obligation, and that a man likes to have his own will, but does not like that his domestic companion should have a will different from his.

We are far from pretending that in modern and civilized times, no reciprocity of obligation is acknowledged on the part of the stronger. Such an assertion would be very wide of the truth. But even this reciprocity, which has disarmed tyranny, at least in the higher and middle classes, of its most

A cartoon from 1870 shows Wall Street brokers Victoria Woodhull and her sister driving a team of their male counterparts.

revolting features, yet when combined with the original evil of the dependent condition of women, has introduced in its turn serious evils.

In the beginning, and among tribes which are still in a primitive condition, women were and are the slaves of men for purposes of toil. All the hard bodily labour devolves on them. The Australian savage is idle, while women painfully dig up the roots on which he lives. An American Indian, when he has killed a deer, leaves it, and sends a woman to carry it home. In a state somewhat more advanced, as in Asia, women were and are the slaves of men for purposes of sensuality. In Europe there early succeeded a third and milder dominion, secured not by blows, nor by locks and bars, but by sedulous inculcation on the mind; feelings also of kindness, and ideas of duty, such as a superior owes to inferiors under his protection, became more and more involved in the relation. But it did not, for many ages, become a relation of companionship, even between unequals. The lives of the two persons were apart. The wife was part of the furniture of home—of the resting-place to which the man returned from business or pleasure. His occupations were, as they still are, among men; his pleasures and excite-

The suffragette movement also supported the right for women to smoke in public.

ments also were, for the most part, among men—among his equals. He was a patriarch and a despot within four walls, and irresponsible power had its effect, greater or less according to his disposition, in rendering him domineering, exacting, self-worshipping, when not capriciously or brutally tyrannical. But if the moral part of his nature suffered, it was not necessarily so, in the same degree, with the intellectual or the active portion. He might have as much vigour of mind and energy of character as his nature enabled him, and as the circumstances of his times allowed. He might write the *Paradise Lost,* or win the battle of Marengo. This was the condition of the Greeks and Romans, and of the moderns until a recent date. Their relations with their domestic subordinates occupied a mere corner, though a cherished one, of their lives. Their education as men, the formation of their character and faculties, depended mainly on a different class of influences.

It is otherwise now. The progress of improvement has imposed on all possessors of power, and of domestic power among the rest, an increased and increasing sense of correlative obligation. No man now thinks that his wife has no claim upon his actions but such as he may accord to her. All

men of any conscience believe that their duty to their wives is one of the most binding of their obligations. Nor is it supposed to consist solely in protection, which, in the present state of civilization, women have almost ceased to need: it involves care for their happiness and consideration of their wishes, with a not unfrequent sacrifice of their own to them. The power of husbands has reached the stage which the power of kings had arrived at, when opinion did not yet question the rightfulness of arbitrary power, but in theory, and to a certain extent in practice, condemned the selfish use of it. This improvement in the moral sentiments of mankind, and increased sense of the consideration due by every man to those who have no one but himself to look to, has tended to make home more and more the centre of interest, and domestic circumstances and society a larger and larger part of life, and of its pursuits and pleasures. The tendency has been strengthened by the changes of tastes and manners which have so remarkably distinguished the last two or three generations. In days not far distant, men found their excitement and filled up their time in violent bodily exercises, noisy merriment, and intemperance. They have now, in all but the very poorest classes, lost their inclination for these things, and for the coarser pleasures generally; they have now scarcely any tastes but those which they have in common with women, and, for the first time in the world, men and women are really companions. A most beneficial change, if the companionship were between equals; but being between unequals, it produces, what good observers have noticed, though without perceiving its cause, a progressive deterioration among men in what had hitherto been considered the masculine excellences. Those who are so careful that women should not become men, do not see that men are becoming, what they have decided that women should be—are falling into the feebleness which they have so long cultivated in their companions. Those who are associated in their lives, tend to become assimilated in character. In the present closeness of association between the sexes, men cannot retain manliness unless women acquire it.

There is hardly any situation more unfavourable to the maintenance of elevation of character or force of intellect, than to live in the society, and seek by preference the sympathy, of inferiors in mental endowments. Why is it that we constantly see in life so much of intellectual and moral promise followed by such inadequate performance, but because the aspirant has compared himself only with those below himself, and has not sought improvement or stimulus from measuring himself with his equals or superiors. In the present state of social life, this is becoming the general condition of men. They care less and less for any sympathies, and are less and less under any personal influences, but those of the domestic roof. Not to be misunderstood, it is necessary that we should distinctly disclaim the belief, that women are even now inferior in intellect to men. There are women who are the equals in intellect of any men who ever lived; and comparing ordinary women with ordinary men, the varied though petty details which compose the occupation of most women, call forth probably as much of mental ability, as the uniform routine of the pursuits which are the habitual occupation of a large majority of men. It is from nothing in the faculties themselves, but from the petty subjects and interests on which alone they are exercised, that the companionship of women, such as their present circumstances make them, so often exercises a dissolvent influence on high faculties and aspirations in men. If one of the two has no knowledge and no care about the great ideas and purposes which dignify life, or about any of its practical concerns save personal interests and personal vanities, her conscious, and still more her unconscious influence, will, except in rare cases, reduce to a secondary place in his mind, if not entirely extinguish, those interests which she cannot or does not share.

Our argument here brings us into collision with what may be termed the moderate reformers of the education of women; a sort of persons who cross the path of improvement on all great questions; those who would maintain the old bad principles, mitigating their consequences. These say, that women should be, not slaves, nor servants, but companions; and educated for that office (they do not say that men should be educated to be the companions of women). But since uncultivated women are not suitable companions for cultivated men, and a man who feels interest in things above and beyond the family circle wishes that his companion should sympathize with him in that interest; they therefore say, let women improve their understanding and taste, acquire general knowledge, cultivate poetry, art, even coquet with science, and some stretch their liberality so far as to say, inform themselves on politics; not as pursuits, but sufficiently to feel an interest in the subjects, and to be capable of holding a conversation on them with the husband, or at least of understanding and imbibing his wisdom. Very agreeable to him, no doubt, but unfortunately the reverse of improving. It is from having intellectual communion only with those to whom they can lay down the law, that so few men continue to advance in wisdom beyond the first stages. The most eminent men cease to improve, if they associate only with disciples. When they have overtopped those who immediately surround them, if they wish for further growth, they must seek for others of their own stature to consort with. The mental companionship which is improving, is communion between active minds, not mere contact between an active mind and a passive. This inestimable advantage is even now enjoyed, when a strong-minded man and a strong-minded woman are, by a rare chance, united: and would be had far oftener, if education took the same pains to form strongminded women which it takes to prevent them from being formed. The modern, and what are regarded as the improved and enlightened modes of education of women, abjure, as far as words go, an education of mere show, and profess to aim at solid instruction, but mean by that expression, superficial information on solid subjects. Except accomplishments, which are now generally regarded as to be taught well if taught at all, nothing is taught to women thoroughly. Small portions only of what it is attempted to teach thoroughly to boys, are the whole of what it is intended or desired to teach to women. What makes intelligent beings is the

A Currier & Ives cartoon from 1869 relegates the men to domestic chores, while the women can come and go as they please.

power of thought: the stimuli which call forth that power are the interest and dignity of thought itself, and a field for its practical application. Both motives are cut off from those who are told from infancy that thought, and all its greater applications, are other people's business, while theirs is to make themselves agreeable to other people. High mental powers in women will be but an exceptional accident, until every career is open to them, and until they, as well as men, are educated for themselves and for the world—not one sex for the other.

In what we have said on the effect of the inferior position of women, combined with the present constitution of married life, we have thus far had in view only the most favourable cases, those in which there is some real approach to that union and blending of characters and of lives, which the theory of the relation contemplates as its ideal standard. But if we look to the great majority of cases, the effect of women's legal inferiority, on the character both of women and of men, must be painted in far darker colours. We do not speak here of the grosser brutalities, nor of the man's power to seize on the woman's earnings, or compel her to live with him against her will. We do not address ourselves to any one who requires to have it proved that these things should be remedied. We suppose average cases, in which there is neither complete union nor complete disunion of feelings and character; and we affirm that in such cases the influence of the dependence on the woman's side, is demoralizing to the character of both.

The common opinion is, that whatever may be the case with the intellectual, the moral influence of women over men is almost salutary. It is, we are often told, the great counteractive of selfishness. However the case may be as to personal influence, the influence of the position tends eminently to promote selfishness. The most insignificant of men, the man who can obtain influence or consideration nowhere else, finds one place where he is chief and head. There is one person, often greatly his superior in understanding, who is obliged to consult him, and whom he is not obliged to consult. He is judge, magistrate, ruler, over their joint concerns; arbiter of all differences between them. The justice or conscience to which her appeal must be made, is his justice and conscience: it is his to hold the balance and adjust the scales between his own claims or wishes and those of another. His is now the only tribunal, in civilized life, in which the same person is judge and party. A generous mind, in such a situation, makes the balance incline against his own side, and gives the other not less, but more, than a fair equality; and thus the weaker side may be enabled to turn the very fact of dependence into an instrument of power, and in default of justice, take an ungenerous advantage of generosity; rendering the unjust power, to those who make an unselfish use of it, a torment and a burthen. But how is it when average men are invested with this power, without reciprocity and without responsibility? Give such a man the idea that he is first in law and in opinion—that to will is his part, and hers to submit; it is absurd to suppose that this idea merely glides over his mind, without sinking into it, or having any effect on his feelings and practice. The propensity to make himself the first object of consideration, and others at most the second, is not so rare as to be wanting where everything seems purposely arranged for encouraging its indulgence. If there is any self-will in the man, he becomes either the conscious or unconscious despot of his household. The wife, indeed, often succeeds in gaining her objects, but it is by some of the many various forms of indirectness and management.

Thus the position is corrupting equally to both; in the one it produces the vices of power, in the other those of artifice. Women, in their present physical and moral state, having stronger impulses, would naturally be franker and more direct than men; yet all the old saws and traditions represent them as artful and dissembling. Why? Because their only way to their objects is by indirect paths. In all countries where women have strong wishes and active minds, this consequence is inevitable: and if it is less conspicuous in England than in some other places, it is because English-women, saving occasional exceptions, have ceased to have either strong wishes or active minds.

We are not now speaking of cases in which there is anything deserving the name of strong affection on both sides. That, where it exists, is too powerful a principle not to modify greatly the bad influences of the situa-tion; it seldom, however, destroys them entirely. Much oftener the bad influences are too strong for the affection, and destroy it. The highest order of durable and happy attachments would be a hundred times more frequent than they are, if the affection which the two sexes sought from one another were that genuine friendship, which only exists between equals in privi-leges as in faculties. But with regard to what is commonly called affection in married life—the habitual and almost mechanical feeling of kindliness, and pleasure in each other's society, which generally grows up between persons who constantly live together, unless there is actual dislike—there is nothing in this to contradict or qualify the mischievous influence of the unequal relation. Such feelings often exist between a sultan and his favourites, between a master and his servants; they are merely examples of the pliability of human nature, which accommodates itself in some degree even to the worst circumstances, and the commonest natures always the most easily.

With respect to the influence personally exercised by women over men, it, no doubt, renders them less harsh and brutal; in ruder times, it was often the only softening influence to which they were accessible. But the assertion, that the wife's influence renders the man less selfish, contains, as things now are, fully as much error as truth. Selfishness towards the wife herself, and towards those in whom she is interested, the children, though favoured by her dependence, the wife's influence, no doubt, tends to counteract. But the general effect on him of her character, so long as her interests are concentrated in the family, tends but to substitute for individual selfishness a family selfishness, wearing an amiable guise, and putting on the mask of duty. How rarely is the wife's influence on the side of public virtue; how rarely does it do otherwise than discourage any effort of principle by which the private interests or worldly vanities of the family can be expected to suffer. Public spirit, sense of duty towards the public good, is of all virtues, as women are now educated and situated, the most rarely to be found among them; they have seldom even, what in men is often a partial substitute for public spirit, a sense of personal honour connected with any public duty. Many a man, whom no money or personal flattery would have bought, has bartered his political opinions against a title or invitations for his wife; and a still greater number are made mere hunters after the puerile vanities of society, because their wives value them. As for opinions; in Catholic countries, the wife's influence is another name for that of the priest; he gives her, in the hopes and emotions connected with a future life, a consolation for the sufferings and disappointments which are her ordinary lot in this. Elsewhere, her weight is thrown into the scale either of the most commonplace, or of the most outwardly prosperous opinions: either those by which censure will be escaped, or by which worldly advancement is likeliest to be procured. In England, the wife's influence is usually on the illiberal and antipopular side: this is generally the gaining side for personal interest and vanity; and what to her is the democracy or liberalism in which she has no part—which leaves her the Pariah it found her? The man himself, when he marries, usually declines into Conservatism; begins to sympathize with the holders of power, more than with its victims, and thinks it his part to be on the side of authority. As to mental progress, except those vulgar attainments by which vanity or ambition are promoted, there is generally an end to it in a man who marries a woman mentally his inferior; unless, indeed, he is unhappy in marriage, or becomes indifferent. From a man of twenty-five or thirty, after he is married, an experienced observer seldom expects any further progress in mind or feelings. It is rare that the progress already made is maintained. Any spark of the *mens divinior* which might otherwise have spread and become a flame, seldom survives for any length of time unextinguished. For a mind which learns to be satisfied with what it already is—which does not incessantly look forward to a degree of improvement not yet reached—becomes relaxed, self-indulgent, and loses the spring and the tension which maintain it even at the point already attained. And there is no fact in human nature to which experience bears more invariable testimony than to this—that all social or sympathetic influences which do not raise up, pull down; if they do not tend to stimulate and exalt the mind, they tend to vulgarize it.

For the interest, therefore, not only of women but of men, and of human improvement in the widest sense, the emancipation of women, which the modern world often boasts of having effected, and for which credit is sometimes given to civilization, and sometimes to Christianity, cannot stop where it is. If it were either necessary or just that one portion of mankind should remain mentally and spiritually only half developed, the development of the other portion ought to have been made, as far as possible, independent of their influence. Instead of this, they have become the most intimate, and it may now be said, the only intimate associates of those to whom yet they are sedulously kept inferior; and have been raised just high enough to drag the others down to themselves.

We have left behind a host of vulgar objections either as not worthy of an answer, or as answered by the general course of our remarks. A few words, however, must be said on one plea, which in England is made much use of for giving an unselfish air to the upholding of selfish privileges, and which, with unobserving, unreflecting people, passes for much more than it is worth. Women, it is said, do not desire—do not seek, what is called their emancipation. On the contrary, they generally disown such claims when made in their behalf, and fall with *acharnement* upon any one of themselves who identifies herself with their common cause.

Supposing the fact to be true in the fullest extent ever asserted, if it proves that European women ought to remain as they are, it proves exactly the same with respect to Asiatic women; for they too, instead of murmuring at their seclusion, and at the restraint imposed upon them, pride themselves on it, and are astonished at the effrontery of women who receive visits from male acquaintances, and are seen in the streets unveiled. Habits of submission make men as well as women servile-minded. The vast population of Asia do not desire or value, probably would not accept, political liberty, nor the savages of the forest, civilization; which does not prove that either of those things is undesirable for them, or that they will not, at some future time, enjoy it. Custom hardens human beings to any kind of degradation, by deadening the part of their nature which would resist it. And the case of women is, in this respect, even a peculiar one, for no other inferior caste that we have heard of have been taught to regard their degradation as their honour. The argument, however, implies a secret consciousness that the alleged preference of women for their dependent state is merely apparent, and arises from their being allowed no choice; for if the preference be natural, there can be no necessity for enforcing it by law. To make laws compelling people to follow their inclination, has not hitherto been thought necessary by any legislator. The plea that women do not desire any change, is the same that has been urged, times out of mind, against the proposal of abolishing any social evil—"there is no complaint"; which is generally not true, and when true, only so because there is not that hope of success, without which complaint seldom makes itself audible to unwilling ears. How does the objector know that women do not desire equality and freedom? He never knew a woman who did not, or would not, desire it for herself individually. It would be very simple to suppose, that if they do desire it they will say so. Their position is like that of the tenants or labourers who vote against their own political interests to please their landlords or employers; with the unique addition, that submission is inculcated on them from childhood, as the peculiar attraction and grace of their character. They are taught to think, that to repel actively even an admitted injustice done to themselves, is somewhat unfeminine, and had better be left to some male friend or protector. To be accused of rebelling against anything which admits of being called an ordinance of society, they are taught to regard as an imputation of a serious offence, to say the least, against the proprieties of their sex. It requires unusual moral courage as well as disinterestedness in a woman, to express opinions favourable to women's enfranchisement, until, at least, there is some prospect of obtaining it. The comfort of her individual life, and her social consideration, usually depend on the good-will of those who hold the undue power, and to possessors of power any complaint, however bitter, of the misuse of it, is a less flagrant act of insubordination than to protest against the power itself. The professions of women in this matter remind us of the State offenders of old, who, on the point of execution, used to protest their love and devotion to the sovereign by whose unjust mandate they suffered. Griselda herself might be matched from the speeches put by Shakespeare into the mouths of male victims of kingly caprice and tyranny: the Duke of Buckingham, for example, in *Henry the Eighth,* and even Wolsey. The literary class of women, especially in England, are ostentatious in disclaiming the desire for equality or citizenship, and proclaiming their complete satisfaction with the place which society assigns to them; exercising in this, as in many other respects, a most noxious influence over the feelings and opinions of men, who unsuspectingly accept the servilities of toadyism as concessions to the force of truth, not considering that it is the personal interest of these women to profess whatever opinions they expect will be agreeable to men. It is not among men of talent, sprung from the people, and patronized and flattered by the aristocracy, that we look for the leaders of a democratic movement. Successful literary women are just as unlikely to prefer the cause of women to their own social consideration. They depend on men's opinion for their literary as well as for their feminine successes; and such is their bad opinion of men, that they believe there is not more than one in ten thousand who does not dislike and fear strength, sincerity, or high spirit in a woman. They are therefore anxious to earn pardon and toleration for whatever of these qualities their writings may exhibit on other subjects, by a studied display of submission on this: that they may give no occasion for vulgar men to say (what nothing will prevent vulgar men from saying), that

An engraving of a suffragette's cabinet meeting.

learning makes women unfeminine, and that literary ladies are likely to be bad wives.

But enough of this; especially as the fact which affords the occasion for this notice, makes it impossible any longer to assert the universal acquiescence of women (saving individual exceptions) in their dependent condition. In the United States, at least, there are women, seemingly numerous, and now organized for action on the public mind, who demand equality in the fullest acceptation of the word, and demand it by a straightforward appeal to men's sense of justice, not plead for it with a timid deprecation of their displeasure.

Like other popular movements, however, this may be seriously retarded by the blunders of its adherents. Tried by the ordinary standard of public meetings, the speeches at the Convention are remarkable for the preponderance of the rational over the declamatory element; but there are some exceptions; and things to which it is impossible to attach any rational

"INDEPENDENCE DAY" OF THE FUTURE.

meaning, have found their way into the resolutions. Thus, the resolution which sets forth the claims made in behalf of women, after claiming equality in education, in industrial pursuits, and in political rights, enumerates as a fourth head of demand something under the name of "social and spiritual union," and "a medium of expressing the highest moral and spiritual views of justice," with other similar verbiage, serving only to mar the simplicity and rationality of the other demands; resembling those who would weakly attempt to combine nominal equality between men and women, with enforced distinctions in their privileges and functions. What is wanted for women is equal rights, equal admission to all social privileges; not a position apart, a sort of sentimental priesthood. To this, the only just and rational principle, both the resolutions and the speeches, for the most part, adhere. They contain so little which is akin to the nonsensical paragraph in question, that we suspect it not to be the work of the same hands as most of the other resolutions. The strength of the cause lies in the support of those who are influenced by reason and principle; and to attempt to recommend it by sentimentalities, absurd in reason, and inconsistent with the principle on which the movement is founded, is to place a good cause on a level with a bad one.

There are indications that the example of America will be followed on this side of the Atlantic; and the first step has been taken in that part of England where every serious movement in the direction of political progress has its commencement—the manufacturing districts of the North. On the 13th of February 1851, a petition of women, agreed to by a public meeting at Sheffield, and claiming the elective franchise, was presented to the House of Lords by the Earl of Carlisle.

(Left) This American cartoon from 1894 predicts the eventual success of the women's rights movement.

Louis Agassiz

Permanence of type? In *evolution*? What type? What permanence? We all
know, or believe we know, that by virtue of the evolutionary process which
underlies all living things, permanence does not exist. Nature, at least that
which takes in living things, and some of what we once classed as inert,
where chemistry is now perceived as still at work, is constantly changing,
never permanent; the types, or as we prefer to say species, which separate
living things are always subject to what we call development, to mutation.
It was once thought that the complex order of living things was an original,
fixed creation. But science is beyond that idea now.

Quite so. But for this very reason it has been thought worthwhile to
reflect upon the implications of the evolutionary view we have adopted.
Such is the excuse for reprinting here an essay by Louis Agassiz, the
nineteenth-century zoologist and paleontologist who notoriously declined
to accept such a view, and on many occasions, as this article in an *Atlantic
Monthly* of 1873, declared his unwillingness to subscribe to Darwin's
theory.

Why? The easy answer is that he thought Darwin, whom he admired,
had nevertheless exceeded his evidence in promulgating his theory of Natural Selection. Agassiz was right. Darwin knew nothing of genes and, as he
acknowledged, could not give a satisfactory explanation of the process of
change in individuals that is required for changes in species. Agassiz did
not object to this on religious grounds any more than did Cardinal Bellarm-
ine to Galileo in that famous interrogation (when Galileo stubbornly insisted that "nevertheless it moves," referring to the passage of the earth
about the sun, he was not so much defying religious authority as holding to
a conclusion of which he felt certain even though he could not prove it, and
the Cardinal, who was a learned man, was accusing him not of bad theology but bad science). Agassiz saw the gap in Darwin's conception, and said

so. He may have felt there was some offense to God in Darwin's idea but that is not the excuse for opposing it here.

Something else seems to have been at work in his mind. The nub of the problem may be the difficulty to which Professor Healey addresses himself elsewhere in this volume in talking about quantum theory. This is, that the theory and the mechanics that arise from that theory are obliged to deal with things such as subatomic particles which can be known only by their motion—cannot be said otherwise with certainty to exist—and that there is some doubt whether what this branch of physics recognizes is matter or simply its own measurements.

So with evolution, which has made of organic nature something which is itself in motion and thus cannot be said to exist in any given sense. There is, after Darwin, no "Nature" apart from an endless (and beginningless?) Coming to Be and Passing Away of things (to use Aristotle's phrase)— unless we say that what endures are the laws by which this process is carried on, and as if our understanding of these was not undergoing constant revision. But this means that there is nothing which can be called a Whole in Nature of which we ourselves are part. And if that is the case there is no framework within which we can define ourselves—what we are, and belong to, and have some kind of responsibility for—but only what in this century we have come to call our existential predicament, which is that we must live without such markers. A sense of Nature as a Whole is very evident in Agassiz, for all that he spent most of his life examining small parts of it, as the skeletal structure of Brazilian fish. Not that he was averse to thinking there was something, indeed much, to be discovered in the natural order; his sense of the mystery of things is evident as well. But for him there is something *there* which cannot cease to *be,* and to which as scientist and man he is committed. It is said that he had read Plato. If so, he may have remembered the Timaeus, where it is maintained that the Cosmos exists both as a whole and in its parts, and that the whole comes, or came, first.

Agassiz (1807–73) was by birth a Swiss and made his scientific reputation in ichthyology, or the study of fish fossils, first at Paris and then at Neuchâtel, where he was professor of natural history. He counted Baron Cuvier, the most eminent ichthyologist of his time, and also Alexander von Humboldt, the German naturalist—both among the great European scientists of the day—among his friends. In 1846 he came to lecture at the Lowell Institute in Boston and afterwards decided to accept an offer from Harvard University, where he remained for the rest of his life, marrying Elizabeth Cabot Cary, a writer and promoter of women's education, in 1850. He was much liked at Harvard, where he worked closely with his students in hands-on study of phenomena, emphasizing the importance of contact with nature and avoiding the use of texts. Thus he revolutionized studies in the sciences he professed, to a point where, from about 1860 to the end of the century, virtually every teacher of natural history in the United States had been one of his pupils. He also created at Harvard the museum of comparative zoology which became a model of its kind.

Evolution and Permanence of Type

Louis Agassiz

Illustrations by Richard Cline

I n connection with modern views of science we hear so much of evolution and evolutionists that it is worth our while to ask if there is any such process as evolution in nature. Unquestionably, yes. But all that is actually known of this process we owe to the great embryologists of our century, Döllinger[1] and his pupils K.E. von Baer,[2] Pander,[3] and others—the men in short who have founded the science of Embryology. It is true there are younger men who have done since, and are doing now, noble work in this field of research; but the glory must, after all, be given to those who opened the way in which more recent students are pressing forward.

The pioneers in the science of Embryology, by a series of investigations which will challenge admiration as long as patience and accuracy of research are valued, have proved that all living beings produce eggs, and that these eggs contain a yolk-substance out of which new beings, identical with their parents, are evolved by a succession of gradual changes. These successive stages of growth constitute evolution, as understood by embryologists, and within these limits all naturalists who know anything of Zoology may be said to be evolutionists. The law of evolution, however, so far as its working is understood, is a law controlling development and keeping types within appointed cycles of growth, which revolve forever upon themselves, returning at appointed intervals to the same starting-point and repeating through a succession of phases the same course. These cycles have never been known to oscillate or to pass into each other; indeed, the only structural differences known between individuals of the same stock are monstrosities or peculiarities pertaining to sex, and the latter are as abiding and permanent as to type itself. Taken together the relations of sex constitute one of the most obscure and wonderful features of the whole organic world, all the more impressive for its universality.

Under the recent and novel application of the terms "evolution" and "evolutionist," we are in danger of forgetting the only process of the kind in the growth of animals which has actually been demonstrated, as well as the men to whom we owe that demonstration. Indeed, the science of Zoology, including everything pertaining to the past and present life and history of animals, has furnished, since the beginning of the nineteenth century, an amount of startling and exciting information in which men have lost sight of the old landmarks. In the present ferment of theories respecting the relations of animals to one another, their origin, growth, and diversity, those broader principles of our science—upon which the whole animal kingdom has been divided into a few grand comprehensive types, each one a structural unit in itself—are completely overlooked.

It is not very long since, with the exception of Insects, all the lower animals were grouped together in one division as Worms, on account of their simple structure. A century ago this classification, established by Linnaeus,[4] was still unquestioned. Cuvier was the first to introduce a classification based not merely upon a more or less complicated organization but upon ideas or plans of structure. He recognized four of these plans in the whole animal kingdom, neither more nor less. However, when this principle was first announced, the incompleteness of our knowledge made it

impossible to apply it correctly in every case, and Cuvier himself placed certain animals of obscure or intricate structure under the wrong head. Nevertheless the law was sanctioned, and gave at once a new aim and impulse to investigation. This idea of structural plans, as the foundation of a natural classification, dates only from the year 1812, and was first presented by Cuvier[5] in the Annals of the Museum in Paris.

About the same time another great investigator, Karl Ernst von Baer, then a young naturalist, Döllinger's favorite and most original pupil, was studying in Germany the growth of the chicken in the egg. In a different branch of research, though bearing equally on the structural relations of organized beings, he, without knowing of Cuvier's investigations, arrived at a like conclusion, namely, that there are four different modes of growth among animals. This result has only been confirmed by later investigators. Every living creature is formed in an egg and grows up according to a pattern and a mode of development common to its type, and of these embryonic norms there are but four. Here, then, was a double confirmation of the distinct circumscription of types, as based upon structure, announced almost simultaneously by two independent investigators, ignorant of each other's work, and arriving at the same result by different methods. The one, building up from the first dawn of life in the embryonic germs of various animals, worked out the four great types of organic life from the beginning; while his co-worker reached the same end through a study of their perfected structure in adult forms. Starting from diametrically opposite points, they met at last on the higher ground to which they were both led by their respective studies.

For a quarter of a century following, the aim of all naturalists was to determine the relations of these groups to one another with greater precision, and to trace the affinities between the minor divisions of the whole animal kingdom. It was natural to suppose that all living beings were in some way or other connected; and, indeed, the discoveries in Geology, with its buried remains of extinct life, following fast upon those of Cuvier in structure and of Von Baer in Embryology, seemed to reveal, however dimly and in broken outlines, a consistent history carried on coherently through all times and extending gradually over the whole surface of the earth, until it culminated in the animal kingdom as it at present exists, with man at its head.

The next step, though a natural result of the flood of facts poured in upon us under the new stimulus to research, led men away from the simple and, as I believe, sound principles of classification established by the two great masters of zoological science. The announcement of four typical divisions in the animal kingdom stirred investigators to a closer comparison of their structure. The science of Comparative Anatomy made rapid strides; and since the ability of combining facts is a much rarer gift than that of discerning them, many students lost sight of the unity of structural design in the multiplicity of structural detail. The natural result of this was a breaking up of the four great groups of Radiates, Mollusks, Articulates and Vertebrates into a larger number of primary divisions. Classifications were multiplied with astonishing rapidity, and each writer had his own system of nomenclature, until our science was perplexingly burdened with synonyms. I may mention, as a sample, one or two of the more prominent changes introduced at this time into the general classification of animals.

The Radiates had been divided by Cuvier into three classes, to which, on imperfect data, he erroneously added the Intestinal Worms and the Infusoria. These classes, as they now stand according to his classification, with some recent improvements, are Polyps (corals, sea-anemones, and the like), Acalephs (jelly-fishes), and Echinoderms (star-fishes, sea-urchins, and holothurians, better known, perhaps, as Beche-de-mer). Of these three classes the two first, Polyps and Acalephs, were set apart by Leuckart and other naturalists as "Coelenterata," while the Echinoderms by themselves were elevated into a primary division. There is, however, no valid ground for this. The plan of structure is the same in all three classes, the only difference being that various organs which in the Polyps and the Acalephs are, as it were, simply hollowed out of the substance of the body, have in the Echinoderms walls of their own. This is a special complication of structural execution, but makes no difference in the structural plan. The organs and the whole structural combination are the same in the two divisions. In the same way Cephalopods, squids and the cuttlefishes, which form the highest class among Mollusks, were separated from the Gasteropods and Acephala, and set apart as a distinct type, because their eggs undergo only a surface segmentation instead of being segmented through and through, as is the case with the members of the two other classes. But this surface segmentation leads ultimately to a structure which has the same essential features as that of the other Mollusks. Indeed, we find also in other branches of the animal kingdom, the Vertebrates for instance, partial or total segmentation, in different classes; but it does not lead to any typical differences there, any more than among Mollusks. Another instance is that of the Bryozoa and Tunicata, which were separated from the Mollusks on account of the greater simplicity of their structure and associated with those simpler Worms in which articulated limbs are wanting. In short, the numerous types admitted nowadays by most zoologists are founded only upon structural complication, without special regard to the plan of their structure; and the comprehensive principle of structural conception or plan, as determining the primary types, so impressive when first announced, has gradually lost its hold upon naturalists through their very familiarity with special complications of structure. But since we are still in doubt as to the true nature of many organisms, such as the sponges and the Protozoa so-called, it is too early to affirm positively that all the primary divisions of the animal kingdom are included in Cuvier's four types. Yet it is safe to say that no primary division will stand which does not bear the test he applied to the four great groups, Radiates, Mollusks, Articulates, and Vertebrates, namely, that of a distinct plan of structure for each.

The time has, perhaps, not come for an impartial appreciation of the views of Darwin,[6] and the task is the more difficult because it involves an equally impartial review of the modifications his theory has undergone at

the hands of his followers. The aim of his first work on The Origin of Species was to show that neither vegetable nor animal forms are so distinct from one another or so independent in their origin and structural relations as most naturalists believed. This idea was not new. Under different aspects it had been urged repeatedly for more than a century by DeMaillet,[7] by Lamarck,[8] by E. Geoffroy St. Hilaire[9] and others; nor was it wholly original even with them, for the study of the relations of animals and plants has at all times been one of the principal aims of all the more advanced students of Natural History; they have differed only in their methods and appreciations. But Darwin has placed the subject on a different basis from that of all his predecessors, and has brought to the discussion a vast amount of well-arranged information, a convincing cogency of argument, and a captivating charm of presentation. His doctrine appealed the more powerfully to the scientific world because he maintained it at first not upon metaphysical ground but upon observation. Indeed it might be said that he treated his subject according to the best scientific methods, had he not frequently overstepped the boundaries of actual knowledge and allowed his imagination to supply the links which science does not furnish.

The excitement produced by the publication of The Origin of Species may be fairly compared to that which followed the appearance of Oken's Natur-Philosophie, over fifty years ago, in which it was claimed that the key had been found to the whole system of organic life. According to Oken,[10] the animal kingdom, in all its diversity, is but the presentation in detail of the organization of man. The Infusoria are the primordial material of life scattered broadcast everywhere, and man himself but a complex of such Infusoria. The Vertebrates represent what Oken calls flesh, that is, bones, muscles, nerves, and the senses, in various combinations; the Fishes are Bone-animals (Knochen-Thiere); the Reptiles, Muscle-animals (Muskel-Thiere); the Birds, Nerve-animals (Nerven-Thiere); the Mammals—with man, combining in his higher structure the whole scheme of organic life, at their head—are Sense-animals (Sinnen-Thiere). The parallelism was drawn with admirable skill and carried into the secondary divisions, down to the families and even the genera. The Articulates were likened to the systems of respiration and circulation; the Mollusks to those of reproduction; the Radiates to those of digestion. The comprehensiveness and grandeur of these views, in which the scattered elements of organic life, serving distinct purposes in the lower animals, are gathered into one structural combination in the highest living being appealed powerfully to the imagination. In Germany they were welcomed with an enthusiasm such as is shown there for Darwinism. England was lukewarm, and France turned a cold shoulder, as she at present does to the theory of the great English naturalist. The influence of Cuvier and the Jussieux was deeply felt in Western Europe, and perhaps saved French naturalists from falling into a fanciful but attractive doctrine, numbered now among the exploded theories of the past.

Darwin's first work, though it did not immediately meet with the universal acceptance since accorded to it, excited, nevertheless, intense and general interest. The circumstance that almost identical views were simultaneously expressed by Wallace,[11] and that several prominent investigators hailed them as the solution of the great problem, gave them double strength; for it seemed improbable that so many able students of nature should agree in their interpretation of facts, unless that interpretation were the true one. The Origin of Species was followed by a second work, The Variation of Animals and Plants under Domestication, to which a third soon succeeded, The Descent of Man. The last phase of the doctrine is its identification with metaphysics in Darwin's latest work on The Expression of the Emotions in Man and Animals. I can only rejoice that the discussion has taken this turn, much as I dissent from the treatment of the subject. It cannot be too soon understood that science is one, and that whether we investigate language, philosophy, theology, history, or physics, we are dealing with the same problem, culminating in the knowledge of ourselves. Speech is known only in connection with the organs of man, thought in connection with his brain, religion as the expression of his aspirations, history as the record of his deeds, and physical sciences as the laws under which he lives. Philosophers and theologians have yet to learn that a physical fact is as sacred as a moral principle. Our own nature demands from us this double allegiance.

It is hardly necessary to give here an analysis of the theory contained in these works of Darwin. Its watchwords, "natural selection," "struggle for existence," "survival of the fittest," are equally familiar to those who do and to those who do not understand them; as well known, indeed, to the amateur in science as to the professional naturalist. It is supported by a startling array of facts respecting the changes animals undergo under domestication, respecting the formation of breeds and varieties, respecting metamorphoses, respecting the dangers to life among all animals and the way in which nature meets them, respecting the influence of climate and external conditions upon superficial structural features, and respecting natural preferences and proclivities between animals as influencing the final results of interbreeding. In the Variation of Animals and Plants under Domestication all that experiments in breeding or fancy horticulture could teach, whether as recorded in the literature and traditions of the subject or gathered from the practical farmers, stock-breeders, and gardeners, was brought together and presented with equal erudition and clearness. No fact was omitted showing the pliability of plants and animals under the fostering care of man. The final conclusion of the author is summed up in his theory of Pangenesis. And yet this book does but prove more conclusively what was already known, namely, that all domesticated animals and cultivated plants are traceable to distinct species, and that the domesticated pigeons which furnish so large a portion of the illustration are, notwithstanding their great diversity under special treatment, no exception to this rule. The truth is, our domesticated animals, with all their breeds and varieties, have never been traced back to anything but their own species, nor have artificial varieties, so far as we know, failed to revert to the wild stock when left to themselves. Darwin's works and those of his followers have added nothing new to our previous knowledge concerning the origin of man and his associates in domestic life, the horse, the cow, the sheep, the dog, or, indeed, of any animal. The facts upon which Darwin, Wallace, Haeckel,[12] and others base their views are in the possession of every well-educated naturalist. It is only a question of interpretation, not of discovery or of new and unlooked-for information.

Darwin's third book, The Descent of Man, treats a more difficult part of the subject. In this book the question of genealogy is the prominent topic. It had been treated already, it is true, in The Origin of Species, but with no special allusion to mankind. The structure was as yet a torso, a trunk without a head. In these two volumes the whole ground of heredity, of qualities transmitted to the new individual by his progenitors, and that of resemblance—whether physical, intellectual, or moral, between mankind and the higher mammalia, and especially between ourselves and our nearest relations, the anthropoid monkeys—are brought out with the fullness of material and the skill of treatment so characteristic of the author. But here again the reader seeks in vain for any evidence of a transition between man and his fellow-creatures. Indeed, both with Darwin and his followers, a great part of the argument is purely negative. It rests partly upon the assumption that, in the succession of ages, just those transition types have dropped out from the geological record which would have proved the Darwinian conclusions had these types been preserved, and that in the living animal the process of transition is too subtle for detection. Darwin and his followers thus throw off the responsibility of proof with respect both to embryonic growth and geological succession.

Within the last three or four years, however, it has seemed as if new light were about to be thrown at least upon one of these problems. Two prominent naturalists announced that they had found indications of a direct structural connection between primary types: in the one case between Mollusks and Vertebrates, in the other between Radiates and Articulates. The first of these views was published by a Russian investigator of great skill and eminence, Kowalevsky.[13] He stated that the Ascidians (the so-called soft-shelled clams) showed, in the course of their growth, a string of cells corresponding to the dorsal cord in Vertebrates. For the uninitiated I must explain that, at one stage of its development, in the upper layer of cells of which the Vertebrate germ consists, there arise two folds which, curving upward and inward, form first a longitudinal furrow and finally a cavity for the nervous centres, the brain and spinal cord, while the lower layer of these cells folds downward to enclose the organs of digestion, circulation, and reproduction. Between these two folds, but on the dorsal side, that is, along the back, under the spinal marrow, arises a solid string of more condensed substance, which develops into the dorsal cord, the basis of the backbone. Kowalevsky describes, in the Ascidians, a formation of longitudinally arranged cells as representing an incipient backbone, running from the middle of the body into the tail, along a furrow of the germ of these animals in which the main nervous swelling is situated. This was hailed as a great discovery by the friends of the transmutation theory. At

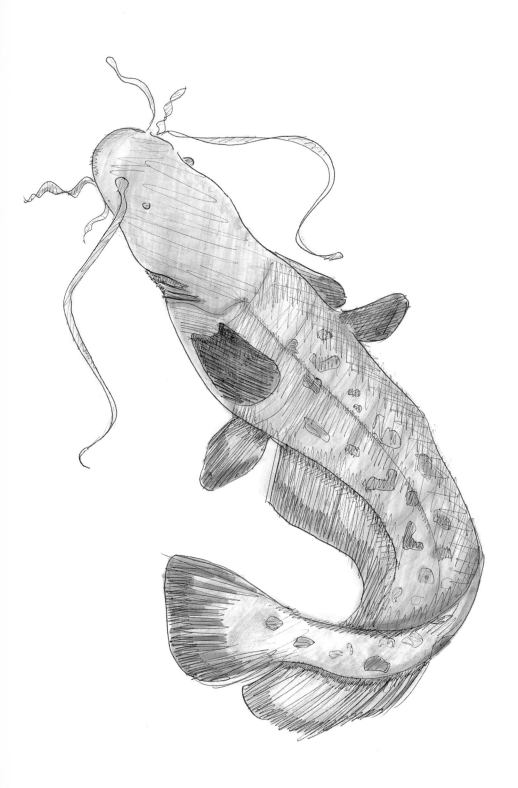

last the transition point was found between the lower and higher animals, and man himself was traced back to the Ascidians. One could hardly open a scientific journal or any popular essay on Natural History, without meeting some allusion to the Ascidians as our ancestors. Not only was it seized upon by the many amateur contributors to the literature of this subject, but Darwin himself, and his ardent followers, welcomed this first direct evidence of structural affinity between the Vertebrates and the lower animals.

The existence of these cells, though never thought of in this light before, was not unknown to naturalists. I have myself seen and examined them, and had intended to say something in this article of their nature and position; but while I was preparing it for the press the subject was taken from me and treated by the hand of a master whom all naturalists venerate. I have received very recently from the aged Nestor of the science of Embryology, K.E. von Baer, to whose early investigations I have already alluded, a pamphlet upon the development of the Ascidians as compared to that of the Vertebrates. There is something touching in the conditions under which he enters the lists with the younger men who have set aside the great laws of typical structure, to the interpretation of which his whole life has been given. He is now very feeble and nearly blind; but the keen, far-reaching, internal sight is undimmed by age. With the precision and ease which only a complete familiarity with all the facts can give, he shows that the actual development of the Ascidians has no true homology with that of the Vertebrates; that the string of cells in the former—compared to the dorsal cord of the latter—does not run along the back at all, but is placed on the ventral side of the body. To say that the first Vertebrates or their progenitors carried their backbones in this fashion is about as reasonable as to say that they walked on their heads. It is reversing their whole structure, and putting their vertebral column where the abdominal cavity should be. Von Baer closes his paper in these words: "It will readily be granted that I have written for zoologists and anatomists; but I may perhaps be blamed for being frequently very circumstantial where a brief allusion would have been sufficient. In so doing, I had the many dilletanti in view, who believe in complete transmutations, and who might be disposed to consider it mere conceit not to recognize the Ascidians as the ancestors of Man. I beg to apologize for some repetitions arising from this consideration for the dilletanti."

The other so-called discovery is that of Haeckel, that star-fishes are compound animals, made up, as it were, of worm-like beings united like rays in one organism. A similar opinion had already been entertained by Duvernoy,[14] and in a measure also by Oken, who described the Echinoderms as Radiate-worms. This doctrine, if true, would at once establish a transition from Radiates to Articulates. There is, in the first place, not the slightest foundation for this assumption in the structure of star-fish. The arms of these animals are made up of the same parts as the vertical zones of a sea-urchin and of all the Radiates, and have no resemblance whatever to the structure of the Worms. Each ambulacral zone of a star-fish or a sea-urchin is strictly homological to a structural segment of an Acaleph or to a radiating chamber of a Polyp. Moreover, the homology between a sea-urchin and a star-fish is complete; if one is an organic unit the other must be also, and no one ever suggested that the sea-urchin was anything but a single organism. In comparing the Radiates with other animals, it is essential to place them in the same attitude, so that we compare like with like; otherwise, we make the mistake of the Russian naturalist, and compare the front side of one animal with the dorsal side of another, or the upper side of one with the lower side of another; thus taking mere superficial resemblance between totally distinct parts for true homologies. In all Mollusks, Articulates, and Vertebrates the parts are arranged along a longitudinal axis; in Radiates alone they are disposed around a vertical axis, like spherical wedges, comparable in some instances to the segments of an orange. This organic formula, for so we may call it, is differently expressed and more or less distinct in different Radiates. It may be built up in a sphere, as in the sea-urchins, or opened out into a star, like the five-finger; it may be in the form of a sac divided internally, as in the sea-anemones, or in that of a disk, channelled or furrowed so as to divide it into equal segments, like the jelly-fish; but upon comparison the same structural elements are found in all. These structural elements bear an identical relation to the vertical axis of the animals. To compare any Radiate with any Articulate is therefore to compare the vertical axis of one animal with the horizontal axis of the other. The parallelism will not bear examination any more than that between the Mollusks and Vertebrates. Even in those holothurians and sea-urchins in which one side of the body is flattened, the structure exhibits the same plan and the parts are arranged in the same way as in all other Radiates, whatever be their natural attitude in the element in which they live; whether they stand upright with the mouth turned upward, or hang down in the reverse position, or crawl about horizontally. In like manner the vertical position of man in no way invalidates the homology of his organization with that of the fishes, reptiles, birds, and mammalia. These two cases are thus far the only instances which have been brought forward to prove actual structural affinity between distinct primary divisions of the animal kingdom.

It is not my intention to take up categorically all the different points on which the modern theory of transmutation is based. Metamorphosis plays a large part in it, and is treated as an evidence of transition from one animal into another. The truth is that metamorphosis, like all embryonic growth, is a normal process of development, moving in regular cycles, returning always to the same starting-point, and leading always to the same end; such are the alternate generations in the lower animals and the metamorphoses in higher ones, as in the butterflies and other insects, or in certain reptiles, frogs and toads, salamanders, and the like. In some of these types the development lasts for a long time and the stages of embryonic growth are often so distinct that, until the connection between them is traced, each phase may seem like a separate existence, whereas they are only chapters in one and the same life. I have myself watched carefully all the successive changes of development in the North American Axolotl, whose recently discovered metamorphoses have led to much discussion in connection with the modern doctrine of evolution. I can see no difference between this and other instances of metamorphosis. Certain organs, conspicuous in one phase of the animal's life, are resorbed and disappear in a succeeding phase. But this does not differ at all from like processes in the toads and frogs, for instance; nor does it even differ essentially from like processes in the ordinary growth of all animals. The higher Vertebrates, including man himself, breathe through gill-like organs in the early part of their life. These gills disappear and give place to lungs only in a later phase of their existence. Metamorphoses have all the constancy and invariability of other modes of embryonic growth, and have never been known to lead to any transition of one species into another.

Another fertile topic in connection with this theory is that of heredity. No one can deny that inheritance is a powerful factor in the maintenance of race and in the improvement of breeds and varieties. But it has never been known that acquired qualities, even though retained through successive generations, have led to the production of new species. Darwin's attractive style is never more alluring than in connection with this subject. His concise and effective phrases have the weight of aphorisms and pass current for principles, when they may be only unfounded assertions. Such is "the survival of the fittest." After reading some chapters of The Descent of Man, could any one doubt, unless indeed he happened to be familiar with the facts, that animals, possessing certain advantages over others, are necessarily winners in the race for life? And yet it is not true that, outside of the influence of man, there are, in nature, privileged individuals among animals capable of holding on to a positive gain, generation after generation, and of transmitting successfully their peculiarities until they become the starting point for another step; the descendants losing at last, through this cumulative process, all close resemblance to their progenitors. It is not true that a slight variation, among the successive offspring of the same stock, goes on increasing until the difference amounts to a specific distinction. On the contrary, it is a matter of fact that extreme variations finally degenerate or become sterile; like monstrosities they die out, or return to their type.

The whole subject of inheritance is exceedingly intricate, working often in a seemingly capricious and fitful way. Qualities, both good and bad, are dropped as well as acquired, and the process ends sometimes in the degradation of the type and the survival of the unfit rather than the fittest. The most trifling and fantastic tricks of inheritance are quoted in support of the transmutation theory; but little is said of the sudden apparition of powerful original qualities which almost always rise like pure creations and are gone with their day and generation. The noblest gifts are exceptional, and are rarely inherited; this very fact seems to me an evidence of something more and higher than mere evolution and transmission concerned in the problem of life.

In the same way, the matter of natural and sexual selection is susceptible of very various interpretations. No doubt, on the whole, Nature protects her best. But it would not be difficult to bring together an array of facts as striking as those produced by the evolutionists in favor of their theory, to show that sexual selection is by no means always favorable to the elimination of the chaff and the preservation of the wheat. A natural attraction, independent of strength or beauty, is an unquestionable element in this problem, and its action is seen among animals as well as among men. The fact that fine progeny are not infrequently the offspring of weak parents and *vice versa* points perhaps to some innate power of redress by which the caprices of choice are counterbalanced. But there can be no doubt that types are as often endangered as protected by the so-called law of sexual selection.

As to the influence of climate and physical conditions, we all know their power for evil and for good upon living beings. But there is, nevertheless, nothing more striking in the whole book of nature than the power shown by types and species to resist physical conditions. Endless evidence may be brought from the whole expanse of land and air and water, showing that identical physical conditions will do nothing toward the merging of species into one another, neither will variety of conditions do anything toward their multiplication. One thing only we know absolutely, and in this treacherous, marshy ground of hypothesis and assumption, it is pleasant to plant one's foot occasionally upon a solid fact here and there. Whatever be the means of preserving and transmitting properties, the primitive types have remained permanent and unchanged—in the long succession of ages amid all the appearance and disappearance of kinds, the fading away of one species and the coming in of another—from the earliest geological periods to the present day. How these types were first introduced, how the species which have successively represented them have replaced one another—these are the vital questions to which no answer has been given. We are as far from any satisfactory solution of this problem as if development theories had never been discussed.

This brings us to the geological side of the question. As a palaeontologist I have from the beginning stood aloof from this new theory of transmutation, now so widely admitted by the scientific world. Its doctrines, in fact, contradict what the animal forms buried in the rocky strata of our earth tell us of their own introduction and succession upon the surface of the globe. Let us therefore hear them;—for, after all, their testimony is that of the eyewitness and the actor in the scene. Take first the type to which we ourselves belong. If it be true that there has been a progressive transmutation of the whole type of Vertebrates, beginning with the lowest and culminating in the highest, the earlier should of course be structurally inferior to the later ones. What then is the lowest* living Vertebrate? Every zoologist will answer, The Amphioxus, that elongated, worm-like Vertebrate whose organization is nothing more than a dorsal cord, with a nervous thread above, and a respiratory and digestive cavity below, containing also the reproductive organs, the whole being clothed in flesh. Yet low as it is in the scale of

---

*I use the terms low and high, throughout, in the zoological sense; with reference to specialization of structure, as comparative anatomists understand it.

life, the Amphioxus is, by virtue of its vertebral column, a member of the same type as ourselves. Next to the Amphioxus come the Myxinoids, structurally but little above them, and the Lamper-eels. These are the animals which Haeckel places at the base of his zoological tree, rooting the whole Vertebrate branch of the animal kingdom in the Amphioxus as the forefather (Stamm-Vater) of the type. Let us look now at the earliest Vertebrates, as known and recorded in geological surveys. They should of course, if there is any truth in the transmutation theory, correspond with the lowest in rank or standing. What then are the earliest known Vertebrates? They are Selachians (sharks and their allies) and Ganoids (garpikes and the like), the highest of all living fishes, structurally speaking. I shall be answered that these belong to the Silurian and Devonian periods, and that it is believed that Vertebrates may have existed before that time. It will also be argued that Myzonts, namely Amphioxus, Myxinoids, and Lamper-eels, have no hard parts and could not have been preserved on that account. I will grant both these points, though the fact is that the Myzonts do possess solid parts, in the jaws, as capable of preservation as any bone, and that these solid parts, if ever found, even singly, would be as significant, for a zoologist, as the whole skeleton. Granting also that Amphioxus-like fishes may have lived and may have disappeared before the Silurian period; the Silurian deposits follow immediately upon those in which life first appeared, and should therefore contain not the highest fishes, but the fishes

next in order to the Myzonts, and these are certainly neither the Ganoids nor the Selachians. The presence of the Selachians at the dawn of life upon earth is in direct contradiction to the idea of a gradual progressive development. They are nevertheless exceedingly abundant in the Palaeozoic beds, and these fossil forms are so similar to the living representatives of the same group that what is true of the organization and development of the latter is unquestionably equally true of the former. In all their features the Selachians, more than any other fishes, resemble the higher animals. They lay few eggs, the higher kinds giving birth only to three, four, or five at a brood, whereas the common fishes lay myriads of eggs, hundreds of thousands in some instances, and these are for the greater part cast into the water to be developed at random. The limitation of the young is unquestionably a mark of superiority. The higher we rise in the scale of animal life the more restricted is the number of offspring. In proportion to this reduction in number, the connection of the offspring with the parent is drawn closer, organically and morally, till this relation becomes finally the foundation of all social organization, of all human civilization. In some Selachians there is an actual organic connection between parent and progeny, resembling the placental connection which marks the embryonic development of the higher Vertebrates. This feature is in harmony with the sexual relations among them; for it is of all facts in their organic history the most curious, that, among Vertebrates, the Selachians are the only ones with whom the connection of sexes recalls that of the human family. Now, these higher fishes being the first representatives of the Vertebrates on earth, or at least those next following their earliest representatives, where do we find the Myzonts, fishes which are structurally inferior to all others, and of which the Amphioxus is the lowest member? They come in during the latest period of our world's history, with what is called the present period, to which we ourselves belong. This certainly does not look like a connected series beginning with the lowest and ending with the highest, for the highest fishes come first and the lowest come last.

The companions of the Selachians in the earlier geological periods, the Ganoids, belong also to the higher representatives of the class of fishes. Some of them have the ball-and-socket vertebral joint of the reptiles and birds, enabling the head to move upon the neck with greater freedom than in the lower fishes. I am aware that these synthetic and prophetic types, which I have myself been the first to point out, and in which features of higher and later groups are combined or hinted at in lower and earlier ones, have been interpreted as transition types. It has even been said that I have myself furnished the strongest evidence of the transmutation theory. This might perhaps be so, did these types follow, instead of preceding, the lower fishes. But the whole history of geological succession shows us that the lowest in structure is by no means necessarily the earliest in time, either in the Vertebrate type or any other. Synthetic and prophetic types have accompanied the introduction of all the primary divisions of the animal kingdom. With these may be found what I have called embryonic types, which never rise, even in their adult state, above those conditions which in higher

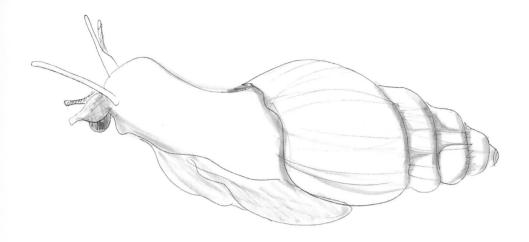

structures are but the prelude to the adult state. It may, therefore, truly be said that a great diversity of types has existed from the beginning.

The most advanced Darwinians seem reluctant to acknowledge the intervention of an intellectual power in the diversity which obtains in nature, under the plea that such an admission implies distinct creative acts for every species. What of it, if it were true? Have those who object to repeated acts of creation ever considered that no progress can be made in knowledge without repeated acts of thinking? And what are thoughts but specific acts of the mind? Why should it then be unscientific to infer that the facts of nature are the result of a similar process, since there is no evidence of any other cause? The world has arisen in some way or other. How it originated is the great question, and Darwin's theory, like all other attempts to explain the origin of life, is thus far merely conjectural. I believe he has not even made the best conjecture possible in the present state of our knowledge.

The more I look at the great complex of the animal world, the more sure do I feel that we have not yet reached its hidden meaning, and the more do I regret that the young and ardent spirits of our day give themselves to speculation rather than to close and accurate investigation.

I hope in future articles to show, first, that, however broken the geological record may be, there is a complete sequence in many parts of it, from which the character of the succession may be ascertained; secondly, that, since the most exquisitely delicate structures, as well as embryonic phases of growth of the most perishable nature, have been preserved from the very early deposits, we have no right to infer the disappearance of types because their absence disproves some favorite theory; and, lastly, that there is no evidence of a direct descent of later from earlier species in the geological succession of animals.

1. Ingnaz Döllinger (1770–1841), one of the most able German embryologists of the early nineteenth century.
2. Karl Ernst Ritter von Baer (1792–1876), Prussian-Estonian embryologist.

3. Christian Pander (1794–1865), Russian embryologist.

4. Carl von Linnaeus (1707–1778), Swedish botanist who established systems to define and name all known plants, animals, and minerals.

5. Baron Georges Cuvier (1769–1832), French zoologist and statesman.

6. Charles Darwin (1809–1882), English naturalist who put forth the theory of evolution by natural selection in his book, *The Origin of Species.*

7. Benoit de Maillet (1656–1738), French scientist involved with geology and oceanography.

8. Jean-Baptist de Monet de Lamarck (1744–1829), pioneer French biologist.

9. E. Geoffroy Saint-Hilaire (1805–1861), French zoologist.

10. Lorenz Oken (1779–1851), German philosopher and natural scientist.

11. Alfred Russel Wallace (1823–1913), English naturalist whose ideas on natural selection (which paralleled Darwin's) were published in *Contributions to the Theory of Natural Selection.*

12. Ernst Haeckel (1834–1919), German zoologist, evolutionist, and supporter of Darwin.

13. Aleksandr Kovalevsky (1840–1901), Russian embryologist and founder of comparative embryology and histology.

14. Georges-Louis Duvernoy (1777–1855), French anatomist and zoologist.

Margaret Mead

Anthropology, the science of man, has origins arguably going back to the eighteenth century when the West began to take notice of peoples in undeveloped parts of the world and decided that their existence raised questions about human nature, or at least human development—a belief that became widespread as a consequence of Darwin's discoveries and writings. Early studies concentrated on physical characteristics, and what is known as physical anthropology, which is biologically based, continues to be a branch of the discipline. But what is called cultural anthropology has become more extensive and in fact dominant, and it is now what most people have in mind when they use the term. It is largely a twentieth century creation, having in fact emanated principally from the teachings of Franz Boas (1858–1942) and his students—among them Ruth Benedict, Margaret Mead, and Edward Sapir—at Columbia University in New York.

Anthropology in this sense deals with the culture of peoples and takes in every aspect of their lives. Early on, there was disagreement among practitioners as to whether "culture" should be understood in the singular or the plural. If the first, then it made sense to think of something called "civilization," in terms of which peoples could be regarded as primitive or advanced. If the second, then there were as many cultures as there were peoples, and none could be regarded as more advanced than any other. Boas took the second view, and the work of his students testified to his influence. Thus Margaret Mead, studying the coming-of-age practices and rituals of Oceanic peoples, argued that these were culturally determined, and that by the same token ours were, too, and are—that there is nothing that can be called "natural" (still less "proper") in such matters. This is now the standard view in cultural anthropology. Indeed, the concept of "nature," or at least "human nature," has been quite superseded in the field by that of "culture" or "cultures," with far-reaching consequences for books and schooling everywhere, and with hardly anyone to recall that the idea of human nature had, and still has, significant meaning. "Nature" itself, however, very much survives in anthropology. Mead had for many years curatorial positions at the Museum of Natural History in New York, where a sense of nature as a whole is seriously observed.

Mead was an active writer and scholar-observer over her long and productive life, publishing books, among them *Coming of Age in Samoa* (1928), *Male and Female* (1949), and *A Rap on Race* with James Baldwin (1971) which were widely read. In the essay reprinted here she speaks of what she calls "applied anthropology" as in her view the part of the discipline that is most deeply involved and responsible. It will be noted that in her argument she rejects the notion of science as concerned with purely objective data, that she believes in the interactive, that she thinks its students must give something to, as well as take something from, what they study, that the sense of cultural identity should not be lost, but that, nevertheless, the need to reconcile the part with the whole—one branch of the human community with all human kind—should not be forgotten. Not that this takes in all or even very much of what she actually says, but it will serve to suggest that what she is really offering is a paradigm for science generally in our time—science, which is so profoundly distrusted in so many places at present (see the essay by Professor Holton elsewhere in this volume), and for the reason, we may guess, that it has not been sufficiently attentive to Mead's manifesto, as it really is.

Mead was herself always much interested in what we call causes—women's rights, childrearing, sexual practice and morals, nuclear proliferation, race relations, drug abuse, population control, environmental pollution, and world hunger. If these concerns seem inconsistent with scientific dignity, we need to read this essay again to see why Mead at least thought they were eminently consistent and indeed inescapable activities and commitments. The scientist, certainly the anthropologist, is in her view a citizen of the world who can no more afford than can the rest of us to ignore what the world is making of itself and not making, what it needs and what it ought to do without. In her view the anthropologist has more responsibilities than the rest of us do, since he, or she, knows much that the rest of us do not about the lives of human beings. It is indeed just the *world* that the anthropologist knows and can tell us about, and not for his own advantage but in disinterested fashion. One sees the absence of this view of things in the report of this year's meeting of the American Association for the Advancement of Science at Washington by Thomas K. Simpson in this volume—a meeting where parochialism seems to have prevailed.

Finally, in this connection it may be added that Margaret Mead was herself elected president of the AAAS in 1973, when she was 72, in recognition of her many contributions to science. She was also awarded—posthumously, in 1979—the Presidential Medal of Freedom, the highest civilian honor which can be given in the United States.

Applied Anthropology: The State of the Art

Margaret Mead

Applied anthropology, as Spicer described it in its early beginnings in the United States, grew out of the concerns of enlightened intellectual entrepreneurs like M.L. Wilson, John Collier, Elton Mayo, and Lawrence K. Frank, who were seeking for new and better ways to care for people, for the land, to reduce injustice, and to develop better social mechanisms. It flourished during World War II, as anthropologists responded with almost complete unanimity to the need to defeat Hitler, and lapsed again as trust in government declined and economic academic opportunities increased. Today, with the shrinking of academic opportunity, interest in applied anthropology is growing again. It remains to be seen whether it will be dominated by career expectations—as so much of medicine, law, and education has been—or be tied, as it was in the past, to a felt need and a felt hope that anthropology can make a real contribution to our life between "...two worlds, one dead, The other powerless to be born."

I think it is important to emphasize that it is as doubtful that applied anthropology, practiced simply as a good, lucrative career, will ever succeed, as it is that research anthropology, with its very peculiar demands on the research worker, will ever attract the mildly motivated or those who are seeking easy, pleasant routes to affluence. Applied anthropology, like the parent discipline, requires a long apprenticeship, extraordinary conditions of execution, and a kind of patience and ability to survive uncertain and often negative results (Mead 1970).

At its most mundane, where the applied anthropologist may live like his academic and professional colleagues, with long, uninterrupted weekends and a guaranteed vacation, it still retains the characteristics of a career—something one would be willing to pay somebody else to let one do if necessary—rather than just a way of making a living. In the field, and under field conditions, applied anthropology is more like the practice of obstetrics without any way of predicting the moment of delivery—a worthwhile, exacting, essentially unpredictable activity, where no office door can be certainly closed behind one. Unless young people care about what can be done and are not merely enamoured of the possible intellectual and monetary rewards of doing it, it leads to frustration, disillusionment, or cynicism. In spite of the current optimism of academicians looking for positions for the large number of students who make their own jobs secure (Bernard and Sibley 1975; Leacock, Gonzalez and Kushner 1974), I believe that everyone thinking of entering the field should ask, in the now unfortunately hackneyed phrase with which John F. Kennedy began his Presidency, not what anthropology will do for you, but how much you are willing to put into anthropology because you care deeply about something that needs to be done.

The satisfaction of intellectual curiosity produces its own rewards, but the practice in the world of power politics and the scrambles for divergent ends are quite another matter. The industrialized world is suffering from the efforts to translate traditional careers of service to society into high incomes, where access to influence, power, and money are both essential and potentially corrupting. The temptation to play God and to cover failures by

(Overleaf) Anthropologist Margaret Mead (left).

various sorts of mumbo jumbo is as ever present as it was when the first shaman palmed his first little stone representation of the "pain" he hoped to banish from his patient's body. And equally, the temptation to substitute good intentions or a fiery sense of the evils in present day society for hard work and real knowledge and competence is as great as it is in other fields where human lives are at stake.

Margaret Mead (center) is pictured here in the native dress of American Samoa.

It is, and will remain a discipline in which the results are uncertain, where—as in politics—accident plays a major role, and the results can never be claimed unequivocally. An earthquake, an epidemic, the removal of appointment of a petty bureaucrat may wreck the most carefully laid plans (Rynkiewich and Spradley 1976). It's an odd mixture, calling for a disciplined mind, but unblunted faith. Those of us who have practiced applied anthropology have done so most successfully when it was a by-product of our commitment to anthropology as a whole, and when the society of which we are a part was stirred by a mixture of fear and hope deep enough to call for personal sacrifice and extraordinary effort (Mead and Metraux 1965). It should appeal to those who believe that the conditions in the world today call for just such an effort, and that their capacities can best be exercised in its practice. We nearly destroyed the practice of medicine by elevating an interest in research into a requirement for entry, and denigrating the impulse to care for the sick. We have turned education into big business with exploited foot soldiers forced into unionizing like mine workers suffering from Black Lung or the consequences of manufacturing some noxious chemical. Anthropology itself has remained less infected by economic ambition or economic exploitation because we were few, idiosyncratic, and only episodically and situationally motivated. It will take strenuous efforts and the kind of sophistication that our discipline should, but so seldom does give us, to keep it so.

There are a variety of ways in which anthropology may be said to be "applied." Definitions vary by the period in which the work was done, the climate of opinion of different eras, the various applied problems on which anthropologists have been asked to work, and the various funding agencies for research and application. Using the broadest possible definition, the term applied anthropology may be said to refer to all anthropological research or writing that takes into account the possible consequences for the well-being of humankind.

The work of a very large number of the founding fathers—Tylor (1960), Brinton (1895), Boas (1962), Radcliffe-Brown (1952), and Malinowski (1945)—was characterized by the general expectation that the conduct of human affairs could be advanced by a greater knowledge of earlier periods of human prehistory or of contemporary variations among existing cultures. The contrasting position, in which the anthropologist disavows all interest in the possible practical effects of the research he is pursuing, has been relatively rare, and the degradation of responsibility in which the anthropologist acts like an engineer using his anthropological skills at the behest of an employer, without taking any responsibility for the goals, had to wait for the last two decades. These are the cases in which ethnolographical knowledge is used simply to obtain the help of a primitive tribe in war, pacify a border people, promote orderly behavior in a refugee camp, or simply modulate conflict between management and labor. All of the social sciences have been involved in this series of debates, and it may be expected that the debates will continue, as the needs of an emerging planetary society become more urgent, the dangers of stifling research that is not mission oriented become more acute, and the skills required of anthropologists as practitioners become more specific (Mead 1962; Thompson 1976).

But historically, anthropologists have concerned themselves implicitly, if not explicitly, with the whole of human history, and studies of any particular area of specialization—the linguistic structure of a lingua franca, human growth or human kinship, the Sioux or the Zulus or European neolithic lake dwellers, the distribution of outriggers or the origins of the arch—as part of the whole human endeavor. Scope and comparison have been essential to the discipline, and we have been somewhat more successful than history in bounding the systems that we study, whether they are periods or culture areas, subcultures, or diasporas. The sense of contrast, depth, and scope is something that the anthropologist brings both to the broadest and to the most specialized and localized concern.

At a second level, anthropological interest has centered on areas that have inevitable connections with questions of national and international policy at any given period of history: the doctrine of the psychic unity of mankind, or the ways in which race differences are and are not socially relevant, unilinear and multilinear evolution, the inevitability or fortuitous nature of invention, the transferability of cultural forms, the capacity of populations to adjust to changing circumstances, the interdependence of cultural forms and ecological and technological conditions. All of these major areas of theoretical interest have had enormous impact on policies— imperialism, decolonialization, neocolonialization, bilateral and multilateral technical assistance, revolution versus gradualism, etc. The convinced exponents of various courses of political action—the "white man's burden," "unalignment," "triage"—will continue to invoke anthropological research in advocating or refuting proposals for action (Mead in press).

Whether or not the interpretation of anthropological data is made by anthropologists themselves, in the stands that they take individually, in identified anthropological associations, or in legislative, judicial, or executive actions, applications will be made. It is for this reason that in the early discussions on ethics in the Society for Applied Anthropology (Mead, Chapple, and Brown 1949), we recognized that an anthropologist, unlike a chemist or a physicist, cannot easily divest himself of his anthropological knowledge and become a simple citizen, devoted to revolution or reaction or a tax law that will favor his own personal interests. It may indeed well be that we will need to invent some way in which an anthropologist who no longer wishes to abide by our traditional recognition of the value of all human beings, all human societies, and all human cultures may publicly and formally divest himself of the earned title of "anthropologist," just as a physician can divest himself of the right to practice, or a priest can relinquish the right to celebrate sacraments.

At Howard University, anthropologists study bones excavated from the African Burial Ground, located in New York City.

When does an anthropological statement about "race" cease to be "abstract" and "theoretical," and become "concrete" and "applied"? Is it when some finding is quoted in a brief before a court, when an individual anthropologist becomes active in the Civil Rights Movement, when an anthropologist becomes the paid executive of a Commission on Civil Rights, or joins the staff of an agency like the Department of Health, Education and Welfare with a responsibility for a declared affirmative action policy? Is it when, as a staff member of UNESCO, he inaugurates discussions on race, or when he acts as an active participant for some agency concerned with

In Botswana, anthropologist Nancy Howell studies the San (bushmen) acquaintance networks. She circulates pictures of the villagers in order to establish how they are all related.

the relationships between nomads and settled populations, Whites and Blacks in an American city, Vietnamese refugees and the host population? It is reasonably clear that the kind of lines that can be drawn here do not provide any clear-cut distinctions. When the American Anthropological Association is faced with resolutions about the alleged views of Herrnstein, the treatment of jungle populations in some South American country, or the dangers of sociobiology, who are the applied anthropologists—the writers of the resolution, those who consider its consequences, or the anthropological employees and members of agencies who receive information about the resolutions?

Similar questions can be raised when anthropological knowledge is applied to questions about human development, human behavior, or human well-being—aging, nutrition, and mental health. So anthropologists may examine, as a pure research problem, some cultural context of one of these defined areas, through the Human Relations Area Files, or pursue their study in the field; they may receive grants from agencies, which require that research be relevant to some mission like rehabilitation, nutrition, or solving the problems of alcoholism. The degree of responsibility of the anthropologist changes as we move from such general mandates to specific task-oriented field research and application in contract activities for a bureau of the Department of Agriculture, for the Agency for International Development, for the United Nations or a Native American Tribal Council.

It is also useful to consider the kind of contribution which anthropologists with different types of skills and experiences can make. The young anthropologist who has finished his course work is prepared to do either library or field research, and to observe the general canons of the anthropological tradition, to treat the people among whom he works or about whom he writes with respect. However, his academic experience has not, except in rare instances, provided him with any skills in human relationships of any sort, although his university experience may have exposed him to some models of good teaching. If he is to work in an applied field, it must be as a team member, where he can learn as well as practice such skills as interviewing, participant observation, and diplomacy. After field trips, preferably at least two, an anthropologist is better prepared to contribute to research designs of multidisciplinary projects, but very often he may still lack any useful knowledge of how to work with members of other disciplines, or how to deal with wider contexts—municipal or national authorities, government agencies, etc. To such orders of participation, we may add the additional role of the senior consultant who has a matured and wide knowledge of the world.

Another way to discriminate between applied and other anthropologists is to describe anything that any kind of anthropologist does as "applied" when his or her knowledge is used for some immediate, mission-oriented, or specific purposes. For example, this might occur when a physical anthropologist is asked to design airplane seats, an archeologist is asked to turn his archeological site into a relief program, a linguist is asked to provide an alphabet so that Navajo children can learn to read and write in Navajo, or an ethnologist is asked to persuade a group of people to give up headhunting or to introduce a public health program on a reservation. But is this enough, or do we need to invoke some further criteria, which the anthropologist brings to such specific tasks?

Here we may choose the kinds of credentials that certify a particular anthropologist's qualification for a specific assignment in terms of skills needed, experience needed, and methods of certifying to the possession of such skills. Or we may choose to certify adherence to some aspect of the whole discipline in which anthropologists may be said to be unique, to differ from the many members of other social science disciplines and other practitioners in such fields as public health, intergroup relations, labor relations, minority education, etc. I will deal with the acquisition of credibility as practitioners in particular skills, later.

At this point, however, I wish to emphasize the unique qualities of anthropologists, which make it possible for them to make a contribution that is distinct from the contribution of other theoretical and applied human science disciplines. I think it may be useful to define anthropological activities, whether practiced by anthropologists or by members of other disciplines who have learned the art, as those activities in which the investigator, research worker, or culture modifier, comes from one culture, subculture, occupational group or class to study another in collaboration with the members of that other group, *to produce a product that neither of them could produce alone.* The anthropologist systematically uses the role of the stranger (Mead 1970; Pelto 1970), and uses the respect in which he holds those about whom he wishes to learn as a research method. In contrast, other social sciences deal with "subjects," "objects," and "consumers"; they see people as "data producing animals," as "respondents," or "members of universes." None of these approaches require the specific kind of collaboration that anthropology has developed (Mead 1956).

This type of peculiarly anthropological work has only slowly been codified as ethics. It has resulted from the circumstance that anthropology has historically developed in the Euro-American world and was practiced among remote and isolated peoples of other physiques; it was impossible for the anthropologist to pretend to be a member of the group he studied. He or she was also almost always dependent upon a relationship of trust between field worker and informant to obtain the kind of data that was needed. Slowly we have evolved an ethic and a rationale for this kind of mutual trust and openness, which stresses the superiority of the data that is so obtained. Although it is a method which has evolved within anthropology (Mead 1961), amid historically determined constraints, it is a method that can be used by any human scientist, and has been used by members of a variety of related disciplines, including geography, psychiatry, sociology, and social psychology.

If we adopted the recognition of this style of work as an essential ingredient of applied anthropology, applied anthropology would be that kind of research or intervention which embodied it. It would be a professional field, which could be practiced also by anyone trained in a related social, biological, or humanistic discipline that used this particular type of cooperation between the investigator or operator and the group with whom he or she works. It includes respect for those with whom one works, recognition of interdependence, purposive avoidance of lying and deceit, and the obligation to take into account the safety, sensitivities, and well-being of those with whom one works. So, in even the rather remote applications, such as the design of airplane seats or the use of an archeological dig for work relief, the physical anthropologist would invoke the responsible cooperation of the pilots and passengers for whom he was designing seats, and the archeologist would insist that those who dug understood the instrumental as well as the archeological reasons for the excavations.

Any kind of accreditation would then relate the specific skills and experience required for a particular task, both to the acceptance of such a standard and to the attainment of specific communication skills, which make its use possible.

We could then go one step further and try to distinguish between practitioners and theoreticians, and designate applied anthropology as any mission-oriented or task-oriented activity in which the well-being of identified individuals, groups, or cultural traditions was involved, as the kind of practice which required not only a general adherence to the anthropological canons, as outlined above, but also the need for apprenticeship training under conditions where supervision and report on learning are possible. The distinction between a well-trained anthropologist with adequate anthropological education and field experience and an "applied anthropologist" would therefore be like the distinction between a PhD in physiology and an MD who specialized in open heart surgery. The findings of the PhD physiologist may affect the future of the entire human race, but no identified lives are in his hands. (It may well be that in time the well-being of students might also be taken into account and the ability to pass examinations and do field research would no longer be the sole criteria for teaching appointments in higher education!) But competence in doing research that is mission-oriented and not designed for any targeted individuals, groups, or cultural traditions, could still be certified academically, taking into account the difference between young, inexperienced anthropologists discussed above, and senior, highly experienced consultants.

So while all anthropologists may be said to be doing work with some possibility of application, there would be a clear distinction between a profession of practitioners and a discipline composed of scholars and scientists without professional credentials—a distinction that exists today between psychologists and clinical psychologists for whom certification is required.

Maintaining these distinctions between different lengths and qualities of experience, and between specific skills and specific apprenticeship training, would help to resolve another ethical problem that has plagued not only anthropology but other practitioners of social intervention from the start—the question of how responsibility is to be assayed and in terms of what overriding values that responsibility is to be executed, in the sense

An anthropologist at a development planning meeting near Battambang, Cambodia.

that physicians are responsible to the overriding value of life (Mead 1962). Where results are always partial, and success and failure are very hard to measure—as is always the case with such practices as education, psychiatry, and social work, as contrasted with surgery, for example—if responsibility is related to experience, and we take measures to see that training and experience are a part of accreditation, then the requirement of responsibility for all foreseeable effects of any act can be built into accreditation. Young anthropologists will automatically be relieved of the responsibilities that may be laid on their seniors—of foreseeing the far-reaching and distant effects of some single applied act, as when a constitution designed for one developing country is inappropriately copied by other developing countries, or a method of culturally accepted self-government designed for an egalitarian community becomes a model for application in a hierarchically organized community. If the discipline of anthropology and a profession of applied anthropology—which does not yet exist—can take responsibility for what their members do, this would go a long way towards resolving these ambiguities.

The other problem—the question of what overriding value can take the place of life in the model of physician, patient, and life—is to a certain extent solved by the emphasis of anthropology upon a holistic approach. Here the Society for Applied Anthropology, which brought together members of several disciplines sharing a common ethic and a common focus on human organization, has insisted on the applied anthropologist's responsibility to a whole—a whole plant including labor and management, a whole program including those administering and the administered, a whole hospital including administration, patients, physicians, and maintenance staff. By interdicting working for a part of any system without consultation and consent from the other parts, this type of overriding value on a whole was introduced. This can be extended to the planet and to the solar system. This again is a value which arose historically from the kind of work the classical field worker was expected to do in bringing back a report on the whole culture, on the assumption that he alone would ever have an opportunity to make that particular study. From responsibility for trying to record a whole culture, it is not difficult to move to responsibility for any whole—nation, continent, solar system—without an understanding of which, a study or intervention is imperfect and may be seriously destructive.

Developments During and Since World War II
and Their Implications for Applied Anthropology

World War II brought together all the possible kinds of applications of anthropology because anthropologists themselves were so deeply committed to the defeat of Hitler. As the years between World War II and the present lengthen, it is continuingly important to emphasize how extraordinary the position of anthropologists was during that period. Our ranks were not torn by the kinds of sympathies for socialism, or alleged sympathies for

Anthropologist David Maybury-Lewis studies the Xavante tribe (Amazonian Indians) of Brazil. The Xavante have adapted more easily to the modern world than other tribes, especially in dealing with the government over land rights issues.

Germany, which disturbed the relationships between Boas and his colleagues in World War I. In World War II, those with ideological leanings towards Eastern European socialism were as deeply involved as those with strong ties to Western Europe. While this was of course true for other disciplines, in the case of anthropology, our central paradigms—the psychic unity of mankind and the value of peoples of all cultures—was under attack, so that our unanimity was overdetermined. Anthropologists with very different skills and specialties were all equally anxious to make a contribution, and at one point in the middle of the War, it was estimated that of the some 303 anthropologists in the United States, over 295 were somehow engaged in making a disciplinary contribution to winning the War.

When the Society for Applied Anthropology was formed, its founders brought together the developing uses of anthropology in modernization, agriculture, Indian Affairs, and industry, with the set of activities directly related to the expected involvement of the United States in the War, which were a part of the work of the Committee for National Morale, in which Gregory Bateson and I were working. Those who were already interested and experienced in what anthropology could do, and had done, joined those who were seeking for ways in which it could be used (Mead 1943; Mead and Metraux 1965).

These preliminary attempts to apply the methods of cultural anthropology and the specific methods of culture and personality to national cultures (Gorer 1970, Mead 1953) and to regional and class divisions of modern cultures, proliferated into a large number of applications: the maintenance of national morale and gathering information for national policies (Mead 1943; Bateson 1942; Mead and Bateson 1941); programs on intergroup

relations (Landes 1965); recommendations for specific policies in dealing with the enemy (Mead and Metraux 1965); methods of qualitative opinion sampling (Metraux 1943; Mead and Metraux 1957); and methods of studying cultures at a distance used during the War for the study of inaccessible enemies or occupied friendly countries, which culminated in a large series of mission-oriented studies for the Office of Naval Research (Guetzkow 1951, Mead and Metraux 1953, Mead and Wolfenstein 1955, Mead and Rand 1951). The type of work that involved identifications of those aspects of culture, or those aspects of character that could be attributed to national institutions has been carried on to the present time (Dillon 1968, Maday 1975), but with very much lessened interest on the part of the anthropological community, and very little receptivity on the part of the governmental agencies that used this type of work during World War II.

(Left) Archaeologists excavate beneath the floor of Saint Blaise's Cathedral in Dubrovnik, Croatia.

These approaches have continued to be of limited use in programs such as the education of foreign service personnel, training for the Peace Corps (Mead 1966; Textor 1966), and interchanges of information between nationals of different countries.

There were other World War II involvements of anthropologists in devising areal institutes after the war, in the survival schools, which prepared pilots for an unplanned descent into areas like New Guinea, in the uses of the Cross Cultural Index, which became the Human Relations Area File (Ford 1969) and the basis for information on inaccessible areas and later for country books. The various councils, the National Research Council, the Social Science Research Council, the American Council of Learned Societies, joined with the Smithsonian Institution in providing a center for anthropological information of all kinds, called the Ethnographic Board. The American Council of Learned Societies conducted an extensive program in language of strategic importance, which later developed into the National Defense Education Act.

This almost total involvement of the discipline of anthropology was then replaced after the War by a growing alienation of human scientists in general, and anthropologists in particular, from working with federal agencies and particularly those government agencies related to international affairs. There is still a very limited participation of anthropologists in the Armed Services (Maday in press). The particular interests of anthropologists that had made them so completely committed during World War II now worked in the opposite direction. Such events as the transformation of bilateral technical assistance into military aid after the Korean War, and the ways in which South East Asian tribal groups were treated, combined to alienate anthropologists. During the Joseph McCarthy period, the remnant of anthropologists still working for the federal government left Washington. Fatigue, weariness with applied work, which had very often proved unrewarding, and a desire to get back to our own disciplinary problems undoubtedly played a part in the general decrease of interest. But as a result of the spreading disenchantment, relatively few anthropologists played an active part in the Civil Rights Movement or the poverty programs of the 1950s and 1960s.

However, there were other fields where activities of the federal government provided new opportunities for application. Under the National Institute for Mental Health, a mission-oriented research and training program was inaugurated, which eventually spent some $20 million training young anthropologists (Maday 1976). Anthropologists were attracted to action research in mental health fields because these meant working with living people. In the early 1950s, some 13% of anthropologists were working in some capacity under the umbrella of mental health, which became the new framework for interdisciplinary research. As the National Institutes of Health multiplied and the interests of the Department of Health, Education and Welfare diversified, openings arose in the study of rehabilitation, alcoholism, urbanization, child health, family life, rural and minority education, etc. However, these have tended to be mission-oriented research rather than anthropology as practice, and there has been little reflection of anthropological attitude at the policy making level of the NIH and HEW bureaucracies (Maday 1976).

While the field of mental health was opening up many opportunities for the domestic application of anthropology, the founding of the United Nations and its specialized agencies offered new opportunities for participation on a global level. The World Federation for Mental Health—of which the Society for Applied Anthropology was a founding member—in cooperation with UNESCO and WHO mediated many of these applications in the

Anthropologists assist in building a well in Equatorial Guinea.

fields of technical assistance, foreign service personnel, crime and delinquency, family life, infant care, and nutrition (Mead 1959).

Within the United Nations itself, Alfred Metraux played a key role in introducing anthropologists and anthropological programs, first at United Nations headquarters, then in UNESCO, where he inaugurated the UNESCO Marbial Valley study in Haiti, in cooperation with the International Labor Office (Metraux, A. 1953). Metraux also initiated the studies on Race and the East-West Program (Wagley 1964). Since his retirement and death, UNESCO's use of anthropologists and liaison with anthropologists has languished. His role points up the importance of key figures within government—like M.L. Wilson and John Collier in the earlier period of applied anthropology—and the necessity for having within the bureaucracy powerful figures who understand the uses to which applied anthropology can be put.

With the series of substantive United Nations Conferences, starting with the UNCAST Conference in 1963 (Mead 1963), a new potential for cooperation with U.N. activities began. This became much more important in the 1970s with the U.N. Conferences on the Environment, Population, Food, the Status of Women, Habitat, and the proposed Conferences on Water, Desertification, and Science and Technology. A new pattern of cooperation has also been developed at the request of the section on anthropology in the American Association for the Advancement of Science, which began with the preparation of a volume on population for the United Nations Conference on Population in Bucharest (AAAS 1975). This initial effort included interviews with over a hundred anthropologists, and now, under the AAAS Office of International Organizations, through contracts with AID, has become a regularized way of including applied anthropology in international activities (Buvinic 1976; Tinker and Bramsen 1976).

Interest in the recording and analysis of visual and auditory communication (Lomax 1968, 1972) has grown to the point that a whole issue of *Human Organization* could be devoted to "media anthropology" (Eiselein and Topper 1976), and the IXth International Congress of Anthropological and Ethnological Sciences could produce a book on *Principles of Visual Anthropology* (Hockings 1975). The National Anthropological Film Center (Sorenson 1974, 1975), is now well established at the Smithsonian, and there is a journal called *Studies in the Anthropology of Visual Communication.* Spearheaded by the development of medical anthropology in the 1950s, one small group after another is forming in education, semiotics, nutrition, dance, etc., with newsletters that connect the growing number of anthropologists specializing in each sub-field. These small specialized groups provide one kind of meeting place between research and applied anthropologists. Another way these same contacts are maintained is in the formation of groups of all the anthropologists in an area, academic and applied, however currently employed, such as that which exists in Tucson today, and which once flourished in New York City. Such groups help anthropologists employed in new fields to maintain a professional identity and to keep an anthropological ethic alive.

Future Activities for Applied Anthropology

The two earlier phases of applied anthropology, before World War II and the period between World War II and 1970, may best be characterized as concerned with change, either directed change or the amelioration or management of the effects of change. With the inauguration in the 1970s of substantive international programs requiring the support of United States agencies, combined with the renewed interest in domestic well-being in 1976, as projected for the Carter-Mondale administration, an increased concentration on goals may be expected—how to attain protection from nuclear proliferation, achieve progressive disarmament, lower pollution, provide for good nutrition, protect the environment, build livable towns, achieve better education and health care, etc. At the same time, there will be more search for new mechanisms; the National Science Foundation programs (Mead 1976b) for the people's participation in science policy, the proposed Science Court (Kantrowitz 1967; Boffey 1976), new uses of media including more extensive stimulation of the various folk communities by the recording of their own music, dance, histories (Lomax in press), occasioned by the Bicentennial programs like the Smithsonian programs in folklife (Mead 1976a) and in Kin and Communities (Smithsonian Institution 1976).

There is one new field—the research industry of profit-making and non-profit-making organizations engaged in contract research primarily for government agencies—which must, I think, be approached with great caution (Wolcott 1975). Some of these organizations use techniques of opinion sampling such as those developed by Likert's Program Research Division in the Department of Agriculture, by H. Passin, J. Bennet, and Jules Henry, and other forms of qualitative analysis, many of which use participation observation (Mead and Metraux, 1953, 1957). These new mushrooming agencies are undertaking the evaluation of ongoing programs and the writing of impact statements, etc. Already we have discussions of the beneficent efforts of such a profit-making agency to protect the anthropologists employed in a five-year evaluation study of a rural school program (Wolcott 1975), and a case study in Rynkiewich and Spradley (1976), where a change in personnel in the contracting bureaucracy meant that all three of the options offered the field workers were virtually unacceptable (Colfer 1976). The question of who is to enforce the recognition of anthropological values, especially of respect for promises made to informants or to the whole population being studied, is a crucial one. It may be that a very powerful profit-making social research agency appears to have such power, but it also would be dependent upon the continuity of personnel. We need a sanctioning agency that is more independent of arbitrary changes; possibly such an agency could be developed within the National Academy of Science, as the anthropological group in the Academy becomes more representative of anthropology as a whole.

For the purposes of this particular discussion, we may divide anthropological research into three stages; the first was the rescue or salvage stage,

in which it was our principal task to record the remnants of existing primitive cultures or vulnerable archeological records of past ones. Anthropologists specializing in salvage activities—which is still of the greatest importance—have only incidental relationships to applied anthropological tasks, and should not be thought of as automatically suited for them, no matter how many years they may have spent in research.

An anthropologist films the daily life of an aboriginal community in Australia.

The second stage, which began with Ruth Bunzel's work on the role of the individual in the Pueblo arts (Bunzel 1929), and my work on adolescence in Samoa (Mead 1928), treated primitive societies as *historically created,* laboratory-like situations in which anthropologists could investigate problems too complex for laboratory experiments. It has been found to be impossible to simulate many crucial aspects of human behavior, and we have relied on these historical accidents to provide us with conditions, which we could not ethically create, or which are so complex that we would have no hope of simulating them, like the relationships within a three-generation family, the interaction over time of a large group of siblings, or the ramifications of different kinds of technological change. Even the very imaginative experiments conducted by the Kurt Lewin group in comparing children reared in different degrees of permissiveness (Lewin, Lippitt, and White 1939), or studying cooperativeness among North End

Bostonians as compared to that among Harvard students relied upon historical differences between groups (French 1941). In general, the cooperation between anthropologists and psychologists proceeds best when the anthropologist takes large questions to the field and addresses them in great detail, after which the psychologist can attempt to devise experiential or clinical explorations (Mead 1942). This works better than the kind of cross-cultural research done by McClelland (1953), Osgood (in press) or Ekman (1973; Mead 1975b), in which the psychologist attempts to apply standardized situations in the field (Adler in press).

Anthropologists who have worked within this framework are on the whole much better fitted for applied work. They have had to establish long-time rapport with village groups, establish relationships with many different kinds of people, and pay at least some attention to the governments that control the people whom they are studying. When an applied anthropology job calls for an understanding of human relationships, which a large proportion of these jobs do, anthropologists who have this kind of field experience would be suitable candidates.

The third stage of anthropology, which we are just entering, is the field of culture building—the systematic attempt to invent new institutions to fill new needs in the international, national, and local scene, in fields like community participation, voluntary services, impact statements, science-court-like procedures (Kantrowitz 1967; Boffey 1976), the interfaces between scientific advisors and administrators, model setting activities, etc. This is a field that very few anthropologists have touched although the need for such new procedures is very urgent, all the way from local telephone hotlines for those who are desperate, to new forms of international organization. Here we need to call again on the developed skills of anthropologists, who have studied historical cultural experiments, to examine the

Anthropology includes the study of languages. Linguist Francesca Merlin works in Highland New Guinea to record a language which has never been written down.

spontaneous, embryonic development of new institutions, and select from among these the essential elements for further development.

Almost all applied anthropological research from the earliest beginnings in the 1930s here in the United States has called for interdisciplinary team work. Modern cultures are too complex for an anthropologist to accomplish very much single-handedly, and situations in which anthropology is to be applied call for a wide range of expertise. But the history of interdisciplinary research and application has been a checkered one (Luszki 1958; Mead and Metraux 1953: Appendix). Paradoxically today, even as such enterprises become rarer, young anthropologists seem more enraptured of a career in which the anthropologist is all alone in a jungle, days away from any communication with the outside world. Comments by anthropologists working as members of teams are filled with self-denigrating phrases like "hired help," "hand maiden," "slave," and "just a cog in a bureaucratic machine." While an experienced anthropologist may become a good research coordinator, anthropologists on the whole are poor administrators, and find it difficult to work with members of other disciplines. Yet it is an anthropological responsibility not only to insist on a holistic approach, a loyalty to the whole that is being studied, but also to provide insights into the place of a particular project and anthropology, itself, in the wider culture (Schwartz 1976).

So in the first phase we learned how to describe a culture, how to make taxonomies, how to use those taxonomies comparatively and, in combination with other disciplines, to correct culture-bound theory, provide very basic information about particular cultures, and characterize culture areas. The results of these early anthropological investigations are represented by the Human Relations Area File and the great variety of studies that have come from these files, reaching their greatest applied usefulness during World War II (Ford 1969; Textor 1967). But the preoccupation in the 1950s and 1960s with mediating culture change, which substantially meant modernization and standardization, has been accompanied by a considerable amount of disciplinary unease.

The post-World War II global demand for and push toward modernization on a Euro-American model, whether that model was socialist or capitalist, was in many ways deeply uncongenial to many anthropologists. The demurrers about the goals of the Society for Applied Anthropology must, I think, be understood in this light, whether we consider the kinds of criticism that came from Sol Tax and his proposals for Action Anthropology (Tax 1952), Oscar Lewis's (1966) concentration on the "culture of poverty," and Charles Valentine's (1968) demand that anthropologists go and live as participant observers in the ghetto, or academic anthropologists who concentrated on kinship and structural analysis. The first group of critics were concerned with the well-being of people—with the need to clothe and feed and educate and care for the burgeoning populations of the world. Too much preoccupation with their culture was seen as handicapping those intervening from other disciplines who were concerned with the same values, essentially harnessing modern technologies for the material well-being of the world's starving millions. For this first group, anthropological qualms about imposing or hastening necessary changes seemed essentially irrelevant. It was not what a people had been, but what they were now that mattered. Their concerns fitted the concerns of their period in which the spread of technology, and later "closing the gap" between developed and developing countries, were primary goals.

But the most deeply held value of American cultural anthropology continued to be that of the diversity of cultures within an essential unity of humankind. Mediating change, ameliorating the consequences of change, postponing or hurrying change—however humanitarian that change might be presented as being—was less congenial. Anthropologists feasted on the explication of cultural differences, as surely as they clung tenaciously to our common biological humanity (Poggie and Lynch 1974).

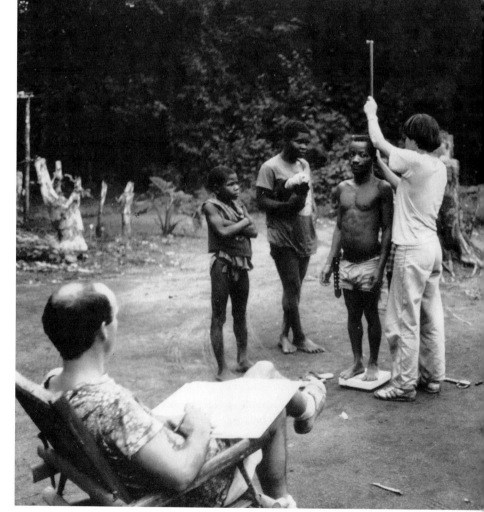

Anthropologists also study the health patterns of indigenous tribes. Here, Elizabeth Ross measures an Efe (pygmy) man in the Ituri rainforest of Zaire. This study, tracking the tribe's height and weight, was performed under the auspices of the Deparment of Nutrition of Zaire.

So this essential distaste for the steamroller effects of technological change was one further reason, beyond the disenchantment with the United States role in the world, for the low representation of anthropology during the 1950s and 1960s in activities connected with technological change. Those who saw the parlous state of the millions who lived in poverty, which the development of civilization had produced, clamored for bread. But most anthropologists, from Ruth Benedict (1934) to Alan Lomax (in press), steadily insisted that man does not live by bread alone and pled for the cultivation of artistic diversities which, once neglected could never be revived, to anthropologists more concerned with the fate of a precariously situated jungle tribe than with the starvation of millions in India or China, maintained their historic dedication to the importance of diversity.

Having recognized the errors and the horrors that have accompanied this

pell-mell westernization, we are now, I believe, entering the new stage—for both research and applied anthropology—of culture building (Mead and Heyman 1975). Out of the ruins of a technological era based on cheap oil and worldwide imperialism, the emphasis is returning to the importance of persisting, indigenous, local groups, within which the necessities of life can be produced near at hand, diversity of culture can be pursued again within a new kind of megalopolis (Mead 1975a), and human beings may again be able to live in face-to-face community relationships. For the first time since the invention of power based on fossil fuels and the trend towards giantism in production—giant power plants, giant factories, giant grain fields and granaries and giant oil tankers—there are technical and economic constraints on size. With the threatened shortage of fossil fuels and the looming dangers of nuclear power proliferation the world is turning towards decentralization, dispersion of populations, ideas of autarchy and self-sufficiency. In the use of solar power, which in some form must be the source of power for the future, there is no economy of scale.

An educational workshop on agriculture is held by field technicians in Bolivia.

But at the same time, the world has become one, communications are global and almost instantaneous, and the dangers of mutual destruction are forcing us towards greater global organization. Whether we consider the need to protect the atmosphere (Mead and Kellogg in press) for new types of urban design within which small multi-generational communities can thrive again (Doxiadis 1974), or the need for continental networks for travel and communication to provide an underpinning for peace-keeping organization, we will have to reshape our older institutions and build new ones.

Culture building on a local and a global scale will make new demands on anthropologists in at least two important ways. To be successful, culture building requires a large amount of social participation by those who are to live within the new forms. Viable institutions grow from a thousand small tentative roots, which struggling communities put out to deal with new necessities. Anthropologists are trained to recognize and identify implicit, covert culture as well as the explicit, overt culture that other disciplines describe.

A pressing and exciting task will be to seek out and cherish the spontaneous changes that are taking place, to study the ways in which new technologies may be adapted to the needs of localization, indigenization and diversification, as cruder technologies were once adapted to massive industrialization. What happens when Eskimos, who cannot read or write, tape-record the promises of a United States senator and send the tapes over hundreds of miles? What happens when a new city finds itself without telephones, but with TV? What happens when the Balinese substitute tape recordings of great orchestras and teach fifty little girls to dance at one time, where before it took an assembled orchestra to give lessons to a trio of chosen dancers? All over the world, peoples are struggling with the question of cultural identity and new viable forms to express it. What happens when the block plans of Civil Defense days are revived as a way of bringing New York City or Philadelphia to life again? What happens when a senatorial committee demands participation of the people in the plans that scientists make for the way in which research money is to be spent? So, in small or large leaps of ten thousand years, readjustments of erstwhile primitive groups or modern, alienated urban populations, groping towards more satisfactory uses of technology and the preservation of cultural identities are a fit and appropriate subject for anthropologists. Institutions, which are devised too formally and artificially, too hurriedly and too ideologically, fail. But institutions, which are homegrown, and then identified in a form in which they can be happily diffused, succeed. This is one new task for anthropologists in the new era. So the task of recognition, description, and identification draws on one set of familiar anthropological skills. There should be easy transitions within traditional anthropological departments in training students in the recognition of such phenomena, now listed under "culture change," or "cultural adjustment" (Edgerton 1971).

The second task for which anthropologists are peculiarly fitted is the problem of planetary or global organization. At present the scales on which contemporary activities are based are all wrong; they are either too large, as when foodstuffs that could be grown at home are shipped around the world, or too small, as when each local township has the right to block a needed highway or refuse the use of its port for needed supplies that must come by sea. The readjustments of scale, and the building of networks of physical and social organization on a continental and global basis is as essential as the protection and cultivation of smaller communities (Mead 1968; Wolfe 1963).

Here we may again turn to the other historical preoccupation of anthropologists—their preoccupation with wholes: whole cultures, whole tribal groups, whole communities. This preoccupation merges easily into General Systems Theory, the kind of theory which, implemented by computers, is necessary for planetary organization. If human civilization is to survive, the present fragmentation of planetary existence must be replaced by types of interlocking, interwoven, sustaining institutions which, instead of promoting lethal conflict, make such destructiveness impossible. Anthropologists have participated from the very beginning of the new interdisciplinary science of cybernetics and the building of General Systems Theory (Foerster 1950–1956; Bateson, M.C. 1972; G. Bateson, 1972; Chapple in press; Laszlo 1973).[3] Cybernetic theory and its systematization into General Systems Theory is an acceptable step for cultural anthropologists, as surely as the identification of cultural diversity uses traditional anthropological skills and interests (Leeds and Foerster in press). When we combine the living models provided by field work with the simulation made possible by computers, and the demands of a world presently in a state of productive disintegration, this new field for anthropology would appear self-evident, congenial, exciting. We have consistently resisted fragmentation; we have consistently insisted on the importance of context (Bateson, G. 1972; Birdwhistell 1970). The future is Now.

Notes

1. The literature on applied anthropology is voluminous. Where a summary article exists, either by myself, or by another anthropologist, I have referred to it rather than to the original source. I have used original sources only where they have not been included yet in the general literature in the field. So, the article on conflict resolution (Mead and Metraux 1965) discusses many of the activities of anthropologists in international relations, but does not include a reference to the discussions at the Anthropological Society of Washington in 1973–74, which has to be cited separately (Maday 1975). When a summary reference is cited, it does not mean that an issue is discussed in detail, but only that the bibliography will contain a specific reference.

2. The Standard works in applied anthropology, as cited by Spicer (in this volume) are as follows:

Arensberg, Conrad and Arthur H. Niehoff
    1964 Introducing Social Change, Chicago: Aldine.
Erasmus, Charles J.
    1961 Man Takes Control. Minneapolis: University of Minnesota Press.
Goodenough, Ward
    1964 Cooperation in Change: An Anthropological Approach to Community
      Development. New York: Russell Sage Foundation.
Leighton, Alexander H.
    1945 The Governing of Men. Princeton: Princeton University Press.
Mead, Margaret, Ed.
    1953 Cultural Patterns and Technical Change. Paris: UNESCO.
Spicer, Edward
    1952 Human Problems in Technological Change. New York: Russell Sage
      Foundation.
Also see, Journal of Applied Anthropology (1941–1949) and Human Organization (1949–), published by the Society for Applied Anthropology.

3. cf. *Behavioral Science,* Journal of the Society for General Systems Research, 1956–, and *General Systems,* Yearbook of the Society for General Systems Research, 1956–.

References Cited

Adler, Lenore L., ed.
    In press Proceedings of the New York Academy of Sciences Conference on Issues in
      Cross-Cultural Research, October 1–3, 1975. Annals of the New York Academy of
      Sciences.
American Association for the Advancement of Science
    1975 The Cultural Consequences of Population Change. Washington, D.C.: The
      Center for the Study of Man, Smithsonian Institution.
Bateson, Gregory
    1942 Morale and National Character. *In* Civilian Morale, Goodwin Watson, ed.
      Pp. 71–91. New York and Boston: Houghton Mifflin.
Bateson, Gregory
    1972 Steps to an Ecology of Mind. San Francisco: Chandler.
Bateson, Gregory and Margaret Mead
    1941 Principles of Morale Building. Journal of Educational Sociology 15:206–220.
Bateson, M.C.
    1972 Our Own Metaphor. New York: Knopf.
Benedict, Ruth
    1934 Patterns of Culture. Boston: Houghton Mifflin.
Bernard, H. Russell and Willis E. Sibley
    1975 Anthropology and Jobs. Washington, D.C.: American Anthropological
      Association.

Birdwhistell, R.L.
1970 Kinesics and Context. Philadelphia: University of Pennsylvania Press.
Boas, Franz
1962 Anthropology and Modern Life. New York: Norton.
Boffey, Philip M.
1976 Science Court: High Officials Back Test of Controversial Concept. Science
194:167–169.
Brinton, Daniel G.
1895 The Aims of Anthropology. Proceedings of the American Association for the
Advancement of Science 44:1–17.
Bunzel, Ruth L.
1929 The Pueblo Potter. Columbia University Contributions to Anthropology No. 8.
New York: Columbia University Press.
Buvinic, Mayra
1976 Women and World Development: An Annotated Bibliography. Washington,
D.C.: Overseas Development Council (AAAS).
Chapple, Eliot D.
in press. Populations of Coupled Non-Linear Oscillators in Anthropological Biology
Systems. Paper presented at the IEEE Systems, Man and Cybernetics Society,
November, 1976.
Colfer, Carol J. Pierce
1976 Rights, Responsibilities and Reports: An Ethical Dilemma in Contract Research.
In Ethics and Anthropology, Michael A. Rynkiewich and James P. Spradly, eds.
Pp. 32–46. New York: John Wiley & Sons.
Dillon, Wilton
1968 Gifts and Nations. The Hague: Mouton.
Doxiadis, C.A., ed.
1974 Anthropolis: City for Human Development. Athens: Athens Publishing Center.
Edgerton, Robert E.
1971 The Individual in Cultural Adaptation: A Study of Four East African Peoples.
Berkeley and London: University of California Press.
Eiselein, E.B. and Martin Topper, eds.
1976 Media Anthropology: A Symposium. Human Organization 35:111–220.
Ekman, Paul, ed.
1973 Darwin and Facial Expression: A Century of Research in Review. New York:
Academic Press.
Foerster, Heinz von, ed.
1950–1956 Cybernetics, 5 Vols. New York: Josiah Macy, Jr. Foundation.
Ford, Clellan S.
1969 Human Relations Area Files: 1949–1969, A Twenty-Year Report. New Haven:
Human Relations Area Files, Inc.
French, John R.P., Jr.
1941 The Disruption and Cohesion of Groups. Journal of Abnormal and Social
Psychology 36:361–377.
Gorer, Geoffrey
1950 The Concept of National Character. Harmondsworth, Middlesex: Penguin
Books.
Guetzkow, Harold, ed.
1951 Groups, Leadership and Men. Pittsburgh: Carnegie Press.
Hockings, Paul, ed.
1975 Principles of Visual Anthropology. The Hague and Paris: Mouton.
Kantrowitz, Arthur
1967 Proposal for an Institution for Scientific Judgment. Science 156:73–764.
Landes, Ruth
1965 Culture in American Education. New York: John Wiley & Sons.
Laszlo, Ervin, ed.
1973 The World System: Models, Norms, Applications. New York: Braziller.
Leacock, Eleanor, Nancie L. Gonzalez, and Gilbert Kushner, eds.
1974 Training Programs for New Opportunities in Applied Anthropology. Washing-

ton, D.C.: American Anthropological Association.

Leeds, Anthony and Heinz von Foerster, eds.
  in press The Potentiality of Systems Theory for Anthropological Inquiry, Wenner
    Gren Conference, May 22, 1965.

Lewin, Kurt, Ronald Lippitt and Ralph K. White
  1939 Patterns of Aggressive Behavior in Experimentally Created "Social Climates."
    Journal of Social Psychology 10:271–299.

Lewis, Oscar
  1966 The Culture of Poverty. Scientific American 215:19–25.

Lomax, Alan, ed.
  1968 Folksong Style and Culture. Washington, D.C.: American Association for the
    Advancement of Science, Symp. Vol. No. 88.

Lomax, Alan
  1972 The Evolutionary Taxonomy of Culture. Science 177:228–239.

Lomax, Alan
  in press An Appeal for Cultural Equity. Journal of Communication.

Luszki, Margaret B.
  1958 Interdisciplinary Team Research: Methods and Problems. National Training
    Laboratories, Research Training Series, 3. New York: New York University Press.

McClelland, D.C., et al.
  1953 The Achievement Motive. New York: Appleton-Century-Crofts.

Maday, Bela C.
  1975 Anthropology and Society. Washington, D.C.: Anthropological Society.

Maday, Bela
  1976 Individual Research Training Support in Anthropology 1964–1976. Anthropo-
    logy Newsletter 17:7–9.

Maday, Bela
  in press Anthropologists in the U.S. Government. Human Organization.

Malinowski, Bronislaw
  1945 The Dynamics of Culture Change. New Haven: Yale University Press.

Mead, Margaret
  1928 Coming of Age in Samoa. New York: Morrow.
  1942 Anthropological Data on the Problem of Instinct. *In* Symposium—Second Col-
loquia on Psychosomatic and Experimental Medicine. Psychosomatic Medicine
    4:396–397.
  1943 The Problem of Changing Food Habits. *In* Report of the Committee on Food
    Habits 1941–1943, Margaret Mead, ed. Pp. 20–31. National Research Washington,
    D.C.: Council Bulletin, No. 108.
  1951 Soviet Attitudes Toward Authority. New York: McGraw-Hill.
  1953 National Character. *In* Anthropology Today: An Encyclopedic Inventory. A.L.
    Kroeber, ed. Pp. 642–667. Chicago: University of Chicago Press.
  1956 Commitment to Field Work. *In* Gladys A. Reichard, 1893–1955. New York:
    Barnard College, pp. 22–27.
  1959 Mental Health in World Perspective. *In* Culture and Mental Health, Marvin K.
    Opler, ed. Pp. 501–516. New York: Macmillan.
  1961 The Human Study of Human Beings. Science 133:163.
  1962 The Social Responsibility of the Anthropologist. Journal of Higher Education
    33:1–12.
  1963 Geneva: Helping the Less Developed Nations—Lessons from the U.N. Confe-
    rence. International Science and Technology 16:86–87.
  1966 Foreword. *In* Cultural Frontiers of the Peace Corps. Robert B. Textor, ed.
    Pp. vii–x. Cambridge, Mass., and London: MIT Press.
  1968 Alternatives to War. *In* War: The Anthropology of Armed Conflict and Aggres-
    sion, Morton Fried, Marvin Harris and Robert Murphy, eds. Pp. 215–228. Garden
    City, New York: Natural History Press.
  1970 The Art and Technology of Field Work. *In* A Handbook of Method in Cultural
    Anthropology, Raoul Naroll and Ronald Cohen, eds. Pp. 246–265. Garden City,
    New York: Natural History Press.
  1975a Statement. *In* Great Lakes Megalopolis: Symposium, Toronto, March 24–27,

1975. Alexander B. Leman and Ingrid A. Leman, eds. P. 12. Ottawa: Ministry of State for Urban Affairs.

1975b Review of Darwin and Facial Expression: A Century of Research in Review, Paul Ekman, ed. Journal of Communication 25:209–213.

1976a Our 200th Birthday: What We Have to Celebrate. *In* 1976 Festival of American Folklife, Smithsonian Institution-National Park Service. Pp. 5–6. New York and White Plains: American Airlines and General Foods.

1976b Statement. National Science Foundation Authorization Legislation, 1976. Hearings: Before the Special Subcommittee on the National Science Foundation of the Committee on Labor and Public Welfare, United States Senate, Ninety-fourth Congress, Second Session on S. 3202, March 1 and 3, 1976. Pp. 184–197. Washington, D.C.: U.S. Government Printing Office.

in press Anthropology and the Climate of Opinion. Annals of the New York Academy of Sciences.

Mead, Margaret, Eliot D. Chapple, and Gordon G. Brown
1949 Report of the Committee on Ethics. Human Organization 8:20–21.

Mead, Margaret and Ken Heyman
1975 World Enough: Rethinking the Future. Boston: Little, Brown.

Mead, Margaret and William Kellogg, eds.
in press The Atmosphere: Endangered and Endangering. Maryland: National Institute of Health, Fogarty International Center.

Mead, Margaret and Rhoda Metraux
1953 The Study of Culture at a Distance. Chicago: University of Chicago Press.

Mead, Margaret and Rhoda Metraux
1957 Image of the Scientist among High School Students: A Pilot Study. Science 126:384–390.

Mead, Margaret and Rhoda Metraux
1965 The Anthropology of Human Conflict. *In* The Nature of Human Conflict. Elton B. McNeil, ed. Pp. 116–138. Englewood Cliffs, N.J.: Prentice Hall.

Mead, Margaret and Martha Wolfenstein
1955 Childhood in Contemporary Cultures. Chicago: University of Chicago Press.

Metraux, Alfred
1953 Applied Anthropology in Government: United Nations. *In* Anthropology Today: An Encyclopedic Inventory. A.L. Kroeber, ed. Pp. 880–894. Chicago: University of Chicago Press.

Metraux, Rhoda
1943 Qualitative Attitude Analysis: A Technique for the Study of Verbal Behavior. *In* The Problem of Changing Food Habits, Report of the Committee on Food Habits 1941–1943. Pp. 86–94. Washington, D.C.: National Research Council Bulletin No. 108.

Osgood, Charles
in press Objective Indicators of Subjective Culture. Annals of the New York Academy of Sciences.

Pelto, Pertti J.
1970 Anthropological Research: The Structure of Inquiry. New York: Harper & Row.

Poggie, John J. and Robert N. Lynch, eds.
1974 Rethinking Modernization: Anthropological Perspectives. Westport and London: Greenwood Press.

Radcliffe-Brown, A.R.
1952 Structure and Function in Primitive Society. London: Cohen and West.

Rynkiewich, Michael A. and James P. Spradley, eds.
1976 Ethics and Anthropology. New York: John Wiley & Sons.

Schwartz, Theodore
1976 Introduction. *In* Socialization as Cultural Communication: Development of a Theme in the Work of Margaret Mead, Theodore Schwartz, ed. Pp. vii–xviii. Berkeley: University of California Press.

Sorenson, E. Richard
1974 Anthropological Film: A Scientific and Humanistic Resource. Science 186:1079–1085.

Sorenson, E. Richard
    1975 Visual Evidence: An Emerging Force in Visual Anthropology, Occasional Paper
        No. 1. Washington D.C.: National Anthropological Film Center.
Tax, Sol
    1952 Action Anthropology. American Indigena 12:103–109.
Textor, Robert B., ed.
    1966 Cultural Frontiers of the Peace Corps. Cambridge, Mass., and London: MIT
        Press.
Textor, R.B., ed.
    1967 Cross-Cultural Summary. New Haven: Human Relations Area Files Press.
Thompson, Laura
    1976 An Appropriate Role for Postcolonial Applied Anthropologists. Human Organi-
        zation 35:1–7.
Tinker, Irene and Michele Bo Bramsen, eds.
    1976 Women and World Development. Washington, D.C.: Overseas Development
        Council (AAAS).
Tylor, Edward
    1960 Anthropology. Ann Arbor: University of Michigan Press.
Valentine, C.A.
    1968 Culture and Poverty: Critique and Counter-Proposals. Chicago: University of
        Chicago Press.
Wagley, Charles
    1964 Alfred Metraux: 1902–1963. American Anthropologist 66:603–613.
Wolcott, Harry, ed.
    1975 Ethnography of Schooling. Human Organization 34:109–215.
Wolfe, Alvin W.
    1963 The African Mineral Industry: Evolution of a Supranational Level of Integra-
        tion. Social Problems 11:153–164.

Comments on Recent Books

In the Absence of Heroines: A Response to Gerda Lerner's *Why History Matters*

Paulette Roeske

Why History Matters
(Oxford University Press, 1997)
Gerda Lerner

 am not a Jew. My dark features and olive complexion, however, have often led people to inquire about my ethnicity, and when they ventured to guess, they first guessed Jew, followed by Italian and Greek—and, if they had dared, mulatto, perhaps, but they did not dare. I always confirmed whatever choice was put forth, although I sometimes corrected Italian to Sicilian. In any case, truth or lie, it is doubtful I would have survived Hitler's tests for racial purity. I was young when it first occurred to me to mislead the line of conjecture—in my early teens, in fact, and working behind the cigar counter in my father's drug store selling cans of Prince Albert, panatelas and corollas, Blackjack chewing gum or Clove, and boxes of Whitman's Samplers. In those days, customers would spend time lounging with their elbows on the high glass counter by the cash register—they had come to purchase a little small talk with their tobacco and candy—and they would ask. I lied because I did not want to admit to the hodgepodge of nationalities that made me just like most Americans. I wanted to be different.

Gerda Lerner in her collection of essays and addresses, *Why History Matters,* writes as a Jew, an agnostic, an immigrant, a woman, a feminist, and a writer and historian, all of them avenues to difference. She speaks eloquently of race, class, and gender, subjects that emerged from her personal struggle with difference in these pieces composed during a seventeen year period between 1980 and 1997. Her struggle gave her her subjects, her vocation: "I am a historian because of my Jewish experience," (p. 5) she tells us in the first essay, "A Weave of Connections." Because she left Austria for Liechtenstein in 1938, a few weeks before *Kristallnacht,* she became a survivor who was charged with keeping memory alive and "History had become an obligation." (p. 12)

"Scapegoat," "outsider," and "tyrannized" are words Lerner uses to describe her experiences, words I understand, can understand, without diminishing the persecution the Jews endured. The ten-year-old child who falls victim to the playground bully has at least a cursory understanding of the terms. Because I lived on the periphery in my own family, I have internalized similar messages that continue to shape my identity. In contrast, my daughter—no one could appear more Aryan—has taken on difference as a young woman by choosing to marry an Orthodox Jew.

Lerner made choices when she refused her *Bat-Mitzvah* and declined to enter a synagogue again for fifty years. "The Nazis robbed me of my mother tongue," she says, "but the rest of the separation, of the violent severing of culture, was my own choice." (p. 48) Such choices heightened her Otherness within her Otherness, which, I suspect, drove her, as one of the voiceless, inward, into a dialogue with the page, that blank and sometimes forgiving surface which one can make reflect one's own point of view. She lived her life. "Now I am old and reconciliation is on my mind," (p. 18) she tells us, after having traveled once again in Germany, relearned her language, and written her way toward an uneasy peace. She points to "having our definition of self made not by ourselves but by others" (p. 15) as the real source of oppression, but who, after all, one might counter, *does* have the luxury of constructing a self? Who is not a product of history, personal, national, and global? And what, if not difference, does history take as its subject as it details events that distinguish moment from moment in time's otherwise linear march?

Most writers welcome the sharp prick of difference as the impetus that turns them to the task of making sense of pain. I think of the Russian poet Irina Ratushinskya in prison scratching her poems with a matchstick into a bar of soap in order to memorize them, or of the poet Gregory Orr turning to the page for release from the emotional prison in which he lived after killing his younger brother in an accidental shooting at age twelve. The lives of writers are often emotionally turbulent—the recluses and alcoholics, the institutionalized, the suicides, all of them different but somehow similar in their difference. Such difference is the source of a vision that is skewed, one that departs from the ordinary, from the most-guessed answers, and pushes down the road toward the anomalous, the shocking, which the writer not so secretly craves. The work of literature is to chronicle the differences within our sameness, otherwise the world would need only one story. Without her acute awareness of her difference, we would not have Gerda Lerner's story.

The past. An odd notion, since it never passes. "We sail with a corpse in the cargo," says Henrik Ibsen, the dark presence of the past coiled in the hold. *Do not forget* is, after all, largely the point of history. In her title essay, Lerner remarks, "The dead continue to live by way of the resurrection we give them in telling their stories." (p. 211) In our writing we memorialize whatever constitutes our personal pasts. If we do not, the particulars will die with us. Perhaps each of us is no more than the sum total of those particulars, since the collective story, the one outlined with a broad-nibbed pen, takes place without us. I failed to record my grandmother's stories: how, for example, as a teenager she sailed from Germany with her clothes in the wicker basket I now keep beside my bed. I told myself that I could write the stories second-hand from my father's memories, but his recent death means that the process of discovery will now become a process of invention. My task as historian has been relegated to acts of the imagination, history's whimsical sister.

To multiply this dilemma many times over is to glimpse Lerner's largest fear: "Civil wars and racist persecutions thrive on selective memory and collective forgetting" (p. 204)—"the Great Forgetting," she calls it—in which whole nations conspire to believe *their* version of history. As every writer knows, it is easy enough to believe any invention constructed in the imagination's fertile and convincing realm, an inclination that makes it possible to perpetuate atrocity. To face up to "what actually happened," Lerner says, (p. 204) precedes healing for both an individual and for a nation. It is likely enough that the act of telling our stories is to heal ourselves, but can we ever know "what actually happened"? And, if we could divine *that*, is it possible to translate accurately experience into language? To think that we can is to forget the inevitable and seductive magic of the word and the fact that the writer is god of the world on the page. Concealment, discovery, and reconciliation (pp. 18, 22) is the happier scenario, a three-step program Lerner describes in "In the Footsteps of the Cathars." Reconciliation is Walt Whitman's big word, in his Civil War poem by the same name, arcing like the democratic sky over the living and the dead, over every man and his enemy. That is what we all would choose, what Lerner has chosen in her work of the last two decades as she approaches her eightieth year.

"In the Footsteps of the Cathars" introduces two of the traveler's familiar responses: the first is predicated on the phrase, *This is where,* as in this is where Marie Antoinette was beheaded, where Thomas à Beckett was struck down, where Joan of Arc was burned, where the emperor's concubines were entombed alive. *This is where* motivates our travel through space, through memory, through history. A second thought is never far behind: *It could have been me,* as in it could have been me occupying that "cozy place of horror," (p. 21) wherever it may be. Because Lerner came so dangerously close to the concentration camps, she lives more intimately with this language than those of us who must reach further to imagine a narrow escape. "What it means to be a Jew—having to look over your shoulder and have your bags packed," (p. 15) casts the notion of travel in a different light. Still, these conversations we hold with ourselves when we travel are reminders that must humanize our perspective, a prerequisite for a writer.

Lerner first turned to poetry, short stories, and novels with an autobiographical inclination in her quest to become an "American writer." After a fifteen-year hiatus from formal education followed by seven additional years of study culminating in a doctorate, she found history. However, only in slow increments did she finally arrive at the notion of telling her own story. Her choice of subjects led her, for example, through a history of black women before she was able to approach what it meant to *her* to be a woman—specifically a woman within the context of Judaism, and a Jew, specifically a Jew who escaped Nazi domination, a number that can only shrink, that is to say compound difference, as time passes. Her journey through the lives of others in order to reach the destination of the self illustrates a writer's usual circuitous route to discovery. How cautiously we must come to ourselves to avoid the shock of the veil torn suddenly away. "It was then by way of American History that I became a successful 'American writer,'" Lerner concludes, (p. 46) making a distinction between the historian and writer, even while acknowledging their happy correspondences.

In her 1982 essay, "The Necessity of History," Lerner itemizes ways in which history satisfies human needs. When speaking of history as encouraging us to "fathom worlds unlike our own," worlds we can then "enter . . . with curiosity and respect," she also describes literature's shared realm. And when she identifies the historian's bid for immortality by maintaining the human continuum, or considers history as an aid to memory, a guide to a personal identity, and a means of ordering the past to shape it into sense, she cites a list identical to the one I discuss with my creative writing students when we talk about why we write poems and stories. But the margin between the disciplines narrows even further when she nods to the historian's interest in evidence but emphasizes "the power to capture the imagination of contemporaries, so as to (make history) seem real to them." History is, in short, "a creative enterprise," (p. 117) when undertaken by, in Lerner's words, the "historian/writer." And what poet or writer would deny that he or she is also a historian?

No less provocative is the role language plays in Lerner's particular history, for every writer has a story to tell about their relationship with language. Psychological complications abound, since Lerner writes in English, her second language. "In translation, one becomes a trickster, too clever by far and too concerned with mastery," she says. "I envy those who live in the power of their own language, who were not deprived of the immediacy by which creativity finds its form." (p. 49) Nevertheless, her language in Part I, "History as Memory," is the highly textured often lyrical language of the poet/writer that privileges feeling. Elsewhere in this collection, her language is frequently surgical, didactic, with little evidence of the woman about whose struggle the reader has come to care. She fluctuates in these essays between the analyst and the creative writer, opposing stances that increasingly find themselves sharing the pages of works of creative nonfiction, specifically in what we could call the new memoir, a genre which began its rise around the same time Lerner wrote the earliest pieces in *Why History Matters*. History *is* story and, as a writer with a handful of published short stories and several novels, at least one of them published, Lerner recognizes the value of the storyteller's art applied to analytical data in the service of education and entertainment, literature's dual objectives as defined by Sir Philip Sidney in his *Defence of Poesy,* written around 1583. Sidney draws the following distinction between the historian and the poet—one, I think, with which Lerner would concur: ". . . the best of the historian is subject to the poet; for whatsoever . . . the historian is bound to recite, that may the poet, if he list, with his imitation make his own, beautifying it both for further teaching and more delighting, as it pleaseth him; having all, from Dante's Heaven to his Hell, under the authority of his pen."

Lerner's mentor was Karl Kraus (1874–1936), an Austrian journalist, playwright, and poet. He was often compared with Juvenal and Jonathan Swift for his use of satire and was renowned for his command of language. Kraus speaks of finding meaning "by tapping along the guiding rope of language," (p. 36) a process with which every poet is intimate. To learn another language then declare its exclusive use is to abandon the parts of the self whose apprehensions are confirmed in language. Lerner *chose,* she says, to be an "American writer," although, as we have seen, she also blames the oppressor for having wrested her language from her. Since the writer writes from the whole of experience, and to the extent that experience is couched in language, Lerner's life began as a young adult when she learned English. Like the women about whom she writes in her comprehensive two-volume *Women and History,* she had no recorded history to which to turn for her models, her heroines. She had to start over. Caught between cultures, between disciplines, driven by differences, her dilemma provokes the old controversy between choice and force at the hand of the oppressor. Had it not been for Hitler, would Lerner the agnostic historian have spent her life as a believing Jew, at home in Austria, writing poems in German? Would they have been any good?

More than history, it is poetry that heals, as evidenced by the moment in "Living in Translation" when Lerner recounts the reconnection with her sister after several strained visits in a description that straddles genres. Separated through immigration when she was eighteen to her sister's twelve, Lerner came to the United States while Nora went first to school in Switzerland, then on to England, and finally to Israel. Lerner becomes her own heroine in her memory of the event as language, which occurred after several decades of separation:

> One of us, I don't know which one, began to hum an Austrian folksong, and then to sing it, in German. The other chimed in, and we found ourselves singing in two voices, the way we had often sung in our childhood. One song followed another—from somewhere long-forgotten by both of us, the childhood songs welled up and broke to the surface. . . . I felt as though suddenly all the barriers between us had broken down; we were children together, as we had always been, and what separated us—the shifts in cultures, the different lifestyles, the separate hard struggles for survival and reconstitution—all of that fell off our shoulders as the common language at last united us. (pp. 43–44)

The two removes of memory and language notwithstanding, we read this account and imagine the two sisters working in the kitchen singing as they wash dishes after dinner, and the reconstructed image is, like much of *Why History Matters,* a moving testament to the power of language: its music, its poetry, its story, its history.

A Need Perceived But Not Met
Krishnan Venkatesh

The Dictionary of Global Culture
(Knopf, 1997)
Kwame Anthony Appiah and Henry Louis Gates, Jr.

t the heart of this enterprise stands a paradox that the editors of this book evoke but flinch from exploring. Explaining the title, the editors rightly point out that cultures have never been separated by impermeable skins or impenetrable walls. Gunpowder, invented in China, made it to Western Europe via the Mongols, Islamic nations, and other peoples; classical Greek learning was "rediscovered" during the Renaissance after having been preserved and nurtured for centuries by Arabic scholars. Awareness of such cross-fertilizations leads to self-knowledge, as well as sating the curiosity.

Cultures have always influenced one another, and their mutual permeability can seem to express a unity that attenuates their differences. Moreover, as the editors of this work point out, the links between far-flung societies have been increased, strengthened, and deepened by colonialism and the reach of modern technology, so that now more than ever "we all participate, albeit from different cultural positions, in a global system of culture" (p. xi) or "a single political, economic, and cultural system." (p. ix) There is no longer any question of our choosing to forge bonds with people from other cultures; like it or not, we are already welded together in one big society, and had better learn to get along with them ungrudgingly and respectfully. To do this, we need to learn something about our neighbors' different cultural backgrounds. Thus, in their introduction, while speaking of "the creation of a global culture," the editors at the same time, and without seeming to notice the shift to the plural, emphasize the need for an "understanding of other cultures."

Such a paradox, while delightful to contemplate and necessary to think through, cannot in itself yield rigorous criteria for the selection of topics in a reference work. Is this to be a dictionary about things common to everybody *qua* participants in the one global culture, or a dictionary about elements from all cultures that everyone should know about, or both? And in the second case, what would that "should" mean? The editors are nebulous on this, as they are in their conception of "culture," which receives no explanation. Aware that "A Dictionary of Global Culture" sounds a little like "A Dictionary of Everything" (albeit "emphasizing the achievement of the non-Western world"), the editors shrewdly disclaim "exhaustiveness" or "representativeness" in their selections with becoming modesty.

The editors themselves refer to their book as a "sampler," a metaphor that suggests a tray full of tasty morsels designed to excite more sustained interest. "We have tried," they say, "to find examples of the great cultural achievements, figures, and events of many cultures, and then to say enough about them to make them interesting and engaging." (p. xii) If I understand their procedure correctly, there were three main stages in the making of this book. First, "scholars *from* other cultures—along with Western scholars *of* other cultures—" were asked for a list of "around fifty of the most important cultural contributions from the region in which they were expert." (p. xii) Then the suggestions were worked over by "a team of researchers," about whom nothing more is said. Finally, these workings-over were written up by "scholars in the field." (p. xii) The book offers no systematic list of specific scholars and their titles; we are simply expected to trust this vague convocation of "experts" and to blame the editors for errors and omissions.

Let us consider the result. In the following pages I shall, as much as possible, allow the Dictionary to speak for itself, and the reader to draw his or her own conclusions.

Opening the book randomly, I discover that the entries under "F" are as follows: *Fanon, al-Fârâbî, Farah, Farrokhzad, Fassbinder, Fatehpur Sikri, Faulkner, Faust, Fellini, Ferré, Fitzgerald (Ella and F. Scott), Flaubert, Fleming (Sir Alexander), Fon, Fonseca, foot-binding, Forbidden City, Forster, Fragonard, St. Francis, Franklin, Franko, French Revolution, Freud, Frye (Northrop), Fuentes, Fulani.* It is easy to carp, and every reader can come up with favorite "F"s more important than Northrop Frye. More significantly, of the "F"s given, roughly a quarter are not historical individuals, and about two-thirds of the historical individuals are from the twentieth century. (We are reminded of Huck Finn: "Moses had been dead a considerable long time; so then I didn't care no more about him; because I don't take stock in dead people.") These proportions seem to hold true for the rest of the book. Clearly, the book as a whole does not express an anthropologist's conception of "culture" and also does not dig very deep down into "the traditions of our species."

What of the content of individual entries? First, I examined various entries on Western figures. The Shakespeare article struck me initially as amateurish, poorly written, and sometimes incorrect until I discovered that it sounds like a garbled rendition of the Micropaedia entry from the 15th edition of the *Encyclopædia Britannica*. For example, while the *Britannica* states that the great tragedies are "enriched by a quality of language that is at once deeply poetical and emotionally expressive while conveying mature philosophical ideas," (*EB:* 10, 690) the *Dictionary of Global Culture* says that the same plays "use deeply poetic and emotionally expressive language to combine highly developed characterizations with compelling philosophical messages." (p. 591) In addition, according to the *Britannica*, "The *Winter's Tale* (1610/11) and *The Tempest* (1611/12) are clearly experimental in their light-hearted and fanciful but basically tragic form" (*EB:* 10, 690–1); while the *Dictionary* states that in these plays "Shakespeare experimented with lighthearted, fanciful language while maintaining a basically tragic theme." (p. 591) There are many other such borrowings and garblings in this entry, including sentences made simply silly by compression or incomprehension: "It was not until after 1599, when his company acquired the Globe Theatre, that he began to introduce the element of human fallibility into his plots in addition to the external and uncontrollable forces that decided his characters' fate." (p. 591) It is hard to believe that this entry was written by an expert.

Thus my first dip into the *Dictionary* did not leave me filled with trust. In my second dip, *Dickens,* I did not consult another reference work but did find this bizarre chronology: "In 1859 he wrote *A Tale of Two Cities,* followed by *Great Expectations* (1860–61), *Bleak House* (1852–53), *Little Dorrit* (1855–57), and *Hard Times* (1854)." (p. 180) Somebody did not think it worthwhile to waste valuable mental energy on the rational ordering of dates.

Faced with such signs of carelessness, I stopped looking up any more Western figures, and turned my view towards the East. No one in any case would use this book to find out about Chaucer or Marlowe; perhaps the entries on things non-Western would be better, I hoped. My optimism proved unfounded.

I first searched in vain for the Chinese classic *Journey to the West,* and also failed to find it under its other common name, *Monkey;* later, however, I stumbled upon it under the Pinyin transliteration of its Chinese name, *Xi You Ji.* As with all reference books arranged alphabetically, one has to know how to spell a word before being able to find it; in this case, one has to know Chinese as well, since the *Dictionary* is in general parsimonious with cross-references. The reader will also not easily locate the Koran, Kahlil Gibran, Salâh al-Dîn, *The Arabian Nights, The Art of War,* or even Moses, although common sense dictates that they must be in there somewhere. The few existing cross-references can be astounding: at *New York Renaissance* we are directed to see *Harlem Globetrotters,* but realize only minutes later that we were supposed to have been directed to *Harlem Renaissance.* In such a slovenly book, even so few cross-references can sometimes seem too many.

There is further chaos with transliteration. The *Taoism* entry mentions the *Dao-de Jing* but goes on to talk about Tao and Te, again taking it for granted that the reader is already sufficiently globally cultured to know about Chinese transliteration systems. Similarly, the honorific *Tzu* or *zi* (different transliterations of the same syllable) is applied inconsistently throughout the dictionary: hence, Lao Tzu, Zhuangzi, Mo Zi. We are informed in *Taoism* that "Te is the embodiment of Tao and describes a state of oneness with nature and its processes," (p. 636) while in *Lao Tzu* Te apparently means "Power."

More disturbing still, the *Taoism* entry evinces the same shoddiness we witnessed with *Shakespeare.* There is too much similarity to the article on Taoism in the Micropaedia and too much evidence of distortion caused by thoughtless paraphrase and compression. For instance, while the *Britannica* defines Tao as "the ineffable, eternal, creative reality which is the source and end of all things," (*EB:* 11, 551) the *Dictionary* calls it "an intangible force that represents the origin and eventual demise of all things in existence." The odd choice of "demise" and the redundant "in existence" both hint at careless paraphrase; on closer analysis, it becomes clear that the writer of this particular entry in the *Dictionary* forgot that "end" might mean "goal" as well as "demise." The entry goes on to describe philosophical Taoism as being "somewhat at odds with" religious Taoism, but never asks why the two concepts are both called Taoism. The same lack of inquisitiveness is manifested in the perplexing conclusion of the entry: "Both the religious and philosophical sects of Taoism were destroyed during the Han Dynasty. Since then, two other sects of Taoism have arisen—the Shang Qing Mao Shan and the Ling Bao traditions. These sects, along with the older sects, continue to have a great influence on Chinese society." (pp. 636–7) So the reader is left asking whether the older sects were destroyed or not destroyed, and what were these two influential traditions? The *Britannica* article, which the *Dictionary* entry closely resembles, answers these questions and fills in other gaps left by the *Dictionary;* for example, it also tells us that only one line of Taoism was destroyed in the Han Dynasty. Once again, then, we find in the *Dictionary* an entry that seems to be a tousled and deranged version of another source.

The Buddhism articles were similarly muddled, although I did not consult other reference works. In other casual dippings, I was alarmed to discover that the *Kamasutra* is a "story, which ostensibly centers on the exploits of a fashionable dandy. . . ." (p. 356) No one who has read the book could say such a thing. By this time, of course, my faith had been shaken, and I had become wary of granting credence to articles on interesting topics that I knew nothing about. Still, I enjoyed reading (under *Quilombo*) about the seventeenth century Republic of Palmáres formed in Brazil by runaway slaves who in turn abducted slaves from Portuguese plantations; and, among other things, I am grateful to be told about the *Ramakien,* the Thai version of the Ramayana. Not surprisingly, the Dictionary offers no bibliographical information or any other way of following up on any interest it may arouse.

As a reference work, then, *The Dictionary of Global Culture* is essentially worthless. As a sampler, the book may have some value, although it will be clear from my examples that the most accurate analogy would be a tray of poorly arranged morsels, some still wrapped in plastic, some mouldy, some carelessly cut, some too sticky to be picked up, and some, alas, half-chewed and half-digested. Better for browsing than for consultation, one of those books meant to be tasted, and tasted cautiously, it is pleased with its own juxtapositions (*Holocaust-Homer-Hong Kong film industry-Hong Lou Meng*) but it is without the lucidity, incisiveness, and originality to delight as a *jeu d'esprit*. The evidence of inattentiveness to organization, content, and derivation suggests that it is not a book meant to be read—in other words, that it is not a book at all—but rather the symbol of a book, a badge of affiliation, a gesture towards a new age and in opposition to an old one. Something of the kind may be needed, and these editors may understand what the need is, but they have failed in their attempt to meet it here.

A Clear and Elegant Account of a Complex Man
Anthony Quinton

The Solitary Self: Jean-Jacques Rousseau in Exile and Adversity
(University of Chicago Press, 1997)
Maurice Cranston

ean-Jacques Rousseau is the only thinker of the modern epoch whose influence is on the same scale as that of John Locke and Karl Marx. Perhaps it is even on a level of its own since it is really much broader than that of the other two. Their domain is essentially the political. Rousseau's is too: he is the prophet of democracy as they are of liberalism and of socialism.

But, as the first great herald of romanticism, he spread himself far beyond the domain of the political into that of imaginative culture and sensibility.

The breadth of his gifts and of the achievements in which they were expressed, is altogether outstanding. He was a political thinker of the first rank (*The Social Contract*); he was an inspired, and by no means visionary, constitution-builder (for Corsica and Poland); he was a radically innovative moralist and social theorist (the two *Discourses*); he was a constructive religious thinker (the *Savoyard Vicar*) and a serious moral critic of Christianity, the author of the first great romantic novel (*Julie, ou, la nouvelle Héloïse*); he was the first educational theorist fully to recognize that children are not simply small adults (*Émile*); he wrote the first true autobiography in which nothing is held back (the *Confessions,* a much less contrived book than Augustine's, is a fascinating, but still edifyingly-intended, tract).

On top of all that, Rousseau was musically talented and expert. He came to Paris with a new musical notation he had devised and which he hoped would bring him fame and fortune. It was received with a polite lack of enthusiasm, but it was at least a foot in the door. He was soon engaged in controversy in defense of free, melodic Italian music against Rameau, the leading French composer, exponent of a more rigid, rule-bound harmonic type of music. To help make his point Rousseau composed an opera, *Le Devin du village,* in accordance with his principles, which was a great success. The king enjoyed it so much he wanted to reward the composer, who refused, as he did all such offers throughout his career, so as not to incur an obligation which might restrict his freedom of thought and action. He contributed articles on music to the *Encyclopédie* and in his later years produced a dictionary of music.

Such a fecund and influential person deserves a substantial biography. It is required, among other things, to serve as a check on the often astonishing contents of the *Confessions*. That is one of the tasks that Maurice Cranston set himself in his three-volume biography, and Rousseau comes out of it pretty well. Where a check is possible, as it quite often is, Rousseau is either vindicated or his errors are innocently explicable and can be attributed to forgetfulness or muddle, but not to any cosmetic intention. Cranston has already written a marvelously researched biography of Locke. In this book, as in that, he has lowered himself into the great lake of correspondence that is available and has come up with an imposing catch of detail. This, like Cranston's *John Locke,* is a "thick" biography, without vague gestures. We are not told what our hero "must have thought when" or "most probably felt as": we are given documented accounts of what he did think and feel.

As with all Cranston's writings, it is extremely well written. The prose just slides sweetly down with quiet elegance, not calling attention to itself either deliberately by artifices or display, or inadvertently by clumsiness or malapropism. The emphasis is fairly exclusively historical. The writings are, for the most part, briefly summarized, but not very lengthily examined or criticized. Such discussion is remitted to a 20-page epilogue—"Rousseau Then and Now"—assembled by Cranston's friend and editor Sanford Lakoff, from various other writings of Cranston's about Rousseau.

The reason for this is that *The Solitary Self,* the third and final volume of Cranston's biography, is only a torso. Maurice Cranston died suddenly late in 1993 with the work unfinished. This volume ostensibly covers the period from 1762, when Rousseau fled from Paris and the violent commotion aroused by *Émile* and *The Social Contract* (which had *both* been published that year, after the glorious success of *Julie* the year before), and his death in 1778 in rural seclusion in France under the protection of the Marquis de Girardin. In fact, only the five years from 1762 to 1765 are covered in detail; the remaining twelve years are polished off at a rate of just over two pages per annum. That is a pity. But the editor's decision is probably wise; a full-scale continuation by another hand would not have worked.

Apart from the astonishment at the scope of Rousseau's powers expressed at the beginning of this review, two other general reactions inspired by this account of Rousseau's life need a mention. The first is the amazement caused by the thought that he was, formally speaking, almost uneducated, apart from a couple of years between the ages of ten and twelve spent studying classics under the tuition of a Protestant pastor. Before that he had spent much of the considerable time he devoted to reading on the trashy romantic novels of which his father was fond. Could this early indulgence explain a certain hectic, gushing quality to his generally excellent prose, so much more heated than the suave mischievousness of Voltaire?

Second, there is the question of the light thrown by a biographical study of this thoroughness on Rousseau's character. It is easy to lump him together with some spectacularly nasty heroes of the intellectual history of mankind: Augustine, Luther, Pascal, Milton, Tolstoy, Wittgenstein. None of these thinkers is known ever to have made a joke and may well never even have seen one. Rousseau, too, never deliberately caused laughter and seems to have emitted it only in moments of animal high spirits as when outwalking younger, less wiry companions. To be fair, he does admit, at times, to finding himself somewhat ridiculous, as indeed he was.

The offence everyone knows about is the dumping of the five illegitimate children he had by his long-term companion, Thérèse Levasseur, at the foundling hospital. His attempts to justify this outrage are pitiful. Essentially he claims they would have a better start in life there than with him. This ghastly act was brought to public notice by Voltaire in 1765 in a pamphlet called *Le Sentiment des citoyens*. He covered his tracks by writing it in the unsophisticated style of a rustic pastor. Rousseau, Cranston suggests, never found out that it was Voltaire's work. He attributed it, with obsessive determination, to a comparatively decent opponent, a young pastor, Jacob Vernes, who had openly criticized his religious views. Cranston is puzzled by Voltaire's unrelenting hostility to Rousseau. It had come to a head with the publication of Rousseau's *Lettre à d'Alembert*, attacking the proposal to institute a theatre at Geneva. No doubt that helped to exacerbate Voltaire's feelings, but the real reason, surely, is competitive jealousy. Voltaire was quite clever enough to see that he was a very much smaller figure than Rousseau, for all his prodigious output. Little of Voltaire is part of an ordinary educated person's mental equipment today, with the exception of *Candide*. Many things ought to be, perhaps—the *Dictionnaire Philosophique* and *The Age of Louis XIV*, for example. But these works, for all their merits, are hardly of the same order as Rousseau's half-dozen major productions.

There is plenty of evidence in Cranston's third volume of Rousseau's moral limitations. He wrote a cold, egotistic letter of condolence to the widow of the Maréchal de Luxembourg, when both had lavishly befriended him. When a cultivated lady with whom he had a flirtatious correspondence sent him her portrait, he sent it back without comment. These are examples of his extraordinary insensitivity; he was far too busy with his own feelings to take any notice of the feelings of others. But readiness to promise various oppressive religious and political authorities to abstain from controversial speech and publication and, usually sooner rather than later, to break the promise, are hardly sins given the nature of the authorities in question.

Rousseau's passionate directness made him attractive to women, but he did not much exploit this power by seducing them. He started quite late erotically, being seduced by Mme de Warens when he was 21. He stayed largely faithful to "Maman," as he quite appropriately called her, until she installed a younger and perhaps more vigorous man in her bed. He then took up with Thérèse Levasseur, the fertile, semi-literate companion who, after many years, thinking of the approach of death, he finally married. She was much less faithful to him, notably with the undiscriminating James Boswell, and quickly married a young groom after Rousseau's death.

He was altogether free from any touch of rapacity. Throughout the 1760's—by which time he was, admittedly, famous—offers of money came flowing in from all directions. But he scrupulously stuck to his principle of independence. He did accept the use of houses, of which a very large number seem to have been available to Rousseau's time, but even then only if he could rent them, at however nominal a charge. The host of people who were anxious to help him and put him up in their homes is some testimony to his personal attractiveness, even allowing for the lavish hospitality of the epoch and the fact that he was a considerable celebrity. By the time the main text of this third volume runs out (1765–66) he was descending into paranoia from a previously manageable sense of persecution. He was a paranoiac with plenty of real and active enemies: Voltaire on one side, most enthusiastic Christians on the other.

He was, on the whole, a moderately impossible person, asking much in the way of loyalty and affection, but only fitfully able to return them. This personal exorbitance penetrates his theoretical writing, which is full of exasperation and overemphasis. That may help to account for the mistaken idea that Rousseau is, in any serious sense of the word, a proponent of totalitarianism. It is, in the first place, an anachronism to ascribe to someone writing in the mid-eighteenth century a conception of government by a party, using the instruments of modern technology to control every detail of the lives of a subject population. Rousseau was not a liberal either, having no concern for the rights of the individual against the community. The small, absolutely democratic states to which he alone thought his political prescriptions applied, might be stuffily oppressive to citizens not part of the ruling consensus, but they would be taken into account. Nevertheless, he was unquestionably a sincere democrat, and the general democratic movement of the nineteenth century is his legitimate political offspring. As John Stuart Mill saw it, liberty and democracy do not guarantee each other, although they are not incompatible. Nor, as the epilogue rightly argues, was Rousseau a nationalist. He was born and spiritually remained a French-speaking Swiss from an area of profound Catholic-Protestant confusion, cutting across linguistic boundaries.

Cranston's three volumes are justified. Rousseau is worth learning about at such length and depth. Of all major thinkers, there is perhaps none about whose personality and real convictions there is more disagreement. This noble work supplies most of the materials for settling it.

The Biological Basis of Society
Deal Hudson

The Origins of Virtue: Human Instincts and the Evolution of Cooperation
(Viking Penguin, 1996)
Matt Ridley

idley's purpose in his well-written book is to discover the roots of human society. How one responds to his investigation will depend upon whether the reader's expectation is elicited primarily by the title or the subtitle. Virtue, in the established sense of a deeply ingrained disposition of character toward morally good action, is not the subject of Ridley's book. Vir-

tue, as employed by Ridley, denotes merely the capacity *of the species* for overcoming selfishness through evolved instincts of trust and benevolence. Thus the reader is advised to concentrate on the subtitle. Ridley's subject, the one that actually matches his expertise, is the evolution of human cooperation, or society, through the process of natural selection.

Indeed, it is a major drawback of this book that the author deals with basic philosophical concepts without a secure knowledge of their traditional meanings. This seriously weakens Ridley's account, in spite of his many insights, about the very issue he wants to elucidate—how it is possible for human beings to put the common good ahead of their own self-interest by creating communities beneficial to everyone.

Likewise, the historical background that Ridley brings to his discussion is not his strong suit; his broad characterizations of great figures and schools of thought lack credible nuance. The proponents of human nature as selfish—Sophists, Augustine, Hobbes, Machiavelli, Huxley—are paired off against those who are held to view human nature as essentially benevolent—Plato, Pelagius, Rousseau, Godwin, and Kropotkin. The tribalism of religious belief is pitted against the equally unrealistic and dangerous convictions of the utopians. Such broad and, often, inaccurate characterizations pervade the book and, while providing a clear context for the debate to unfold, leave the reader uncertain about the author's grasp of the deeper moral and political issues he wishes to address. For example, Ridley accuses religion of fostering global war and death, seemingly without awareness that the totalitarian dictatorships of the twentieth century have been responsible for more deaths than any religious institutions in recorded human history.

Ridley would probably welcome this correction: His findings challenge both utopian sentimentalism and the Hobbesian prostration of fallen human nature before the Leviathan. The truth about human nature, Ridley argues, lies somewhere in between the extremes of selfishness and altruism: Human beings are self-interested, as demanded by their genetic material, yet this primal instinct has worked itself out, evolved, in socially beneficial ways. Through trial and error, human beings have realized that "no man is an island" and have developed, through adaptation, those sociable instincts necessary to living together. Subject to rational reflection over the centuries, human self-interest became ameliorated into the often fragile and unpredictable interdependence we call human society. Only female human beings, we are told, inexplicably, are fully trustworthy; somehow they have evolved beyond the males in their ability to live in an open society. (p. 169)

Ridley, who is trained in economics, in addition to anthropology and zoology, is determined to account for the fact of human cooperation in the light of two parallel foci: The weight afforded to self-interest in Adam Smith's economics and the discovery of "the selfish gene" in biology. The influence of both these theories have conspired to portray humanity in a univocal and unflattering light, one that, if unchallenged, will exacerbate the free market excesses of the past. Ridley wants to save economic principles of Adam Smith from a reduction to the justification of greed. Highlighting Adam Smith's account of human cooperation, Ridley argues that commerce and trade are far superior to religion in providing evidence of human cooperation at its best. Smith's analysis of the division of labor, "perhaps the least appreciated insight in the whole history of ideas" (p. 44), and regarded as the capacity to create more and better goods through specialization, is the case in point—"the sums of all our efforts are greater than they would be if each of us had to be a jack of all trades." (p. 41)

At the same time, Ridley wants to show that the latest genetic theory, the argument that human benevolence serves the interest of our hereditary gene pool, does not make necessary hoarders of us all. His use of the latest research from evolutionary biology and cultural anthropology persuasively advances his argument that instincts of cooperation and the pursuit of a common good are an evolved trait of our human nature. Ridley tries to show what human beings and animals have in common, what they do not, and what can be learned from both. He insists that only a "Martian" would refuse to learn what animals have to teach human beings about their nature. Fortunately Ridley does not make the basic blunders exposed by Mortimer J. Adler in *The Difference of Man and the Difference It Makes*—he strongly implies a difference in kind rather than degree between human and animal intelligence, although he does not seem aware of the problem this poses for evolutionary theory. (He does not address the issue of how this degree of intelligence could have evolved.) In fact, Ridley insists that the reason for the relative success of the human species is the ability, based upon its unique intelligence, to bend the genetic instinct of self-interest to the necessity of social cooperation. Human beings have become so adept at this over the centuries that we can safely say that the instinct of trust has become part of human nature.

It is also to Ridley's credit that he does not shy away from the political ramifications of his thesis. Some of Ridley's political applications are surprising. Although he corrects the abuse of Adam Smith "nostrums of neo-classical economics" (p. 146), Ridley warns against relying upon the government to create virtue. "We are not so nasty that we need to be tamed by intrusive government, nor so nice that too much government does not bring out the worst in us. . . ." (p. 262) Much of contemporary politics, with its reliance on large government solutions are out of touch with human nature. (p. 258) Government intervention, such as nationalizing lands to preserve resources, destroys personal incentive and gets in the way of cooperation. Ecological problems are best addressed by the people whose lives and livelihood are directly affected by them. By nationalizing ecologically threatened resources, the commons are taken out of the hands of the people with the incentives to take care of them. Ridley's data shows that nationalization actually creates the very problems that governmental ownership seeks to redress. Individuals have shown that they will react rationally to incentives, while those in favor of nationalization have overlooked the unwritten rules that local communities developed over generations to protect their limited resources. (p. 232) Some of Ridley's most interesting pages are devoted to debunking various ecological myths, employed by "eco-optimists," lauding the prelapsarian harmony of human beings and nature found in the prehistoric man, Native Americans, the Hawaiian, and Samoan islanders.

Aristotelians will welcome Ridley's confident return to the subject of human nature; they will notice that his concept of nature remains wedded to an evolutionary, or Hegelian, context. This is what makes it possible for Ridley to trace the acquisition of a trust instinct in human nature. In other words, Ridley conflates what Aristotle would term the difference between first and second nature, the nature common to all individuals in species, and the nature that is acquired on the basis of repeated action and developed habit. Ridley talks about second nature as human nature because he views it as long-term development of traits made possible by human intelligence. The kind of natural selection at work through human evolution is not matched by those of other animals, even the higher primates. "[The human brain] is equipped with special faculties to enable it to exploit reciprocity, to trade favors and to reap the benefits of social living." (p. 131) The success of the human species is due to the development of social instincts.

Ridley treats human nature in this manner because the only other factor of first nature he acknowledges is "our masters—the genes." (p. 249) These genes, following the work of George Williams, William Hamilton, and Richard Dawkins, are selfish, and it required centuries of rational response to life in the world to develop a cooperative instinct to ameliorate the effect of the selfish gene. "Selfish genes sometimes use selfless individuals to achieve their ends." (p. 20)

Ridley deliberates at great length on why people are nice to each other using the so-called "prisoner's dilemma": Two prisoners can give evidence against the other one and receive a reduced sentence. If neither gives evidence they both would be convicted on a lesser charge, but if one gives evidence, called "defecting," that one would be markedly better off than the other. Given all the alternatives, both are better off defecting since the reward for defecting is greater than cooperating. In other words, someone is going to get the biggest piece of the pie, just by reaching for it first, so why shouldn't it be me! The issue raised by the dilemma, according to Ridley, is not strictly speaking moral, it is one of rational calculation: How individuals can be led by self-interest to serve a greater good. At first glance, the prisoner's dilemma suggests that there is no rational basis for cooperation since the outcome of defection is always greater than cooperation.

However, decades of games theory research on the prisoner's dilemma reveals that different factors vary the approach to the game. If the game is played over a period of time, agents inevitably develop a pattern of cooperation that results in more even distribution of rewards. In addition, players begin to recognize the kind of person they are playing against, distinguishing those who are sociable from those who are not. As Ridley puts it, the virtuous recognize the virtuous to their mutual benefit. (p. 147) In spite of the logic leading inevitably to self-interested action, human beings choose to be nice to one another. For Ridley, this provides proof of his thesis that self-interested individuals instinctively put aside their own selfish desires for the sake of another, for reciprocity, for the sake of the common good. "Our minds have been built by selfish genes, but they have been built to be social, trustworthy and cooperative. That is the paradox this book has tried to explain." (p. 249)

Ridley's lack of familiarity with classical virtue theory spoils an otherwise interesting series of comments on the importance of emotion. In his opinion, emotions make human agents dependable; they enable us to make commitments to long-term action. "Emotions mediate between our inner calculator and our outer behaviour." (p. 136) Ridley does not seem to recall that the virtues, from Aristotle to Aquinas, ensure the proper ordering of emotion to provide the smooth and predictable functioning of morally responsible actions. Ridley completely ignores the role of the will and choice in this respect, making the assumpion that emotion is somehow made intentional by intelligence without the intermediate steps provided by human volition.

The reason for these leaps in moral psychology surely springs from Ridley's unquestioned faith in genetic appetite and natural selection. The necessity for personal volition crumbles before the overwhelming process of evolutionary change. The trait of human cooperation "simply develops within us as we mature, an ineradicable predisposition, to be nurtured by teaching or not as the case may be. And why? Because natural selection has chosen it to enable us to get more from social living." (p. 66) Ridley has created a kind of contemporary Averroism, except this time a single will expresses itself through individuals, not a single mind. Individual choice is ruled out because natural selection has made all these choices for us. Virtue is no longer acquired by the individual through action, as his or her acquired dispositions, but belongs to the species as a whole *through the agency of natural selection.*

The trouble with all this, of course, is that it leaves up in the air how a person recognizes and accounts for those people with whom it is safe to play the prisoner's dilemma. In Ridley's view individuals are not trustworthy, the species has become trustworthy—there is no account of why one individual is trustworthy and another is not, except in terms of their emotional commitments.

If Ridley is right about this, and I think he is, when he makes the statement that "trust is . . . a form of social capital" (p. 250) then his account is badly weakened by his inability to deal with individual differences. If it is essential, as Ridley thinks, to distinguish between the "hawks" and the "doves," (p. 70) then it is important to know why some individuals actualize the species potency for trust and others do not. Put in Ridley's terms, he fails to explain why some individuals translate their calculations to emotional commitments and others do not. Ridley does not pursue this question in *The Origins of Virtue* because he does not appear to view individuals as having very much control over the acquisition of moral characteristics. Presumably the answer to that question would enable us to encourage the nurturing of these dispositions not just in the species but in individuals.

On Reading
Otto Bird

Samuel Johnson and the Life of Reading
(The Johns Hopkins University Press, 1997)
Robert DeMaria, Jr.

*Augustine the Reader: Meditation, Self-Knowledge,
and the Ethics of Interpretation*
(Harvard University Press, 1996)
Brian Stock

hese two books deal with writers who are famous as readers. One is about that "great Cham of literature," as Samuel Johnson was called in eighteenth century England, according to his biographer James Boswell (*GBWW* I: 44, 97; II: 41, 97); the other treats of the father of the church in the fourth to fifth century who left a detailed account of his reading in his *Confessions,* and who in the treatise *On Christian Doctrine,* produced the earliest book on "How to Read." Both the latter are in *GBWW* I: 18; II: 16.

Notwithstanding their common theme, the two books under review are as different from one another as their subjects were in life and work. DeMaria's is relatively slight, with modest documentation in the form of notes. It is an off-shoot of the immense research the author did in writing two previous works on Johnson: *Johnson's Dictionary and the Language of Learning* (1987) and *The Life of Samuel Johnson: A Critical Biography* (1995). The purpose of this slighter work aims to show how Johnson classified and evaluated the many types of reading he engaged in, and to cite particular examples of these types.

The task that Brian Stock set for himself in *Augustine the Reader* was much more ambitious: to expound and analyze "Augustine's attempt to lay the theoretical foundation for a reading culture" and thereby "give birth to the West's first developed theory of reading." (p. 1) To this end, Stock has not only studied the many works that Augustine produced but also the vast secondary literature on the subject. As a result, almost a third of his book consists of notes, a great many in Augustine's Latin, as backing for points made in the text.

Let us consider first, how and what Johnson read, not just the various types of books, but the degree of attention he gave to each and the extent of the reading community that he thereby entered. DeMaria, using Johnson's own language, distinguishes four types or ways of reading: (1) study or hard reading; (2) perusal; (3) mere reading; and (4) curious reading. Each merits consideration for the insight it gives into reading itself.

Study, or hard reading, is the most serious, attentive, even energetic kind. Johnson was a man of his age in holding that its principal books consisted in the Bible and the Greek and Latin classics. Reading the Bible, however, was unique in that its aim was not so much critical understanding as it was as a means to spiritual and moral edification. Although Johnson studied it in Greek and Latin—translating, commenting, meditating—its community, at least potentially, consisted of all Christians. Intense reading of classical literature, he told Boswell, began as a boy: "not voyages and travels, but all literature, Sir, all ancient writers, all manly; though but little Greek." (*GBWW* I: 44, 11; II: 41, 11) He also followed Humanist practice in his fondness for aphorisms, of which Erasmus provided thousands in his collection, *Adagia.* Such a liking fed Johnson's predilection in reading for extracting the complete thought, most valuable for a lexicographer in his need for examples of verbal usage. It was also a valuable practice for an extremely desultory reader, leafing through many books in the course of a single day.

The reading community of classical literature was less extensive than that of the Bible, of course, being limited to readers of Greek and Latin. Most restricted of all hard reading is what DeMaria calls "coterie reading." In Johnson's case this comprised his liking for Neo-Latin poetry, since the number of writers and readers there was very small. A modern example of coterie reading is found in the devotees of the Bloomsbury group of London in the 1920s.

The variety of reading as "perusal" is indicated by a statement in the preface to Johnson's *Dictionary.* "I applied myself to the perusal of our writers; and noting whatever might be of use to ascertain or illustrate a word or phrase, accumulated in time the materials of a dictionary." It is a form of reading that is careful and attentive, though somewhat easier than study, and directed to a special definite purpose. The books consulted most for perusal reading consist of dictionaries, encyclopaedias, reference works, self-help books, how-to books. Unlike hard reading, perusal calls for suspension of criticism and evaluation, as the reader trustingly seeks for what he is after.

By "mere" reading Johnson understood the kind that is given to such material as newspapers, advertisements, tickets, and playbills. As DeMaria notes, the emergence of the newspaper in Johnson's day marked a new period in the history of reading. Mere reading is neither hard reading nor that of self-help, but such as to fill the gap between the latter and narrative fiction, which belongs in the fourth type. "News" has to possess some degree of credibility, although the amount may vary. Yet it demands no such trust as that of self-help and allows greater irresponsibility in both writer and reader than do either of the first two types. Its reading public is also wider and more common.

"Curious," the name for the fourth type of reading, is defined in Johnson's *Dictionary* as "inquisitive, desirous of information, addicted to inquiry." Hence, curious reading finds its best representative in fiction. Johnson evaluated it as the lowest form of reading. Yet he himself engaged in it and appreciated especially the *Iliad, Don Quixote, The Pilgrim's Progress,* and *Robinson Crusoe.*

The four ways of reading should not be equated with any one genre or form of literary material. Any book can be read in all four ways. This is true even of the Bible, Johnson's preferred example of hard reading, since it can be read for self-help, fiction, even news, as shown by the title for *Gospel* in Greek—*evangelion,* meaning good news.

Turning now to Stock's *Augustine the Reader,* we face a more difficult task. The text is divided into two parts: I Confessions 1–9, and II, The Ethics of Interpretation. The first analyses and explicates what Augustine writes of his reading in the first nine books of his *Confessions.* In part II, Stock draws upon the remaining books of the *Confessions* as well as on many other works to present Augustine's theory of reading.

Regarding particular instances of his reading, it is enough here to sum-marize those that Augustine claimed marked the most important changes in his life. Of his early schooling he notes that he loved Latin, had to memo-rize much of Virgil's *Aeneid,* but also enjoyed the epic (*GBWW* I: 18, 6; II: 16, 7). The first significant change he singles out came from reading the *Hortensius,* a dialogue by Cicero (no longer extant) containing an exhorta-tion to the life of philosophy. Augustine writes, "it altered my outlook on life," the last words of which are *Mutavit affectum* (affection, disposition) (*GBWW* I: 18, 14–15; II: 16, 18–19). It made a change in thought, emotion, ambition: his first conversion by a book. Augustine then tried reading the Sacred Scriptures but was turned away by their style, which he considered barbaric.

The next significant change in Augustine's reading came when he was called to Milan as city orator and heard the sermons of Ambrose, Catholic bishop of that city. From Ambrose's interpretation of Scriptures, Augustine learned that his inability to read them came from taking them too literally, especially the Old Testament, where they should be read figuratively or spiritually; for as St. Paul declared (II Cor. 3. 6): "The Letter killeth, but the Spirit giveth life." Yet Augustine confesses that he was still unable to conceive of a spiritual substance (*GBWW* I: 18, 34; II: 16, 42–43).

He was able to overcome the remaining obstacle in his materialism through reading "some of the books of the Platonists, translated from Greek into Latin," presumably the Neoplatonist writer Plotinus. Augustine recounts his discovery by quoting the Prologue to the Gospel of St. John and noting what doctrines he found in the Plotinus contrasted with what was *not* there, especially the incarnation of Christ and his life among men (*GBWW* I: 18, 47; II: 16, 60–61).

The most decisive in its effect of all Augustine's readings up to the time he writes of came from a reading of St. Paul. He was in a garden in Milan with his friend Alypius, weeping in great anguish. He hears childish voices saying "Take it and read, take it and read." Answering the command, he takes up the book at hand, Paul's "Epistle to the Romans," and reads: "Not in revelling and drunkenness, not in lust and wantonness, not in quarrels and rivalries, arm yourselves with (*induite,* put on) the Lord Jesus Christ; spend no more thought on nature and nature's appetites." A more literal translation of these final words is: "and make not provision for the flesh in concupiscence." Augustine, much given to such sin at that time, reads no further. He writes that his heart filled with light of confidence and all the darkness of doubt vanished, so that he "no longer desired a wife or placed any hope in this world" but would instead devote himself to a life in religion (*GBWW* I: 18, 61; II: 16, 77).

Stock asks us to consider that in writing the *Confessions* Augustine was thinking of his life—past, present, and future—as though he were interpreting a text. Its literal meaning consisted of the events he had experienced in the past and was recalling in the present of his writing about it, while its spiritual meaning lay in the matters that were potential or about to occur in the future.

In the book's second part, entitled "The Ethics of Interpretation," Stock traces the development of Augustine's thought on this matter through a number of his analytical writings that consider it, especially his works *On the Teacher, First Catechetical Instruction* (the first catechism in the West), *The Utility of Believing,* and the treatise *On Christian Doctrine,* which is the earliest work that discusses how to read a book, the book in this case being the Bible. Stock notes that the assumption underlying discussion of these works is that to talk about literature is to talk about ethical matters, i.e., serious consideration regarding the good. Such is Augustine's belief, as well as Johnson's.

The serious and complex way in which Augustine looked upon reading is evident from the three-fold organization of his work on reading the Bible: (1) Books 1–3 of *On Christian Doctrine* concern the discovery of truth, whereas Book 4 concerns teaching and preaching the truth found. (2) The distinction between signs and the things of which they are the signs divides Books 2–3, concerning the nature, kinds, and interpretation of signs, from Book 1 devoted to things or realities. (3) Throughout all four books Augustine stresses the distinction between the merely useful and the truly enjoyable, since reading at most is only a means leading beyond itself to a truth that can be enjoyed. The ultimate rule to be followed in reading the scriptures, Augustine declares, is a rule of love:

> "Whoever, then, thinks that he understands the Holy Scriptures, or any part of them, but puts such an interpretation on them as does not tend to build up this twofold love of God and our neighbour, does not yet understand them as he ought." (*GBWW* I: 18, 634–35; II: 16, 715)

Stock's primary interest lies in the psychology of reading, and in particular in how Augustine in writing as well as reading seeks a knowledge of self. One of the most impressive of his self-discoveries lies in his anticipation of Descartes' *Cogito. Cogito ergo sum* (I think, therefore I am), the French philosopher declared, maintaining that it provides the foundation stone for the erection of modern philosophy. (*GBWW* I: 31, 51; II: 28, 275) Augustine's version of this occurs in his treatise *On the Trinity,* where he explores how images of the triune God can be found in inner trinities within the mind. According to Stock, Augustine's *Cogito,* the proof that the mind knows itself, is accomplished in four steps:

1. The mind knows what it is to know, since it knows things other than itself.
2. The mind, even if it does not know itself, still knows itself as a state of knowing.
3. Since it is impossible for another mind to know this knowing, then to the extent that the mind knows that it knows, it knows itself.
4. In seeking itself, therefore, the mind already knows itself.

Augustine is then able to reconsider the maxim "Know thyself." The standard interpretation given by the Stoic philosophers was that one should live according to nature. For Augustine, this means the mind should live in accord with nature, understood as "ordered to its nature" by being ruled by God, who is above it, and to rule over the corporeal, which is below it.

Augustine the Reader is immensely rewarding. A review can indicate but a few of its riches. By focussing upon reading and its psychology, it opens up an entirely new approach to the understanding of Augustine's thought, as well as of reading itself.

Leo Strauss and Judaism

George Anastaplo

Jewish Philosophy and the Crisis of Modernity
(State University of New York Press, 1997)
Leo Strauss (edited by Kenneth Hart Green)

> Oh, that is not true; I mean, that is simply not true . . .
> Oh, God! That is, I think, really unfair.
> —Leo Strauss (February 4, 1962)

My 1974 eulogy of one of my teachers, Leo Strauss (1899–1973), was not well received by some of my former fellow students. One of their complaints seems to have been that I made too much of his Jewishness. I had said, for example,

> My limitations, even as the mere reporter I here
> try to be, should be acknowledged at the outset
> of these recollections: I was a quarter century Leo Strauss's junior; I was never an intimate of his; and I am neither Jewish nor conventionally conservative, both of which conditions did tend to promote intimacy with him. . . .

It should be evident, when I speak of Mr. Strauss and Judaism, that I do presume to speak of matters which I can glimpse only at a distance, if at all. Even so, as I have indicated, the outsider can recognize that there is something here to be investigated by a competent student. Thus, Mr. Strauss could acknowledge publicly that there was a disproportion between the "primitive feelings" he always retained from his Orthodox upbringing [in Germany] and the "rational judgment" guided in him by philosophy. [Anastaplo, *The Artist as Thinker* (Ohio University Press, 1983), pp. 254–70.]

Now, a generation later, I am intrigued to see Kenneth Hart Green's collection of materials which very much testifies to Professor Strauss's lifetime interest in, if not even devotion to, Jewish things. Green is "a competent student" of these matters. My observations about the significance of Strauss's Jewishness are generously noticed by the editor of this carefully-annotated collection. He can refer to my 1974 Strauss eulogy, understandably, as "a provocative article." (p. 476)

Much more of Strauss's "Jewish writings" is scheduled to come. Green opens his preface with these announcements (pp. xi–xii):

> The following is a collection of essays and lectures written by Leo Strauss in the field of modern Jewish thought, which have been gathered together for the first time. It is meant to offer the reader an introduction to the enormous range of Strauss's Jewish interests. In doing so, I have been guided by two intentions: first, to present the best of Strauss's shorter writings on modern Jewish thought; and second, to present a comprehensive view of how Strauss expressed himself as a modern Jewish thinker. . . . I have included only those works of Strauss that were produced in the years following 1945. The reason for excluding all but the later writings is simply that this is merely one of five volumes to appear in a State University of New York Press series, "The Jewish Writings of Leo Strauss" (series editor, K.H. Green). The series will consist of the following volumes: the early German Jewish writings, 1921–32; a new translation of *Philosophy and Law* (1995); Strauss's writings on Moses Mendelssohn; Strauss's writings on Moses Maimonides; and the present work.

Almost all of the score of pieces in this *Jewish Philosophy* collection have been previously published. Those pieces are collected by Green in seven parts: I. Essays in Modern Jewish Thought; II. Studies of Modern Jewish Thinkers; III. Lectures on Contemporary Jewish Issues; IV. Studies on the Hebrew Bible; V. Comments on Jewish History; VI. Miscellaneous Writings on Jews and Judaism; VII. Autobiographical Reflections.

My point of departure in this cursory review is provided by the items in Green's Part III, the two lectures given by Strauss forty or so years ago at the Hillel Foundation Jewish Student Center at the University of Chicago. Until recently, those two Hillel House lectures, which were delivered by Strauss from notes, were available only in unpublished transcriptions of tape recordings, which transcriptions evidently were never reviewed by him. The lectures are "Freud on Moses and Monotheism" (1958) and "Why

We Remain Jews: Can Jewish Faith and History Still Speak to Us?" (1962). A personal Jewishness is more on the surface in these lectures than it is in almost all other materials Strauss had published or had anticipated publishing. This is particularly so in the question period following upon the "Why We Remain Jews" lecture. It is from that question period, for example, that the epigraph for this book review is taken.

One can be reminded here of the materials that may best illuminate the mode of thought of this remarkable scholar, the transcriptions of many of his courses during his two decades (1949–1968) at the University of Chicago. (One can be reminded also of what is said in Plato's *Phaedrus* about the superiority of living speech to unresponsive writing.) Those transcriptions, too, were never reviewed by Strauss. But the master teacher may be seen at work there, especially in the extended discussions that would often occupy much of each meeting of his classes. Green notices that those course transcriptions "do perhaps convey something of his charm, humor, and power as a teacher." (p. xii)

It is to be regretted that those of us who attended Strauss's University of Chicago classes have not yet managed to have those transcriptions reviewed for their many errors. He recognized that those course transcriptions might be published some day, and he agreed, in several conversations with me, that he should write something which would serve, in effect, as their introduction, explaining particularly the difference between materials prepared for publication and the sort of thing that may be said and done in the classroom. I do not believe he ever wrote that explanation, which would no doubt have included a thoughtful elaboration upon what I have just said. Perhaps someone as learned, energetic, and careful as Green could now put the Strauss course-transcriptions in proper shape, consulting with the Strauss students who happen to be still available.

The two Hillel House lectures I have referred to reveal Leo Strauss as a loyal Jew, standing for a manly refusal to abandon one's people, which is consistent with his youthful dedication to political Zionism. (See p. 505.) The distinctiveness of the Bible is very much in evidence here, as is Strauss's insistence upon the unique contributions made by Judaism to the development of standards of righteousness, if not also of rationality, in the Western World. (See, for example, *Deuteronomy* 4: 6.) Also evident are the passions Strauss was capable of when caught up in an inquiry into things, whether philosophical or personal, which mattered to him. Such inquiry may be seen throughout this fine collection. But however superior Strauss may have considered Judaism (in its rootedness in rationality as well as in righteousness) to the religions of the world, he never seemed to suggest that sensible Gentiles with "religious" inclinations should try to become Jews. Is it then primarily a matter of chance (if not of providence) who is, and hence who should remain, a Jew? Consider on the Noahide laws for the non-Jews, Elijah Banamozegh, in *Israel and Humanity* (New York: Paulist Press, 1994), e.g., p. 237 where it is said "There are . . . innumerable scriptural texts following the election of Israel which portray God speaking and acting as the God of all mankind, watching over the destinies of every people . . . . [A] radical forsaking by God of virtually the entire human race in order to attach Himself exclusively to a tiny people [as some suppose] is a hypothesis as monstrous as it is improbable."

There may be a problem with the term "Jewish Philosophy" used in the title of Green's collection of Strauss' writings. One may wonder whether a mode of thought is properly called *philosophy* if it is distinctively Jewish (or, for that matter, if it is distinctively Christian or Buddhist or whatever). Green seems very much aware of this problem. Even more intriguing is the question whether one can be fully a Jew, in the traditional sense, if one is truly a philosopher. Strauss was reluctant to call himself, or anyone else he knew personally, a philosopher. He was obliged to distinguish between the rare philosopher and, for example, the many members of philosophy departments in this country and abroad. Related to this question is the concern about what the failure to be an observant Jew does to one's condition, if not to one's status, as a descendant of Abraham, Isaac, and Jacob. Strauss recognized this concern during his 1962 "Why We Remain Jews" question period (p. 344):

> I believe—and I say this without any disrespect to any orthodox Jews—
> that it is hard for people, for most Jews today, to believe in verbal inspira-
> tion (I mean, in verbal inspiration of the Torah), and in the miracles—or
> most of the miracles—and other things. I know that. My friend Rabbi
> [Monford] Harris is not here, but I am in deep sympathy with what he
> means by a "postcritical Judaism." I think that it offers a perfectly legiti-
> mate and sensible goal, namely to restate the essence of Jewish faith in a
> way which is by no means literally identical with, say, Rambam's "Creator
> of the world," or with something of this kind—I mean, with any traditional
> statement of principles. That is not the point. But a Judaism which is not
> belief in the "Creator of the world," that has problems running through it.

The reference here to "Rambam" is to Moses Maimonides (1135–1204). (See, on Gershom Scholem and the mysticism underlying Jewish rationalism, Hayim G. Perelmuter, *Harvest of a Dialogue* [KTAV Publishing House, 1997], p. 119f.)

This kind of inquiry has even been taken so far as to erupt from time to time in a controversy, since Leo Strauss's death, as to whether he was an "atheist." Such has been alleged recently in a somewhat hostile manner by one scholar (Patrick Glynn, in *God: The Evidence* [Rocklin, Calif.: Forum, 1997], pp. 12–14, 171–73). Far friendlier arguments, but perhaps to somewhat the same effect, have been made by a few of Strauss's students. Other students have delivered stout rejoinders to such talk. It *was* observed, during Strauss's lifetime, that he made many of his students, both Jews and Gentiles, take their religious heritage seriously. It could also be observed that he spoke morally (or, as we say, "responsibly") about what completes or transcends morality.

Strauss, in considering what the charge of "atheism" can mean, reminded students of the precepts of natural theology. Even more critical here, it seems to me, is what he had to say, again and again, about the relation of Reason to Revelation, if not also about the Idea of the Good. Consider how this relation was put by one of his devoted students:

> The most impressive alternative to philosophy in the life of Leo Strauss is summed up by the name of a city, Jerusalem, the holy city. What if the one thing most needful is not philosophic wisdom, but righteousness? The notion of the one thing most needful, Mr. Strauss argued, is not defensible if the world is not the creation of the just and loving God. Neither philosophy nor revealed religion, he argued, can refute one another; for, among other reasons, they disagree about the very principles or criteria of proof. . . . This mutual irrefutability and tension between philosophy and biblical revelation appear to him to be the secret of the vitality of Western Civilization. (Laurence Berns, "Leo Strauss," The College [St. John's College], April 1974, p. 5)

Would not anyone who takes seriously this kind of juxtaposition of Biblical revelation and philosophy have to concede that a reasoned atheism is impossible? That is, does not a *reasoned* atheism imply that Biblical revelation has, in effect, been refuted, something which Strauss had good reason to believe could never be done?

Strauss made invaluable contributions in showing what Judaism and Jewish things, including, of course, the Bible carefully read, contribute to the thought of the West. Gentiles may be more apt to notice, than are Jews these days, that Christianity can be understood as a remarkable consequence of the combination of Judaism and Greekness (or philosophy). Put another way, Christianity, which has helped both preserve and discipline philosophy across millennia, can be seen as a Jewish sect for Gentiles, albeit a sect suspected, if not considered heretical, by the observant Jew.

These derivations from, and the influences of, Judaism can be generally appreciated. What does not seem to be sufficiently appreciated, I venture to add, is how much Judaism, as something to be taken seriously in and by the modern world, relies upon Christianity, illuminated as well as distorted as Judaism has come to be, for many of us, by the great tradition of Christian theology and dependent as Judaism now is upon the political influence of that Christendom which once subjected it to many uncharitable trials. (See pp. 13–14.) This is illustrated most dramatically perhaps by the extent to which the patronage of a still-Christian United States has made it possible for the country of Israel ("a tiny people") to emerge and survive. The long-term consequences of Israel for Jews, and for their ability to probe deeply into and to speak frankly about issues which they have had to approach with caution for millennia, can be profound.

That Strauss was much more sensitive to the questions I have raised than most of us are ever likely to be is illustrated by his pioneering work in both Maimonides and Machiavelli (who could celebrate the political prowess of Moses). One can see in Strauss's Hillel House "Freud" lecture his concern about the threats to Judaism and the Mosaic community posed by secularized Jewish intellectuals. Strauss recognized, as we have noticed, the power of Maimonides's going to the roots of the differences between the philosopher and the man of faith. At these roots is, among other things, a divergence in opinion as to whether the world had a beginning in time—that is, whether, instead of being eternal, the world was created by God out of nothing.

These questions and other similar matters are usefully considered in *Jewish Philosophy and the Crisis of Modernity*. Professor Green's instructive introduction to this volume concludes with the following paragraphs (p. 48):

> Strauss came to maintain that the search for wisdom in the midst of our contemporary crisis seems to require us to return to the original sources of our wisdom. Over and above everything else, this meant in Strauss's mind that we need especially to turn to the Hebrew Bible, the most fundamental Jewish source, in order to consider whether this book contains a unity of forgotten knowledge that had provided us with our first light, and with an unrefuted truth that we can still recover.

> Just as Maimonides focused on the Hebrew Bible in order to meet the medieval philosophic challenge and the crisis it provoked, Strauss believed that modern Jews should return to studying the Hebrew Bible as one book with one teaching about God, man, and the world. As this suggests, Strauss thought that we are in need of its essential teaching about God, man, and the world. As this suggests, Strauss thought that we are in need of its essential teaching—blurred by tradition and obscured by modern critique—which we must try to grasp afresh. This is because, to Strauss, it is only in the original sources of our wisdom that true wisdom may reside and can best be rediscovered.

It makes sense that the editorial mind evident in these remarks has produced a collection which should be well received not only by Leo Strauss's students. (See, for an expanded version of this book review, Anastaplo, "Law and Literature and the Bible," *Oklahoma City University Law Review*, 23, Appendix B, 1998.)

Maxwell for All
Daniel Siegel

Maxwell on the Electromagnetic Field: A Guided Study
(Rutgers University Press, 1997)
Thomas K. Simpson

ames Clerk Maxwell is not as well known as he should be; a mention of "Maxwell" will elicit responses concerning the antique car or the coffee, rather than the nineteenth-century Scottish physicist (b. Edinburgh 1831, d. Cambridge 1879) whose principal writings on electromagnetic theory are presented in this edition. Physicists, however, hold

Maxwell in a position of reverence—just behind Newton and Einstein—for his profound contributions in two principal areas: First, as a pioneer of kinetic-molecular theory, he introduced the probability distribution of molecular speeds, thus laying the foundation of statistical mechanics and providing crucial background for twentieth-century treatments of the world of atoms and molecules and the science of heat and energy. Second, as a pioneer of electromagnetic field theory, Maxwell established, in the set of equations that bear his name, the foundation of modern electromagnetic theory and the background of relativity theory; further, in his identification of light as an electromagnetic phenomenon, Maxwell provided the theoretical basis for Heinrich Hertz's experiments on electromagnetic waves in 1887–88, leading to radio, television, radar, and related technologies. Beyond this, Maxwell made important contributions to the theory of color vision, the mathematics of vector quantities, the theory of Saturn's rings, and the foundations of cybernetic control. Last but not least, Maxwell was a very likable person—earnest, dedicated, and sincere in his work and personal life, but not at all a dour Scotsman: his jokey correspondence and humorous poems still afford comic relief for scholars working on his papers.

In bringing Maxwell's work on electromagnetic theory to a broader public, Thomas K. Simpson has chosen a Great Books approach, presenting extensive excerpts from Maxwell's three major scientific papers (of 1855, 1861–62, and 1864–65) dealing with the electromagnetic field concept, and adding to these a substantive introduction, running notes on the text, followup discussions of important themes, and a postscript and epilogue. Drawing on his many years of teaching in the Great Books program at St. John's College in Annapolis and Santa Fe, Simpson achieves a level of success in explicating these texts for a broad audience that is, frankly, amazing. This is not to say that he makes it easy—understanding Maxwell is never easy—but he does make it feasible.

Simpson's effort is part of a larger project: the Guided Studies of Great Texts in Science program of the National Endowment for the Humanities, which has supported editions of Galileo, Newton, Mendel, Einstein, and many others, including this one on Maxwell. The contribution of this NEH project to the general understanding of science as a human enterprise has been immense, and NEH is to be commended for the effort. (I must admit, I am biased in favor: NEH supported my own edition of an Einstein text under this program; look for it in your bookstore soon.) A group of these studies, including this one by Simpson, has been published by Rutgers University Press in a series entitled Masterworks of Science: Guided Studies of Great Texts in Science.

Maxwell, in his scientific work, was pursuing not only physical truth, but also a metaphysical agenda, Simpson argues; in this, Maxwell was one of the last of the line of old-fashioned natural philosophers who were as much interested in the broad, philosophical implications of their work as in technical issues (pp. 174, 366). In particular, Maxwell was interested in the question of the *intelligibility* of explanations of electromagnetic phenomena, as over and above the question of mere technical adequacy. The alternative and preexisting approach to electromagnetic phenomena, which involved the notion of electrical and magnetic systems acting on each other directly at a distance, was technically and mathematically quite successful: it enabled the calculation and prediction of electromagnetic effects to a high degree of accuracy. Maxwell, however, was not interested merely in technical and formal success. He was interested in *understanding* the interactions of electromagnetic systems: What happens, Maxwell asked, in the spaces between the electrical and magnetic bodies, in order to transmit the forces from one to the other? Maxwell's answer to this question, following the lead of his countryman Michael Faraday, was the concept of invisible electric and magnetic fields existing in the spaces between the visible electrical and magnetic objects. Simpson's vision of the matter merits quotation at some length:

> Maxwell in rejecting the stark but efficient formalism of action-at-a-distance equations is on the track of *being:* he wants to know what really *exists*. Even in this he is not simply a neutral inquirer. He is driven by a faith that the world must be of a certain sort, coherent in a way which admits understanding in terms of a complete chain of cause and effect. Here must lie the real significance of his search for a theory of the field. He is determined to tell a story of electromagnetism that will not only serve to predict all the phenomena, but will fill the world with intelligible connective links. To do this would be to restore the vision of the world as *cosmos,* in the old sense of a whole harmonious with its parts and commensurate with human understanding. (p. 139)

Indeed, argues Simpson, this conception of the field, "understood not literally and physically, but in its power as metaphor, becomes an invitation to a sense of membership in a world perceived as cosmos." With this, Simpson goes beyond the explication of Maxwell's vision to an exploration of its hermeneutic possibilities (pp. 367, xviii).

The intelligible connections or causal chains that Maxwell envisioned to connect electromagnetic effects at distant locations were modeled in mechanical terms, in different ways in each of Maxwell's three major papers. First, in 1855, Maxwell presented a picture of the electromagnetic field in terms of a moving fluid: the flow lines of this fluid were taken to correspond to the field lines. Maxwell characterized this mechanical representation as a mere analogy: its purpose was as a mnemonic aid, rather than as an account of what the reality of the field might be. In Maxwell's second paper, of 1861–62, however, he ventured something more: whereas in the previous paper he had been "using mechanical illustrations to assist the imagination, but not to account for the phenomena," here, in contrast, his aim was "to examine magnetic phenomena ... to determine what ... motions of a [mechanical] medium are capable of *producing* the ... phenomena observed" (p. 144, emphasis mine).

This was to be a full causal account. But the mechanism of the field that Maxwell managed to construct was so artificial that one might doubt whether it was realistically intended: in the fully developed model, Maxwell envisioned space as filled with a cellular medium. Inside each cell was a parcel or blob of elastic material; the cell walls were envisioned as consisting of monolayers of small spherical particles (Figure 2, from p. 162). Rotations of the elastic blobs inside the cells were taken to represent magnetic fields; the small spherical particles were to act as ball bearings, providing frictionless contact between the rotating elastic blobs. When these small particles moved—as they would when neighboring elastic blobs had different rotational velocities, corresponding to varying magnetic fields—the moving particles would constitute an electric current. The functional success of the model was impressive. With this "molecular vortex" model (so named because the rotating parcels of etherial material were originally envisioned as vortices in a fluid), Maxwell was able to model successfully all classes of electromagnetic phenomena. (Simpson provides an excellent overview of the six different categories of electromagnetic phenomena known at the time, pp. 22–52.)

Beyond this, Maxwell was able, on the basis of this model, to go beyond the known phenomena to arrive at two startling and highly significant novelties: First, he was able to conclude that one of the known electromagnetic equations had to be modified through the introduction of a new term called the displacement current. This modification of an experimental equation on the basis of purely theoretical arguments stands as a shining example in the history of physics of the power of theoretical ideas: the modified equation, which serves to complete the set of "Maxwell's equations" and make it a coherent mathematical system, has remained the keystone of Maxwellian electrodynamics ever since, sustained in both the scientific use and the technological application of electromagnetic theory. Second, on the basis of this model, Maxwell first concluded that light was an electromagnetic phenomenon; from this followed the concept of electromagnetic waves and the foundations of 20th-century communications technology. The heuristic value of the model was thus immense. But does this mean that Maxwell really believed in the model as physical reality or truth: did he really think that space was filled with elastic blobs and ball bearings? This question has bedevilled historians of Maxwell's electromagnetic theory over the years.

The answer that Simpson gives to this question illustrates the strengths, but also perhaps some of the weaknesses of the Great Books approach, in which primary texts—presenting the words of the historical figures involved—constitute the central reading material, as opposed to the approach of the synthetic historical narrative, in which the story is told primarily in the words of the historian. On the one hand, the nuanced reply that Simpson gives to the question of Maxwell's realism is far superior in sophistication and historical verisimilitude to most of what has been offered in synthetic historical narratives over past decades. The consensus view—informed as it has been by a 20th-century retrospective sensibility—has been that Maxwell's vortex model is bizarre and ridiculous, and that he could not have believed in it as a realistic physical hypothesis. In this view, the vortex model of 1861–62 is to be lumped with the flow model of 1855 as another mere analogy, without realistic or explanatory intent. Simpson, however, in a Great Books vein, pays more attention to the texts. While the writers of historical narratives have opportunity to select textual evidence to support preconceived views, the Great Books analyst cannot so easily exercise that option: if one is presenting and commenting on extensive and continuous textual passages, one has to pay attention to all of the words in those passages, rather than selecting according to taste. Looking at the texts in this way, Simpson comments that, in contrast to the merely illustrative and geometrical model of 1855, which had no explanatory power, Maxwell was now presenting a "physical" account, a "theory," "pursu[ing] the question whether any imaginable physical system could *accomplish* what electromagnets and pith balls are regularly observed to do," by actually "produc[ing]" (Maxwell's word) the mechanical forces involved (pp. 139–40, emphasis mine).

Relatedly, Maxwell here was concerned, at least in part, with a "probable" hypothesis; he was "think[ing] more earnestly about reality." In fact, as Simpson's analysis recognizes, Maxwell assigned different status to the different parts of the model, as concerns realistic intent: The idea of rotating parcels of etherial material, whose rotations were to represent magnetic fields, was a "hypothesis" that was "probable"; the idea of the ball-bearing particles, on the other hand, was a "more questionable move, qualifying as a 'suggestion' rather than a hypothesis" (pp. 174–75, 197). Again, as stated earlier, the Great Books approach here supports a more nuanced treatment of this material, with greater historical verisimilitude, than the more traditional treatment of Maxwell's model-building by the writers of historical narratives.[1]

But there is also a limitation associated with the Great Books approach, as compared with the historical narrative: if the Great Books approach is to be practiced with integrity, the emphasis must be on what is actually found in the texts, rather than on ancillary and contextual material that the presenter may want to bring forward. Certainly in the teaching situation—at St. John's or elsewhere—nothing will stifle discussion more quickly than having the teacher claim to explicate the "real" meaning of the texts, on the basis of contextual material to which the students do not have direct access: if contextual material is determinative, then what is the use of reading the texts presented and attempting to arrive at opinions concerning their meaning? As a result, context winds up being somewhat deemphasized, and this can be a loss.

In the case of Maxwell's models, the texts that Simpson presents in this publication—chosen for a combination of centrality, accessibility, and brevity—lead to an emphasis on the imaginative and nonrealistic aspects of Maxwell's molecular-vortex model. Thus, in the third and last (1864–65) text that Simpson presents, Maxwell had given up the model in favor of a much more abstract approach, and the implication seems to be that the model had been, finally, rejected, having functioned for Maxwell primarily as an imaginary, "playful" construct, whose purpose was as a "way

station ... along the course of Maxwell's investigations," leading ultimately
to a more abstract formulation of field theory:

> A playful mind is at work. ...Maxwell indulges in the invention of wheels
> and gears to fill the vacuum and do his bidding in a way that Rube
> Goldberg might envy. The reader must be the judge, but I submit that
> Maxwell has tongue in cheek here and does not seriously intend that the
> devices he conjures up would in fact be found to exist in the form he is
> describing. ... Maxwell is claiming latitude ... to pursue the question
> whether any *imaginable* physical system could accomplish what electro-
> magnets and pith balls are regularly observed to do (pp. 140, 175).

The emphasis here is thus on an *imaginable* system, showing that a connected, field-theoretic account is *possible,* rather than on realistic intent.

The reader, however, might judge differently if made aware of some of
the broader context, including the following elements: the origins of the
model in the work of William Thomson (later Lord Kelvin), who regarded
the model as realistic, and whose opinion in this was applauded by Maxwell; the continuing efforts by Maxwell to detect the magnetic rotations
through direct mechanical experiments; the arguments in favor of magnetic
rotations that Maxwell made on the basis of the mathematics of linear and
rotational vectors and the observed properties of electric currents and magnetic polarity; the later reappearance of the molecular-vortex model in
Maxwell's *magnum opus* on field theory, the *Treatise on Electricity and
Magnetism,* in 1873; and Maxwell's continuing statements in favor of
magnetic rotations in a variety of his popular writings.[2] Proper attention to
this contextual material would motivate a shift in the balance of historical
judgment to a greater emphasis on the realistic intent of Maxwell's hypothesis of molecular vortices.

And what of it? What difference does it make whether Maxwell really
believed in the magnetic rotations? In Simpson's epilogue, he offers
thoughtful reflections on the meaning of the story of Maxwell and field
theory: It was Maxwell's dedicated, "passion[ate]," "unswerving," "driving
inner conviction," according to Simpson, that impelled Maxwell toward a
complete, coherent, intelligible field theory. This achievement then brought
in train an unexpected bonus, the electromagnetic theory of light: "It is as if
the cosmos had rewarded Maxwell for his labors in the creation of field
theory with the solution of the mystery of light as a prize." Maxwell's
exercise in mechanical modeling was a part of this driving quest for coherence and intelligibility, and it was the thoroughness, care, and dedicated
effort invested in the model that brought forth the bonus, the identification
of light as an electromagnetic phenomenon.[3] The full historical record,
indeed, shows that it was because Maxwell regarded this mechanical model
as in significant part realistic that he invested so much effort in it, thus
making possible its successes. To continue Simpson's metaphor, Maxwell's
reward for pursuing coherence and intelligibility so doggedly and cre-
atively in the mechanistic context was to achieve a result that ultimately
transcended the nineteenth-century mechanistic context, enduring as "one

of the truly great works of western science," and furnishing the basis for a large segment of twentieth-century science and technology (pp. 363–367).

1. For the traditional treatment, see, for example, John Hendry, *James Clerk Maxwell and the Theory of the Electromagnetic Field* (Bristol: Adam Hilger, 1986), and Ivan Tolstoy, *James Clerk Maxwell: A Biography* (Chicago: University of Chicago Press, 1982), esp. pp. 77–78, 121–124. Concerning the latter, see, further, Daniel Siegel, Review of Ivan Tolstoy, *James Clerk Maxwell,* and Martin Goldman, *The Demon in the Aether,* in *Physics Today,* 1985, 38:66–67.

2. Daniel M. Siegel, *Innovation in Maxwell's Electromagnetic Theory: Molecular Vortices, Displacement Current, and Light* (New York: Cambridge University Press, 1991), pp. 29–55.

3. Siegel, *Innovation,* esp. pp. 120–143.

Future More Vivid:
A Review of Freeman Dyson's *Imagined Worlds*
Thomas K. Simpson

Imagined Worlds
(Harvard, 1997)
Freeman Dyson

reeman Dyson is a lover of science fiction, and in his new book *Imagined Worlds* several classics of that art, among them *The Time Machine* of H.G. Wells, J.B.S. Haldane's *Daedalus,* and Aldous Huxley's *Brave New World,* play important roles. Yet when Dyson, himself a noted scientist with long experience in space technologies and the engineering of nuclear energy, turns his own mind to speculation upon the far future of mankind the result is by no means a matter of mere entertainment. By reading a book such as *Imagined Worlds*, we are taught to take science fiction seriously. As Dyson points out early in the work, it is our lot as humans to live in a number of time-frames simultaneously; but he evidently feels we do not do this very well. We are too occupied with what I think we might call the *hybris* of the short-term. *Imagined Worlds* is calling our attention to the immense importance of keeping our possible futures more vividly in view. In the course of his book Dyson carries us through seven sets of nested futures, ranging in scale from ten to a million years and beyond, so that we may be said to be looking, under his considered guidance, from the present moment outward toward the end of time.

By its very title, Dyson's is admittedly a work of imagination, but he draws on his own long experience as a working scientist in the age of nuclear energy and space exploration, to bring into the balance a special appreciation of what responsible engineering can achieve at its best. Speculations into the long future are weighed against such evidence as we have of symmetric time spans in the past, so that although he pretends to no certainty, Dyson is able to gauge persuasively the broad nature of a future we would do well to expect. The resulting work is no mere scene-painting, but a call to a new order of civic thought in which informed visions extended over an immense range of time come to bear intensely upon judgments we must make at the present moment.

Imagined Worlds is a brief work, and its style is often informal, verging even on the chatty; yet its message is of a sort which in another time would have been uttered by choruses weaving choriambs before the altar of Dionysus. These are messages of prospect and doom, addressed to ourselves and often painful to read. Dyson never lets us forget that we are speaking, not about *other people,* but always about ourselves in a future tense. It is of ourselves, our own children and our children's children through untold generations of whom Dyson is bringing us word. When he speaks of the colonization of the Moon, asteroids and perhaps Mars in 100 years; and then in 1000 years of the occupancy of the Solar System, and ultimately, in perhaps 100,000 years, of "the greening of the Galaxy" it is of our seed whose destiny he is prophesying. He sees the human species diversifying, and in time flowing into new forms we cannot now imagine. The future vision returns to us as a *present question:* do we understand ourselves today sufficiently to endure such futures without losing what we most prize as the essence of our humanity? With such reminders of transience, past and future thoughts fold back upon the present, to press more strongly the questions of today. Dyson speaks warmly of the ethical character of responsible engineering, and of the world community of scientists, and it is no contradiction to say that despite its grounding in science and engineering, the burden of *Imagined Worlds* bears ultimately on critical issues of ethics, politics, and society.

Some of the challenges which Dyson foresees constitute immediate practical problems in which all the citizenry of the Earth inherently hold a common interest. We are, for example, under ongoing threat of catastrophic destruction through collision with any one of the myriad other bodies with which we share the Solar System, whether asteroids and small comets whose orbits about the sun can be determined, or larger comets travelling in orbits so immense that the arrival of each must come as a surprise to earthly observers. This is not a hazard about which we hear much, but it is well known, and ever-present. Earth is currently at risk, and it behooves us to begin taking protective measures without delay. These require first an appropriate system of surveillance, and then engineering provision to deflect the orbit of the comet or asteroid. The surveillance systems as he describes them will require major outlay, on the order of that already planned for the Earth Observer System (EOS). Dyson is ready here, as elsewhere, with a practical engineer's proposal for the countermeasures we should plan to take—not the use of hydrogen bombs, a recommendation of which he is highly suspicious, but of "mass-drivers," a more economical means of delivering momentum to the oncoming body sufficient to deflect it from its course. With proper surveillance we might expect some 100 years' warning of a collision event, which is about the length of time we might need to implement our countermeasures. We see here an instance of the present need for very-long-range commitment of resources to which Dyson's perspective is now calling our attention.

Technologies, Dyson points out, take something on the order of 100 years to ripen to general adoption, as we have experienced in the instances of steam or electrical engineering, the internal combustion engine or the science of flight. As he looks forward to appraise the technologies of fifty years hence, Dyson selects two as dominant, genetic engineering and artificial intelligence. Many of us might have supposed these fields, already familiar today, would ripen much sooner: but Dyson means that somewhere on the order of the hundred-year span they will become the routine working modes of civilized society. In the case of genetic engineering, this means that science will have mastered the "grammar and syntax" of the genetic code, and will be enabled not only to doctor specific genes and traits, but to create new genetic compositions at will. Thus what seem now rather esoteric ethical questions concerning the management of limited elements of our genetic structure will open out into an entirely new attitude in our relationship to living forms. We must inevitably think more largely, more earnestly and better, about present questions of genetic manipulation if we see them in terms of a far more daunting future prospect. Dyson has no belief in our ability to prevent these developments; improvements, he says, will be sure to occur in spite of attempted controls. But we can take thought and give guidance. Far more is at issue than we might have thought, and today's questions may take new forms, when seen through the lens of the distant future.

Dyson is alarmed by the unmistakable tendency of technologies in our present form of society to serve the interests of the rich increasingly at the expense of the poor of the world. Under the continued aegis of an unrestrained free-market economy, he foresees a world split even further. His book is therefore an earnest appeal to his readers to re-think our social forms to avoid a doom otherwise lying directly in our path. He does not endorse the pessimistic fantasy of Wells' *Time Machine,* in which a ruling class has become enfeebled and childlike while a serving class, literally driven underground, has been shaped genetically into apelike managers of machines. Yet it is hard to find in the pages of this book any recipe by which such a social disaster can be prevented, beyond some underlying confidence of Dyson's in the innate resourcefulness of mankind.

Dyson is no utopian, and has no use for bureaucracies or autocratic measures—looking to Tolstoy's *War and Peace,* he separates "Napoleonic" solutions of social problems from those he terms "Tolstoyean," which rely rather on the concurrent initiatives of resourceful individuals than on plans and regulations formulated from above. He holds no hope for world government, or for the end of the strife among nations under which the world suffers today. At the same time, however, it is clear from his text that things cannot be allowed to continue without some fresh and coordinated social thought. He if vigorously opposed to imposed "ideologies," yet he is a person of strong principles according to which social actions need to be carried out on a broad scale. He thus walks a fine line between individuality on the one hand, and intelligent social planning on the other, leaving us with the sense that new social forms need to be contrived which implement collective planning and governance without impeding spontaneous initiatives.

Dyson disapproves of the conclusion of Huxley's *Brave New World*, in which the human voice is silenced in its encounter with a complete and controlling regime of technology. There, "old-fashioned ideas" encounter only derision and scorn on the part of these people for whom "human dignity and tragedy have no meaning." (p. 125) In Dyson's view, both Wells and Huxley have got their science fiction wrong, precisely because they have underestimated the human—in effect, they have answered the *present question* wrongly. As a corrective to this problem, he quotes Saul Bellow:

> We do not, we writers, represent mankind adequately. We do not think well of ourselves. We do not think amply about what we are. ...The pictures they offer no more resemble us than we resemble the reconstructed reptiles and other monsters in a museum of paleontology. We are much more limber, versatile, better articulated; there is much more to us; we all feel it. (p. 129)

Holding to the symmetry of his nesting of times, Dyson asserts "the best way to predict the future of human society is to study the past," (p. 128) and concludes

> The past shows us that humans are an ungovernable crowd, averse to logic and discipline. It is unlikely that any totalitarian world government of the future, or any dogmatically imposed system of beliefs, will last longer than the theoretic utopias of the past. (p. 128)

"As every parent and grandparent knows," he adds, "human children are born rebels." (p. 130)

His own projections, therefore, are not those of Wells or Huxley, and even as he looks on the thousand-year scale to technologies still more disturbing to our sense of ourselves, such as the direct communication of human minds through the technology of *radiotelepathy*, he holds to his own view of the importance of the human, and of the self and its privacy, as we know it today. As, in this same millennial future, what is now preliminary space exploration has become the human occupancy of the solar system, he urges the importance of preserving the old Earth as a *museum* in which these values are remembered:

> If we are to survive through a long future, we must stay in contact with our long past. It is not only for aesthetic reasons that we should preserve the earth as a cultural museum. The earth with its millions of species will offer to our descendants an object-lesson in the art of living. It will give them a reality check which they will need more and more, the further they move away from it. (p. 161)

Imagined Worlds must be thought of as a preliminary work. It sets us thinking in a mode with which we are unfamiliar, that of serious and practical thought about the long future; it challenges us to find ways to incorporate such prospective thoughts into our immediate practical lives, whose horizon is commonly so short. Freeman Dyson has here succeeded in the first, crucial task: to make these future prospects so vivid that they from now on haunt our so limited sense of what is real and of practical importance.

Indeed, it may be that the most important word in *Imagined Worlds* is the little pronoun "we," which recurs in various striking contexts. He is willing to say that "we" emerged from pre-human forms some million years ago, and that "we" will on the scale of some hundreds of years populate the Solar System. He foresees that "we" will become more than one human species and that as we move into space in "the greening of the Galaxy" we will live beyond contact with one another, to evolve apart in genetically isolated islands of the galaxy. At the same time, he invests great credit in us, his present-day readers, in supposing that it will be possible to rise to the thoughts and actions to which these future scenarios are summoning us. There is, then, beyond the unity which binds humanity in time, this other "we"—the one which makes of us, as intelligent occupants of Earth at this present moment, one community with a common fate.

Dyson has written from one perspective; the rest of us must now respond with informed fictions of our own, drawing upon whatever competence each of us is able to summon. *Imagined Worlds* has reminded us that we are a species in flux; if we have a "nature," then, we must think of it as a linking principle and a sense of historic direction, rather than any fixed body of limits, habits or ways. We are perhaps still only in the first stages of learning what it will mean, to be "human." We live at present in midst of unbelievable violence and irrational strife, all under the dominance of the savage concept of "war." There is no more reason to believe that we can never escape this curse, than to have once supposed that we might never fly, or now, that we would never colonize the Solar System. Engineering thinking may be easier than devising social or political controls, but it is clearly essential that we bring the same level of studied thought to envisioning the social forms of a more peaceful and rational world; indeed, the two projects are ultimately one.

We need, then, more such studies of "imagined worlds"—not only on the part of the scientists, but from many points of view. These imaginings can no longer be toyed with as idle fictions; Freeman Dyson has placed them on our present plate. Here is work for all of us; the world in all its scope is our estate, its inheritors, our children, and their children's children. The future can be foreseen, but it is not *given,* it can be shaped. We cannot manage a world in space if we cannot do a better job of governing our world at home, today, on our familiar Earth.

The Great Ideas Today 1961–1998

This is a thirty-eight-year cumulative index of *The Great Ideas Today,* 1961–1998. It is arranged in sections: AUTHORS, SUBJECTS, and TITLES. The entries under SUBJECTS are in five categories: HISTORY, ECONOMICS, POLITICS, AND SOCIAL SCIENCE; LITERATURE AND THE ARTS; PHILOSOPHY AND RELIGION; SCIENCE AND MATHEMATICS; and BOOK REVIEWS. Titles in capital letters are of works that appeared in "Additions to the Great Books Library" as reprinted works, distinct from original articles. The year listed after each work refers to the issue of *The Great Ideas Today* in which it appeared.

AUTHORS

Abraham, William J. The State of Christian Theology in North America. 1991: 242–286.

Ackerman, Diane. On Discovery, The Healing Power of Nature, and The Value of Poetry. 1998: 272–292.

Adams, Henry. "The Dynamo and the Virgin" from THE EDUCATION OF HENRY ADAMS. 1980: 452–460.

Addams, Jane. THE SETTLEMENT HOUSE. 1989: 406–431.

Adler, Mortimer J. A Catechism for Our Times. 1969: 79–97.

—. A COMMENTARY ON ARISTOTLE'S *NICO-MACHEAN ETHICS.* 1988: 290–311.

—. The Confusion of the Animalists. 1975: 72–89.

—. A Disputation on the Future of Democracy (Argument, Reply, and Discussion). 1978: 8–29, 60–70.

—. The End of the Conflict Between Capitalism and Communism. 1990: 224–275.

—. Ethics: Fourth Century B.C. and Twentieth Century A.D. 1988: 274–287.

—. The Idea of Dialectic. 1986: 154–177.

—. Minds and Brains: Angels, Humans, and Brutes. 1982: 2–14.

—. Natural Theology, Chance, and God. 1992: 287–301.

—. A Philosophical Problem to Be Solved. 1993: 329–332.

—. Philosophy in Our Time. 1982: 238–255.

—. "Reality and Appearances" from TEN PHILOSOPHICAL MISTAKES. 1990: 318–323.

—. The Transcultural and the Multicultural. 1991: 227–240.

—. Two Approaches to the Authors of the Great Books. 1986: 178–183.

Adler, Mortimer J., and Wayne F. Moquin. Hans Küng: *Does God Exist?* 1981: 188–203.

Adzhubei, Alexei. America from Far and Near. 1964: 4–29.

Agassiz, Louis. EVOLUTION AND PERMANENCE OF TYPE. 1998: 382–403.

Ahern, James F. Democratic Control and Professional Restraint. 1972: 58–71.

SUBJECTS

History, Economics, Politics, and Social Science

PHILOSOPHY AND RELIGION

SCIENCE AND MATHEMATICS

TITLES

PICTURE CREDITS